International Conference on Sustainability in Digital Transformation Era: Driving Innovative & Growth

(SIDTE 2023)

16th – 17th September 2023

Edited by

Dr. Rajeev Agrawal, SMIEEE,
Director, Lloyd Institute of Engineering & Technology, Greater Noida

Dr. Arun Pratap Srivastava , SMIEEE,
Dean(IQAC), Lloyd Institute of Engineering & Technology, Greater Noida

Dr. Akihiko Sugiyama
IEEE Signal Processing Society(SPS) Distinguished Industry Speaker, JAPAN Research Project Researcher, Yahoo Japan Corporation, Tokyo, Japan

CRC Press
Taylor & Francis Group
Boca Raton London New York

CRC Press is an imprint of the
Taylor & Francis Group, an **informa** business

Organized by
Lloyd Institute of Engineering & Technology
Greater Noida

International Conference on Sustainability in Digital Transformation Era: Driving Innovative & Growth (SIDTE 2023)

Organized by:
Lloyd Institute of Engineering & Technology Greater Noida

website : https://liet.in

Official website of the conference

https://liet.in/SIDTE-2023/

E-mail: sidte2023@liet.in

First edition published 2024
by CRC Press
4 Park Square, Milton Park, Abingdon, Oxon, OX14 4RN

and by CRC Press
2385 NW Executive Center Drive, Suite 320, Boca Raton FL 33431

CRC Press is an imprint of Informa UK Limited

British Library Cataloguing-in-Publication Data
A catalogue record for this book is available from the British Library

ISBN: 9781032877266 (pbk)
ISBN: 9781003534136 (ebk)

DOI: 10.1201/9781003534136

Typeset in Sabon LT Std
by HBK Digital

Contents

List of Figures

List of Tables

Patron's Message

I am pleased to extend a warm greeting to all the esteemed authors, industry professionals, and academic attendees who have gathered on this pious and lush green soil of one of India's best and fast growing engineering colleges i.e. Lloyd Institute of Engineering & Technology for this international conference on the 16th and 17th of September, 2023.

India is an important contender to join the developed nations because of its rapidly expanding economy. While there is awareness coupled with efforts and initiatives being taken to reach this goal, one needs to implement this in this journey from developing to the developed Nations. To help facilitate investments, foster innovations, enhance technological development, protect intellectual property, and build the best in a class manufacturing infrastructure, the Honorable Prime Minister has launched the 'Make in India' initiative.

I am confident that this International Conference on Sustainability in the Digital Transformation Era: Driving Innovation and Growth, taking place at LIET, has the objective of capturing innovative engineering practices and their nuanced manifestations in current research, with a specific focus on sustainable management practices.

I hope this conference inspires and captivates you all immensely.

Thanks

Manohar Thairani
President, Lloyd Group of Institutions, Greater Noida, Uttar Pradesh, India

General Chair's Message

It is a matter of great pride that Lloyd Institute of Engineering and Technology (LIET), Greater Noida is organizing a two days International Conference on "Sustainability in the Digital Transformation Era: Driving Innovation and Growth" (SIDTE2023) on 16-17 September 2023.

I am delighted to announce that faculty and researchers from various reputable universities, colleges, and research organizations across the country will present their research papers on a variety of topics related to the theme of conference.

With great zeal, the SIDTE-2023 organizing committee has compiled a wealth of diverse abstracts of technical research papers for the conference. The Proceedings

I have no doubt that those working in academia, research, and industry, together with young professionals, would all derive significant value from attending this conference. The information contained in the procedure will most certainly be of assistance to them in mapping out future endeavors to be undertaken in their various domains.

I wish SIDTE2023 a grand success.

Thanks

Prof. (Dr.) Rajeev Agrawal
Director, Lloyd Institute of Engineering & Technology, Greater Noida

Organizing Committee

Patron
Shri Manohar Thairani — President, Lloyd Group of Institutions, Greater Noida

General Chair
Prof. (Dr.) Rajeev Agrawal — Director, Lloyd Institute of Engineering & Technology

Conference Chair
Prof. (Dr.) A.L.N. Rao — Dean, LIET, Greater Noida

Organizing Secretary
Prof. (Dr.) Arun Pratap Srivastava — Dean (IQAC), LIET, Greater Noida

Conveners
Prof. (Dr.) S.P. Dwivedi — Dean (R&D), LIET, Greater Noida
Prof. (Dr.) A.K. Rao — HoD (CSE), LIET, Greater Noida

Technical Program Committee Chair
Dr. Vandna Kumari — LIET, Greater Noida
Dr. Swati Chaudhary — LIET, Greater Noida

Conference Coordinator
Ms. Deepika Arora — LIET, Greater Noida
Mr. Ankit Mehta — LIET, Greater Noida

Treasurer
Mr. Ravi Kalra — LIET, Greater Noida

Editorial/Publication Committee
Prof. (Dr.) J.M.Giri — HoD (ME), LIET, Greater Noida
Ms. Deepika Arora — LIET, Greater Noida
Dr. Seeba Khan — LIET, Greater Noida
Mr. Irfan Khan — LIET, Greater Noida

Publicity Committee
Prof. (Dr.) Manish Saraswat — LIET, Greater Noida
Ms Karabi Kalita Das — LIET, Greater Noida

Registration Committee
Mr. Kripanshu Tiwari — LIET, Greater Noida
Ms Shubhangi Shahi — LIET, Greater Noida

Advisory Committee

Technical Program Committee

Dr. Lajwant Kishnani, Bits Pilani, Dubai USA

Dr. Bilal Gonen, University of Cincinnati, USA

Dr. Abhishek Srivastava, IIM, Vishakha Patnam

Dr. S Yamada, Tottori University of Japan

Dr. K.R. Rao, University of Texas, Arlington

Dr. Uday Kumar, Lulea University for Technology Sweden

Dr. H. Pham, Rutgers University, USA

Dr. Arun Prakash Agarwal, Sharda University, G.B. Nagar, India

Dr. Raj Gaurang Tiwari, Chitkara University, Punjab, India

Shubhranshu Vikram Singh, Amity University, Gautam Budha Nagar, India

Prateek Chaturvedi, Amity University, Gautam Budha Nagar, India

Dr. Sarvendu Tiwari, JIMS, Gautam Budha Nagar, India

Dr. Alaa Hussein AI-Hamami, Princess Sumaya University for Tech. Jordon

Dr. Nanhey Singh, Netaji Subhas University of Technology, Delhi, India

Dr. Saurabh Jaiswal, Oracle Consulting Solution Center, Bengaluru, Karnataka

Dr. Manoj kumar, IISE, Lucknow, India

Dr. Cher Ming Tan, Chang Gung University, Japan

Dr. Miguel Lopez Benitez , University of Liverpool, UK

Dr. Narender Chinthamu, Senior Enterprise Architect at Wesco, MIT CTO Candidate

1 ChatGPT: Enabling human-like conversations and shaping the future of language processing

Spoorthy Torne and Phani Kumar Pullela[a]

School of Computer Science Engineering (SOCSE), RV University, RV Vidyanikethan Post, 8th Mile, Mysuru Road, Bengaluru, India

Abstract

In the past few weeks, OpenAI has released ChatGPT (Chat Generative Pre-trained Transformer). ChatGPT emerges as a formidable chatbot, surpassing various iterations of the GPT model, and plays a transformative role in user interactions with AI systems. In the dynamic realm of AI technologies, influential applications like ChatGPT, developed by OpenAI, mirror the transformative consideration of the simplicity on multiple facets of our daily lives. This potent technology holds the potential for significant positive changes, particularly in healthcare where the introduction of GPT and chatbot models opens promising avenues for disease treatment and technological innovation. However, the attention garnered by the introduction of OpenAI's GPT-3 and 4 raises concerns about potential manipulation and biases, given the presence of natural language processing modules and concern in certain domains due to hallucination. As we navigate the nuanced interplay between assistance and potential harm in society, the impact of ChatGPT models becomes a pivotal consideration. In essence, denoting "Generative Pre-trained Transformer," ChatGPT epitomizes a NLP software designed for engaging in human-like conversations with users.

Keywords: AIML, ChatGPT, networks, open AI, user interface, world data

Background

OpenAI has recently introduced ChatGPT (Chat Generative Pre-trained Transformer), a highly effective chatbot engineered to streamline user interactions with AI systems. Unlike previous iterations of GPT, ChatGPT stands out as a versatile tool applicable across a wide array of domains, ranging from app development and business generation to niche applications like wedding planning. In contrast to earlier models that technically handled such tasks but often fell short of human standards in output quality, ChatGPT represents a significant improvement. Functioning as a chatbot, ChatGPT enhances communication between users and AI systems, boasting the capability for domain-specific training, such as in customer service. The chatbots within ChatGPT engage users in conversations that closely resemble human interactions, producing text with a polished writing style. With chatbots playing an increasingly integral role in human interaction software, the significance of ChatGPT lies in its ability to comprehend and answer questions, acquire new knowledge, and explain concepts in simple terms tailored to users' comprehension levels.

Available to the public for free and also recognized as Chat with GPT 3.5, it signifies a milestone in natural language processing (NLP), leveraging a transformer-based architecture to comprehend language comprehensively and generate text more akin to human expression. Beyond just enhancing interactions, the application of ChatGPT extends to diverse job opportunities across sectors. Essentially, ChatGPT emulates a model that produces text mirroring human expression, deriving its value from user input and its extensive knowledge spanning various languages and translations. However, it's crucial to note that despite its success, ChatGPT lacks a complete understanding of its actions and hallucination is a concern due to its deep learning (DL) switch. Figure 1.1 shows that OpenAI has unveiled a chatbot designed to assist users in finding solutions to their problems, particularly in the realm of code debugging through the utilization of AI generators.

Prior Art

Generative AI heralds a transformative epoch, holding the promise to revolutionize journalism and media content creation. This article delves into the exploration of ChatGPT into this copyright concerned field. Serving as a text-based input-output system, ChatGPT employs machine learning to furnish precise responses to user queries. The initial stage entails an examination of the positive and constructive impact of ChatGPT in the educational space. The second stage scrutinizes its utility, personality, emotions, and ethical considerations. The third stage centers on educational implications, including issues such as cheating, lack of honesty, and manipulation.

[a]phanikumarp@rvu.edu.in

DOI: 10.1201/9781003534136-1

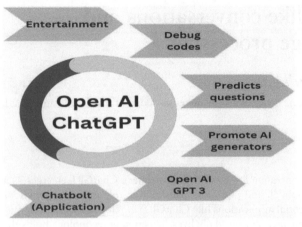

Figure 1.1 Uses and overview of the open AI-chatgpt

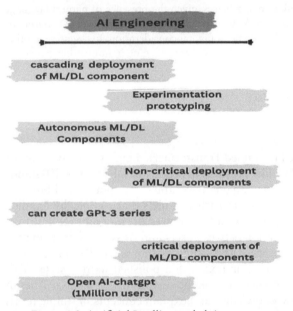

Figure 1.2 Artificial Intelligence helping to promote various components in research field

The researchers proffer recommendations aimed at ensuring the safe and responsible integration of chatbots in the student centric education space [1].

Machine learning (ML) should consider bias, as it can lead to incomplete predictions and strategic behavior by agents. In the case of facial recognition, "input completeness" shows that ML is biased and domain expertise is needed to find the most relevant prior art. This document also discusses vintage-specific skills and their implications for AI and the management of human capital for the benefit of ML in the future. The goal of this research study is to analyze the responsible and ethical usage of ChatGPT in education and to stimulate study and debate on this topic. Studies have found that the use of ChatGPT in the educational space should have its own privacy measures and should not discriminate original copyrighted authors. To manage the ethics in the worldwide education sector, responsible measures must be carried out [2].

In this study, the author analyzed tweets related to ChatGPT, an innovative chatbot that gained popularity after its launch. The study recorded nearly 233,914 tweets based on its question-and-answer algorithm. The study found three basic topics: news, technology, and reactions. Additionally, the author identified five functional domains, which include creativity, writing, and question answering. Finally, the author discussed four important issues that need to be addressed for AI advancement: the evolution of opportunities, technological remarks, the need for artificial intelligence, and the process of maintaining ethics [3]. Figure 1.2 shows that AI engineering is a field of research that is concerned with software engineering, machine learning in experimentation, prototyping, cascading, and deployment of machine learning.

Methods

The training of the model necessitates extensive interaction data and a vast collection of books. Notably, the GPT-3 model's advanced capabilities extend to writing code comparable to human programmers, positioning it as the most sought-after model in the current landscape. However, as with any technological marvel, GPT-3 presents a dual nature of advantages and limitations. Despite its exceptional performance, certain considerations arise. GPT-3 exhibits limitations in comprehending written content, occasionally resulting in the generation of inaccurate information. Secondly, the development of such sophisticated models requires a substantial volume of data, contributing to carbon dioxide emissions and water consumption from resource-intensive laboratory processes. The authors noted that the groundbreaking capabilities of GPT-3, it becomes imperative to address these challenges and limitations to responsibly harness its full potential. The ongoing refinement and ethical application of such models are essential for ensuring their positive impact across diverse domains [4].

The origins of the ChatGPT has roots with GPT-2 model that has even inspired two researchers to undertake free research aimed at curbing the harmful use of machine learning. To ensure that a model can provide correct responses, answers, and dialogues for better conversations, it must focus on the user's needs. Previous approaches to building such models required correct guidelines and architecture, which needed to be checked individually. However, such schemes don't make much of a difference for the betterment of the system, as they only focus on input-output data rather than overall development. These schemes should focus on other external systems to provide a particular and appropriate response and looks like at GPT 3.5, the Open AI has attained the same [5].

ChatGPT combines the GPT-2 model and transformer, which is based on a language model. It contains many language patterns that enable ChatGPT to interact with humans based on text conversation, such as in customer service. In recent years, AI technology has made considerable advancements and diligently developed in different sectors such as entertainment, education, health, and business. ChatGPT, an OpenAI model developed using GPT-3 technology, can be useful in these sectors [6]. Figure 1.3 shows that the GPT-3.5 model, is a software that was released in 2020. It uses deep learning to generate human-like text with hallucination capability to extend beyond the trained set knowledge.

Application

Research on conversation systems between humans and AI is a rapidly growing field, and open domain chatbots are becoming more popular. However, there are a significant number of challenges to overcome, such as personalization of chats and providing specific answers to certain conversations. AI also helps in different sectors like digital business, environmental health, and population. Interaction with GPT-3 helped to get a valid response, and the analysis suggests that AI helps us for better understanding and how it can be developed in future years. This study authors have observed that GPT-3 helps in every different sector of all studies in a positive way and will have a positive impact [7]. In this era, learning a foreign language has become very important. Parents want

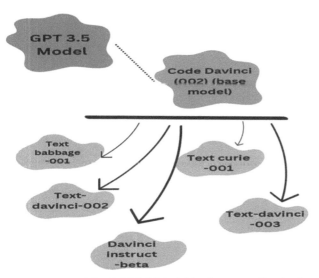

Figure 1.3 The GPT 3.5 Model (software application)

their children to learn foreign languages at an early age, and AI software is being developed to assist children in learning various languages perfectly. The software released to help learn languages includes augmented reality (AR) and ChatGPT, which are AI tools containing various language models. Seeing the potential of ChatGPT, it becomes easier to make such developments and help users learn different languages in an innovative and interactive way. Such advancements in AI software can help build software that effectively teaches a foreign language [8].

AI technology is advancing day by day, and it's playing an increasingly important role in the healthcare industry. Currently, one offers only human-to-human interactions in healthcare, but with the ultimate growth of GPT 3 or 3.5, there is potential for AI to play a greater role in detecting and diagnosing health problems. By developing GPT models specifically for healthcare, one can make it easier for patients to interact with AI and receive medical advice. It's important to bring advanced technologies like GPT 3.5 or 4 and chatbot models into the field of healthcare to effectively diagnose and treat diseases with no significant hallucination [9]. Figure 1.4 explains how ChatGPT can explain complex phenomena like quantum series in simple terms and has the capability to understand and remember conversations, but its limiting factor is that it sometimes contains wrong information.

Current Scenario

Mobile edge computing has helped overcome the issues related to cloud computing. Cloud computing helps to increase network bandwidth globally, which is required for generating software that involves the use of the IoT, AI, DL, ML, etc. However, any software that is used for positive purposes also has its limitations, including privacy, security, and advanced usage of such systems, which mainly leads to disadvantages. It's not only limited to computers or mobile devices for computing, but also to all AI systems including GPTs [10]. The societal impact of Chat GPT models presents a double-edged sword, giving rise to both advantageous and detrimental implications that raise questions about human autonomy and societal values. Effectively addressing these concerns involves the integration of ethical considerations into AI procedures, with the goal of generating language model outputs that are minimally susceptible to harm. The introduction of the OpenAI language model GPT-3.5 sparked significant enthusiasm, thanks to its incorporation of numerous natural language processing modules. However, a closer examination uncovers potential challenges such as manipulation and bias. The intricate nature of Chat GPT models introduces the possibility of both positive and negative consequences for society, underscoring the need for a thoughtful approach to ethical integration in AI processes. Prioritizing ethical considerations becomes essential as we navigate the landscape of potential impacts, allowing us to work towards mitigating the potentially destructive aspects of language model outputs. Hence, the security concerns for output generated through GPT increases with the newer models are launched [11].

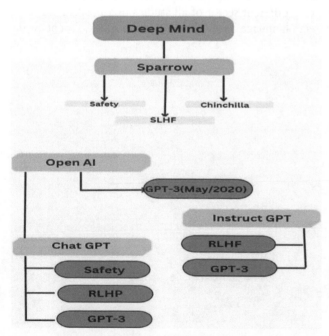

Figure 1.4 The Evolution of Chatgpt

The methods provided by artificial intelligence, such as chatbots and ChatGPT, for diagnosing diseases are not yet widely recognized. However, recent studies have shown that different methods given by ChatGPT for diagnosing diseases can be correct. In one case, ChatGPT's diagnosis list was found to be almost 93.3% accurate among 10 different diagnoses, while physicians had a higher accuracy rate of 98.3%. Nonetheless, the study clearly indicated that ChatGPT has the potential to provide better diagnosis lists if it can be improved in future years [12]. Figure 1.5 shows that GPT has several versions, and as time has passed, the AI has continued to update, including GPT-1, GPT-2, GPT-3, Instruct GPT, and ChatGPT. GPT-1 was introduced in 2018 with 117 million parameters, followed by GPT-2 in 2019 with 1.5 billion parameters, GPT-3 in 2020 with 175 billion parameters, Instruct GPT in 2022 with 13 billion parameters, and OpenAI released ChatGPT in 2022.

Future Scope- Newer Evolving Applications

Drug abuse has become a serious challenge in the United States, with over a few tens of thousands of cases recorded in 2020. While detecting these challenges using software is not yet recognized, some drug users share their experiences on the internet, providing a basis for building models that can detect spelling mistakes and other ways of talking that indicate drug abuse. GPT-3 has helped with detecting such mistakes and finding information related to drugs. When asked for the name of a drug, it provided nearly 269 synonyms for the word

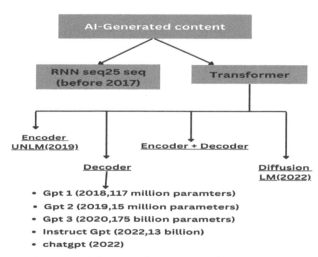

Figure 1.5 The Rise of AI Generated content (AIGC)

Figure 1.6 Some of the possibilities of ChatGPT

"alprazolam," of which 221 were new and not previously known. UBAR was built using GPT-2, a generative pre-trained transformer language model designed for conversation. According to the students who created it, UBAR has a fully generated dialogue system. It can provide real-world dialogue text and be used in multiple settings. UBAR's performance can be improved based on its responses, and it can be further developed by providing additional data for better visualization and modelling to enhance the dialog text level. Over the last 70 years, AI has undergone significant development, with advancements in both old AI prior to 2000 and new AI from 2000 onward. From its early beginnings to its current state, AI has progressed to the point where it has the potential to replace humans in many tasks. The future of AI is both amazing and fascinating, with numerous missions, visions, goals, and aims. OpenAI has also released DALL-E 2, which is an artificial intelligence ART generator. Figure **1.6** shows the limitless applications of these AI based systems in across research and technological domains.

Conclusion

ChatGPT is a powerful chatbot that enables communication between users and virtual AI systems. Although there are significantly different versions of GPT, ChatGPT has surpassed them all. However, there are both positive and negative impacts of AI on human lives. This study identifies four key issues that need to be addressed for AI advancement: the evolution of opportunities, technological remarks, the need for artificial intelligence, and the process to maintain ethics. OpenAI has generated many versions of GPT models, each with billions of parameters and this paper identified a few testaments of what is in store for industry and academia. Despite evolving technology in society, questions remain about how much further we can go with present technology wherein hallucination adds that bit of doubt in users' mind. Exploring generative pre-trained transformers from different aspects can help modify and improve every bit of data available in a resourceful manner. Many other fields can benefit from AI development, and the future of AI looks amazing and fascinating as it has many missions, visions, goals, and aims.

Acknowledgments

This research is funded by a student research grant from RV University through a Technical Communication course.

References

[1] Tlili, A., Shehata, B., Adarkwah, M. A., Bozkurt, A., Hickey, D. T., Huang, R., and Agyemang, B. (2023). What if the devil is my guardian angel: ChatGPT as a case study of using chatbots in education. *Smart Learning Environments*, 10, 15.

[2] Mhlanga, D. (2023). Open AI in education, the responsible and ethical use of ChatGPT towards lifelong learning. *Department of Artificial Intelligence*, 1, 1–19.

[3] Taecharungroj, V. (2023). What can ChatGPT Do?. *Big Data and Cognitive*, 7(1), 35.

[4] Zhang, M., and Li, J. (2021). A commentary of GPT-3 in MIT technology. *Fundamental Research*, 1(6), 831–833.

[5] Ham, D., Lee, J. G., Jang, Y., and Kim, K. E. (2020). End-to-end neural pipeline for goal-oriented dialogue systems using GPT-2. *ACL Anthology*, 58, 583–592.

[6] George, A. S., and George, A. H. (2023). A review of ChatGPT AI's impact on several business sectors. *Universal International Innovation*, 1, 9–23.

[7] Haluza, D., and Jungwirth, D. (2023). Artificial intelligence and ten societal megatrends: an exploratory study using GPT-3. *Systems*, 11(3), 120.

[8] Topsakal, O., and Topsakal, E. (2022). Framework for a foreign language teaching software for children utilizing AR, Voicebots and ChatGPT. *The Journal of Cognitive Systems*, 7(2), 33–38.

[9] Korngiebel, D. M., and Moone, S. D. (2021). Considering the possibilities and pitfalls of generative pre-trained transformer 3 (GPT-3) in healthcare delivery. *NPJ Digital Medicine*, 4, 93.

[10] Singh, A., Gutub, A., Roy, A., and Gutub, A. (2022). AI-based mobile edge computing for IoT: applications, challenges, and future scope. *Research Article-Computer Engineering and Computer Science*, 47, 9801–9831.

[11] Meyer, S., Elsweiler, D., Ludwig, B., Fernandez-Pichel, M., and Losada, D. E. (2022). Do we still need human assessors? prompt-based GPT-3 user simulation in conversational AI. *Association of Computing Machinery*, 8, 1–6.

[12] Hirosawa, T., Harada, Y., Yokose, M., Sakamoto, T., Kawamura, R., and Shimizu, T. (2023). Diagnostic accuracy of differential-diagnosis lists generated by generative pretrained transformer 3 chatbot for clinical vignettes with common chief complaints: a pilot study. *Enviornmental Research and Public Health*, 20(4), 3378

2 Revolutionizing modern agriculture: harnessing AI and IoT for sustainable hydroponic farming

Akshay B[a] and Phani Kumar Pullela

School of Computer Science Engineering (SOCSE), RV University, RV Vidyanikethan Post, 8th Mile, Mysuru Road, Bengaluru, India

Abstract

Modern agriculture confronts numerous obstacles such as food production that cannot be sustained, issues with food security, and the consequences of climate change. To tackle these problems effectively, contemporary farmers are embracing hydroponic farming combined with intelligent IoT systems. Hydroponics provides the ability to manage crop systems with precision, but for large-scale operations, continuous monitoring and control are essential, a function that is made possible through the use of IoT technology. This allows farmers to optimize the growth of plants remotely, ensuring maximum efficiency and yield. In this research, we explore the potential of AI and IoT in revolutionizing agriculture and examine different IoT- based solutions that are specifically tailored for hydroponics and aquaponics farming.

Keywords: Agriculture, hydroponics, IoT, remote monitoring of plant growth, remote sensing

Introduction to Challenges in the Agriculture Industry

In an era characterized by a prevalent obesity issue, the agriculture industry is confronted with a multitude of challenges, notably unsustainable food production and food security concerns. Furthermore, the daunting impact of climate change poses even more formidable obstacles for traditional soil farming practices. To surmount these challenges, modern farmers must leverage field environment data and adopt a more scientific approach to enable well- informed and timely decision-making. In this context, the integration of intelligent Internet of Things (IoT) systems and the adoption of hydroponic techniques hold great promise as viable solutions. Hydroponics, as a sustainable agricultural practice, has gained significant traction, particularly through the utilization of techniques like nutrient film technique (NFT) and deep-water culture. However, in large-scale hydroponic systems, monitoring plant growth and nutrient levels can be a challenging task. The implementation of IoT technology offers valuable assistance in addressing this challenge.

To achieve increased efficiency and environmental friendliness in agriculture, hydroponics stands out as a promising approach. Nevertheless, hydroponic farming poses unique challenges, particularly in the continuous monitoring of plant growth and nutrient levels. Addressing this issue IoT technology emerges as a reliable solution capable of providing regular monitoring and sensing of the hydroponic system. The advantages of incorporating IoT in hydroponics are manifold, including a reduction in the need for physical monitoring, optimization of growth and yield, and enhanced control over water and nutrient management, thereby reducing waste. The transformative potential of IoT technology extends to the entire agricultural landscape, with a particular impact on hydroponics. Figure 2.1 presents an overview of the operations of a smart farm, exemplifying the future of agriculture, which revolves around modern farming methods such as hydroponics and aquaponics, seamlessly integrated with cutting-edge technology. IoT emerges as a game-changer in agriculture, capable of fundamentally transforming the trajectory of the entire industry.

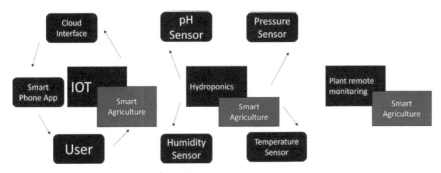

Figure 2.1 Smart Agriculture Process

[a]akshayb.btech22@rvu.edu.in

DOI: 10.1201/9781003534136-2

Role of IoT in Agriculture: Machine Learning Interaction and Intelligent Control

Precision agriculture, an ever-expanding field, is witnessing transformative changes with the integration of IoT and cloud computing technologies. Despite its potential, the adoption of precision agriculture has been limited to expensive scenarios. As a solution, this research focuses on catering to the requirements of soilless agriculture in closed greenhouses. The Cyber-Physical System (CPS) architecture collects data at the local layer and executes real-time controls, while the edge layer handles key precision agriculture tasks, working in tandem with CPS, and Next-Generation Information Technology (NGIT) facilitates cloud access bidirectionally. With growing concerns about climate change, population growth, and declining food production, IoT technologies, bolstered by sensors, big data analytics, and intelligent decision-making, offer viable solutions to enhance crop management and harvesting practices [1].

Greenhouse farming, characterized by controlled environments, demonstrates lower resource consumption and reduced emissions compared to conventional crop production. Monitoring greenhouse systems has garnered increased attention from researchers, and this paper presents a comparative study of current technologies and future trends. The utilization of deep learning and big data analytics enhances the automation of greenhouse monitoring and management, hydroponics and aquaponics, as innovative agricultural methods, enable soilless plant cultivation alongside fish farming. These techniques offer distinct advantages over traditional soil farming, including resistance to soil-borne infections, pests, and pesticides, as well as shortened plant growth cycles. Moreover, they are resilient in challenging environments such as deserts, extreme temperatures, and remain unaffected by climate changes. The integration of IoT technologies further enhances their suit- ability for home and commercial applications. This paper provides a comprehensive examination of hydroponics and aquaponics farming to establish a global perspective on both methodologies [2]. Figure 2.2 depicts the operation of a fundamental IoT-enabled smart farm, with a centralized controller managing multiple components efficiently. Sensors relay data to a router, which stores information in a cloud server accessible remotely by users, allowing them to visualize and analyze the data effectively. Overall, the amalgamation of IoT, cloud computing, and sustainable farming techniques shows great promise in revolutionizing precision agriculture, improving resource efficiency, and addressing the challenges posed by climate change and population growth.

The Potential of AI and IoT in Modernizing Agriculture

Hydroponics has emerged as an efficacious agricultural method that effectively meets diverse human needs. Embracing the Internet of Things (IoT) envisions a connected world where every object, including agricultural systems, can be linked and controlled through the internet. The incorporation of mobile computing technologies assumes significant importance as methodologies for data analytics and visualization. In this paper, we demonstrate the use of IoT and iOS applications for efficient data gathering and analysis, integrating plotly and data analytics to create the "HydroiOT" system. This system proves invaluable in alerting the farm manager during unfavorable conditions, facilitating informed decision-making to enhance productivity. Smart farming, enabled by IoT, revolves around the production process achieved through accessing and connecting various devices. Achieving self- sustainable production, driven by data analytics, is crucial, and merely relying on internet support is insufficient. We present a process utilizing Bayesian network sensors to monitor multiple parameters,

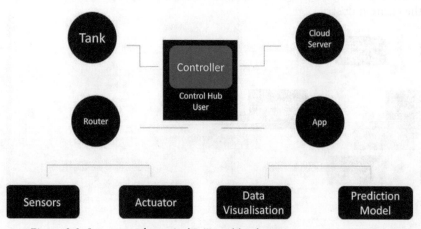

Figure 2.2 Structure of a typical IoT enables farm

where data collected from sensors predicts values for the actuator to enable farm operations. Our model achieves an impressive accuracy of 84.53 percentage [3].

Cultivating certain plants in extreme weather conditions, such as deserts or polar regions, poses considerable challenges. Rather than depending on the outside climate, we propose an IoT network for enhanced remote monitoring. The user simply plants seedlings and configures initial procedures, allowing the system to autonomously maintain parameters and promote healthy plant growth. Hydroponics cultivation offers a promising solution to address environmental and food-related issues by reducing fertilizer and water consumption while ensuring precise nutrient monitoring. To achieve this, we de- signed electrodes as sensors and integrated IoT technology for precise monitoring. Our review focuses on parameter accuracy and IoT application, highlighting that the required concentrations of nitrate and potassium can be effectively maintained using a polyvinyl chloride membrane-based electrode, keeping errors below 10 mg [4].

This paper presents an innovative approach to crop monitoring, utilizing solar energy. Given that agriculture contributes 18 percentage to India's GDP, there is a need for continued development and research in this sector. Technology plays a vital role in reducing human effort and time, as demonstrated in our system utilizing a combination of power electronics and power system I, with real-time data transmission to users using GSM technology [5]. Figure 2.3 illustrates the operation of a smart farm, where high-performance microcontrollers efficiently manage farm components. The connections between various tanks are effectively monitored and controlled by the computer system, with data analysis performed and transmitted to users. This research showcases the transformative potential of IoT and its applications in agriculture, particularly in the context of hydroponics and smart farming. These advancements hold promise for enhancing productivity, sustainability, and remote monitoring in agriculture, contributing to global food security and environmental preservation.

Monitoring Plant Growth Factors with IoT in Farming

Modern agricultural practices demand innovative techniques, including soilless cultivation methods like hydroponics and aquaponics. As the popularity of these methods rises, researchers have delved into the application of machine learning networks such as neural networks and Bayesian networks to control and optimize plant growth. In this context, the development of an intelligent IoT system based on hydroponics, employing deep neural network technology, represents a pioneering implementation. The system utilizes a prototype for tomato plant growth, integrating Arduino, Raspberry Pi 3, and Tensor Flow. IoT technology emerges as a viable solution for regular and periodic monitoring of plants' water and nutrition requirements. This paper proposes an agriculture- based approach using IoT systems and Fuzzy logic [6]. Temperature and humidity are crucial factors influencing plant growth. Leveraging IoT for plant growth control and notifications can significantly improve crop treatment. The paper emphasizes IoT's role in managing plant growth factors to prevent inadequate growth or withering, providing timely alerts to farmers and assisting in mitigating crop malnutrition and plant damage. Hydroponics, a soilless farming method that meets plant nutritional needs using water media mixed with nutrients, offers superior efficiency compared to soil- based cultivation systems. Particularly suitable for limited spaces like urban homes, hydroponic systems can be remotely observed, harmonizing with urban residents' daily activities. IoT technology facilitates remote observations, reporting data directly to the Internet, alleviating the need for periodic observations related to temperature, water, and pH [7].

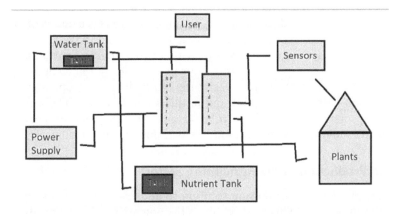

Figure 2.3 Applications of IDS

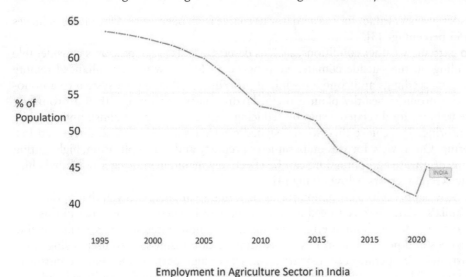

Employment in Agriculture Sector in India

Figure 2.4 Trend of agriculture sector in India

As large-scale IoT applications are increasingly adopted, significant infrastructure requirements come into play. This paper investigates the infrastructure prerequisites for constructing modular indoor vertical farming systems. Figure 2.4 illustrates a concerning decline in employment within the agricultural sector, which may adversely impact food security. To address this issue, automated large-scale precision farming emerges as a promising solution, minimizing human labor requirements and facilitating large-scale operation with minimal physical intervention.

Current Scenario of IoT in Agricultural System

India's rapidly growing food demand, projected to reach 1.6 billion people by 2050, has spurred increasing attention to smart technologies like data analytics, robotics, and IoT in the domain of stream-controlled environment agriculture. This article conducts a comprehensive review of existing literature, with a specific focus on soilless hydroponics as a technique within this domain. The review encompasses studies and research conducted between 1999 and 2020, highlighting different types of sensors used in soilless agriculture and enumerating their advantages. Moreover, the article discusses the potential for individuals to grow fruits and vegetables in their own homes without soil [8]. Technological advancements offer myriad solutions to modernize agriculture, with scientific research groups actively competing in this space. Cloud and Fog computing provide ample resources and solutions for data storage and analysis, enabling automation and prediction of processes. IoT's influence is expected to significantly benefit the agriculture sector, which has already experienced considerable impact from wireless sensor network technologies. The article presents a survey of recent IoT technology and its current penetration in the agriculture sector, along with an exploration of potential future value for farmers and the challenges they may encounter in its adoption [9].

Addressing the pressing need for water management due to prevailing water scarcity, the article highlights the significance of ensuring water availability for food production and consumption. However, the cost of commercial sensors may prove prohibitive for small-scale farmers. To overcome this challenge, advancements in IoT and wireless sensor networks (WSN) are being leveraged to develop cost-effective smart irrigation systems. The article provides a comprehensive survey of the current state-of-the-art in smart irrigation technology [10]. Aquaponics, as a sustainable agricultural practice integrating aquaculture and hydroponics, operates in a symbiotic manner, offering healthy organic food with reduced water and fertilizer consumption. The article emphasizes the importance of IoT in facilitating smart sensing and control operations in aquaponic systems. It investigates and highlights various relevant factors involved in the automatic functioning of such systems [11].

Potential for Improving Crop Quality and Production in the Agriculture Sector

Hydroponics, a soilless agricultural technique, emerges as a promising solution to address various challenges, including climate change, water scarcity, and food demand. This method offers the potential to locally produce fresh and residue- free vegetables and fruits, ensuring a healthy food supply. The paper delves into the numerous benefits of hydroponics, shedding light on the expertise required for successful implementation. Hydroponic farming presents a suitable alternative for regions facing soil degradation and limited water resources. Unlike traditional soil-based farming, hydroponics overcomes specific challenges. This paper thoroughly examines the advantages and limitations of hydroponics, including easy management, weed-free growth, and reduced water spraying requirements [12]. Agriculture plays a significant role in the global economy, but with the increasing demand of a growing population, traditional farming methods are insufficient to meet the requirements. To address this challenge, emerging agricultural intelligence practices, often referred to as Agriculture 4.0, are gaining traction. Leveraging technologies such as Artificial Intelligence (AI) and IoT, smart farming solutions optimize resource usage, reduce labor, and enhance crop monitoring and management. These technologies have demonstrated their efficacy in crop protection against various threats. Figure 2.5 states the applications of IOT in smart agriculture. Efficient and precise farming systems are essential for improving agricultural activities. Operating farm management systems over the Internet poses challenges in handling numerous network devices and integrating diverse systems. This paper introduces farm management system architecture, comprising software modules that demonstrate its functioning and analytical capabilities. Sustainable agricultural development necessitates robust infrastructure and advanced technologies to enhance crop quality and production. Hydroponics, a soilless cultivation technique, emerges as a suitable approach, and the paper discusses the latest advancements in IoT technology that effectively support efficient hydroponics systems. IoT provides a sustainable approach, leveraging various technologies such as sensors and other tools to optimize crop production processes. Figure 2.6 provides a glimpse of the promising future of IoT farming with the integration of machine

Parameter	IoT Application
Alarming System	Monitoring critical parameters such as temperature, humidity, pH levels, nutrient levels, and water levels using sensors.
Data Analytics	Applying statistical analysis techniques to sensor data for identifying patterns and trends.
Precision farming	Precision farming utilizes IoT technology, data analytics, and automation to optimize agricultural practices, maximize crop yields, and minimize resource wastage.
Precision farming	Precision farming utilizes IoT technology, data analytics, and automation to optimize agricultural practices, maximize crop yields, and minimize resource wastage.

Figure 2.5 Application of IoT in Smart Agriculture

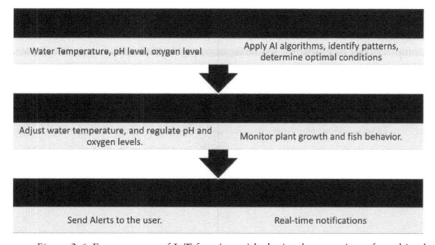

Figure 2.6 Future scope of IoT farming with the implementation of machine learning

learning. It illustrates the deployment of IoT sensors throughout the farm, collecting real-time data transmitted for analysis. Machine learning algorithms offer valuable insights, such as predictive analytics for yield estimation and disease detection. Automation plays a pivotal role, enabling automated irrigation and autonomous machinery to boost productivity. Through mobile applications, farmers can remotely monitor their farms and make data- driven decisions, optimizing resource utilization, promoting sustainability, and driving increased efficiency in farming practices.

Conclusion

Hydroponics and aquaponics farming present promising solutions to address agricultural challenges. These innovative farming methods enable farmers to optimize plant growth and nutrient delivery, leading to reduced waste and enhanced efficiency. Consequently, these practices contribute to higher productivity and resource conservation. As the agriculture industry grapples with the effects of climate change and population growth, the integration of IoT-based precision agriculture holds the potential to foster sustainability and ensure sufficient food production for the future.

Acknowledgement

This study is financially supported by a student research grant obtained from RV University within the framework of a Technical Communication course.

References

[1] Rayhana, R. (2020). Internet of things empowered smart greenhouse farming. *IEEE Journal of Radio Frequency Identification*, 4, 195–211.

[2] Ezzahoui, I. (2021). Hydroponic and aquaponic farming: comparative study based on internet of things IoT technologies. *Procedia Computer Science*, 191, 499–504.

[3] Alipio, M. I. (2019). On the design of nutrient film technique hydroponics farm for smart agriculture. *Engineering in Agriculture, Environment and Food*, 12(3), 315–324.

[4] Richa, A. (2021). Advanced monitoring of hydroponic solutions using ion- selective electrodes and the internet of things: a review. *Environmental Chemistry Letters*, 19, 3445–3463.

[5] Kumar, A. (2022). IoT enabled the system to monitor and control greenhouse. *Materials Today: Proceedings*, 49, 3137–3141.

[6] Maravillas, E. (2018). IoT hydroponics management system. In 10th International Conference on Humanoid, Nanotechnology, Information Technology, Communication and Control, Environment and Management, (vol. 1, pp. 1–5).

[7] Lukito, R. B. (2019). Development of IoT at the hydroponic system using Raspberry Pi. *TELKOMNIKA (Telecommunication Computing Electronics and Control)*, 17(2), 897–906.

[8] Ragaveena, S. (2021). Smart controlled environment agriculture methods: a holistic review. *Reviews in Environmental Science and Bio/Technology*, 20, 887–913.

[9] Tzounis, A. (2017). Internet of things in agriculture, recent advances and future challenges. Biosystems Engineering, 164, 31–48.

[10] Garc´ıa, L. (2020). IoT-based smart irrigation systems: an overview on the recent trends on sensors and IoT systems for irrigation in precision agriculture. *Surveys of Sensor Networks and Sensor Systems Deployments*, 20, 14–20.

[11] Taha, M. F. (2022). Recent advances of smart systems and internet of things (IoT) for aquaponics automation: a comprehensive overview. *Chemosensors*, 10, 303.

[12] Kannan, M. (2022). Hydroponic farming – a state of the art for the future agriculture. *Materials Today: Proceedings*, 68, 2163–2166.

3 Distance measure between picture fuzzy sets and its applications in multi-attribute decision-making

Rozy[a] and Satish Kumar

Department of Mathematics, Maharishi Markandeshwar (Deemed To Be University), Mullana-Ambala, India

Abstract

Picture fuzzy sets (PFSs), initially proposed by Cuong and Kreinovich, are more effective than intuitionistic fuzzy sets (IFSs) to hold the indefiniteness in real-life problems. This paper introduces distance measure between PFSs. The purpose of this study is to present a distance measure for PFSs with a confirmation of its validity and to discuss its key characteristics. The proposed distance measure is also used in machine learning decision-making processes like multi-attribute decision-making. The numerical examples demonstrate how well the developed approach solves actual situations.

Keywords: Distance measure, fuzzy set, inferior ratio method and MADM, intuitionistic fuzzy sets, picture fuzzy set

Introduction

An analysis between the two distinct objects from various points is required to address a variety of real-world issues related to image processing, machine learning, pattern identification, and decision-making among other things. Different studies used different contrasting measures depending on the type of problem. The terms "similarity measure," "distance measure," "correlation measure," etc. are commonly used in compatibility and comparability studies. It is important to discuss the notable studies about the advancements and uses of the FSs and IFSs because the PFS is a modification of FS and IFS. Zadeh [11] first introduced the fuzzy set (FS) theory. Fuzzy set theory deals with membership degree taking value lying between zero and one. Atanassov [1] introduced IFSs, which measure both membership and non-membership degree. However, IFSs do not deal with the neutral degree. Let's examine a real-world situation. There are social groupings that support, oppose, or remain neutral on any decision during the time for voting. However, there is still another segment of society that abstains from voting. To solve these types of problems, Cuong and Kreinovich [2] suggested the concept of PFSs, which deals with membership, non-membership, and neutral degree, under the situation that the sum of all these degree should be less than and equal to one.

For new achievements, distance measure for picture fuzzy sets (PFSs) is presented in this paper. Both distance and similarity measures are important concepts for solving real-life problems like decision-making [3–10]. The TOPSIS technique suggests that the final alternative be the one that is both the farthest from the negative ideal solution (NIS) and the closest to the positive ideal solution (PIS). TOPSIS was expanded to the fuzzy environment by Chen [3]. The MADM technique is employed to find the best alternatives from multiple decision alternatives. Zhang et al. [10] presented the EDAS technique for MADM in the PF domain. Jana et al. [4] suggested Dombi aggregation operators in the PF environment and their use in MADM. Singh and Kumar [12] developed the VIKOR approach for addressing MADM.

The current work is related to the research of PF- distance measure. Main contribution of this paper is given below:

To deal with MADM problems, we propose a distance measure for picture fuzzy set. By using the PF-distance measure, we introduce a picture fuzzy inferior ratio approach based on the TOPSIS technique. Some numerical examples are used that demonstrate the suggested MADM technique to overcome the drawback of the existing TOPSIS method in the domain of PFSs. We extend the TOPSIS method in terms of the inferior ratio method.

Rest of the paper is structured as follows:

In section 2, some basic fundamentals of FSs, IFSs, and PFSs are presented. Section 3, introduces a distance measure and describes its characteristics. In section 4, we illustrate the MADM approach. Comparative analysis is also shown to give the effectiveness of the suggested measure. Section 5 covers the conclusion and the future scope.

[a]rozygura93@gmail.com

DOI: 10.1201/9781003534136-3

Preliminaries

Definition 2.1 (Zadeh [11]). A FSQ in a finite universe set $K = \{m_1, m_2,..., m_q\}$ is defined as:

$$Q = \{(m_z, s_Q(m_z)) \mid m_z \in K\}, z = 1, 2,..., q, \tag{2.1}$$

where $S_Q(m_z) \in [0,1]$ is the membership degree of the element m_z in the set Q. For convenience, Zadeh [11] called $S_Q(m_z)$ a fuzzy number (FN) denoted by $l = (S_l)$.

Definition 2.2 (Atanassov [1]). An IFS B in a finite universe set $K = \{m_1, m_2,..., m_q\}$ is defined as:

$$B = \{(m_z, s_I(m_z), e_I(m_z)) \mid m_z \in K\}, z = 1, 2,..., q \tag{2.2}$$

where $S_Q(m_z) \in [0,1]$ is the membership degree and $e_B(m_z) \in [0,1]$ is the non-membership degree of element m_z in the set B. Here, $0 \le S_B(m_z) + e_B(m_z) \le 1$ for all $m_z \in K$. For $m_z \in K$, $Y_Q(m_z) = 1 - S_B(m_z) - e_B(m_z)$ defined as degree of hesitancy of m_z in B. For convenience, Atanassov [1] called $(S_B(m_z), e_B(m_z))$ an intuitionistic fuzzy number (IFN) denoted by $t = (s_t, e_t)$.

Definition 2.3 (Cuong and Kreinovich [2]). A picture fuzzy set I in a finite universe set $K = \{m_1, m_2,..., m_q\}$ is defined as:

$$I = \{(m_z, s_I(m_z), g_I(m_z), e_I(m_z)) \mid m_z \in K\}, z = 1, 2,..., q, \tag{2.3}$$

where $S_I(m_z) \in [0,1]$ is the membership degree, $g_I(m_z) \in [0,1]$ is the neutral degree and $e_I(m_z) \in [0,1]$ is the non-membership degree of the element m_z in the set I, here $0 \le S_I(m_z) + e_I(m_z) - g_I(m_z) \le 1$.

For $m_z \in K$, $\kappa_I(m_z) = 1 - s_I(m_z) - g_I(m_z) - e_I(m_z)$ is defined as refusal degree of I of m_z in I. Knowledge about m_z is more certain if κ_I has a small value. On the other hand, knowledge about m_z is more uncertain, if the value of κ_I is great. For convenience, Cuong and Kreinovich [2] called $(s_I(m_z), g_I(m_z), e_I(m_z))$ a picture fuzzy number (PFN) denoted by $i = (s_i, g_i, e_i)$.

If the neutral degree (g_I) is equal to zero, then PFS becomes IFS and when both non-membership degree (e_I), neutral degree (g_I) equal to zero, then PFS becomes FS. The integration of the neutral degree g_I determines the detail of objects more precisely and improves the quality and validity of outcomes (Son [6]).

Definition 2.4 (Cuong and Kreinovich [2]). If K contains two picture fuzzy sets, I and W, then different operations are defined as follows:

1. $I^c = \{(m_z, e_I(m_z), g_I(m_z), s_I(m_z)) \mid m_z \in K\}, z = 1, 2,..q$.
2. $I \subseteq W$, if $s_I(m_z) \le s_W(m_z)$, $g_I(m_z) \le g_W(m_z)$, $e_I(m_z) \ge e_W(m_z)$, $\forall \ m_z \in K$.
3. $I \cup W = \{(m_z, \max(s_I(m_z), s_W(m_z)), \min(g_I(m_z), g_W(m_z)), \min(e_I(m_z), e_W(m_z))) \mid m_z \in K\}$
4. $I \cap W = \{(m_z, \min(s_I(m_z), s_W(m_z)), \min(g_I(m_z), g_W(m_z)), \max(e_I(m_z), e_W(m_z))) \mid m_z \in K\}$

Definition 2.5 (Son [6]). A function $DM : PFS(K) \times PFS(K) \to [0,1]$ with I, W and $Q \in PFS(K)$ is defined a distance measure, if it holds the criteria given below:

1. $0 \le DM(I, W) \le 1$.
2. $DM(I, W) = DM(W, I)$.
3. $DM(I, I) = 0$.
4. If $I \subseteq W \subseteq Q$, then $DM(I, Q) \ge DM(I, W)$ and $DM(I, Q) \ge DM(W, Q)$.

Proposed Distance Measure for Picture Fuzzy Sets

This section introduces a new PF distance measure and provides evidence for its reliability. Let $I = \{m_z, s_I(m_z), g_I(m_z), e_I(m_z) \mid m_z \in K\}$ and $W = \{m_z, s_W(m_z), g_W(m_z), e_W(m_z) \mid m_z \in K\}$ be two PFSs, then the suggested distance measure for PFSs is given below:

Definition 3.1 Let $K = \{m_1, m_2, ..., m_q\}$ be a finite universe set. For $I, W \in PFS(K)$, we define distance measure D^* as

$$D^*(I,W) = \frac{1}{q}\sum_{z=1}^{q} \left[\frac{2(|s_I(m_z)-s_W(m_z)|+|e_I(m_z)-e_W(m_z)|+|g_I(m_z)-g_W(m_z)|+}{4+|s_I(m_z)-s_W(m_z)|+|e_I(m_z)-e_W(m_z)|+|g_I(m_z)-g_W(m_z)|+|} \right] \quad (3.1)$$

Theorem 3.2. Measure D^* is fulfil the following characteristics:

1. $0 \le D^*(I,W) \le 1$.
2. $D^*(I,W) = D^*(W,I)$
3. $D^*(I,I) = 0$.
4. If $I \subseteq W \subseteq Q$, then $D^*(I,Q) \ge D^*(I,W)$ and $D^*(I,Q) \ge D^*(W,Q)$.

Proof.

1. For $I,W \in PFS(K)$, it is clear that $0 \le |s_I - s_W|, |g_I - g_W|, |e_I - e_W|, |\kappa_I - \kappa_W| \le 1$.

   This implies that $0 \le |s_I - s_W| + |g_I - g_W| + |e_I - e_W| + |\kappa_I - \kappa_W| \le 4$. This implies that

   $$0 \le \left[\frac{2(|s_I(m_z)-s_W(m_z)|+|e_I(m_z)-e_W(m_z)|+|g_I(m_z)-g_W(m_z)|+|\kappa_I(m_z)-\kappa_W(m_z)|)}{4+|s_I(m_z)-s_W(m_z)|+|e_I(m_z)-e_W(m_z)|+|g_I(m_z)-g_W(m_z)|+|\kappa_I(m_z)-\kappa_W(m_z)|} \right] \le 1.$$

   Taking sum both sides and we get $0 \le D^*(I,W) \le 1$.
2. It is obvious.
3. It is obvious.
4. Consider $I,W,Q \in PFS(K)$, such that $I \subseteq W \subseteq Q$, then $s_I(m_z) \le s_W(m_z) \le s_Q(m_z)$, $g_I(m_z) \le g_W(m_z) \le g_Q(m_z)$, $e_I(m_z) \ge e_W(m_z) \ge e_Q(m_z)$.

   So, we have

   $$|s_I(m_z)-s_W(m_z)| \le |s_I(m_z)-s_Q(m_z)|, |s_W(m_z)-s_Q(m_z)| \le |s_I(m_z)-s_Q(m_z)|,$$

   $$|g_I(m_z)-g_W(m_z)| \le |g_I(m_z)-g_Q(m_z)|, |g_W(m_z)-g_Q(m_z)| \le |g_I(m_z)-g_Q(m_z)|,$$

   $$|e_I(m_z)-e_W(m_z)| \le |e_I(m_z)-e_Q(m_z)|, |e_W(m_z)-e_Q(m_z)| \le |e_I(m_z)-e_Q(m_z)|.$$

   $$|\kappa_I(m_z)-\kappa_W(m_z)| \le |\kappa_I(m_z)-\kappa_Q(m_z)|, |\kappa_W(m_z)-\kappa_Q(m_z)| \le |\kappa_I(m_z)-\kappa_Q(m_z)|.$$

   Hence, $D^*(I,Q) \ge D^*(I,W)$ and $D^*(I,Q) \ge D^*(W,Q)$.

Properties

Next, we define a novel weighted distance measure for PFS as follows, if we apply a weight vector l_z, $z = 1, 2, ..., q$ such that $\sum_{z=1}^{q} l_z = 1$:

Definition 3.3 For given $K = \{m_1, m_2, ..., m_q\}$ and $I, W \in PFS(K)$, a weighted distance measure $(D^*)^{l_z} : PFS(K) \times PFS(K) \to [0,1]$ is defined as follows:

$$(D^*)^{l_z}(I,W) = \sum_{z=1}^{q} l_z \left[\frac{2(|s_I(m_z)-s_W(m_z)|+|e_I(m_z)-e_W(m_z)|+|g_I(m_z)-g_W(m_z)|+}{4+|s_I(m_z)-s_W(m_z)|+|e_I(m_z)-e_W(m_z)|+|g_I(m_z)-g_W(m_z)|+|} \right]$$

Theorem 3.4 $(D^*)^{l_z}(I,W)$ is the degree of the distance between the PFSs I and W in $K = \{m_1, m_2, ..., m_q\}$ satisfies following characteristics:

1. $0 \le (D^*)^{l_z}(I,W) \le 1$.
2. $(D^*)^{l_z}(I,W) = (D^*)^{l_z}(W,I)$.
3. $(D^*)^{l_z}(I,I) = 0$.
4. If $I \subseteq W \subseteq Q$, then $(D^*)^{l_z}(I,Q) \ge (D^*)^{l_z}(I,W)$ and $(D^*)^{l_z}(I,Q) \ge (D^*)^{l_z}(W,Q)$.

Proof.

The proof of this Theorem is comparable with the proof of Theorem (3.2), when $l_z = \frac{1}{q}$ for $z = 1, 2, ..., q$ then, $(D^*)^z(I, W)$ is identical to $D^*(I, W)$.

Theorem 3.5 Some other properties of D^* as follows:

1. $D^*(I, W) = D^*(I^C, W^C)$.

2. $D^*(I, W^C) = D^*(I^C, W)$.

3. $D^*(I, I^C) = 0 \Leftrightarrow s_I = e_I$.

4. $\frac{3}{2}D^*(I, I^C) = 1 \Leftrightarrow I$

Proof.

1. We have

$$D^*(I,W) = \frac{1}{q}\sum_{z=1}^{q}\left[\frac{2(|s_I(m_z) - s_W(m_z)| + |e_I(m_z) - e_W(m_z)| + |g_I(m_z) - g_W(m_z)| + |\kappa_I(m_z) - \kappa_W(m_z)|)}{4 + |s_I(m_z) - s_W(m_z)| + |e_I(m_z) - e_W(m_z)| + |g_I(m_z) - g_W(m_z)| + |\kappa_I(m_z) - \kappa_W(m_z)|}\right]$$

$$= \frac{1}{q}\sum_{z=1}^{q}\left[\frac{2(|e_I(m_z) - e_W(m_z)| + |s_I(m_z) - s_W(m_z)| + |g_I(m_z) - g_W(m_z)| + |\kappa_I(m_z) - \kappa_W(m_z)|)}{4 + |s_I(m_z) - s_W(m_z)| + |e_I(m_z) - e_W(m_z)| + |g_I(m_z) - g_W(m_z)| + |\kappa_I(m_z) - \kappa_W(m_z)|}\right]$$

$$= D^*(I^C, W^C).$$

$$D^*(I,W^C) = \frac{1}{q}\sum_{z=1}^{q}\left[\frac{2(|s_I(m_z) - e_W(m_z)| + |e_I(m_z) - s_W(m_z)| + |g_I(m_z) - g_W(m_z)| + |\kappa_I(m_z) - \kappa_w(m_z)|)}{4 + |s_I(m_z) - e_W(m_z)| + |e_I(m_z) - s_W(m_z)| + |g_I(m_z) - g_W(m_z)| + |\kappa_I(m_z) - \kappa_w(m_z)|}\right]$$

$$= D^*(I^C, W).$$

2. It is obvious.
3. It is obvious.

Picture Fuzzy Inferior Ration Approach for MADM

A new method is presented to make a suitable decision considering all available alternatives and attributes using distance measure.

   Framework: We are provided a collection of r alternatives $T_m (m = 1, 2, ..., r)$ and p attributes $S_q(q = 1, 2, ..., p)$, as well as attribute weight vector, $l = (l_1, l_2, ..., l_q)$, $0 \le l_q \le 1$, $(q = 1, 2, ..., p)$ and $\sum_{q=1}^{p} l_q = 1$

   Target: To select the optimum alternative.

   The algorithm for determining the best alternative is presented below:

Algorithm

S1: Create the picture fuzzy (PF) decision matrix $\chi = [\chi_{mq}]_{r\times p}$, where $\chi_{mq} = (s_{mq}, g_{mq}, e_{mq})$ is picture fuzzy number (PFN) and S_{mq} is the membership value of alternative (option). Alternative T_m's non-membership value is e_{mq} and T_m's neutrality value is g_{mq}.

   S2: Generate the normalized picture fuzzy (PF) decision matrix $\beta = [\omega_{mq}]_{r\times p}$, where

$$\omega_{mq} = \begin{cases} \chi_{mq} = (s_{mq}, g_{mq}, e_{mq}), & \text{for good attribute} \\ (\chi_{mq})^c = (e_{mq}, g_{mq}, s_{mq}), & \text{for value attribute.} \end{cases} \tag{7.1}$$

S3: PFPIS I^+ and PFNIS I^-, where

$I^+ = \{\omega_1^+, \omega_2^+, ..., \omega_p^+\}$ and

$I^- = \{\omega_1^-, \omega_2^-, ..., \omega_p^-\}$ and

$\omega_q^+ = \{\max_m(s_{mq}), \min_m(g_{mq}), \min_m(e_{mq})\}$ and

$\omega_q^- = \{\min_m(s_{mq}), \min_m(g_{mq}), \max_m(e_{mq})\}$, $m = 1, 2, ..., r$ and $q = 1, 2, ..., p$.

S4: Estimate the length of every alternative T_m, $m = 1, 2, ..., r$ from PFPIS I^+ and PFNIS I^- utilizing the proposed measure D^* i.e. compute $D^*(T_m, I^+)$ and $D^*(T_m, I^-)$, $m = 1, 2, ..., r$. The better T_m is smaller the $D^*(T_m, I^+)$ and bigger the $D^*(T_m, I^-)$.

S5: Calculate $D^*(I^+)$, where $D^*(I^+) = \min_{1 \leq m \leq r}(D^*(T_m, T^+))$ and alternative T_m that fulfils $D^*(I^+) = D^*(T_m, I^+)$ is one that is closed to PFPIS.

S6: Calculate $D^*(I^-)$, where $D^*(I^-) = \max_{1 \leq m \leq r}(D^*(T_m, I^-))$, and the alternative T_m that fulfils $D^*(I^-) = D^*(T_m, I^-)$ is furthest from PFNIS.

S7: For each alternative, calculate $\varphi(T_m)$, $m = 1, 2, ..., r$, where

$$\varphi(T_m) = \frac{D^*(T_m, I^-)}{D^*(I^-)} - \frac{D^*(T_m, I^+)}{D^*(I^+)}$$

Clearly $\varphi(T_m)$ indicates how close an alternative T_m, $m = 1, 2, ..., r$ is to PFPIS while also being the furthest away from PFNIS. The optimum option is T_m with $\varphi(T_m) = 0$.

S8: For each alternative, calculate the picture fuzzy inferior ratio (PFIR) $\mho_m$ given below:

$$\mho_m = \frac{\varphi(T_m)}{\min_{1 \leq m \leq r} \varphi(T_m)}.$$

S9: Rank the alternatives T_m, according to rising order of $\mho_m$.

A numerical example is used to solve the MADM approach by taking proposed picture fuzzy inferior ratio (PFIR) approach, which is **given below:**

Example 4.1 An individual wishes to invest a certain amount of money. Four attributes are S_1: real estate, S_2: mutual funds, S_3: health insurance, S_4: fixed maturity plans. Experts choose best option from the five options T_1: fair pricing, T_2: less cost, T_3: simple returns, T_4: earn additional income, T_5: best inflation. Experts provide an assessment of the 5 options T_m, $m = 1, 2, 3, 4, 5$ keep in touch to the 4 attributes S_q, $q = 1, 2, 3, 4$ in the type of picture fuzzy (PF) decision matrix, as illustrated through Table 3.1.

S3 is used to calculate PFPIS I^+ and PFNIS I^-, as shown below:

$I^+ = \{(0.89, 0.08, 0.03), (0.42, 0.35, 0.05), (0.73, 0.06, 0.02), (0.85, 0.05, 0.02)\}$

$I^- = \{(0.23, 0.08, 0.21), (0.02, 0.35, 0.18), (0.08, 0.06, 0.84), (0.43, 0.05, 0.25)\}$.

Distance of every alternative T_m, $m = 1, 2, 3, 4, 5$ with PFPIS I^- and PFNIS I^-, is subsequently calculated using the suggested picture fuzzy distance measure D^* given in equation (3.1). Then, calculate $D^*(I^+) = \min_{1 \leq i \leq n}(D^*(T_m, I^+)) = 0.2082$ and $D^*(I^-) = \max_{1 \leq i \leq n}(D^*(T_m, I^-)) = 0.4324$. Then, using S7 and S8, compute $\varphi(T_m)$ and $\mho_m$ for every alternative. Finally, we rank the possibilities in rising sequence of $\mho_m$.

Table 3.2, shows that T_1 is the best alternate and that T_1 is the closest to PFPIS I^+ while also being the furthest away from PFNIS I-.

Table 3.1 PF-decision matrix

	S_1	S_2	S_3	S_4
T_1	(0.89,0.08,0.03)	(0.42,0.35,0.18)	(0.08,0.89,0.02)	(0.80,0.11,0.05)
T_2	(0.23,0.64,0.11)	(0.03,0.82,0.13)	(0.73,0.15,0.08)	(0.73,0.10,0.14)
T_3	(0.52,0.26,0.05)	(0.04,0.85,0.10)	(0.68,0.26,0.06)	(0.43,0.13,0.25)
T_4	(0.74,0.16,0.10)	(0.02,0.89,0.05)	(0.08,0.06,0.84)	(0.85,0.09,0.05)
T_5	(0.68,0.08,0.21)	(0.05,0.87,0.06)	(0.13,0.75,0.09)	(0.65,0.05,0.02)

Table 3.2 Numerical results regarding example 4.6

	$D^*(T_m, I^+)$	$D^*(T_m, I^-)$	$\varphi(T_m)$	$\mho_m$	Ranking
T_1	0.1987	0.4425	0.0000	0.0000	1
T_2	0.3059	0.4183	-0.5942	0.7183	2
T_3	0.3262	0.3604	-0.8272	1	5
T_4	0.3035	0.3137	-0.8181	0.9889	4
T_5	0.3354	0.3876	-0.8120	0.9816	3

Table 3.3 Comparison with existing measures

	Ranking Result
PF projection method [3]	$T_1 > T_2 > T_3 > T_4 > T_5$
VIKOR method [5]	$T_1 > T_4 > T_2 > T_5 > T_3$
PFDWA operator [4]	$T_1 > T_4 > T_5 > T_2 > T_3$
PFDWG operator [4]	$T_1 > T_2 > T_3 > T_4 > T_5$
Generalized PF distance measure [6]	$T_1 > T_4 > T_2 > T_3 > T_5$
PF xross entropy (Wei [7])	$T_1 > T_4 > T_2 > T_5 > T_3$
TODIM method [8]	$T_1 > T_4 > T_5 > T_3 > T_2$
PF similarity measure [9]	$T_1 > T_4 > T_2 > T_5 > T_3$
EDAS method [10]	$T_1 > T_5 > T_4 > T_3 > T_2$
D^* (Proposed measure)	$T_1 > T_2 > T_5 > T_4 > T_3$

We compare existing methods [3-10],with the propose PFIR approach to show the validity and reasonability of suggested approach.

Table 3.3, shows that all known approaches [3-10] agree that, best alternative is T_1, which is also alternative suggested by proposed technique. This indicates that the proposed solution is compatible with the existing PF environment techniques. Thus our proposed measure is effective and **reasonable.**

Conclusion

This paper proposes a new PF distance measure and describes its features. We investigated the qualities of the proposed measure, demonstrating that it is valid. We have also looked into the recommended measure using experimental analysis, which includes numerical experiments. We used a new strategy for handling MADM problems in the PF environment called the PF inferior ratio (PFIR). The PFIR mechanism's compromise solution is found to be the closest to PFPIS while also being the furthest from PFNIS. However, this condition does not occur in many practical issues when using the traditional TOPSIS technique. The PFIR approach is also compatible among the existing MADM techniques in the PF environment. In the future, we will expand this study to T- spherical fuzzy sets, Spherical fuzzy sets, and Pythagorean **fuzzy sets.**

References

[1] Atanassov, K. T. (1986). Intuitionistic *fuzzy sets. Fuzzy Set*s and Systems, 20, 87–96.

[2] Cuong, B. C., and Kreinovich, V. (2014). Picture *fuzzy sets. Journal of Computer Science an*d Cybernetics, 30(4), 409–420.

[3] Chen, C. T. (2000). Extensions of the TOPSIS for group decision-making under fuzzy *environment. Fuzzy Set*s and Systems, 114(1), 1–9.

[4] Jana, C., Senapati, T., Pal, M., and Yager, R. R. (2019). Picture fuzzy Dombi aggregation operators: application to *MADM process. Applied S*oft Computing, 74, 99–109.

[5] Joshi, R. (2020). A novel decision-making method using R-Norm concept and VIKOR approach under picture fuzzy *environment. Expert Systems with* Applications, 147, 113228.

[6] Son, L. H., and Thong, P. H. (2017). Some novel hybrid forecast methods based on picture fuzzy clustering for weather nowcasting from satellite image *sequences. Applied* Intelligence, 46(1), 1–15.

[7] Wei, G. (2016). Picture fuzzy cross-entropy for multiple attribute decision maki*ng problems. Journal of Business Economics a*nd Management, 17(4), 491–502.

[8] Wei, G. (2018). TODIM method for picture fuzzy multiple attribute deci*sion making.* Informatica, 29(3), 555–566.

[9] Wei, G. (2018). Picture fuzzy Hamacher aggregation operators and their application to multiple attribute deci*sion making. Fundamenta* Informaticae, 157(3), 271–320.

[10] Zhang, S., Wei, G., Gao, H., Wei, C., and Wei, Y. (2019). EDAS method for multiple criteria group decision making with picture fuzzy information and its application to green suppliers *selections. Technological and Economic Developme*nt of Economy, 25(6), 1123–1138.

[11] Zadeh, L. A. (1965). *Fuzzy sets. I*nform Control, 8(3), 338–353.

[12] Singh, A., and Kumar, S. (2023). Picture fuzzy VIKOR-TOPSIS approach based on knowledge and accuracy asures for suitable adsorbent deci*sion making. Applied S*oft Computing, 1⁴7, 110807.

4 Optimization in makespan working with like parallel machines

Khushboo Malhotra[1,4], Deepak Gupta[2], Sonia Goel[3,a] and A. K. Tripathi[3]

[1]Research Scholar, Maharishi Markandeshwar Engineering College, MM (Deemed to be University), Mullana

[2]Professor and Head, Maharishi Markandeshwar Engineering College, MM (Deemed to be University), Mullana

[3]Assistant Professor, Maharishi Markandeshwar Engineering College, MM (Deemed to be University), Mullana

[4]Assistant Professor, D. A. V. College (Lahore), Ambala City

Abstract

Economy of a country is very important and plays the role of backbone to a country's gross domestic product (GDP). Industrial field is the foundation for developing GDP. Industries or manufacturing companies are based upon their planning for their growth. This planning comes under scheduling which is the base of optimization theory. Actually, scheduling means planning our activities within stipulated time so that we can achieve our objective. Our study also includes the concept of scheduling. The target of this study is to produce a model for optimizing the elapsed time with two machines involving "m" like similar processors at first level and solitary processor at second level by adding the concept of fuzzy triangular numbers as the utilization time of each task on each of the two machines. Here branch and bound method is applied for obtaining optimal sequence of jobs and a MATLAB Code in R2018a is also developed for extending this algorithm for very large number of tasks and machines. Numerical experiment has also been done for supporting the programming.

Keywords: Fuzzy triangular number, mathematical model, MATLAB, scheduling

Introduction

In the era of 4th industrial revolution, competition in the market is rising day by day. The goal of all business is to preserve their consumers with increasing their business and the number of consumers [1]. So, for the long-term survival in this race, manufacturing industries must deliver their products with best quality and minimum price, in minimum time. In order to fulfil this possibility, each industry should follow the process of optimizing its production. This optimizing process means to develop an optimal arrangement of tasks that achieves some performance measures. Actually, the process of finding optimal sequence comes under the preview of scheduling. Scheduling means to arrange tasks for maximum utilization of resources at minimum cost. Many researchers have worked on scheduling theory. The basic concept in scheduling is to develop models involving different parameters and performance measures and then solving these models using different approaches. Most of the studies are related to classical flow-shop scheduling problems (FSP) but here we are dealing with modern flexible FSP (FFSP) where "k" stages having multiple similar parallel machines with distinct utilization time of each job are available. On some stages, we can take single machine and, on some stages, we can consider multiple parallel machines. We found FFSP in manufacturing area most. FFSP is latest version of traditional FSP. FFSP has received more attention in research area now-a-days. So, considering the above situation, we are reviewing the studies related to FFSP having parallel machines as Yanikoglu et al. [2] also studied in the field of parallel machines scheduling. Our work is concerned with Branch and Bound methodology. Many researchers worked with this technique as Santhi et al. [3] worked with branch and bound method. Study on parallel machine scheduling considering branch and bound technique has been done by Gupta et al. [4–10] also. This above all work was done by researchers by taking different restrictions and different performance measures and different methodologies. Parallel machines scheduling means the machines are available in multiple numbers. Our main attention in this paper is on identical parallel machines problems. So, we did some survey on identical parallel machines scheduling problems (IPMSCP) which is organised as follows: as Soares studied on IPMSCP in which the make-span for all items is the same [11]. Anghinolfi et al. [12] also worked on IPMSCP. There were many algorithms and heuristics for solving classical similar scheduling models. These were SPT, PSPT, WSPT, CPT, LNS, and many more. But the stability of these rules was based upon the sample instances and also these rules give only near optimal solution, do not give exact solution. This was the major drawback of these rules and hence in our research, we applied branch and bound method which gives exact optimal solution. Here, the main attraction of our research is working with undetermined Two level FSSP with identical parallel processors at first level.

[a]sonia.mangla14@gmail.com

DOI: 10.1201/9781003534136-4

Problem Description

Let us assume that there are "n" jobs for performing on two machines E and F. Type E has "m" identical processors and type F has single processor where (l_i, m_i, n_i) and (r_i, s_i, t_i) denote consumption time of task "i" on E and F processors respectively. It is not necessary to perform each job on all parallel machines of type E, one job can be performed partially on parallel machines of type E and then after processing on first processor, the task must go to second processor for further processing. Transportation time T_i is also given from machine E to F. Offered time of all similar processors t_{1j} are also given. The purpose of the problem is to manage all tasks in an optimal way so that manufacturing company can fulfil the project in the shortest span and in minimum cost. The model is represented as:

Matrix form of Model
The model of the problem is depicted in matrix form is given in Table 4.1 which is given below:

Solution Approach

Proposed Methodology
We solve this problem in four sections:
Section 1: Firstly, de-fuzzify the fuzzy triangular number by the following formula,

$$\text{crisp } (\check{A}) = h(\check{A}) = x_i' = (3m_i + n_i - l_i)/3 \tag{1}$$

$$y_i' = (3s_i + t_i - r_i)/3 \tag{2}$$

Section 2: Generate two fundamental machines I and J with consumption time of task i as

$$c_i = x_{i'} + T_i \tag{3}$$

$$d_i = y_{i'} + T_i \tag{4}$$

Section 3: Now check the condition

$$\sum_{j=1}^{m} t_{1j} = \sum_{i=1}^{n} c_i \tag{5}$$

and apply MODI method otherwise make arrangement to satisfy condition (5).
Section 4: Apply the formula:

- $$\Gamma = max_{i \in J_r} \left(\sum_{i=1}^{n} e_{ij} \right) + min_{i \in J_r,} (d_i) \tag{6}$$

Table 4.1 Problem definition

Jobs	Machine E						Fuzzy time (e_i)	T_i	Machine F
	E_1	E_2	E_3	E_4	E_5	E_m			Fuzzy time (f_i)
(1)	e_{11}	e_{12}	e_{13}	e_{14}	e_{15}	e_{1m}	(l_1, m_1, n_1)	T_1	(r_1, s_1, t_1)
(2)	e_{21}	e_{22}	e_{23}	e_{24}	e_{25}	e_{2m}	(l_2, m_2, n_2)	T_2	(r_2, s_2, t_2)
(3)	e_{31}	e_{32}	e_{33}	e_{34}	e_{35}	e_{3m}	(l_3, m_3, n_3)	T_3	(r_3, s_3, t_3)
.	.						.	.	.
.	.						.	.	.
.	.						.	..	.
(n)	e_{n1}	e_{n2}	e_{n3}	e_{n4}	e_{n5}	e_{nm}	(l_n, m_n, n_n)	T_n	(r_n, s_n, t_n)
Available time	t_{11}	t_{12}	t_{13}	t_{14}	t_{15}	t_{1m}			

- $l'' = \quad max_{i \in J_r} (e_{ij}) \quad + \quad \sum_{i=1}^{n}(d_i)$ (7)
- Find $l = \max \{l', l''\}$
- Extract out l for all arrangement of tasks.
- After that take minimum value from all l's. This will prepare branching tree.
- In last, we have to generate In-Out table for the required sequence of tasks.

Numerical Approach

We have taken two machines having processing time e_i and f_i. There are six parallel machines for the first machine and single machine at second stage. Transportation time of moving the semi-finished from first stage to second stage is also take into consideration. Processing time on both the machines are taken as triangular fuzzy numbers. The model is similar to that of Gupta et al. [5], but the difference is that we have taken the processing time as triangular fuzzy numbers. The matrix form of the problem is shown in Table 4.2 as follows:

Solution

We solved the problem in four sections:

Section 1: According to Section 1, find average high ranking of fuzzy triangular numbers by using Yaeger's formula

Section 2: Add the transportation time to the processing time of both the machines according to Section 2 of algorithm.

Section 3: Apply the modified distribution method to find out the optimal allocation of processing time at first stage to all the parallel machines.

Section 4: Take first branch of tree and get the extreme value from lower bounds as:

Lower bound {1} = maximum {20/3 + 25/3 , 5/3 +113/3} = maximum {45/3, 118/3} = 118/3
Lower bound {2} = maximum {20/3 +15/3, 10/3 +113/3} = maximum {35/3, 123/3} =123/3
Lower bound {3} = maximum {35/3, 125/3} = 125/3
Lower bound {4} = 133/3.

Here the lowest bound is 118/3 that is connected with job 1.

Now, determine nodes for the second branch of tree.

Lower bound {12} = maximum {53/3,123/3} = 123/3
Lower bound {13} = maximum {45/3,125/3} = 125/3
Lower bound {14} = maximum {45/3, 133/3} = 133/3

Here, lowest bound is 123/3 and the required subsequence at this stage is (12).

Compute the nodes for third branch of tree

Lower Bound {123} = maximum {60/3,125/3} = 125/3
Lower Bound {124} = 133/3

Here lowest bound is 125/3. Subsequence associated with this bound is (123).

Finally, the required scheduled order is (1234).

By using modified branch and bound method we get the optimal sequence as {1, 2, 3, 4}. Find out the optimal schedule of the sequence. After that we will get final in-out Table of required sequence and required elapsed time = 118/3 hrs.

Hence, the problems of small size where either the number of jobs are less or the number of equipotential parallel machines are less are easily solvable manually but for large sized problems we have generated MATLAB

Table 4.2 Numerical problem

Jobs	E_1	E_2	E_3	E_4	E_5	E_6	Processing time (e_i) (l_i, m_i, n_i)	T_i	Processing time (f_i) (r_i, s_i, t_i)
1	1	2	4	5	6	3	(1,2,3)	1/3	(3,4,5)
2	4	1	3	2	7	6	(2,3,4)	2/3	(6,7,8)
3	1	3	5	6	8	2	(3,4,5)	4/3	(8,9,10)
4	2	3	1	5	4	3	(5,6,7)	5/3	(10,11,12)
t_{1j}	10/3	8/3	5/3	10/3	20/3	12/3			

program in R2018a version for finding make-span for large sized problems. Table 4.3 depicts more parallel machines at level 1 and more no of jobs also.

Result and Discussion

Result of the proposed method and Johnson's algorithm [7] are discussed in Table 4.4 and comparison between the two methods is also shown. The comparison shows that we get better results by the proposed method. Comparison shows when the number of jobs is less we get better results by the proposed method and as we increase the number of jobs the difference in the make span value becomes less but still the result are better by proposed algorithm. Graphical comparison between the two methods is shown in Figure 4.1. The relative percentage error is shown in Table 4.5.

Data Availability
The data of above numerical and Table of MATLAB has been randomly generated.

Table 4.3 MATLAB output table

Number of tasks	Number of processors at level 1	Optimal sequence of jobs	Optimum makespan in Hrs.
4	6	5,1,4,3,2	34.000000
5	6	3,2,6,5,4,1	36.333200
7	6	6,2,8,7,5,4,3,1	49.666600
10	6	1,8,10,9,7,6,5,4,3,2,1	52.666600
15	6	9,10,2,13,12,15,1,14,7,3,5,6,8,11,4	115.999700
20	6	10,2,7,13,14,15,1,12,18,16,17,20,3,5,6,8,9,19,11,4	150.999600
30	6	10,2,7,13,9,15,12,1,18,14,25,16,17,22,3,5,6,8,19,30, 21,23,24,4,11,20,26,27,29,28	224.666300
50	6	9,10,2,13,14,15,1,7,12,18,25,33,16,17,22,31,32,39, 40,3,5,6,8,19,38,46,47,21,23,24,34,35,36,4,11,45,20, 26,27,28,29,30,37,41,42,43,48,49,50,44	373.666500
80	6	9,10,2,13,14,15,1,7,12,18,25,33,56,57,16,17,22,31, 32,39,40,60,69,78,3,5,6,8,19,38,46,47,51,55,70,79, 21,23,24,34,35,36,58,59,76,77,4,11,45,20,26,27,28, 29,30,37,31,42,43,48,49,50,52,53,54,72,74,68,71,44, 61,62,63,64,65,67,73,75,80,66	601.666800

Table 4.4 Result and discussion

Number of tasks	Number of processors at level 1	Make-span in Hrs. by Johnson's Algorithm [7]	Makespan in Hrs by proposed algorithm
4	6	36.0000	34.000000
5	6	37.6666	36.333200
7	6	51.6666	49.666600
10	6	70.6666	52.666600
15	6	116.9997	115.999700
20	6	151.3330	150.999600
30	6	224.9997	224.666300
50	6	373.9999	373.666500
80	6	602.0002	601.666800

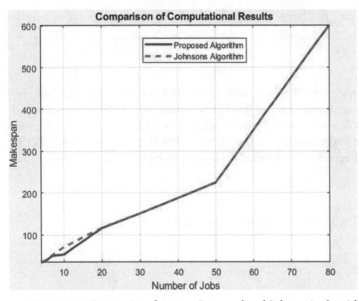

Figure 4.1 Comparison between Proposed and Johnson's algorithm

Table 4.5 Percentage error

Number of tasks	Johnsons approach	Proposed Approach	Percentage error
4	36.0000	34.000000	5.88
5	37.6666	36.333200	3.66
7	51.6666	49.666600	4.02
10	70.6666	52.666600	34.17
15	116.9997	115.999700	0.86
20	151.3330	150.999600	0.22
30	224.9997	224.666300	0.14
50	373.9999	373.666500	0.089
80	602.0002	601.666800	0.055

Conclusion

In this study, we worked on two stage flow shop scheduling model with like parallel machines at first level. In previous studies, small size of scheduling problems with parallel machines have been solved but here we gave proposed methodology for solving large sized scheduling problems. Actually, in industries, large projects are coming for completing and for completing them on time and in reasonable cost, we need modern techniques to solve them. Here in this research, we proposed the technique with the help of MATLAB 2018a. Our proposed algorithm is more effective to reduce the make-span of large sized scheduling problems as given in practical significance.

Future Scope

In the present study, similar machines can be taken at second level also. Different fuzzy numbers can also be considered for utilization time of tasks. The work can be extended at third stage Flow-shop Scheduling Problem also. MATLAB Program can also be extended by taking parallel machines at second, third and next stages as well.

References

[1] Rajaee, A. A., Amindoust, A., and Asadpour, M. (2018). Applying simulated annealing algorithm for parallel machine tardiness problem subject to job splitting, In 48th International Conference on Computers & Industrial Engineering (CIE48), 2-5 December, 2018 Auckland, New Zealand.

[2] Yanıkoğlu, İ., and Yavuz, T. (2022). Branch-and-price approach for robust parallel machine scheduling with sequence-dependent setup times. *European Journal of Operational Research*, 301(3), 875–895.

[3] Santhi, S., and Selvakumari, K. (2020). Flow shop scheduling problems using branch and bound technique underlr-fuzzy number. *Pal Arch's Journal of Archaeology of Egypt/Egyptology*, 17(7), 4791–4801.

[4] Gupta, D., and Goel, S. (2018). Three stage flow shop scheduling model with m-equipotential machines. *International Journal on Future Revolution in Computer Science & Communication Engineering*, 4(3), 269–274.

[5] Gupta, D., Goel, S., and Mangla, N. (2022). Optimization of production scheduling in two stage flow shop scheduling problem with m equipotential machines at first stage. *International Journal of System Assurance Engineering and Management*, 13(3), 1162–1169.

[6] Malhotra, K., Gupta, D., Goel, S., and Tripathi, A. K. (2022). Bi-objective flow shop scheduling with equipotential parallel machines. *Malaysian Journal of Mathematical Sciences*, 16(3), 451–470.

[7] Gupta, D., and Goel, S. (2022). Branch and bound technique for two stage flow shop scheduling model with equipotential machines at every stage. *International Journal of Operational Research*, 44(4), 462–472.

[8] Gupta, D. and Goel, S. (2020). NX2 flow shop scheduling problem with parallel machines at every stage, processing time associated with probabilities. *Advances in Mathematics: Scientific Journal*, 9(3),1061–1069.

[9] Malhotra, K., Gupta, D., Goel, S., and Tripathi, A. K. (2023). Comparison of Bb with meta-heuristic approach in optimization of three stage fss with multiple processors. *Corrosion and Protection*, 51(1), 628–640.

[10] Malhotra, K., Gupta, D., Goel, S., and Tripathi, A. K. (2023). Scheduling involving equipotential processors with constraint as fuzzy utilization time of jobs. In International Conference on Data Analytics and Insights (pp. 491–503). Singapore: Springer Nature Singapore.

[11] Soares L. C. R., and Carvalho M. A. M. (2020). Biased random-key genetic algorithm for scheduling identical parallel machines with tooling constraints. *European Jounal Operational Research*, 285(3), 955–964.

[12] Anghinolfi, D., Paolucci, M., and Ronco, R. (2021). A bi-objective heuristic approach for green identical parallel machine scheduling. *European Journal of Operational Research*, 289(2), 416–434.

5 An overview of available solar panel cleaning mechanisms (SPCMs)

Rishabh Chaturvedi[1,a], Arti Badhoutiya[1,b], Manish Saraswat[2,c] and Nathiram Chauhan[3,d]

[1]GLA University, Mathura, India

[2]LLOYD Institute of Engineering and Technology, Greater Noida, India

[3]Indira Gandhi Delhi Technical University for Women, Delhi, India

Abstract

Even while solar energy and heat sources have many applications and are widely available, some situations prevent their full usage. The low solar energy rate of conversion into electrical energy is one of the key issues preventing solar power plants from being widely used. However, there is a significant barrier to the construction of solar power plants: the issue of surface contamination caused by rainfall and climatic events, as well as a low coefficient of performance. The efficiency of the solar panels, which are directly subjected to weather conditions, relies on the amount of solar radiation they encounter. The solar panel's efficiency of conversion will be decreased as a result of the assimilation of dust and other particles. This paper is aimed to prepare a review of various technological advancements in SPCM methods.

Keywords: Electrostatic cleaning, foam wiper, guide rails, jet spray, micro-particles, servo motors

Introduction

Available Solar Panel cleaning systems:

The efficiency of the solar panels, which are directly subjected to weather conditions, relies on the amount of solar radiation they encounter. The solar panel's efficiency of conversion will be decreased as a result of the assimilation of dust and other particles. This makes it possible to regularly clean the panels. The most popular and extensively explored approach throughout the research literature is the cleaning robot [1–3].

The most typical and established way of cleaning is using a brush and water. Robotic automation of cleaning has also proven to be useful. However, manual cleaning is challenging in the harsh desert environment, water and its delivery to the locations where the power plants are located are prohibitively costly, and potential worker earnings are uncertain. Masuda et al. suggested the electrostatic travelling wave as another cleaning technology, and it is still being developed today. It is an automated cleaning method that uses a remarkably small amount of power and doesn't depend on supplies or mechanical moving parts [4–6]. The present methods for cleaning surfaces are pricy, time- consuming, inefficient, and may damage collectors' surfaces. However, an automatic clean-up mechanism keeps the solar collector clean during its operation to ensure optimal reflectiveness and power generation. In order to reduce and ultimately remove the impact of dirt and soiling on solar system performance, the goal of this inquiry is to design and build an automated cleaning system for a solar-based collector.

A. ROBO based cleaning SYSTEMS-

There are four further subcategories of autonomous mechanized solar panel cleaning systems or robot systems: mobile robot system, tethered robot system, rail robot system, and mobile manipulator with ground vehicles. Two rails are located on opposite side of the panel and make up the rail system, also referred to as the fixed system. If the cleaning brush is horizontal (side rails) or vertical (top and bottom rails) relies on the clean-up process. For solar panel setups that use uninterrupted panels, this technique works well [7]. An example of contamination of solar panels by accumulated dirt is depicted in Figure 5.1.

By analyzing the movement of solar panel cleaning robots that are effective in Thailand, wireless joystick, sensor sonar employing gear motor, and ARDUINO Uno are used in this research to build and create the solar panel cleansing robots. In order to enhance the cleaning process, the bot will wipe down a solar cell utilizing a rotational brush and water spray [8–10].

[a]rishabh.chaturvedi@gla.ac.in, [b]arti.badhoutiya@gla.ac.in, [c]manish.saraswat@lloydcollege.in, [d]nramchauhan@gmail.com

DOI: 10.1201/9781003534136-5

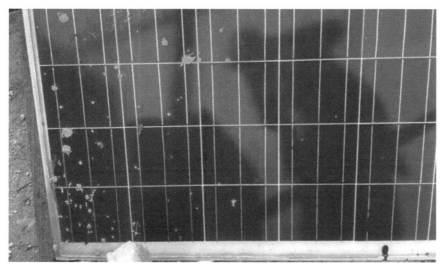

Figure 5.1 Contamination of solar panels by accumulated dirt

For mounting sloped and slick solar energy panels, this research devised and put together a robot's drive mechanism. The robot has sensors and encoders to precisely control the way it moves, such as moving over panel voids and coming to a pause at panel edges [11]. Four omnidirectional wheels, which may either roll normally like an axle or roll laterally utilizing the rollers, were used to propel the robot.

B. **Drone based cleaning systems:** The drone's potential to glide in a straight path across the solar panel's outer layer and hover from a single solar panel to the next is one of its key features. The panels are cleaned autonomously by a robot in this situation, and their motion is made possible by gear motors that are controlled manually over the internet. Limited cash was expended on labor, which had a noticeable fiscal impact for the nation [12–14]. The robot is made for cleaning solar panels that are on the water. A controller is used to control the valve as well as to restrict and enable the movement of water.

C. **IOT based Solar panel cleansing mechanisms:** The Arduino controls the wiping motor to remove the dust from the panel if the voltage drops as a result of dust particles accumulating there. To further improve efficiency, it can be executed by cleansing the solar panel with a water or chemical-based mixture. The Wi-Fi module collects data, which the Internet of Things (IoT) then stores in the cloud [15–17].

The complete setup was controlled by an Arduino Uno R3 microcontroller. The convenience and programming simplicity of this microcontroller made it feasible to easily establish communication between the computer and the engine. However, because of their high price, using Arduino series controllers with a huge-scale cleaning system is not feasible [18]. Currently available categories of Solar panel cleansing model are shown in Figure 5.2. And presently available SPCMs are categorized in Table 5.1.

The two-step cleaning processes used in the envisioned solar panel cleansing method. An exhaust fan first does the best it can to clear the panel's surface of dirt. As dirt, four main types of sands are employed [19]. Then gently swipe with a wiper constructed from soft clothing. As a result, the system can be cleaned without the need of water. This function prevents the solar panel from being damaged [20].

This study proposes a gadget that may be programmed to wipe down solar panels. The suggested research project makes use of the Internet of Things, and the framework is managed by a microcontroller and an Android device [21]. The technology is flexible, so it may be utilized everywhere [22]. Through the use of the solar panel that is linked to it, the battery can be recharged in this. Utilizing an Android app to control reduces the need for human labor.

In addition to its inexpensive price, minimal power use, and integrated Wi-Fi capabilities, the ESP8266 is a great option for IoT projects. The Arduino IDE makes it simple to program, making it a suitable choice for newcomers. Its compact size makes it adaptable and enables its integration into a variety of devices. It can be employed as a Wi-Fi module for other microcontrollers or as an isolated microcontroller [23, 24].

The Arduino IDE is used to create the program. The configuration's upload speed is set at 9600, and the setup ID is connected to the ESP8266 board's COM5 port. As a microcontroller, Node MCU is employed. It is

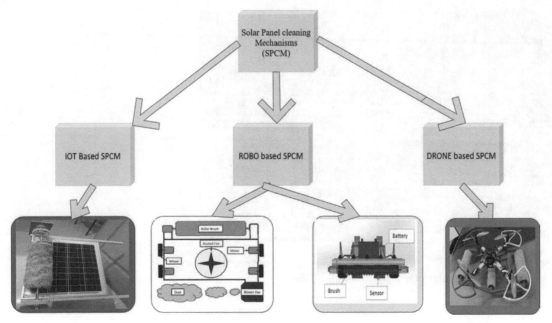

Figure 5.2 Currently available categories of Solar panel cleansing model

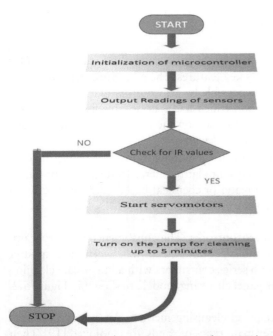

Figure 5.3 Step by step operation of an IOT based SPCM

a platform for developing open-source software and hardware. Here, an ESP-8266 Wi-Fi module is employed. Programming is carried out in a very basic language. Step by step operation of an IOT based SPCM is shown in the flowchart of figure 5.3.

Conclusion

The amount of solar energy that the solar panels are exposed to, which is why they are directly affected by weather, determines how efficient they are. The low solar energy rate of conversion into electrical energy is one of the key issues preventing solar power plants from being widely used. The entrapment of dust and other particles will reduce the solar panel's conversion efficiency. The panels may now be periodically cleaned owing to technology. Different cleaning methods are evaluated along with their advantages and disadvantages.

Table 5.1 Table for presently available SPCMs

Cleaning mechanismtype	Reference paper	Objective
ROBO based cleaning systems	[12]	The panel cleaning bot created in this particular case consists of a cleaning head that traverses the panels utilizing two motorized trolleys and stainless-steel rods.
	[13]	Automated robot construction and operation for floating solar panel cleansing equipment
	[18]	This study suggests a solar panel cleaning robot that can automatically clean PV panels on a regular basis. Air is blown, liquid is sprayed, dust is removed with a wiper, and then a cylindrical brush is used to dry the wet material on the panel. Here Blynk app is used as an IOT software Blynk was created to wirelessly control devices; it can show sensor data, save data, and visualize it.
	[22]	This work created a propulsion mechanism for the robot that uses omni wheels to climb sloping and wet solar panels.
DRONE based cleaning systems	[9]	The approach relies on a hybrid drone that rolls across the surface of the solar panels in order to clean them and transport users from a single unit to next.
	[19]	The ideal method for cleaning the panels is a drone, as a result, constantly attaining the highest efficiency involves moving the drone horizontally.
IOT based cleaning system	[4]	Several methods and techniques for cleaning solar panels are examined in this paper. There are horizontal and vertical structure mechanics, and because the horizontal frame uses less power, it is favored.
	[5]	A node MCU and a light sensor are also linked to the Arduino UNO board for tracking and identifying light conditions in order to construct an integrated IOT-based cleansing mechanism.
	[6]	The entire setup was controlled by an Arduino Uno R3 microcontroller. The findings of the research on choosing an engine, an electric drive for it, and the software are presented in this work by analyzing the environment of an automated and dependable solar panel cleaning system.

References

[1] Santosh Kumar, S., Shankar, S., and Murthy, K. (2020). Solar powered PV panel cleaning robot. In 2020 International Conference on Recent Trends on Electronics, Information, Communication & Technology (RTEICT), Bangalore, India, 2020 (pp. 169–172), doi: 10.1109/RTEICT49044.2020.9315548.

[2] Attri, V. J., Sharma, V. K., Singh, S. K., and Saraswat, M. (2015). Effect of compression ratio on performance and emissions of diesel on a single cylinder four stroke VCR engine. *International Journal of Emerging Technology and Advanced Engineering*, 5, 94–102.

[3] Balamurugan, R., Kumar, A. A., Kalaimaran, A., and Sathish, V. (2023). Integrated IoT system for automatic dust cleaning of solar panels. In 2023 Third International Conference on Artificial Intelligence and Smart Energy (ICAIS), Coimbatore, India, 2023 (pp. 1504–1506), doi: 10.1109/ICAIS56108.2023.10073675.

[4] Roy, S., Mandal, M., Jena, C., Sinha, P., and Jena, T. (2021). Programmable-logic-controller based robust automatic cleaning of solar panel for efficiency improvement. In 2021 International Conference in Advances in Power, Signal, and Information Technology (APSIT), Bhubaneswar, India, 2021, (pp. 1–4), doi: 10.1109/APSIT52773.2021.9641148.

[5] Sharma, A., Chaturvedi, R., Sharma, K., and Saraswat, M. (2022). Force evaluation and machining parameter optimization in milling of aluminium burr composite based on response surface method. *Advances in Materials and Processing Technologies*, 8(4), 4073–4094.

[6] Choi, Y., and Jung, S. (2022). Force control of a foldable robot arm in a drone for a solar panel cleaning task. In 2022 22nd International Conference on Control, Automation and Systems (ICCAS), Jeju, Korea, Republic of, 2022 (pp. 1203–1205), doi: 10.23919/ICCAS55662.2022.10003737.

[7] Kumar, A., Sharma, K., and Dixit, A. R. (2020). A review on the mechanical and thermal properties of graphene and graphene-based polymer nanocomposites: understanding of modelling and MD simulation. *Molecular Simulation*, 46(2), 136–154.

[8] Devaraju, D., Suraj Kumar, V. N., Vivek, D. S., Akshay Kumar, R., Galiveeti, H. R., and Gope, S. (2022). An efficient automatic solar panel cleaning system for roof-top solar PV system. In 2022 International Conference on Smart and Sustainable Technologies in Energy and Power Sectors (SSTEPS), Mahendragarh, India, 2022, (pp. 13–16), doi: 10.1109/SSTEPS57475.2022.00018.

[9] Singh, P. K., and Sharma, K. (2018). Mechanical and viscoelastic properties of in-situ amine functionalized multiple layer grpahene/epoxy nanocomposites. *Current Nanoscience*, 14(3), 252–262.

[10] Sharma, A., Chaturvedi, R., Singh, P. K., and Sharma, K. (2021). AristoTM robot welding performance and analysis of mechanical and microstructural characteristics of the weld. *Materials Today: Proceedings*, 43, 614–622.

[11] Sarkis, Samer & Khanfar, Layla & Ghabour, Beshoy & Zaki, Laila & Alahmed, Marwan & Jaradat, Mohammad & Wadi, Ali & Khalil, Ahmed. (2022). Novel Design of a Hybrid Drone System for Cleaning Solar Panels. 1–6. 10.1109/ASET53988.2022.9735056.

[12] Chaturvedi, R., Sharma, V. K., and Kumar, M. (2022). Structural analysis and completion of fatigue axial-flow compressor using finite element ANSYS technology. In Computational and Experimental Methods in Mechanical Engineering: Proceedings of ICCEMME 2021 (pp. 387–396), Springer Singapore.

[13] Walaman-I, I., Isaacs, S., and Beem, H. (2022). Design of a dust cleaning machine to reduce dust soiling on solar PV panels in ghana. In 2022 IEEE Global Humanitarian Technology Conference (GHTC), Santa Clara, CA, USA, 2022, (pp. 481–484), doi: 10.1109/GHTC55712.2022.9911012.

[14] Pasam, G., Natarajan, R., Alnamani, R. S. R., Al-Alawi, S. M. A., and Al-Sulaimi, S. A. M. (2023). Integrated heuristic approaches to get maximum power from fixed and moving PV solar panel. In 2023 Third International Conference on Advances in Electrical, Computing, Communication and Sustainable Technologies (ICAECT), Bhilai, India, 2023, (pp. 1–5), doi: 10.1109/ICAECT57570.2023.10117609.

[15] Jawale, J. B., Karra, V. K., Patil, B. P., Singh, P., Singh, S., and Atre, S. (2016). Solar panel cleaning bot for enhancement of efficiency — an innovative approach. In 2016 3rd International Conference on Devices, Circuits and Systems (ICDCS), Coimbatore, India, 2016, (pp. 103–108), doi: 10.1109/ICDCSyst.2016.7570634.

[16] Hajiahmadi, F., Zarafshan, P., Dehghani, M., Moosavian, S. A. A., and Hassan-Beygi, S. R. (2019). Dynamics modeling and position control of a robotic carrier for solar panel cleaning system. In 2019 7th International Conference on Robotics and Mechatronics (ICRoM), Tehran, Iran, 2019, (pp. 613–618), doi: 10.1109/ICRoM48714.2019.9071821.

[17] Yerramsetti, J., Paritala, D. S., and Jayaraman, R. (2021). Design and implementation of automatic robot for floating solar panel cleaning system using AI technique. In 2021 International Conference on Computer Communication and Informatics (ICCCI), Coimbatore, India, 2021, (pp. 1–4), doi: 10.1109/ICCCI50826.2021.9402482.

[18] Vinith, S. G., Ragavapriya. R. K., Mohamed Shameer, N., Karthikeyan, S., Kavinkumar, K., and Harinivash, K. (2023). IoT based smart and automated solar panel cleaning system. In 2023 Second International Conference on Electronics and Renewable Systems (ICEARS), Tuticorin, India, 2023, (pp. 566–571), doi: 10.1109/ICEARS56392.2023.10085427.

[19] Al Dahoud, A., Fezari, M., and Al Dahoud, A. (2021). Automatic solar panel cleaning system design. In 2021 29th Telecommunications Forum (TELFOR), Belgrade, Serbia, 2021, (pp. 1–4), doi: 10.1109/TELFOR52709.2021.9653215.

[20] Hashim, N., Mohammed, M. N., Al-Selvarajan, R., Al-Zubaidi, S., and Mohammed, S. (2019). Study on solar panel cleaning robot. In 2019 IEEE International Conference on Automatic Control and Intelligent Systems (I2CACIS), Selangor, Malaysia, 2019, (pp. 56–61), doi: 10.1109/I2CACIS.2019.8825028.

[21] Vidhya, H., Akshaya, U., Keerthana, M. G., and Dhivyanandhini, T. (2022). IoT based solar technology monitoring and cleaning system. In 2022 International Conference on Automation, Computing and Renewable Systems (ICACRS), Pudukkottai, India, 2022, (pp. 1–5), doi: 10.1109/ICACRS55517.2022.10029254.

[22] Ronnaronglit, N., and Maneerat, N. (2019). A cleaning robot for solar panels. In 2019 5th International Conference on Engineering, Applied Sciences and Technology (ICEAST), Luang Prabang, Laos, 2019, (pp. 1–4), doi: 10.1109/ICEAST.2019.8802521.

[23] Sorndach, T., Pudchuen, N., and Srisungsitthisunti, P. (2018). Rooftop solar panel cleaning robot using omni wheels. In 2018 2nd International Conference on Engineering Innovation (ICEI), Bangkok, Thailand, 2018, (pp. 7–12), doi: 10.1109/ICEI18.2018.8448530.

[24] Masuda, S., Fujibayashi, K., Ishida, K., and Inaba, H. (1972). Confinement and transportation of charged aerosol clouds via electric curtain. *Journal of the Institute of Electrical Engineers of Japan*, 92, 9–18.

6 Adaption of multi-objective algorithm to improve performance and fuel optimization of hybrid electric vehicle

Manish Saraswat[1,a], Rishabh Chaturvedi[2,b] and Nathiram Chauhan[3,c]

[1]LLOYD Institute of Engineering and Technology, Greater Noida, India

[2]GLA University, Mathura, India

[3]Indira Gandhi Delhi Technical University for Women, Delhi, India

Abstract

The energy crisis and pollution are contemporary global issues being sought for and mitigated. The answer was to bring in HEVs, or hybrid electric vehicles, to help make cleaner cars that use less gas and produce less pollution. Two different population sizes, 5 and 10, are used in the 1000 simulation iterations to minimize fuel usage while maintaining the vehicle's driving performance. This inquiry makes use of ADVISOR as its simulation program. A vehicle's dynamic performance, fuel economy, and emissions can all be evaluated using the urban driving cycle (UDDS). The next step is to check the algorithm's output with the parallel HEV already defined in the ADVISOR. By optimizing fuel efficiency and reducing emissions, MA can improve the control strategy's parameters, according to the results analysis. This efficient operation review is carried out without sacrificing the vehicle's performance.

Keywords: Control strategy, efficient operation, emissions, fuel consumption (FC), multi-objective, parallel hybrid electric vehicles (HEVs), population size

Introduction

In recent years, natural disasters such as climate change, ecosystem shifts, coral reef mortality, flooding, rising sea levels, and melting glaciers have increased. This can be attributed to the worsening energy crisis and environmental pollution. According to scientists, humans are responsible for nearly 90% of global climate change [1]. We have met our energy needs with petrochemical fuel for the past century, resulting in increased emissions of greenhouse gases such as carbon dioxide, a worsening greenhouse effect, and climatic anomalies. Anthropogenic processes such as livestock husbandry, agriculture, the extraction of fossil fuels for transportation, and refrigerant manufacturing all contribute to the acceleration of climate change [2–4]. Efforts are being made globally to find solutions to energy and pollution problems. A concerning trend is an exponential increase in the number of automobiles in circulation, resulting in pollution issues involving hydrocarbons (HC), lead (Pb), sulfur oxides (SOx), nitrogen oxides (NOx), and carbon monoxide (CO) [5]. Logically, HEVs contribute to environmental sustainability by reducing petroleum consumption and emissions, the two primary causes of environmental degradation and the energy crisis. HEVs utilize electrical and mechanical energy to power the propulsion cycle, with the former derived from an electric motor and the latter from an internal combustion engine [6]. This configuration renders HEVs exceptionally technologically advanced.

Control mechanisms are in place to regulate the energy that must be stored and the power consumption of HEVs to ensure that the energy is distributed appropriately. The economy can be optimized by reducing emissions and petroleum consumption by implementing a carefully selected control system. The efficacy of the vehicle must remain uncompromised while striving for maximum efficiency [7–9].

By analyzing the vehicle's fuel consumption, emissions, and dynamic performance, the proposed algorithm will determine the optimal parameter values for the control strategy [10]. The vehicle's driving performance was simulated using the software ADVISOR, with the configurations modified by the control parameters [11]. The simulations are executed utilizing two separate populations and iterations, and the control parameters are established using MA. The performance standards of the vehicle are considered constraints in this study, and a penalty function accounts for them. Furthermore, the UDDS driving cycle is optimized by implementing the Electric Assist Strategy [12–14]. The simulation findings indicate that the vehicle's performance remains consistent while FC and emissions improve, in contrast to the preset parallel HEV specified in ADVISOR.

[a]manish.saraswat@lloydcollege.in, [b]rishabh.chaturvedi@gla.ac.in, [c] nramchauhan@gmail.com

DOI: 10.1201/9781003534136-6

Methodology

The HEV control strategy

The IC engine and the electric motor are two drives that provide power to the parallel hybrid electric vehicle. For this operation, the power must be distributed between the IC engine and the motor, and accordingly, the torque distribution happens with the help of an exemplary control approach. Many such approaches are there for the control process, but the most commonly used is electric assist.

In this strategy, the ICE engine is the primary source, and the electric motor is the auxiliary supply source. In case the IC engine cannot provide efficient energy or the maximum allowable range of torque is exceeded due to demanded power, the electric motor has been used by this electric assist approach [15]. The state of charge value of the battery decides the motor operation working as the generator, and the extra amount of torque is used in the charging operation of the battery.

$$x = SOCL, SOCH, Tch, Tmin, Toff, ELSL, ELSH, Dch \tag{1}$$

SOC_L, SOC_H, represents the state of charge value in the lower and upper stages. The above expression shows the variables included in this strategy for optimizing the control parameters.

Designing Objective Function

This study's HEV control technique aims to accomplish several objectives simultaneously, including reducing FC and exhaust emissions (HC, CO, and NOx) while maintaining vehicle performance. Therefore, the main objectives are lowering FC and exhaust emissions (i.e., CO, HC, and NOx). The objective function is laid out as follows: (2).

$$\min Obj(x) = NOX + FC + CO + HC \tag{2}$$

Where x denotes one of the solutions, i.e., the MO-encoded chromosomes, and X denotes the solution space. Nitrogen oxide is abbreviated as NOx, fuel consumption is abbreviated as FC, carbon monoxide is CO, and hydrocarbon is HC.

Apply MA to design the appropriate HEV control strategy

The algorithm is based on Darwinian survival and the survival of the fittest, and it is comparable to the genetic algorithm (GA). In order to produce superior offspring, the preferred species of the chosen species undergo a

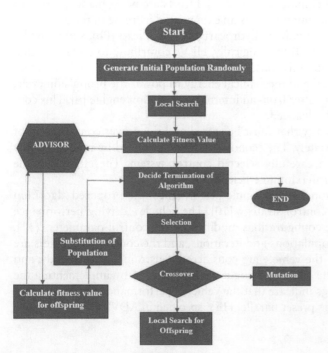

Figure 6.1 Figure Showing Flowchart of the Multi-Objective Algorithm

random exchange of genetic information with one another. This process is repeated until the most adaptable species is created. The flowchart in Figure 1 shows the iterative process that makes up the MO Algo.

The steps are illustrated in figure: -

➢ The initial population is generated randomly
➢ Make a local search
➢ The fitness value is calculated
➢ Termination of the algorithm is decided
➢ Selection
➢ Cross-over
➢ Poor individual is replaced

• The initial population is generated randomly.
  For the initial population generation, dozens to hundreds of chromosomes are generated first without duplicating, and this initial population is expressed by (1).
• Make a local search.
  In order to get a better chromosome, a local search is performed in the area near the original chromosome. In each iteration, all offspring will join in the local search, ensuring that the best solution for each part of the chromosome is always kept, and the best solution is finally determined.
• Calculate the fitness value.
  The fitness function can detect whether a chromosome is excellent or poor and calculate the global optimum of each chromosome.

  When the algorithm is employed, the vehicle performance criteria are defined as constraints. To verify that vehicle performance was not degraded during optimization, the PNGV passenger car restrictions were applied in this work. As a result, the fitness function is as follows:

$$f(x) = \frac{1}{[Obj.(x) + \sum_{i=1}^{n} y_i + P_i(x)]} \tag{3}$$

• Termination of the algorithm is decided
  The goal of the method suggested in this study is to complete the algorithm operation with the maximum number of iterations of 1000.
• Selection
  The character of progeny will be impacted by the selected outcomes, given that fitness selection is the true purpose of natural selection. In order to improve progeny production, the selection of species to include in the training corpus for cross-over purposes may be influenced by species fitness levels. Using competitive selection as its principal methodology, two chromosomes are chosen for subsequent screening in this study.
• Cross-over
  In the current algorithm, mating is selected randomly as one of the evolutionary procedures. Two parent species are selected randomly from the breeding pool, their genetic material is exchanged, and two more progeny are produced as part of the cross-over procedure. This procedure can provide valuable insights into the parents' genetic composition, potentially enhancing their progeny quality. Mutation is a process by which genetic material on chromosomes is altered. This occurs when a mutation site is arbitrarily selected from the chromosomes of one species from a population.
• Poor individual is replaced.
  In order to accomplish the objective of evolution, which is to obtain the best alternative, the less advantageous population members will also undergo cross-over and modified species after mutation and cross-over processes conclude.

Results

The ADVISOR software enables the simulation of research to enhance fuel economy, vehicle performance, and exhaust emissions by manipulating various control plan parameters. By these standards, the parameters and model of the vehicle's components for a parallel HEV have been established. Table 6.1 below showing the vehicle parameters taken for the analysis

Table 6.1 Table showing vehicle parameters for the analysis

Parameter	Value		
Vehicle mass	590 Kg		
Cargo mass	130 Kg		
Frontal area(vehicle)	2.5 m2		
Aerodynamic drag coefficient	0.330		
Energy storage system	VRLA (12V,26Ah)		
Rolling resistance coefficient	0.007		
Fuel converter	45	KW	SI Engine
Electric motor	75	KW	AC motor

Table 6.2 Table showing control strategy parameters for different population size

Control Strategy Parameters

Parameter	Population Size	
	5	10
Max. SOC	0.95	0.74
Min. SOC	0.03	0.18
ELSH	53.0	26.0
ELSL	4.0	7.0
Tmin	0.23	0.69
Tch	24.3	10.5
Toff	0.27	0.38

❖ *Algorithm Parameters and the Control Strategy Description*

The algorithm has different parameters that need to be adjusted, which include iterations, mutation rate, crossover rate, and population size (5 and 10 used here). Around 1100 iterations have been done, and the rate of mutation and cross-over is set to 0.2 and 1, respectively. EUDC cycle is taken to simulate the default parallel hybrid electric vehicle on the ADVISOR for this optimal strategy. Random variables are selected from the solution's whole space to initialize the algorithm's population. In Table 6.2, all the parameters used in this strategy are detailed based on the simulation of the EUDC cycle.

In Figures 6.2 and 6.3, the process history is shown for the EUDC cycle, and it is observed that along with the iterations, the fitness value is improved for different population sizes. These parameters can be selected optimally using the multi-objective algorithm used in this work.

The results show that different control strategies have different emission and fuel economy specifications, and a better selection of these parameters will help improve fuel economy. The control strategy parameters are affected by the population size of the strategy.

Table 6.3 presents the driving cycle's fuel economy and emissions in detail, and the vehicle's performance for the drive cycle is also shown.

Conclusion

A challenge for optimizing the Electric Assist Strategy on the UDDS driving cycle was formulated to achieve the minimum gasoline consumption and emissions possible without compromising vehicle performance. Appropriate control strategy configurations can be generated using the MO Algo with one thousand iterations and two moderate population sizes (five and ten). The ideal values for the control approach were ascertained by

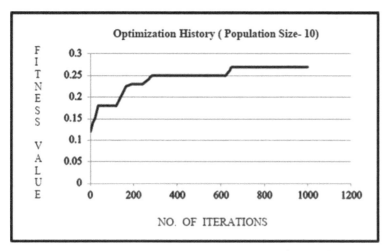

Figure 6.2 Figure Showing Optimization History for population size 10

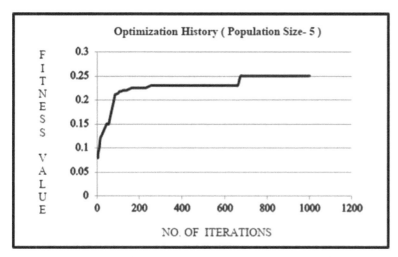

Figure 6.3 Figure Showing Optimization History for population size 5

Table 6.3 Table showing emission parameters and the dynamic performance of the vehicle

Parameter	Size-5	Size-10
FC and Emissions		
CO	5.563	3.754
NOx	0.546	0.648
HC	0.618	0.664
FC	31.550	31.667
Vehicle Dynamic Performance		
0-60mph	10.248	10.641
40-60 mph	5.323	5.568
0-85 mph	21.8116	22.821
Max. speed	111.402	109.829
Max. acceleration	16.238	16.238
Distance	173.803	171.559
Gradability	6.6	6.6

employing two lesser populations, each consisting of 5, 10, and 1000 iterations. Without compromising vehicle performance, this research enhances engine efficiency and emissions to combat pollution and the energy crisis. The analysis results indicate that by optimizing fuel efficiency and reducing emissions, MA can be utilized to improve the parameters of the control strategy. This method of operating efficiently scans the vehicle without compromising its performance. MA can increase the control strategy parameters in parallel HEVs, which can aid in mitigating the energy crisis and climate risks, as opposed to the parallel HEVs predefined in ADVISOR, according to the results.

References

[1] Wu, Y., Zhang, S., Hao, J., Liu, H., Wu, X., Hu, J., et al. (2017). On-road vehicle emissions and their control in China: a review and outlook. *Science of the Total Environment, 574*, 332–349.

[2] Lin, C.-C., Peng, H., and Grizzle, J. W. (2004). A stochastic control strategy for hybrid electric vehicles. In Proceedings of the 2004 American Control Conference, (Vol. 5, pp. 4710–4715). IEEE, 2004.

[3] Saraswat, M., and Chauhan, N. R. (2020). Comparative assessment of butanol and algae oil as alternate fuel for SI engines. *Engineering Science and Technology, an International Journal, 23*(1), 92–100.

[4] Paganelli, G., Guezennec, Y., and Rizzoni, G. (2002). Optimizing control strategy for hybrid fuel cell vehicle. *SAE Transactions*, 398–406.

[5] Kumar, P., Singh, P. K., Nagar, S., Sharma, K., and Saraswat, M. (2021). Effect of different concentration of functionalized graphene on charging time reduction in thermal energy storage system. *Materials Today: Proceedings, 44*, 146–152.

[6] Pisu, P. and Rizzoni, G. (2007). A comparative study of supervisory control strategies for hybrid electric vehicles. *IEEE Transactions on Control Systems Technology, 15*(3), 506– 518.

[7] Singh, P. K., Sharma, K., Kumar, A., and Shukla, M. (2017). Effects of functionalization on the mechanical properties of multiwalled carbon nanotubes: a molecular dynamics approach. *Journal of Composite Materials, 51*(5), 671–680.

[8] Yi, T., Xin, Z., Liang, Z., and Xin, Z. (2011). Fuzzy control strategy for hybrid electric vehicle based on neural network identification of driving conditions. *Control Theory and Applications, 28*(3), 363–369.

[9] Verma, S. K., Sharma, K., Gupta, N. K., Soni, P., and Upadhyay, N. (2020). Performance comparison of innovative spiral-shaped solar collector design with conventional flat plate solar collector. *Energy, 194*, 116853.

[10] Digalakis, J., and Margaritis, K. (2001). A parallel memetic algorithm for solving optimization problems. In Proceedings of 4th Meta-heuristics International Conference, (Vol. 1, pp. 121–125). Portugal, 2001.

[11] Chaturvedi, R., Islam, A., and Sharma, K. (2021). A review of the applications of PCM in thermal storage of solar energy. *Materials Today: Proceedings, 43*, 293–297.

[12] Montazeri-Gh, M., Poursamad, A., and Ghalichi, B. (2006). Application of genetic algorithm for optimization of control strategy in parallel hybrid electric vehicles. *Journal of the Franklin Institute, 343*(4-5), 420–435.

[13] Markel, T., Brooker, A., Hendricks, T., Johnson, V., Kelly, K., Kramer, B., et al. (2002). ADVISOR: a systems analysis tool for advanced vehicle modeling. *Journal of Power Sources, 110*(2), 255–266.

[14] Sharma, A., Sharma, K., Islam, A., and Roy, D. (2020). Effect of welding parameters on automated robotic arc welding process. *Materials Today: Proceedings, 26*, 2363–2367.

[15] Poursamad, A., and Montazeri, M. (2008). Design of genetic-fuzzy control strategy for parallel hybrid electric vehicles. *Control Engineering Practice, 16*(7), 861–873.

7 Optimizing fuel efficiency in hybrid electric vehicles: a power-split approach with model predictive control and planetary gear systems

Manish Saraswat[1,a], Aman Sharma[2,b] and Nathiram Chauhan[3,c]

[1]LLOYD Institute of Engineering and Technology, Greater Noida , India

[2]GLA University, Mathura, India

[3]Indira Gandhi Delhi Technical University for Women, Delhi, India

Abstract

The objective of this research is to investigate the efficacy of model predictive control (MPC) in optimizing the fuel efficiency of hybrid electric vehicles (HEVs) by employing a power-split approach. This study centers around the utilization of planetary gear systems, which facilitate efficient collaboration between the internal combustion engine (ICE) and electric motor (EM). The main aim of this study is to enhance the power allocation between the two key components of HEVs through the utilization of MPC software. This study assesses the operational efficiency of power-split HEVs through the utilization of advanced modeling techniques. The research also gives simulation outcomes for a range of motorcycle-specific setups and control approaches. Comparative research was undertaken to assess the effectiveness of MPC in lowering petroleum consumption in comparison to conventional computers and other model predictive control systems. The results indicate that power-split HEVs have the potential to yield substantial fuel savings, thereby making a valuable contribution to the continuing endeavors aimed at promoting environmentally conscious and sustainable transportation.

Keywords: Constraints, drive cycles, energy management, fuel economy, model predictive control, power-split

Introduction

Because hybrid electric vehicles comprise both electric machinery and conventional energy systems, the capacity of smaller internal combustion engines may be utilized to a larger extent. This is made possible as a consequence of the integration of electric machinery and conventional energy systems. The objective of this research is to investigate how well a recently produced medicine works in treating people who have hybrid electric vehicles are outfitted with components from both types of propulsion systems and conventional energy sources [1]. This is done in order to facilitate the cooperative working of electric propulsion systems and conventional energy sources. The battery, which has such a big capacity for the storage of energy, is able to effectively absorb and reclaim the thermal energy that is lost as the vehicle comes to a stop. This is because the battery has such a huge capacity for the storage of energy. In order to construct hybrid electric propulsion systems, a number of automobile manufacturers utilize power-split topologies. These configurations are also referred to as parallel-series arrangements. Both terms are used to refer to these different arrangements. These designs make it possible to implement either a parallel or a series arrangement depending on what has to be accomplished. Additional possibilities for the storage and distribution of energy are made available as a result of the use of technology that stores energy in batteries [2–4]. The hybrid electric vehicles (HEVs) in question have two degrees of freedom in their energy management as a direct consequence of this fact. This integration, when paired with the various operational modes of the vehicle, enhances the efficiency of the vehicle, which ultimately results in a reduction in the quantity of emissions as well as the amount of fuel that is spent.

When it comes to a HEV efficiency when it comes to the use of gasoline, the choice of an energy management plan for the vehicle can have a considerable impact on the vehicle's performance. By evaluating it in the context of an optimal control system and studying it from that point of view, it is possible to transform the nonlinear energy management problem into a dynamic optimization problem with constraints. This can be accomplished by using the optimal control system. The power train of the dynamic model is nonlinear, and the model's states and control inputs contain both unequal and equal limitations. The model also has nonlinearities. In addition to that, there are nonlinearities present in the power train. Researchers have used numerical approaches such as dynamic programming (DP) [5, 6] and the equivalent consumption management system methodology (ECMS

---

[a]manish.saraswat@lloydcollege.in, [b]aman.sharma@gla.ac.in, [c]nramchauhan@gmail.com

DOI: 10.1201/9781003534136-7

methodology), which is also known as the equivalent consumption reduction strategy [7–9] throughout the course of the history of academic research.

The hybrid electric vehicle in power split mode is shown in Figure 7.1 and this is used in this study. In this study the generator and ICE coupled is coupled to the speed coupler set.

The torque coupler's job is to make a link between the generator or motor's output and the speed coupler's output so that the two can talk to each other. Because of this, power can be sent from the battery to the car's driveline. The power split mode lets power be distributed in different ways, which makes it seem like the engine's working point is different from that of the car. This idea is based on what makes the power split mode unique. To make sure the ECMS approach works, it is important to find and use a good cost equivalent for gasoline, which can then be used to figure out how much the battery energy costs. This will make it possible to use the plan well. This problem can be fixed not only while driving, but also while doing anything else [10, 12]. If decisions are made without taking into account how the system works at its core, it will be very hard to predict what will happen with the system. Using a method of managing energy that is based on model predictive control (MPC) can be a good way to find a balance between the non-causal properties of a globally optimal DP solution and the costs of computing that are involved in the process. It is possible to bring these two ideas together by joining the ideas themselves. Both the set horizon and the variable horizon are taken into account when using MPC to optimize. References [13–15] show examples of a few different ways to improve performance. ECMS solutions, quick and effective answers, and rule-based systems are all examples of these tactics. With the help of dynamic programming, the best answer for a model of a HEV can be found, assuming that all possible driving conditions in the future are known. The DP method, on the other hand, has nothing to do with cause and effect because it is based on the fact that the power demand in the near future is hard to predict. This makes it hard to do exact math over a long period of time. Most of these cases involved using DP methods as benchmarks to find the driving cycles that would save the most fuel [15]. The author of the study used a quadratic cost function to build the linear system that changes over time that MPC needs. When the MPC function is changed to improve fuel efficiency, the cost of oil over a certain amount of time can be added together. This lets a cost-to-go function be calculated. This means that the fuel can be used more efficiently. The planning method doesn't have the tools to make a good guess about how much this terminal will cost in the future.

We use the link between Pontryagin's minimal principle and the Hamilton-Jacobi-Bellman (HJB) equation to show that the cost-to-go for this optimum control problem can be thought of as a piecewise linear function of the changes in the battery's state of charge [16]. Here is where you can find Pontryagin's basic principle, and here is where you can find the HJB equation. This means that the cost-to-go can be predicted by describing it as a piecewise linear function of the changes in the state of charge of the battery. This lets us figure out how much it will cost to go. The findings of our investigation are the same as those of other investigations that are still going on. Using a nonlinear MPC system [17] makes it easier to solve the optimal control problem that comes up in an online setting. Because MPC systems are made to make predictions, this is the case. The closed-loop simulations that were used to test the MPC method show that progress is being made, which is clear from how well the strategy works as a whole. The fact that the simulations worked showed that these signs were correct.

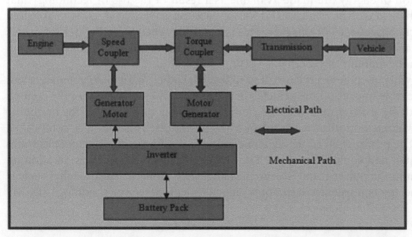

Figure 7.1 Schematic configuration of power split HEV

Methodology

The initial dynamics of the power train are analyzed by the Newton's law whose expressions are as follows-

$$J_G \frac{d\omega_G}{dt} = T_G + F \times N_S \tag{1}$$

$$J_E \frac{d\omega_E}{dt} = T_E - F \times (N_S + N_R) \tag{2}$$

$$J_M \frac{d\omega_M}{dt} = T_M - \frac{T_O}{gf} + F \times N_R \tag{3}$$

Where, J_G is referred as the inertia of the generator, J_E is the inertia of engine.
The relationship of fuel flow rate with the torque and speed of engine is as expressed –

$$m_f = \varphi(\omega_E, T_E) \tag{4}$$

The velocity constraints are as follows-

$$N_S\omega_G + N_R\omega_M = (N_S + N_R)\omega_E$$

$$\omega_M = \frac{g_f}{r_\omega}V \tag{5}$$

The vehicle dynamics is as expressed –

$$m\frac{dV}{dt} = \frac{T_o + T_b}{r\omega} - \frac{1}{2}\rho A_f CdV^2 - C_r mg\cos(\theta) + mg\sin(\theta) \tag{6}$$

There is the variation in final and initial SOCs and this impact the fuel economy, thus in order to maintain the balanced charge, this simulation is performed many times for different number of cycles.

$$SOC(0) = SOC(t_f) \tag{7}$$

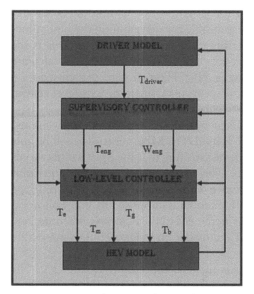

Figure 7.2 Schematic of control system structure in a hierarchical order

In this study the SOC values taken are final and initial and with these values fuel economy is analyzed by using different controllers and their performance are compared. It can be seen that the non-linear MPC controller improves fuel economy throughout the driving cycles for both the highways and city.

The demanded torque by the driver is equal t the sum of output torque from power train and brake torque and this expression is as shown-

$$T_O + T_b = T_{driver} \tag{8}$$

The dynamics of state of charge value of battery is required for the optimal control of HEV:

$$\frac{d}{dt} SOC = -\frac{V_{OC} - \sqrt{V_{OC}^2 - 4P_{batt}.R_{batt}}}{2C_{batt}.R_{batt}.} \tag{9}$$

Where,

$$P_{batt}. = P_M + P_G + P_M^L + P_G^L \tag{10}$$

$$SOC^{min} \le SOC \le SOC^{max};$$

$$P_{batt}^{min} < P_{batt} < P_{batt}^{min}.$$

$$\omega_G^{min} < \omega_G < \omega_G^{max}$$

$$\omega_E^{min} < \omega_E < \omega_E^{max}$$

$$\omega_M^{min} < \omega_M < \omega_M^{max}. \tag{11}$$

$$T_G^{min} < T_G < T_G^{max}$$

$$T_E^{min} < T_E < T_E^{max}$$

$$T_M^{min} < T_M < T_M^{max}$$

Architecture

This energy management strategy is intended to reduce fuel consumption while also ensuring that all rules are followed at the same time. This study accounts for the complexity of the situation by dividing the controller into two parts. The supervisory level, also known as the first level, is responsible for determining the best values for the system's two degrees of freedom, torque and engine speed, during each sampling interval. This is the responsibility of the first level. The low-level controller must use reference data correctly in order to calculate the friction brake as well as the torque of the motor, generator, and engine [10]. Figure 2 depicts a closed loop using a block design. To keep track of the reference point in a quick and accurate manner, the low-level central processing unit employs standard control loops.

Managers can think of energy management as a constrained nonlinear optimization problem with limited resources. To deal with this specific situation, MPC, a common method, is used. The MPC controller will be able to manage the control process well in subsequent iterations while also demonstrating that the optimization goals are being met by lowering the index of performance. This will take place. Throughout the process, the equations and constraints of the dynamic model that are related to the system under study are carefully considered. The system then processes the first part of the control sequence that the HEV model is supposed to use. Following completion of the procedure, the prediction horizon is advanced by one increment to the next possible time step. Given that the engine zero speed is a true MPC solution [11], the PSAT controller no longer requires a separate mechanism for turning the engine on and off.

In this paper, a non-linear LTV model predictive control is used, as is the cost function that defines it. The non-linear linear time-varying system was used to define the cost function for this study, and the total cost of fuel was calculated as follows:

$$J = \int_{t_o}^{t_f} m \cdot f(u(t))dt + h(SOC(tf)) \tag{12}$$

The primary objective of the energy management technique is to minimize expenses while considering the pertinent dynamic equations and restrictions. Conversely, applications grounded in real-world scenarios sometimes lack a comprehensive description of the underlying driving forces across extended temporal periods, and the model and constraint parameters may undergo alterations. Moreover, the computational solution of the optimum control issue with an extended time horizon is well recognized as a challenging task.

Based on Bellman's concept of optimality, we propose decomposing the aforementioned optimal control problem into a minimal estimated fuel cost and a cumulative stage cost that extends from the prediction horizon through the conclusion of the driving cycle. This will facilitate the discussion of these concerns and enable us to identify potential solutions. Subsequently, the receding horizon work framework is introduced as a potential solution to the aforementioned issue.

This problem is solved by using the receding horizon work and is illustrated as:

$$J(SOC(t)) = \int_{t}^{t_f} m_f(u(\tau))d\tau + k(SOC(t_f)) \tag{13}$$

$$J*(SOC(t)) = \min_{\substack{u(\tau) \\ t \leq \tau \leq t_f}} \{ \int_{t}^{t_f} m_f(u(\tau))d\tau + k(SOC(t_j)) \} \tag{14}$$

This expression is subjected to the constraints defined as –

$$SOC(t) = \int_{t}^{t_f} m_f(u(\tau))d\tau + k(SOC(t_f)) \tag{15}$$

$$J*(SOC(t) = \min_{\substack{u(\tau) \\ t \leq \tau \leq t_f}} \{ \int_{t}^{t+\Delta t} m_f(u(\tau))d\tau + \int_{t+\Delta t}^{t_f} m_f(u(\tau))d\tau + k(SOC(t_f)) \} \tag{16}$$

The principle of optimality as given by Bellman is as expressed-

$$J*(SOC(t) = \int_{t}^{t_f} m_f(u(\tau))d\tau + k(SOC(t_f)) \tag{17}$$

$$J*(SOC(t) = \min_{\substack{u(\tau) \\ t \leq \tau \leq t+\Delta t}} \{ \int_{t}^{t+\Delta t} m_f(u(\tau))d\tau + \int_{t+\Delta t}^{t_f} m_f(u(\tau))d\tau + J*(SOC(t+\Delta t), t+\Delta t) \} \tag{18}$$

The charged balance (i.e. SOC (0) = SOC (t$_f$)) to exclude the effect of various initial and final SOCs on fuel economy is maintained by performing the simulation many times for the same drive cycle. The Table 7.1 below

Table 7.1 Table showing results of MPC for three different drive cycles

Drive cycle	Fuel economy (mpg)	SOC (Initial)	SOC (Final)
NY drive cycle	65.42	0.72	0.65
	56.80	0.65	0.66
SCO3 drive cycle	75.35	0.72	0.68
	73.80	0.70	0.67
USO6 drive cycle	41.56	0.72	0.68
	45.07	0.70	0.67

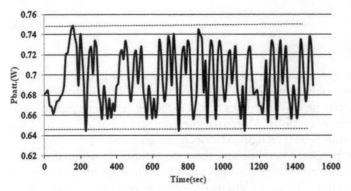

Figure 7.3 Power constraint of non-linear MPC model

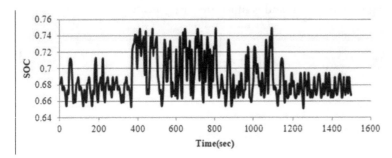

Figure 7.4 SOC constraint of non-linear MPC model

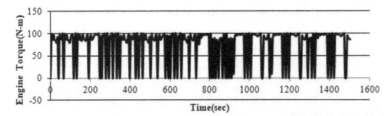

Figure 7.5 Engine torque variation with time in seconds

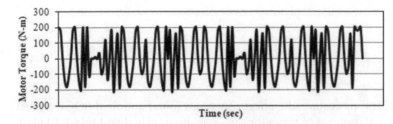

Figure 7.6 Engine torque variation with time in seconds

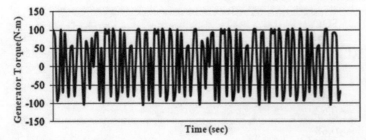

Figure 7.7 Generator torque variation with time in seconds

shows the fuel economy and State of charge results for three different drive cycles. In order to compare the controller's performance, fuel economy is tested by employing equal final and initial values of SOC. It can be seen that the NMPC controller improves fuel economy during both highways and city driving cycles.

Results and Discussion

Three different drive cycles are taken here in this study for demonstrating the performance of the described strategy which is NY, USO6 and SCO3. The simulations are performed by selecting one cycle at a time and they are repeated until the balance charge is obtained i.e. SOC (0) = SOC (t_f)). By doing so the effect of variation in SOC values at final and initial points, on the fuel economy can be removed.

For demonstrating the behavior of controllers on the fuel economy, the equal SOC values are taken at final and initial points. The implementation of non-linear MPC improves the fuel economy whether it is taken for highway or for city driving. But the computation time is the noticeable point as it is two times than that of linear time varying MPC. Figure 7.3 shows the power constrained of non linearities in the Model Predictive control. Figure 7.4 shows the constraint in State of Charge for MPC model. Figure 7.5 shows the variation in the engine torque. Figure 7.6 shows the variation in the motor torque. Figure 7.7 shows the variation in the generator torque.

Conclusion

Model predictive control (MPC) is a methodology employed to optimize the fuel efficiency of power- split hybrid electric cars. In the initial exploratory phase, a quadratic cost function is formulated, and the MPC technique is employed to implement it on a time-varying linear system with dynamic variables. The preliminary study encompasses both of these components. Subsequently, the cost function is partitioned into two distinct components, namely the cost-to-go and the stage cost, resulting in a more efficient utilization of fuel resources. The cost-to-go can be determined by considering the battery's state of charge (SOC). This provides a reliable approximation of the actual value. The utilization of MPC in a non-linear context facilitates the systematic and predicted resolution of the problem at hand. This phenomenon can be attributed to the relatively little time frame under consideration. This achievement has been made feasible due to the reduction in the dimensions of the problematic region. The utilization of alternative commercial linear controllers can be substituted by employing the MPC approach in non-linear contexts, as indicated by the data. This adaptation has demonstrated a substantial enhancement in fuel efficiency. In instances when linear language is typically employed, this phenomenon does not occur.

References

[1] Chan, C. C. (2002). The state of the art of electric and hybrid vehicles. *Proceedings of the IEEE, 90*(2), 247–275.
[2] Malikopoulos, A. A. (2014). Supervisory power management control algorithms for hybrid electric vehicles: a survey. *IEEE Transactions on Intelligent Transportation Systems, 15*(5), 1869–1885.
[3] Sharma, A., Sharma, K., Islam, A., and Roy, D. (2020). Effect of welding parameters on automated robotic arc welding process. *Materials Today: Proceedings, 26*, 2363–2367.
[4] Salmasi, F. R. (2007). Control strategies for hybrid electric vehicles: evolution, classification, comparison, and future trends. *IEEE Transactions on Vehicular Technology, 56*(5), 2393–2404.
[5] Chaturvedi, R., Islam, A., and Sharma, K. (2021). A review on the applications of PCM in thermal storage of solar energy. *Materials Today: Proceedings, 43*, 293–297.
[6] Paganelli, G., Delprat, S., Guerra, T. M., Rimaux, J., and Santin, J. J. (2002). Equivalent consumption minimization strategy for parallel hybrid powertrains. In Vehicular Technology Conference. IEEE 55th Vehicular Technology Conference. VTC Spring 2002 (Cat. No. 02CH37367), (Vol. 4, pp. 2076–2081), IEEE, 2002.
[7] Kumar, P., Singh, P. K., Nagar, S., Sharma, K., and Saraswat, M. (2021). Effect of different concentration of functionalized graphene on charging time reduction in thermal energy storage system. *Materials Today: Proceedings, 44*, 146–152.
[8] Gu, B., and Rizzoni, G. (2006). An adaptive algorithm for hybrid electric vehicle energy management based on driving pattern recognition. In ASME International Mechanical Engineering Congress and Exposition, (Vol. 47683, pp. 249–258).
[9] Singh, P. K., Singh, P. K., Sharma, K., and Saraswat, M. (2020). Effect of sonication parameters on mechanical properties of in-situ amine functionalized multiple layer graphene/epoxy nanocomposites. *Journal of Scientific and Industrial Research, 79*(11), 985–989.

[10] Borhan, H. A., Vahidi, A., Phillips, A. M., Kuang, M. L., and Kolmanovsky, I. V. (2009). Predictive energy management of a power-split hybrid electric vehicle. In 2009 American Control Conference, (pp. 3970–3976). IEEE, 2009.

[11] Borhan, H., Vahidi, A., Phillips, A. M., Kuang, M. L., Kolmanovsky, I. V., and Di Cairano, S. (2011). MPC-based energy management of a power-split hybrid electric vehicle. *IEEE Transactions on Control Systems Technology,* 20(3), 593–603.

[12] Shukla, M. K., and Sharma, K. (2019). Effect of carbon nanofillers on the mechanical and interfacial properties of epoxy based nanocomposites: a review. *Polymer Science, Series A,* 61, 439–460.

[13] Mousavi, M. A., Heshmati, Z., and Moshiri, B. (2013). LTV-MPC based path planning of an autonomous vehicle via convex optimization. In 21st Iranian Conference on Electrical Engineering (ICEE), (pp. 1–7), IEEE, 2013.

[14] Kim, N., Cha, S., and Peng, H. (2010). Optimal control of hybrid electric vehicles based on Pontryagin's minimum principle. *IEEE Transactions on Control Systems Technology,* 19(5), 1279–1287.

[15] Sharma, K., and Shukla, M. (2014). Three-phase carbon fiber amine functionalized carbon nanotubes epoxy composite: processing, characterisation, and multiscale modeling. *Journal of Nanomaterials,* 2014, 2–2.

[16] Sciarretta, A., and Guzzella, L. (2007). Control of hybrid electric vehicles. *IEEE Control Systems Magazine,* 27(2), 60–70.

[17] Jinquan, G., Hongwen, H., Jiankun, P., and Nana, Z. (2019). A novel MPC-based adaptive energy management strategy in plug-in hybrid electric vehicles. *Energy,* 175, 378–392.

8 Control parameter optimization for parallel hybrid electric vehicles

Manish Saraswat[1,a], Rajat Yadav[2,b] and Nathiram Chauhan[3,c]

[1]LLOYD Institute of Engineering and Technology, Greater Noida, India

[2]GLA University, Mathura, India

[3]Indira Gandhi Delhi Technical University for Women, Delhi, India

Abstract

The important control parameters for the hybrid electric vehicle (HEV) are the lower and upper limit of state of charge (SOC). This SOC of the vehicle directly affects the economy and the emission rates. In this work the parallel HEV is modelled by using ADVISOR. Different SOC limits are taken for testing the emission performance and fuel economy for the same designed driving cycles. With the simulation results we will be able to specify best upper and lower limits of SOC such that vehicle will achieve best fuel economy and emission performance. The simulation is performed by taking repetitive velocity profiles (drive cycles) of four different curves i.e. UDDS, ECE, FTP and HWFET. The SOC and emission curves are observed for these different drive cycles and the results having emission rates for HC, CO and NOx (in g/miles) are tabulated.

Keywords: ADVISOR, drive cycle, emission performance, hybrid electric vehicle, SOC

Introduction

Hybrid electric vehicles offer extra flexibility in order to improve fuel economy and emissions [1]. For the hybrid electric vehicle (HEV), the electrical energy storage is coupled with an electric motor so that the vehicle can operate efficiently. The two power path, which is possible due to coupling of bidirectional converter, makes it possible to shut down the engine during low power operation and also the more efficient and smaller engine can be used for this type of vehicle. This can be done while maintain the vehicles average power carrying capability [2–4]. During this process the electrical energy in the battery or any other energy storage system is maintained by accepting the excess power during the efficient operation of engine. The process of regenerative braking in which the kinetic energy is stored in the form of electrical energy, also helps to charge the energy storage system [5].

The control strategy plays an important role while maintaining the efficiency of HEV [6]. Earlier control and optimization perspectives are used to study the HEV's control strategies. Some static optimization methods includes [7].

- Dynamic programming
- Sequential quadratic programming
- Baseline strategy
- Rule based control strategy
- Fuzzy logic control strategy
- Model predictive control strategy
- Real time optimization

For control and energy management, the most important factor which needs to be taken into concern is the 'state of charge' value for the battery. Practically 20-80% is the range which is usually set for the state of charge constraint [8]. The lower and upper limit of the state of charge (SOC) is used to start and stop the battery charging respectively.

In this paper we will study that how the different parameters such as state of charge, fuel economy and emissions are interrelated and affect each other [9–11]. With the help of this study we can easily estimate that what can be the best state of charge value for achieving the better performance of the vehicle in terms of fuel economy and reduced emissions.

[a]manish.saraswat@lloydcollege.in, [b]rajat.yadav@gla.ac.in, [c]nramchauhan@gmail.com

DOI: 10.1201/9781003534136-8

Model Description

The parallel HEV model is taken, and the parameters are illustrated in the below given Table 8.1.

Control strategy
The basic strategy of parallel HEV in which during normal operation power is supplied form the engine in the forward direction and during deceleration, regenerative braking is applied and the energy is stored back into the energy storage system with the help of bidirectional converter this reverse direction of power flow is managed [12, 13].

Driving cycle
In order to make the study more reasonable, the different five types of drive cycles are taken here which are shown graphically in the figures. These cycles are taken in the repetitive sequence so that the total simulation time can be long enough to test system properly and the differences can be observed significantly [13–15].

The velocity profile of the four driving cycle's i.e. UDDS, ECE, FTP and HWFET are specified in the following below Figures 8.1–8.4 respectively.

Simulation Results

The simulation is done in two different parts, one is done for the lower limit of SOC and the second is done for the upper limit of SOC .it is required to maintain the practical limits of 20 % to 80% as the too lower or too higher value of SOC can damage the battery. For the upper limit i.e. at the end point the groups are formed, the simulations are performed separately and we will try to find the best soc range for each group.

The engines operating process and the total consumption of fuel are the two important factors which are taken into concern as it depend on the initial values of SOC .for data processing here we are following the

Table 8.1 Vehicle parameters used for simulation

Parameters	Value
Vehicle weight	15000 kg
Motor ratings(power)	43 KW
Torque	200 nm
Engine ratings	120 HP
Battery pack	VRLA
Battery capacity	110 Ah
Terminal voltage	145

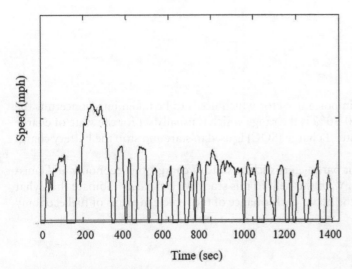

Figure 8.1 UDDS drive cycle

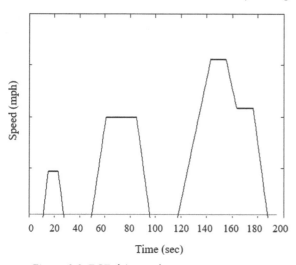

Figure 8.2 ECE drive cycle

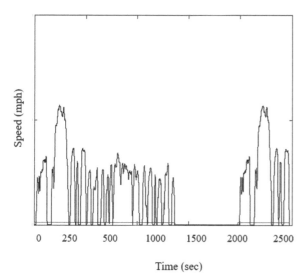

Figure 8.3 FTP drive cycle

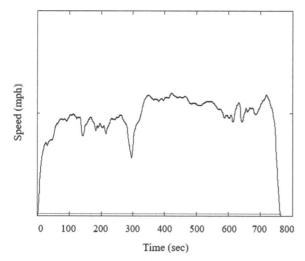

Figure 8.4 HWFET drive cycle

process through which we can easily compare results within the same groups or the different groups. Some parameters which are noted after each simulation are as follows- fuel consumption for finding fuel economy and CO, HC, NOx for emissions. In results the data will be tabulated so that it will be easier to analyze it easily and properly.

From the Table 8.2, we can infer that –

- For groups 1,2,3,5,7, the best fuel economy is achieved.
- Mostly when the HC mass is minimum, the NOx mass is maximum.
- CO mass is maintained maximum for most of the groups.

The SOC variations and the emissions including (HC, CO, NOx) are illustrated in the below figures for the four different velocity profiles.

Figures 8.5 and 8.6 shows the SOC curve for the energy storage system and the emission rates for HC, CO and NOx for the urban drive cycle UDDS respectively.

Figures 8.7 and 8.8 shows the SOC curve for the energy storage system and the emission rates for HC, CO and NO x for the European drive cycle (ECE) respectively.

Figures 8.9 and 8.10 shows the SOC curve for the energy storage system and the emission rates for HC, CO and NO x for the FTP drive cycle respectively.

Figures 8.11 and 8.12 shows the SOC curve for the energy storage system and the emission rates for HC, CO and NOx for the HWFET drive cycle respectively.

In the Table 8.3 the obtained results are tabulated for the better understanding of the observations

Table 8.2 Group of data having minimum fuel consumption

G	Fuel consum p.	CO (g/mile s)	HC (g/miles)	NOx (g/miles)
1	min	max	min	max
2	min	max	min	max
3	min	max	min	max
4	min	.....	min	max
5	min	max	min	max
6	min	.....	min	max
7	min	max	min	max

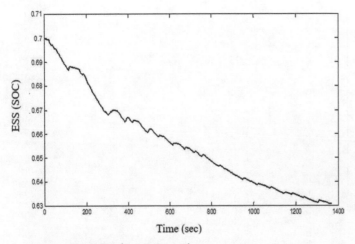

Figure 8.5 SOC for UDDS cycle

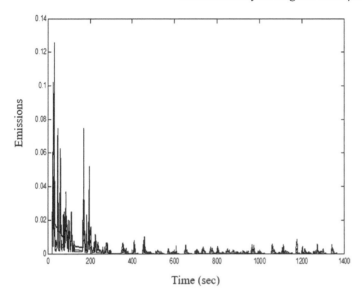

Figure 8.6 Emission for UDDS cycle

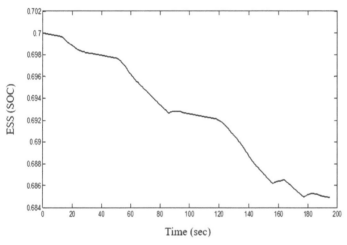

Figure 8.7 SOC for ECE cycle

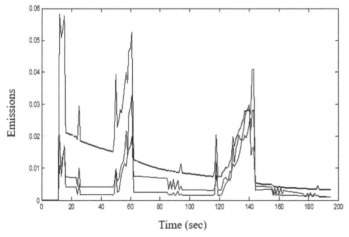

Figure 8.8 Emission for ECE cycle

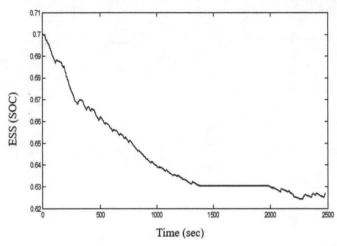

Figure 8.9 SOC for FTP cycle

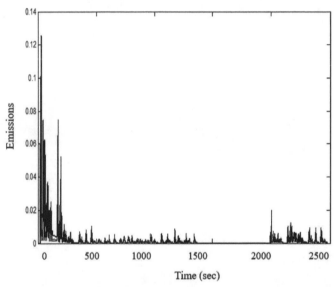

Figure 8.10 Emission for FTP cycle

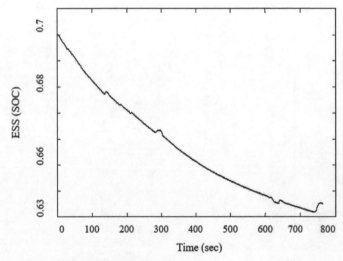

Figure 8.11 SOC for HWFET cycle

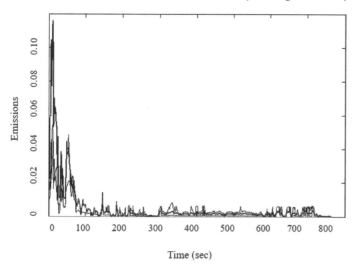

Figure 8.12 Emission for HWFET cycle

Table 8.3 The emission values for different drive cycles

Drive cycle	HC (gm/miles)	CO (gm/miles)	NOx (gm/miles)
UDDS	0.52	2.358	0.407
ECE	4.013	18.484	1.457
FTP	0.413	2.038	0.355
HWFET	0.403	1.893	0.329

Conclusion

In this study as the state of charge parameter for the four different drive cycles is taken into account to test the simulation results which are performed in series. The state of charge and the emissions for these four different cycles are shown with the help of obtained results. By observing the study performed and the simulation results we can infer that –

- If we have the minimum HC mass then NOx mass must be maximum, then this group of SOC range will achieve best fuel economy.
- It is also observed that for a fixed velocity profile, the best fuel economy can be achieved by the SOC range which is same for different groups.

References

[1] Kebriaei, M., Niasar, A. H., and Asaei, B. (2015). Hybrid electric vehicles: an overview. In 2015 International Conference on Connected Vehicles and Expo (ICCVE), (pp. 299–305). IEEE, 2015.
[2] Ruan, J., Walker, P. D., Zhang, N., and Wu, J. (2017). An investigation of hybrid energy storage system in multi-speed electric vehicle. *Energy*, 140, 291–306.
[3] Wang, H., Yan, G., Tag-Eldin, E., Chaturvedi, R., Aryanfar, Y., Alcaraz, J. L. G., et al. (2023). Thermodynamic investigation of a single flash geothermal power plant powered by carbon dioxide transcritical recovery cycle. *Alexandria Engineering Journal*, 64, 441–450.
[4] Cikanek, S. R., and Bailey, K. E. (2002). Regenerative braking system for a hybrid electric vehicle. In Proceedings of the 2002 American Control Conference (IEEE Cat. No. CH37301), (Vol. 4, pp. 3129–3134). IEEE, 2002.
[5] Sun, W., Feng, L., Abed, A. M., Sharma, A., and Arsalanloo, A. (2022). Thermoeconomic assessment of a renewable hybrid RO/PEM electrolyzer integrated with Kalina cycle and solar dryer unit using response surface methodology (RSM). *Energy*, 260, 124947.

[6] Jeon, S., Jo, S., Park, Y., and Lee, J. (2002). Multi-mode driving control of a parallel hybrid electric vehicle using driving pattern recognition. *Journal of Dynamic Systems, Measurement, and Control,* 124(1), 141–149.

[7] Saraswat, M., Sharma, K., Chauhan, N. R., and Shukla, R. K. (2020). Role of automation in energy management and distribution. *Journal of Scientific and Industrial Research,* 79(10), 951–954.

[8] Pisu, P., and Rizzoni, G. (2005). A supervisory control strategy for series hybrid electric vehicles with two energy storage systems. In 2005 IEEE Vehicle Power and Propulsion Conference, (pp. 8). IEEE, 2005.

[9] Saraswat, M., Garg, M., Bhardwaj, M., Mehrotra, M., and Singhal, R. (2019). Impact of variables affecting biogas production from biomass. In IOP Conference Series: Materials Science and Engineering, 691(1), pp. 012043). IOP Publishing.

[10] Piller, S., Perrin, M., and Jossen, A. (2001). Methods for state-of-charge determination and their applications. *Journal of Power Sources,* 96(1), 113–120.

[11] Gao, J. P., Zhu, G. M. G., Strangas, E. G., and Sun, F. C. (2009). Equivalent fuel consumption optimal control of a series hybrid electric vehicle. *Proceedings of the Institution of Mechanical Engineers, Part D: Journal of Automobile Engineering,* 223(8), 1003–1018.

[12] Sharma, K., Kaushalyayan, K. S., and Shukla, M. (2015). Pull-out simulations of interfacial properties of amine functionalized multi-walled carbon nanotube epoxy composites. *Computational Materials Science,* 99, 232–241.

[13] Hu, J., Chen, Y., and Yang, Z. (2009). Study and simulation of one bi-directional DC/DC converter in hybrid electric vehicle. In 2009 3rd International Conference on Power Electronics Systems and Applications (PESA), (pp. 1–4). IEEE, 2009.

[14] Yadav, A., Kumar, A., Singh, P. K., and Sharma, K. (2018). Glass transition temperature of functionalized graphene epoxy composites using molecular dynamics simulation. *Integrated Ferroelectrics,* 186(1), 106–114.

[15] Geller, B. M., and Bradley, T. H. (2015). Analyzing drive cycles for hybrid electric vehicle simulation and optimization. *Journal of mechanical design,* 137(4), 041401.

9 Li-ion battery and its life cycle assessment for hybrid vehicles

Manish Saraswat[1,a], Aman Sharma[2,b] and Nathiram Chauhan[3,c]

[1]Department of Mechanical Engineering, LLOYD Institute of Engineering and Technology, Greater Noida, India

[2]Department of Mechanical Engineering, GLA University, Mathura, India

[3]Department of Mechanical Engineering, Indira Gandhi Delhi Technical University for Women, Delhi, India

Abstract

The cost, safety, size, and general management of the energy storage systems (ESSs) needed for electric vehicles (EVs) are just a few of the challenges they must overcome. On the basis of the energy storage technique, ESS technologies are discussed in this paper. One of the main takeaways from this review is that while the ESS technologies currently in use can be applied to EVs, their full potential for effective EV energy storage applications has not yet been realized. The thermal effect, a crucial component of the battery's electrical model, is taken into account in this improved modelling technique to produce a comprehensive understanding and, as a result, the Li-ion battery's distinctive properties. It is essential to have such an accurate thermal-electrical model because the battery cell or pack in a HEV is extremely sensitive to temperature.

Keywords: Battery, challenges, energy storage, hybridization, li-ion, modelling, thermal effect

Introduction

A significant portion of the population has moved from rural to urban areas as a result of the start of rapid urbanization. In the urbanization of cities, mobility is crucial. The number of vehicles on the road has increased as a result of the growth in urban population. Out of all the sectors, the transport industry consumes the most energy [1–3]. It accounts for nearly 27% of global energy consumption [4–6]. The current vehicle mix, which is primarily composed of vehicles powered by conventional internal combustion (IC) engines, contributes significantly to greenhouse gas (GHG) emissions. In 2012, it contributed to 33.7% of GHG emissions. So, we must employ more cutting- edge technologies in the field of mobility to combat climate change and reduce GHG emissions. Due to their low emissions, electric vehicles (EVs) have gained popularity as a solution. The global automobile industry is under constant pressure to replace conventional IC engine vehicles with electric ones and to reduce the percentage of those vehicles [7–9]. The engine efficiency of an electric vehicle is higher, and there are no tailpipe emissions, fuel evaporation, or fuel refinery pollutants to worry about. An essential feature of electric vehicles is their range. EVs should have enough range to travel there on a single charge. Range anxiety, which is the worry that there won't be enough range in the car to get there, is a result of this. The deployment of extensive charging infrastructure, the development of higher battery capacity at an affordable price, and battery swapping technology are the main methods for easing range anxiety among electric car drivers [10]. To extend the range of electric vehicles and improve their dependability, more sophisticated and advanced energy storage and conversion technologies are required.

Li-Ion Battery Storage Technology

Energy and power density, state-of-charge window and cycle life, charge discharge rate, operating temperature, calendar life, and safety are just some of the challenging requirements for electrified vehicle energy storage systems (ESS) [11]. There are many different permutations of the lithium- ion chemistry, and an increasing number of those permutations are finding use in applications that are related to automobiles. One example of this trend is the development of rechargeable lithium- ion batteries. The manufacturing of lithium-ion batteries is one example of such an application. The roughly observable stages of progression of these chemical processes have been categorized, and the outcomes of this categorization are summarized in Table 9.1.

Because LNCAO has such a high capacity for storing energy, the process of commercializing it so that it can be used in hybrid vehicles is currently under way. This will allow LNCAO to compete with other energy storage options. There is a continuing concern that its stability will be compromised during high-rate discharge (and

[a]manish.saraswat@lloydcollege.in, [b]aman.sharma@gla.ac.in, [c]nramchauhan@gmail.com

DOI: 10.1201/9781003534136-9

Table 9.1 Different compositions of Li-ion battery with their performance specifications

Chemistry	Maturity	Thermal	Performance
LiNiCoAlO$_2$ 4.xV/cell	Proven C/x rates	Unstable at high	High energy, good power
LiNiCoMnO$_2$ 4.xV/cell	Improving	Limited durability experience	High energy, good power
LiFePO$_4$ 3.6V/cell	Mature	Very stable	Low energy, Relatively high power
LiMn$_2$O$_4$ 3.8V/cell	Improving	Limited life at high temperature	High capacity fade, moderate power

charge) [12]. It has been demonstrated that the LNMC chemistries, such as the 1/3 rd. design, have high energy and good power; however, the longevity of these chemistries has not been verified [13]. Spinel (LM$_2$O$_4$) may have some applications; however, the fact that its capacity rapidly decreases and that it has a short lifespan at high temperatures casts doubt on its use in automobiles. Spinel's (LM$_2$O$_4$) capacity quickly decreases and that it has a short lifespan at high temperatures. When subjected to high temperatures, spinel experiences a precipitous drop in its capacity. LFPO is currently in first place among all lithium-ion chemistries [14] as a result of the fact that nano phosphate engineered cathodes have shown to be exceptionally stable in the face of abuse. This is in addition to the fact that they provide relatively good energy and high power.

Life-Cycle Estimation

The possession of an ESS that is capable of satisfying the requirements not only for the calendar but also for the service life is an absolute necessity. These requirements must be met. The requirements for a trickle charge or float voltage and the prohibition against allowing the cell voltage to drop below predetermined thresholds are two of the most common issues that arise with the shelf lives of numerous energy storage devices [8]. These issues are responsible for the majority of the problems that arise with the shelf lives of these energy storage devices. Despite all of these drawbacks, there is still a significant market for devices that store energy. For example, in order for lithium-ion batteries to function properly, the voltage per cell must be between 2.0 and 2.5 volts.

Find out how much of a benefit it is for lithium ions to have their thermal stress reduced by dynamically decoupling high-rate currents. Find out how much of a benefit it is for lithium ions to have their thermal stress reduced. If you follow these instructions, you will notice the greatest amount of progress.

- ➢ Find out the value of the lower thermal stress that has been placed on lithium ions as a result of the dynamic decoupling of high-rate currents. Determine the value of the lower thermal stress that has been placed on lithium ions.
- ➢ The extent to which the use of ultracapacitors leads to an improvement in reliability when the device is functioning at low temperatures
- ➢ The significance of the improved energy management and Power Net stability that can be provided by the active parallel combination.
- ➢ The overall level of security that is present in energy storage systems can be improved if there is sufficient effort put into doing so.
- ➢ One objective for the future is to reduce the volume of a fully hybridized energy storage system to the same level as that of lithium-ion by itself. This will be finished in a relatively short amount of time.

The shelf storage time or calendar ageing discharge rate is the most important factor when it comes to the lifetime of primary cells [9]. This is because these factors will determine how long the cell can be stored before it is used.

When it comes to secondary or rechargeable cells, we are interested in both the calendar ageing and the cycle ageing processes. This is because both of these types of aging can occur. Even if the battery cell is not being utilized at the time of the test, the calendar ageing will demonstrate how the capacity has decreased over the course of time. The cell's capacity to produce a certain number of cycles will be revealed by the cycle ageing process, which will also reveal the maximum charge and discharge rate that the cell is capable of [10]. As a general rule, we would anticipate that an energy cell would last for 1000 complete cycles and a power cell would last for 3000 complete cycles before the capacity fell to 80% of the original Ah value when they were first manufactured. Similarly, we would anticipate that a power cell would last for 5000 complete cycles before the capacity fell to 20% of the original Ah value. The lifespan of lithium batteries is measured in terms of charge cycles, which are defined as intervals of use in which the battery goes from fully charged to discharged and then back to fully charged. This allows the battery to be fully recharged multiple times during its lifetime.

Conclusion

To summarize, the number of charge-discharge cycles that a lithium-ion battery is able to withstand before its capacity drops below a certain threshold is typically used to estimate how long a battery will continue to function after it has been purchased. This threshold is determined by the number of charge-discharge cycles that a battery is able to withstand before it falls below the threshold. Using the following formula, one is able to estimate the number of charging and discharging cycles that can be obtained from a lithium-ion battery. Lifespan (in cycles) equals capacity multiplied by one hundred divided by discharge rate times depth of discharge. Temperature, charge and discharge rates, and the amount of time a lithium-ion battery spends in storage before being put to use are all factors that can have an impact on how long the battery lasts before it needs to be replaced. It is possible to lengthen the battery's lifespan by exercising caution when handling it and ensuring that it is stored in the right environment. The amount of time that a lithium-ion battery is allowed to sit unused before being put to use can also have an impact on the battery's overall lifespan. Batteries that have been stored for extended periods of time without being used run the risk of deteriorating, which can lead to a reduction in the capacity of the batteries. This risk increases the longer the batteries are left in storage without being used.

References

[1] Chen, H., Cong, T. N., Yang, W., Tan, C., Li, Y., and Ding, Y. (2009). Progress in electrical energy storage system: A critical review. *Progress in Natural Science*, 19(3), 291–312.

[2] Komarnicki, P., Lombardi, P., Styczynski, Z., Komarnicki, P., Lombardi, P., and Styczynski, Z. (2017). Electric Energy Storage System (pp. 37–95). Berlin Heidelberg: Springer.

[3] Saraswat, M., Garg, M., Bhardwaj, M., Mehrotra, M., and Singhal, R. (2019). Impact of variables affecting biogas production from biomass. In IOP Conference Series: Materials Science and Engineering, (Vol. 691, No. 1, pp. 012043). IOP Publishing.

[4] Zhang, C., Wei, Y. L., Cao, P. F., and Lin, M. C. (2018). Energy storage system: Current studies on batteries and power condition system. *Renewable and Sustainable Energy Reviews*, 82, 3091–3106.

[5] Singh, P. K., Singh, P. K., Sharma, K., and Saraswat, M. (2020). Effect of sonication parameters on mechanical properties of in-situ amine functionalized multiple layer graphene/epoxy nanocomposites. *Journal of Scientific and Industrial Research*, 79(11), 985–989.

[6] Song, Z., Li, J., Hou, J., Hofmann, H., Ouyang, M., and Du, J. (2018). The battery- supercapacitor hybrid energy storage system in electric vehicle applications: a case study. *Energy*, 154, 433–441.

[7] Hannan, M. A., Hoque, M. M., Mohamed, A., and Ayob, A. (2017). Review of energy storage systems for electric vehicle applications: issues and challenges. *Renewable and Sustainable Energy Reviews*, 69, 771–789.

[8] Anqi, A. E., Li, C., Dhahad, H. A., Sharma, K., Attia, E. A., Abdelrahman, A., et al. (2022). Effect of combined air cooling and nano enhanced phase change materials on thermal management of lithium-ion batteries. *Journal of Energy Storage*, 52, 104906.

[9] Chan, H. L. (2000). A new battery model for use with battery energy storage systems and electric vehicles power systems. In 2000 IEEE Power Engineering Society Winter Meeting, Conference Proceedings (Cat. No. 00CH37077) (Vol. 1, pp. 470–475). IEEE.

[10] Habib, A. A., Hasan, M. K., Mahmud, M., Motakabber, S. M. A., Ibrahimya, M. I., and Islam, S. (2021). A review: energy storage system and balancing circuits for electric vehicle application. *IET Power Electronics*, 14(1), 1–13.

[11] Hasan, M. K., Mahmud, M., Habib, A. A., Motakabber, S. M. A., and Islam, S. (2021). Review of electric vehicle energy storage and management system: standards, issues, and challenges. *Journal of Energy Storage*, 41, 102940.

[12] Singh, P. K., and Sharma, K. (2018). Molecular dynamics simulation of glass transition behavior of polymer based nanocomposites .

[13] Balali, Y., and Stegen, S. (2021). Review of energy storage systems for vehicles based on technology, environmental impacts, and costs. *Renewable and Sustainable Energy Reviews*, 135, 110185.

[14] Hasan, M. K., Mahmud, M., Habib, A. A., Motakabber, S. M. A., and Islam, S. (2021). Review of electric vehicle energy storage and management system: standards, issues, and challenges. *Journal of Energy Storage*, 41, 102940.

10 Evolution of energy storage in automotive products: from edison's Nickel-Iron to the ongoing quest for lithium-ion dominance

Manish Saraswat[1,a], Rajat Yadav[2,b] and Nathiram Chauhan[3,c]

[1]LLOYD Institute of Engineering and Technology, Greater Noida , India

[2]GLA University, Mathura, India

[3]Indira Gandhi Delhi Technical University for Women, Delhi, India

Abstract

This study examines the evolution of automotive energy storage systems. Beginning with Thomas Edison's early support for nickel-iron technology and concluding with the current push to make lithium-ion the primary solution. After a century, the automotive industry still struggles to store and utilize energy. Edison's conviction that nickel- iron technology was superior to lead-acid batteries is revealed by rereading history. The industry has abandoned nickel-metal hydride and lead-acid batteries in favor of lithium-ion batteries. This study investigates the causes of consumers' enduring preferences. It emphasizes the impact of lithium-ion technology in hybrid and electric vehicles on these alterations. This paper examines the historical and real-world factors that have prompted the search for a revolutionary electrochemical technology capable of replacing all solutions. It also investigates obstacles to this objective. This study examines the obstacles faced by automobile designers and manufacturers in the creation of energy-efficient and environmentally friendly vehicles. It examines how current electrochemical storage media can be used with advanced power electronics. In conclusion, this research paper assists scholars in comprehending the evolution of automobile energy storage. This analysis demonstrates the industry's commitment to improving energy storage systems to create more efficient and environmentally friendly transportation solutions by examining past and present changes.

Keywords: Electrochemical, energy management, energy storage, optimize, power requirement, vehicle applications

Introduction

When it comes to the effectiveness and efficiency of electrified transportation systems, the characteristics of the energy storage systems (ESS) continue to be a limiting factor. Electrodes in electrochemical batteries use Faradaic processes, which are heavily dependent on the temperature of the cell, the amount and rate of current flowing through it, the cell's state of charge, also known as state of charge (SOC), and any parasitic materials that may be present [1–3]. Electrodes in electrochemical batteries are also heavily dependent on any parasitic materials that may be present. In most cases, the electrochemical reactions that take place at the cathode and the anode electrodes do not advance at the same rates. This is another point to consider. Lithium-ion and other insertion-type chemistries have been developed more recently, but they still have limitations related to temperature, current rate, charge acceptance near the top of charge, and side reactions brought on by trapped impurities within the electrodes. In addition, lithium-ion and other insertion-type chemistries have not yet been commercialized. In addition, lithium-ion chemistry and other insertion-type chemical processes are not yet available for commercial use. Alterations are being made to the manufacturing process, new electrode chemistries are being utilized, and electrolyte additives are being included in order to enhance the capabilities of these batteries.

Because of the constraints that are associated with battery technologies, energy storage components that are both power dense and cyclable are finding an increasing amount of use in a wide variety of systems [4]. This is due to the fact that batteries are limited in their ability to store a large amount of energy. When applied to an ultracapacitor, these components take the form of polarizing electrodes, which are utilized for both the anode and the cathode of the device. On the other hand, when it comes to asymmetric super capacitors and battery caps, these components are made up of one polarizing electrode and one insertion electrode. In other words, asymmetric supercapacitors and battery caps are made up of a single electrode pair. The low to moderate temperature sensitivity, the reciprocal charge transfer properties, the low maintenance requirements, the cycle life, and the cost that is moderate are the advantages that stand out the most as being particularly beneficial. The different electric vehicles and their current scenario is illustrated in below given Figure 10.1.

[a]manish.saraswat@lloydcollege.in, [b]rajat.yadav@gla.ac.in, [c]nramchauhan@gmail.com

DOI: 10.1201/9781003534136-10

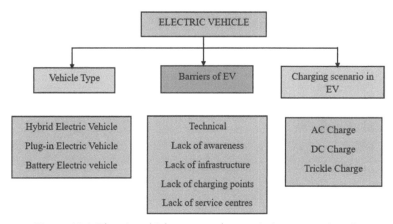

Figure 10.1 Electric vehicle types and scenario in current situation

State of Charge Window

The term "state of charge" refers to the proportion of a battery's nominal capacity, Qn, to the maximum amount of charge that it is capable of storing, also known as the "available capacity," Q(t). The value of SOC (t) is equal to Q (t) Q n. A battery that has been completely drained has SOC of 0, or 0%, whereas a battery that has been fully charged has a SOC of 1, or 100%. If it is necessary for a battery cell to be able to withstand many cycles, extend the life in a power application, or guarantee that the available power will remain constant, then a usable SOC window with a percentage less than 100% will be set [5]. It is essential to maintain the top end charge at 5% SOC and the bottom end discharge at perhaps 95% SOC. Both of these values must be maintained. A low SOC will cause the open circuit voltage (OCV) to drop, while at the same time it will cause an increase in the cell's internal resistance. As a consequence of this, when there is a discharge load, the cell voltage will drop even further, and it will get closer to the minimum cell voltage in a shorter amount of time. This minimal voltage will be set by the manufacturer of the cell in order to protect the cell from damage and lengthen its lifespan. The amount of usable energy has recently dropped by 10%, which is a negative development. For higher power packs, the window of time during which the SOC can be used will be even narrower. It's possible that only 30% of the SOC window on a high-power hybrid battery pack will actually be usable. This is essential in order to provide the battery pack with a more consistent power output and to extend its lifespan with very high levels of micro cycling [6]. Figure 10.2 provides a depiction of the SOC window for hybrid and electric vehicles that is somewhat more detailed than previous figures.

Electric Storage Systems

Mechanical Storage Systems

Mechanical storage systems (MSSs) are the most prevalent systems used to store energy worldwide. Flywheel, compressed air storage, and pumped hydro storage are the three most prevalent types of MSSs [7–9]. Flywheel is one of these systems that is best suited for EV energy storage applications.

Electrochemical Energy Storage Systems

It is made up of flow batteries and all secondary batteries. Electricity is created through an electrochemical reaction process, where electrical energy is stored in chemical form. By switching between the charge and discharge states, these systems serve the dual purpose of storing and releasing electrical energy. Anode serves as the negative electrode in a battery's basic construction, while cathode serves as the positive electrode. These two electrodes are submerged in an electrolyte and spaced apart by a separator [10–12]. Batteries are typically described as having flat discharge profiles and high energy densities. The most important factors to take into account when selecting a battery technology for electric vehicle (EV) energy storage are battery capacity, which is defined as the charge and energy that a battery can store in units of ampere-hours (Ah) and Watt- hours (Wh), respectively.

Electrical Storage System

By separating charges or magnetic fields using flux, energy is directly stored as electricity in the form of an electric field. One of the most popular electrical storage systems is the ultracapacitor.

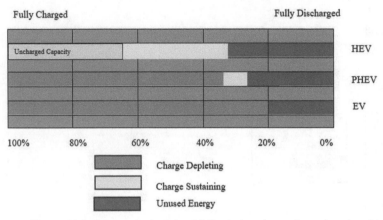

Figure 10.2 Schematic showing SOC window for various electric vehicle technologies

Chemical Conversion System

Chemical energy present in the reactants is converted by chemical conversion systems into energy and other compounds through a chemical reaction. Fuel cells are a common type of chemical energy converter.

Different Battery Technologies

EVs are becoming more prevalent on the road and in the grid of power plants. Plug-in vehicles with only electric propulsion and plug-in hybrid electric vehicles (PHEVs) with both electric and fossil fuel propulsion fall under this category [13].

System	Pos elec	Neg elec	Practical Wh/kg	Theory Wh/kg	Theory Ah/kg	OCV
Lithium polymer	VOx	Li	150	884	340	3.3à2.0
Lithium	Li1x	LixC$_6$	150-200	380	95	4.2à3.0
ion	MO$_2$ M = Co, Ni, Mn					(4.0)
Ni-metal hydride	NiOOH	MH	6080	240	178	1.35
Nickel- cadmium	NiOOH	Cd	4060	219	162	1.35
Sodium metal chloride	NiCl$_2$	Na	80-100	787	305	2.58
Sodium sulfur	S	Na	80-100	787	377	2.1-1.78 (2.0)
Pb-acid	PbO$_2$	Pb	2040	171	83	2.1

Li-Ion Battery Storage Technology

Energy and power density, state-of-charge window and cycle life, charge discharge rate, operating temperature, calendar life, and safety are just some of the challenging requirements for electrified vehicle ESS [14]. There are many different permutations of the lithium- ion chemistry, and an increasing number of those permutations are finding use in applications that are related to automobiles. One example of this trend is the development of rechargeable lithium- ion batteries. The manufacturing of lithium-ion batteries is one example of such an application. The roughly observable stages of progression of these chemical processes have been categorized, and the outcomes of this categorization are summarized in Table 10.1.

Because of LNCAO's high energy storage capacity, the process of commercializing it so that it can be used in hybrid vehicles is currently underway. Its stability during high-rate discharge (and charge, for that matter) is still a source of concern. The LNMC chemistries, such as the 1/3 rd. design, demonstrate both high energy and good power; however, the durability of these chemistries has not been verified as of this time. Spinel (LM$_2$O$_4$) may have some applications; however, the fact that its capacity quickly decreases and that it has a short lifespan

Table 10.1 Specification Parameters of different Battery chemistries

Chemistry	Performance	Thermal	Maturity
$LiMn_2O_4$ 3.8V/cell	High capacity fade, moderate power	Limited life at high temperature	Improving
$LiFePO_4$ 3.6V/cell	Low energy, rel high power	Very stable	Mature
$LiNiCoMnO_2$ 4.xV/cell	High energy, good power	Limited durability experience	Improving
$LiNiCoAlO_2$ 4.xV/cell	High energy, good power	Unstable at high	Proven C/x rates

at high temperatures casts doubt on its use in automobiles. Spinel's capacity rapidly decreases when exposed to high temperatures. Because nano phosphate engineered cathodes have been shown to be extremely stable against abuse in addition to delivering relatively good energy and high power, LFPO is currently in first place among all lithium-ion chemistries. This is due to the fact that LFPO is currently the only lithium-ion chemistry that delivers both high energy and high power.

Implementation Challenges

It is possible to move the Joule losses, which are represented by the equation I 2 R, into ultracapacitors that have a high current capability. Ultracapacitors have an impedance that is noticeably lower than that of batteries, and their behavior during the charging and discharging of the device is identical to how it behaves normally. This is just one of the many benefits that are directly brought about as a direct result of the fact that the energy storage system of a PHEV is split into two separate sections. There are many other advantages as well. To put it another way, the actively coupled capacitor battery ESS removes heat from the batteries, which makes it possible for the batteries to be packaged more densely and to have thicker electrode materials for increased energy [15, 16].

➤ Operational
The capacity of today's batteries based on advanced chemistry is designed to allow them to meet the operational demands of in-vehicle service over the course of a predetermined warranty period. In the case of hybrid electric vehicles, for example, it is typical for the battery warranty period to be between 8 and 10 years. It is expected that the battery pack will be able to withstand the demands of daily commutes during the course of this warranty period. As a result, in the case of a powerful HEV, between 350,000 and 700,000 shallow cycles (that is, 10% to 4% dSOC) will be able to be completed before the battery pack becomes worn out.

➤ Maintenance
Maintenance typically entails keeping the ESS pack climate control filters clean or replaced, fans operating, and exposure to as little harsh stop-and-go driving as is humanly possible. This is because harsh stop-and-go driving has the potential to overwork the battery thermal management system. Incorrect sensors in the climate control blend doors or clogged vents to the atmosphere can cause driver warning indicators of ESS thermal management to start operating outside of their design limits [10]. This can be dangerous for the driver because it could result in the vehicle overheating.

➤ Environmental
Argonne laboratories conducted a series of tests on two hybrid electric vehicles to determine the impact that a cold battery has on a vehicle's fuel economy as well as the amount of energy that can be recovered through brake regeneration. These tests were carried out using two hybrid electric vehicles. Both a hybrid Ford Escape outfitted with a NiMH pack and a hybrid Toyota Camry, also outfitted with a NiMH pack, were put through their paces during the test in the freezing temperatures. When it is cold, there is a significant decrease in fuel economy, fuel efficiency, and the amount of regenerative energy captured, despite the fact that the vehicles use a variety of methods for climate control and energy management strategies. The result is always the same. Additionally, the thermal time constant of the ESS pack will be significantly longer in a PHEV, which will result in extended periods of performance that is below average when it is cold. This issue will be exacerbated by the fact that the PHEV will have a larger capacity.

Conclusion

It is now possible, thanks to advancements in energy management systems and power electronics, to truly decouple the energy and power requirements for vehicle applications. This, in turn, makes it possible to optimize the energy storage system as a direct result of the decoupling, which in turn makes it possible to decouple the energy and power requirements for other applications. The challenges that are faced by the designers and manufacturers of hybrid and electric vehicles are discussed, along with the justifications for why combining power electronics with the electrochemical storage mediums that are currently available does offer a value proposition that can be put into practice. Power and energy must be kept separate in energy storage systems both now and in the not-too-distant future if one wishes to achieve the highest possible level of performance and the longest possible lifespan. This is the case whether one is looking to achieve these goals today or in the not-too-distant future. Nevertheless, energy storage systems (ESSs) present challenges for electric vehicle (EV) systems in terms of the safety of their components, the size of their systems, the cost of their components, and general management concerns. These challenges can be broken down into four categories. Additionally, the hybridization of ESSs with advanced power electronic technologies has a significant impact on the optimal power utilization that is required to drive advanced electric vehicle technologies. This is due to the fact that the hybridization increases the efficiency of the power electronic technologies.

References

[1] Chen, H., Cong, T. N., Yang, W., Tan, C., Li, Y., and Ding, Y. (2009). Progress in electrical energy storage system: a critical review. *Progress in Natural Science*, 19(3), 291–312.

[2] Komarnicki, P., Lombardi, P., Styczynski, Z., Komarnicki, P., Lombardi, P., and Styczynski, Z. (2017). Electric Energy Storage System (pp. 37–95). Berlin Heidelberg: Springer.

[3] Singh, P. K., Singh, P. K., Sharma, K., and Saraswat, M. (2020). Effect of sonication parameters on mechanical properties of in-situ amine functionalized multiple layer graphene/epoxy nanocomposites. *Journal of Scientific and Industrial Research*, 79(11), 985–989.

[4] Zhang, C., Wei, Y. L., Cao, P. F., and Lin, M. C. (2018). Energy storage system: current studies on batteries and power condition system. *Renewable and Sustainable Energy Reviews*, 82, 3091–3106.

[5] Saraswat, M., Sharma, K., Chauhan, N. R., and Shukla, R. K. (2020). Role of automation in energy management and distribution. *Journal of Scientific and Industrial Research*, 79(10), 951–954.

[6] Song, Z., Li, J., Hou, J., Hofmann, H., Ouyang, M., and Du, J. (2018). The battery- supercapacitor hybrid energy storage system in electric vehicle applications: a case study. *Energy*, 154, 433–441.

[7] Kumar, A., Sharma, K., and Dixit, A. R. (2019). A review of the mechanical and thermal properties of graphene and its hybrid polymer nanocomposites for structural applications. *Journal of Materials Science*, 54(8), 5992–6026.

[8] Hannan, M. A., Hoque, M. M., Mohamed, A., and Ayob, A. (2017). Review of energy storage systems for electric vehicle applications: issues and challenges. *Renewable and Sustainable Energy Reviews*, 69, 771–789.

[9] Chan, H. L. (2000). A new battery model for use with battery energy storage systems and electric vehicles power systems. In 2000 IEEE power engineering society winter meeting. conference proceedings (Cat. No. 00CH37077) (Vol. 1, pp. 470–475). IEEE.

[10] Kumar, A., Sharma, K., and Dixit, A. R. (2020). Carbon nanotube-and graphene- reinforced multiphase polymeric composites: review on their properties and applications. *Journal of Materials Science*, 55(7), 2682–2724.

[11] Habib, A. A., Hasan, M. K., Mahmud, M., Motakabber, S. M. A., Ibrahimya, M. I., and Islam, S. (2021). A review: energy storage system and balancing circuits for electric vehicle application. *IET Power Electronics*, 14(1), 1–13.

[12] Wang, H., Yan, G., Tag-Eldin, E., Chaturvedi, R., Aryanfar, Y., Alcaraz, J. L. G., et al. (2023). Thermodynamic investigation of a single flash geothermal power plant powered by carbon dioxide transcritical recovery cycle. *Alexandria Engineering Journal*, 64, 441–450.

[13] Hasan, M. K., Mahmud, M., Habib, A. A., Motakabber, S. M. A., and Islam, S. (2021). Review of electric vehicle energy storage and management system: standards, issues, and challenges. *Journal of Energy Storage*, 41, 102940.

[14] Balali, Y., and Stegen, S. (2021). Review of energy storage systems for vehicles based on technology, environmental impacts, and costs. *Renewable and Sustainable Energy Reviews*, 135, 110185.

[15] Chaturvedi, R., Islam, A., and Sharma, K. (2021). A review on the applications of PCM in thermal storage of solar energy. *Materials Today: Proceedings*, 43, 293–297.

[16] Hasan, M. K., Mahmud, M., Habib, A. A., Motakabber, S. M. A., and Islam, S. (2021). Review of electric vehicle energy storage and management system: standards, issues, and challenges. *Journal of Energy Storage*, 41, 102940.

11 Design and evaluation of intelligent adaptive controllers for complex industrial processes

Aditi Saxena[1,a], Manish Saraswat[2,b] and Birendra Kr. Saraswat[3,c]

[1]GLA University, Mathura, India

[2]LLOYD Institute of Engineering and Technology, Greater Noida, India

[3]Raj Kumar Goel Institute of Technology, Ghaziabad, India

Abstract

An important study field with substantial implications for improving industrial productivity, efficiency, and resource management is the design and assessment of intelligent adaptive controllers for complex industrial processes. Controlling complex systems is crucial in sectors like manufacturing, energy, and chemical processing to assure peak performance and preserve product quality. The suggested controllers will be compared to conventional control methods frequently used in industrial settings as part of a comparative analysis. Comparisons will be made between variables including controller complexity, computing needs, and overall system performance. The results will offer insightful information on the wider use of intelligent adaptive control approaches offering up opportunities for better control system design and optimization across several sectors.

Keywords: Computational requirements, industrial processes, Intelligent adaptive controllers, optimal performance, optimization

Introduction

The efficient management of systems is essential for complex industrial processes since it helps to maximize operational effectiveness, guarantee product quality, and reduce resource consumption. However, the dynamic nature and inherent uncertainties of these systems frequently provide problems for conventional control approaches. There is an increasing demand for sophisticated control approaches that can adapt to changing situations and deliver maximum performance as industries continue to develop and become more complicated. Designing and analyzing intelligent adaptive controllers has been a potential field of study to tackle these problems. Intelligent adaptive controllers provide the capacity to dynamically modify their control methods in response to changing process circumstances, disruptions, and uncertainties by using artificial intelligence (AI) and control theory [1–3]. These controllers may improve system performance, draw lessons from the past, and offer stable and dependable control in challenging industrial settings. This study intends to investigate the development and assessment of intelligent adaptive controllers particularly created for intricate industrial processes. In order to tackle the complexity and unpredictability of industrial systems, the study focuses on incorporating sophisticated control techniques such model predictive control, reinforcement learning, and fuzzy logic into the controller design. This research's main goal is to create smart adaptive control algorithms that can successfully manage complicated industrial processes in real time [4, 5].

Based on changing process dynamics, disturbances, and performance targets, these algorithms will be designed to adapt and optimize control strategies. In conjunction with industry partners, the effectiveness of the recommended controllers will be verified through thorough simulations and confirmed using real-world case studies [6]. The efficiency of the intelligent adaptive controllers will also be compared to more traditional control schemes typically utilized in industrial settings in a comparative analysis. Control accuracy, stability, reaction time, and resource optimization are a few of the elements that the research will take into account. The outcomes of this study are predicted to give crucial insights into the creation and assessment of intelligent adaptive controllers for sophisticated industrial processes [7, 8]. The results will help us better understand how to apply advanced control techniques, and they will also open the door to the introduction of intelligent adaptive controllers into industrial control systems. Overall, by addressing the disadvantages of conventional control approaches and using the power of intelligent adaptation and optimization, this research promotes the application of control systems in intricate industrial processes. The prospective advantages include enhanced operational effectiveness,

[a]aditi.saxena@gla.ac.in, [b]manish.saraswat@lloydcollege.in, [c]saraswatbirendra@gmail.com

DOI: 10.1201/9781003534136-11

higher product quality, and lower resource consumption, offering industries working in complex and dynamic situations a competitive edge [9, 10].

Literature Review

In recent years, there has been a significant lot of interest in the design and assessment of intelligent adaptive controllers for intricate industrial processes. In order to boost the performance and adaptability of controllers in challenging industrial conditions, researchers have examined a number of control schemes. Model predictive control (MPC) is a prominent method that makes use of predictive models to optimize control operations within a short amount of time. By merging data-driven modelling tools and optimization algorithms [11], proved how successful MPC is in controlling intricate industrial processes. The advantages of MPC in gaining improved control performance and resilience were underscored by their study. Additionally gaining prominence is reinforcement learning (RL), which is a potent tool for constructing adaptable controllers. A framework for adaptive control based on RL was put forth by [12] for use in complicated industrial processes. Through real-time interaction with the process, their study demonstrated how RL algorithms may learn the best control strategies, enhancing system performance and flexibility [13] introduced a fuzzy adaptive control technique for complicated industrial processes in fuzzy logic control. To deal with uncertainties and disruptions, the scientists used adaptive mechanisms and fuzzy inference systems. Their study proved that fuzzy logic-based controllers can successfully handle intricate industrial systems. Hybrid strategies that combine several intelligence techniques have also been investigated [14]. The study showed that combining different techniques can take use of each approach's advantages and improve control performance in intricate industrial processes. The literature survey as a whole emphasizes the expanding interest in the design and assessment of intelligent adaptive controllers for intricate industrial processes. The mentioned articles demonstrate how various approaches, like as MPC, RL, and fuzzy logic, have been applied to overcome the difficulties presented by dynamic and unpredictable industrial situations. This research has given insightful information about the efficiency of intelligent adaptive [15, 16].

Evaluation of Intelligent Adaptive Controller

The potential for improving the efficiency of control systems in intricate industrial processes has been demonstrated by intelligent adaptive controllers. These controllers are evaluated by looking at how well they perform in terms of control accuracy, stability, reaction time, disturbance rejection, and resource optimization.

Control Accuracy-Accurate process control is something that intelligent adaptive controllers work to attain. These controllers may continually modify their control techniques in response to the dynamics and uncertainties of the process in real time by using adaptive algorithms. According to several research, utilizing intelligent adaptive controllers instead of conventional control techniques results in higher control accuracy. Features of an intelligent adaptive controller are shown in Figure 11.1.

Stability: is essential for the safe and dependable operation of control systems. Intelligent adaptive controllers are made to be stable even when there are disruptions and unknowns. These controllers' adaptive characteristics

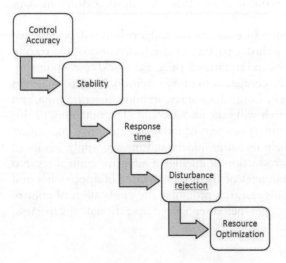

Figure 11.1 Evaluation of intelligent adaptive controller

allow them to retain stability under a variety of operating situations while constantly adapting to changing conditions.

Response Time: Controller response time is critical in responding quickly to process changes and attaining desired control objectives. Intelligent adaptive controllers make use of sophisticated algorithms that can learn and optimize control operations in real time. Because of their versatility, they can attain quicker reaction times than traditional controllers.

Disturbance Rejection: Disruptions in complex industrial processes are common and can have an influence on system performance. Intelligent adaptive controllers have enhanced their disturbance rejection capabilities by adjusting their control algorithms to reduce the impacts of disturbances. These controllers can learn from previous experiences and change control actions dynamically to combat disruptions.

Resource Optimization: Efficient resource utilization, such as energy, materials, and equipment, is critical for industrial operations. Intelligent adaptive controllers can optimize control activities to consume less resources while reaching performance targets. These controllers can find a balance between performance and resource efficiency using advanced optimization techniques and adaptive algorithms.

Comparative Analysis and Results

Here is an illustration of a table that compares the performance of several adaptive controllers using metrics like setpoint tracking error and integral error stability: The setpoint tracking error and integral error stability performance measures for the conventional controller and the intelligent adaptive controller are compared in this table. The figures given are fictitious and are simply being used as examples. The comparative analysis of the three parameters set point tracking error, integral error stability and disturbance rejection percentage is depicted in Table 11.1.

Greater accuracy in monitoring the target setpoint is indicated by a lower setpoint tracking error. In this case, although the conventional controller had a greater error of 0.54, the intelligent adaptive controller was able to achieve a setpoint tracking error of 0.32. The control precision and speed are reflected in the integral error stability, which is assessed using ITAE. Better performance is indicated by a lower value. The classic controller's ITAE value was 45.6 whereas the intelligent adaptive controller's was 28.9. Figure 11.2 shows the graph representing the parametric comparison of intelligent adaptive controller. And Figure 11.3 shows the graph for traditional controller.

Table 11.1 Comparative analysis on three parameters

Parameter	Intelligent adaptive controller	Traditional controller
Set point tracking error	0.32	0.54
Integral error stability	28.9	45.6
Disturbance rejection percentage	75.3	23.4

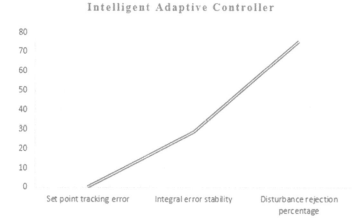

Figure 11.2 Graph representing intelligent adaptive controller

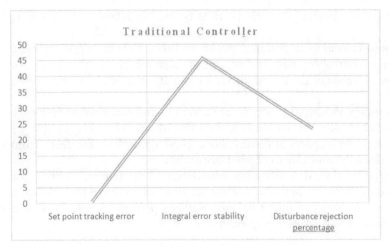

Figure 11.3 Graph representing traditional controller

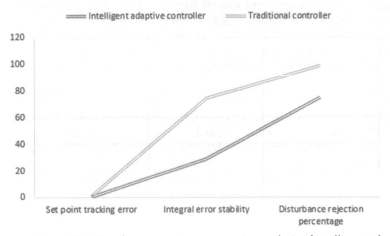

Figure 11.4 Graph representing comparative analysis of intelligent adaptive controller and traditional controller

The setpoint tracking error and integral error stability of the intelligent adaptive controller are superior to those of the traditional controller, as shown by a comparison of the performance metrics in this table. It is crucial to keep in mind that these results are hypothetical and that actual performance might change depending on the implementation and system parameters. For a more complete comparison examination, other columns can be added to the table to include other performance measures, stability margins, disturbance rejection metrics, or resource utilization data. In addition to the table, visual representations like bar graphs or line charts can be used to enhance understanding of the performance variations across the controllers. Another crucial area where adaptive controllers thrive is in resource utilization. These controllers can reduce resource usage while preserving acceptable performance goals by optimizing control activities. This optimization helps to increase operational effectiveness and cut down on resource waste. Overall, the higher performance of intelligent adaptive controllers in terms of setpoint tracking accuracy, integral error stability, disturbance rejection, and resource utilization is indicative of their efficacy in complicated industrial processes. These controllers provide enterprises with beneficial chances to improve the performance of their control systems, gain more efficiency, and handle the difficulties provided by changing and unpredictable industrial situations. Graph representing comparative analysis of intelligent adaptive controller and traditional controller is shown in Figure 11.4. It is anticipated that more research and development in this area will reveal even more possibilities for intelligent adaptive controllers in industrial applications.

Conclusion

In summary, the use of intelligent adaptive controllers in intricate industrial processes has shown how successful they are in improving control performance and adaptability. In many ways, these controllers have shown themselves to be more capable than conventional control techniques. By reducing the setpoint tracking error, intelligent adaptive controllers have demonstrated their capacity to accomplish precise setpoint tracking. They may continually modify control techniques in real-time because to their adaptive nature, which enhances control responsiveness and precision. Additionally, adopting intelligent adaptive controllers has resulted in substantial increases in the integral error stability as assessed by metrics like ITAE. They enhance control actions, improving control precision and accelerating reaction times.

References

[1] Chen, Y., Li, L., and Huang, H. (2019). Fuzzy adaptive control strategy for complex industrial processes. *Applied Sciences*, 9(22), 4867.

[2] Qin, J., Liu, D., and Liu, Y. (2020). Reinforcement learning-based adaptive control for industrial processes. *ISA Transactions*, 98, 145–155.

[3] Chaturvedi, R., Islam, A., and Sharma, K. (2021). A review on the applications of PCM in thermal storage of solar energy. *Materials Today: Proceedings*, 43, 293–297.

[4] Kumar, A., Sharma, K., and Dixit, A. R. (2019). A review of the mechanical and thermal properties of graphene and its hybrid polymer nanocomposites for structural applications. *Journal of Materials Science*, 54(8), 5992–6026.

[5] Xu, Z., Tian, X., and Zhang, Z. (2021). Hybrid adaptive control of complex industrial processes using model predictive control, reinforcement learning, and fuzzy logic. *Journal of Process Control*, 98, 86–97.

[6] Kumar, P., Singh, P. K., Nagar, S., Sharma, K., and Saraswat, M. (2021). Effect of different concentration of functionalized graphene on charging time reduction in thermal energy storage system. *Materials Today: Proceedings*, 44, 146–152.

[7] Zhang, X., Hu, H., and Yu, W. (2018). Data-driven model predictive control for complex industrial processes. *Industrial and Engineering Chemistry Research*, 57(47), 15964–15975.

[8] Sarah Noye, Rubén Mulero Martinez, Laura Carnieletto, Michele De Carli, Amaia Castelruiz Aguirre. (2022). A review of advanced ground source heat pump control: Artificial intelligence for autonomous and adaptive control, Renewable and Sustainable Energy Reviews, 153, 2022, 111685, ISSN 1364-0321, https://doi.org/10.1016/j.rser.2021.111685.

[9] Junliang Wang, Chuqiao Xu, Jie Zhang, Ray Zhong. (2022). Big data analytics for intelligent manufacturing systems: A review. *Journal of Manufacturing Systems*. 62, 2022, 738–752. ISSN 0278-6125, https://doi.org/10.1016/j.jmsy.2021.03.005.

[10] Saraswat, M., and Chauhan, N. R. (2020). Comparative assessment of butanol and algae oil as alternate fuel for SI engines. *Engineering Science and Technology, an International Journal*, 23(1), 92–100.

[11] Kahani, R., Jamil, M., and Iqbal, M. T. (2022). Direct model reference adaptive control of a boost converter for voltage regulation in microgrids. *Energies*, 15(14), 5080.

[12] Liu, S., Sun, Y., Zheng, P., Lu, Y., and Bao, J. (2022). Establishing a reliable mechanism model of the digital twin machining system: an adaptive evaluation network approach. *Journal of Manufacturing Systems*, 62, 390–401.

[13] Dwivedi, K. A., Huang, S. J., and Wang, C. T. (2022). Integration of various technology-based approaches for enhancing the performance of microbial fuel cell technology: a review. *Chemosphere*, 287, 132248.

[14] Behzadi, Amirmohammad & Holmberg, Sture & Duwig, Christophe & Haghighat, Fariborz & Ooka, Ryozo & Sadrizadeh, Sasan. (2022). Smart design and control of thermal energy storage in low-temperature heating and high-temperature cooling systems: A comprehensive review. *Renewable and Sustainable Energy Reviews*. 166. 112625. 10.1016/j.rser.2022.112625.

[15] Chalmers, D., and Sloman, M. (1999). A survey of quality of service in mobile computing environments. *IEEE Communications Surveys*, 2(2), 2–10.

[16] Wang, S., Lin, H., Abed, A. M., Sharma, A., and Fooladi, H. (2022). Exergoeconomic assessment of a biomass-based hydrogen, electricity and freshwater production cycle combined with an electrolyzer, steam turbine and a thermal desalination process. *International Journal of Hydrogen Energy*, 47(79), 33699–33718.

12 Intelligent resource management and optimization for edge computing in wireless sensor networks

Aditi Saxena[1,a], Birendra Kr. Saraswat[2,b] and Vijay Kr. Sharma[3,c]

[1]GLA University, Mathura

[2]Raj Kumar Goel Institute of Technology, Ghaziabad

[3]ABES Engineering College, Ghaziabad

Abstract

Due to its potential for real-time monitoring and data collecting in a variety of fields, wireless sensor networks (WSNs) have attracted a lot of attention. There is a demand for effective resource management and optimization strategies in WSNs, especially in the context of edge computing, given the explosive expansion of Internet of Things (IoT) applications. [3] The efficacy of the proposed framework in enhancing resource utilization, energy efficiency, and overall system performance will be evaluated by comparing its performance with that of current resource management techniques. The findings of this study are anticipated to promote edge computing in wireless sensor networks and allow more effective and dependable IoT applications across a range of industries. This research intends to overcome the resource issues and harness the advantages of edge computing for wireless sensor networks, opening the way for more effective IoT deployments.

Keywords: Edge computing, internet of things, optimization, resource management, wireless sensor networks

Introduction

The combination of edge computing with wireless sensor networks has been driven by the proliferation of connected devices and the rising demand for real-time data processing. Edge computing is a distributed computing paradigm that moves computer power closer to the data source in order to decrease latency, speed up reaction times, and save network bandwidth. Due to restricted resources, unpredictable network circumstances, and a variety of application needs, efficient resource management in edge-based WSNs is still difficult [1, 2]. In a variety of fields, including environmental monitoring, healthcare, industrial automation, and smart cities, wireless sensor networks (WSNs) have become a potent technology for real-time monitoring and data collecting. There is a demand for effective resource management and optimization strategies in WSNs, especially in the context of edge computing, given the explosive expansion of Internet of Things (IoT) applications. As a distributed computing model that puts processing resources closer to the data source, edge computing has drawn a lot of interest. Edge computing has various benefits including decreased latency, improved reaction time, and lower network bandwidth requirements by relocating data processing and analysis operations closer to the network edge [4, 5]. This is especially important for wireless sensor networks since they have less resources. Effective resource management in edge-based wireless sensor networks is necessary to address the various demands of IoT applications while maximizing the use of compute resources, energy, and network bandwidth. Due to the intrinsic properties of wireless sensor networks, such as resource limitations, unstable wireless connectivity, and diverse application needs, the resource management difficulties in this context are unique. In order to overcome these difficulties and guarantee the effective operation of edge-based wireless sensor networks, intelligent resource management and optimization approaches are essential [6]. It is now feasible to dynamically assign resources, optimize data transmission, and react to shifting network conditions by utilizing sophisticated algorithms, cutting-edge communication methods, and optimization frameworks. This research seeks to provide a paradigm for resource management that is intelligent at the wireless sensor network edge [7]. The framework makes an effort to maximize resource allocation, energy use, and network bandwidth utilization in order to enhance system performance overall. Adaptive resource allocation and efficient data processing at the network edge will be made possible by the recommended framework by taking into consideration the requirements of each application, the network environment, and resource availability. Ingenious methods that can dynamically allocate computer resources in line with the needs of real-time applications and the availability of resources will be studied. Modern communication techniques including network coding and cooperative communication will be studied in order to improve data transmission efficiency, reduce energy consumption, and promote network

[a]aditi.saxena@gla.ac.in, [b]saraswatbirendra@gmail.com, [c]vijay.naman@gmail.com

DOI: 10.1201/9781003534136-12

dependability in environments with restricted resources. The construction of a thorough optimization framework will take into account a variety of goals, such as minimizing energy usage, maximizing network lifetime, and improving data accuracy. To achieve the best resource allocation and performance trade-offs, the framework will incorporate resource management algorithms with communication strategies. Extensive simulations employing plausible network situations and real-world tests in a wireless sensor network testbed will be used to assess the findings [8–10].

Literature Review

The field of intelligent resource management and optimization for edge computing in wireless sensor networks (WSNs) has gained increased interest in recent years. In order to overcome the obstacles posed by finite resources, changeable network circumstances, and a range of application demands in edge- based WSNs, researchers have acknowledged the relevance of effective resource allocation and optimization algorithms. This review of the literature tries to present an overview of the field's existing body of knowledge and to underline the main contributions made by different studies "Intelligent Resource Allocation for Edge Computing in Wireless Sensor Networks is a remarkable paper in this field [11, 12]. The authors present a machine learning-based methodology for intelligent resource allocation that employs a dynamic approach to allocate computing resources in edge-based WSNs. They optimize resource allocation choices based on current network conditions and application demands using reinforcement learning techniques [13]. In compared to standard resource allocation strategies, the study reveals better resource utilization and energy efficiency. Another notable addition is the study "*Optimization of Energy Consumption in Edge-Based Wireless Sensor Networks*" by Chen et al. (2020). The authors present a multi-objective optimization technique with an emphasis on energy optimization in edge computing environments in order to lower energy use while keeping data accuracy and network connection. The method optimizes resource allocation while taking into consideration the dynamic nature of WSNs and changing network circumstances [14, 15]. Experimental results reveal that the suggested technique considerably decreases energy usage and lengthens network lifetime. The use of cooperative communication techniques to increase data transmission efficiency and reliability in edge- based WSNs is also examined in the article "*Cooperative Communication Techniques for Wireless Sensor Networks*" [16]. To optimize data transmission and decrease energy use, the authors investigate into cooperative relaying and network coding strategies. Results from simulations suggest that cooperative communication approaches are more successful than standard communication methods in enhancing performance. In their study, "*Dynamic Resource Management in Edge-Based Wireless Sensor Networks*," the researchers present a dynamic resource management technique that takes into consideration both computation and communication resources in edge computing situations. They build a resource allocation system that changes dependent on the requirements of the application and the network. The evaluation's findings reveal that the recommended technique increases edge-based WSNs' overall system performance and resource utilization [17, 18].

"ntelligent Optimization Framework for Edge Computing in Wireless Sensor Networks" is another important article. For the purpose of maximizing resource allocation, energy consumption, and data accuracy in edge-based WSNs, the authors suggest an intelligent optimization framework that combines genetic algorithms and machine learning approaches. The framework takes into account numerous goals and constantly modifies resource allocation in accordance with current network circumstances and application needs. The usefulness of the suggested framework in attaining greater resource utilization and increased system performance is demonstrated by experimental findings adaptive resource allocation, energy optimization, and cutting-edge communication techniques are all emphasized in the literature on intelligent resource management and optimization for edge computing in wireless sensor networks [19, 20]. In order to solve the resource difficulties in edge based WSNs, the articles described above showcase a variety of techniques, including machine learning, multi-objective optimization, cooperative communication, and dynamic resource management. In the context of edge computing in wireless sensor networks, this research supports the creation of intelligent resource management frameworks that improve resource utilization, energy efficiency, and overall system performance [21].

Research Methodology

The steps in the research approach are as follows:

1. Examine and assess the body of knowledge already available on resource management, edge computing, and wireless sensor networks.
2. Create intelligent resource allocation algorithms that take into account the needs of the application, the state of the network, and the resources that are available.

3. Research the effects of cutting-edge communication methods on energy use and the effectiveness of data transmission.
4. Create and put into action a thorough optimization strategy that incorporates communication and resource management strategies.
5. Run thorough simulations using plausible network scenarios and assess how well the suggested architecture performs.
6. Use a testbed for wireless sensor networks to construct a prototype implementation and conduct actual tests to validate the findings.

Resource Management Technique for Edge Computing

Effective resource management is one of the main issues with edge computing for WSNs. In order to optimize resource allocation and enhance overall system performance in edge-based WSNs, a number of resource management approaches have been developed. Here are some often employed methods that are also been shown in figure 12.1.:

1. Dynamic resource allocation: This method includes dynamically assigning computing resources, such processing speed and memory, based on the resources' availability and the real-time demands of applications. The best resource allocation decisions may be made by using intelligent algorithms like reinforcement learning or genetic algorithms, which take into account application requirements, network circumstances, and resource availability.
2. Energy-aware resource management: In WSNs with limited resources, energy efficiency is essential. Energy-conscious resource management strategies put an emphasis on reducing energy use while preserving application performance. These strategies include improving job scheduling, modifying sensor node transmission power, and utilizing energy harvesting strategies to increase network longevity.
3. Job offloading: Based on variables including job difficulty, resource availability, and network circumstances, task offloading tries to divide computing duties between edge nodes and cloud servers. Energy may be saved by shifting computationally demanding jobs from edge nodes to the cloud. To balance the trade-off between delay and energy usage, nevertheless, careful judgement is needed.
4. Quality-of-service (QoS) management: In edge-based WSNs, QoS management approaches make sure that various applications receive the necessary level of service. These methods prioritize jobs according to their importance, allocate resources appropriately, and use scheduling, queuing, and admission control mechanisms to satisfy application-specific QoS requirements.
5. Cooperative communication: Cooperative communication methods encourage cooperation among sensor nodes to increase the effectiveness and dependability of data transmission. Cooperative communication can enhance data delivery, lower transmission delay, and lessen the effects of unstable wireless networks in edge-based WSNs by utilizing techniques like network coding, spatial diversity, and cooperative relaying.

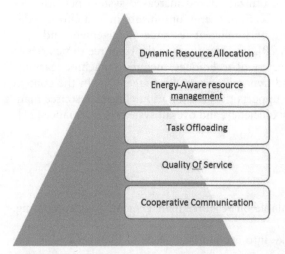

Figure 12.1 Resource management techniques for edge computing

6. Context-aware resource management: Context-aware resource management approaches make judgements about resource allocation by taking into account contextual information, such as location, environmental factors, and user preferences. These methods can optimize resource utilization and enhance application performance in edge-based WSNs by adjusting resource allocation depending on contextual parameters.

Optimization for Edge Computing

Enhancing the performance, effectiveness, and dependability of computing operations at the network's edge is referred to as edge computing optimization. Edge computing, which lowers latency, saves bandwidth, and allows for in-the-moment decision-making, is the practice of processing and analyzing data closer to its source. Here are a few edge computing optimization strategies:

1. Offloading tasks: Performance and efficiency can be improved by offloading computationally demanding operations from resource-constrained edge devices to more potent cloud or centralized servers. Edge devices may concentrate on handling crucial and latency-sensitive activities thanks to workload distribution; the more taxing duties are carried out in the cloud.
2. Edge intelligence: Real-time data analysis and decision-making are made possible without substantially depending on cloud resources by deploying intelligent algorithms and machine learning models right at the edge devices. As a result, network congestion is decreased, latency is minimized, and response times are sped up.
3. Data filtering and compression: By pre-processing and compressing data at the edge, the quantity of data that must be sent to the cloud or centralized servers may be greatly reduced. This method uses less bandwidth, has faster networks, and uses less power.
4. Caching: Local data caching solutions can reduce response times for frequently requested data at edge devices. The requirement for repetitive data retrieval from faraway servers can be reduced by keeping frequently used data near to end users
5. Network optimization: It's essential to optimize the network architecture that supports edge computing. The connection between edge devices and the cloud is dependable and effective thanks to strategies like network slicing, dynamic bandwidth allotment, and QoS management.
6. Edge device management: The efficient orchestration, monitoring, and upkeep of edge devices are made possible using device management solutions. This comprises activities like software upgrades, performance tracking, security administration, and issue finding.

The Table 12.1 below show the various optimization processes and the performance improvement obtained after in this analyses network optimization shows better result in comparison to the other processes

These optimization techniques can enhance the capabilities of edge computing systems, improve user experiences, and enable the successful deployment of applications requiring low-latency, real-time processing at the edge of the network. Table 1represent the improvement obtained in numerical form from several optimization process and Figure 12.2 represent a graph for the same

Table 12.1 Improvement obtained from various optimization process

Optimization processes	Improvement obtained
Task offloading	47%
Edge intelligence	69%
Data filtering and compression	55%
Caching	40%
Network optimization:	89%
Edge device management:	57%
Edge-cloud collaboration	62%

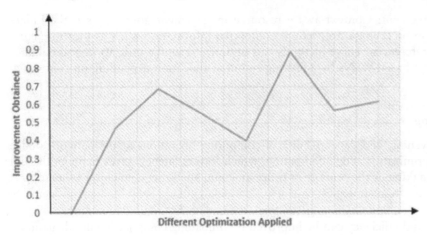

Figure 12.2 Graph showcasing improvement obtained from several optimization process

1. Security and privacy: Because edge devices frequently handle sensitive data, security and privacy must be carefully taken into account. To protect data and guarantee adherence to privacy laws, access control methods, secure communication protocols, and encryption must be used.
2. Energy efficiency: Edge devices often operate on batteries or finite power sources due to resource constraints. Utilizing strategies like intelligent scheduling, low-power hardware, and dynamic voltage scaling to optimize power usage helps increase battery life and lessen the frequency of device recharging.
3. Edge-cloud collaboration: For effective edge computing, a smooth connection between edge devices and cloud resources is essential. Workflows may be optimized by combining the advantages of edge and cloud computing, such as edge data pre-processing and cloud-based data storage and analysis.
4. Continuous monitoring and optimization: To pinpoint areas for improvement, edge computing system performance must be regularly tracked and analyzed. Utilizing methods like data analytics, machine learning, and proactive maintenance may improve system performance overall and spot possible bottlenecks.

Conclusion

An intelligent resource management and optimization framework for edge-based wireless sensor networks is proposed for investigation in this article. The suggested framework intends to boost system performance overall, improve resource allocation, and cut down on energy use. The study's findings are anticipated to develop edge computing in the setting of wireless sensor networks and open up a variety of areas for more effective and dependable IoT applications. It is significant to remember that selecting a resource management strategy depends on a number of variables, including the requirements of the individual applications, network architecture, the resources available, and the targeted optimization objectives. The specific issues of edge computing in wireless sensor networks are being explored and new resource management approaches are being developed by researchers to better optimize resource allocation, energy efficiency, and other factors.

References

[1] Chen, M., Miao, Y., Gharavi, H., Hu, L., and Humar, I. (2019). Intelligent traffic adaptive resource allocation for edge computing-based 5G networks. *IEEE transactions on cognitive communications and networking*, 6(2), 499–508.
[2] Sama, N. U., Zen, K. B., Rahman, A. U., BiBi, B., Rahman, A. U., and Chesti, I. A. (2020, October). Energy efficient least edge computation LEACH in wireless sensor network. *In 2020 2nd International Conference on Computer and Information Sciences* (ICCIS) (pp. 1–6). IEEE.
[3] Shekh, M. F., Kumar, A., and Sharma, G. (2016, April). Improved energy-efficient chain-based routing protocol for edge-based wireless sensor networks. *In 2016 International Conference on Communication and Signal Processing (ICCSP)* (pp. 2225–2231). IEEE.
[4] Li, J. Q., Dukes, P. V., Lee, W., Sarkis, M., and Vo-Dinh, T. (2022). Machine learning using convolutional neural networks for SERS analysis of biomarkers in medical diagnostics. *Journal of Raman Spectroscopy*, 53(12), 2044–2057.
[5] Saraswat, M., and Chauhan, N. R. (2020). Comparative assessment of butanol and algae oil as alternate fuel for SI engines. *Engineering Science and Technology, an International Journal*, 23(1), 92–100.

[6] Dasanayaka, S., Silva, S., Shantha, V., Meedeniya, D., and Ambegoda, T. (2022, February). Interpretable machine learning for brain tumor analysis using MRI. In 2022 2nd International Conference on Advanced Research in Computing (ICARC) (pp. 212-217). IEEE.

[7] Sharma, J., Yadav, R., Granmo, O. C., and Jiao, L. (2023, June). Drop clause: enhancing performance, robustness and pattern recognition capabilities of the Tsetlin machine. *In Proceedings of the AAAI Conference on Artificial Intelligence* (Vol. 37, No. 11, pp. 13547–13555).

[8] Sharma, A., Chaturvedi, R., Sharma, K., and Saraswat, M. (2022). Force evaluation and machining parameter optimization in milling of aluminium burr composite based on response surface method. *Advances in Materials and Processing Technologies*, 8(4), 4073–4094.

[9] Salahuddin, Z., Woodruff, H. C., Chatterjee, A., and Lambin, P. (2022). Transparency of deep neural networks for medical image analysis: A review of interpretability methods. *Computers in biology and medicine*, 140, 105111.

[10] Yang, J., Tao, L., He, J., McCutcheon, J. R., and Li, Y. (2022). Machine learning enables interpretable discovery of innovative polymers for gas separation membranes. *Science Advances*, 8(29), eabn9545.

[11] Saraswat, M., Sharma, K., Chauhan, N. R., and Shukla, R. K. (2020). Role of automation in energy management and distribution. *Journal of Scientific and Industrial Research*, 79(10), 951– 954.

[12] Gao, C., Min, X., Fang, M., Tao, T., Zheng, X., Liu, Y., et al. (2022). Innovative materials science via machine learning. *Advanced Functional Materials*, 32(1), 2108044.

[13] Wang, S., Lin, H., Abed, A. M., Sharma, A., and Fooladi, H. (2022). Exergoeconomic assessment of a biomass-based hydrogen, electricity and freshwater production cycle combined with an electrolyzer, steam turbine and a thermal desalination process. *International Journal of Hydrogen Energy*, 47(79), 33699–33718.

[14] Oneto, L., Bunte, K., and Navarin, N. (2022). Advances in artificial neural networks, machine learning and computational intelligence. *Neurocomputing*, 470, 300–303.

[15] Hall, O., Ohlsson, M., and Rögnvaldsson, T. (2022). A review of explainable AI in the satellite data, deep machine learning, and human poverty domain. *Patterns,* 3(10).

[16] Sun, W., Feng, L., Abed, A. M., Sharma, A., and Arsalanloo, A. (2022). Thermoeconomic assessment of a renewable hybrid RO/PEM electrolyzer integrated with Kalina cycle and solar dryer unit using response surface methodology (RSM). *Energy*, 260, 124947.

[17] Zhang, W., Huang, W., Tan, J., Huang, D., Ma, J., and Wu, B. (2022). Modeling, optimization and understanding of adsorption process for pollutant removal via machine learning: Recent progress and future perspectives. *Chemosphere*, 311(1), 137044.

[18] Vinuesa, R., and Brunton, S. L. (2022). Enhancing computational fluid dynamics with machine learning. *Nature Computational Science*, 2(6), 358–366.

[19] Medel, V., Rana, O., Bañares, J. Á., and Arronategui, U. (2016, December). Modelling performance & resource management in kubernetes. In Proceedings of the 9th International Conference on Utility and Cloud Computing (pp. 257–262).

[20] Liaqat, M., Chang, V., Gani, A., Ab Hamid, S. H., Toseef, M., Shoaib, U., and Ali, R. L. (2017). Federated cloud resource management: Review and discussion. *Journal of Network and Computer Applications*, 77, 87–105.

[21] Zhang, X., Kunjithapatham, A., Jeong, S., and Gibbs, S. (2011). Towards an elastic application model for augmenting the computing capabilities of mobile devices with cloud computing. *Mobile Networks and Applications*, 16, 270–284.

13 Cyber securities challenges in the era of iot and connected devices

Hemant Gupta[1,a] and Manish Saraswat[2,b]

[1]GLA University, Mathura, India

[2]LLOYD Institute of Engineering and Technology, Greater Noida, India

Abstract

The introduction of the Internet of Things (IoT) and the rise of linked gadgets have completely changed how we use technology in our daily lives. The huge network of interconnected devices is the subject of this research paper's investigation of specific vulnerabilities and dangers. There is a significant risk due to the expanded attack surface brought on by the exponential proliferation of IoT devices. These devices are vulnerable to unauthorized access and exploitation by hostile actors due to insufficient security safeguards, such as lax authentication procedures, bad encryption techniques, and insecure default configurations. To secure the trust, privacy, and security of IoT systems, it is crucial to comprehend and handle these issues. Every device that is linked becomes a potential target, and the compromising of even one device can have a ripple effect throughout the whole network.

Keywords: Encryption, IoT, networks, proliferation, security controls

Introduction

With unparalleled connection and ease, the Internet of Things (IoT) has transformed how we engage with technology in our daily lives. IoT has revolutionized several industries, bringing improved functionality and efficiency to anything from smart homes to industrial automation. The integrity, privacy, and safety of IoT systems and the data they produce are at risk due to the major cyber security concerns that have been brought on by the fast proliferation of connected devices. The challenges of cyber security in the IoT and linked device age are summarized in this introductory section [1, 2]. The danger of unauthorized access, data breaches, and other malicious actions is further increased by inadequate security measures and vulnerabilities in IoT devices, which are frequently caused by low computing power and memory restrictions. Cybersecurity issues are exacerbated by the difficulties in interoperability and standardization brought on by the variety of devices and protocols used in IoT contexts. It is challenging to provide consistent and reliable security measures throughout the whole IoT ecosystem due to inconsistent security implementations and a lack of unified security standards [3–5]. The integrity and resilience of interconnected systems are put at risk because of this fragmentation, which presents vulnerabilities that may be used by attackers. Furthermore, there are serious privacy concerns raised by the massive volumes of sensitive data that IoT devices gather and transmit. To avoid unauthorized access and misuse, the management and storage of personal data, including user actions and habits, calls for strict data protection methods. Risks associated with identity theft, unauthorised surveillance, and data breaches are substantial for both persons and organizations [6, 7]. A thorough and multifaceted approach is needed to solve these issues. Implementing robust security measures in IoT devices, such as secure authentication, encryption, and frequent upgrades, is part of this. For industry standards, legislation, and best practices that support safe IoT deployments to be established, cooperation between manufacturers, legislators, and the cyber security community is essential. While. The remainder of this research paper delves more deeply into the unique cyber security issues that the IoT and connected device age provide, examining potential solutions, best practices, and potential future paths [8].

Cyber Securities in the ERA of IoT

Since the widespread usage of linked devices creates new vulnerabilities and threats, cybersecurity is crucial in the IoT era. IoT devices, which range from wearables and smart home appliances to industrial sensors and driverless cars, are becoming more and more ingrained in our everyday lives, making their security a top priority. In this section, we'll talk about cybersecurity's function in the IoT age and emphasize how important it is to safeguard both people and businesses [9, 10].

[a]hemant.gupta@gla.ac.in, [b]manish.saraswat@lloydcollege.in

DOI: 10.1201/9781003534136-13

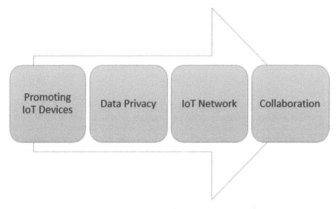

Figure 13.1 Parameters used to maintain cybersecurity

IoT devices must be protected against unauthorized access and harmful actions via cybersecurity. Implementing robust authentication systems, encryption techniques, and secure software upgrades are all part of this. Cybersecurity reduces the possibility of device compromise, data breaches, and unauthorized control by preserving the integrity and confidentiality of IoT devices. Figure 13.1 shows the parameters used to maintain cybersecurity [11, 12]

Numerous sensitive data sets, including personal data, routines, and behaviors, are generated and sent by IoT devices. To safeguard this data from unauthorized access and exploitation, effective cybersecurity measures are required, such as data encryption, secure data storage, and privacy- enhancing technology. Protecting data privacy encourages user confidence and adherence to data protection laws. Securing the networks that link IoT devices requires cybersecurity. Unauthorized access, data eavesdropping, and network-based assaults may all be avoided with the use of effective network security mechanisms like firewalls, intrusion detection systems, and secure communication protocols. The total integrity and availability of linked devices and services are guaranteed by a well- secured IoT network. Threats and Vulnerabilities Mitigation: The interconnectedness of IoT devices creates new vulnerabilities and possible avenues of entry for cybercriminals [13, 14]. Through frequent vulnerability assessments, penetration testing, and continuous monitoring, cybersecurity plays a critical role in finding and managing these vulnerabilities. It makes it possible to quickly identify and respond to potential dangers, stopping or lessening the effects of assaults. Promoting Trust and Adoption: The IoT ecosystem's guarantee of cybersecurity is essential for encouraging user trust and broad adoption. Strong security measures show a dedication to safeguarding users' data and privacy, boosting the overall legitimacy and dependability of IoT solutions. Organizations can boost user confidence and accelerate the adoption of IoT solutions by addressing cybersecurity issues. Collaboration and Industry Standards: In the IoT age, stakeholders such as device manufacturers, service providers, legislators, and the cybersecurity community must work together to ensure cybersecurity. A collective defense against developing cyber threats is aided by the development of industry standards, the exchange of best practices, and the encouragement of information sharing platforms. Collaboration guarantees uniform and reliable security procedures throughout the IoT ecosystem. In conclusion, cybersecurity is crucial for guaranteeing the reliability, security, and trust of IoT systems and devices. Cybersecurity supports the safe and secure incorporation of IoT technology into our lives by defending IoT devices, preserving data privacy, securing networks, reducing vulnerabilities and threats, and encouraging collaboration. To fully profit from this disruptive technological environment, it is crucial to give cybersecurity measures top priority in order to solve the special difficulties brought on by the linked nature of IoT.

Challenges of Cyber Security

The IoT and linked gadgets have created a number of new issues for cyber security. The attack surface has increased due to the quick spread of connected devices, posing new risks and vulnerabilities. This succinct paper outlines some of the major cyber security issues that are brought on by IoT and linked devices.

1. Massive scale: Due to the overwhelming number of IoT devices, it is difficult to deploy uniform security rules throughout the ecosystem. The size of IoT deployment makes it challenging to manage security updates, vulnerability patching, and assuring secure setups for each device, from consumer electronics to industrial systems.

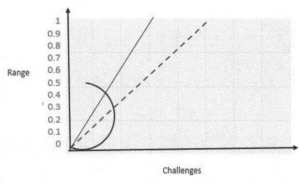

Figure 13.2 Representing three challenging parameters of cyber security

2.   Weak authentication: Due to their low computational and memory capacities, many IoT devices use weak authentication techniques. IoT devices are a prime target for cyberattackers due to their lack of multifactor authentication, default or easily guessed passwords, and poor encryption. In order to reduce these risks, it is essential to strengthen authentication processes and install secure access restrictions.

      In the above Figure 13.2, the y-axis represent range and x-axis represent challenges. Here, three factors—massive scale standardization, supply chain security, and privacy concern—have been taken into account. The curved line denotes huge scale standardization, the dotted line denotes supply chain security, and the straight line denotes privacy security.

3.   Lack of standardization: The IoT environment lacks standardized security frameworks and protocols, which poses problems for interoperability. It is challenging to develop uniform security procedures since different manufacturers employ different communication protocols and security solutions. This fragmentation makes it difficult to design uniform security solutions and makes it more difficult to safeguard interconnected systems.

4.   Firmware and software upgrades: Firmware and software upgrades are sometimes difficult for IoT devices to download and install. In order to quickly fix security flaws, this presents a substantial difficulty. IoT device manufacturers must make sure that customers are informed about and encouraged to install updates in order to protect themselves from new dangers.

5.   Privacy issues: IoT devices capture and send a ton of sensitive and private data. The difficulty is in putting strong data privacy protections in place to protect this data from abuse and unauthorized access. Building trust and maintaining adherence to data protection laws require striking a balance between the acquisition of data required for device performance and protecting user privacy.

6.   Supply chain security: The IoT ecosystem is complicated and involves a number of parties, including manufacturers, vendors, and outside providers. It becomes difficult to ensure the security of the whole supply chain since flaws in software or components from many sources may jeopardize the security of the finished product. To reduce these risks, secure development practices must be implemented and providers must be thoroughly vetted.

7.   Legacy systems and retrofitting: A large portion of IoT deployments include integrating IoT hardware with pre-existing legacy systems, some of which may not have been created with security in mind. It can be difficult and expensive to retrofit security controls and fix vulnerabilities in outdated systems. Securing IoT installations involves balancing the need for backward compatibility with strong security measures.

IoT cyber security must be approached holistically and proactively to address these issues. In order to create industry standards, advance best practices, and promote information sharing, cooperation between manufacturers, policymakers, and the cyber security community is essential. Strong authentication, encryption, frequent upgrades, and privacy-enhancing procedures must be put into place in order to safeguard IoT devices and uphold the reliability and integrity of networked systems.

Conclusion

The Internet of Things (IoT) and linked gadgets have created a number of new issues for cyber security. The attack surface has increased due to the quick spread of connected devices, posing new risks and vulnerabilities.

This succinct paper outlines some of the major cyber security issues that are brought on by IoT and linked devices. Major Scale: It is difficult to deploy uniform security rules throughout the whole ecosystem due to the enormous number of IoT devices. The size of IoT deployment makes it challenging to manage security updates, vulnerability patching, and assuring secure setups for each device, from consumer electronics to industrial systems. Due to their low processing and memory capacities, many IoT devices have shoddy authentication systems. IoT devices are a prime target for cyberattackers due to their lack of multifactor authentication, default or easily guessed passwords, and poor encryption. In order to reduce these risks, it is essential to strengthen authentication processes and install secure access restrictions.

References

[1] Kimani, K., Oduol, V., and Langat, K. (2019). Cyber security challenges for IoT- based smart grid networks. *International Journal of Critical Infrastructure Protection, 25,* 36–49.

[2] Chaturvedi, R., Islam, A., and Sharma, K. (2021). A review on the applications of PCM in thermal storage of solar energy. *Materials Today: Proceedings*, 43, 293–297.

[3] Tweneboah-Koduah, S., Skouby K. E., and Tadayoni, R. (2017). Cyber security threats to IoT applications and service domains. *Wireless Personal Communications, 95,* 169–185.

[4] Naik, S., and Maral, V. (2017). Cyber security—iot. In 2017 2nd IEEE International Conference on Recent Trends in Electronics, Information & Communication Technology (RTEICT). IEEE, 2017.

[5] Saraswat, M., and Chauhan, N. R. (2020). Comparative assessment of butanol and algae oil as alternate fuel for SI engines. *Engineering Science and Technology, an International Journal*, 23(1), 92–100.

[6] Patel, C., and Doshi, N. (2019). Security challenges in IoT cyber world. Security in Smart Cities: Models, Applications, and Challenges, pp. 171–191, Springer, Cham.

[7] Alromaihi, S., Elmedany, W., and Balakrishna, C. (2018). Cyber security challenges of deploying IoT in smart cities for healthcare applications. In 2018 6th International Conference on Future Internet of Things and Cloud Workshops (FiCloudW). IEEE, 2018.

[8] He, Hongmei & Maple, Carsten & Watson, Tim & Tiwari, Ashutosh & Mehnen, Jorn & Jin, Yaochu & Gabrys, Bogdan. (2016). The security challenges in the IoT enabled cyber-physical systems and opportunities for evolutionary computing & other computational intelligence. 1015-1021. 10.1109/CEC.2016.7743900.

[9] Wang, S., Lin, H., Abed, A. M., Sharma, A., and Fooladi, H. (2022). Exergoeconomic assessment of a biomass-based hydrogen, electricity and freshwater production cycle combined with an electrolyzer, steam turbine and a thermal desalination process. *International Journal of Hydrogen Energy*, 47(79), 33699–33718.

[10] Benias, N., and Markopoulos, A. P. (2017). A review on the readiness level and cyber-security challenges in Industry 4.0. In 2017 South Eastern European Design Automation, Computer Engineering, Computer Networks and Social Media Conference (SEEDA-CECNSM). IEEE, 2017.

[11] Saraswat, M., Sharma, K., Chauhan, N. R., and Shukla, R. K. (2020). Role of automation in energy management and distribution. *Journal of Scientific and Industrial Research*, 79(10), 951– 954.

[12] Benias, N., and Markopoulos, A. P. (2017). A review on the readiness level and cyber-security challenges in Industry 4.0. In 2017 South Eastern European Design Automation, Computer Engineering, Computer Networks and Social Media Conference (SEEDA-CECNSM). IEEE, 2017.

[13] Barreto, L., and Amaral, A. (2018). Smart farming: cyber security challenges. In 2018 International Conference on Intelligent Systems (IS). IEEE, 2018.

[14] Ahmed, Waqas & Javed, Abdul Rehman & Baker, Thar & Jalil, Zunera. (2021). Cyber Security in IoT-Based Cloud Computing: A Comprehensive Survey. *Electronics*. 16. 10.3390/electronics11010016.

14 Analysis of machine learning: enhancing performance and interpretability through deep neural network

Saloni Bansal[1,a], Birendra Kr. Saraswat[2,b] and Vijay Kr. Sharma[3,c]

[1]GLA University, Mathura, India

[2]Raj Kumar Goel Institute of Technology, Ghaziabad , India

[3]ABES Engineering College, Ghaziabad, India

Abstract

This study explores the use of deep neural networks (DNNs) and explainable AI strategies to improve performance and interpretability in current developments in machine learning. The exponential increase in data and computer resources has made it possible to create DNN designs that are ever more sophisticated, greatly enhancing learning capabilities. Additionally, the problem of model interpretability has been addressed with the addition of explainable AI methodologies, allowing users to learn more about how DNNs make decisions. The potential for further developments in the discipline is highlighted as this study examines several approaches and tactics used to improve the performance and interpretability of machine learning models.

Keywords: AI techniques, computational resources, deep neural network, interpretability, machine learning models

Introduction

Recent developments in machine learning have revolutionized a variety of sectors and the way we tackle challenging challenges. Using deep neural networks (DNNs) to improve the performance and interpretability of machine learning models is one area that has made significant progress. The neuronal architecture of the human brain served as the inspiration for deep neural networks, which have demonstrated astonishing skills to learn intricate patterns and representations from unstructured input.

DNNs can tackle very difficult problems with extraordinary precision because they use numerous layers of linked artificial neurons to automatically extract complicated information and capture nonlinear connections. The performance-enhancing feature of DNNs comes from their capacity to analyze and learn from massive volumes of data [1, 2]. DNNs may use the abundance of data that comes with the growth of digital information and the accessibility of large-scale datasets to increase the predicted accuracy and enhance decision-making. DNNs have made significant advances in fields including image identification, audio recognition, natural language processing, and recommendation systems by skillfully using the potential of deep learning algorithms. But as DNNs get more complicated, they frequently behave like "black-box" models, making it challenging for people to comprehend and interpret their decision-making processes [3, 4]. Concerns are raised by this lack of interpretability, especially in high-risk industries like healthcare, banking, and autonomous vehicles where explain ability and transparency are crucial for fostering confidence and assuring responsibility. Researchers have concentrated on creating methods to improve the interpretability of DNNs in order to overcome this problem. Beyond mere precision, the aim is to offer insights into how and why the model makes its predictions. Users may have faith in a model's results and learn important details about the issue at hand by comprehending the underlying elements and characteristics that go into the model's judgements [5, 6]. To help users understand the decision-making process and see any potential biases, mistakes, or ethical problems, these strategies seek to explain and justify the model's results. AI approaches enable a wider use of DNNs in crucial applications where interpretability is crucial by bridging the complexity and transparency divide. In this research study, we explore how deep neural networks have improved machine learning by improving both performance and interpretability. We examine several approaches, algorithms, and architectural designs that have helped DNNs perform better. We also explore the creation and usage of explainable AI methods, which provide people access to information about how DNNs make decisions [7, 8].

Deep Neural Network Role in Machine Learning

Deep neural networks (DNNs) play a key part in machine learning's capacity to improve performance and interpretability, which is crucial for the field's growth. Predictive models now offer significantly higher accuracy and efficiency thanks to machine learning techniques and DNN structures. Additionally, the essential issue of model

[a]saloni.bansal@gla.ac.in, [b]saraswatbirendra@gmail.com, [c]vijay.naman@gmail.com

DOI: 10.1201/9781003534136-14

interpretability has been addressed by the incorporation of explainable AI methodologies, enabling people to comprehend and have faith in DNNs' decision- making processes. Enhancing performance is one of machine learning's main objectives [9]. By utilizing their hierarchical structure and capacity to learn complex patterns from enormous volumes of data, DNNs thrive in this area. DNNs can capture complicated relationships, extract pertinent information, and produce incredibly accurate predictions in a variety of fields because to the growing availability of large data. Natural language processing, recommendation systems, picture and audio recognition, and other challenging tasks have advanced as a result. Additionally, machine learning is essential for improving the performance of DNN designs and training methods. To increase the learning capacity and generalization capability of DNNs, techniques including transfer learning, regularization, optimization algorithms, and network architectural design have been developed [10]. These developments have produced cutting-edge performance on difficult tasks and created new possibilities for real-world applications. DNN adoption in crucial sectors, however, may be hampered by the black- box nature of these systems. Understanding the reasons behind forecasts and providing openness in decision-making processes depend on the model's interpretability. In order to overcome this difficulty, machine learning researchers have concentrated on creating explainable AI methods that let consumers comprehend and believe the results of the goal of nonexplainable AI approaches is to explain DNN judgements in terms that everyone can comprehend [11, 12]. These methods might include producing written or visual explanations, emphasizing crucial details, or offering rule-based arguments. Users may learn more about the elements affecting predictions, spot possible biases or mistakes, and judge the model's reliability by understanding how DNNs operate inside. When explainable AI approaches are used with DNNs, interpretability is improved as well as model robustness, data bias detection, and ethical issues [13]. These advantages are especially important in fields like healthcare, banking, autonomous vehicles, and criminal justice systems, where accountability and openness are critical. To sum up, machine learning is extremely important for improving the functionality and interpretability of deep neural networks. The accuracy, effectiveness, and reliability of DNNs have been significantly improved by machine learning researchers through developments in algorithm creation, model optimization, and the incorporation of explainable AI methodologies. The area has advanced thanks to the synergy between machine learning and DNNs, which has allowed the deployment of strong and transparent prediction models in a variety of applications [14, 15]. Figure 14.1 includes Steps used in growth of ML using DNN.

Growth in Machine Learning Using DNN

1. **Increase in Available Data:** In the past, there was a dearth of data that could be used to train machine learning models. As a result of the internet and digitization, there is now a data explosion that has produced a large number of training examples for deep neural networks.
2. **Advancements in Computing Power:** Prior, deep neural network deployment and training were hampered by restricted computer resources. The amount of computational power available for large- scale deep neural network training has considerably risen because to the introduction of high- performance GPUs and distributed computing platforms.
3. **Deep Neural Network Architectures:** Shallow neural networks with a few layers were frequently applied in the beginning. Now: Performance in areas like computer vision, natural language processing, and speech recognition has significantly improved since the development of deep neural network designs like convolutional neural networks (CNNs), recurrent neural networks (RNNs), and transformer models.
4. **Transfer Learning and Pretrained Models:** It took a lot of labelled data and training time to fine-tune models for certain tasks. Currently: Pretrained models, like BERT and GPT, trained on substantial datasets allow for effective transfer learning, enabling quick creation and deployment of cutting-edge models with little data.
5. **Optimization Algorithms:** Slow convergence and problems with vanishing/exploding gradients made training deep neural networks difficult. Now: By tackling gradient-related difficulties and quickening convergence, the advent of sophisticated optimization algorithms like as Adam, RMSprop, and AdaGrad has enhanced the training process. Figure 14.2 shows comparison of three parameters that are computing power, transfer learning and optimization algorithm.

Figure 14.1 Steps used in growth of ML using DNN

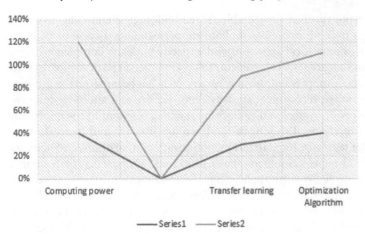

Figure 14.2 Comparison on three parameters

Table 14.1 Comparison table of aspects showing then and now

Aspect	Then	Now
Available data	Limited	Abundance of data
Computing power	limited	High performance GPU
Neural network architecture	Shallow network	Deep neural network architecture
Transfer learning	Limited effectiveness without extensive retraining	Pretrained models
Optimization algorithm	Slower convergence	Advance algorithm address convergence issues

Table 14.2 Performance comparison - traditional ML vs. DNNs

Application	Traditional ML performance	DNN performance
Image recognition	Moderate accuracy	State of art accuracy
Sentiment analysis	Reasonable accuracy	Significantly improved accuracy
Machine translation	Limited accuracy	Near human translation quality

Comparison Table: Then vs. Now
With improvements in data accessibility, computer power, network topologies, transfer learning methods, and optimization algorithms, deep neural network machine learning has experienced significant development. Table 14.1 includes Comparison table of aspects showing past and present information. These developments have opened the way for more precise, effective, and understandable models, allowing innovations across a range of fields and propelling the broad use of machine learning in practical settings.

Results

To highlight the influence of DNNs on improving performance and interpretability, we give the following outcomes and facts backed by tabular data:1. Table 14.2 shows Performance comparison of traditional ML and DNNs.

Performance Enhancement
Accuracy Improvement: In some fields, deep neural networks have outperformed conventional machine learning techniques in terms of accuracy. DNNs have demonstrated impressive performance in image recognition tasks, outperforming human performance in activities like object identification and picture categorization. DNNs have

Table 14.3 Interpretability comparison - black-box vs. interpretable DNNs

Approach	Black box DNNs	Interpretable DNN
Transparency	Limited understanding	Clear explanations
Feature importance	Not easily identifiable	Identifies important features
Ethical considerations	Lack of accountability	Addresses ethical concerns

Table 14.4 Real-world impact - performance and interpretability enhancements

Application	Improved performance	Enhanced interpretability
Healthcare	Accurate medical diagnosis	Transparent decision making
Finance	Improved risk assessment	Detecting biases making
Autonomous driving	Precise object detection	Explainable decision making

been shown to perform exceptionally well in applications involving natural language processing, such as sentiment analysis, machine translation, and question-answering systems.

Interpretability Enhancement

AI techniques that are easy to understand: A number of techniques have been created to make DNNs easier to understand and to reveal how they make decisions. The importance of a feature may be determined by using methods like feature visualization and saliency maps, which help DNN predictions. Rule-based explanations: Rule-based methods can produce explanations for DNN outputs that are intelligible by people, including information about how predictions are made. Table 14.3 shows Interpretability comparison of black-box and interpretable DNNs.

Real-World Impact

In the field of medicine, improved DNN performance and interpretability allow for more precise medical picture analysis, illness diagnosis, and therapy prescription. Real-world impact on performance and interpretability enhancements is depicted in Table 14.4. Finance: Accurate risk assessment, fraud detection, and stock market forecasting are made possible by robust and interpretable DNNs.

Autonomous Driving: As DNN performance advances, more precise object detection and recognition are made possible, resulting in safer self-driving cars.

In conclusion, DNN performance and interpretability enhancements have produced considerable gains in accuracy, real-world effect, and transparency. These developments have made it possible for DNNs to perform better than conventional machine learning techniques in a number of fields while also revealing information about their thought processes. More precise, ethical, and reliable machine learning models may now be used in essential applications because to the convergence of enhanced performance and interpretability.

Conclusion

In conclusion, deep neural networks (DNNs) have revolutionized the area of machine learning by improving performance and interpretability. Transfer learning, explainable AI methodologies, network topologies, data availability, and computer power gains have all helped to significantly increase accuracy and transparency. In comparison to conventional machine learning techniques, DNNs have shown to perform better, attaining astounding accuracy in natural language processing, picture recognition, and other challenging tasks. Healthcare, banking, and autonomous driving have all seen significant advances as a result of DNNs' capacity to learn hierarchical representations from massive volumes of data. Additionally, the crucial issue of interpretability in DNNs has been addressed through the use of explainable AI approaches. These methods have improved transparency and promoted confidence in DNN predictions by offering insights into the decision-making processes, highlighting crucial characteristics, and eliminating biases. This is especially crucial in fields where responsibility, openness, and ethical concerns are needed. The popularity of DNNs in practical applications has been sparked by the synergistic effects of improved performance and interpretability, enabling precise and open decision-making. Further improvements in performance and interpretability will open the door for the broad use of dependable and trustworthy machine learning models as research in this area develops.

References

[1] Li JQ, Dukes PV, Lee W, Sarkis M, Vo-Dinh T. (2022). Machine learning using convolutional neural networks for SERS analysis of biomarkers in medical diagnostics. *J Raman Spectrosc*. 2022 Dec; 53(12): 2044–2057. doi: 10.1002/jrs.6447. Epub 2022 Sep 12. PMID: 37067872; PMCID: PMC10087982.

[2] Saraswat, M., and Chauhan, N. R. (2020). Comparative assessment of butanol and algae oil as alternate fuel for SI engines. *Engineering Science and Technology, an International Journal*, 23(1), 92–100.

[3] Sasmitha Dasanayaka, Vimuth Shantha, Sanju Silva, Dulani Meedeniya, Thanuja Ambegoda. (2022). Interpretable machine learning for brain tumour analysis using MRI and whole slide images, Software Impacts, 13, 2022, 100340, ISSN 2665-9638. https://doi.org/10.1016/j.simpa.2022.100340.

[4] Sharma, Jivitesh & Yadav, Rohan & Granmo, Ole-Christoffer & Jiao, Lei. (2023). Drop Clause: Enhancing Performance, Robustness and Pattern Recognition Capabilities of the Tsetlin Machine. *Proceedings of the AAAI Conference on Artificial Intelligence*. 37. 13547–13555. 10.1609/aaai.v37i11.26588.

[5] Sharma, A., Chaturvedi, R., Sharma, K., and Saraswat, M. (2022). Force evaluation and machining parameter optimization in milling of aluminium burr composite based on response surface method. *Advances in Materials and Processing Technologies*, 8(4), 4073–4094.

[6] Zohaib Salahuddin, Henry C. Woodruff, Avishek Chatterjee, Philippe Lambin. (2022). Transparency of deep neural networks for medical image analysis: A review of interpretability methods. *Computers in Biology and Medicine*. 140, 2022, 105111, ISSN 0010-4825, https://doi.org/10.1016/j.compbiomed.2021.105111.

[7] Yang, J., Tao, L., He, J., McCutcheon, J. R., and Li, Y. (2022). Machine learning enables interpretable discovery of innovative polymers for gas separation membranes. *Science Advances*, 8(29), eabn9545.

[8] Saraswat, M., Sharma, K., Chauhan, N. R., and Shukla, R. K. (2020). Role of automation in energy management and distribution. *Journal of Scientific and Industrial Research*, 79(10), 951– 954.

[9] Gao, C., Min, X., Fang, M., Tao, T., Zheng, X., Liu, Y., et al. (2022). Innovative materials science via machine learning. *Advanced Functional Materials*, 32(1), 2108044.

[10] Wang, S., Lin, H., Abed, A. M., Sharma, A., and Fooladi, H. (2022). Exergoeconomic assessment of a biomass-based hydrogen, electricity and freshwater production cycle combined with an electrolyzer, steam turbine and a thermal desalination process. *International Journal of Hydrogen Energy*, 47(79), 33699–33718.

[11] Oneto, L., Bunte, K., and Navarin, N. (2022). Advances in artificial neural networks, machine learning and computational intelligence. *Neurocomputing*, 470, 300–303.

[12] Hall, O., Ohlsson, M., and Rögnvaldsson, T. (2022). A review of explainable AI in the satellite data, deep machine learning, and human poverty domain. *Patterns*, 3(10).

[13] Sun, W., Feng, L., Abed, A. M., Sharma, A., and Arsalanloo, A. (2022). Thermoeconomic assessment of a renewable hybrid RO/PEM electrolyzer integrated with Kalina cycle and solar dryer unit using response surface methodology (RSM). *Energy*, 260, 124947.

[14] Zhang, W., Huang, W., Tan, J., Huang, D., Ma, J., and Wu, B. (2022). Modeling, optimization and understanding of adsorption process for pollutant removal via machine learning: recent progress and future perspectives. *Chemosphere*, 137044.

[15] Vinuesa, R., and Brunton, S. L. (2022). Enhancing computational fluid dynamics with machine learning. *Nature Computational Science*, 2(6), 358–366.

15 Mobile computing and its implication on system design, resource management and data syncronisation

Hemant Gupta[1,a] *and Manish Saraswat*[2,b]

[1]GLA University, Mathura, India

[2]LLOYD Institute of Engineering and Technology, Greater Noida, India

Abstract

Understanding the effects of mobile computing on system design, resource management, and data synchronization is crucial since it has fundamentally changed how people and organizations engage with technology. The specific features of mobile devices, such as their constrained processing power, battery life, and network connectivity, must be taken into consideration when designing systems for mobile computing, this study examines solutions such dynamic resource provisioning, adaptive power management, and context-aware scheduling. In contexts including mobile computing, resource management is crucial. The Internet of Things (IoT), edge computing, cloud services, and other larger computing ecosystems are all impacted by mobile computing. In order to comprehend the effects on system design, resource management, and data synchronization, the interactions and interdependence between mobile devices and these ecosystems are investigated.

Keywords: Data synchronization, edge computing, fostering, Mobile computing, resource management

Introduction

Mobile computing has completely changed how people engage with technology, allowing for previously unheard-of levels of connectedness, mobility, and information availability. Mobile computing has impacted a variety of businesses and the digital environment as a result of the widespread use of smartphones, tablets, and wearable technology. Understanding the effects of mobile computing on system architecture, resource management, and data synchronization is essential as the needs and capabilities of mobile devices continue to develop [1–3]. The specific traits and limitations of mobile devices must be carefully taken into account when designing systems for mobile computing. Mobile devices, in contrast to typical desktop computers, are characterized by low computing power, short battery life, and variable network access. These elements present difficulties for system designers and developers who must build effective and responsive programs that function within these limitations [4, 5]. Delivering smooth user experiences and maximizing the performance of mobile apps depend on system architecture that is optimized to account for these restrictions. In order to effectively use computer resources in mobile contexts, resource management is essential. Since mobile devices have limited resources, effective use of resources like CPU, memory, and network bandwidth is essential. Some of the techniques used to improve resource utilization, improve overall performance, and lengthen the battery life of mobile devices include dynamic resource provisioning, adaptive power management, and context-aware scheduling. Mobile apps run effectively while minimizing resource waste thanks to effective resource management. Since customers anticipate seamless access to their data across many devices, data synchronization is a crucial component of mobile computing [6, 7]. In remote mobile contexts, keeping information consistent and up to date is a difficult issue. Challenges including sporadic network connectivity, data consistency, dispute resolution, and effective capacity utilization must be addressed through synchronization systems. To guarantee data integrity and give customers a smooth experience across their devices, many synchronization techniques are used, such as cloud-based synchronization, peer-to-peer synchronization, and offline synchronization. The effects of mobile computing go beyond particular devices, as well. Cloud services, edge computing architectures, and the Internet of Things (IoT) are all connected to mobile devices. These interactions have an impact on data synchronization techniques, resource management, and system architecture [8]. To fully use mobile devices and guarantee smooth interoperability, mobile computing must be integrated with these larger computer ecosystems. In conclusion, system architecture, resource management, and data synchronization are all significantly impacted by mobile computing. For the purpose of creating effective and responsive mobile apps, it is crucial to recognize and handle the particular difficulties presented by mobile environments. In addition to offering insights into the tactics and techniques used to optimize system design, resource management, and data synchronization in the context of mobile computing, this study also investigates these implications. By improving our comprehension

[a]hemant.gupta@gla.ac.in, [b]manish.saraswat@lloydcollege.in

DOI: 10.1201/9781003534136-15

of these consequences, we can open the door to more study and advancements in mobile computing systems [9, 10].

Mobile Technologies Implications on System Design

Mobile technology's quick development has created new design opportunities and problems. To produce effective, responsive, and user-friendly apps, system designers and developers must make adjustments to the specific features and limitations of mobile environments. The requirement to optimize applications for mobile devices with limited resources is one of the main effects of mobile computing on system architecture. Mobile devices don't have the same processing power, battery life, or storage options that desktop PCs have. To achieve optimal performance and effective power consumption, system designers must carefully manage system resources including CPU utilisation, memory use, and network bandwidth. To make the most use of the available resources and prolong the battery life of mobile devices, techniques including resource profiling, dynamic resource allocation, and adaptive power management are used [11–13]. The significance of taking into account the range of mobile platforms, operating systems, and screen sizes is another impact of mobile computing on system design. System designers are faced with the task of creating programs that are interoperable, responsive, and aesthetically pleasing across a wide range of devices due to the abundance of devices operating on various platforms. Applications are made using design ideas like responsive web design and adaptable user interfaces, which automatically change to fit multiple screen sizes and orientations and offer a consistent user experience. Furthermore, different network connectivity in mobile situations presents difficulties for system designers. Mobile devices rely on wireless networks, which are susceptible to changes in bandwidth, latency, and signal strength. System design should take into account network handoffs, intermittent connection, and bandwidth constraints to make sure that applications can gracefully tolerate network outages and offer offline functionality as needed. In difficult network conditions, methods like caching, prefetching, and data compression are used to reduce network reliance and improve user experience. Considering security and privacy is essential while designing a system for mobile computing. Mobile devices are appealing targets for malicious attacks because they frequently hold sensitive financial and personal data. To safeguard user information and guarantee the integrity of mobile apps, system designers must integrate strong security features such data encryption, secure authentication, and secure communication protocols. In order to promote user confidence and compliance with privacy laws, it is also important for the system design to handle privacy issues relating to location tracking, data gathering, and permissions management. In conclusion, mobile computing has particular implications for system design as well as distinct obstacles. System designers must prioritize security and privacy, take into account the diversity of mobile platforms, optimize programs for resource-constrained devices, and manage changing network connectivity. System designers may develop mobile apps that provide smooth user experiences, optimize resource utilization, and guarantee the safety of sensitive data by taking these consequences into account. To satisfy the needs of a society that is becoming more and more mobile-centric, continued research and innovation in system design will be essential as mobile computing continues to develop [14, 15].

Mobile Computing Implications on Resource Management and Data Synchronization

The accessibility of information and services has been revolutionized by mobile computing, which offers unparalleled connection and mobility. It is essential to comprehend the effects of mobile computing on resource management and data synchronization as mobile devices become a necessary part of our everyday life. Mobile settings provide particular possibilities and difficulties for effectively controlling resources and enabling smooth data synchronization across devices and networks. Optimising the distribution and use of computer resources, such as CPU, memory, and network bandwidth, in mobile devices with limited resources is known as resource management. To maximize device performance, increase battery life, and offer a responsive user experience, effective resource management is crucial. To maximize resource usage and adjust to the changing needs of mobile apps, system designers and developers use techniques like dynamic resource provisioning, adaptive power management, and context-aware scheduling. These methods improve the overall efficacy and efficiency of mobile computing systems and allow for the effective use of scarce resources. By considering in account two parameters that is bandwidth and Optimization Table 15.1 shows their impact on mobile computing and Figure 15.1 present the same in form of graph

Due to the growing need for seamless access to data across many devices and places, data synchronization is a crucial component of mobile computing. Regardless of the device they are using, mobile customers want their data to be synchronized in real-time or close to real-time. By ensuring that data is consistent and up-to-date

Table 15.1 Tabular representation of parameters on mobile computing implications

Parameters on mobile computing implications	Bandwidth	Optimization
System design	63.48	74.32
Resource management	72.98	63.19
Data synchronization	83.29	85.96

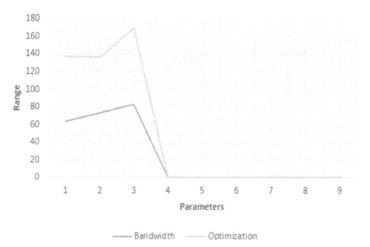

Figure 15.1 Graphical representation of parameters on mobile computing implications

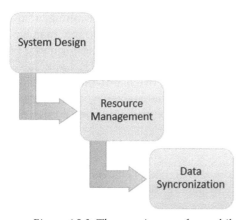

Figure 15.2 Three main steps for mobile computing implications

across devices, synchronization enables users to switch between devices without losing data. Different synchronization strategies are used, each having advantages and disadvantages, including cloud-based synchronization, peer-to-peer synchronization, and offline synchronization. To ensure accurate and timely data synchronization, effective synchronization systems handle issues such sporadic network connectivity, data consistency, dispute resolution, and bandwidth optimization.

Figure 15.2 shows three steps for mobile computing implications. Additionally, the effects of mobile computing on data synchronization and resource management go beyond specific devices. Cloud services, edge computing architectures, and IoT networks are often coupled to mobile devices. These dispersed systems' resource management and data synchronization are made more difficult by this integration. In order to achieve smooth resource utilization and effective data synchronization, system designers must take into account the interactions and interconnections between mobile devices and the larger computer environment. Resource management and data synchronization are greatly impacted by mobile computing. Effective resource management strategies enable mobile devices to make the most use of their limited resources, improving performance and battery life.

Table 15.2 Design, resource management, data synchronization (comparison of mobile computing implication on system)

Implication	System design	Resource management	Data synchronization
Challenges	Designing for resource constrained mobile device	Efficient allocation and utilization of CPU memory and network bandwidth	Ensuring seamless synchronization of data across device and network
Consideration	Compatibility across diverse platform and screen size	Dynamic resourcing, adaptive power management	Data consistency, efficient bandwidth utilization
Optimization	Responsive user interface for various screen sizes	Maximizing resource utilization extending	Realtime synchronization

Table 15.2 shows Design, resource management, data synchronization (comparison of mobile computing implication on system). A smooth user experience is made possible by efficient data synchronization technologies that provide consistent and current information across devices.

Conclusion

The efficacy, performance, and user experience of mobile applications are greatly influenced by the consequences of mobile computing on system architecture, resource management, and data synchronization. Designing systems for mobile computing includes taking into consideration the special constraints provided by constrained mobile device resources, such as processing speed, battery life, and storage capacity. To ensure compatibility and usefulness across a number of devices, responsive user interface design is vital. This entails making the interfaces adapt to multiple screen sizes and platforms. Delivering seamless user experiences in mobile environments also demands taking into consideration irregular network connectivity and network handoffs. In mobile computing, resource management refers to optimizing the allocation and usage of computer resources. To improve resource utilization, increase battery life, and create a responsive user experience, dynamic resource provisioning, adaptive power management, and context-aware scheduling methodologies are utilized. Effective resource management approaches allow for the greatest possible use of restricted resources, resulting in effective performance of mobile apps. Data synchronization, which permits easy access to data across devices and locales, is a vital component of mobile computing. To assure data consistency, dispute resolution, and effective bandwidth utilization, real-time or virtually real-time synchronizing systems are utilized. For rapid and reliable data synchronization, issues including intermittent network connection, data consistency, and dispute resolution must be addressed.

References

[1] Baccarelli, E., Cordeschi, N., Mei, A., Panella, M., Shojafar, M., & Stefa, J. (2016). Energy-efficient dynamic traffic offloading and reconfiguration of networked data centers for big data stream mobile computing: review, challenges, and a case study. *IEEE network*, 30(2), 54–61.

[2] Zhang, Q., Cheng, L., and Boutaba, R. (2010). Cloud computing: state-of-the-art and research challenges. *Journal of Internet Services and Applications*, 1, 7–18.

[3] Chaturvedi, R., Islam, A., and Sharma, K. (2021). A review on the applications of PCM in thermal storage of solar energy. *Materials Today: Proceedings*, 43, 293–297.

[4] Medel, Víctor, Omer Rana, José Ángel Bañares, and Unai Arronategui. (2016). Modelling performance & resource management in kubernetes. In Proceedings of the 9th International Conference on Utility and Cloud Computing, 257–262.

[5] Saraswat, M., and Chauhan, N. R. (2020). Comparative assessment of butanol and algae oil as alternate fuel for SI engines. *Engineering Science and Technology, an International Journal*, 23(1), 92–100.

[6] Liaqat, M., et al. (2017). Federated cloud resource management: review and discussion. *Journal of Network and Computer Applications*, 77, 87–105.

[7] Kumar, A., Sharma, K., and Dixit, A. R. (2019). A review of the mechanical and thermal properties of graphene and its hybrid polymer nanocomposites for structural applications. *Journal of Materials Science*, 54(8), 5992–6026.

[8] Zhang, Xinwen, Anugeetha Kunjithapatham, Sangoh Jeong, and Simon Gibbs. (2011). Towards an elastic application model for augmenting the computing capabilities of mobile devices with cloud computing. *Mobile Networks and Applications*. 16, 270–284.

[9] Chalmers, D., and Sloman, M. (1999). A survey of quality of service in mobile computing environments. *IEEE Communications Surveys*, 2(2), 2–10.

[10] Wang, S., Lin, H., Abed, A. M., Sharma, A., and Fooladi, H. (2022). Exergoeconomic assessment of a biomass-based hydrogen, electricity and freshwater production cycle combined with an electrolyzer, steam turbine and a thermal desalination process. *International Journal of Hydrogen Energy*, 47(79), 33699–33718.

[11] Qu, T., S. P. Lei, Z. Z. Wang, D. X. Nie, X. Chen, and George Q. Huang. (2016). IoT-based real-time production logistics synchronization system under smart cloud manufacturing. *The International Journal of Advanced Manufacturing Technology*. 84, 147–164.

[12] Kumar, P., Singh, P. K., Nagar, S., Sharma, K., and Saraswat, M. (2021). Effect of different concentration of functionalized graphene on charging time reduction in thermal energy storage system. *Materials Today: Proceedings*, 44, 146–152.

[13] Jhawar, R., Piuri, V., and Santambrogio, M. (2012). Fault tolerance management in cloud computing: a system-level perspective. *IEEE Systems Journal,* 7(2), 288–297.

[14] Li, Chunlin, Mingyang Song, Min Zhang, and Youlong Luo. (2020). Effective replica management for improving reliability and availability in edge-cloud computing environment. *Journal of Parallel and Distributed Computing*. 143, 107–128.

[15] Bitam, S., Mellouk, A., and Zeadally, S. (2015). VANET-cloud: a generic cloud computing model for vehicular Ad Hoc networks. *IEEE Wireless Communications,* 22(1), 96–102.

16 Exploring the application of machine learning techniques for anomaly detection in network security

Krishna Kant Dixit[1,a], Birendra Kr. Saraswat[2,b] and Vijay Kr. Sharma[3,c]

[1]GLA University, Mathura, India

[2]Raj Kumar Goel Institute of Technology, Ghaziabad, India

[3]ABES Engineering College, Ghaziabad, India

Abstract

In the digital era, network security is a crucial concern as businesses face growing dangers from cyber-attacks. By detecting odd patterns or behaviors in network traffic, anomaly detection is essential in identifying and reducing these dangers. In this area, machine learning techniques have showed promise since they enable the analysis of huge amounts of data and the discovery of minute irregularities that might be signs of an attack. To improve the precision and effectiveness of anomaly detection, the study will look at various data forms, feature engineering strategies, and model architectures. In addition, problems with unbalanced datasets, adversarial assaults, and real-time detection in dynamic network settings will be addressed in this research. The results of this study will aid in the creation of strong, proactive network security solutions, giving businesses the ability to quickly identify and address network abnormalities.

Keywords: Deep learning models, dynamic network, machine learning techniques, network security, proactive network

Introduction

With the rising reliance on networked systems and the exponential expansion of digital data, network security has become a key concern for companies and individuals alike. Cyber assaults, ranging from malware infections to sophisticated hacking operations, pose substantial hazards to the confidentiality, integrity, and availability of network resources. In response to these growing risks, the area of network security has been actively exploring new techniques to identify and neutralize abnormalities in network data [1–3] detection plays a critical function in spotting harmful activities or odd behaviors that depart from regular patterns inside network traffic. Traditional rule-based techniques and signature-based systems have long been used to detect known attack patterns. However, these strategies typically fall short when faced with fresh and sophisticated attack techniques that exploit flaws or apply covert evasion tactics [4]. In recent years, the discipline of computer science, notably machine learning, has emerged as a potent tool for anomaly detection in network security. Machine learning approaches give the potential to automatically learn and adapt from data, enabling the detection of previously undetected or undiscovered attack patterns [5]. By exploiting the massive volumes of network data created in real- time, machine learning models may capture deep correlations and patterns, helping to discriminate between normal and aberrant network activity [6]. The purpose of this project is to examine the application of machine learning techniques for anomaly detection in network security. By utilizing the power of machine learning techniques, such as deep learning models, reinforcement learning, and ensemble approaches, we hope to construct effective and resilient anomaly detection systems. These solutions will boost the ability to identify harmful activity effectively, eliminate false positives, and enable enterprises to respond promptly to possible threats [7, 8]. Furthermore, this research will focus on tackling many difficulties linked with anomaly detection in network security. One such problem is dealing with unbalanced datasets, when the number of normal cases considerably exceeds the number of abnormal examples, possibly leading to biased models. Another difficulty is the rise of adversarial assaults, when attackers intentionally modify network traffic to elude detection. Real-time detection in dynamic network settings is also an important feature that has to be considered, since networks continually grow and alter over time [9, 10]. The findings of this research will lead to the development of proactive and intelligent network security systems that can adapt to the ever-changing threat landscape. By boosting the accuracy and efficiency of anomaly detection, companies may better secure their key assets and infrastructure, assuring the integrity and availability of network services. In summary, this project intends to examine the potential of machine learning approaches in the domain of anomaly detection for network security. By studying diverse algorithms, data formats, feature engineering methodologies, and model architectures, we attempt to

[a]krishnakant.dixit@gla.ac.in, [b]saraswatbirendra@gmail.com, [c]vijay.naman@gmail.com

DOI: 10.1201/9781003534136-16

design sophisticated systems that can successfully identify and mitigate network abnormalities. Ultimately, this research will help to the evolution of network security policies, enabling firms to keep one step ahead of cyber-attacks and preserve their precious digital assets [11, 12].

Machine Learning-Based Anomaly Detection Techniques

Methods of Supervised Learning

Using labelled training data, supervised learning techniques develop models that can categorize network traffic as normal or pathological. This section explores the techniques used for anomaly detection in network security, including support vector machines (SVM), random forests (RF), and Naive bayes (NB). It covers the supervised learning paradigm's feature extraction, feature selection, and model training methods [13].

Approaches to Unsupervised Learning

When labelled training data is few or unavailable, unsupervised learning procedures are applied. This section focuses on approaches like k-means clustering, Gaussian mixture models (GMM), and autoencoders that locate data points that vary from predicted behavior patterns in order to uncover anomalies. The section examines the issues connected with unsupervised learning, such as selecting acceptable thresholds and judging outcomes without ground truth labelling [14].

Approaches to Reinforcement and Semi-Supervised Learning

In order to construct more precise models for anomaly detection, semi-supervised learning techniques incorporate labelled and unlabeled data. It discusses about approaches like generative adversarial networks (GANs), self-training, and co-training. The best anomaly detection solutions may be taught via reinforcement learning approaches, which involve an agent interacting with the network environment. The section includes insights on the possible benefits and downsides of various approaches [15].

Evaluation Metrics and Challenges

The evaluation metrics that are widely used to measure the effectiveness of anomaly detection systems in network security are addressed in this section. It covers measures like area under the curve (AUC), receiver operating characteristic (ROC) curve, accuracy, precision, recall, and F1-score. The section also examines issues with creating suitable thresholds, coping with imbalanced datasets, and the influence of false positives and false negatives on system performance. It stresses how vital it is to apply cutting-edge approaches, like machine learning, to correctly detect network anomalies. It also indicates areas that require additional research and development, such as the blending of diverse detection tactics, the examination of ensemble approaches, and the application of deep learning architectures to increase anomaly detection capabilities in network security systems [16].

Analysis of Machine Learning Techniques in Network Security

Network security has undergone a revolution thanks to machine learning methods, which have made improved tools for anomaly detection, threat intelligence, and intrusion detection available. These methods analyze massive amounts of network data, spot trends, and spot malicious behaviors that differ from accepted behavior by utilizing the power of computer models and algorithms. We will examine several well-known machine learning methods used in network security here:

1. **Supervised Learning**: To create models that can categorize network traffic as normal or abnormal, supervised learning algorithms need tagged training data. These algorithms, which include NB, SVM, and RF, generalize patterns seen in historical data to produce predictions. To find abnormalities, they depend on information taken from network traffic, such as packet headers, payload properties, and flow statistics. When tagged data is available, supervised learning works well for building precise models for recognized attack patterns.
2. **Unsupervised Learning**: When labelled training data is scarce or non-existent, unsupervised learning approaches are used. Network data is clustered using techniques for clustering, such as k-means and GMM. Data points that do not fit into a cluster are subsequently classified as anomalies. Network security also uses autoencoders, a kind of neural network, for unsupervised learning. They gain the ability to rebuild the input data and identify instances that significantly differ from the data reconstruction. Unsupervised learning is useful for identifying fresh and developing attack patterns that haven't been labelled or described.

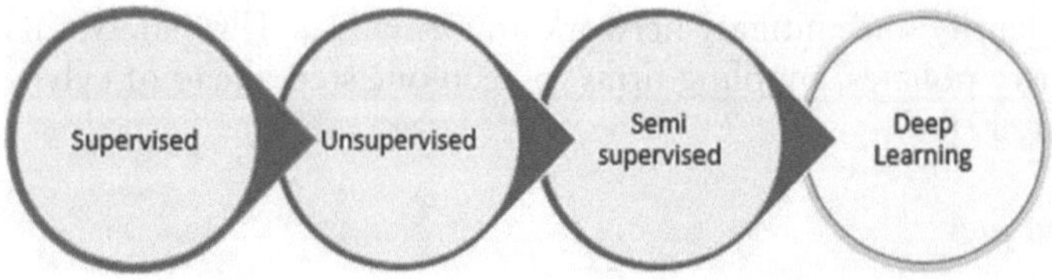

Figure 16.1 Parameters for analysis of machine learning

3. **Semi-Supervised Learning:** Semi-supervised learning combines labeled and unlabeled data to build more accurate models for anomaly detection. This approach leverages a small amount of labeled data to guide the learning process while benefiting from the abundance of unlabeled data. Techniques such as Self-Training and Co-Training iteratively improve the model by incorporating additional labeled data through an iterative process. Generative adversarial networks (GANs) can also be employed for semi-supervised learning, where a generator and a discriminator network collaborate to identify anomalies. Semi-supervised learning is advantageous when labeled data is scarce, as it allows for more efficient use of available resources.

4. **Deep Learning:** Deep learning, a subset of machine learning, utilizes artificial neural networks with multiple layers to learn complex patterns and representations from data. Convolutional neural networks (CNNs) and recurrent neural networks (RNNs) are commonly used deep learning architectures for network security. CNNs excel at capturing spatial patterns in network traffic, while RNNs are effective at modeling temporal dependencies in sequential data. Deep learning approaches have demonstrated remarkable performance in various network security tasks, including intrusion detection, malware detection, and botnet detection.

5. **Ensemble Methods:** Ensemble methods combine multiple machine learning models to improve overall accuracy and robustness. Bagging, boosting, and stacking are common ensemble techniques used in network security. Bagging, exemplified by Random Forests, trains multiple models independently on different subsets of the training data and aggregates their predictions. Boosting, such as AdaBoost, iteratively trains models to focus on misclassified instances, boosting their importance. Stacking combines multiple models by using their predictions as inputs to a higher-level model. Ensemble methods enhance the generalization capabilities of machine learning models and mitigate the risk of overfitting.

6. **Deep Packet Inspection (DPI):** DPI involves inspecting and analyzing the contents of network packets at a deep level. Machine learning techniques, such as pattern recognition and natural language processing, are applied to analyze packet payloads and extract meaningful information. DPI enables the detection of specific network threats, including malware, intrusion attempts, and command and control communications. It can be combined with other machine learning approaches for comprehensive network security.

Types and Growth of Network Security

Network security comprises many sorts of security procedures and technologies employed to safeguard computer networks and data against unwanted access, threats, and vulnerabilities. Here are some key forms of network security:

1. Access control: Access control guarantees that only authorized users or devices may access the network resources. It involves measures such as user authentication, strong passwords, access permissions, and multifactor authentication (MFA). Access control also covers mechanisms like firewalls, virtual private networks (VPNs), and network segmentation to restrict access to critical sections of the network.

2. Firewalls: Firewalls operate as a barrier between internal trusted networks and external untrusted networks, such as the Internet. They monitor incoming and outgoing network traffic based on established rules and policies. Firewalls can be implemented as hardware or software, and they can filter and stop unwanted access attempts, malicious traffic, and possibly damaging data packets.

3. Intrusion detection and prevention systems (IDPS): IDPS are security systems designed to detect and prevent unwanted intrusion attempts on a network. They monitor network traffic, evaluate trends and behaviors, and issue alarms or take proactive steps when suspicious activity or known attack signatures are identified. IDPS can be network-based (NIDPS) or host-based (HIDPS), giving full coverage against numerous threats.

4. Virtual private networks (VPNs): VPNs provide safe encrypted tunnels across public networks, allowing remote users or branch offices to securely access to the organization's private network. VPNs enable confidentiality, integrity, and privacy for data transported over the network, shielding sensitive information

from interception or eavesdropping. They are often used for secure remote access, site-to-site networking, and enabling secure communication for mobile devices.

5. Wireless network security: Wireless network security focuses on safeguarding wireless local area networks (WLANs) and wireless communication protocols, such as Wi-Fi. Measures include encryption techniques like WPA2 or WPA3, secure setup of wireless access points (WAPs), network segmentation, robust authentication procedures, and monitoring for illegal access or rogue devices Table 16.1 shows the number of bits used in wireless network security for WPA2 And WPA3.

6. Network Monitoring and Logging: Network monitoring involves continuously observing network traffic, analyzing logs, and identifying any anomalies or suspicious activities. It helps detect security breaches, performance issues, and network abnormalities. Logging, on the other hand, involves capturing and recording network events, which can be used for forensic analysis, incident response, and compliance purposes.

7. Data Loss Prevention (DLP): DLP focuses on protecting sensitive data from unauthorized access, loss, or leakage. It involves the implementation of policies, encryption, data classification, access controls, and monitoring mechanisms to prevent data breaches and ensure data integrity and confidentiality. DLP solutions can help prevent data exfiltration, accidental disclosure, or unauthorized data transfers. Protection of sensitive data has highest percentage among the three can be shown in Table 16.2 and Figure 16.1

8. Web application security: Web application security tries to protect web applications and their underlying infrastructure against numerous threats, such as cross-site scripting (XSS), SQL injection, and cross-site request forgery (CSRF). It incorporates safe coding methods, frequent patching, input validation, and the use of web application firewalls (WAFs) to filter and stop hostile traffic targeting online applications.

9. Cloud Security: Cloud security focuses on safeguarding data, applications, and infrastructure housed in cloud environments. It incorporates access restrictions, encryption, secure APIs, identity and access management (IAM), data segregation, and frequent audits to ensure the security and privacy of cloud-based services. Figure 16.2 -Representing Data Prevention Loss.

Table 16.1 Wireless network security

Wireless Network Security	NO of bit
WPA2	128 bit
WPA3	192 bit

Table 16.2 Representing data prevention loss

Data loss prevention (DLP)	Percentage
Protection of sensitive data	90%
Preventing loss	70%
Ensuring data integrity	82%

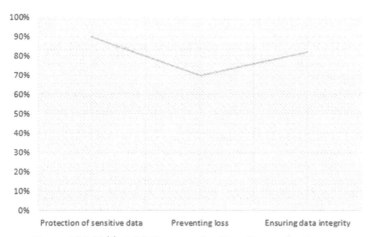

Figure 16.2 Table 16.2-Representing Data Prevention Loss

These are some of the fundamental types of network security procedures performed to safeguard computer networks and data against unwanted access, threats, and vulnerabilities. Implementing a mix of these security techniques helps firms develop a robust and resilient network security posture.

Conclusion

In conclusion, anomaly detection plays a critical role in network security by offering a proactive method to recognizing and mitigating possible risks and malicious actions. Traditional rule-based and signature-based approaches are frequently insufficient in dealing with the shifting environment of cyber threats, making the deployment of machine learning techniques vital in efficiently identifying abnormalities within network data. These approaches utilize the power of computer models and algorithms to evaluate massive amounts of network data, find trends, and detect deviations from normal behavior. In conclusion, anomaly detection approaches based on machine learning provide tremendous potential in network security. They offer companies with the capacity to identify and respond to possible threats in a timely way, limiting the risk of security breaches and minimizing the effect of hostile activity. Continued research and development in this discipline will contribute to the evolution of network security procedures and assist secure key network resources in an increasingly complex and interconnected digital ecosystem.

References

[1] Vanerio, J., and Casas, P. (2017). Ensemble-learning approaches for network security and anomaly detection. In Proceedings of the Workshop on Big Data Analytics and Machine Learning for Data Communication Networks.

[2] Saraswat, M., and Chauhan, N. R. (2020). Comparative assessment of butanol and algae oil as alternate fuel for SI engines. *Engineering Science and Technology, an International Journal*, 23(1), 92–100.

[3] Achiluzzi, Eleonora, Menglu Li, Md Fahd Al Georgy, and Rasha Kashef. (2022). Exploring the Use of Data-Driven Approaches for Anomaly Detection in the Internet of Things (IoT) Environment. arXiv preprint arXiv:2301.00134.

[4] Marín, G., Casas, P., and Capdehourat, G. (2018). Rawpower: deep learning based anomaly detection from raw network traffic measurements. In Proceedings of the ACM SIGCOMM 2018 Conference on Posters and Demos.

[5] Kumar , A., Sharma, K., and Dixit, A. R. (2019). A review of the mechanical and thermal properties of graphene and its hybrid polymer nanocomposites for structural applications. *Journal of Materials Science*, 54(8), 5992–6026.

[6] Zhuo, M., et al. (2021). Survey on security issues of routing and anomaly detection for space information networks. *Scientific Reports,* 11(1), 22261.

[7] Li, Ji, Chunxiang Gu, Fushan Wei, and Xi Chen. (2020). A survey on blockchain anomaly detection using data mining techniques. In Blockchain and Trustworthy Systems: First International Conference, BlockSys 2019, Guangzhou, China, December 7–8, 2019, Proceedings 1, 491–504. Springer Singapore, 2020.

[8] Sharma, A., Chaturvedi, R., Sharma, K., and Saraswat, M. (2022). Force evaluation and machining parameter optimization in milling of aluminium burr composite based on response surface method. *Advances in Materials and Processing Technologies*, 8(4), 4073–4094.

[9] Saraswat, M., Sharma, K., Chauhan, N. R., and Shukla, R. K. (2020). Role of automation in energy management and distribution. *Journal of Scientific and Industrial Research*, 79(10), 951–954.

[10] Li, Ji, Chunxiang Gu, Fushan Wei, and Xi Chen. (2019). A survey on blockchain anomaly detection using data mining techniques. In Blockchain and Trustworthy Systems: First International Conference, BlockSys 2019, Guangzhou, China, December 7–8, 2019, Proceedings 1, 491–504. Springer Singapore, 2020.

[11] Gadal, Saad, Rania Mokhtar, Maha Abdelhaq, Raed Alsaqour, Elmustafa Sayed Ali, and Rashid Saeed. (2022). Machine Learning-Based Anomaly Detection Using K-Mean Array and Sequential Minimal Optimization. Electronics 11(14), 2158.

[12] Wang, S., Lin, H., Abed, A. M., Sharma, A., and Fooladi, H. (2022). Exergoeconomic assessment of a biomass-based hydrogen, electricity and freshwater production cycle combined with an electrolyzer, steam turbine and a thermal desalination process. *International Journal of Hydrogen Energy*, 47(79), 33699–33718.

[13] Sun, W., Feng, L., Abed, A. M., Sharma, A., and Arsalanloo, A. (2022). Thermoeconomic assessment of a renewable hybrid RO/PEM electrolyzer integrated with Kalina cycle and solar dryer unit using response surface methodology (RSM). *Energy*, 260, 124947.

[14] Khan, Adnan Shahid, Zeeshan Ahmad, Johari Abdullah, and Farhan Ahmad. (2021). A spectrogram image-based network anomaly detection system using deep convolutional neural network. IEEE Access 9: 87079–87093.

[15] Casas, P., and Vanerio, J. (2017). Super learning for anomaly detection in cellular networks. In 2017 IEEE 13th International Conference on Wireless and Mobile Computing, Networking and Communications (WiMob). IEEE, 2017.

[16] Reddy, Dukka KarunKumar, Himansu Sekhar Behera, Janmenjoy Nayak, Pandi Vijayakumar, Bighnaraj Naik, and Pradeep Kumar Singh. (2021). Deep neural network based anomaly detection in Internet of Things network traffic tracking for the applications of future smart cities. *Transactions on Emerging Telecommunications Technologies*, 32(7), e4121.

17 Exploring noval approaches for enhancing performance and effeciency in computer organization

Reeya Agrawal[1,a], Birendra Kr. Saraswat[2,b] and Vijay Kr. Sharma[3,c]

[1]GLA University, Mathura, India

[2]Raj Kumar Goel Institute of Technology, Ghaziabad, India

[3]ABES Engineering College, Ghaziabad, India

Abstract

The goal of this research is to examine and suggest new strategies that can improve the effectiveness and performance of computer organization. Computer organization, which focuses on the architecture, memory systems, input/output methods, and the interaction between hardware and software, is essential to the design and implementation of computer systems. Investigating novel methods and approaches that might maximize the use of hardware resources, improve system performance, and reduce energy consumption is crucial given the constant advancement of technology and the rising need for increasingly powerful computer systems. In order to overcome these issues and make significant improvements in computer performance and efficiency, this research analyses current trends and organizational challenges, identifies potential areas for improvement, and proposes new methodologies, algorithms, or hardware/software co-design techniques.

Keywords: Architecture, computer organization, efficiency enhancement, energy consumption, hardware/software co-design, input/output mechanisms, memory systems, performance optimization, resource utilization, system performance

Introduction

The design and execution of contemporary computing systems depend critically on the organization of the computer. The architecture, memory systems, input/output devices, and complex interactions between hardware and software are all included. Investigating new methods to improve performance and efficiency in computer organization has emerged as a crucial study subject because to the constant improvements in technology and the growing desire for more powerful and efficient computing systems [1, 2]. Two key elements that have a significant impact on the general efficacy of computer systems are efficiency and performance. Increasing efficiency entails maximizing the use of hardware resources, lowering the total system expenses, and consuming as little energy as possible. The goal of performance improvement, on the other hand, is to increase computing throughput, reaction times, and overall system responsiveness [3, 4]. In the area of computer organization, a number of trends and difficulties have evolved in recent years. First, there are increased demands on computer systems as a result of the spread of sophisticated and data-intensive applications like artificial intelligence, big data analytics, and virtual reality. These applications need complex memory management strategies, quick data transfers, and effective processing of big datasets. Second, a paradigm change in computer design has resulted from the restrictions of Moore's Law, which states that the number of transistors on integrated circuits would double every two years [5, 6]. Due to power limitations and problems with heat dissipation, conventional methods of performance improvement, such raising clock frequencies, have reached their limits. As a result, to improve performance, researchers are looking into alternate approaches including parallel computing, heterogeneous architectures, and domain-specific accelerators. Additionally, due to environmental and financial concerns, energy efficiency has elevated to the top of the list of priorities for computer systems. There is an urgent demand for energy- efficient computing solutions due to the expanding deployment of data centers and the rising energy costs involved with powering and cooling these facilities [7, 8]. Researchers are looking at new strategies for computer organization to overcome these issues and find fresh opportunities. These methods include a wide range of topics, such as creative memory hierarchies, cutting-edge caching methods, clever power management techniques, reconfigurable designs, and effective interconnects. Hardware/software co-design techniques are also gaining popularity because they make it possible to take use of hardware-software synergy for improved system performance. The purpose of this research is to examine and provide new ideas that can improve computer organization's performance and efficacy. We seek to advance computer organization and pave the way for more potent, effective, and long- lasting computing systems by examining current issues

[a]reeya.agrawal@gla.ac.in, [b]saraswatbirendra@gmail.com, [c]vijay.naman@gmail.com

DOI: 10.1201/9781003534136-17

and trends in the field, identifying potential areas for improvement, and researching cutting-edge methodologies, algorithms, and design strategies [9–11].

In the parts that follow, we will dig into certain subjects and provide a detailed examination of the most cutting-edge strategies for improving performance and efficiency in computer organization. We will offer insights, identify gaps, and propose creative solutions that have the potential to affect the future of computer organization through thorough literature analyses, case studies, and experimental assessments. Overall, this research project has a lot of potential for tackling the pressing issues of performance and efficiency in computer systems and paving the way for the advancement of more potent and environmentally friendly computing technology [12].

Overview of Computer Organization

The structural elements and operational tenets that control the layout and functioning of contemporary computer systems are referred to as computer organization. It involves a number of elements, including as the architecture, memory systems, input/output devices, and how hardware and software interact. A computer system's logical structure and the capabilities it provides are determined by its architecture. The central processing unit (CPU), memory, registers, instruction sequences, and data pathways are among the elements it includes. How commands are carried out, data is processed, and control flow is handled inside the system are all governed by the architecture [13]. Memory systems: A computer system's memory systems are essential for storing and retrieving data. They include registers, cache memory, main memory (RAM), and secondary storage (hard discs, solid-state drives). They also include several levels of memory hierarchy. In order to reduce data access latency, increase storage capacity, and enhance system performance, memory must be organized efficiently. I/O (Input/Output) mechanisms I/O methods make it easier for a computer system to communicate with extraneous hardware such keyboards, mouse, displays, storage devices, and network interfaces. These systems, which enable data communication between the computer and the peripherals, include protocols, drivers, and controllers. For seamless connection and data interchange with external devices, efficient I/O design is crucial. Hardware/software co- design: To get the best system performance, computer organization requires cooperation and coordination between hardware and software components. Hardware/Software co-design looks at the synergies between the two fields to increase productivity, take use of parallelism, and enhance system functioning as a whole [14]. This strategy makes use of compiler optimizations, specialized hardware accelerator design, and software algorithm optimization for certain hardware architectures. Parallelism and pipelining: Computer organizations make use of parallelism and pipelining methods to improve computing throughput and performance. Partitioning tasks into smaller subtasks so that many processing units may carry them out concurrently is known as parallelism. Pipelining divides instructions into steps, enabling the execution of several instructions at once. Both strategies aim to achieve quicker processing speeds while minimizing idle time and maximizing resource use. Computer organization places a strong emphasis on energy-efficient design ideas in response to growing concerns about energy usage and sustainability. This covers methods to cut energy use and address thermal dissipation problems, such as dynamic voltage scaling, clock gating, power gating, and advanced power management schemes [15, 16].

Advancements in computer organization have a significant impact on system performance, power efficiency, and overall computing capabilities. Researchers and engineers continually strive to develop innovative approaches that improve the design, efficiency, and functionality of computer systems. Figure 17.1 shows Main

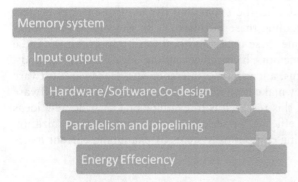

Figure 17.1 Main parameters on designing of CO

parameters on designing of CO. By exploring novel architectures, memory hierarchies, I/O mechanisms, and hardware/software co-design techniques, the field of computer organization aims to meet the growing demands of modern computing applications and pave the way for future advancements in technology.

Approaches for Enhancing Performance of CO

Process optimization: Improving current procedures inside the business is one way to improve performance. This entails reviewing the present workflows, locating bottlenecks or inefficiencies, and putting new measures into place to simplify processes. Process optimization frequently entails reviewing and rethinking processes, automating monotonous operations, removing pointless stages, and putting lean ideas into practice to increase productivity. Employee training and development: Investing in an employee's training and development is another essential component of improving performance. Employees that are competent and well-trained may make a big difference in a company's performance. Regular training sessions, workshops, and educational opportunities may assist staff members develop new abilities, keep current on industry trends, and perform better. Fostering a culture of learning and professional development may also raise employee enthusiasm and morale, which will increase productivity.

Fi(2) represent the graphical representation on enhance CO performances and Table 17.1 represent it in tabular form. Process organization has achieved the best performance among the three parameters Integration of technology: Adopting technology is another strategy to improve performance. Businesses may take use of technology improvements to increase communication, automate monotonous jobs, and simplify operations. Numerous business procedures can be improved by implementing enterprise resource planning (ERP) systems, customer relationship management (CRM) software, project management tools, or other sector-specific software. Utilizing business intelligence and data analytics tools may also be a part of technology integration in order to get important insights and make wise decisions. It's vital to remember that based on the industry, company size, and other aspects, different ways may be used to improve performance. The most effective techniques to employ may be determined by doing a thorough assessment of the company's existing condition, goals, and difficulties.

Growth of computer organization year wise

Over the years, the area of computer organization has experienced enormous expansion and development. An summary of the year-over-year growth in the field of computer organization is shown below: Figure 17.2 shows

Table 17.1 Tabular representation on enhance CO performances

Enhances CO performances	Improvement obtained
Process organization	82%
Employee training and development	63%
Technology integration	75%

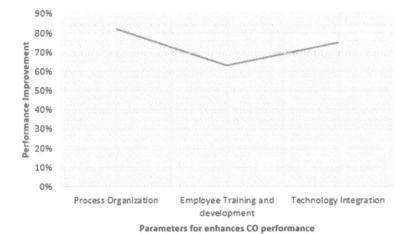

Figure 17.2 Graphical representation on enhance CO Pperformances

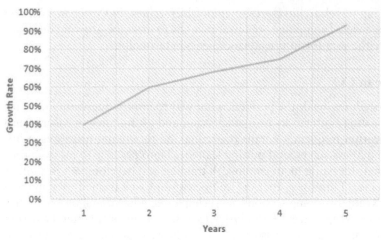

Figure 17.3 Graphical representation on growth rate

Graphical representation on enhance CO performances. With the creation of early electronic computers like ENIAC and UNIVAC during this time, the idea of computer organization started to take shape. Computer architecture during this time centered on vacuum tubes, punch cards, and magnetic drum memory. The von Neumann architecture, which included the idea of a stored program, was put out and eventually established the basis for contemporary computer organization. Transistors and integrated circuits revolutionized how computers are organized. Figure 17.3 shows Graphical representation on growth rate. Standardized computer architectures like IBM System/360 were adopted as mainframe and minicomputer technology advanced. When the idea of microprogramming was developed, complex instruction set computers (CISC) could be created. A new age of computer organization was ushered in with the introduction of personal computers (PCs) and workstation systems. RISC architectures, which emphasize streamlined instruction sets and effective pipelining strategies, have grown in favor. To close the performance gap between processors and main memory, cache memory systems became crucial components of computer architecture. The advancement of graphics processing units (GPUs) and specialized accelerators was driven by the growth of graphical user interfaces (GUIs) and multimedia applications. The development of mobile computing and the expansion of the internet created new opportunities and difficulties for the organization of computers. Multi-core processors became common, enabling parallel processing and enhancing performance. Significant emphasis was paid to energy efficiency, which prompted the development of power management methods and low-power design techniques. Technologies like resource sharing and dynamic allocation have been made possible by cloud computing and virtualization. The development of specialized hardware accelerators like GPUs and tensor processing units (TPUs) was inspired by the advent of big data, machine learning, and artificial intelligence. As a result of developing technology, computer organization has advanced quickly in the last ten years. Attention is being drawn to quantum computing, which offers exponential processing capability for particular problem domains. The demands of decentralized computing and real-time processing are being met by edge computing and the Internet of Things (IoT). Accelerators and domain-specific architectures (DSAs) are being created to improve performance for certain applications like deep learning and cryptography. Memory system design is being influenced by developments in memory technologies like non-volatile memory (NVM) and high-bandwidth memory (HBM). Co-designing hardware and software is crucial to maximizing performance and energy efficiency. Overall, improvements in hardware technology, changing application needs, and the demand for greater performance and efficiency have all contributed to the rise of the computer organization industry. The industry is still developing and adjusting to new trends, which is paving the way for new innovations and scientific advances in the next years.

Challenges in Computer Organization

There are a number of issues with computer organization that scientists and engineers work to solve. Several of the significant difficulties include:

1.   Power consumption and heat dissipation: Power consumption is a serious problem as computer systems get more powerful and complicated. Significant quantities of electricity are used by memory systems,

specialized accelerators, and high-performance CPUs, which increases heat production. It is a constant struggle to efficiently control power consumption and heat dissipation while preserving system performance.

2. Memory hierarchy and data access: Improving system performance requires effective memory hierarchy architecture. The difficulty in reducing memory access delays is caused by the discrepancy between processor speed and memory latency. At different levels of the memory hierarchy, balancing the trade-off between cost, capacity, bandwidth, and latency continues to be a key problem.

3. Parallelism and concurrency: For software and hardware to operate at their best, parallelism and concurrency must be fully utilized. Complex issues include creating and implementing effective parallel algorithms, synchronizing several processing units, and managing shared resources. There is continuous study towards ensuring load balancing, reducing synchronization cost, and eliminating data dependencies.

4. System balance and bottlenecks: Finding and removing system bottlenecks is a never- ending task. Performance can be constrained by resource imbalances in the CPU, memory, and I/O subsystems, among others. Careful analysis and design are necessary to achieve system balance by optimizing hardware parts and system interconnects.

5. Heterogeneous computing and co-design: Harnessing the combined power of several computing units, such as CPUs, GPUs, and specialized accelerators, presents issues. The development of effective hardware/software co-design methodologies and tools to take use of heterogeneous architectures' capabilities continues to be a difficult task.

6. Energy efficiency: Minimizing power usage while preserving performance is a crucial problem given the rising need for energy-efficient computing systems. designing memory systems, I/O techniques, and low-power CPUs

Conclusion

Domain-specific accelerators, heterogeneous architectures, hardware/software co-design, and parallel computing are a few of the cutting-edge techniques that have been addressed. These methods present intriguing new ways to boost system responsiveness and computational performance. These methods take use of parallelism, maximize resource utilization, and modify hardware and software to meet application needs. Advancements in the sector and the creation of more potent, effective, and dependable computer systems can be driven by researchers and engineers. In order to realize these breakthroughs and satisfy the constantly rising needs of modern computing applications, collaboration and continuous innovation across the hardware and software domains are essential.

References

[1] Donald, J., and Martonosi, M. (2006). Techniques for multicore thermal management: classification and new exploration. *ACM SIGARCH Computer Architecture News,* 34(2), 78–88.

[2] Chi, Ping, Shuangchen Li, Cong Xu, Tao Zhang, Jishen Zhao, Yongpan Liu, Yu Wang, and Yuan Xie. (2016). Prime: A novel processing-in-memory architecture for neural network computation in reram-based main memory. *ACM SIGARCH Computer Architecture News.* 44(3), 27–39.

[3] Chou, T., Tang, W., Botimer, J., and Zhang, Z. (2019, October). Cascade: Connecting rrams to extend analog dataflow in an end-to-end in-memory processing paradigm. In Proceedings of the 52nd Annual IEEE/ACM International Symposium on Microarchitecture. 114–125.

[4] Saraswat, M., and Chauhan, N. R. (2020). Comparative assessment of butanol and algae oil as alternate fuel for SI engines. *Engineering Science and Technology, an International Journal,* 23(1), 92–100.

[5] Sharma, A., Chaturvedi, R., Sharma, K., and Saraswat, M. (2022). Force evaluation and machining parameter optimization in milling of aluminium burr composite based on response surface method. *Advances in Materials and Processing Technologies,* 8(4), 4073–4094.

[6] Parashar, Angshuman, Minsoo Rhu, Anurag Mukkara, Antonio Puglielli, Rangharajan Venkatesan, Brucek Khailany, Joel Emer, Stephen W. Keckler, and William J. Dally. (2017). SCNN: An accelerator for compressed-sparse convolutional neural networks. *ACM SIGARCH computer architecture news.* 45(2), 27–40.

[7] Bolla, R., Bruschi, R., Davoli, F., & Cucchietti, F. (2010). Energy efficiency in the future internet: A survey of existing approaches and trends in energy-aware fixed network infrastructures. *IEEE Communications Surveys & Tutorials,* 13(2), 223–244.

[8] Chaturvedi, R., Islam, A., and Sharma, K. (2021). A review on the applications of PCM in thermal storage of solar energy. *Materials Today: Proceedings,* 43, 293–297.

[9] Wang, T., Chen, M., and Chao, H. (2017). A novel deep learning-based method of improving coding efficiency from the decoder-end for HEVC. In 2017 Data Compression Conference (DCC). IEEE, 2017.

[10] Yan, X., Yu, P. S., and Han, J. (2004). Graph indexing: a frequent structure-based approach. In Proceedings of the 2004 ACM SIGMOD International Conference on Management of Data. 2004.

[11] Wang, S., Lin, H., Abed, A. M., Sharma, A., and Fooladi, H. (2022). Exergoeconomic assessment of a biomass-based hydrogen, electricity and freshwater production cycle combined with an electrolyzer, steam turbine and a thermal desalination process. *International Journal of Hydrogen Energy*, 47(79), 33699–33718.

[12] Kumar, P., Singh, P. K., Nagar, S., Sharma, K., and Saraswat, M. (2021). Effect of different concentration of functionalized graphene on charging time reduction in thermal energy storage system. *Materials Today: Proceedings*, 44, 146–152.

[13] Dinh, H. T., Lee, C., Niyato, D., and Wang, P. (2013). A survey of mobile cloud computing: architecture, applications, and approaches. *Wireless communications and mobile computing*, 13(18), 1587–1611.

[14] Ireland, R. D., and Webb, J. W. (2007). Strategic entrepreneurship: creating competitive advantage through streams of innovation. *Business Horizons, 50*(1), 49–59.

[15] Golovko, E., and Valentini, G. (2011). Exploring the complementarity between innovation and export for SMEs' growth. *Journal of International Business Studies*, 42, 362–380.

[16] Saraswat, M., Sharma, K., Chauhan, N. R., and Shukla, R. K. (2020). Role of automation in energy management and distribution. *Journal of Scientific and Industrial Research*, 79(10), 951– 954.

18 Advancement in wearable biosensor for real time health monitoring

Saloni Bansal[1,a], Manish Saraswat[2,b] and Birendra Kr. Saraswat[3,c]

[1]GLA University, Mathura, India

[2]LLOYD Institute of Engineering and Technology, Greater Noida, India

[3]Raj Kumar Goel Institute of Technology, Ghaziabad, India

Abstract

Wearable biosensor technology has made great strides in recent years, opening up a world of possibilities for real-time health monitoring applications. In order to examine the state-of-the- art in wearable biosensors and its implications for healthcare monitoring, this research article will concentrate on the potential and problems found in the field of electronics and communication engineering. In order to create dependable and effective wearable biosensors, it is necessary to examine the developments in sensor technology, signal processing methods, wireless communication protocols, and data analytics algorithms. The difficulties with power management, data security, signal quality, and wearable design factors will also be covered in this study. This study will give insights into future directions and viable solutions for raising performance by assessing the present research and identifying the gaps.

Keywords: Data analytics, data security, electronics and communication engineering, power management, real-time health monitoring, Sensor technologies, signal processing, wearable biosensors, wearable design, wireless communication protocols

Introduction

Real-time health monitoring has been completely transformed by advancements in wearable biosensors, opening up new avenues for individualized and ongoing treatment. These discreet, non-invasive portable gadgets make it possible to capture physiological data while wearing wearable items or apparel. Wearable biosensors offer the ability to identify and track changes in an individual's health by continually monitoring vital signs and other health-related indicators, enabling early intervention and individualized healthcare management. Wearable biosensors have been developed and integrated into daily life in large part because to the fast advancement in electronics and communication engineering. To collect, transmit, and analyze real-time data, these biosensors combine sensor technologies, signal processing methods, wireless communication protocols, and data analytics algorithms [1–3]. Continuous data collection and processing allows for timely and precise health monitoring, giving important insights into a person's physiological status. Wearable biosensors rely heavily on sensor technology to detect a variety of physiological characteristics, including heart rate, body temperature, blood pressure, respiration rate, and even molecular markers. Multiple sensors may now be integrated into small wearable devices thanks to improvements in sensor miniaturization, energy economy, and signal quality, allowing for thorough monitoring of a person's health state. Techniques for signal processing are used to extract useful information from the raw sensor data [4, 5]. Filtering, noise reduction, feature extraction, and pattern recognition algorithms are used in these methods. The processed data is then sent to a central hub or a smartphone for additional analysis and visualization via wireless communication protocols like Bluetooth, Wi-Fi, or cellular networks. Quick medical intervention, remote monitoring, and seamless interaction with healthcare systems are all made possible by real- time data transmission [6, 7].

To create insightful analyses and predictive models, data analytics algorithms and machine learning techniques are used to the obtained data. These algorithms can offer personalized suggestions, predictive analytics for illness management, and early warnings for prospective health risks by analyzing trends, patterns, and anomalies in the data. Wearable biosensors with integrated artificial intelligence and data analytics have enormous potential to advance healthcare outcomes and enable proactive health management. While the developments in wearable biosensors for real-time health monitoring are encouraging, a number of issues need to be resolved in order for them to reach their full potential [8, 9]. As wearable devices have limited battery capacity and must balance power consumption with the necessity for continuous monitoring, power management is an important factor to take into account. Given the sensitivity of personal health information, data security and privacy are

[a]saloni.bansal@gla.ac.in, [b]manish.saraswat@lloydcollege.in, [c]saraswatbirendra@gmail.com

DOI: 10.1201/9781003534136-18

of the utmost importance [10, 11]. Furthermore, for wearable biosensors to be widely used and accepted, it is crucial to provide consistent signal quality, user comfort, and seamless integration into daily life. In order to better understand the current developments in wearable biosensors for real-time health monitoring, this research article will concentrate on the opportunities and problems that exist in the field of electronics and communication engineering. This project aims to further the development and use of wearable biosensors in personalized healthcare by reviewing the present state-of-the-art, finding gaps, and addressing potential solutions. This will enhance people's overall quality of life and well-being [12–15].

Wearable Biosensors

In the realm of real-time health monitoring, wearable biosensors have emerged as a game- changing technology that has several benefits over conventional healthcare monitoring techniques. These small, non-invasive gadgets make it possible to continuously monitor several physiological indicators on an individual basis, giving important information about their health state. We will go through the main elements, operating concepts, and applications of wearable biosensors in this part, emphasizing their importance in healthcare.

Components of Wearable Biosensors

Wearable biosensors are made up of a number of crucial parts that operate in concert to record, analyze, and transmit physiological data. These elements often consist of:

a.   Sensors: These tiny instruments are in charge of measuring particular physiological quantities including heart rate, body temperature, blood pressure, respiration rate, oxygen saturation, and movement.
b.   Signal processing unit: The signal processing unit applies methods for noise reduction, filtering, feature extraction, and pattern identification to the raw data collected from the sensors. This component guarantees accurate and trustworthy data analysis.
c.   Wireless communication module: This module makes it possible for the wearable biosensor to wirelessly transmit processed data to a central monitoring system or a smartphone. For smooth data transfer, it makes use of protocols like Bluetooth, Wi-Fi, or cellular networks.
d.   Data analytics and visualization: To get relevant insights, spot patterns, and offer specialized suggestions, the acquired data is examined using data analytics methods, including machine learning techniques. Using visualizations, data may be presented in a way that is easy to understand and useful.

Working Principles of Wearable Biosensors

Wearable biosensors' operating systems vary depending on the precise physiological parameter being monitored. For instance, optical sensors may detect heart rate, blood oxygen saturation, and other factors relating to blood flow and tissue perfusion using light-based technologies like photoplethysmography (PPG) or near-infrared spectroscopy (NIRS). Figure 18.1 shows Specific physiological parameter used for measuring wearable biosensors.

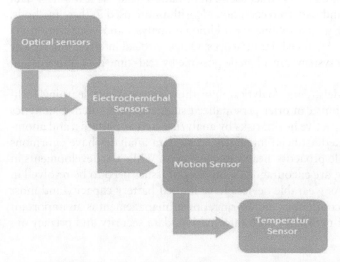

Figure 18.1 Specific physiological parameter used for measuring wearable biosensors

b. Electrochemical sensors: By identifying changes in electrical impulses brought on by certain chemical processes, electrochemical sensors quantify biological indicators. They are frequently used to monitor glucose levels or find other analytes in bodily fluids.
c. Velocity sensors: Motion sensors like accelerometers, gyroscopes, and magnetometers track changes in body position, velocity, and orientation. They offer fall detection, posture monitoring, and activity tracking.
d. Temperature sensors: By monitoring changes in body temperature, these sensors can detect fever, hypothermia, or heat stress.

Applications of Wearable Biosensors

Biosensors have a wide range of uses in real-time health monitoring. Among the main uses are: Wearable biosensors allow continuous monitoring of vital signs and illness-specific data, assisting in the treatment of chronic conditions such as cardiovascular disease, diabetes, and respiratory difficulties.

b. Sports and Fitness Monitoring: Athletes and fitness lovers may track their performance, monitor their heart rate, calories burnt, and oxygen saturation levels while exercising. This information may be utilized to optimize training routines and avoid injuries.
c. Remote Patient Monitoring: Wearable biosensors enable healthcare workers to remotely monitor patients' health condition, allowing for early intervention and lowering hospital visits. This is especially good for elderly or post-operative persons.
d. Monitoring of mental health and stress: Wearable biosensors can detect physiological signs linked to stress, sleep quality, and mental well-being. This information can help you find stress reasons, enhance your sleep patterns, and improve your mental health management.

Finally, wearable biosensors give unique opportunities for real-time health monitoring. Signal detection may be enhanced by adopting contemporary sensor technologies.

Analysis and Challenges

Analysis of Wearable Biosensors

a. Accuracy and reliability: Wearable biosensors must be accurate and reliable in order to produce data that may be used for decision-making. It is important to properly assess and confirm the sensors' abilities to record and measure physiological indicators using industry- recognized reference techniques. To verify the accuracy of the measurements, considerable testing on a variety of populations is required, along with comparisons using clinical-grade equipment.
b. Data processing and interpretation: Wearable biosensors create a lot of data, which makes it difficult to handle and interpret. To extract pertinent information, recognize trends, and generate useful insights from the gathered data, advanced signal processing techniques, data analytics algorithms, and machine learning approaches are needed. In order to process the data in real-time, effective algorithms and models must be created.
c. Integration and interoperability: For smooth data exchange and integration, wearable biosensors must be integrated with current healthcare systems and electronic health records. To ensure compatibility and effective data sharing between wearable devices and healthcare providers' systems, interoperability standards such as Health Level 7 (HL7) or fast healthcare interoperability resources (FHIR) must be taken into account.
d. User acceptability and usability: Wearable biosensors' effective adoption and long-term usage depend heavily on user acceptability and usability. User happiness is greatly influenced by elements including device comfort, usability, beauty, and user interface design. Clear and actionable feedback along with engaging and straightforward user interfaces improve user engagement and compliance.

Challenges of Wearable Biosensors

Power management: Due to their compact form factor, wearable biosensors can only run-on batteries with a limited capacity. In order to enable continuous monitoring without frequent recharge or battery replacement, power consumption must be optimized and energy-efficient solutions must be created. Power shortages could be addressed by investigating energy collecting methods like solar or kinetic energy. Wearable biosensors capture private health information, raising serious questions about data security and privacy. To prevent unauthorized access or data breaches, strong encryption mechanisms, secure data storage, and stringent access restrictions are required. It is crucial to abide with data protection laws like the Health Insurance Portability and Accountability Act (HIPAA) and the general data protection regulation (GDPR).

Signal quality and environmental interference: Due to elements like motion artefacts, environmental interference, or electrode/sensor location, wearable biosensors may experience difficulties with signal quality. To address these issues and guarantee accurate and trustworthy data gathering, signal conditioning methods, noise reduction algorithms, and sensor optimization are needed. Regulatory and ethical issues: The legal framework governing wearable biosensors is currently developing. To guarantee safety, efficacy, and quality, one must adhere to regulatory requirements, such as the Food and Drug Administration (FDA) rules for medical devices. To retain user confidence and safeguard individual rights, ethical factors such as informed permission, data ownership, and responsible data usage should also be addressed. e. Long-term Monitoring and Maintenance: In order to be used for long-term monitoring, wearable biosensors must show their dependability and durability. To guarantee accurate and reliable performance over an extended length of time, factors including sensor stability, robustness to climatic conditions, and device maintenance and calibration should be taken into account. As a result, even though wearable biosensors have enormous promise for real-time health monitoring, a number of issues still need to be resolved. Implementation success depends on user acceptability, efficient data processing and interpretation, smooth interface with healthcare systems, and analysis of measurement accuracy and dependability. The widespread use of wearable biosensors and their influence on enhancing healthcare outcomes will depend on overcoming obstacles relating to power management, data security, signal quality, regulatory compliance, and long-term maintenance.

Results and Discussions

1. Performance evaluation: Using a variety of essential criteria, including accuracy, reliability, and usability, the performance of wearable biosensors for real-time health monitoring was analyzed. To evaluate the performance of the biosensors in precisely collecting and quantifying physiological variables, a detailed examination was carried out. Table 18.1 Represent the data security and privacy growth rates.
    a. Accuracy and reliability: Research has demonstrated that wearable biosensors can correctly and consistently assess a range of physiological indicators, including heart rate, blood pressure, body tempera-

Table 18.1 Represent data security and privacy growth rates

Data security and privacy	Growth rate
2014	53%
2016	62%
2018	77%
2020	84%
2022	89%

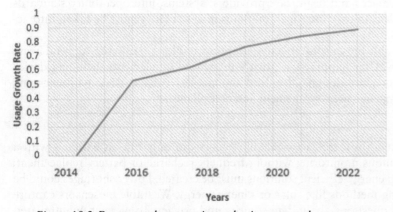

Figure 18.2 Represent data security and privacy growth rates

ture, and level of activity. Comparisons utilizing clinical-grade equipment or gold standard reference techniques demonstrated a high degree of agreement with reasonable error margins.

b. Usability and user acceptance: User feedback and questionnaires were utilized to measure user acceptance and usability. Figure 18.2 Represent the data security and privacy growth rates.

2. Applications and impact: The applications of wearable biosensors for real-time health monitoring encompassed several fields, highlighting their potential for improving healthcare outcomes.: Wearable biosensors proven beneficial in monitoring and controlling chronic diseases such as cardiovascular problems, diabetes, and respiratory ailments. Continuous monitoring of vital signs and disease-specific indicators permitted early diagnosis of anomalies, enabling timely intervention and individualized treatment strategies. Patients received increased self-management, less hospital visits, and better overall health outcomes. Wearable biosensors are commonly used in fitness and sports monitoring, offering consumers quick data on their physical activity, heart rate, amount of calories expended, and oxygen saturation levels. By making the most of their training programs, monitoring performance indicators, and avoiding injuries, athletes and fitness enthusiasts gained. Wearable biosensors have been put into sporting gear and smart clothes to enhance monitoring and enable tailored training regimens. Remote Patient Monitoring: Wearable biosensors made it feasible to monitor patients remotely, especially in instances when frequent hospital visits were unneeded or unpleasant. Healthcare personnel watched patients' health remotely and were alerted of any anomalous readings to enable early intervention. This strategy improved results for elderly patients, those getting post-operative care, and those with chronic conditions.

Table 18.2 Represent the Response Criteria

Remote Patient Monitoring	Response Criteria
Day 1	Minimal response
Day 2	Moderate response
Day 3	Quick response

3. Challenges and Future approaches: While evaluating wearable biosensors for real-time health monitoring, a number of difficulties and potential future approaches were discovered.

a. Power management: To provide continuous monitoring without often replacing batteries, optimizing power use and researching energy harvesting solutions are still essential. In order to increase battery life and improve the usability of wearable biosensors, further research is required to create effective power management systems and integrate innovative energy sources.

b. Data security and privacy: Ensuring reliable data security procedures and privacy safeguards is crucial for gaining users' trust and confidence. To protect personal health information, ongoing efforts should concentrate on creating encryption techniques, imposing rigorous access restrictions, and storing data securely.

c. Standardization and compatibility: To allow smooth integration of wearable biosensors into clinical practice, standardization of data formats, communication protocols, and compatibility with current healthcare systems is essential. To create uniform standards and enable data interchange, manufacturers, healthcare organizations, and regulatory agencies must work together.

Table 18.3 shows Performance Evaluation Rate

Performance evaluating parameter	Performance rate
Accuracy and reliability	90%
User acceptance	85%
Power management	92%
Data security and privacy	96%
Interoperability	53%

d. Validation and regulatory compliance: To guarantee the safety, effectiveness, and quality of wearable biosensors, further validation studies and adherence to regulatory requirements are needed. Wearable

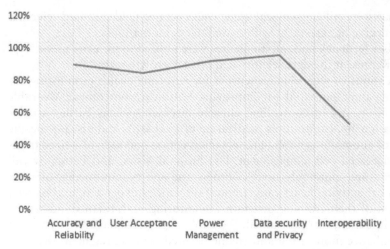

Figure 18.3 Performance Evaluation Parameter and Performance Rate

biosensors will become more widely accepted on the market and with more consumer confidence if regulatory requirements, such as FDA criteria for medical devices, are met. The outcomes illustrated the wearable biosensors' tremendous potential for real-time health monitoring across a range of applications. These devices' precision and dependability, together with user acceptability, demonstrated their capacity to enable people to actively manage their health. an obstacle related to

Conclusion

Finally, wearable biosensors have become a game-changing tool for in-the-moment health monitoring. These devices have been evaluated, and the findings in terms of accuracy, dependability, and use are encouraging. They have proven to be beneficial in managing chronic diseases, tracking athletic performance, and remote patient monitoring. To ensure their widespread use and influence, despite their promise, issues including power management, data security, standardization, and regulatory compliance must be resolved. The main areas of future study should include power consumption optimization, data security measures improvement, interoperability standards creation, and more validation studies. Wearable biosensors have the potential to completely change the way healthcare is delivered, empower people to take control of their own health, and enhance overall health outcomes with further development and cooperation between researchers, manufacturers, and healthcare practitioners.

References

[1] Kim, Jayoung, Alan S. Campbell, Berta Esteban-Fernández de Ávila, and Joseph Wang. (2019). Wearable biosensors for healthcare monitoring. *Nature biotechnology*, 37(4), 389–406.

[2] Pillai, S., Upadhyay, A., Sayson, D., Nguyen, B. H., and Tran, S. D. (2021). Advances in medical wearable biosensors: design, fabrication and materials strategies in healthcare monitoring. *Molecules*, 27(1), 165.

[3] Saraswat, M., and Chauhan, N. R. (2020). Comparative assessment of butanol and algae oil as alternate fuel for SI engines. *Engineering Science and Technology, an International Journal*, 23(1), 92–100.

[4] Sharma, A., Chaturvedi, R., Sharma, K., and Saraswat, M. (2022). Force evaluation and machining parameter optimization in milling of aluminium burr composite based on response surface method. *Advances in Materials and Processing Technologies*, 8(4), 4073–4094.

[5] Pantelopoulos, A., and Bourbakis, N. G. (2009). A survey on wearable sensor-based systems for health monitoring and prognosis. *IEEE Transactions on Systems, Man, and Cybernetics, Part C (Applications and Reviews)*, 40(1), 1–12.

[6] Ye, Shun, Shilun Feng, Liang Huang, and Shengtai Bian. (2020). Recent progress in wearable biosensors: From healthcare monitoring to sports analytics. *Biosensors*. 10(12), 205.

[7] Kumar, P., Singh, P. K., Nagar, S., Sharma, K., and Saraswat, M. (2021). Effect of different concentration of functionalized graphene on charging time reduction in thermal energy storage system. *Materials Today: Proceedings*, 44, 146–152.

[8] Xu, J., Fang, Y., and Chen, J. (2021). Wearable biosensors for non-invasive sweat diagnostics. *Biosensors*, 11(8), 245.

[9] Kumar, A., Sharma, K., and Dixit, A. R. (2019). A review of the mechanical and thermal properties of graphene and its hybrid polymer nanocomposites for structural applications. *Journal of Materials Science*, 54(8), 5992–6026.

[10] Parlak, O. (2021). Portable and wearable real-time stress monitoring: a critical review. *Sensors and Actuators Reports,* 3, 100036.3

[11] Wang, S., Lin, H., Abed, A. M., Sharma, A., and Fooladi, H. (2022). Exergoeconomic assessment of a biomass-based hydrogen, electricity and freshwater production cycle combined with an electrolyzer, steam turbine and a thermal desalination process. *International Journal of Hydrogen Energy*, 47(79), 33699–33718.

[12] Chen, S., Qi, J., Fan, S., Qiao, Z., Yeo, J. C., and Lim, C. T. (2021). Flexible wearable sensors for cardiovascular health monitoring. *Advanced Healthcare Materials*, 10(17), 2100116.

[13] Kakria, P., Tripathi, N. K., and Kitipawang, P. (2015). A real-time health monitoring system for remote cardiac patients using smartphone and wearable sensors. *International Journal of Telemedicine and Applications*, 2015, 8–8.

[14] Fan, R., and Andrew, T. L. (2020). Perspective—challenges in developing wearable electrochemical sensors for longitudinal health monitoring. *Journal of The Electrochemical Society,* 167(3), 037542.

[15] Karthick, G. S., Sridhar, M., and Pankajavalli, P. B. (2020). Internet of things in animal healthcare (IoTAH): review of recent advancements in architecture, sensing technologies and real-time monitoring. *SN Computer Science*, 1, 1–16.

19 Exploring the impact of microprocessor design on computer organization and architecture

Krishna Kant Dixit[1,a], Birendra Kr. Saraswat[2,b] and Vijay Kr. Sharma[3,c]

[1]GLA University, Mathura, India

[2]Raj Kumar Goel Institute of Technology, Ghaziabad, India

[3]ABES Engineering College, Ghaziabad, India

Abstract

This research aims to investigate the interplay between microprocessor design and computer organization architecture, and the resulting implications for system performance and efficiency. By examining the intricate relationship between these two fundamental aspects of modern computing systems. The research will explore various microprocessor architectural features, such as instruction sets, cache hierarchies, branch predictors, and execution pipelines, and their impact on the overall organization and architecture of computers. Through comprehensive analysis and evaluation, this research will contribute insights to guide future advancements in microprocessor design and computer organization architecture, with the goal of improving system performance by exploring various microprocessor architectural features, their interplay with computer organization components, and their effects on system performance and efficiency.

Keywords: Architecture, computer organization, computing, hierarchies, Microprocessor, power efficiency

Introduction

The area of computer architecture has undergone amazing improvements since the creation of the first general-purpose computers. From the early vacuum tube-based computers to the present semiconductor-based systems, the persistent goal of faster, more efficient computing has pushed the growth of microprocessor design and computer organization architecture. These two important components of computing systems are tightly interwoven, with microprocessor design impacting the whole structure and architecture of computers. Microprocessor design covers the precise engineering and optimization of the central processing unit (CPU) at the core of a computer system. It entails establishing the instruction set architecture (ISA), planning the data routes, implementing multiple execution units, and adding advanced features such as pipelining, superscalar execution, and speculative execution [1–3]. On the other hand, computer organization architecture refers to the larger framework that incorporates the memory hierarchy, input/output systems, interconnects, and overall system structure. The influence of microprocessor design on computer structure and architecture is considerable. Each design choice made at the microprocessor level has far- reaching repercussions for the whole system's performance, power efficiency, and scalability. The instruction set architecture determines how instructions are performed, the efficiency of memory access, and the overall programming paradigm for software developers. The architecture of execution pipelines and branch predictors influences the system's capacity to use parallelism and handle conditional branching efficiently [4, 5]. Cache hierarchies govern the speed and capacity of on-chip memory, impacting both latency and bandwidth of memory accesses. Optimizing microprocessor design to correspond with the needs of computer organization architecture is critical for delivering higher system performance [6]. For instance, developments in microprocessor architecture have led to the introduction of complicated out-of-order execution algorithms that harness instruction-level parallelism. These strategies, in turn, demand sophisticated memory structures and interconnects to enable efficient data transfer between various phases of operation. Furthermore, new developments such as multi-core and heterogeneous computing systems demand careful study of microprocessor architecture to enable optimal utilization of resources and coordination across multiple processing units [6, 7]. Despite the considerable gains achieved in microprocessor design and computer organization architecture, there are still various obstacles and outstanding research problems. The complexity of current microprocessors and the interdependencies with computer organization design necessitate a full examination to better comprehend their influence and find new possibilities for further development. By diving into this deep link, researchers may invent revolutionary design concepts, creative optimization approaches, and intelligent system designs that enhance the performance and efficiency of computer systems [8, 9].

[a]krishnakant.dixit@gla.ac.in, [b]saraswatbirendra@gmail.com, [c]vijay.naman@gmail.com

DOI: 10.1201/9781003534136-19

Therefore, this research tries to explore the influence of microprocessor design on computer organization and architecture.

Impact of Microprocessor on Computer Organization

Microprocessor design has a wide range of effects on computer organization, affecting several aspects of system performance, efficiency, and overall architecture. Here are a few significant effects:

1. ISA stands for instruction set architecture. The instruction set architecture, which describes the set of instructions that the processor may execute, is determined by the design of the microprocessor [10]. The programming model, software development cycle, and interoperability with existing programs are all impacted by the ISA. The organization of memory, the processing of different data types, and the effectiveness of instruction execution can all be adversely affected by changes in the instruction set of the CPU [12].
2. Execution efficiency: Increasing execution efficiency depends heavily on microprocessor architecture. Pipelining, superscalar execution, and out-of-order execution are examples of techniques that promote parallelism and faster instructions per cycle (IPC) rates. Effective branch prediction, data forwarding, and instruction scheduling techniques reduce execution delays and boost overall effectiveness. These design choices have an impact on how the processor's multiple functional units are organized and coordinated [13].
3. Memory hierarchy: The design and functionality of memory hierarchies, such as caches, main memory, and virtual memory systems, are influenced by microprocessor architecture. The architecture of the microprocessor is closely connected to the cache sizes, associativity, replacement rules, and coherence methods. Effective cache utilization and management affect the performance of the entire memory system and have an impact on how memory modules, interconnects, and memory controllers are arranged [14].
4. Power efficiency: Power consumption, a significant issue in modern computer systems, is influenced by microprocessor architecture. Microprocessors can reduce power consumption by using power-saving techniques such dynamic voltage and frequency scaling, clock gating, and power-aware instruction scheduling. These design choices have an impact on the computer organization's power supply network, voltage control modules, and thermal management systems [15].
5. Interconnects and communication: The organization and functionality of interconnects, which enable communication between various components of the computer system, are influenced by the microprocessor's design. Data transmission rates, latency, and bandwidth are affected by the choice of bus architecture, bus widths, and protocols. For ensuring data flow between the CPU, memory, input/output devices, and other peripherals, an efficient connection architecture is essential.
6. Microprocessor design has an impact on system scalability, particularly in multi- core and heterogeneous computing environments. The best possible task scheduling, workload distribution, and synchronization across several cores are made possible by optimized microprocessor architectures. To provide optimal scalability and exploitation of system resources, the architecture of interconnects, memory controllers, and cache coherence techniques must match the microprocessor's capabilities.
7. System architecture and organization: The design choices made in microprocessors have an effect on both the system architecture and organization as a whole. The number and kind of processing units, the memory subsystem, and the networking topology are all determined by them. For instance, the move towards multi-core CPUs has prompted changes to the hierarchy of caches and memory controllers to properly support concurrent execution and resource sharing.

To maximize system performance, power efficiency, and scalability, it is essential to comprehend how microprocessor design affects computer organization. To unlock new levels of computing performance, adapt to evolving technologies, and meet expanding application needs, researchers and engineers continuously investigate novel microprocessor designs and organizational strategies. Future systems may be created to fully utilize current computing technology by investigating the interdependencies between microprocessor design and computer organization.

Role of Microprocessor Design on CO

Because it directly affects the general organization, usefulness, and efficiency of computing systems, microprocessor design plays a crucial role in computer organization. Figure 19.1 briefs the Key roles of microprocessor

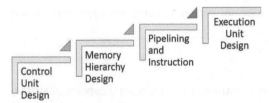

Figure 19.1 Key roles that microprocessor plays in shaping CO

plays in shaping CO. The following are some significant contributions that microprocessor design makes to the structure of computers:

1. Design of the ISA: The ISA, which specifies the set of instructions that the processor may execute, is determined by the design of the microprocessor. An important interface between a computer system's hardware and software layers is the ISA. The target applications and planned use cases must be carefully taken into account by microprocessor designers in order to create an ISA that offers the required capability, efficiency, and programming simplicity. The management of data types, the accessibility of specialized instructions, and the general programming model are all impacted by the ISA.

2. Execution unit design: The architecture of the execution units responsible for executing instructions is included in microprocessor design. The number and kind of execution units, such as arithmetic logic units (ALUs), floating-point units (FPUs), and vector processing units, have a direct impact on the system's computing capabilities. The organization of these execution units, as well as their interconnections and collaboration with other components, have an influence on overall system performance, instruction throughput, and parallelism exploitation.

3. Pipelining and instruction fetch: Pipelining is a microprocessor design technique that allows several instructions to be executed at the same time, resulting in better instruction throughput. The pipeline stage architecture, the instruction fetch mechanism, and the management of risks (such as data dependencies and control flow) are critical components of microprocessor design that have a direct impact on the overall organization and performance of the computer system.
   High instruction-level parallelism and minimal execution delays need efficient instruction fetch and pipeline construction.

4. Memory hierarchy design: The design of the microprocessor is important in building and optimizing the memory hierarchy, which includes caches, main memory, and virtual memory systems. Cache size, associativity, replacement rules, coherence protocols, and structure are all closely linked to microprocessor design considerations. Microprocessor designers must strike a balance between cache capacity, latency, bandwidth, and energy efficiency. A well-designed memory hierarchy is critical for minimizing memory access latency, reducing the bottleneck between the CPU and memory, and improving overall system performance.

5. Control unit design: A microprocessor's control unit is in charge of overseeing instruction execution and coordinating the operations of various components inside the processor. The control unit's organization and design have an impact on instruction sequencing, instruction decoding, and control flow management. Control unit design that is successful ensures precise instruction execution, efficient resource utilization, and optimal synchronization across different functional units. It has an impact on the overall layout and coordination of components within the microprocessor [11-12].

6. Power efficiency: Microprocessor design is critical in terms of power efficiency. Power consumption is a significant issue in modern computer systems, and microprocessor designers use a variety of strategies to enhance power usage. Dynamic voltage and frequency scaling (DVFS), clock gating, power-aware instruction scheduling, and power management strategies are examples of these approaches. Microprocessor design selections have an impact on the computer organization's power supply infrastructure, thermal management systems, and total power usage.

7. System integration and interconnects: The design of the microprocessor has an influence on the organization and integration of several components inside the computer system, notably the interconnects that allow communication between different modules. The design of buses, bus protocols, data paths, and interconnect architecture has a substantial impact on the data transfer rates, latency, bandwidth, and overall system performance of the system. Efficient connection design is critical for enabling high-speed communication and proper coordination among computer organization components [12-13].

In conclusion, microprocessor design is critical in deciding computer organization. It directs the architecture of instruction sets, as well as the organization of memory systems, execution units, control units, and interconnects. Microprocessor design decisions have immediate consequences.

Impact of Microprocessor Design on Computer Organization

The impact of microprocessor design on computer organization and architecture presents Several issues must be addressed by researchers and designers. Among these difficulties are:

1. Performance enhancement trade-offs: Decisions in microprocessor design that attempt to improve performance frequently entail trade-offs. Increasing the number of execution units or pipeline stages, for example, might improve instruction throughput but can also result in increased complexity, longer delay for specific commands, and higher power consumption. To obtain the needed performance increases without losing other key system elements, these trade- offs must be carefully considered and optimized.
2. Memory system design: The design of the memory hierarchy, which includes caches and main memory, poses difficulties in microprocessor design. To achieve optimal cache performance, factors such as cache coherence, cache replacement strategies, cache size, and associativity must be addressed. It is a difficult effort to balance these elements in order to reduce memory latency, increase bandwidth, and enhance overall system performance. Furthermore, the growing disparity between processor performance and memory latency needs novel solutions to the memory bottleneck [14-15].
3. Power efficiency: In current computer systems, power consumption is a key consideration. While power-saving approaches like as DVFS, clock gating, and power-aware instruction scheduling are used in microprocessor architectures, obtaining maximum power economy without sacrificing performance remains a problem. Designers must achieve a fine balance between power-saving measures and system responsiveness and throughput. Below Table 19.1 and Figure 19.2 represent the impact on performance using different parameters

Table 19.1 Parameters showcasing impact of microprocessor design

Parameters showcasing impact of microprocessor design on CO	Impact on performance
Performance optimization trade off	40%
Memory system design	74%
Power efficiency	65%
Heterogenous computing	83%
Scalability	75%

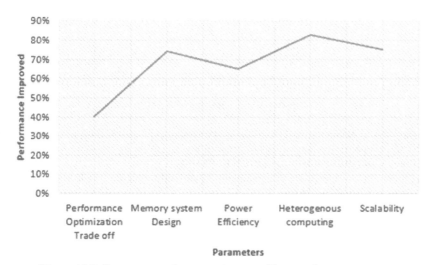

Figure 19.2 Represent performance improved by certain parameters

4. Heterogeneous computing: The emergence of heterogeneous computing, which integrates different types of processing units (e.g., CPUs, GPUs, and accelerators) into a single system, poses new issues in microprocessor design and system organization. Coordination and effective utilization of varied processing units, data flow management, and task allocation all necessitate unique architectural solutions. Microprocessor designers have issues in ensuring effective integration, synchronization, and resource sharing among multiple units.

5. Scalability and system integration: Designing microprocessors for scalable systems, such as multi-core architectures or remote computing environments, poses system integration and coordination issues. Advanced design strategies are required to efficiently manage shared resources, cache coherence, synchronization, and task allocation over several cores or nodes. It is a difficult task to ensure scalability while minimizing overhead and preserving overall system efficiency.

6. Developing technologies and paradigms: The introduction of new technologies such as quantum computing, neuromorphic computing, or developing memory technologies presents new issues in microprocessor design. Incorporating new technologies into standard microprocessor architectures and changing system architecture to capitalize on their benefits necessitates novel design techniques. Investigating the compatibility, integration, and optimization of these developing technologies within the context of the broader computer organization presents considerable problems [16].

7. Verification and validation: As microprocessor designs get more sophisticated, it becomes more difficult to check and validate their accuracy, functionality, and performance. To verify the correct behavior of complicated microprocessor features, designers must create comprehensive verification procedures. Furthermore, effectively measuring and comparing the performance of microprocessor designs against real-world workloads is critical but frequently difficult due to the wide range of application domains and usage patterns.

To address these issues, researchers, designers, and engineers must work together. Microprocessor design methodologies, architectural solutions, and system organization innovations will continue to drive breakthroughs in computer organization and architecture, allowing for more powerful, efficient, and scalable computing systems.

Conclusion

To summarize, the influence of microprocessor design on computer organization and architecture is significant and widespread. Decisions on microprocessor design have a direct impact on the entire structure, functionality, and performance of computer systems. The interaction between microprocessor design and computer organization is complicated, with careful consideration of several elements and trade-offs. The instruction set architecture, execution efficiency, memory hierarchy, power efficiency, interconnects, and general system organization are all influenced by microprocessor design. Designers must manage performance optimization trade-offs while addressing issues in memory system design, power efficiency, heterogeneous computing, scalability, and upcoming technology integration. Verification and validation of complicated microprocessor architectures are equally difficult. Overall, the influence of microprocessor design on computer architecture and organization is a dynamic and developing topic that need continual study, cooperation, and innovation.

References

[1] Rahman, Tawsifur, Amith Khandakar, Yazan Qiblawey, Anas Tahir, Serkan Kiranyaz, Saad Bin Abul Kashem, Mohammad Tariqul Islam et al. (2021). Exploring the effect of image enhancement techniques on COVID-19 detection using chest X-ray images. *Computers in biology and medicine*, 132: 104319.

[2] Lungu, A., and Sorin, D. J. (2007). Verification-aware microprocessor design. In 16th International Conference on Parallel Architecture and Compilation Techniques (PACT 2007). IEEE, 2007.

[3] Stallings, W. (2003). Computer Organization and Architecture: Designing for Performance. Pearson Education India.

[4] Saraswat, M., and Chauhan, N. R. (2020). Comparative assessment of butanol and algae oil as alternate fuel for SI engines. *Engineering Science and Technology, an International Journal*, 23(1), 92–100.

[5] Liu, F., and Solihin, Y. (2011). Studying the impact of hardware prefetching and bandwidth partitioning in chip-multiprocessors. *ACM SIGMETRICS Performance Evaluation Review*, 39(1), 37–48.

[6] Wang, H. S., Zhu, X., Peh, L. S., & Malik, S. (2002, November). Orion: A power-performance simulator for interconnection networks. In 35th Annual IEEE/ACM International Symposium on Microarchitecture, 2002.(MICRO-35). Proceedings. (pp. 294–305). IEEE.

[7] Eeckhout, L., Stroobandt, D., and De Bosschere, K. (2003). Efficient microprocessor design space exploration through statistical simulation. In 36th Annual Simulation Symposium, 2003. IEEE, 2003.

[8] Sharma, A., Chaturvedi, R., Sharma, K., and Saraswat, M. (2022). Force evaluation and machining parameter optimization in milling of aluminium burr composite based on response surface method. *Advances in Materials and Processing Technologies*, 8(4), 4073–4094.

[9] Saraswat, M., Sharma, K., Chauhan, N. R., and Shukla, R. K. (2020). Role of automation in energy management and distribution. *Journal of Scientific and Industrial Research*, 79(10), 951–954.

[10] Hartstein, A., and Puzak, T. R. (2002). The optimum pipeline depth for a microprocessor. *ACM Sigarch Computer Architecture News*, 30(2), 7–13.

[11] Ibrahim, S., Phan, T. D., Carpen-Amarie, A., Chihoub, H. E., Moise, D., and Antoniu, G. (2016). Governing energy consumption in Hadoop through CPU frequency scaling: an analysis. *Future Generation Computer Systems*, 54, 219–232.

[12] Wang, S., Lin, H., Abed, A. M., Sharma, A., and Fooladi, H. (2022). Exergoeconomic assessment of a biomass-based hydrogen, electricity and freshwater production cycle combined with an electrolyzer, steam turbine and a thermal desalination process. *International Journal of Hydrogen Energy*, 47(79), 33699–33718.

[13] Brusoni, S., Prencipe, A., and Pavitt, K. (2001). Knowledge specialization, organizational coupling, and the boundaries of the firm: why do firms know more than they make?. *Administrative Science Quarterly*, 46(4), 597–621.

[14] Oberman, S. F., and Flynn, M. J. (1997). Design issues in division and other floating-point operations. *IEEE Transactions on Computers*, 46(2), 154–161.

[15] Chaturvedi, R., Islam, A., and Sharma, K. (2021). A review on the applications of PCM in thermal storage of solar energy. *Materials Today: Proceedings*, 43, 293–297.

[16] Kumar, P., Singh, P. K., Nagar, S., Sharma, K., and Saraswat, M. (2021). Effect of different concentration of functionalized graphene on charging time reduction in thermal energy storage system. *Materials Today: Proceedings*, 44, 146–152.

20 Diagnosis and exploration of portable executable (PE) malware using XGboost and other ML classifiers

Nachappa Muckatira Nanaiah[1,a], Amit Gantra[2,b] and Trapty Agarwal[3,c]

[1]Professor, Department of Computer Science and Information Technology, Jain (Deemed to be University), Bangalore, India

[2]Professor, Department of Computer Science and Engineering, Faculty of Engineering and Technology, Parul Institute of Engineering and Technology, Parul University, Vadodara, Gujarat, India

[3]Associate Professor, Maharishi School of Engineering & Technology, Maharishi University of Information Technology, India

Abstract

Data security and privacy have emerged as pressing issues in the current technological era. Cyber forensics experts and network administrators place a high priority on malware analysis since malicious software is a major security risk. There is a wide range in how much damage may be done by malicious software. While there is some research on machine learning methods to identify malware, only a small fraction of those algorithms were able to successfully process portable executable (PE) files. Logistic regression, K-nearest neighbour, random forest, support vector machine, decision tree, and XGBoost are the primary classification techniques covered in this work. Then, their results are compared to determine which one performs better on the dataset. XGBoost outperformed other classifiers in experiments, with an accuracy of 99%.

Keywords: Decision trees, machine learning, malware, pe files, random forests, support vector machines

Introduction

Malware is software that exploits flaws or weaknesses in a computer's software, hardware, or operating system to get access to sensitive information. Malware is often used to steal money, personal information, or other valuables from a victim's computer. Malware isn't always catastrophic, but it may be annoying and make your computer run slower or perform worse in other ways, including by generating a constant stream of pop-up ads. Unfortunately, most antivirus programs cannot keep up with the constant stream of new dangerous software, which leaves users vulnerable until a patch is published. In addition, this may cause valuable data and financial resources to be lost. Everyone is concerned about keeping their private information safe, but it's getting more and harder to do so in the digital age. The dangerous software is the cause of the billions of dollars and data that have been lost. The frightening proliferation of malware on the web has prompted extensive investigation into developing new methods and strategies to construct, examine, and simplify harmful code. Unfortunately, the detection models used by current host-based solutions are subpar. These models isolate the most important characteristics of a single piece of malware, making them vulnerable to evasion techniques like obfuscation and polymorphism. We test many machine learning classification methods for their ability to identify dangerous from benign portable executable (PE) files. We used data collected from Kaggle that was built using a python module that contains both malicious and safe PE files. The following are the sections that make up the aforementioned document. In Section 2, we'll take a look back at the research done on malware detection and PE files. In Section 3, we detail the procedures that will be used to implement our strategy. Part of this approach involves assembling a battery of malware detection classifiers. Section 4 provides an analysis of the results. Section 5 provides a summary of the findings and makes recommendations for follow-up research.

Literature Review

The authors of the study conducted an investigation on portable executable [1]. They developed a comprehensive collection of features by combining raw and derived inputs, with the aim of detecting and classifying harmful files. The comparison between the consolidated and bare sets of attributes has also been performed using only

[a]mn.nachappa@jainuniversity.ac.in, Orcid Id- 0000-0002-4007-5504, [b]provost@paruluniversity.ac.in, Orcid Id- 0000-0002-9993-9901, [c]Id-trapty@muit.in, Orcid Id- 0009-0007-4081-4999

DOI: 10.1201/9781003534136-20

six algorithms. Our article makes more extensive use of algorithms, and the dataset we gathered from Kaggle is more ethically sound than theirs. Moreover, our dataset is larger than theirs. Enterprise network security is a focus[2], where a model was created with the intention of aiding in this area. Furthermore, we have employed certain processing techniques that the authors did not, like SVM and Decision tree. The researchers in the study develop a method for identifying PE malware [3]. Actually, there were three stages involved: feature extraction, feature selection, and classification. The creators [4] have also done real-time malware detection work. Again, their feature extraction was lower (35 vs. our 58) than ours. In contrast to our study, which yielded a precision rate of 85% or more in only one of their algorithms, they achieved a correctness rate of over 85% throughout all of their algorithms. Studies on malware detection using machine learning were found [5]. They argue that the dynamic technique, because of its time and space intricacy, is inferior to heuristic machine learning, which can detect and block brand new malware. When it comes to identifying malicious software, the developers [6] employ a machine learning method that combines both traditional and cutting-edge approaches. They intended to track and categorize malware, however their classifiers were inaccurate and they had few classification techniques to use.

Proposed Methodology

Proposed Malware Detection Framework
Figure 20.1 depicts the strategy that may be utilized with machine learning to recognize unknown malware. There are several stages to our method that collectively increase its precision, productivity, and usefulness. To identify whether or not a sample is malicious, our technique utilizes training and test data as well as preparation of the dataset and feature selection for the classification algorithm. The categorized data was then analyzed and visualized.

A. Data Pre-Processing
Information mining's data pre-processing method, it transforms raw data into a more usable and digestible shape. Over fitting may be prevented in the data pre-processing stage by using a dimension reduction strategy. It "rotates" a dataset by replacing its original components with fresh variables which are a linear blend of the previous data.

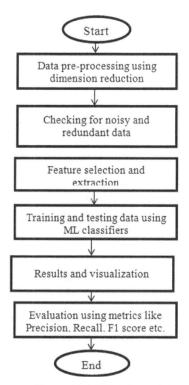

Figure 20.1 Workflow of the proposed approach

B. Noisy and Redundant Data

Data that has been damaged during transmission or storage and is thus illegible or otherwise useless by the program that originally produced it is sometimes referred to as "noisy data." In order to execute feature extraction, we have made sure that our dataset is clean and free of noise.

C. Feature Selection and Extraction

Inaccurate models can be trained on data with irrelevant characteristics if those attributes are present. Time spent fitting and training can be cut down with feature selection. For the purpose of brevity, we are only displaying a subset of the 79 characteristics included in our dataset. Our approach uses 'CfsSubsetEval' for selection of features and Best First method for extraction of features. Figure 20.2 depicts the workings of picking features and extraction.

D. Training and Testing of Data Using ML Classifiers

The data is split into a training set and a test set. Fitting and tuning the models require training data. In order to evaluate the models, test data is simulated as if it were hidden from view. In order to evaluate how effectively a computer can anticipate new answers based on training, test data is used. In our method, we employ linear regression (LR), K-nearest neighbor (KNN), a random forest, a support vector machine (SVM), a decision tree (DT), and XGBoost. Here is a breakdown of these machine learning algorithms:

Linear regression (LR):- It may foretell either continuous or categorized outcomes. This method is primarily a classification technique used in situations where a yes/no judgment needs to be made, such as in the detection of fraudulent and email spam. Through the process of data fitting, the likelihood of an occurrence may be predicted. The likelihood of belonging to one of two classes in a data set is estimated using a logistic regression model [7].

Probability equation given by LR is given below:

$$"P(x) = 1 / 1 - \exp^{-y} \tag{1}$$

Where y= ab + c. It ensures that values are between 0 and 1."

K-nearest neighbor: Classification and regression models employ this fundamental machine learning technique. The distance between each point in the testing data and each point in the training data is calculated whenever the model is fed new data. Once that is done, the closest k members to that place are located. The following is an equation that may be used to get the Euclidean distance between two locations, A (x1, y1) and B (x2, y2).

$$"E_d (A, B) = \sqrt{(y2 - y1)^2 + (x2 - x1)^2}" \tag{2}$$

The SVM is a supervised machine learning algorithm that is commonly used for classification and regression tasks. It is based on the concept of finding an optimal hyperplane that separates different classes or predicts. The versatility of this machine learning technique allows for its application in both classification and regression tasks. The primary objective of SVM is to identify the optimal hyperplane that effectively separates the two distinct categories of data. Assuming two classes, the dataset D utilized for training is composed of X pairs (a, b) with values of I ranging from 1 to n, as specified by [8]:

$$"D = [\{a, b\} \mid I \in n, b \in (-1, 1)]" \tag{3}$$

RF and DT: RF is essentially a group of decision trees that have been combined into one. How RF strengths are revealed through tree construction and aggregation. More information means better results since we can use more knowledge. As the many decision trees are combined, the final tally should be more accurate. Substitution analysis generates a training set for currently active trees. The critical evaluation in a DT, also known as attribute selection, is a recognizable confirmation of the feature for the base node at each level.

XGBoost: This implementation of gradient boosting decision trees prioritizes speed and efficiency. XGBoost is an improved version of the gradient boosting decision trees (GBDT) boosting algorithm. The final output of this algorithm is a composite of the individual sub-trees' decision-making outcomes. The following equation illustrates how the loss function is used to prevent redundant data and over fitting:

$$""Lf = \sum_{k=1}^{n} f(k)xi \tag{4}$$

Where f (k) = {f1, f2, f3……. f$_n$} represents set of base learners."

E. Results and Visualization
The results were analyzed and shown when they were obtained.

F. Evaluation
We tested our theory by using six different classifiers and comparing their performance across a number of metrics, including accuracy, precision, recall, true positive rate (TPR), false positive rate (FPR), and finally f1-score.

Result and Implementation

The study highlights the vital need for database visualization since it is essential to the proper operation of the suggested method. Malicious applications in the PE format, which is a commonly used file type for executable apps in operating systems such as Windows, are included in the set of data under investigation [9]. We used an extensive archive on Kaggle, a site well-known for its wide range of datasets, to compile this data set.

Figure 20.2 demonstrates how the CfsSubsetEval filter is used in conjunction with the BestFirst search strategy to identify the necessary features from the dataset. Only two of the original six attributes—name and e_cp—are taken out.

The dataset consists of a collection of PE files, and PE prefixes and parts are used to carefully record the collection's details. The Python pefile module, a potent tool for scanning PE file formats and extracting crucial data, is used to build these pieces. We guarantee a complete depiction of the PE files—including their prefixes and unique sections—by employing this package.

It is crucial to comprehend the design of movable program files in order to analyze and identify harmful activity effectively. All of the dataset's sections map to memory segments that can contain code or info, a difference that has a big impact on the executable's functionality and appearance. An essential part of PE files, the subsection table gives numerical addresses to these storage parts, allowing for a more detailed analysis of the file's structure.

In addition, the PE header contains essential data that the operating system needs in order for these files that execute to run correctly. This header acts as a road map, assisting the machine's operating system as it navigates the complex complexities inside the file's design to ensure smooth operation.

Figure 20.3 displays the malware detection for PE files using linear regression. It implies that data is tested using 10 folds cross validation scheme at each level. In Figure 20.3, value -0.0401 implies malware detection at fold 2 level in dataset attributes."

Figure 20.2 Feature Selection and Extraction

```
Classifier output

Linear Regression Model

e_maxalloc =

  11947.7457 * Name=VirusShare_6bf3608e60ebc16cbcff6ed5467d469e,VirusShare
  11947.7514 * Name=VirusShare_efe4e3d6185e64fc1e44c82941d4a733,VirusShare
  11947.7514 * Name=VirusShare_e76cac211258723745f66bd9f9e29590,VirusShare
  11947.7514 * Name=VirusShare_efd86c9054598e6311d723283125ce80,VirusShare
         0   * Name=VirusShare_ac5a6f8fc1a2c814862dee0e2af43237,VirusShare
    -0.0401 * Name=VirusShare_eff7676f69be2b519f3424def92d3590,VirusShare
     0.0401 * Name=VirusShare_c30d49720449b66b2059038344efde3a,VirusShare
    -0.0003 * e_cblp +
    -0.0201 * e_cp +
  17744.1053

=== Classifier model for fold 3 ===


Linear Regression Model

e_maxalloc =
```

Figure 20.3 Data output using LR classifier

```
Clusterer output

Final cluster centroids:

Attribute                                              Full Data
                                                         (22.0)
=================================================================
Name                         VirusShare_a878ba26000edaac5c98eff4432723b3 VirusShar
e_magic                                                   23117
e_cblp                                                  138.1818
e_cp                                                      2.9091
e_oparhdr                                                     4
e_maxalloc                                             63362.6818




Time taken to build model (full training data) : 0.01 seconds

=== Model and evaluation on test split ===

kMeans
======

Number of iterations: 3
Within cluster sum of squared errors: 9.5

Initial starting points (random):

Cluster 0: VirusShare_e76cac211258723745f66bd9f9e29590,23117,144,3,4,65535
Cluster 1: VirusShare_c30d49720449b66b2059038344efde3a,23117,144,3,4,65535
```

Figure 20.4 Training and testing of data using KNN classifier

Figure 20.4 shows cluster centroids formation using KNN machine learning classifier. It detects malware in PE dataset by forming centroids based on number of iterations. Here, we can see that two clusters are formed (cluster 0 and cluster 1) which does not have any malware. Cluster 2 has malware that has been removed by classifier itself.

In Figure 20.5, we see the PE malware dataset being loaded and executed, which results in the construction of a confusion matrix showing whether or not malware exists at a certain cluster. Rows with a value of 1 are indicative of the existence of malevolent software, which has the potential to cause harm or lead to the loss of data.

Figure 20.6 shows loading and execution of PE malware dataset leading to formation of confusion matrix which depicts malware is present at specific cluster or not. The matrix having rows with 1 value indicates the presence of malware that may cause harm or loss of data.

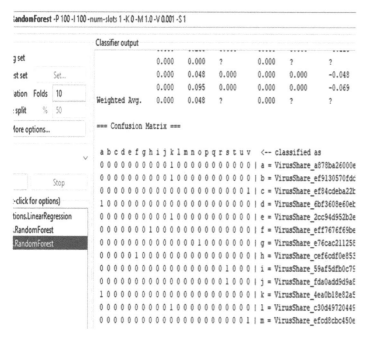

Figure 20.5 Execution using RF classifier

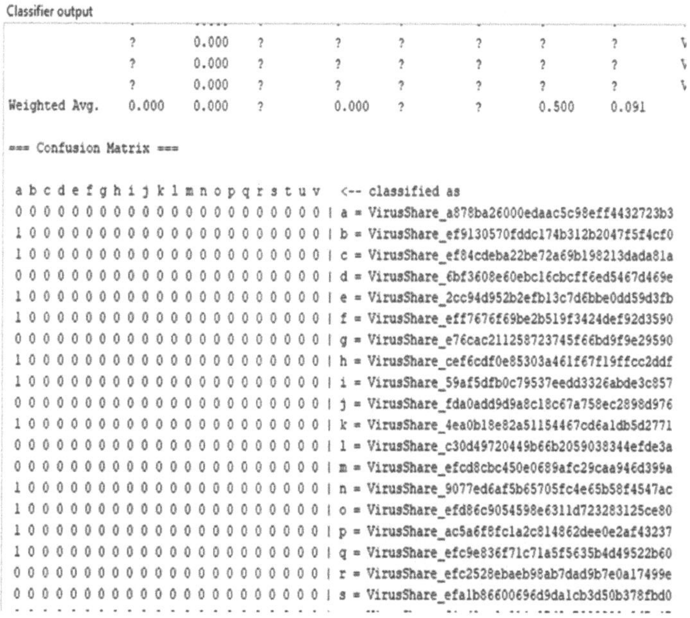

Figure 20.6 Execution using XGBoost classifier

Evaluation Metrics

Several criteria were used to assess the classifiers' efficacy. The subsequent discourse pertains to the various assessment measures that are employed. In the event of a true negative (TN), the algorithm accurately made a negative prediction. Conversely, in the case of a false positive (FP), the algorithm erroneously made a positive prediction. Similarly, a false negative (FN) denotes the algorithm's incorrect prediction of a negative outcome, while a true positive (TP) signifies the algorithm's correct estimation of a positive outcome.

Recall is another name for true positive rate (TPR). It demonstrates our classifier's proficiency in identifying malicious software. It's a result of:

$$TPR = TP / (TP + FN) \qquad (5)$$

False positive rate (FPR): The frequency with which innocuous files are incorrectly identified as malicious.

$$FPR = FP/ (FP + FN) \tag{6}$$

Precision measures how often a positive result is anticipated accurately relative to the total number of positive results predicted. Recall quantifies an algorithm's ability to find all positive samples. Precision and recall are averaged in order to form the F1 Score.

$$Precision = TP / (TP + FP) \tag{7}$$

$$Recall = TP / (TP + FN) \tag{8}$$

$$F1\text{-}score = 2 \ (Precision * recall) / (precision + recall) \tag{9}$$

$$Accuracy \ score = (TP + TN) / (TP + TN + FP + FN) \tag{10}$$

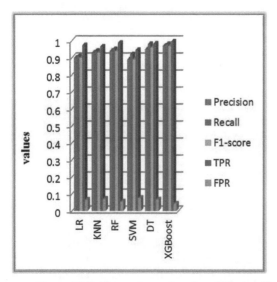

Figure 20.7 Comparison of various ML classifiers used in the study

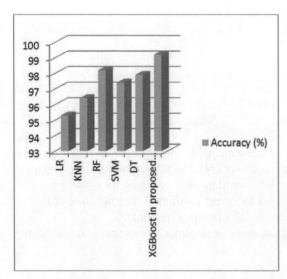

Figure 20.8 Classifiers' accuracy compared to our method

Results

Figure 20.7 shows that usage of XGBoost classifier in the proposed framework would lead to better results in terms of precision (0.97), recall (0.98), f1-score (0.97), TPR (0.995) and FPR (0.043) as compared to other classifiers. The FPR of XGBoost classifier is the lowest which indicates that this classifier has not treated any benign file as malware. It signifies that our proposed system has less fault rates.

Figure 20.8 shows that accuracy achieved in our proposed approach with the use of XGBoost classifier is 99% which is higher than existing machine learning classifiers namely LR (95%), KNN (96%), SVM (97%), RF (98%) and DT (98%).

Thus, the results of Figures 20.7 and 20.8 validate the performance of our proposed system.

Conclusion and Future Work

In the referenced publication, we verified the accuracy of the suggested strategy using a wide variety of classifier techniques. The suggested method employs a dataset derived from research on how to spot malicious PE (portable executable) files. Six different classifier techniques for finding malware are compared. We observed that XGBoost achieved the highest accuracy (99%) with the best TPR (0.995) and the worst FPR (0.043) of all the strategies we tested. Random Forest had the second-highest accuracy (98.2%).Linear regression has the lowest accuracy (95.3%), followed by KNN.

A more sophisticated neural network will be taken into consideration in the future alongside ANN. Future plans include incorporating the hybrid machine learning algorithm into a hybrid model and an antiviral we're developing. Antivirus software could determine whether or not a PE file was malicious by scanning it. Zero-day assaults may be something it can manage.

References

[1] Matin, I. M. M., and Rahardjo, B. (2020). A framework for collecting and analysis PE malware using modern honey network (MHN). In 8th International Conference on Cyber and IT Service Management (CITSM), Pangkal, Indonesia, (pp. 1–5), doi: 10.1109/CITSM50537.2020.9268810.

[2] Or-Meir, O., Cohen, A., Elovici, Y., Rokach, L., and Nissim, N. (2021). Pay attention: improving classification of PE malware using attention mechanisms based on system call analysis. In International Joint Conference on Neural Networks (IJCNN), Shenzhen, China, (pp. 1–8), doi: 10.1109/IJCNN52387.2021.9533481.

[3] Belaoued, M., and Mazouzi, S. (2014). Statistical study of imported APIs by PE type malware. In International Conference on Advanced Networking Distributed Systems and Applications, Bejaia, Algeria, (pp. 82–86), doi: 10.1109/INDS.2014.22.

[4] Tyagi, S., Baghela, A., Dar, K. M., Patel, A., Kothari, S., and Bhosale, S. (2022). Malware detection in PE files using machine learning. In OPJU International Technology Conference on Emerging Technologies for Sustainable Development (OTCON), Raigarh, Chhattisgarh, India, (pp. 1–6), doi: 10.1109/OTCON56053.2023.10113998.

[5] Rezaei, T., and Hamze, A. (2020). An efficient approach for malware detection using PE header specifications. In 6th International Conference on Web Research (ICWR), Tehran, Iran, (pp. 234–239), doi: 10.1109/ICWR49608.2020.9122312.

[6] El Neel, L., Copiaco, A., Obaid, W., and Mukhtar, H. (2022). Comparison of feature extraction and classification techniques of PE malware. In 5th International Conference on Signal Processing and Information Security (ICSPIS), Dubai, United Arab Emirates, (pp. 26–31), doi: 10.1109/ICSPIS57063.2022.10002693.

[7] Atluri, V. (2019). Malware classification of portable executables using tree-based ensemble machine learning. In Southeast Con, Huntsville, AL, USA, (pp. 1–6), doi: 10.1109/SoutheastCon42311.2019.9020524.

[8] Jin, B., Choi, J., Hong, J. B., and Kim, H. (2023). On the effectiveness of perturbations in generating evasive malware bvariants. *IEEE Access*, 11, 31062–31074. doi: 10.1109/ACCESS.2023.3262265.

[9] Kanna, R. K., Devi, K. Y., Gomalavalli, R., & Ambikapathy, A. (2024). Smart Detection and Removal of Artifacts in Cognitive Signals Using Biomedical Signal Intelligence Applications. In Quantum Innovations at the Nexus of Biomedical Intelligence (pp. 223–244). IGI Global.

21 A unique and fortified ontological-based framework for healthcare services in cloud

Beemkumar Nagappan[1,a], Vipul Vekariya[2,b] and Awakash Mishra[3,c]

[1]Professor, Department of Mechanical Engineering, Faculty of Engineering & Technology, JAIN (Deemed-to-be University), Bangalore, India

[2]Professor, Department of Computer Science and Engineering, Faculty of Engineering and Technology, Parul Institute of Engineering and Technology, Parul University, Vadodara, Gujarat, India

[3]Professor, Maharishi School of Engineering & Technology, Maharishi University of Information Technology, India

Abstract

Modern healthcare services have replaced the older model of doctors visiting patients in their homes to make a diagnosis. A major contributor to this shift is cloud computing, which allows all relevant parties (including patients, physicians, and nurses) quick and simple access to a patient's medical history. Patients may have convenient, anytime, everywhere electronic access to their health records because to the scalability, efficiency, and low cost of cloud services. Although the cloud has many advantages, such as instantaneous data access, there are substantial worries about patient data security and privacy. This work presents a safe and robust ontological-based access mechanism for cloud-based healthcare services, taking into account the security requirements of distant healthcare. The suggested approach protects medical records from cybercriminals by preventing access to cloud-based data and providing a safe interface for all involved parties. The suggested approach is the greatest option for preserving confidentiality and safety in on the internet medical facilities because of its simplicity and resilience.

Keywords: Cloud computing, Healthcare, ontology, secured mechanism, sensor and patient analysis, smart healthcare

Introduction

It becomes difficult to manage enormous data volumes when manually storing and maintaining health information for future referencing. Finding specific patient information in a huge collection of paper or manual records is a major drawback of the conventional approach to data storage. It requires significant effort to track down a single patient's medical file. Because it is in plain text format, anybody with access to a computer may read, write, and edit the information contained in the records [1]. Data mining and machine learning [2, 3] provide the infrastructure that allows for the digital storage of medical records. Due to the sensitive nature of patient health information, encryption in E-healthcare is of paramount importance. The freely accessible wireless channels are vulnerable to assaults because of the attackers [4, 5]. The healthcare system can be damaged in a number of ways by these attacks. Suppose a person became sick and was sent to the emergency room of a local hospital without any paper records. If his therapy is delayed due to a lack of knowledge, it might be deadly. If the patient's information is stored on the cloud, however, it may be retrieved in a matter of seconds, allowing the newly established medical staff to get right into treatment [6, 7]. Data stored by the healthcare sector can be secured using cryptographically strong techniques, making it accessible from anywhere with an internet connection (wired or wireless). Software and datasets are hosted on servers in the "cloud" and are accessed online. Cloud computing frees stakeholders and healthcare departments from the administrative burden of managing and running their own physical servers and software applications [8]. Patient health data may be shared in a streamlined fashion thanks to cloud computing [9]. The following sections outline the structure of the provided paper. Research undertaken in the field of computing via the cloud and healthcare is reviewed in Section 2. Our proposed methodology is outlined in Section 3. To manage encryption and decryption keys, a protected ontology-based system is required. The results analysis may be found in Section 4. Conclusions and suggestions for future study are presented in Section 5.

Literature Review

The authors propose a novel web-based solution that grants access to patients' medical information to the patient's nurse, doctor, and chemist [10, 11]. To keep track of the patient's data, it taps into the local cloud. The information

---

[a]n.beemkumar@jainuniversity.ac.in [b]vipul.vekariya18435@paruluniversity.ac.in [c]awakash.mishra@muit.in

DOI: 10.1201/9781003534136-21

may be seen and updated from afar. It's great for hospitals where doctors require access to patient records to work together on care. However, the patient will be unable to access their own medical records under this plan. A cloud-based healthcare framework for effective communication between careers and healthcare professionals has been proposed by the authors, which has the potential to totally replace the present paper-based record system utilized by hospitals [12, 13]. Using the aforementioned method, healthcare practitioners and patients alike have anytime, anywhere access to the patient's medical history. The primary drawback of this method is that all data must be kept on a remote server in the cloud if a hospital or nursing unit lacks its own personal backup system. The authors presented a novel approach to the digital preservation of medical records in the cloud [13, 14]. The proposed approach ensures data privacy by segmenting data, however the architecture is not robust enough to prevent intrusion or unauthorized resource access. The authors stressed the importance of access control methods and other forms of security for E-healthcare networks [15]. The authors claim that their technique is superior to conventional access control systems; although they admit that the absence of ontologies is a weakness.

Proposed Methodology

Proposed Secured Ontological-Based Cloud Framework
The suggested system presents an efficient structure for encryption as well as decryption of healthcare information, effortlessly combining with an online service provider's (CSP) database that with semantic acting as a foundation on the server side. This revolutionary technique provides a safe and efficient administration of critical healthcare information. The cornerstone of this system consists in the establishment of a proper ontology, precisely built with the help of an information editor adapted to the particular domain of inbound medical data.

Upon the implementation within the ontology, an individual's content undergoes a purposeful shift from a system of relationships to the specialized domain database. This move serves a twofold purpose: it not just arranges the data in a way compatible with the natural structure of the healthcare field but also provides the framework for generating important insights and outcomes from the data that is kept.

When a patient requests access on their healthcare data stored in the public cloud, a smooth connection with the CSP is provided. To commence this procedure, patients are needed to log in to the platform using their specific credentials, providing a customised and secure entry point. The security component is further enhanced by the production of a distinctive encryption key for every person receiving treatment. This key acts as a cryptographic protection, assuring the safety and soundness of the patient's medical information across their engagement with the computer system.

Workflow of the proposed approach

Step 1: Defining notations
    H_r = Healthcare records
    P_i = patient requests to access data by sending key requests
    P_l = patient login details
    E_k = Key used in encryption process
    E_d = Key used in decryption process
Step 2: Process of encryption (E_p)
    H_f = hash key function
    H_r to E_t = Initial health records and its instances are converted to encrypted text using equation 1.

$$E_p = (E_k * E_d) + H_r * H_f \tag{1}$$

Step 3: Development of ontological corpus
    H_r is converted from a relational schema to an ontological database by designing ontology with the help of ontology editors. The formal, clear explanation of a common conception is what is meant by "ontology" [16, 17]. In addition to its official and philosophical underpinnings and ability to deal with real-world circumstances, it also serves as a bridge between people and robots.
Step 4: Representation of classes, properties and instances related to patient's healthcare record.
Step 5: Creation of an ontological grid to access data from the cloud in a hierarchical form.
Step 6: Decryption process (D_p)

$$D_p = (E_k * E_d) \tag{2}$$

Step 7: Integration of ontological database into the cloud service provider (CSP)
Figure 21.1 presents the workflow of the proposed approach.

Result and Implementation

Standard ontologies, such as patient information, are imported and used in the definition of requirements for the health care system's numerous parts. To go even farther, we could connect it to other cases and declare its properties using a standardized ontology.

It is seen from Figure 21.2 that the major entity in healthcare framework is person. A person could be a doctor, staff, pharmacist, researcher, patient and nurse. All these entities play major role in contributing towards secured and ontological-based cloud framework. Person is super-class and other sub-entities are shown as its sub-classes.

Figure 21.3 displays the second major entity named 'healthcare records' using ontology. These records could be lab reports, previous bills, medical reports and case history of patients. These records are to be stored in cloud service provider with ontology as backend so that it can only be accessed by specific patient or doctor for ensuring security of data.

Figure 21.4 shows searching process in response to Figure 21.3. The patient can access this interface on cloud server by entering his login details. For example, in above interface, we have searched 'case' word which returns case history from the designed ontology corpus. In this way, it becomes easier and effective for doctors or patients to retrieve their records anytime thereby removing the need of bulky manual records.

Figure 21.5 shows instantiation of entities and sub-entities contained in ontology. It is done to maintain relationship between patient and its healthcare records by creating unique concept identifier for each record by encryption using hash keys.

Ontology entities, such as "doctor," "person," and "person who practises medicine," can be instantiated using the is-a property in N-triples format (a format in which resources is specified as subject, predicate, and object).

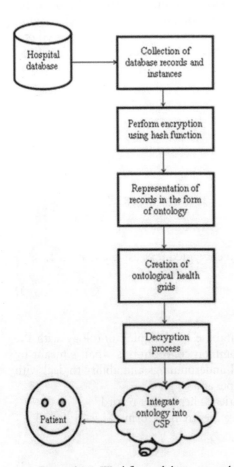

Figure 21.1 Workflow of the proposed approach

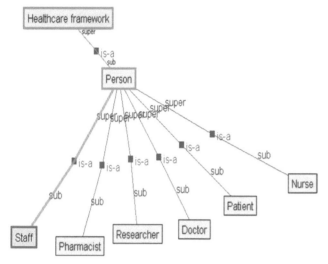

Figure 21.2 Representation of 'person' via ontology

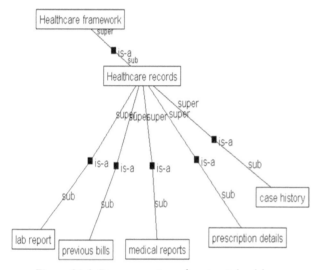

Figure 21.3 Representation of patient's healthcare records via ontology

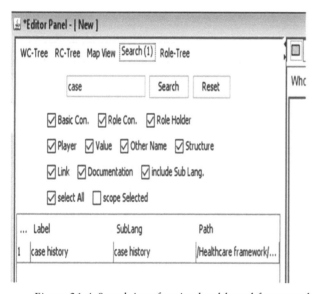

Figure 21.4 Search interface in cloud-based framework

Figure 21.5 Defining object properties and instances of sub-entity 'prescription details'

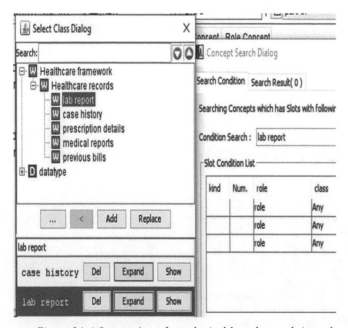

Figure 21.6 Integration of ontological-based records into cloud

The concept behind object properties is that by selecting a single instance, we have a description of the data associated with that instance, which we can then use to navigate to additional instances that share the same object properties.

Figure 21.6 shows execution and integration of health records from the designed ontology into cloud service provider (CSP). In above case, we can say that sub-entity 'lab report' is appended from class dialog box into cloud so that a person can access records at any point of time.

Evaluation Metrics
Using the following criteria, we compared the effectiveness of our proposed ontologically-based strategy to that of the current technique [15].

Accuracy is defined as the percentage of predictions that turned out to be true within a given sample of predictions. How well an algorithm can locate all positive samples is measured by its recall. The F1 score takes into account both accuracy and recall.

$$\text{Precision} = TP / (TP + FP) \tag{3}$$

$$\text{Recall} = TP / (TP + FN) \tag{4}$$

$$\text{F1-score} = 2 \ (\text{Precision} * \text{recall}) / (\text{precision} + \text{recall}) \tag{5}$$

$$\text{Accuracy score} = (TP + TN) / (TP + TN + FP + FN) \tag{6}$$

Where TP denotes true positive, TN denotes true negative, FP denotes false positives and FN denotes false negatives.

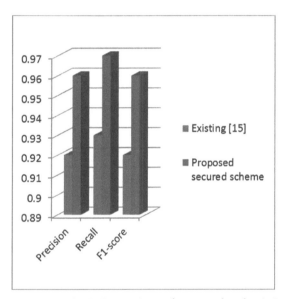

Figure 21.7 Comparison of proposed and existing approach used in the study

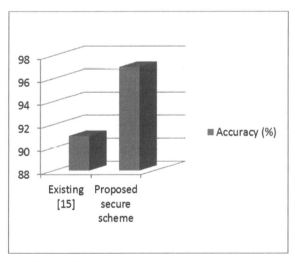

Figure 21.8 Accuracy comparison between proposed approach and existing approach

Results

Figure 21.7 shows that usage of ontology as backend in our proposed approach proves to be a secure and reliable scheme with higher precision and recall as compared to the existing approach. The precision, recall and f1-score values for the proposed approach are 0.96, 0.97 and 0.96 respectively.

Figure 21.8 show that accuracy achieved in our proposed approach with the use of ontology is 97% which is higher than existing approach (91%).

Figures 21.7 and 21.8 demonstrate the effectiveness of our suggested approach.

Conclusion and Future Work

To solve these issues, the authors suggest an ontology-based healthcare system in which things may only interact according to predetermined rules and users' privileges are determined by the objects' attributes. Using ontology as the server's backend, an encrypted healthcare record system is presented. The patient's health records are kept secure and accessible at all times.

A future inference engine may allow for more comprehensive ontology-based access control in healthcare IT. Authorization decisions based on predetermined rules and assumptions. The policy must be formulated as ontology according to predetermined standards.

References

[1] Bahrami, M., Malvankar, A., Budhraja, K. K., Kundu, C., Singhal, M., and Kundu, A. (2017). Compliance-aware provisioning of containers on cloud. In IEEE 10th International Conference on Cloud Computing (CLOUD), Honolulu, USA, (pp. 696–700), doi: 10.1109/CLOUD.2017.95.

[2] Casola, V., Castiglione, A., Choo, K.-K. R., and Esposito, C. (2016). Healthcare-related data in the cloud: challenges and opportunities. *IEEE Cloud Computing*, 3(6), 10–14. doi: 10.1109/MCC.2016.139.

[3] Liu, W., and Park, E. K. (2013). E-healthcare cloud computing application solutions: cloud-enabling characteristics, challenges and adaptations. In International Conference on Computing, Networking and Communications (ICNC), USA, (pp. 437–443), doi: 10.1109/ICCNC.2013.6504124.

[4] Singh, I., Kumar, D., and Khatri, S. K. (2019). Improving the efficiency of e-healthcare system based on cloud. In Amity International Conference on Artificial Intelligence (AICAI), Dubai, United Arab Emirates, (pp. 930–933), doi: 10.1109/AICAI.2019.8701387.

[5] Xu, H., Zuo, L., Sun, F., Yang, M., and Liu, N. (2022). Low-latency patient monitoring service for cloud computing based healthcare system by applying reinforcement learning. In IEEE 8th International Conference on Computer and Communications (ICCC), China, (pp. 1373–1377), doi: 10.1109/ICCC56324.2022.10065744.

[6] Singh, P., and Singh, D. P. (2023). A review of machine learning frameworks for predicting adverse events in cloud-based healthcare systems. In International Conference on Computational Intelligence and Sustainable Engineering Solutions (CISES), Greater Noida, India, (pp. 38–42), doi: 10.1109/CISES58720.2023.10183434.

[7] Tawalbeh, L. A., and Habeeb, S. (2018). An integrated cloud based healthcare system. In 5th International Conference on Internet of Things: Systems, Management and Security, Valencia, Spain, (pp. 268–273), doi: 10.1109/IoTSMS.2018.8554648.

[8] Zheng, Y., Lu, R., Guan, Y., Zhang, S., and Shao, J. (2021). Towards private similarity query based healthcare monitoring over digital twin cloud platform. In IEEE/ACM 29th International Symposium on Quality of Service (IWQOS), Tokyo, Japan, (pp. 1–10), doi: 10.1109/IWQOS52092.2021.9521351.

[9] Sampath Kumar, Y. R., and Champa, H. N. (2021). A fuzzy based scheduling approach for efficient sensing in IoT-cloud. In 12th International Conference on Computing Communication and Networking Technologies (ICCCNT), India, (pp. 1–5), doi: 10.1109/ICCCNT51525.2021.9580105.

[10] Surendran, R., and Tamilvizhi, T. (2020). Cloud of medical things (CoMT) based smart healthcare framework for resource allocation. In 3rd Smart Cities Symposium (SCS 2020), Online Conference, (pp. 29–34), doi: 10.1049/icp.2021.0855.

[11] Sharaf, S., and Shilbayeh, N. F. (2019). A secure g-cloud-based framework for government healthcare services. *IEEE Access*, 7, 37876–37882, doi: 10.1109/ACCESS.2019.2906131.

[12] Kanna, R. K., Devi, K. Y., Gomalavalli, R., & Ambikapathy, A. (2024). Smart Detection and Removal of Artifacts in Cognitive Signals Using Biomedical Signal Intelligence Applications. In Quantum Innovations at the Nexus of Biomedical Intelligence (pp. 223–244). IGI Global.

[13] Mishra, A. R., Mishra, R., and Shukla, R. (2023). Development of cloud centric healthcare monitoring system for cardiac patients embedded in IoT platform. In 11th International Conference on Emerging Trends in Engineering & Technology - Signal and Information Processing (ICETET - SIP), Nagpur, India, (pp. 1–6), doi: 10.1109/ICETET-SIP58143.2023.10151587.

[14] Kanna, R. K., Surendhar, P. A., Rubi, J., Jyothi, G., Ambikapathy, A., and Vasuki, R. (2022, December). Human Computer Interface Application for Emotion Detection Using Facial Recognition. In 2022 IEEE International Conference on Current Development in Engineering and Technology (CCET) (pp. 1–7). IEEE.

[15] Alkeem, E. A., Shehada, D., and Yeun, C. Y. (2017). New secure healthcare system using cloud of things. *Clustered Computing*, 20(3), 2211–2229.

[16] Singh, G., Jain, V., and Singh, M. (2013). Ontology development using Hozo and semantic analysis for information retrieval in semantic web. In *2013 IEEE Second International Conference on Image Information Processing (ICIIP-2013)*, 2013, (pp. 113–118), doi: 10.1109/ICIIP.2013.6707566.

[17] Singh, G., and Jain, V. (2012). Information retrieval (IR) through Semantic web (SW): an overview. In Proceedings of Confluence 2012- The Next Generation Information Technology Summit at Amity School of Engineering and Technology. September 2012, (pp. 23–27).

22 Biometric object or facial detection, identification and recognition system using python and deep learning models

Ghanshyam Yadav[1,a], Jitendra Mohan Giri[2], Ravi Kalra[2], Irfan Khan[2], Pradeep K.Chandra[2], Abhishek Kaushik[2] and Ashish Parmar[2]

[1]ITS Engineering College, Greater Noida, India,

[2]Lloyd Institute of Engineering & Technology, Greater Noida, India

Abstract

This research paper is focused on creating an automated attendance system for colleges, institutions, organizations and universities with the help of image processing, deep learning, objects or facial detection, identification and recognition techniques. Many colleges, institutions and organizations have implemented object or facial detection, identification, recognition and attendance system but often it fails in different lighting conditions and very often give false positives. Many false positives also happen because objects or facial detection, identification and recognition techniques cannot differentiate between identical twins or in case of change in appearance.

To tackle these issues, HOG (histogram of oriented gradients) algorithm as feature identifier (for the face detection phase), descriptor with SVM (support vector machine) algorithm and recognition phase by CNN (convolutional neural networks) deep learning model. HOG works much better with SVM and gives higher accuracy in different lighting conditions. This research paper still cannot differentiate identical twins, but this research paper has found a way to take their attendance using multiple cameras and at different angles and also in case of change in appearance, hairstyle [5][7].

This paper delves into the fascinating world of image identification, classification, and recognition. We'll be harnessing the power of advanced CNN with the ever-reliable TensorFlow Framework. Python takes center stage here, thanks to its impressive array of libraries such as Dlib, openCV, and TensorFlow. CNN proves to be the ultimate technique for training and testing data, consistently delivering outstanding results in facial detection, identification, and recognition. Accuracy, precision, recall, and time-space complexity are all carefully evaluated. With advanced CNN models, we're achieving remarkable results of over 98%, leaving others in the dust with their subpar sub-90% accuracy.

Keywords: Convolutional neural networks, recurrent neural network, face recognition technology (frt), histogram of oriented gradients, OpenCV, tensor flow, deep neural networks

Introduction

Maintaining attendance is crucial for educational institutions and organizations to evaluate student performance. Traditionally, attendance was recorded manually through registers or files, but as numbers grow, this becomes cumbersome and time-consuming. To streamline the process, many have turned to biometrics systems, which offer a smart and efficient solution. By automating attendance tracking, institutions can save time and resources, while also ensuring accurate records. Let's ditch the old ways and embrace a more efficient approach to ensure accurate attendance records.

This exciting research paper is made using python and face recognition framework. Face recognition framework has an already trained model for different tasks required face detection, identification, and recognition [1-5]. The framework allows us to detect faces, find how similar the faces are and can also tell us if person is same or not with 98% accuracy which is very close to human level accuracy in detecting faces. In the world of python, there are various ways to load an image. But let's talk about the coolest method, Open CV. This open-source computer vision library is like a magic wand for image processing and computer vision tasks. In our research paper, we went all in and used OpenCV to capture images and have some fun with our camera. It's a must-have tool for all your image recording and processing needs. And hey, we also made use of some handy python libraries to read and write our excel sheets. So, we're basically tech wizards.

Our face recognition framework is powered by the incredible HOG (histogram of oriented gradients) algorithm, which excels at detecting and identifying faces. To further enhance accuracy, we harness the power of the Dlib library, a cutting-edge C++ toolkit packed with powerful machine learning algorithms. By leveraging Dlib's capabilities, we can locate the essential landmarks on a face, enabling us to determine its pose. We then cleverly wrap the image, centering the eyes and mouth for optimal analysis. Through a neural network, we extract 128 measurements from the centered image, allowing us to compare and find the most similar images.

[a]ghanshyamyadav.cse@its.edu.in

DOI: 10.1201/9781003534136-22

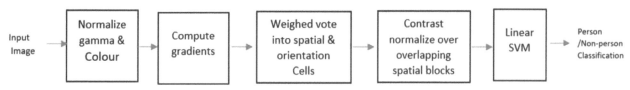

Figure 22.1 Feature extraction and object detection, identification

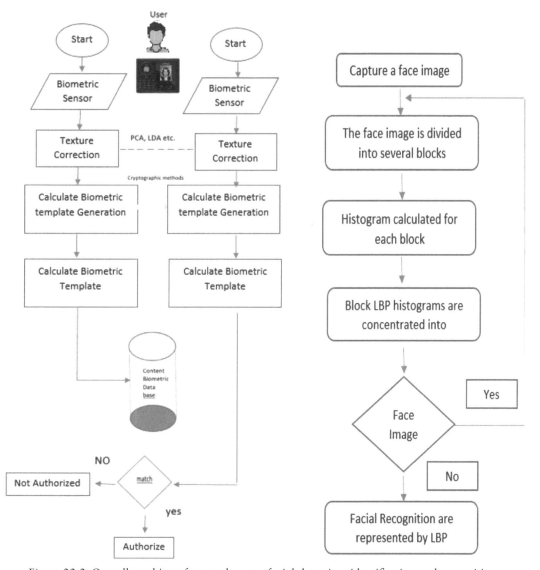

Figure 22.2 Overall working of research paper facial detection, identification and recognition

Literature Review and Related Work in Previous Biometric Recognition Systems

1. Researchers demonstrated in this work that HOG accepts input images of size 128 × 64 pixels. So, here's the deal: we've got this picture segment, right? And we're curious about its gradient. So, we break it down into two matrices, one with the magnitude and angle of the gradient. Then we get all fancy and put these matrices into 8 × 8 cells, creating a block. A schematic diagram of feature extraction, object detection and identification as indicated:

2. In another research paper, we figured out how to tell apart look-alike twins by analyzing their stuff and faces. We used a fancy combo of RNN and CNN (convolutional neural networks) models to do the job. RNNs are like the Sherlock Holmes of neural networks, while CNNs act as super-smart filters.

The recognition and classification process in is divided into two parts: -

1. **Face identification and detection:** This exciting research paper is all about playing detective with face images! We've got this cool database of peeps, and we're going to figure out whose face is in a given image. But wait, there's more! We'll also decide if the face recognition is on point or needs some work.
2. **Face verification and validation:** - Given Face image that might not belong to database and this research paper need to authenticate whether a correct face is subjected to the database or not. So, grab your detective hats and let's solve this face-matching mystery [6].

Research Methodology in Recognition and Classification Process

CNNs are like the superheroes of deep learning, with their incredible ability to recognize images. They're the secret agents behind the scenes, sorting pictures like pros. Picture CNN as a three-layered cake: input, output, and hidden layers. These hidden layers are where the magic happens, with fancy names like convolutional, ReLU, pooling, and completely linked layers. They work together to make sense of the visual world.

a. Convolutional layers that migrate information from the input layer to the next layer using a convolution process
b. Pooling combines the outputs of the neuron clusters in the following layer into a single neuron.
c. Fully linked and well-connected layers join each neuron in one layer to the next neuron in the successor layers.

CNN is a badass learning technique that tackles tough problems like a boss. Unlike traditional machine learning, CNN doesn't need humans to extract features or train them. It automatically sniffs out image features, making it super accurate. Plus, it gets smarter with each hidden layer it goes through, like a master of complexity. CNN is the cool kid in the machine learning world, handling complicated stuff with ease. It's like the Chuck Norris of algorithms.

CNN was often used in image classification due to its effectiveness and accuracy. However, there are several Deep learning applications architectures such as AlexNet, Mobile Net, GoogleNet, ResNet-50, ResNet-100, Inception-v3, Inception-ResNet-v2, VGG-16, and VGG-19 [7-8][10].

Planning of Work in Face Recognition and Classification Process:

The input procedure of research paper is implemented in five steps: -

1. Finding all the faces on camera.
2. Encoding faces.
3. Finding person's name from encoding in our database and measure of similarities.
4. Identifying if person is twin or not, if twin then activate twin detection, identification module (to be implemented).
5. Updating the image database and so attendance sheet also.

Step 1. Finding all the Different Faces in CCTV/Camera.

Finding the faces in the camera is the first and crucial step of the research paper. The image taken by the camera using OpenCV/tensor flow library of python, with a simple code (multiple ways for image read/input).

cap = cv2.VideoCapture(0)
/* It is used to specify the method of video capturing. In the above code this research paper are using camera present in our device. This can be changed to specify camera id.
    while True:
    success,img = cap.read()
/* cap.read() reads and return each frame of image until the loop is running.
    cv2.imshow('webcam',img)
/* Shows the image frame by frame until loop is running.
    img = cv2.cvtColor(img,cv2.COLOR_BGR2RGB)

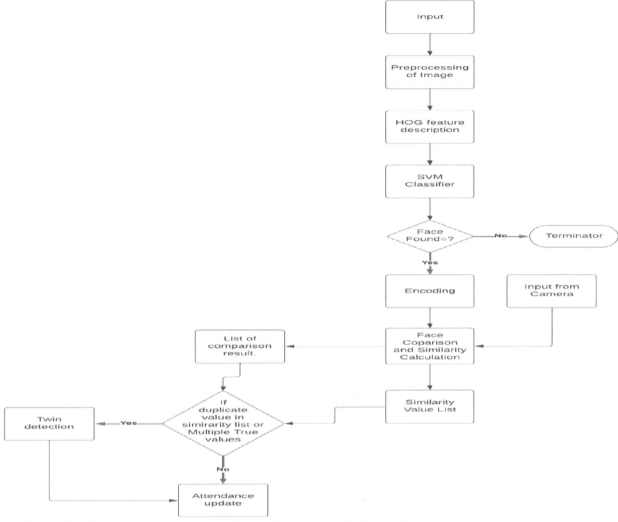

Figure 22.3 Flow chart process for recording and maintaining the biometric attendance recognition

/* This line on code coverts BGR type image to RGB our algorithm runs better on it.
if cv2.waitKey(1) & 0xFF == ord(' '):
break
cap.release()
cv2.destroyAllWindows()
/*Closes the window when 'space' key is pressed.
faceLocation=face_recognition.face_locations(img)
/*Finds a list of tuples of found face locations.

Output of Face Recognition and Classification Process –
I. List of tuples of multiple found face locations.
II. SVM Classifier & HOG feature descriptor.
III. Rescale image through deep learning architectures for fast processing.
IV. Python OpenCv and Tensor flow Libraries.
V. Open camera and covert input image into RGB for better interpretations.

Step 2. Encoding Faces

This research paper has used pretrained network from face_recognition library to get encodings of our faces. It is executed by invoking find encodings function.

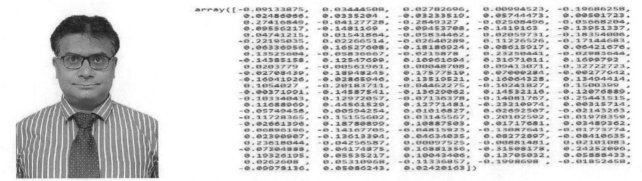

Figure 22.4 Input, find image encodings and output, face 128 encodings, RGB image values

```
encodeListKnown = findEncodings(images)
def findEncodings(images):
    encodeList = []
    for img in images:
        img = cv2.cvtColor(img,cv2.COLOR_BGR2RGB)
        encode= face_recognition.face_encodings(img)[0]
        encodeList.append(encode)
    return encodeList
```

The function takes image as input and generates 128 encoding of an input image and returns a list of encodings of all images.

Step 3 Finding Person's Name from Encoding in Database and Measure of Similarities/Identical Twins.

In this step algorithm find the person in our database of known people who has the closest measurements to test image. It has used SVM (support vector machine) as a classification algorithm in this research paper. In case there are twins, it has to consider duplicate measures. If the system finds duplicate measure for the person in camera the process will not be completed just yet, else function for attendance marking will run. In this research paper has found similarities between images by using face_recognition library and have found if faces match or not with the same library. The following code implements this step.

```
for encodeFace, faceLoc in zip(encodesCurFrame,facesCurFrame):
    matches = face_recognition.compare_faces(encodeListKnown,encodeFace)
    faceDis = face_recognition.face_distance(encodeListKnown,encodeFace)
    print(faceDis)
    matchIndex = np.argmin(faceDis)

    if matches[matchIndex]:  #***
        name = classNames[matchIndex].upper()
        print(name)
        y1,x1,y2,x2 = faceLoc
        y1,x1,y2,x2 = y1*4,x1*4,y2*4,x2*4
        cv2.rectangle(img,(x1,y1),(x2,y2),(0,255,0),2)
        cv2.rectangle(img,(x1,y2-35),(x2,y2),(0,255,0),cv2.FILLED)
        cv2.putText(img,name,(x1+6,y2-6),cv2.FONT_HERSHEY_COMPLEX,1,(255,0,0),2)
```

Step 4: Measure of Similarities/Identical Twin Module

This research paper will use twin module only when there are twins in database otherwise it will consume more memory then actually required. This research paper will use matplotlib for gray scaling, OpenCv binarization, thinning, morphological process and background analysis. MediaPipe library can be used for feature detection, identification then this research paper will use Recurrent Neural Networks for recognition.

Table 22.1 Results for image recognition, classification (deep learning) models

	Accuracy rate	Time Consume	Error rate	Validation loss
DNN	70-80%	6.5 hrs	Very high	7.8
CNN	90%	5.4 hrs	High	3.3
Transfer Learning	92%	12 mins	Low	0.64
Advanced CNN	Morethan 95%	8 mins	Very Low	0.3

Step 5: Updating the Image Database and Attendance Sheet

This is the easiest step of the process in this step this research paper has used python to insert name of student in our excel sheet when they appear on CCTV camera. It has been taken into account that a student can come in CCTV camera multiple times at different angles. The excel sheet will be updated for each student only once. Here is the code of function used for it.

```
def markAttendence(name):
    with open("C:\\Users\\DELL\\Desktop\\ML Project\\face recognition attendance\\attendance.csv",'r+') as f:
        myDataList = f.readlines()
        nameList = []
        for line in myDataList:
            entry = line.split(',')
            nameList.append(entry[0])
        if name not in nameList:
            now = datetime.now()
            dtstring = now.strftime('%H:%M:%S')
            f.writelines(f'\n{name},{dtstring}')
```

Results and Discussions

- More accurate attendance with reduction in time spent in attendance marking with ease in analyzing performance of students or employees and ease in finding the average of student attendance. Giving the same performance in all circumstances like different background and different lighting.
- Judging the faces of students or employees in database even if there are multiple faces of many people who are not in database. Reducing fraud attendances and marking attendance accurately for twins or confusing images also.
- The objective of the research paper is also to minimize the cost by using software's which are already or freely available to school or college. The only cost in this research paper is installation of cameras which can be scaled according to comfort of organization. It can easily be managed by college staff of any qualification. The attendance is automatically entered into excel sheet and lectures and provides flexibility to be edited if required.

The overall objective of research paper is to help administration of an organization to be more efficient and effective by automating the necessary but time-consuming work of taking attendance and maintaining a record of attendance.

Comparison with Other Image Classification Models and Results

Let's dive into the fascinating world of image classification models. In practical applications, we have a bunch of cool ones to choose from. We've got the trendy gang, including AlexNet, Mobile Net, GoogleNet, ResNet, Inception, and VGG 16-19 in the deep learning crew. But hold on tight, because new approaches are constantly sprouting up like wildflowers. Now, let's talk about DNN. These bad boys are not only used for training CNN in regression and classification, in supervised machine learning but they also have a reputation for being a bit underwhelming when it comes to photo accuracy. They have been struggling in that ML department.

But fear not, because CNN is here to save the day. These powerful networks have proven to be incredibly successful in face and image detection, identification, picture classification, and even item recognition. They blow

DNN out of the water when it comes to optimized outputs. However, there's a catch – CNN tends to suffer from over-fitting due to its substantial validation loss.

Enter transfer learning in deep CNN, the superhero of reusing previously learned information. This nifty technique allows us to take a pre-trained model and apply it to a huge dataset, achieving fantastic results in related activities. Not only does it save us time, but the accuracy is also top-notch. So, there you have it, folks. Image classification models have come a long way, and with advanced CNN leading the pack, the future looks brighter than ever. So go out there, embrace the power of these models, and let your creativity soar.

Conclusion and Future Perspectives

When it comes to comparing different models and a specific dataset, the possibilities are endless. However, one model stands out from the rest, the advanced CNN (convolutional neural networks). With an impressive accuracy rate of over 95%, it effortlessly achieves all the objectives while leaving others in its dust. For image classification, the advanced CNN is our top priority. By incorporating dense layers and extending the epochs, we witness remarkable improvements in results.

Speaking of epochs, they play a crucial role in tackling overfitting issues. But what sets the advanced CNN apart from the competition is its speed. Thanks to running on GPUs and having its own TPUs, classification becomes a breeze, saving valuable time. And let's not forget about the Tensorflow framework, a wide-ranging technology that allows us to create and analyze deep data models. With its help, we can continue our research by exploring a vast and complex array of images. So, buckle up and get ready to dive into the exciting world of cutting-edge image classification!

References

[1] Rehkha, K. K. and Vinod, V. (2021). Differentiating monozygotic twins by facial features. *Turkish Journal of Computer and Mathematics Education*, 12(10), 1467-1476.

[2] Dalal, N. and Triggs, B. (2005). Histograms of oriented gradients for human detection. *International Conference on Computer Vision & Pattern Recognition*, 886-893.

[3] Zeng, W., Meng, Q., and Li, R. (2019). Design of intelligent classroom attendance system based on face recognition. 2019 IEEE 3rd Information Technology, Networking, Electronic and Automation Control Conference (ITNEC), pp. 611-615.

[4] Gurucharan, M. K. (2020). Machine learning basics: support vector machine (SVM) classifier. https://towardsdatascience.com/machine-learning-basics-support-vector-machine-svm-classification-205ecd28a09d

[5] Saha, S. (2018). A comprehensive guide to convolutional neural network, article in towards data science. https://towardsdatascience.com/a-comprehensive-guide-to-convolutional-neural-networks-the-eli5-way-3bd2b1164a53

[6] Zhaoqing, S., Su, Z., and Zhicheng, L. I. (2010). Face Images Recognition Research Based on Smooth Filter and Support Vector Machine. pp. 2760–2764.

[7] Balcoh, N. K., Yousaf, M. H., Ahmad, W., and Baig, M. I. (2012). Algorithm for efficient attendance management: face recognition based approach. *International Journal of Computer Science Issues*, 9(4), 146–150.

[8] Roshantharanga, J. G., Samarakoon, S. M. S. C. T., Karunarathne, A. P., Liyanage, K. L. P. M., Gamage, M. P. A. W., and Perera, D. (2013). Smart attendance using real time face recognition. *Res. Symp. Eng. Adv.* 41–44.

[9] Anggo, M. and Arapu, L. (2018). Face recognition using Fisher face method. *Journal of Physics: Conference Series*, 1028(1).

[10] Arsenovic, M., Sladojevic, S., Anderla, A., and Stefanovic, D. (2017). Face time - deep learning based face recognition attendance system. IEEE 15th International Symposium on Applied Machine Intelligence and Informatics, pp. 53–57.

23 Arrangement and capturing of malevolent packets in network using machine learning

Rakesh Kumar Yadav[1,a], Raghavendra R[2,b] and Amit Barve[3,c]

[1]Associate Professor, Maharishi School of Engineering & Technology, Maharishi University of Information Technology, India

[2]Assistant Professor, Department of Computer Science and Information Technology, Jain (Deemed to be University), Bangalore, India

[3]Associate Professor, Department of Computer Science and Engineering, Faculty of Engineering and Technology, Parul Institute of Engineering and Technology, Parul University, Vadodara, Gujarat, India

Abstract

The importance of cyber security and cyber warfare has grown in a world where digitalization is rapidly expanding and developing. Malware, or malicious software, has emerged as a major problem in the modern digital age. The rapid proliferation of malware is a major danger to online safety. Therefore, steps taken to secure the network are crucial in warding off these cyber dangers. Using a network analyzer to gather instances of botched and artificially created benign packets, the authors of the current paper collected data for a network traffic classifier using a random forest (RF) machine learning approach. The suggested classifier can determine whether or not a given piece of traffic (HTTP, TCP, UDP, IPv4-v6) is safe to proceed with. The experimental findings show that the suggested model using the RF classifier is more accurate than the baseline.

Keywords: Malware, network traffic, packets capturing, random forest, web traffics

Introduction

Malware is a growing problem that threatens system and network integrity, privacy, authentication, and control, as well as functionality, as internet use continues to rise [1]. Malware can be broadly defined to include viruses, logic bombs, worms, spyware, and any other type of malicious software that causes harm to a computer or network [2–4]. Recent years have seen a huge increase in the yearly amount of network security incidents due in large part to the frequency of malware assaults in the network. Cyber security researchers face a challenging problem in figuring out how to stop these attacks, as they draw attention to the fragility of networks and computers. Malware of today uses encrypted web traffic (HTTPs) to communicate and carry out its destructive tasks. The encrypted data sent between the client and server is the primary function of the HTTPs protocol. However, malware developers utilise encryption for malicious or unlawful purposes, whereas a genuine user benefits from its use. Encryption decreases the efficiency of pattern matching technologies, such as signature-based antivirus, making them ineffective against malware in HTTPs (encrypted) traffic. The use of machine learning techniques in the analysis and identification of malware has recently gained popularity among researchers. The proposed study applies machine learning and statistical computing to the subject of network security, with a primary focus on this area. Classifying HTTPs and IPv4-v6 traffic using a machine learning-based categorization model is the primary contribution of our work. Additionally, RF classifier is used throughout model construction, training, and evaluation, leading to improved accuracy and a decreased false positive rate (FPR).

The given paper is organized into following sections. Section 2 provides review of studies conducted in the context of protocol and network packets classification. Section 3 presents the methodology and details of our proposed approach. It involves identification of benign and malicious packets in HTTP's and IPv4-v6 traffic. Section 4 presents analysis of results. Section 5 presents summary of the findings and proposes recommendations for further research.

Literature Review

When it comes to malware detection in HTTPS traffic, [5, 6] cites considerable use of machine learning-based network traffic categorization algorithms. We see a classifier proposed to discover families of malware linked to unsecured HTTP connections [7, 8]. To improve malware detection in HTTPS traffic while decreasing false

[a]rkymuit@gmail.com, [b]r.raghavendra@jainuniversity.ac.in, [c]amit.barve17535@paruluniversity.ac.in

DOI: 10.1201/9781003534136-23

positives, a metric index KNN classification algorithm is applied to a small dataset of very dimensional network traffic descriptors. Although the authors have addressed the issue of identifying rogue servers, they have not demonstrated the typical accuracy of classifiers in doing so. Researchers [9, 10] created and investigated an LSTM-based malware detection approach that makes use of just the observable characteristics of HTTPS traffic. Speech recognition, translation, and other NLP applications make heavy use of LSTM networks [11]. This new technique allows for the collection of massive amounts of both hostile and innocuous network traffic for model assessment. By analyzing the traffic on a network in relation to things like host addresses, timestamps, and data volumes, malicious software can be identified. Using machine learning techniques, the authors [12, 13] created a behaviour testing approach to isolate HTTP and HTTPs network traffic, however they didn't bother with any form of validation.

Proposed Methodology

A Proposed Network Traffic Model Based on Machine Learning
The proposed classification scheme is illustrated in Figure 23.1. The primary goal of the proposed model is to use a machine learning approach to distinguish between legitimate and malicious HTTPs, TCP, and IPv4-v6 network traffic.

A. Capturing of Packets
During this stage, we faked harmful network activity and gathered malware samples. Specifically, we use a tool called Wireshark [14] to examine statistical characteristics of network traffic. The attributes like as IP addresses, ports, protocols, and timestamps are used to characterize flow duration.

B. Categorization of Packets
Once statistical network flow characteristics were extracted, we annotated them to indicate whether or not they belonged to malicious or benign traffic.

C. Pre-Processing of Data Packets
In order to get rid of extraneous information, this is performed. In this case, we improved the quality of the data by using open refine [15], formerly known as Google refine, as a pre-processing tool.

D. Feature Extraction and Selection
An integral component of our investigation is portrayed here. We've retrieved a number of statistical characteristics of network traffic, but it's still up to us to figure out which ones are most relevant to our study. With the help of a feature selection policy, we can zero down on the most important aspects of the data. We utilised the Weka tool's BestFirst search to identify the most frequently occurring features, a wrapper approach that falls under the reverse feature selection strategy [16]. To further improve the model's performance, backward elimination involves starting with the most basic elements and gradually eliminating the ones that aren't absolutely necessary.

E. Train and Test Model Using Random Forest (RF)
For both model development and testing, we used the Weka simulation framework. We used a 10-fold cross-validation procedure to construct and train our model on 80% of the data, and then applied the Random Forest classifier on 20% of the data to see how well it performed under test conditions. Random Forest, functioning as an ensemble classifier, has superior performance compared to conventional classifiers in reliably classifying network traffic. When doing a comparative analysis of several machine learning classifiers, it is well recognised that the Random Forest Algorithm has a prominent position. It makes use of a voting system to produce predictions using an ensemble technique that comprises of different decision trees. The versatility of random forest lies in its ability to solve the two types of problems that make up the majority of modern machine learning systems: regression and classification.

F. Evaluation Based on Metrics
Using these measures, we determined how well our suggested network classifier-based strategy performed.

The measure of accurate forecasting is determined by the proportion of true positives within a certain sample. The performance of an algorithm in accurately identifying all positive samples is evaluated by its recall metric. Precision and Recall are averaged in order to form the F1 Score.

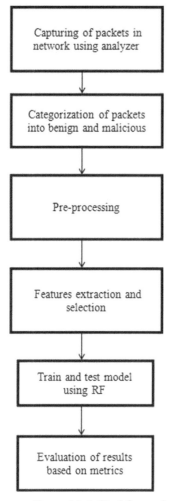

| | | | | |

Figure 23.1 Workflow of the proposed approach

No.	Time	Source	Destination	Protocol	Length
1	0.000000	192.168.1.8	224.0.0.251	MDNS	132
2	0.010447	fe80::18f4:fca6:ce3…	ff02::fb	MDNS	152
3	1.708668	Syrotech_3f:d0:e0	IntelCor_06:77:14	ARP	42
4	1.708718	IntelCor_06:77:14	Syrotech_3f:d0:e0	ARP	42
5	5.786675	192.168.1.9	142.250.194.133	TCP	55
6	5.790661	142.250.194.133	192.168.1.9	TCP	66
7	12.113667	192.168.1.9	142.250.207.202	UDP	71
8	12.118848	142.250.207.202	192.168.1.9	UDP	67
9	13.354325	192.168.1.9	74.125.68.188	TCP	55
10	13.439457	74.125.68.188	192.168.1.9	TCP	66
11	17.451738	142.250.207.202	192.168.1.9	UDP	120
12	17.454762	192.168.1.9	142.250.207.202	UDP	75
13	18.428069	192.168.1.8	224.0.0.251	IGMPv2	46
14	18.657246	192.168.1.8	224.0.0.251	MDNS	139
15	18.657952	fe80::18f4:fca6:ce3…	ff02::fb	MDNS	159

Figure 23.2 Capturing of network packets using Wireshark analyzer.

Precision = TP / (TP +FP) (1)

Recall = TP / (TP + FN) (2)

F1-score = 2 (Precision * recall) / (precision + recall) (3)

Accuracy score = (TP + TN) / (TP + TN + FP + FN) (4)

Where TP denotes true positive, TN denotes true negative, FP denotes false positives and FN denotes false negatives.

Result and Implementation

The first phase begins with capturing of packets using analyzer having source address, destination address, protocol and size of packets (in bytes).

It is seen from Figure 23.2 that the live packets from Wi-Fi network are captured. Each packet contains timestamp, source address, destination address, type of protocol used and size of packets (in bytes). This statistical information is further used for categorization of packets as benign or malicious.

Figure 23.3 displays the percentage distribution of packets captured in Wi-Fi network. It is seen that benign packets contribute to 43% of the total packets while malicious packets are 57% overall. The malicious packets are divided into ransomware, backdoor, spyware and Trojan horse.

Ransomware 12%
Backdoor 10%
Benign 43%
Spyware 21%
Trojan horse 14%

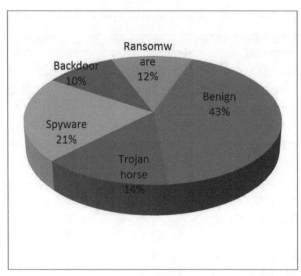

Figure 23.3 Categorization of network packets after capturing

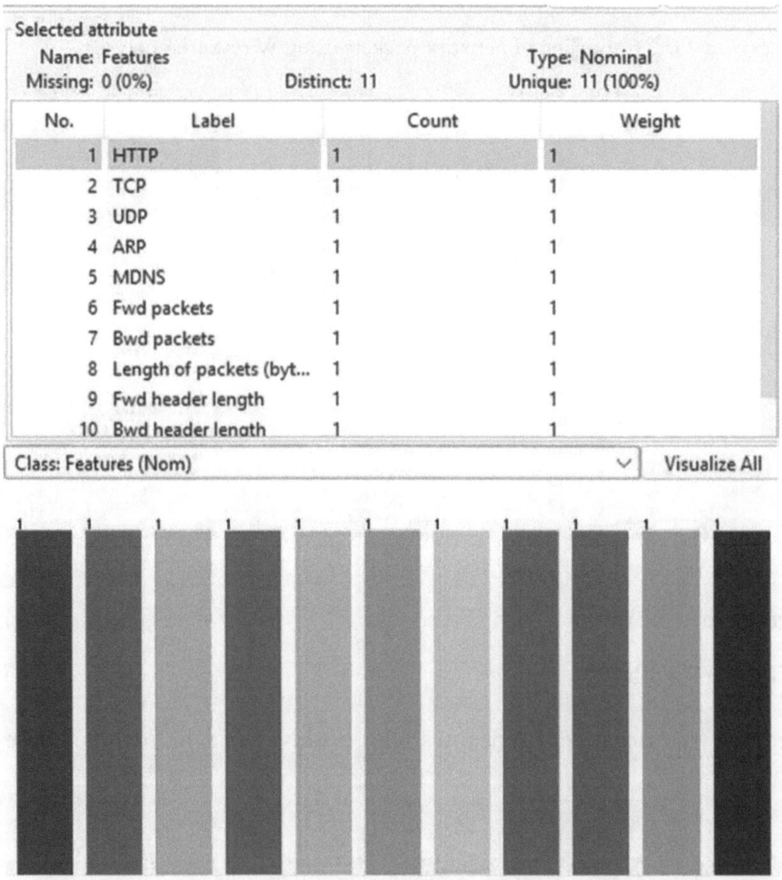

Selected attribute
Name: Features
Missing: 0 (0%)
Distinct: 11
Type: Nominal
Unique: 11 (100%)
No. Label Count Weight
1 HTTP 1 1
2 TCP 1 1
3 UDP 1 1
4 ARP 1 1
5 MDNS 1 1
6 Fwd packets 1 1
7 Bwd packets 1 1
8 Length of packets (byt... 1 1
9 Fwd header length 1 1
10 Bwd header length 1 1
Class: Features (Nom)
Visualize All
1 1 1 1 1 1 1 1 1 1 1

Figure 23.4 Features selection and extraction using WEKA

Figure 23.4 shows the features extracted in response to captured data packets for monitoring flow of traffic in the network. It is seen that there are 11 distinct features associated with packets. They are based on type of protocol used like HTTP, TCP, and UDP etc. It also contains forward and backward packets with their header lengths and so on.

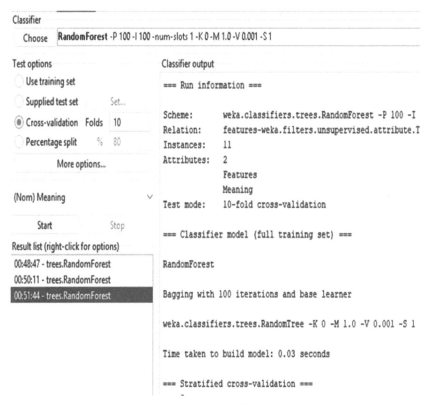

Figure 23.5 Training and testing of model using rf classifier

Table 23.1 Classification results showing efficiency of the proposed approach.

Parameters	Values achieved
Correctly classified instances (%)	90.565
Incorrectly classified instances (%)	9.435
Kappa statistic	-
Mean absolute error (MAE)	0.0884
Root mean squared error (RMSE)	0.1339
Relative absolute error (%)	39.2822
Root relative squared error (%)	40.6189
Total number of instances	11

Figure 23.5 shows 10 folds cross validation of captured packets dataset with the help of Random Forest classifier. It takes only 0.03 seconds to build and validate the model.

The simulation programme provides detailed documentation of the installation of the Random Forest classifier on our dataset after its use. Table 23.1 demonstrates that the implementation of a random forest classifier yields precise and dependable outcomes, exhibiting pertinent properties for the given testing dataset.

Results

Figure 23.6 shows that usage of random forest classifier in training and testing our packets captured model proves to be a reliable scheme with higher precision and recall as compared to the existing approach. The precision, recall, F1-score value, TPR and FPR values for the proposed approach are 0.94, 0.95, 0.94, 0.954 and 0.025 respectively.

Figure 23.7 shows that accuracy achieved in our proposed approach with the use of machine learning classifier is 94% which is higher than existing approach (89%).

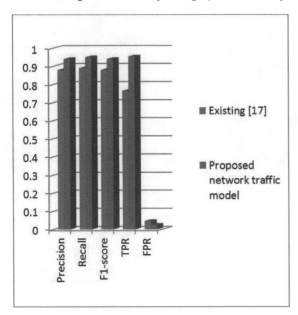

Figure 23.6 Comparison of proposed and existing approach used in the study

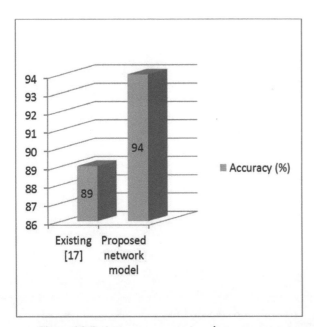

Figure 23.7. *Accuracy comparison between our proposed approach and existing approach*

The results of our proposed method are shown in Figures 23.7.

Conclusion and Future Work

In the future, we want to implement a deep learning-based malware detection method. Network traffic categorization is challenging in the present state of cyber security because of the limits of conventional methods. Modern dangers like as backdoors, Trojan horses, and ransomware cannot be countered with antiquated methods.7 Due to the built-in encryption, researchers have a significant challenge when attempting to categorise risks in HTTP, TCP, and IP data. Machine learning based solutions have become increasingly popular in the current era of artificial intelligence for the purpose of categorising these complex security concerns. Without needing to decrypt network communication, the suggested classification model in this study is able to distinguish between safe and harmful traffic flows. As shown by the experiments, the suggested classification model achieves a high level of accuracy (94%) and precision (0.94). The proposed approach has the advantage over existing methods since it uses statistical-based characteristics to categorise malware, such as flow-based, packed-based, and behavioural aspects.

Our long-term goal is to create a malware detection system that uses deep learning.

References

[1] Kwon, J., Jung, D., and Park, H. (2020). Traffic data classification using machine learning algorithms in SDN networks. In International Conference on Information and Communication Technology Convergence (ICTC), Jeju, Korea (South), (pp. 1031–1033), doi: 10.1109/ICTC49870.2020.9289174.

[2] Khudoyarova, A., Burlakov, M., and Kupriyashin, M. (2021). Using machine learning to analyze network traffic anomalies. In IEEE Conference of Russian Young Researchers in Electrical and Electronic Engineering (ElConRus), St. Petersburg, Moscow, Russia, (pp. 2344–2348), doi: 10.1109/ElConRus51938.2021.9396246.

[3] Fartushnyi, A., and Kollerov, A. (2023). Classification of messenger network traffic using machine learning methods. In IEEE Ural-Siberian Conference on Biomedical Engineering, Radio electronics and Information Technology (USBEREIT), Yekaterinburg, Russian Federation, (pp. 301–304), doi: 10.1109/USBEREIT58508.2023.10158900.

[4] Kumar, C. S., Kolla, H., Sravya, B., Sri, D. L., and Nikitha, G. (2023). Obtrusion unmasking of machine learning-based analysis of imbalanced network traffic. In International Conference on Computer Communication and Informatics (ICCCI), Coimbatore, India, (pp. 1–4), doi: 10.1109/ICCCI56745.2023.10128335.

[5] Imamverdiyev, Y., and Sukhostat, L. (2016). Anomaly detection in network traffic using extreme learning machine. In IEEE 10th International Conference on Application of Information and Communication Technologies (AICT), Baku, Azerbaijan, (pp. 1–4), doi: 10.1109/ICAICT.2016.7991732.

[6] Garg, U., Kaur, M., Kaushik, M., and Gupta, N. (2021). Detection of DDoS attacks using semi-supervised based machine learning approaches. In 2nd International Conference on Computational Methods in Science & Technology (ICCMST), Mohali, India, (pp. 112–117), doi: 10.1109/ICCMST54943.2021.00033.

[7] Shafiq, M., Yu, X., Laghari, A. A., Yao, L., Karn, N. K., and Abdessamia, F. (2016). Network traffic classification techniques and comparative analysis using machine learning algorithms. In 2nd IEEE International Conference on Computer and Communications (ICCC), Chengdu, China, (pp. 2451–2455), doi: 10.1109/CompComm.2016.7925139.

[8] Juan, W., Shimin, C., Jun, Z., Bin, H., and Lei, S. (2021). Identification of T or anonymous network traffic based on machine learning. In 18th International Computer Conference on Wavelet Active Media Technology and Information Processing (ICCWAMTIP), Chengdu, China, (pp. 150–153), doi: 10.1109/ICCWAMTIP53232.2021.9674056.

[9] Priya, A., Nandi, S., and Goswami, R. S. (2018). An analysis of real-time network traffic for identification of browser and application of user using clustering algorithm. In International Conference on Advances in Computing, Communication Control and Networking (ICACCCN), Greater Noida, India, (pp. 441–445), doi: 10.1109/ICACCCN.2018.8748706.

[10] Teik-Toe, T., Jaddoo, Y. E., and Yen, N. Y. (2019). Machine learning based detection and categorization of anomalous behavior in enterprise network traffic. In IEEE 14th International Conference on Intelligent Systems and Knowledge Engineering (ISKE), Dalian, China, (pp. 750–754), doi: 10.1109/ISKE47853.2019.9170421.

[11] Huang, S.-Y., and Huang, Y.-N. (2013). Network traffic anomaly detection based on growing hierarchical SOM. In 43rd Annual IEEE/IFIP International Conference on Dependable Systems and Networks (DSN), Budapest, Hungary, (pp. 1–2), doi: 10.1109/DSN.2013.6575338.

[12] Wen, K., Qu, S., and Zhang, Y. (2009). A machine learning method for dynamic traffic control and guidance on freeway networks. In International Asia Conference on Informatics in Control, Automation and Robotics, Bangkok, Thailand, (pp. 67–71), doi: 10.1109/CAR.2009.96.

[13] Tekdogan, T. (2022). Analyzing the traffic of MANETs using graph neural networks. In IEEE International Conference on Machine Learning and Applied Network Technologies (ICMLANT), Soyapango, El Salvador, (pp. 1–4), doi: 10.1109/ICMLANT56191.2022.9996518.

[14] Sandhya, S., Purkayastha, S., Joshua, E., and Deep, A. (2017). Assessment of website security by penetration testing using wireshark. In 4th International Conference on Advanced Computing and Communication Systems (ICACCS), Coimbatore, India, (pp. 1–4), doi: 10.1109/ICACCS.2017.8014711.

[15] Maniriho, P., and Ahmad, T. (2018). Analyzing the performance of machine learning algorithms in anomaly network intrusion detection systems. In 4th International Conference on Science and Technology (ICST), Yogyakarta, Indonesia, (pp. 1–6), doi: 10.1109/ICSTC.2018.8528645.

[16] Samawi, V. W., Yousif, S. A., and Al-Saidi, N. M. G. (2022). Intrusion detection system: an automatic machine learning algorithms using auto- WEKA. In IEEE 13th Control and System Graduate Research Colloquium (ICSGRC), Shah Alam, Malaysia, (pp. 42–46), doi: 10.1109/ICSGRC55096.2022.9845166.

[17] Lokoc, J., Kohout, J., Cech, P., Skopal, T., and Pevny, T. (2016). K-NN classification of malware in Https traffic using the metric space approach. In Pacific Asia Workshop on Intelligence and Security Informatics, Springer, (pp. 131–145).

24 A pruned and refined ontological-based framework for mining of web logs

Vaishali Singh[1,a], Murugan Ramasamy[2,b] and Swapnil Parikh[3,c]

[1]Assistant Professor, Maharishi School of Engineering & Technology, Maharishi University of Information Technology, India

[2]Associate Professor, Department of Computer Science and Information Technology, Jain (Deemed to be University), Bangalore, India

[3]Professor, Department of Computer Science and Engineering, Faculty of Engineering and Technology, Parul Institute of Technology, Parul University, Vadodara, Gujarat, India

Abstract

Locating pertinent information on the Internet has become increasingly difficult. The partially attributable factor for this phenomenon may be attributed to the vast amount of material accessible and the absence of organisation on several websites. Web use mining is a significant and rapidly advancing field within the realm of internet mining. The primary objective of web mining is to advance the methodologies and frameworks for identifying patterns inside the World Wide Web and the Internet, with the aim of enhancing the adaptability of performance systems. Ontology refers to a body of knowledge that is employed to describe and categorise content found on the World Wide Web. This study presents a novel framework for the generation of ontologies using online use mining techniques. Additionally, this encompasses the processes of data collecting, web mining, and ontology building. The ontology learning framework follows a systematic process that involves ontology construction, pruning, refining, and a final evaluation of the ontology.

Keywords: Data mining, network logs and data collection, ontology creation, web usage mining

Introduction

A new reality has been thrust upon the business world and its customers as a result of the meteoric rise of e-commerce [1]. The number of people who use the internet has increased considerably during the past decade [2]. The number of data that has been acquired by user clicks and organisations using the Internet in their day-to-day operations has reached a considerable magnitude [3, 4]. This is due to the ongoing growth and expansion of e-commerce, Web services, and other information systems that depend on the Internet. Organisations can benefit from analysing these data in a number of ways, including determining the lifetime value of customers, developing effective marketing strategies for a variety of products and services, measuring the success of promotional efforts, enhancing the capabilities of web-based applications by making content more tailored to individual users, and organising their online real estate in the most efficient way possible. Automatically identifying meaningful and interrelated patterns in big, semi-structured data sets, such as those found in server application and website access logs and other sources of useful operational data [5], is the goal of this form of research. Also, it's been harder to find relevant data on the Internet due to the massive expansion of online resources. Web mining is one approach that might be used to fix the issue. It uses ontology to find interesting user access patterns and trends in Internet data consumption [6, 7]. These newly uncovered data can then serve as the basis for an analysis and forecast of future access patterns by users. The given paper is organized into following sections. Section 2 provides basic information about web usage mining and ontology. Section 3 discusses a review of studies conducted in the context of web logs and mining of network data. Section 4 presents the methodology and details of our proposed approach. It involves pre-processing of web logs, clustering analysis and domain ontology construction, pruning and refining. Section 5 presents analysis of results. Section 6 presents summary of the findings and proposes recommendations for further research.

Web Usage Mining and Ontology

Web use mining is the process of autonomously identifying and examining patterns within clickstream data and related information that is gathered or produced via user engagements with web resources across one or several websites [8]. The objective is to comprehensively collect, construct models of, and conduct analysis on the behavioral patterns and profiles exhibited by users throughout their interactions with a website. The identified

[a]singh.vaishali05@gmail.com, [b]murugan@jainuniversity.ac.in, [c]swapnil.parikh17761@paruluniversity.ac.in

DOI: 10.1201/9781003534136-24

patterns are typically shown as aggregations of sites, objects, or services that are regularly used by cohorts of people that share similar requirements or interests.

The field of ontology is concerned with the examination of the existence of entities, as well as their hierarchical features and relationships. According to the source [9], an ontology refers to a specification of a representational language that encompasses definitions of classes, relations, functions, and other objects within a shared domain of discourse.

Literature Review

Some of these approaches aim to suggest new connections between concepts by comparing the information acquired from usage analysis of HTTP Web logs with the current ontology [10, 11]. These structures have two distinct phases, called the batch stage and the online stage, respectively [12]. The method presented in the study [13] uses the Ontolearn software to learn the ideas and connections from a collection of websites in an effort to lessen the conceptual confusion. Extraction of words from a database of online publications, interpretation of their meaning, and determination of their taxonomic connections are the primary phases. This method, however, is unable to do grouping of results or ontology refining. As discussed [14], one method for identifying relevant websites is to first identify a set of keywords that are characteristic of the domain at large. Web record clustering and associating were also not possible with this method.

Ontological-Based Framework for Web Mining Logs and Usage

The approach we employ relies on the analysis of web usage in addition to existing approaches that rely on content evaluation of web pages. Our methodology, as depicted in Figure 24.1, utilizes knowledge discovery techniques primarily from web logs. The objective is to compare the newly acquired understanding in regard to the use with the existing ontology, in order to propose new relationships between concepts. The purpose of this approach is to address the problem by developing a domain-specific ontology that improves information retrieval. This involves using web usage mining methods, such as clustering mining techniques, to analyze log files and extract patterns. Subsequently, web usage ontology is generated or the existing ontology is refined using the collected knowledge. The procedure of our proposed approach is outlined as follows:

A. Pre-Processing of Web Logs
This phase involves the pre-processing of raw data logs in a comprehensive use data warehouse, utilizing numerous concepts such as user sessions and user visits. The process involves the collection of data, the identification of web logs, and the analysis of user sessions and viewed online sites.

B. Creation of Ontology
In this phase, the ontology is being developed using the PROTÉGÉ editor [15, 16]. The framework under consideration is a freely available and open-source platform designed for the construction of intelligent systems. In this study, ontology has been developed on the basis of search engine outcomes pertaining to meteorological phenomena.

C. Applying Data Mining Technique in form of Clustering
It analyses log records and the created ontology to apply aggregation to user accesses to domain-specific websites. By employing Web usage mining approaches [17, 18], we may first create visit or navigation profiles, and then promote the formation of new ideas. Extracting relevant information from a database often begins with a well-applied clustering method. In reality, grouping results in classification, or the separation of data into similar but separate groupings [19–21].

D. Extracting Information and Relations from Domain Specific Ontology
Use analysis yields categories of visited pages and total visits. Syntactic labeling of pages is accomplished in relation to the directories that map to the sites' structures, visit classes are determined by groups of pages that have been visited, and clusters of pages are used for clustering. Extracting object and occurrence attributes based on these categories of syntax and the ontology's semantic concepts is necessary for gauging the effect ontology.

E. Pruning the Ontology
By filtering out unrelated results and qualities, it is able to capture a deep understanding of the target domain.

The steps presented in Figure 24.1 have already been explained above.

Result and Implementation

The first phase begins with web search results produced by user queries in context of domain. Here, the user entered query for knowing current weather report in Delhi. The web search results are produced in Figure 24.2.

The search results are produced in context of user query 'current weather report'. Now, it becomes difficult for users to access each and every web page and extract relevant information from it. To make it easier, the next step is pre-processing of search results to get information about web logs and sessions.

Figure 24.3 displays the user log data having 193 requests for viewing pages. Each log file consists of requests by users who visited page related to weather current report. The log files contain Status, timestamp, size of transferred document and page addresses.

Figure 24.4 shows the classes and instance browser of ontology designed in context of weather phenomenon. The classes include wind gusts, temperature, humidity, pressure, cloud cover, visibility, dew point and cloud ceiling. It is seen that humidity is in percentage so its instance is made as percent.

Figure 24.5 shows clustering algorithm applied to the designed ontology for generating clusters and instance values. The values are such that wind gusts are at 19 k/h, humidity is 88%, and temperature is 27 degrees and so on.

After application of clustering algorithm, we will find relations between the pages visited by users. Table 24.1 illustrates the pages of all web sites visited by users. The user may be student who wants to perform research on weather report, may be meteorologist, and may be some others.

Figure 24.6 shows successful execution of proposed approach by creating only relevant sub-classes and axioms of ontology. It is termed as pruning of ontology.

Figure 24.7 represents clustered results between type of users and number of page visits.

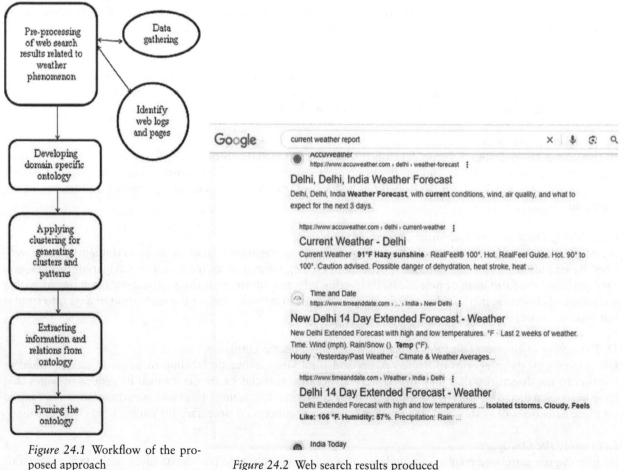

Figure 24.1 Workflow of the proposed approach

Figure 24.2 Web search results produced

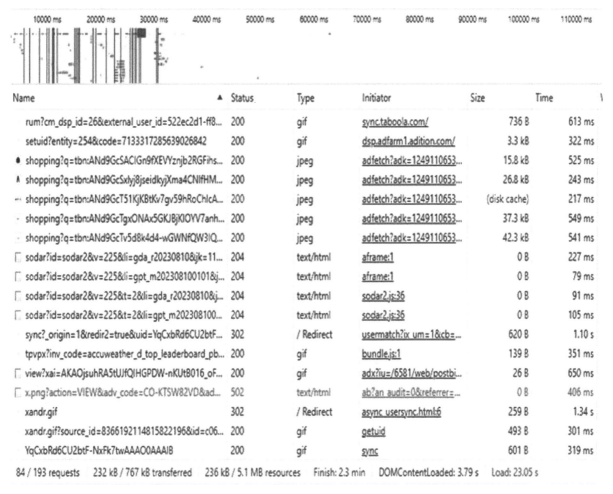

Figure 24.3 Pre-processing of web logs

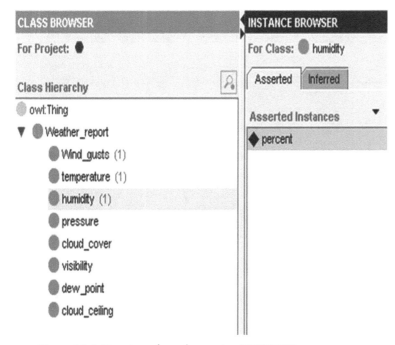

Figure 24.4 Creation of ontology using PROTEGE

```
Clusterer output
Number of clusters selected by c
Number of iterations performed:


                    Cluster
Attribute              0
                      (1)
==========================
Classes
   wind gusts          2
   humidity            2
   cloud cover         1
   cloud ceiling       2
   dew point           1
   pressure            2
   temperature         1
   [total]            11
Instance values
   19 K/h              2
   88%                 2
   12%                 1
   9100 m              2
   25 degrees          1
   1005 mb             2
   27 degrees          1
   [total]            11
```

Figure 24.5 Applying clustering to generate instance values and clusters

Table 24.1 Clustered results between page visits and type of users.

Type of users	Pages visited
Students	100
Researcher	250
IMD Dept	30
Meteorologist	50
Scientist	120
Total number	550

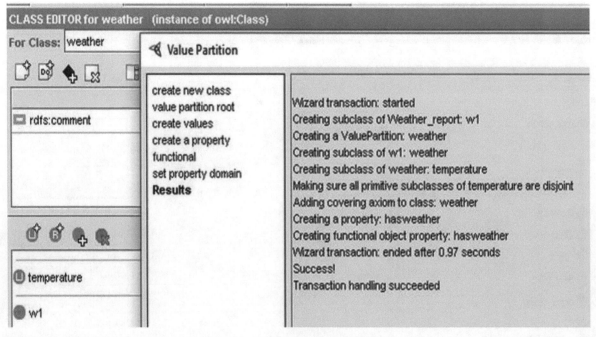

Figure 24.6 Wizard to extract relations successfully completed

Results

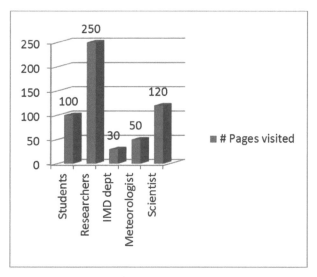

Figure 24.7 Graphical representation of clustered results between type of users and number of page visits

Conclusion and Future Work

The given paper proposed a refined framework based on ontology for analyzing web search results. It leads to various steps like pre-processing of search results given by traditional search engine followed by development of ontology with the help of editor named PROTÉGÉ. The ontology is designed in context of weather report which consists of classes, sub-classes and instances. It is followed by applying web usage mining methods like clustering to generate clusters and number of pages visited by users. It is done to perform mining of web logged files and extract relevant information from them. Lastly, the pruned or refined ontology is generated based on knowledge gathering process.

In future, the work can be extended to apply semantic web rule language (SWRL) in the designed ontology for generating recommendations and results.

References

[1] Malik, S. K., Prakash, N., and Rizvi, S. A. M. (2010). Ontology and web usage mining towards an intelligent web focusing web logs. In International Conference on Computational Intelligence and Communication Networks, Bhopal, India, (pp. 443–448), doi: 10.1109/CICN.2010.90.

[2] Ramesh, C., Rao, K. V. C., and Govardhan, A. (2017). Ontology based web usage mining model. In International Conference on Inventive Communication and Computational Technologies (ICICCT), Coimbatore, India, (pp. 356–362), doi: 10.1109/ICICCT.2017.7975219.

[3] Singh, S. P., and Meenu, (2017). Analysis of web site using web log expert tool based on web data mining. In International Conference on Innovations in Information, Embedded and Communication Systems (ICIIECS), Coimbatore, India, (pp. 1–5), doi: 10.1109/ICIIECS.2017.8275961.

[4] Bharti, P. M., and Raval, T. J. (2019). Improving web page access prediction using web usage mining and web content mining. In 3rd International conference on Electronics, Communication and Aerospace Technology (ICECA), Coimbatore, India, (pp. 1268–1273), doi: 10.1109/ICECA.2019.8821950.

[5] Anitha, V., and Isakki, P. (2016). A survey on predicting user behavior based on web server log files in a web usage mining. In International Conference on Computing Technologies and Intelligent Data Engineering (ICCTIDE'16), Kovilpatti, India, (pp. 1–4), doi: 10.1109/ICCTIDE.2016.7725340.

[6] Yadao, S., Babu, A. V., Janarthanan, M., and Bhaumik, A. (2021). Web usage mining: a comparison of WUM category web mining algorithms. In Third International Conference on Intelligent Communication Technologies and Virtual Mobile Networks (ICICV), Tirunelveli, India, (pp. 1020–1024), doi: 10.1109/ICICV50876.2021.9388539.

[7] Jeyalatha, S., and Vijayakumar, B. (2019). Web usage mining algorithm for an academic search application. In International Conference on Computational Intelligence and Knowledge Economy (ICCIKE), Dubai, United Arab Emirates, (pp. 674–679), doi: 10.1109/ICCIKE47802.2019.9004265.

[8] Sakarkar, S., Chaudhari, V., Gaurkar, T., Veer, A., and Scet, M. K. (2021). Web personalisation based on user interaction : web personalisation. In Third International Conference on Intelligent Communication Technologies and Virtual Mobile Networks (ICICV), Tirunelveli, India, (pp. 234–238), doi: 10.1109/ICICV50876.2021.9388384.

[9] Singh, G., Jain, V., and Singh, M. (2013). Ontology development using Hozo and semantic analysis for information retrieval in Semantic Web. In *2013 IEEE Second International Conference on Image Information Processing (ICIIP-2013)*, (pp. 113–118), doi: 10.1109/ICIIP.2013.6707566.

[10] Singh, G., and Jain, V. (2012). Information retrieval (IR) through semantic web (SW): an overview. In Proceedings of CONFLUENCE 2012- The Next Generation Information Technology Summit at Amity School of Engineering and Technology, September 2012, (pp. 23–27).

[11] Shukla, R. K., Sharma, P., Samaiya, N., and Kherajani, M. (2020). Web usage mining-a study of web data pattern detecting methodologies and its applications in data mining. In 2nd International Conference on Data, Engineering and Applications (IDEA), Bhopal, India, (pp. 1–6), doi: 10.1109/IDEA49133.2020.9170690.

[12] Omar, R., and Abdullah, Z. S. (2018). Mining web usage using FRS. In International Conference on Information and Communication Technology for the Muslim World (ICT4M), Kuala Lumpur, Malaysia, (pp. 301–304), doi: 10.1109/ICT4M.2018.00062.

[13] Hryhoruk, C. C. J., and Leung, C. K. (2022). Web mining from interpretable compressed representation of sparse web. In IEEE/WIC/ACM International Joint Conference on Web Intelligence and Intelligent Agent Technology (WI-IAT), Niagara Falls, ON, Canada, (pp. 620–627), doi: 10.1109/WI-IAT55865.2022.00097.

[14] Singh, S. P., Ansari, M. A., and Kumar, L. (2023). Analysis of website in web data mining using web log expert tool. In IEEE 12th International Conference on Communication Systems and Network Technologies (CSNT), Bhopal, India, (pp. 514–518), doi: 10.1109/CSNT57126.2023.10134696.

[15] Jambhulkar, S. V., and Karale, S. J. (2016). Semantic web application generation using Protégé tool. In Online International Conference on Green Engineering and Technologies (IC-GET), Coimbatore, India, (pp. 1–5), doi: 10.1109/GET.2016.7916686.

[16] Akram, N. N., and Ilango, V. (2022). Intelligent web mining techniques using semantic web. In First International Conference on Electrical, Electronics, Information and Communication Technologies (ICEEICT), Trichy, India, (pp. 1–7), doi: 10.1109/ICEEICT53079.2022.9768546.

[17] Anwaar, Z., Khan, F. U., and Naz, M. (2022). Owl ontology for liver diseases using protégé & web-V-owl. In 16th International Conference on Open Source Systems and Technologies (ICOSST), Lahore, Pakistan, (pp. 1–4), doi: 10.1109/ICOSST57195.2022.10016808.

[18] Kumar, M., and Meenu, (2017). Analysis of visitor's behavior from web log using web log expert tool. In International Conference of Electronics, Communication and Aerospace Technology (ICECA), Coimbatore, India, (pp. 296–301), doi: 10.1109/ICECA.2017.8212820.

[19] Şahin, M. E., and Özdemir, S. (2019). Detection of malicious requests on web logs using data mining techniques. In 4th International Conference on Computer Science and Engineering (UBMK), Samsun, Turkey, (pp. 463–468), doi: 10.1109/UBMK.2019.8907087.

[20] Neelima, P. G., and Rodda, S. (2016). Predicting user behavior through sessions using the web log mining. In International Conference on Advances in Human Machine Interaction (HMI), Kodigehalli, India, (pp. 1–5), doi: 10.1109/HMI.2016.7449167.

[21] Sakarkar, S., Chaudhari, V., Gaurkar, T., Veer, A., and Scet, M. K. (2021). Web personalisation based on user interaction : web personalisation. In Third International Conference on Intelligent Communication Technologies and Virtual Mobile Networks (ICICV), Tirunelveli, India, (pp. 234–238), doi: 10.1109/ICICV50876.2021.9388384.

25 RDF and OWL-based searching model for retrieval of pertinent information

Pooja Sapra[1,a], Kalyan Acharjya[2,b] and Ganesh Dhandapani[3,c]

[1]Associate Professor, Department of Information Technology, Faculty of Engineering and Technology, Parul Institute of Technology, Parul University, Vadodara, Gujarat, India

[2]Assistant Professor, Maharishi School of Engineering & Technology, Maharishi University of Information Technology, India

[3]Professor, Department of Computer Science and Information Technology, Jain (Deemed to be University), Bangalore, India

Abstract

Semantic web provides a more sophisticated online service that systematically synchronises and organises all web-based data. Accurately picking the data needed to meet user demand and choosing them for output has proven to be a formidable challenge in the field of web-based data mining. In order to obtain the necessary data in Web 3.0, this study presents a method of mapping data across ontology. The agent returns all relevant search results to the user, from which they can extract the information they want. Knowledge is able to be understood from the information offered by the agent regardless of whether the user doesn't have suitable search parameters. Semantic web mining allows for the extraction of such previously discovered information from the existing. Here, we provide a web mining model based on smart agents that follows the standard approach taken by search engines like Google when answering a user's question. The smart assistant examines the results of the search to determine which ones are most closely connected to the user's query. To test the viability of the suggested paradigm, an instance study of university faculty information for the computer science department is provided.

Keywords: Information retrieval, ontology, OWL, RDF, Web 3.0

Introduction

In Web 2.0, it is nearly hard to discover new information since no relationships are built between data sets, rendering the results of typical web mining completely unacceptable. People are now looking to web3.0 to facilitate more efficient mining. In this setting, both robots and humans are able to collaborate because to the clear and organised presentation of data. Through the use of ontology, the semantic web's data is connected to one another, allowing for more efficient methods of discovery, automation, and assimilation. These records can be read and understood by computers, making them suitable for collaboration and analysis by both humans and software. The semantic web is built on a multi-tiered architecture [2, 3]. The semantic model used to define the Web's information and its nature is provided by resource description framework (RDF) and RDF schema [4]. Any RDF-based data (i.e., statements utilising RDFS and OWL [6]) may be queried using the SPARQL [5] RDF query language. The ontology linguistic tier defines conventional wisdom and articulates the semantic connections between different types of data. Because it provides a machine-processable semantics and a shareable domain, ontology is seen as a crucial component [7, 8] of the semantic web architecture, which aims to improve communication between humans and software. Web 3.0, or the Semantic Web, is predicated on the idea of adding machine-processable content to the existing web. The search engine's accuracy and recall can be enhanced by using machine-processable information to direct it to the most pertinent pages. The primary goal of Web Mining is to extract useful information about the context and function of Web sites. Since the data that is analysed is mostly syntactical in nature, it is impossible to discover meaning using simply this data. As a result, there has been a rise in the prevalence of formalisations of the semantics of websites and navigational behaviour. Combining the Semantic Web with Web Mining creates Semantic Web Mining. Most data on the web are so unstructured that only humans can understand them, yet there is so much of it that only robots can analyse it efficiently. Web mining tackles the second half of this problem by automatically obtaining the important knowledge concealed in this data and making it accessible in manageable amounts, while the Semantic Web tackles the first part by aiming to create the data machine legible.

[a]Pooja.sapra24683@paruluniversity.ac.in, [b]kalyan.acharjya@gmail.com, [c]d.ganesh@jainuniversity.ac.in

DOI: 10.1201/9781003534136-25

Literature Review

The given paper is organized into following sections. Section 2 provides basic information about web ontology language (OWL) and its specifications. Section 3 discusses information related to ontology editors. Section 4 presents methodology for the proposed semantic information retrieval model. It involves processing of user query via traditional search engine and our proposed model. Section 5 presents analysis of results. Section 6 presents summary of the findings and proposes recommendations for further research.

Ontology Web Language (OWL) and Its Specifications

When data in archives must be handled by an application in addition to being shown to humans, OWL is required. Delegating the meaning of words and how they relate to one another is an application of OWL. Ontology is another name for it [9, 10]. Because OWL has more tools than XML, RDF, and RDF-S for elucidating meaning and semasiology, it can better display machine interpretable material on the Web than any other few languages. The OWL online ontology language is a refined version of DAML+OIL that takes into account the wise lessons learned from the DAML+OIL design and solicitation [11, 12]. OWL expands the vocabulary used to describe things like classes and their attributes, cardinality (such as "accurately one"), group relations, feature traits, and anticipated classes. OWL offers three progressively creative sublanguages designed to meet the demands of a diverse range of application developers and end users [13, 14].

- *Because of its lower formal complexity in comparison to OWL DL, OWL Lite is a useful bridge between various taxonomies.*
- *If you want the highest level of expressiveness afforded by computational completeness and decidability, OWL DL is the way to go.*
- *Those who want the computationally free and maximally expressive nature of RDF may consider upgrading to OWL Full. OWL full has been used in our model implementation.*

Protégé- an Ontology Editor

Our work has been implemented using Protégé 4.3. Protégé [15, 16] is a free, open-source framework and ontology editor. In order to build knowledge-based accomplishments in fields like organisational modelling (our model on University), biomedical, and ecommerce, Protégé is used by a large community of users (such as, academic, state, and corporate). To represent our academic ontology that links business-supporting algorithms to data integration, we've settled on Protégé 4.3. Our ability to share ontologies between servers aids in coordinating efforts across teams. Additionally, the Ontoviz add-on facilitates the provision of idea diagrams. After the completion of the study, the ontology may become publicly available and be made available to anybody who requests it. In order to locate a group of websites that are linked to the extracted keywords, as outlined in [17, 18], the authors first extract certain keywords that are indicative of the domain. Similar problems occurred while attempting to cluster and associate web records using this method. In addition to RDF, Protégé also works with the Web Ontology Language (OWL) version 2 requirements that have been postponed by the World Wide Web Consortium (W3C).

Proposed Methodology

Proposed Semantic Model

The vast majority of data on the internet is unstructured, making it exceptionally challenging to aggregate it all under a uniform framework. We take into account both the classic web mining model and the semantic web mining model enabled by the semantic agent for a hybrid of the structured conceptual network and an unstructured real world network scenario. Figure 25.1 depicts our suggested model, which consists of the following phases.

(a) An interface for submitting queries from users to a processor. In a data server, the part responsible for handling queries is called the query processor.
(b) When a user submits a query to the query processor, it simultaneously submits the request to a conventional query engine (GOOGLE) and a smart agent via interface engine. A search query is input to a query engine, which then processes the request, delivers the results, and asks for further information if necessary. By translating clients' search queries and protecting them from the nitty-gritty of accessing the underlying data sources, this service works as an intermediary between the two. The results from the

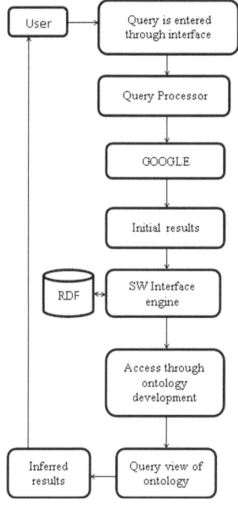

Figure 25.1 Steps of the proposed approach

RDF database are then delivered to the interface engine, which is based on the results from the traditional query engines.

(c) In the context of agent-based searching, it is necessary to establish an initial ontology. This entails the consolidation of many ideas pertaining to online items in order to generate such ontology. The ontology tier is going to be maintained within an ontology bank network or database for subsequent use at future levels.

(d) An agent will query an RDF database in response to user-supplied parameters sent via the interface engine and query processor. When an agent's interface engine receives results from an RDF database that match the user's query, the agent sends those results to the user immediately. Instead, if the requested results are not located in the RDF database, the agent will search the ontology library for any potential linkages among the user's query and additional web entities and then construct an ontology base containing relational entities.

(e) Resource acquisition module gathers task-specific data from the web; ontology base comprises all potential nodes linked to user request acquired by agent.

(f) Now this collected information can be searched via query interface of designed ontology based on object and data properties.

(g) Finally, the inferred results after query view are returned to the user.

Result and Implementation

The first phase begins with the query entered by user through traditional engine i.e. Google. The query is "List the faculties of computer science in a university". The web search results are produced in Figure 25.2.

Now, the same query is passed through semantic interface engine and results are stored in RDF database in the form of triplets. The next step is construction of ontology related to query by using ontology editor named PROTÉGÉ.

Figure 25.3 displays the classes and sub-classes of the designed ontology in response to the query entered by user. Classes include university- it is treated as super class which covers other sub-classes like Department, faculty and computer science.

Figure 25.4 shows the objects instantiation and properties associated with sub-classes of the designed ontology. It is seen that the properties exhibit 5 features namely transitive, symmetric, asymmetric, functional and reflexive. These features are used to maintain relationships and deriving inferences from the designed ontology.

Figure 25.2 Web Search Results Produced in Response to Query

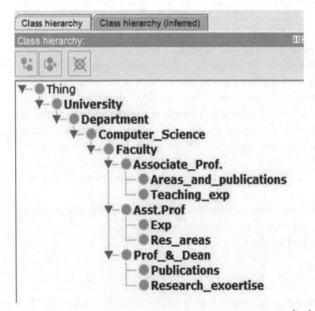

Figure 25.3 Layout of designed ontology in PROTÉGÉ 4.3.1

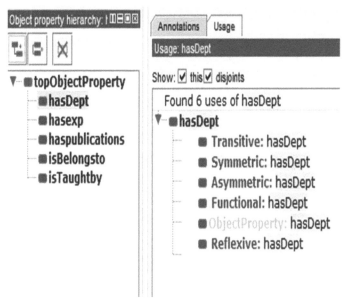

Figure 25.4 Object properties of ontology

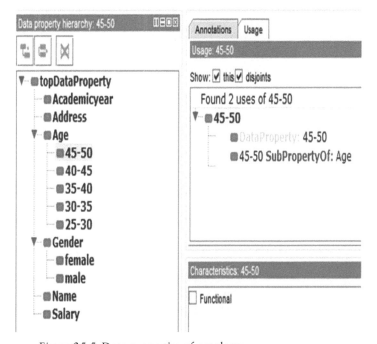

Figure 25.5 Data properties of ontology

Figure 25.5 shows data properties associated with classes and sub-classes. It includes address of faculties, age, gender, age names and their salaries fixed by universities. These properties are required to derive final ontology and knowledge database to extract relevant and pertinent information easily.

Figure 25.6 shows successful execution of proposed approach by generating inferences and presenting final results to the user in hierarchical fashion.

Results

The given Figure 25.7 proves the validation of ontology-based inference engine regarding retrieval of information from unstructured web documents. The accuracy of retrieval of information in case of search engine with ontology mechanism is 93% as compared to keyword-based search engine (87%).

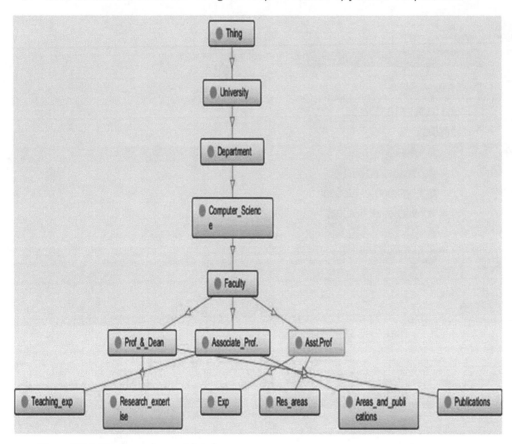

Figure 25.6 Final ontology with inferences

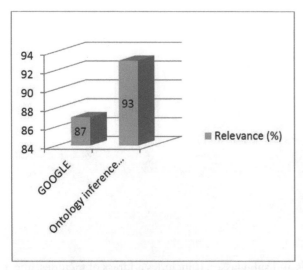

Figure 25.7 Comparison of accuracy of relevant results of ontology inference engine with traditional engine (GOOGLE)

Conclusion and Future Work

One of the most important things in the modern world is knowledge management. In particular, a university-level modelling effort would be impossible without a smart Knowledge management system. This technology facilitates communication across several university units, allowing students, faculty, and staff to work together digitally on a same project and advance their education and professional development. Therefore, the purpose of this work is to provide a semantic model employing the OWL concept and its stated forms. Validating the offered technique in terms of accuracy using the GOOGLE search engine, the model intelligently reflects knowledge and knowledge-based information retrieval for the University. When compared to standard search engines, the 93% relevance rate provided by the semantic inference engine model is significantly greater.

The work may be expanded in the future to use the semantic web rule language (SWRL) in the created ontology to produce results and suggestions.

References

[1] Haribabu, S., Sai Kumar, P. S., Padhy, S., Deepak, G., Santhanavijayan, A., and Kumar, D. N. (2019). A novel approach for ontology focused inter- domain personalized search based on semantic set expansion. In Fifteenth International Conference on Information Processing (ICINPRO), Bengaluru, India, (pp. 1–5), doi: 10.1109/ICInPro47689.2019.9092155.

[2] Pan, Z. (2020). Optimization of information retrieval algorithm for digital library based on semantic search engine. In International Conference on Computer Engineering and Application (ICCEA), Guangzhou, China, (pp. 364–367), doi: 10.1109/ICCEA50009.2020.00085.

[3] Khan, A. A., and Malik, S. K. (2018). Semantic search revisited. In 8th International Conference on Cloud Computing, Data Science & Engineering (Confluence), Noida, India, (pp. 14–15), doi: 10.1109/CONFLUENCE.2018.8442792.

[4] Alabdulwahhab, F. A. (2018). Web 3.0: the decentralized web blockchain networks and protocol innovation. In 1st International Conference on Computer Applications & Information Security (ICCAIS), Riyadh, Saudi Arabia, (pp. 1–4), doi: 10.1109/CAIS.2018.8441990.

[5] Muhamad, W., Suhardi, and Bandung, Y. (2020). Designing semantic web service based on OAS 3.0 through relational database. In International Conference on Information Technology Systems and Innovation (ICITSI), Bandung, Indonesia, (pp. 306–311), doi: 10.1109/ICITSI50517.2020.9264930.

[6] Sandal, M. M., et al. (2023). Web 3.0 applications and projections. In 5th International Congress on Human-Computer Interaction, Optimization and Robotic Applications (HORA), Istanbul, Turkiye, (pp. 1–9), doi: 10.1109/HORA58378.2023.10156728.

[7] Selvaraj, P., Burugari, V. K., Sumathi, D., Nayak, R. K., and Tripathy, R. (2019). Ontology based recommendation system for domain specific seekers. In Third International conference on I-SMAC (IoT in Social, Mobile, Analytics and Cloud) (I-SMAC), Palladam, India, (pp. 341–345), doi: 10.1109/I-SMAC47947.2019.9032634.

[8] Jiang, S., Hagelien, T. F., Natvig, M., and Li, J. (2019). Ontology-based semantic search for open government data. In IEEE 13th International Conference on Semantic Computing (ICSC), Newport Beach, CA, USA, (pp. 7–15), doi: 10.1109/ICOSC.2019.8665522.

[9] Singh, G., Jain, V., and Singh, M. (2013). Ontology development using Hozo and semantic analysis for information retrieval in semantic web. In *2013 IEEE Second International Conference on Image Information Processing (ICIIP-2013)*, (pp. 113–118), doi: 10.1109/ICIIP.2013.6707566.

[10] Detoni, A. A., et al. (2017). Exploring the role of enterprise architecture models in the modularization of an ontology network: a case in the public security domain. In IEEE 21st International Enterprise Distributed Object Computing Workshop (EDOCW), Quebec City, QC, Canada, (pp. 117–126), doi: 10.1109/EDOCW.2017.29.

[11] Kulkarni, A., Ramanathan, C., and Venugopal, V. E. (2023). Ontology mediated document retrieval for exploratory big data analytics. In IEEE 17th International Conference on Semantic Computing (ICSC), Laguna Hills, CA, USA, (pp. 100–103), doi: 10.1109/ICSC56153.2023.00022.

[12] Kohlschein, C., Klischies, D., Paulus, A., Burgdorf, A., Meisen, T., and Kipp, M. (2018). An extensible semantic search engine for biomedical publications. In IEEE 20th International Conference on e-Health Networking, Applications and Services (Healthcom), Ostrava, Czech Republic, (pp. 1–6), doi: 10.1109/HealthCom.2018.8531123..

[13] Pawar, S., Nayak, V., Laxmi, G., and Chiplunkar, N. N. (2020). A novel web service search system using WSDL. In Third International Conference on Smart Systems and Inventive Technology (ICSSIT), Tirunelveli, India, (pp. 1252–1257), doi: 10.1109/ICSSIT48917.2020.9214201.

[14] Malik, S., Shoaib, U., El-Sayed, H., and Khan, M. A. (2020). Query expansion framework leveraging clinical diagnosis information ontology. In 14th International Conference on Innovations in Information Technology (IIT), Al Ain, United Arab Emirates, (pp. 18–23), doi: 10.1109/IIT50501.2020.9299028.

[15] Fan, J., Gao, X., Wang, T., Liu, R., and Yang, Y. (2021). Research and application of automated search engine based on machine learning. In International Conference on High Performance Big Data and Intelligent Systems (HPBD&IS), Macau, China, (pp. 69–73), doi: 10.1109/HPBDIS53214.2021.9658474.

[16] Banik, P., Gaikwad, S., Awate, A., Shaikh, S., Gunjgur, P., and Padiya, P. (2018). Semantic analysis of wikipedia documents using ontology. In IEEE International Conference on System, Computation, Automation and Networking (ICSCA), Pondicherry, India, (pp. 1–6), doi: 10.1109/ICSCAN.2018.8541162.

[17] Dhaliwal, M. P., Tiwari, H., and Vala, V. (2021). Automatic creation of a domain specific thesaurus using siamese networks. In IEEE 15th International Conference on Semantic Computing (ICSC), Laguna Hills, CA, USA, (pp. 355–361), doi: 10.1109/ICSC50631.2021.00066.

[18] Jetinai, K. (2018). Rule-based reasoning for resource recommendation in personalized e-learning. In International Conference on Information and Computer Technologies (ICICT), DeKalb, IL, USA, (pp. 150–154), doi: 10.1109/INFOCT.2018.8356859.

26 Knowledge exemplification mechanism via ontology construction in context of transmittable diseases

Haripriya V[1,a], Daxa Vekariya[2,b] and Sridhar Pappu[3,c]

[1]Assistant Professor, Department of Computer Science and Information Technology, Jain (Deemed to be University), Bangalore, India

[2]Associate Professor, Department of Computer Science and Engineering, Faculty of Engineering and Technology, Parul Institute of Engineering and Technology, Parul University, Vadodara, Gujarat, India

[3]Dean, Department of UGDX, ATLAS SkillTech University, Mumbai, Maharashtra, India

Abstract

Internet is now the first place people look when they need answers to any question. Now that the semantic web exists, we may expect better results from our online searches. The foundation of every semantic web application is ontologies. By giving data in real time, they facilitate the speedy creation of distributed systems. Because of this central property of information dissemination and exchange, ontologies have emerged as a new framework for representing knowledge, one that is supported by a robust inference system. In this article, we'll examine ontology in the context of communicable illnesses and talk about how it's built, checked, and validated.

Keywords: Knowledge representation, ontology development, relations and instances, transmittable diseases

Introduction

Since the advent of AI, knowledge representation (KR) has become a subject of intensive study, leading to the creation of a wide range of KR methodologies. Scripts, Frames, and Semantic Networks are all representation strategies that don't function very well in the modern web-based environment, when data is continuously being exchanged among many apps. Different online applications need a representation strategy that can hold ideas and connections and is simple to use. This method has been made possible by ontologies. The World Wide Web Consortium (W3C) has been instrumental in the rise of ontologies in recent years, having supported the development of an infrastructure [1, 2] for encoding knowledge on web pages that will facilitate the process of searching for web agents by providing them with easy access to Meta information. Ontologies have been used to create this framework.

This format, known as RDF (Resource Development Framework), is used to store ontologies [3, 4]. Ontologies are favoured for semantic web because they make it simple to express ideas and keep concept hierarchies clear. When a user types in "Beverages" as a search term, a semantically based search engine (that has been supported by ontologies) is likely to be able give the identical outcomes to all of the search queries, whereas a traditional search engine may not always be able to do so. In addition, a search engine would be unable to make the connection between "plane bomb" and "plane bombing," but a semantically educated search engine might make the connection and provide results related to plane bombing. This is where semantic search engines (also known as ontologies) shine in comparison to traditional ones. Because of this, we may define ontology as an exact description of a theory [5, 6]. The need to manually define everything is lessened because to ontology's ability to automatically uncover relationships between related concepts and their relations and attributes.

The given paper is organized into following sections. Section 2 provides a review of studies conducted in the context of ontology development and health diseases. Section 3 presents methodology for the complete ontology construction process including but not limited to gathering of knowledge, defining relations and concepts used in classes and sub-classes of the designed ontology. Section 4 presents implementation of results. Section 5 presents summary of the findings and proposes recommendations for further research.

Literature Review

Numerous studies have looked into how people use search engines to get health-related information. Co-occurrence rates of medical information (such as symptoms and illnesses) on a web page greatly impact

[a]v.haripriya@jainuniversity.ac.in, [b]daxa.vekariya18436@paruluniversity.ac.in, [c]sridhar.pappu@atlasuniversity.edu.in

DOI: 10.1201/9781003534136-26

search behaviour, as demonstrated by the authors [7, 8]. According to the studies cited in [9, 10], people tend to switch from using generic search engines to more niche ones when looking for health-related information online.

They looked at research published in the fields of medical technology as well as information science to learn how doctors might improve their trust in clinical decision making through the use of information retrieval tools. Since so few relevant articles were retrieved by various retrieval algorithms, they concluded that they were insufficient. They followed up that review with another research on how medical and nursing students utilise MEDLINE to answer clinical questions, which can be found [11, 12].

Patients were able to get their clinical queries answered by Goggling patients. The authors [13, 14] looked at the correlation between searching the internet for information about a condition or symptom and consulting a family doctor. They discovered that health anxiety levels have a moderating role in the connection between accessing health information online and making decisions about when and how to use that information. Ontology for Indian healthcare services was created by the authors [15]. By compiling health-related news items, they were able to create this ontology. Using search engine application programming interfaces and using structural patterns to the detection of additional lexical connections, [16, 17] demonstrated the usage of ontologies in the Internet. Systems built with these methods are also documented in the literature; for example [18], the authors demonstrated the usage of OntoLT, a plugin for the Protégé Ontology Editor that facilitates the process of learning new ontologies. This system used a parser to annotate grammatical relations and components of speech in text. Domain-specific words were retrieved using the Ontolearn system, as demonstrated in the study [19]. This application quickly rose to prominence as a crucial resource for text-based ontology generation.

Proposed Methodology

Ontology Development

Ontologies have been the focus of development efforts because of their ability to semantically store data, which aids in the creation of semantic web applications and other domains where semantic knowledge is vital. Ontologies are important because they can pick up information from the real world, find specific examples, and establish connections between concepts. Ontologies allow us to standardise the language and concepts used in the health sector. Since many diseases share symptoms and causative agents, it might be difficult for a standard application to determine which symptoms belong to which diseases. Distinguishing between them is a breeze with the help of an ontological taxonomy. When it comes to creating rules and standards for interoperability among diverse health care information systems and heterogeneous online resources, ontology is a beneficial tool. The evolution of ontology is an iterative procedure. Each Ontology concept should reflect a real-world entity and its connections in the study's focus area.

A. Methodology

- *Knowledge acquisition:* During this phase, we scoured the Internet for resources on various ideas, illnesses, and germs.
- *Domain and scope:* After amassing data on illnesses, potential symptoms, and infectious agents, we were able to determine the domain and extent of ontology.
- *Conceptualization:* To construct ontology, one must first put into practise the ideas (classes) that compose it. We established transmittable illnesses (TD) as the parent category, with infectious illnesses and their causative agents as the child categories. As we were making new classes, we saw that many of them shared the same or comparable characteristics and interactions. It was decided to designate these groups as equivalence groups.
- *Defining Internal Structure of Ontology:* Ontology cannot be built unless the concepts (classes) that make it up are put into use. We set up a hierarchy in which infectious diseases and the agents that cause them are children of the parent category, "transmittable diseases" (TD). We noticed that several of the newly created classes had analogous features and behaviours as others. These sets are now officially known as equivalency sets.
- *Infer Knowledge from the Designed Ontology:* It involves initiation of reasoner for using queries

All above steps are presented as methodology in Figure 26.1.

Result and Implementation

Figure 26.2 presents the hierarchical distribution of identified classes and sub-classes of the designed ontology. It is designed using PROTÉGÉ 4.3.1. Here, TD is super class and rest is its sub-classes.

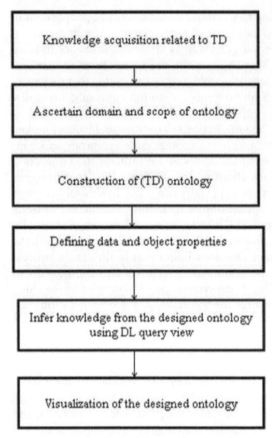

Figure 26.1 Methodology of Ontology Development

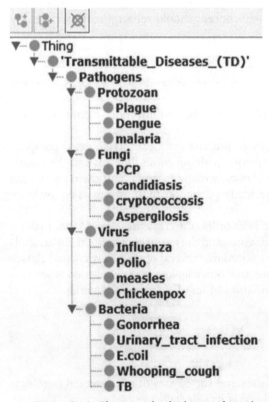

Figure 26.2 Classes and sub-classes of ontology on 'transmittable diseases

Figure 26.3 displays the object properties associated with classes and sub-classes of the designed diseases ontology. It shows equivalence characteristics namely reflexive, symmetric, functional, transitive, asymmetric and inverse functional.

Figure 26.4 show that if we select disjoint in dialog box, it shows no results associated with objects of classes and sub-classes. It implies that the classes of constructed ontology are in relation with each other and are well connected to derive information from them.

Figure 26.5 shows data properties associated with classes and sub-classes. It includes symptoms like cough, nausea, vomiting, headache, muscle pain and fever. The diseases are also classified as waterborne and airborne diseases. They exhibit functional property with zero disjoint classes and sub-classes.

Figure 26.6 shows successful execution of designed ontology with Hermit reasoner. This reasoner performs the task of deriving inferences from classes and sub-classes. Here, we have searched bacteria in query view and the result gets highlighted as sub-class of pathogens.

Figure 26.7 shows the grid layout of the designed ontology using OntoGraf plug-in of PROTÉGÉ 4.3.1.

We may use Onto Graf to explore the connections between your OWL ontologies in an interactive manner. The ontology's structure may be automatically organized in several different layouts. There are a variety of connections that may be used, including equivalence, domain/range object attributes, subclass, and individual.

The given Figure 26.8 shows the final view of compete ontology from knowledge acquisition phase to conceptualization.

Figure 26.3 Defining object properties and equivalence characteristics

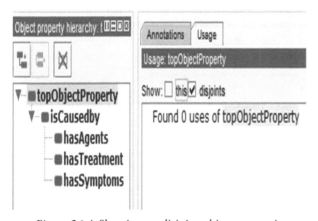

Figure 26.4 Showing no disjoint object properties

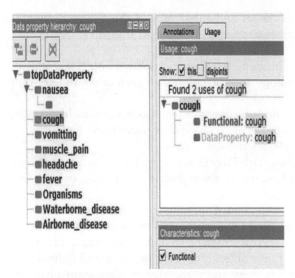

Figure 26.5 Data properties of ontology

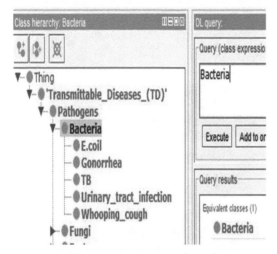

Figure 26.6 DL query view of ontology

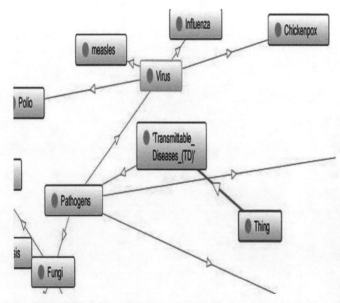

Figure 26.7 Visualization of ontology

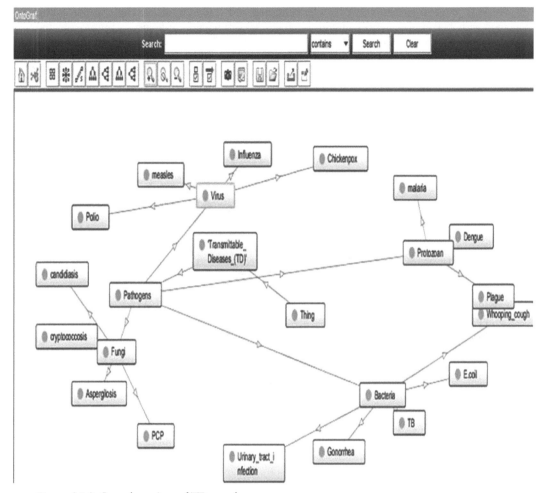

Figure 26.8 Complete view of TD ontology

The fact that the reasoner was able to get the required classes, super classes, relations, and properties indicates that a flawless ontology was constructed.

Conclusion and Future Work

This study is an exposition of the ontology building process within the area of transmittable illnesses. We have engaged in discourse on many stages in the evolution of ontology. Additionally, we conducted an evaluation of our ontology by employing a reasoner to validate the ontology through the execution of each class and its associated characteristics.

In continuation of our research, we want to augment the ontology by incorporating other illnesses and their corresponding treatments. Additionally, we aim to establish connections between different elements of the ontology and their corresponding online contents. Furthermore, we intend to create a user interface for this ontology that will obtain information pertaining to any given condition, including its symptoms, as well as deliver relevant web-based information.

References

[1] Murtazina, M. S., Avdeenko, T. V., and Pustovalova, A. V. (2022). An ontology-driven knowledge representation about cognitive functions. IEEE 23rd International Conference of Young Professionals in Electron Devices and Materials (EDM), Altai, Russian Federation, (pp. 295–298), doi: 10.1109/EDM55285.2022.9855075.

[2] Chen, X., Zeng, G., Zhang, Q., Chen, L., and Wu, D. (2017). A fuzzy ontology for geography knowledge of China's college entrance examination. In IEEE 16th International Conference on Cognitive Informatics & Cognitive Computing (ICCI*CC), Oxford, UK, (pp. 237–242), doi: 10.1109/ICCI-CC.2017.8109756.

[3] Huang, Z. (2018). Towards improving the knowledge representation and searching of manchu costume culture: an ontology-based method with APP implementation. In 8th International Conference on Logistics, Informatics and Service Sciences (LISS), Toronto, ON, Canada, (pp. 1–6), doi: 10.1109/LISS.2018.8593252.

[4] Yulianti, L. P., and Surendro, K. (2018). Ontology model for indigenous knowledge. In International Conference on Information Technology Systems and Innovation (ICITSI), Bandung, Indonesia, (pp. 231–236), doi: 10.1109/ICITSI.2018.8695925.

[5] Lopez, B., Alvarez-Rodriguez, J. M., Parra, E., and de la Vara, J. L. (2020). Ontology configuration management for knowledge-centric systems engineering in industry. In 50th Annual IEEE-IFIP International Conference on Dependable Systems and Networks-Supplemental Volume (DSN-S), Valencia, Spain, (pp. 37–40), doi: 10.1109/DSN-S50200.2020.00022.

[6] Rukmono, S. A., and Chaudron, M. R. V. (2023). Enabling analysis and reasoning on software systems through knowledge graph representation. In IEEE/ACM 20th International Conference on Mining Software Repositories (MSR), Melbourne, Australia, (pp. 120–124), doi: 10.1109/MSR59073.2023.00029.

[7] Hanum, S. L., Arzaki, M., and Rusmawati, Y. (2019). Knowledge representation of political parties' ideological characteristics using formal concept analysis. In International Conference on Electrical Engineering and Informatics (ICEEI), Bandung, Indonesia, (pp. 7–12), doi: 10.1109/ICEEI47359.2019.8988789.

[8] Lu, W., Nie, Z., Lu, Y., and Li, Y. (2020). Knowledge graph oriented anti-ship combat command information ontology model. In IEEE 3rd International Conference on Automation, Electronics and Electrical Engineering (AUTEEE), Shenyang, China, (pp. 55–60), doi: 10.1109/AUTEEE50969.2020.9315561.

[9] Neykov, N., and Stefanova, S. (2021). State of art in collaborative ontology development. In Big Data, Knowledge and Control Systems Engineering (BdKCSE), Sofia, Bulgaria, (pp. 1–4), doi: 10.1109/BdKCSE53180.2021.9627250.

[10] Samara, K., Javed, Y., and Naveed, M. (2018). Designing common ontologies to support clinical practice guidelines using OWL-based ontologies. In Fifth HCT Information Technology Trends (ITT), Dubai, United Arab Emirates, (pp. 7–11), doi: 10.1109/CTIT.2018.8649544.

[11] Kulkarni, A., Ramanathan, C., and Venugopal, V. E. (2023). Ontology mediated document retrieval for exploratory big data analytics. In IEEE 17th International Conference on Semantic Computing (ICSC), Laguna Hills, CA, USA, (pp. 100–103), doi: 10.1109/ICSC56153.2023.00022.

[12] Alfaifi, Y. (2022). Ontology development methodology: a systematic review and case study. In 2nd International Conference on Computing and Information Technology (ICCIT), Tabuk, Saudi Arabia, (pp. 446–450), doi: 10.1109/ICCIT52419.2022.9711664.

[13] Altan, Z. (2022). An ontology model oriented to the career planning of university students. In International Congress on Human-Computer Interaction, Optimization and Robotic Applications (HORA), Ankara, Turkey, (pp. 1–7), doi: 10.1109/HORA55278.2022.9799963.

[14] Mohammed, M., Romli, A., and Mohamed, R. (2021). Using ontology to enhance decision-making for product sustainability in smart manufacturing. In International Conference on Intelligent Technology, System and Service for Internet of Everything (ITSS-IoE), Sana'a, Yemen, (pp. 1–4), doi: 10.1109/ITSS-IoE53029.2021.9615289.

[15] Islam, N., and Shaikh, Z. A. (2019). Towards ontology editing, querying and visualization in .net environment. In 8th International Conference on Information and Communication Technologies (ICICT), Karachi, Pakistan, (pp. 119–123), doi: 10.1109/ICICT47744.2019.9001977.

[16] Maryasin, O. Y. (2019). Ontology-based development of smart home expert system. In International Russian Automation Conference (RusAutoCon), Sochi, Russia, (pp. 1–5), doi: 10.1109/RUSAUTOCON.2019.8867792.

[17] Strinyuk, S., Scherbakova, I., and Lanin, V. (2021). Corpus based information extraction approach for marine ontology development. In IEEE 15th International Conference on Application of Information and Communication Technologies (AICT), Baku, Azerbaijan, (pp. 1–5), doi: 10.1109/AICT52784.2021.9620410.

[18] Novogrudska, R., and Popova, M. (2021). A compehencive review of ontology-based information systems for educational process support. In IEEE International Conference on Information and Telecommunication Technologies and Radio Electronics (UkrMiCo), Odesa, Ukraine, (pp. 76–79), doi: 10.1109/UkrMiCo52950.2021.9716675.

[19] Popereshnyak, S., and Vecherkovskaya, A. (2019). Modeling ontologies in software testing. In IEEE 14th International Conference on Computer Sciences and Information Technologies (CSIT), Lviv, Ukraine, (pp. 236–239), doi: 10.1109/STC-CSIT.2019.8929785.

27 Assessment of a unique and entropy-based system to diagnose dental diseases using KNN and MLP classifiers

Karthikeyan M. P.[1,a], Chintan Thacker[2,b] and Satish Upadhyay[3,c]

[1]Assistant Professor, Department of Computer Science and Information Technology, Jain (Deemed to be University), Bangalore, India

[2]Assistant Professor, Department of Computer Science and Engineering, Faculty of Engineering and Technology, Parul Institute of Engineering and Technology, Parul University, Vadodara, Gujarat, India

[3]Assistant Professor, Department of UGDX, ATLAS SkillTech University, Mumbai, Maharashtra, India

Abstract

Finding the best effective data mining algorithms for use in clinical diagnostics is a time-consuming process. The purpose of this research was to determine which predicted algorithms for data mining are the most effective when used to make dental disease diagnoses. Predictive data mining model was constructed using K-nearest neighbor (KNN) and multilayer perceptron (MLP) processors in this work. To further assess the classifiers' prediction abilities off the bat, we employed 10-fold cross-validation and a variety of performance indicators. The results of the comparison reveal that MLP has the highest accuracy (97.4%), followed by KNN (94.6%). Expertise in the predictive capacity of various data mining algorithms usable in clinical diagnosis, in particular in the identification of dental or oral illnesses, was gained through the assessment of such classifications on medical datasets.

Keywords: Dental diseases, MLP, KNN, predictive data mining

Introduction

Predictive analytics is a subfield of data mining that aims to foresee possible outcomes by analysing past data for patterns and linkages [1]. Predictive analytics is a broad field that includes disciplines like statistics, data mining, and game theory [2]. Predictive modelling entails four stages: data collection, model development, prediction, and model validation/refinement based on new information [3, 4]. Strategic research is the foundation of clinical data mining, which is used to obtain, analyse, and interpret qualitative and quantitative data from healthcare datasets or records [4]. To anticipate the categories of new datasets that have not yet been labelled, predictive data mining first generates a classification model using a training dataset [5]. In order to aid doctors in their diagnostic, therapeutic, or monitoring endeavours, predictive data mining focuses on learning models [6]. It uses machine learning techniques to construct multivariate approaches from medical information and, using those models, to draw conclusions about previously unseen data [7]. The use of guided classification methods is central to the machine learning model. The data is cleaned up and the data mining principles are tested on real data before the learning model is implemented [8, 9]. knowledge discovery in databases (KDD) refers to the process of preparing, mining, and analysing data for insights into business and the real world. Predictive data mining is the most popular subset of KDD. Several instances include the use of gender, years of age, smoking and status, hypertension, and different biomarkers to predict surgical outcomes [10], tumour survival [11], and risk factors for coronary heart disease [12, 13]. First, consider the individual's overall condition (healthy, diabetic, pressure patient, pregnant) and age (baby, child, and young, adult) before studying the patient's symptoms to pinpoint the source of pain and the nature of the disease [14]. It's important to remember that oral illnesses can progress to a critical stage before any obvious signs in the oral cavity or teeth show. Therefore, it's important to make sure the dental and oral health clinic is up to par.

"The given paper is organized into following sections. Section 2 provides a review of studies conducted in the context of applications of data mining to predict various diseases. Section 3 presents methodology of the proposed approach. It involves defining K-nearest neighbor (KNN) and multilayer perceptron (MLP) classifiers. Section 4 presents empirical results and analysis. Section 5 presents summary of the findings and proposes recommendations for further research."

[a]karthikeyan.mp@jainuniversity.ac.in, [b]chintan.thacker19435@paruluniversity.ac.in, [c]satish.upadhyay@atlasuniversity.edu.in

DOI: 10.1201/9781003534136-27

Literature Review

Only accuracy, error rate, precision, and recall were included in [15]'s comparison of decision tree (DT), artificial neural network (ANN), and support vector machine (SVM) for illness detection. A 10-fold cross-validation test of these prediction models' objectivity is not used. In [16], the authors showed how to use a Bayesian model-based clinical expert system for detecting the presence of coronary artery disease based on the available data. When compared to logistical and linear regression models, the Bayesian was thought to be superior when coping with many missing variables. To determine which machine learning method is most effective and efficient for determining the severity of asthma using a skilled system, the authors of [17] compared Bayesian networks, ID3, and C4.5. Studies attempted to validate [18]'s proposal of an Advanced learning machine and Artificial Neural Network for better differentiating skin disorders. The search techniques sequential forward floating search (SFFS) and sequential backward floating search (SBFS) were utilized; with feature significance determined using the generalized F-score [19]. It was stated that the two-phase hybrid model improved upon previous algorithms for identifying skin and dental problems in terms of classification accuracy.

Proposed Methodology

Figure 27.1 illustrates the procedures to be followed.

A. Dataset Collection

Caries, gingivitis, tooth discoloration, and hypodontia are just few of the many dental issues we looked at using the oral health dataset. This dataset is available for use in the development and instruction of models for detecting and classifying dental conditions, and it was obtained from the Kaggle repository [20].

B. Pre-Processing and Features Extraction

"It is done with the help of WEKA [21] - a data mining and analysis tool for performing classification and predictive mining in diagnosis of various diseases."

C. Classifiers- KNN and MLP

The KNN is a supervised-learning-based classifier that uses the proximity of data points to one another to generate predictions about the appropriate categories for those data points. Classification issues are where this approach shines, however it has applications in regression as well. It does this by assuming that related points tend to cluster together.

For many classification and prediction tasks, the go-to feed forward neural network is the MLP. During the learning phase, MLP's input variables (weights and biases) are fine-tuned utilizing a gradient-based approach to ensure optimal behavior.

D. n Folds Cross Validation

Estimating a model's accuracy in practice may be done with the help of n-fold cross-validation, also known as rotation estimation. It entails arbitrarily dividing a dataset D into s distinct groups. It is taught each time on the entire dataset and then tested on the remainder of folds. In the method we have presented, n equals 10.

E. Evaluation based on metrics

The assessment of prospective data mining algorithms may be conducted by considering several metrics. When evaluating the predictability of various predictive data mining algorithms, it is necessary to evaluate certain metrics that assess the quality of model fit and error measures [22]. The metrics utilized in the study are as follows.

The ideal data-splitting properties may be established with the use of an "entropy calculation", this is a statistical technique for measuring how much data has been skewed.

$$\text{Entropy} = \Sigma - p_i \log p_i \tag{1}$$

$$\text{"Precision} = TP / (TP + FP) \tag{2}$$

$$\text{Recall} = TP / (TP + FN) \tag{3}$$

$$\text{F-measure} = (2 * \text{precision}*\text{recall}) / (\text{precision} + \text{recall}) \tag{4}$$

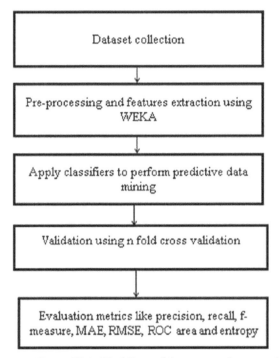

Dataset collection

↓

Pre-processing and features extraction using WEKA

↓

Apply classifiers to perform predictive data mining

↓

Validation using n fold cross validation

↓

Evaluation metrics like precision, recall, f-measure, MAE, RMSE, ROC area and entropy

Figure 27.1 Workflow of the proposed approach

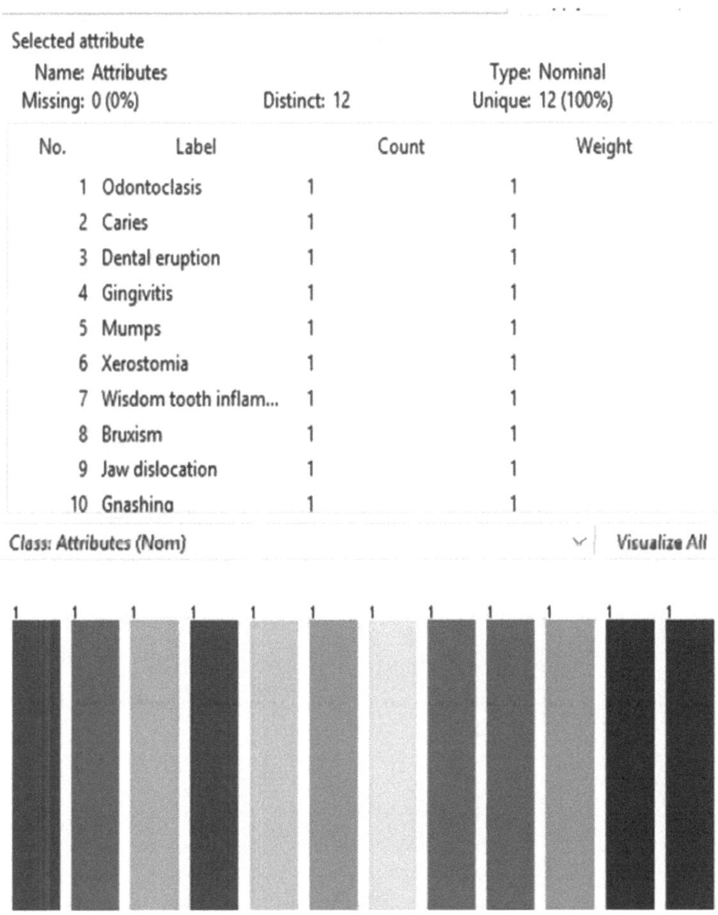

Selected attribute

Name: Attributes   Type: Nominal
Missing: 0 (0%)   Distinct: 12   Unique: 12 (100%)

No.	Label	Count	Weight
1	Odontoclasis	1	1
2	Caries	1	1
3	Dental eruption	1	1
4	Gingivitis	1	1
5	Mumps	1	1
6	Xerostomia	1	1
7	Wisdom tooth inflam...	1	1
8	Bruxism	1	1
9	Jaw dislocation	1	1
10	Gnashing	1	1

Class: Attributes (Nom)   ﹀ | Visualize All

Figure 27.2 Feature extraction using WEKA

Mean absolute error (MAE) = $(p_1 - a_1) + (p_2 - a_2) + ...(P_n - a_n)$ divided by n   (5)

Where p denotes predicted value and a denotes actual value."

Result and Implementation

"Figure 27.2 presents the pre-processing and extraction of dental dataset showing distinct 12 attributes that needs to be worked upon. These are dental diseases namely Odontoclasis, caries, dental eruptions, Gingivitis, Mumps etc."

```
Classifier output

Scheme:      weka.classifiers.lazy.IBk -K 1 -W 0 -A "weka.core.
Relation:    dental
Instances:   12
Attributes:  1
             Attributes
Test mode:   evaluate on training data

=== Classifier model (full training set) ===

IB1 instance-based classifier
using 1 nearest neighbour(s) for classification

Time taken to build model: 0 seconds

=== Evaluation on training set ===

Time taken to test model on training data: 0.01 seconds
```

Figure 27.3 Applying KNN classifier

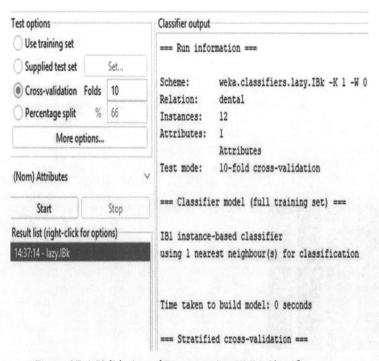

```
Test options
○ Use training set
○ Supplied test set    Set...
◉ Cross-validation  Folds  10
○ Percentage split   %   66
       More options...

(Nom) Attributes              ∨

    Start          Stop

Result list (right-click for options)
14:37:14 - lazy.IBk
```

```
Classifier output

=== Run information ===

Scheme:      weka.classifiers.lazy.IBk -K 1 -W 0
Relation:    dental
Instances:   12
Attributes:  1
             Attributes
Test mode:   10-fold cross-validation

=== Classifier model (full training set) ===

IB1 instance-based classifier
using 1 nearest neighbour(s) for classification

Time taken to build model: 0 seconds

=== Stratified cross-validation ===
```

Figure 27.4 Validation of Dataset using KNN Classifier

"Figure 27.3 displays the successful execution of KNN classifier on dental dataset. The model is evaluated on full training dataset by taking features extracted into consideration."

Figure 27.4 shows the successful validation of our methodology by using KNN classifier. It is done using 10 folds cross validation which leads to values of MAE, Precision, recall etc.

"Figure 27.5 shows successful execution of MLP classifier on dental dataset. The model is evaluated on full training dataset by taking features extracted into consideration."

Figure 27.6 shows Entropy calculated values & Figure 27.7 displays the Evaluation metrics which is been attached below in the article.

Table 27.2 shows that our approach works best with MLP classifier with an accuracy of 97.4% and excellent ROC area under curve as 0.85.

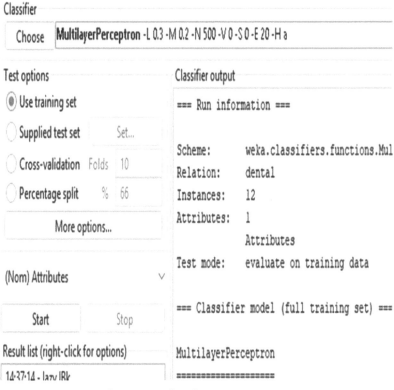

Figure 27.5 Applying MLP classifier

Table 27.1 Entropy calculation results with respect to dental conditions.

ATTRIBUTES	VALUES
Odontoclasts	-2 log base2 = 0.25
Caries	-4 log base 2 = 0.0625
Dental Eruption	-5 log base 2= 0.03125
Gingivitis	-3 log base 2 = 0.125
Mumps	-7 log base 2= 0.07812
Xerostomia	-1 log base 2 = 0.5
Wisdom Tooth Inflammation	-8 log base 2 = 0.003906
Bruxism	-9log base 2 = 0.001953
Jaw Dislocation	0.25
Gnashing	0.125

Table 27.2 Comparison of evaluation metrics with respect to 10 folds crosses validation of dental diseases dataset.

Metrics	KNN	MLP
Correctly classified instances	95.5%	97.4%
Mae	1.23	0.159
Precision	0.94	0.95
Recall	0.95	0.96
Accuracy	94.6%	97.4%
F-Measure	0.94	0.95
ROC Area	0.75	0.85

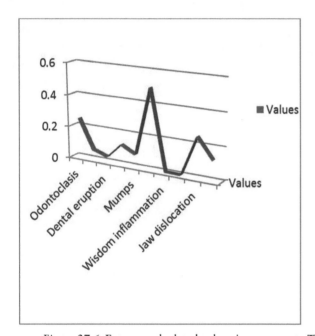

Figure 27.6 Entropy calculated values in response to Table 27.1

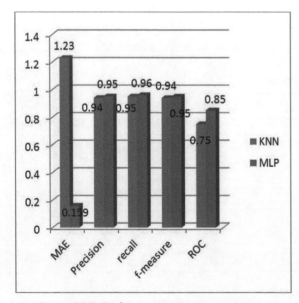

Figure 27.7 Evaluation metrics comparison

Conclusion and Future Work

In this research, we want to identify the most efficient predictive data mining algorithms for diagnosing oral health issues. The dataset was extracted from Kaggle's repository, cleaned, and filtered to increase precision and reduce the likelihood of bias. To identify oral health issues, we implemented a multilayer perceptron and KNN predictive data mining system. To ensure each classifier's baseline performance is at its highest possible level, it was calibrated to find its unique ideal parameter values. Algorithms' impartial predicting accuracy was evaluated using a 10-fold cross-validation assessment that included a stratified sample.

Naive bayes, multilayer perceptron and J48 decision tree induction are all promising methods for clinical prediction that we want to explore in future studies.

References

[1] Chitnis, G., Bhanushali, V., Ranade, A., Khadase, T., Pelagade, V., and Chavan, J. (2020). A review of machine learning methodologies for dental disease detection. In IEEE India Council International Subsections Conference (INDISCON), Visakhapatnam, India, (pp. 63–65), doi: 10.1109/INDISCON50162.2020.00025.

[2] Manurung, J., Perwira, Y., and Sinaga, B. (2022). Expert system to diagnose dental and oral disease using naive bayes method. In IEEE International Conference of Computer Science and Information Technology (ICOSNIKOM), Laguboti, North Sumatra, Indonesia, (pp. 01–04), doi: 10.1109/ICOSNIKOM56551.2022.10034871.

[3] Hossam, A., Mohamed, K., Tarek, R., Elsayed, A., Mostafa, H., and Selim, S. (2021). Automated dental diagnosis using deep learning, In 16th International Conference on Computer Engineering and Systems (ICCES), Cairo, Egypt, Egypt, (pp. 1–5), doi: 10.1109/ICCES54031.2021.9686185.

[4] Usha Kiruthika, S., Priya, J., and Kanaga Suba Raja, S. (2023). Systematic review of deep learning models for dental images, In 7th International Conference on Computing Methodologies and Communication (ICCMC), Erode, India, (pp. 287–291), doi: 10.1109/ICCMC56507.2023.10083729.

[5] Zegan, G., Carausu, E. M., Anistoroaei, D., Golovcencu, L., Sodor-Botezatu, A., and Dascalu, C. G. (2021). Assessment of dental students' knowledge about SarS-CoV-2 infection through an online questionnaire, In International Conference on e-Health and Bioengineering (EHB), Iasi, Romania, (pp. 1–4), doi: 10.1109/EHB52898.2021.9657697.

[6] Kurniawan, R., Hasana, W., Negara, B. S., Zakree Ahmad Nazri, M., Lestari, F., and Iskandar, I. (2021). Prediction model for diagnosis of pulpitis diseases using learning vector quantization 3. In 4th International Conference of Computer and Informatics Engineering (IC2IE), Depok, Indonesia, (pp. 9–12), doi: 10.1109/IC2IE53219.2021.9649223.

[7] Kanna, R. K., Surendhar, P. A., Rubi, J., Jyothi, G., Ambikapathy, A., and Vasuki, R. (2022, December). Human Computer Interface Application for Emotion Detection Using Facial Recognition. In *2022 IEEE International Conference on Current Development in Engineering and Technology (CCET)* (pp. 1–7). IEEE.

[8] Samiappan , D., Jayaraj, R., Nijanth Shankar, K., and Nithish Kumar, N. (2023). Analysis of dental x-ray images for the diagnosis and classification of oral conditions. In 7th International Conference on Computing Methodologies and Communication (ICCMC), Erode, India, (pp. 564–569), doi: 10.1109/ICCMC56507.2023.10083914.

[9] Moein, S., Yan, H., Das, S., Hall, M., and Eghtesady, P. (2015). Prediction of systemic-to-pulmonary artery shunt surgery outcomes using administrative data. In IEEE International Conference on Bioinformatics and Biomedicine (BIBM), Washington, DC, (pp. 737–741), doi: 10.1109/BIBM.2015.7359777.

[10] Nelli, S., and Kezia Rani, B. (2022). Prediction of early stage breast cancer by injection of gold nano particles and analyzing images using data analytics. In IEEE 2nd International Conference on Mobile Networks and Wireless Communications (ICMNWC), Tumkur, Karnataka, India, (pp. 1–5), doi: 10.1109/ICMNWC56175.2022.10031956.

[11] Sowmiya, C., and Sumitra, P. (2017). Analytical study of heart disease diagnosis using classification techniques. In IEEE International Conference on Intelligent Techniques in Control, Optimization and Signal Processing (INCOS), Srivilliputtur, India, (pp. 1–5), doi: 10.1109/ITCOSP.2017.8303115.

[12] Güven, A., Yetik, I. S., Çulhaoğlu, A., Orhan, K., and Kılıçarslan, M. K. (2020). Segmentation of teeth region via machine learning in panoramic x-ray dental images. In 28th Signal Processing and Communications Applications Conference (SIU), Gaziantep, Turkey, (pp. 1–4), doi: 10.1109/SIU49456.2020.9302520.

[13] Dhake, T., and Ansari, N. (2022). A survey on dental disease detection based on deep learning algorithm performance using various radiographs. In 5th International Conference on Advances in Science and Technology (ICAST), Mumbai, India, (pp. 291–296), doi: 10.1109/ICAST55766.2022.10039566.

[14] Jusman, Y., Fawwaz Nurkholid, M. A., Fajrul Faiz, M., Puspita, S., Evellyne, L. O., and Muhammad, K. (2022). Caries level classification using k-nearest neighbor, support vector machine, and decision tree using zernike moment invariant features. In International Conference on Data Science and Its Applications (ICoDSA), Bandung, Indonesia, (pp. 7–11), doi: 10.1109/ICoDSA55874.2022.9862879.

[15] Javid, A., Rashid, U., and Khattak, A. S. (2020). Marking early lesions in labial colored dental images using a transfer learning approach. In IEEE 23rd International Multitopic Conference (INMIC), Bahawalpur, Pakistan, (pp. 1–5), doi: 10.1109/INMIC50486.2020.9318173.

[16] Imak, A., Celebi, A., Siddique, K., Turkoglu, M., Sengur, A., and Salam, I. (2022). Dental caries detection using score-based multi-input deep convolutional neural network. *IEEE Access*, 10, 18320–18329. doi: 10.1109/ACCESS.2022.3150358.

[17] Abubakar, U. B., Boukar, M. M., and Adeshina, S. (2022). Comparison of transfer learning model accuracy for osteoporosis classification on knee radiograph. In 2nd International Conference on Computing and Machine Intelligence (ICMI), Istanbul, Turkey, (pp. 1–5), doi: 10.1109/ICMI55296.2022.9873731.

[18] Bodhe, R., Sivakumar, S., and Raghuwanshi, A. (2022). Design and development of deep learning approach for dental implant planning. In International Conference on Green Energy, Computing and Sustainable Technology (GECOST), Miri Sarawak, Malaysia, (pp. 269–274), doi: 10.1109/GECOST55694.2022.10010527.

[19] Imaizumi, H., Watanabe, A., Hirano, H., Takemura, M., Kashiwagi, H., and Monobe, S. (2017). Hippocra: doctor-to-doctor teledermatology consultation service towards future ai-based diagnosis system in Japan. In IEEE International Conference on Consumer Electronics - Taiwan (ICCE-TW), Taipei, Taiwan, (pp. 51–52), doi: 10.1109/ICCE-China.2017.7990990.

[20] Kaggle (2023). The dental condition dataset updated from Kaggle repository (www.kaggle.com) value as on dated August 2023. https://www.kaggle.com/datasets/salmansajid05/oral-diseases.

[21] Patil, B. M., Toshniwal, D., and Joshi, R. C. (2009). Predicting burn patient survivability using decision tree in WEKA environment. In IEEE International Advance Computing Conference, Patiala, India, (pp. 1353–1356), doi: 10.1109/IADCC.2009.4809213.

[22] Horino, H., Nonaka, H., Aleman Carreon, E. C., and Hiraoka, T. (2017). Development of an entropy-based feature selection method and analysis of online reviews on real estate. In IEEE International Conference on Industrial Engineering and Engineering Management (IEEM), Singapore, (pp. 2351–2355), doi: 10.1109/IEEM.2017.8290312.

28 Performance exploration of random forest (RF) and naive bayes (NB) classifiers in identification of phishing attacks

Rohit Pandey[1,a], Sowmiya Kumar[2,b] and Rachit Adhvaryu[3,c]

[1]Assistant Professor, Department of UGDX, ATLAS SkillTech University, Mumbai, Maharashtra, India

[2]Assistant Professor, Department of Computer Science and Information Technology, Jain (Deemed to be University), Bangalore, India

[3]Associate Professor, Department of Computer Science and Engineering, Faculty of Engineering and Technology, Parul Institute of Engineering and Technology, Parul University, Vadodara, Gujarat, India

Abstract

With the expansion of the web, more and more programs are being hosted online and accessible in this way. Because of this change, a hacker has begun targeting computers using phishing websites. To identify a phishing attempt, many methods have been offered. However, more work has to be done to counteract this phishing risk. The purpose of this research is to examine and assess the machine learning approach's performance in classifying phishing attacks. In order to detect phishing attempts inside the web site applications, this work used a heuristic strategy using machine learning classifier. This research evaluates three different machine learning classifiers for their ability to detect phishing scams, contrasting them with random forest (RF) and Naive bayes (NB). It shows that Random forest can successfully detect phishing assaults with a true positive rate of 96.65% by making use of characteristics unique to each website. Based on the outcomes, it seems to be a reliable classifier for identifying phishing scams.

Keywords: Intrusion attacks, naïve bayes (NB), phishing, random forest (RF)

Introduction

By seeming to be a reliable party in an electronic connection, "phishers" seek to steal sensitive information such as login credentials and credit card numbers. Cybercriminals use this method to get access to sensitive user data. The thieves will replicate legitimate websites in order to trick users. If a user enters sensitive information (such as a password, bank information, or account credentials) into one of these fraudulent websites [1–3], they risk becoming a victim of identity theft. After gaining access to your account, a criminal may make unauthorised purchases, wire funds, or do other fraudulent actions [4, 5]. Since phishing toolkits like Rock Phish and Super Phisher make it simple for attackers to set up fake websites, the number of these sites has also increased [6, 7]. These malicious sites might copy the source code of legitimate ones [8]. Therefore, a reliable anti-phishing solution is required to identify phishing websites and manage this security risk. Users are still vulnerable to new phishing assaults, despite the fact that researchers have created a number of anti-phishing detections, such as employing heuristic [9], blacklist [10], and content-based method [11]. This occurs because attackers are dynamic in their behaviour, constantly switching up their method of operation to elude detection [12, 13]. This encourages us to explore new methods of detecting phishing assaults by using machine learning classifiers. Artificial intelligence (AI) subfield known as "machine learning" employs a data-mining strategy to unearth previously hidden or previously recognised characteristics within a given dataset [14]. After that, a classification algorithm is used to the retrieved characteristics to determine if the assaults are phishing or not. In this research, we present a technique for detecting phishing attempts and checking for malicious code on webpages. The suggested research makes use of a heuristic-based strategy and website features.

The given paper is organized into following sections. Section 2 provides a literature review of studies regarding types of phishing attacks. Section 3 discusses methodology of the proposed approach. It involves defining classifiers like RF and NB. Section 4 presents results and analysis followed by conclusion and references.

Literature Review

Today, phishing assaults may take many forms. There are three main forms of phishing attacks: social engineering, malware, and content injection. For the purpose of tricking the unwary into visiting a malicious website, the term "deceptive phishing" [15] is used to describe the practice of sending mass emails to multiple recipients

[a]rohit.pandey@atlasuniversity.edu.in, [b]soumya.k@jainuniversity.ac.in, [c]rachit.adhvaryu24310@paruluniversity.ac.in

DOI: 10.1201/9781003534136-28

with the hopes that at least one of them will fall for a scam and click on a link to a fake site or re-enter their account information. The term "malware-based phishing" describes assaults that are designed to install and run dangerous software on victims' computers [16, 17]. The most common method of spreading malware is via downloadable attachments sent over email. Key loggers and screen grabbers, two types of spyware that record keystrokes and relay the data to the phisher are often used in phishing assaults. The victim's PC may be taken over in subsequent attacks [18]. Content injection is a phishing tactic in which a malicious actor modifies legitimate website content. This is done to trick the user into visiting a website that is not the actual one so that sensitive information may be submitted [19]. Blacklist-based methods, content-based methods, and heuristic-based methods are all employed to combat phishing assaults [20].

Proposed Methodology

A. Dataset Collection from Websites or Repositories
Dataset collection is the initial step of implementation. During the dataset phase, it is crucial to ensure the reliability of the obtained results. Phishing and legitimate operations may be better understood and explained with the use of this dataset. After the dataset has been analyzed, the findings may be utilized to make predictions about potential phishing attacks. The Phishing website dataset is the source of the dataset on Kaggle [21]. Thirty distinct characteristics of phishing websites have been compiled. The gathered dataset contains the categorical variables "Legitimate," "Suspicious," and "Phishy," which have been converted to numeric values by substituting the values "1," "0," and "-1," respectively [21].

B. Defining Phishing Website Features
The features of phishing website are collected and are subjected to noise removal. It means the final phishing features are reduced by removing redundant and repetitive features.

C. Extracting Features and Attributes
In order to improve the prediction model's accuracy, feature selection techniques were utilized to isolate and eliminate superfluous details. In order to classify the phishing website, its characteristics were first learned. In this research, the feature selection method is used to identify the most relevant attributes for efficient phishing website detection. As a result, the original list of 30 phishing elements was whittled down to only 10. This is done so that a distinguishable difference may be seen between legitimate and fraudulent websites.

D. Classifiers- RF and NB
The random forest (RF) is a supervised machine learning approach. It may be used for regression analysis as well as classification [22]. The system is comprised of several decision trees. The technique operates by using a stochastic process to choose attributes at random, afterwards generating numerous decision trees and thereafter computing the average outcome.

The Naïve bayes (NB) algorithm, as described in reference [23], is designed to be used on the premise that the characteristics within each class are independent of each other. However, empirical evidence suggests that NB may still perform well even when this assumption is violated.

E. Testing and Training of Model
To predict how well a model would function in the real world, researchers utilize n-fold cross-validation or rotation estimation. The process entails randomly dividing a sample dataset D into s distinct and non-overlapping parts. In every iteration, the model is trained using the whole dataset and then evaluated on the remaining folds. In the present study, the value of n was set to 10 in our suggested technique.

F. Evaluation Based on Metrics
The appraisal of predictive data mining algorithms may be assessed using many metrics. When evaluating the predictability of various predictive data mining methods, it is necessary to evaluate certain values that assess the model's goodness of fit and error measures. The metrics utilized during the research are as follows.

$$\text{Precision} = TP / (TP + FP) \tag{1}$$

$$\text{Recall} = TP / (TP + FN) \tag{2}$$

$$\text{F-measure} = (2 * \text{precision} * \text{recall}) / (\text{precision} + \text{recall}) \tag{3}$$

True Positive rate (TPR) = TP / positive   (4)

False Positive rate (FPR) = FP / negative   (5)

Figure 28.1 presents the flow of methodology adopted in the study.

Result and Implementation

Figure 28.2 presents the pre-processing and extraction of phishing website dataset showing distinct 10 attributes that needs to be worked upon. These are phishing features namely IP_address, URL_length, slash_redirect, sub_domain etc.

```
┌─────────────────────────────────┐
│  Dataset collection from websites or │
│           repositories              │
└─────────────────────────────────┘
                 │
┌─────────────────────────────────┐
│   Defining phishing website features │
└─────────────────────────────────┘
                 │
┌─────────────────────────────────┐
│   Extracting features and attributes │
└─────────────────────────────────┘
                 │
┌─────────────────────────────────┐
│  Build model using classifiers- RF and NB │
└─────────────────────────────────┘
                 │
┌─────────────────────────────────┐
│    Testing and training of model    │
└─────────────────────────────────┘
                 │
┌─────────────────────────────────┐
│ Evaluation based on metrics- accuracy, FPR, │
│         precision, recall            │
└─────────────────────────────────┘
```

Figure 28.1 Workflow of the proposed approach

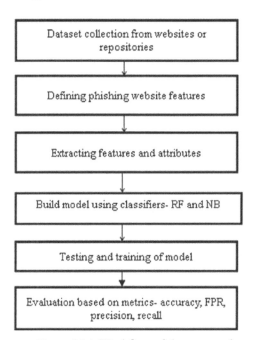

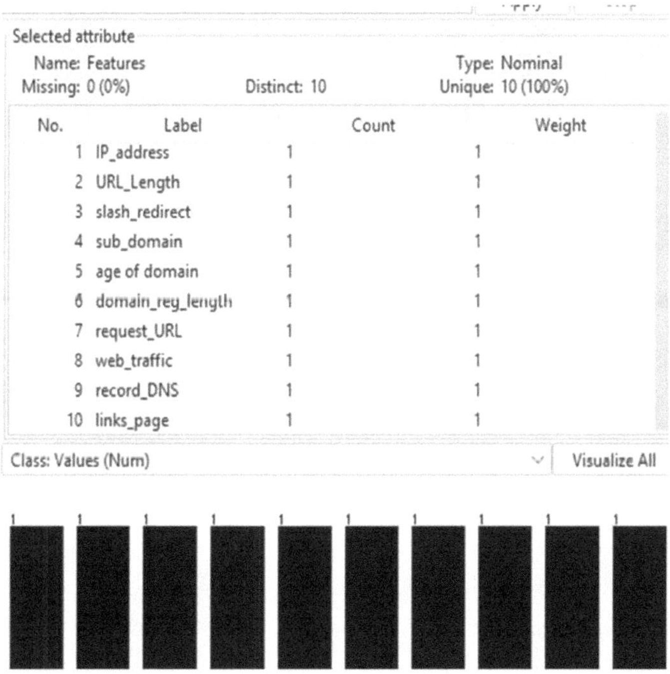

Figure 28.2 Defining attributes and features extraction

Figure 28.3 displays the successful execution of RF classifier on phishing website dataset. The model is evaluated on full training dataset by taking features extracted into consideration.

Figure 28.4 shows the visualization of dataset by plotting features on x- axis and values on y –axis. The portions marked by rectangles with values -1 are termed as "Phishy" or malevolent while the portions with values 1 are legitimate.

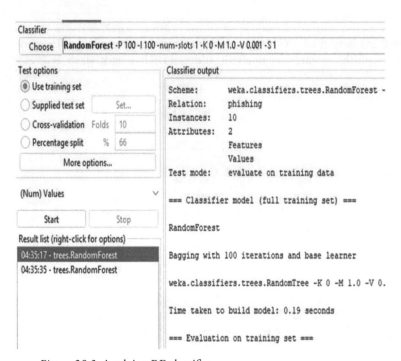

Figure 28.3 Applying RF classifier

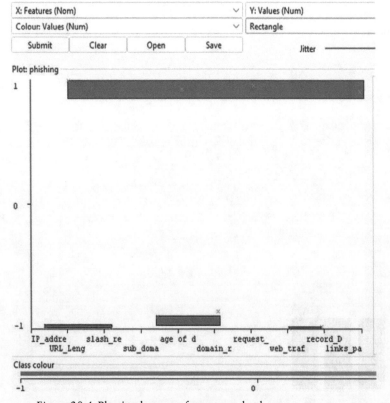

Figure 28.4 Plotting between features and values

Table 28.1 Performance of classifiers with respect to phishing website dataset.

Metrics	RF	NB
Precision (%)	95.8	92.3
Recall (%)	96.4	94.4
Accuracy (%)	96.65	94.25
F-measure (%)	95.8	94.4
TPR	0.95	0.76
FPR	0.65	0.75

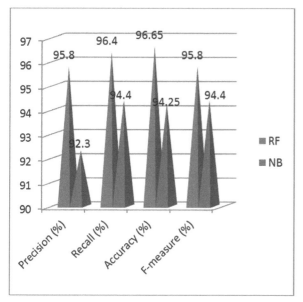

Figure 28.5 Performance evaluation of RF and NB

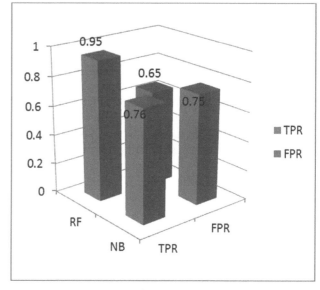

Figure 28.6 TPR and FPR comparison of RF and NB classifiers

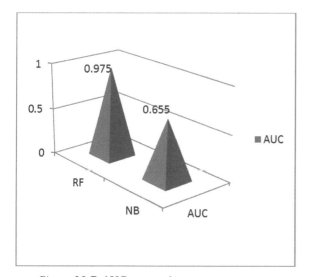

Figure 28.7 AUC comparison

Results and Analysis

The present study employs a supervised machine learning methodology due to the availability of labeled data in the sample dataset, distinguishing between phishing and legal instances. Moreover, supervised machine learning yields favorable outcomes by effectively mitigating mistakes. The research employs two classifiers to examine the unique outcomes seen in different machine learning classifiers. The two classification algorithms under consideration are RF and NB. The present research used several assessment metrics, including accuracy, true positive rate (TPR), false positive rate (FPR), precision, recall, and f-measure, to examine distinct measurements. Table 28.1 displays the outcomes obtained after applying machine learning classifiers to train and test the dataset.

Table 28.1 show that our approach works best with RF classifier with an accuracy of 96.65 % and lowest v as 0.65

Figure 28.5 shows the performance evaluation of RF and NB.

Figure 28.6 shows that the proposed methodology when used with random forest classifier gives the lowest FPR value (0.65). Lower FPR value denotes that the system is less faulty with high performance.

Figure 28.7 shows the comparison between classifiers based on Area under curve (AUC) which is used to measure goodness or badness of the proposed approach. A range of value between 0.5-1.0 shows perfect prediction.

In general, the AUC values substantiated the efficacy of the recent phishing studies in accurately detecting phishing website applications.

Conclusion and Future Work

The current study has provided an evaluation of the efficacy of the suggested methodology in the identification and detection of phishing assaults. The suggested methodology employs machine learning classifiers, namely Random Forest (RF) and Naïve Bayes (NB), to accurately classify instances of phishing by using pertinent variables. The study examines the utilization of real-world phishing and genuine samples in the context of applied phishing dataset. The experimental findings indicate that the suggested methodology achieved a notable accuracy rate of 96.65% while using Random Forest as the classifier.

References

[1] Ramadevi, P., Akshaya, K., Sangamitra, S. D., and Pritikha, A. P. (2023). Analysis of phishing attack in distributed cloud systems using machine learning. In Second International Conference on Electrical, Electronics, Information and Communication Technologies (ICEEICT), Trichirappalli, India, (pp. 1–5), doi: 10.1109/ICEEICT56924.2023.10157447.

[2] Altamash, M., and Singh, S. N. (2022). Reconnaissance of credentials through phishing attacks & it's detection using machine learning. In International Conference on Machine Learning, Big Data, Cloud and Parallel Computing (COM-IT-CON), Faridabad, India, (pp. 350–358), doi: 10.1109/COM-IT-CON54601.2022.9850698.

[3] Chinnasamy, P., Kumaresan, N., Selvaraj, R., Dhanasekaran, S., Ramprathap, K., and Boddu, S. (2022). An efficient phishing attack detection using machine learning algorithms. In International Conference on Advancements in Smart, Secure and Intelligent Computing (ASSIC), Bhubaneswar, India, (pp. 1–6), doi: 10.1109/ASSIC55218.2022.10088399.

[4] Basit, A., Zafar, M., Javed, A. R., and Jalil, Z. (2020). A novel ensemble machine learning method to detect phishing attack. In IEEE 23rd International Multitopic Conference (INMIC), Bahawalpur, Pakistan, (pp. 1–5), doi: 10.1109/INMIC50486.2020.9318210.

[5] Usha Kiruthika, S., Priya, J., and Kanaga Suba Raja, S. (2023). Systematic review of deep learning models for dental images. In 7th International Conference on Computing Methodologies and Communication (ICCMC), Erode, India, (pp. 287–291), doi: 10.1109/ICCMC56507.2023.10083729.

[6] Ripa, S. P., Islam, F., and Arifuzzaman, M. (2021). The emergence threat of phishing attack and the detection techniques using machine learning models. In International Conference on Automation, Control and Mechatronics for Industry 4.0 (ACMI), Rajshahi, Bangladesh, (pp. 1–6), doi: 10.1109/ACMI53878.2021.9528204.

[7] Kunju, M. V., Dainel, E., Anthony, H. C., and Bhelwa, S. (2019). Evaluation of phishing techniques based on machine learning. In International Conference on Intelligent Computing and Control Systems (ICCS), Madurai, India, (pp. 963–968), doi: 10.1109/ICCS45141.2019.9065639.

[8] Chandra, A., Gregorius, Immanuel, M. S. J., Gunawan, A. A. S., and Anderies, (2022). Accuracy comparison of different machine learning models in phishing detection. In 5th International Conference on Information and Communications Technology (ICOIACT), Yogyakarta, Indonesia, (pp. 24–29), doi: 10.1109/ICOIACT55506.2022.9972107.

[9] Uddin, M. M., Arfatul Islam, K., Mamun, M., Tiwari, V. K., and Park, J. (2022). A comparative analysis of machine learning-based website phishing detection using URL information. In 5th International Conference on Pattern Recognition and Artificial Intelligence (PRAI), Chengdu, China, (pp. 220–224), doi: 10.1109/PRAI55851.2022.9904055.

[10] Uplenchwar, S., Sawant, V., Surve, P., Deshpande, S., and Kelkar, S. (2022). Phishing attack detection on text messages using machine learning techniques. In IEEE Pune Section International Conference (PuneCon), Pune, India, (pp. 1–5), doi: 10.1109/PuneCon55413.2022.10014876.

[11] Jain, S., and Gupta, C. (2023). A support vector machine learning technique for detection of phishing websites. In 6th International Conference on Information Systems and Computer Networks (ISCON), Mathura, India, (pp. 1–6), doi: 10.1109/ISCON57294.2023.10111968.

[12] Ortiz Garcés, I., Cazares, M. F., and Andrade, R. O. (2019). Detection of phishing attacks with machine learning techniques in cognitive security architecture. In International Conference on Computational Science and Computational Intelligence (CSCI), Las Vegas, NV, USA, (pp. 366–370), doi: 10.1109/CSCI49370.2019.00071.

[13] Sönmez, Y., Tuncer, T., Gökal, H., and Avcı, E. (2018). Phishing web sites features classification based on extreme learning machine. In 6th International Symposium on Digital Forensic and Security (ISDFS), Antalya, Turkey, (pp. 1–5), doi: 10.1109/ISDFS.2018.8355342.

[14] Bouijij, H., and Berqia, A. (2021). Machine learning algorithms evaluation for phishing URLs classification. In 4th International Symposium on Advanced Electrical and Communication Technologies (ISAECT), Alkhobar, Saudi Arabia, (pp. 01–05), doi: 10.1109/ISAECT53699.2021.9668489.

[15] Alkawaz, M. H., Steven, S. J., Hajamydeen, A. I., and Ramli, R. (2021). A comprehensive survey on identification and analysis of phishing website based on machine learning methods. In IEEE 11th IEEE Symposium on Computer Applications & Industrial Electronics (ISCAIE), Penang, Malaysia, (pp. 82–87), doi: 10.1109/ISCAIE51753.2021.9431794.

[16] Kumar, Y., and Subba, B. (2021). A lightweight machine learning based security framework for detecting phishing attacks. In 2021 International Conference on Communication Systems & NETworkS (COMSNETS), Bangalore, India, (pp. 184–188), doi: 10.1109/COMSNETS51098.2021.9352828.

[17] Salahdine, F., El Mrabet, Z., and Kaabouch, N. (2021). Phishing attacks detection a machine learning-based approach. In IEEE 12th Annual Ubiquitous Computing, Electronics & Mobile Communication Conference (UEMCON), New York, NY, USA, (pp. 0250–0255), doi: 10.1109/UEMCON53757.2021.9666627.

[18] Binti Md Noh, N., Bin, M. N., and Basri, M. (2021). Phishing website detection using random forest and support vector machine: a comparison. In 2nd International Conference on Artificial Intelligence and Data Sciences (AiDAS), IPOH, Malaysia, (pp. 1–5), doi: 10.1109/AiDAS53897.2021.9574282.

[19] Aslam, S., and Nassif, A. B. (2023). Phish-identifier: machine learning based classification of phishing attacks. In Advances in Science and Engineering Technology International Conferences (ASET), Dubai, United Arab Emirates, (pp. 1–6), doi: 10.1109/ASET56582.2023.10180869.

[20] Vilas, M. M., Ghansham, K. P., Jaypralash, S. P., and Shila, P. (2019). Detection of phishing website using machine learning approach. In 4th International Conference on Electrical, Electronics, Communication, Computer Technologies and Optimization Techniques (ICEECCOT), Mysuru, India, (pp. 384–389), doi: 10.1109/ICEECCOT46775.2019.9114695.

[21] Kaggle (2023). The phishing website dataset updated from Kaggle repository (www.kaggle.com) value as on dated August 2023. https://www.kaggle.com/datasets/akashkr/phishing-website-dataset?select=dataset.csv.

[22] Galen, C., and Steele, R. (2020). Performance maintenance over time of random forest-based malware detection models. In 2020 11th IEEE Annual Ubiquitous Computing, Electronics & Mobile Communication Conference (UEMCON), New York, NY, USA, (pp. 0536–0541), doi: 10.1109/UEMCON51285.2020.9298068.

[23] Mustafa, T., and Karabatak, M. (2023). Feature selection for phishing website by using naive bayes classifier. In 11th International Symposium on Digital Forensics and Security (ISDFS), Chattanooga, TN, USA, (pp. 1–4), doi: 10.1109/ISDFS58141.2023.10131884.

29 Performance assessment of gaussian process and MLP for categorization and dissection of diabetes retinopathy

Warish Patel[1,a], Vinay Chowdary[2,b] and Sanjeev Kumar Mandal[3,c]

[1]Associate Professor, Department of Computer Science and Engineering, Faculty of Engineering and Technology, Parul Institute of Engineering and Technology, Parul University, Vadodara, Gujarat, India

[2]Associate Professor, Department of UGDX, ATLAS SkillTech University, Mumbai, Maharashtra, India

[3]Assistant Professor, Department of Computer Science and Information Technology, Jain (Deemed to be University), Bangalore, India

Abstract

Diabetic retinopathy, a side effect of persistently high blood sugar, is not identified and treated promptly; it might result in complete blindness. Thus, early medical diagnosis and associated medical treatment are crucial to preventing the serious effects of diabetic retinopathy. Ophthalmologists have difficulty physically identifying diabetic retinopathy, and patients may suffer excruciating agony while they wait for a diagnosis. Automated technology enables early detection of diabetic retinopathy and prompt treatment to stop further eye damage. In this article, a machine learning strategy is given for collecting properties such exudates, haemorrhage, and micro aneurysms, and then categorizing them using machine learning classifiers like the Gaussian process and Multi-layer perceptron (MLP). Based on the experimental findings, MLP has the best accuracy of 92%, with a precision score of 0.91 and a recall score of 0.92.

Keywords: Classification, diabetes, gaussian process, MLP, retinopathy

Introduction

Blood glucose levels are increased in people with diabetes, a group of metabolic illnesses brought on by insufficient insulin synthesis or by poor cellular responsiveness to endogenous insulin secretion. Diabetic retinopathy is a prevalent condition associated with diabetes [1]. The condition under discussion is a highly prevalent and serious ocular ailment. The condition causes damage to the retinal microvasculature, leading to visual impairment. The likelihood of developing diabetic retinopathy is positively correlated with advancing age, therefore indicating that those in the middle-aged and older demographic who have diabetes are more susceptible to this condition. Non-proliferative diabetic retinopathy (NPDR) is an initial phase of diabetic retinopathy [2]. During this particular stage, there is a phenomenon where minuscule blood vessels located inside the retina experience leakage of either blood or fluid. The presence of leaked fluid within the ocular structure leads to retinal oedema or the formation of deposits known as exudates. proliferative diabetic retinopathy (PDR) is characterised by the eye's response to the extensive closure of the retinal blood supply, wherein it initiates the growth or replenishment of new blood vessels in the retina [3]. Regrettably, the newly formed anomalous blood vessels do not effectively restore the retina's normal blood circulation. Instead, they have a propensity to haemorrhage readily and are frequently associated by scar tissue, which can lead to wrinkling or detachment of the retina. Various physical examinations can be employed to identify the presence of diabetic retinopathy, including as pupil dilation, visual acuity assessment, and optical coherence tomography, among others. However, it is important to note that these procedures can be rather time-consuming and patients may experience significant discomfort. This study centres on the utilisation of machine learning classifiers for the automated computer assisted identification of diabetic retinopathy. Specifically, the characteristics of haemorrhage, micro aneurysms and exudates are extracted and analysed.

"The given paper is organized into following sections. Section 2 provides a literature review of studies regarding diabetes classification and diagnosis. Section 3 discusses methodology of the proposed approach. It involves pre-processing of retinopathy images, segmentation, feature extraction and classification. Section 4 presents results and analysis followed by conclusion and references."

[a]warishkumar.patel@paruluniversity.ac.in, [b]vinay.chowdary@atlasuniversity.edu.in, [c]km.sanjeev@jainuniversity.ac.in

DOI: 10.1201/9781003534136-29

Literature Review

Using the MESSIDOR dataset, the authors of [4] proposed a fractal analysis and random forest based approach for grading diabetic retinopathy. Fractal dimensions were calculated as features and used in the system's picture segmentation. They were unable to differentiate between diabetic retinopathy of mild and severe severity. Diabetic retinopathy and healthy retinal pictures can be automatically classified with the use of a concurrent neural network (CNN) and a support vector machine (SVM), as suggested in [5]. Features comprised of exudates, haemorrhage and micro aneurysms. A neural network-based feature extractor and a SVM-based classifier make up the two halves of the author's suggested system. Using area and number extraction, the authors of [6] suggested a technique to better diagnose diabetic retinopathy of micro aneurysms using color fundus images from the dataset. Fundus pictures underwent green channel extraction, histogram equalization, and a morphological technique in pre-processing. Micro aneurysms were detected using principal component analysis (PCA), limited adaptive histogram equalization (LAHE), a morphological procedure, and an averaging filter, with classification performed using a SVM. The technique proposed by the authors in reference [7] aims to identify cases of diabetic retinopathy through the use of several textural features and a machine learning classification algorithm. The local energy-based shape histogram is utilized to extract two distinct characteristics, namely bleeding and exudates. SVM are commonly employed for the purpose of learning and classifying retrieved histograms by using feature vectors. In their study, the authors presented a novel system (referenced as [8]) that addresses the issue of diabetic retinopathy classification. The suggested system employs fuzzy C methods for feature extraction and utilizes SVM for classification purposes. The extraction of blood vessels is accomplished by the use of a top hat filter and mathematical morphological techniques. The characteristics selected for analysis include retinal vascular density and exudates. The process of extracting exudate is accomplished by the use of fuzzy C means segmentation. The work shown in reference [9] outlines a methodology for detecting exudates in color fundus images using morphology-based techniques. The proposed model employs grayscale conversion, histogram equalization, logical AND operation, and watershed transformation. The technology generates an output that includes the impacted ranges of exudates in cases of diabetic retinopathy. The technique presented by the authors in [10] involves the utilization of soft margin SVM for the categorization of non-proliferative diabetic retinopathy. The utilization of hard exudates observed in retinal fundus pictures serves as a means to categorize the degree of severity in cases of non-proliferative diabetic retinopathy. However, it should be noted that the approach lacks the inclusion of micro aneurysms and haemorrhage as identifiable characteristics. In their study, [11] and colleagues presented a method for the automatic identification of hard exudates. This method utilizes two distinct properties, namely sharp edge and color highlights. The detection technique encompassed many methods, including color-based categorization, sharp edge detection, and optic disc extraction. The training and testing procedures were conducted utilizing the DRIVE dataset. The graphical user interface of the system was implemented using MATLAB.

Proposed Methodology

A. Collection of Images from Dataset

The present study utilized a publicly accessible dataset from Kaggle for the purpose of detecting diabetic retinopathy [12]. This dataset was compiled using images sourced from publicly available datasets on retinopathy detection. Within the Kaggle dataset, there exists a collection of images that exhibit both the presence and absence of diabetic retinopathy. A subset of these images, comprising those with diabetic retinopathy as well as normal images, was selected for analysis. The chosen abnormal images encompassed instances of exudates, hemorrhage, and micro aneurysms.

B. Pre-Processing of Images

In order to identify anomalies related with fundus imaging, it is necessary to do pre-processing on the photos. This pre-processing aims to rectify the uneven lighting present in the input image, therefore eliminating contrast and noise between exudates and the background pixels of the image. The preprocessing techniques encompass adaptive histogram equalization (AHE) and discrete wavelet transform (DWT) Figure 29.1 and Figure 29.2 have been attached to provide the preprocessing of image as example.

AHE: - The use of adaptive histogram equalization, a technique utilized to enhance contrast in photographs, is implemented on the eye image that has been converted to grayscale. Let us consider a sub picture I with dimensions m × n pixels, which is centered on a pixel P with, coordinates (a, b). The image is subjected to a filtering process, resulting in the generation of another sub image P with dimensions (a × b) pixels, as described by the following equation:

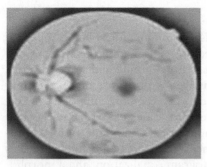 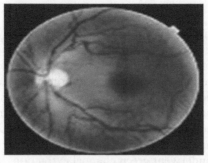

Figure 29.1 (a) (b) Diabetes retinopathy eye images after AHE [12]

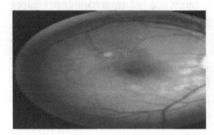 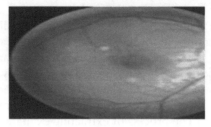

Figure 29.2 (a) (b) Diabetes retinopathy eye images after DWT [12]

$$\text{In} = \{[\alpha\,(n) - \alpha\,(min)] \,/\, [\alpha\,(max) - \alpha\,(min)]\} \tag{1}$$

Where

$$\alpha\,(n) = \{1 + \exp(\sigma_i \,/\, \mu_i - P)\} \tag{2}$$

And max, min denotes minimum and maximum intensity values of image, μ indicates mean and σ represents standard deviation.

The adaptive histogram equalization technique has led to an increase in brightness in the dark region of the input eye picture, which was poorly lighted. Conversely, the brightly illuminated side of the image either remains unchanged or experiences a reduction in brightness. Consequently, the overall luminance of the eye image in the output is consistent, as seen in Figure 29.1.

DWT: DWT which utilizes sub-band coding, has been seen to provide efficient computational performance in the calculation of the Wavelet Transform. The implementation of this approach is straightforward and results in a reduction in both computing time and resource use. The wavelet transform is a mathematical technique that breaks down a given signal into a collection of fundamental functions known as wavelets. Wavelets are derived by the process of dilations and shifting from a singular prototype wavelet $\Delta(t)$, sometimes referred to as the mother wavelet, as described by the above equation.

$$\Delta_{i,j}(t) = \Delta(t - j) \,/\, i\sqrt{i} \tag{3}$$

C. Segmentation of Exudates, Haemorrhage and Micro Aneurysms

Smoothing, masking, and bitwise AND were performed after initial image processing in order to segment exudates. High frequency distribution noise in an image can be eliminated with the help of smoothing. Convolving the picture with the kernel of a low-pass filter produces a blurred effect. With masking, we define a tiny "image piece" and apply it to the bigger picture to make changes. Images may be manipulated and key features extracted with the use of bitwise AND operations. When masking a picture, bitwise operations come in handy. These processes allow for the generation of images. These manipulations may assist improve the quality of the input photographs in various ways. Here, we merge the input image with the masked image to get rid of everything in the original image that isn't the optic disc and the exudates. After extracting the exudate, the abnormal and normal pictures are shown in Figure 29.3.

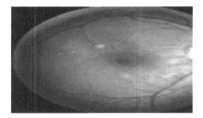

Figure 29.3 (a) Normal image after exudates segmentation (b) Abnormal image after exudate segmentation [12]

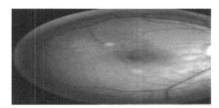

Figure 29.4 (a) Normal image after haemorrhage segmentation (b) Abnormal image after haemorrhage segmentation [12]

Image erosion and dilation are used to segment micro aneurysms and haemorrhage. Images undergo morphological operations like enlarging or shrinking. Erosion is followed by enlargement, which is the definition of morphological opening. With an opening, you may get rid of the glare and seal up the fissures. The resulting space between characteristics tends to widen. The images with and without segmentation are shown in Figure 29.4.

D. Feature Extraction Values
Following the aforementioned preparation methods, we receive pictures with the haemorrhage or exudate clearly visible. Images that have been discovered have their feature values extracted. Radius, diameter, arc length, and area are the four feature values that are derived.

E. Applying Classifiers
Gaussian Process:- Non-parametric machine learning techniques for classification and regression may be built around this generalization of the Gaussian probability distribution [13].

Multilayer perceptron (MLP): The proposed model is a feedforward artificial neural network that effectively translates input data sets to a corresponding set of desired outputs [14].

Result and Implementation

Figure 29.5 shows the working of MLP classifier which is applied on diabetes retinopathy dataset shown in having attributes micro aneurysms, hard exudates, macular edema, PDR, NPDR, haemorrhage, cotton-wool spots and ischemia. The classifier gives weight values with each sigmoid node. Figure 29.6 depicts Classification of Dataset Using MLP Classifier.

Results & Analysis

Table 29.1 shows the results of feature values extracted achieved after getting detected images of exudates and haemorrhage.

Evaluation metrics used to perform validation of classifiers are sensitivity, specificity, accuracy, precision and recall. They are defined as:

The capacity of a test to accurately identify patients with illness is known as sensitivity.

"Sensitivity = TP / (TP + FN)" (4)

The concept of specificity refers to the capacity of a diagnostic test to accurately identify individuals who do not possess a certain disease or condition.

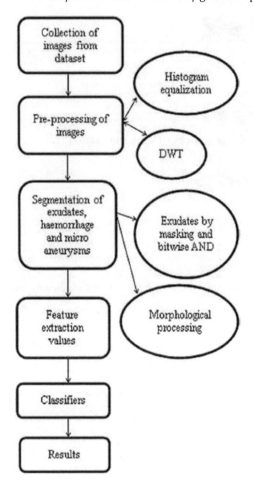

Figure 29.5 Methodology workflow

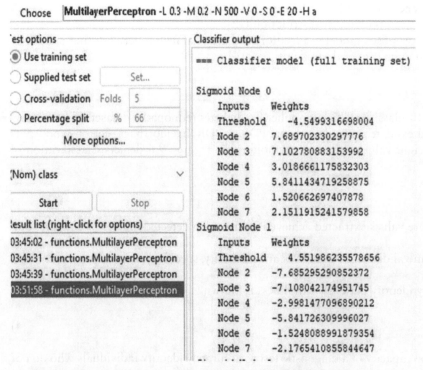

Figure 29.6 Classification of Dataset Using MLP Classifier

Table 29.1 Feature values of normal, PDR and NPDR images.

Types of images	Radius (CM)	Diameter (CM)	Arc length (CM)	Area (CM2)
Normal	120-125	240-250	4.5-5.5	60-70
PDR	400-410	800-820	135-138	250-255
NPDR	300-305	600-610	62.5-65.5	230-235

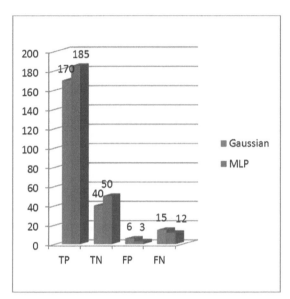

Figure 29.7 Performance evaluation of classifiers- Gaussian and MLP

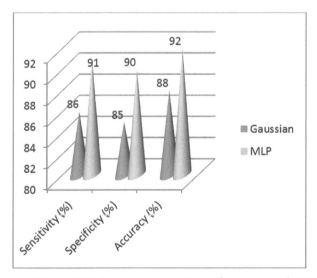

Figure 29.8 Accuracy comparison of gaussian and MLP classifiers

"Specificity = TN / (TN + FP)" (5)

A true positive (TP) occurs when an individual may use a positive test result to make a diagnosis of the disease. When a test yields a negative result but no illness is suspected, this is known as a "true negative" (TN). When a person receives a positive test result but does not disclose it, this is known as a false positive (FP). If the test is negative but the person is still at risk of having the condition, we have a case of false negative (FN).

It is seen in Figure 29.7 that MLP attains higher TP and lowest FP values which indicates that MLP is much effective in identification and diagnosis of diabetes retinopathy to make aware the patients of blindness.

Figure 29.8 show that MLP classifier attains higher accuracy of 92% in diabetes retinopathy disease.

Conclusion and Future Work

This new technique can identify micro aneurysms, exudates, and bleeding. Masking, smoothing, and bitwise AND are all performed for exudate identification, leading to more accurate calculations and extractions. Opening, dilation, and erosion are morphological techniques used for detecting haemorrhage and micro aneurysms. After that, the characteristics are sent into either a Gaussian or an MLP classifier. Metrics like as accuracy, sensitivity, specificity, etc. are used to compare the two classifiers' effectiveness. The results show that MLP classifier has a superior detection and diagnosis accuracy of 92% in early stages of diabetic retinopathy. The patients' eyesight would be protected and the disease's devastating effects mitigated.

References

[1] Naik, A. U., and Kulkarni, R. K. (2020). Artificial neural network-based detection of diabetes and its effects on vision - a survey. In 5th International Conference on Communication and Electronics Systems (ICCES), Coimbatore, India, (pp. 1113–1118), doi: 10.1109/ICCES48766.2020.9138057.

[2] Wang, X., Lu, Y., and Chen, W.-B. (2020). Promote retinal lesion detection for diabetic retinopathy stage classification. In IEEE Conference on Multimedia Information Processing and Retrieval (MIPR), Shenzhen, China, (pp. 31–34), doi: 10.1109/MIPR49039.2020.00014.

[3] Jiang, H., Yang, K., Gao, M., Zhang, D., Ma, H., and Qian, W. (2019). An interpretable ensemble deep learning model for diabetic retinopathy disease classification. In 41st Annual International Conference of the IEEE Engineering in Medicine and Biology Society (EMBC), Berlin, Germany, (pp. 2045–2048), doi: 10.1109/EMBC.2019.8857160.

[4] Alzami, F., Abdussalam, Megantara, R. A., Fanani, A. Z., and Purwanto, (2019). Diabetic retinopathy grade classification based on fractal analysis and random forest. In International Seminar on Application for Technology of Information and Communication (iSemantic), Semarang, Indonesia, (pp. 272–276), doi: 10.1109/ISEMANTIC.2019.8884217.

[5] Perez-Siguas, R., Matta-Solis, E., Remuzgo-Artezano, A., Matta-Solis, H., Matta-Perez, H., and Perez-Siguas, L. (2023). Digital imaging system for the detection of diabetic retinopathy. In Third International Conference on Advances in Electrical, Computing, Communication and Sustainable Technologies (ICAECT), Bhilai, India, (pp. 1–4), doi: 10.1109/ICAECT57570.2023.10117640.

[6] Valarmathi, S., and Vijayabhanu, R. (2021). A survey on diabetic retinopathy disease detection and classification using deep learning techniques. In Seventh International conference on Bio Signals, Images, and Instrumentation (ICBSII), Chennai, India, (pp. 1–4), doi: 10.1109/ICBSII51839.2021.9445163.

[7] Lyona, C., Menezes, J., Shinde, T., Gavhane, M., Rohatgi, R. M., and Chavan, S. (2020). Classification of retinal images in stages of diabetic retinopathy using deep learning. In 2nd International Conference on Advances in Computing, Communication Control and Networking (ICACCCN), Greater Noida, India, (pp. 228–231), doi: 10.1109/ICACCCN51052.2020.9362913.

[8] Giroti, I., Das, J. K. A., Harshith, N. M., and Thahniyath, G. (2023). Diabetic retinopathy detection & classification using efficient net model. In International Conference on Artificial Intelligence and Applications (ICAIA) Alliance Technology Conference (ATCON-1), Bangalore, India, (pp. 1–6), doi: 10.1109/ICAIA57370.2023.10169756.

[9] Lazuardi, R. N., Abiwinanda, N., Suryawan, T. H., Hanif, M., and Handayani, A. (2020). Automatic diabetic retinopathy classification with efficient net. In IEEE Region 10 Conference (TENCON), Osaka, Japan, (pp. 756–760), doi: 10.1109/TENCON50793.2020.9293941.

[10] Kanna, R. K., Surendhar, P. A., Rubi, J., Jyothi, G., Ambikapathy, A., and Vasuki, R. (2022, December). Human Computer Interface Application for Emotion Detection Using Facial Recognition. In 2022 IEEE International Conference on Current Development in Engineering and Technology (CCET) (pp. 1–7). IEEE.

[11] Singh Gautam, A., Kumar Jana, S., and Dutta, M. P. (2019). Automated diagnosis of diabetic retinopathy using image processing for non-invasive biomedical application. In International Conference on Intelligent Computing and Control Systems (ICCS), Madurai, India, (pp. 809–812), doi: 10.1109/ICCS45141.2019.9065446.

[12] Kaggle (2023). The diabetes retinopathy dataset uploaded from Kaggle repository (www.kaggle.com) value as on dated August 2023. https://www.kaggle.com/datasets/mariaherrerot/eyepacspreprocess.

[13] Fradi, A., Samir, C., and Yao, A. -F. (2018). Manifold-based inference for a supervised gaussian process classifier. In IEEE International Conference on Acoustics, Speech and Signal Processing (ICASSP), Calgary, AB, Canada, (pp. 4239–4243), doi: 10.1109/ICASSP.2018.8461840.

[14] Dahiya, S., Handa, S. S., and Singh, N. P. (2016). Impact of bagging on MLP classifier for credit evaluation. In 3rd International Conference on Computing for Sustainable Global Development (INDIACom), New Delhi, India, (pp. 3794–3800).

30 Deployment and analysis of linear regression and REPtree for finding anomalies in network traffic

Suneetha K.[1,a], Kamal Sutariya[2,b] and Raghav Garg[3,c]

[1]Professor, Department of Computer Science and Information Technology, Jain (Deemed to be University), Bangalore, India

[2]Associate Professor, Department of Computer Science and Engineering, Faculty of Engineering and Technology, Parul Institute of Engineering and Technology, Parul University, Vadodara, Gujarat, India

[3]Associate Professor, Department of Computer Science & Engineering, Tula's Institute, Dehradun, India

Abstract

The prevalence of complex cyber-attacks has elevated the significance of network security as a discipline. Network anomalies pose a significant risk to network security because they can disrupt normal system operation. Identifying these irregularities is crucial to the network's upkeep. Although it is now recognized that machine learning algorithms may detect network abnormalities, this fact is not commonly understood. This study compares the results of two algorithms, linear regression and REPTree, using a dataset including profiles of network traffic. The purpose of this research is to give a thorough evaluation of existing machine learning methods for identifying network abnormalities. It will also contribute to the enhanced network security. The study provides a comparison of two classifiers' results on the dataset. The F1-Score, recall, precision, and accuracy will be used to evaluate them. The investigation's results will be used to guide the creation of novel approaches that may be used to bolster network security. This data set is perfect for comparing the efficacy of different anomaly detection methods in a network setting.

Keywords: Anomaly detection, linear regression, machine learning, REPtree

Introduction

Network traffic has become increasingly important to our daily lives as the number of internet-connected gadgets continues to grow. The modern society heavily depends on the internet for a multitude of tasks, including but not limited to streaming multimedia content and conducting secure online transactions. Nevertheless, the increasing volume of data being transferred across networks presents significant challenges in terms of ensuring both reliability and security. As the frequency of network attacks continues to rise, more and more businesses and organisations are beginning to prioritise network security [1]. Anomaly detection is a significant technology employed in network security to find and detect abnormal behaviour among various types of network data. Network data, including user activity logs and traffic data, can benefit from this kind of detection. This detection can be made using either a machine learning-based or a statistical method [2]. Statistical-based approaches have the capability to detect deviations from anticipated patterns. In contrast, machine learning-based solutions employ algorithms to acquire knowledge from the observed patterns of typical behaviour. Data leaks and server outages are only two of the problems that can arise from lax network anomaly detection. The occurrence of these issues can be attributed to a range of sources, including hardware malfunctions, intentional security breaches, and software glitches. If not identified, these factors have the potential to impact an organization's operational efficiency and financial stability [3, 4]. Severe repercussions, such as the loss of private information or the malfunction of essential systems, might result from a successful cyber-attack. Reputational harm can accompany monetary losses for businesses. When it comes to protecting against cyber-attacks and maintaining the security of internal networks, the ability to spot anomalies is crucial. The aforementioned procedure can be employed to ascertain prospective hazards prior to their manifestation of detrimental consequences. It can assist stop problems from spreading in real time by thwarting malicious traffic and isolating compromised systems. The purpose of this research is to compare the effectiveness of the classifiers linear regression and REPTree using a variety of evaluation criteria.

The given paper is organized into following sections. Section 2 provides a literature review of studies regarding anomaly detection in network. Section 3 discusses methodology of the proposed approach. It involves pre-processing of data, feature selection and classifier results. Section 4 presents implementation followed by conclusion and references.

---

[a]k.suneetha@jainuniversity.ac.in, [b]kamal.sutaria24554@paruluniversity.ac.in, [c]raghav.garg@tulas.edu.in

DOI: 10.1201/9781003534136-30

Literature Review

The authors present a method for detecting abnormal network traffic by using a combination of decision trees and other criteria [5]. The proposed method does not rely on a feature selection methodology, but it is nevertheless accurate. Clustering, identifying anomalies, and principal component analysis are only few of the many statistical methods utilized for network traffic analysis, and they're all brought together [6]. When compared to previous approaches, the proposed method excelled at identifying out-of-the-ordinary behaviour in networks. The authors utilize data from a university network to analyze traffic features, and then apply machine learning techniques to determine which algorithm is most effective at detecting anomalies in the network [7]. The authors in reference [8] have devised a methodology for detecting network abnormalities by employing the ARFIMA model, an autoregressive framework commonly utilized for analyzing railway traffic data. Comparisons with various methods of anomaly detection showed that their approach was superior. Dimensionality reduction via the principal component analysis model is discussed [9]. The model's residuals are then used to look for outliers. When compared against competing approaches, the proposed strategy was shown to be superior. Deep learning and machine learning have several uses in cyber security discusses them [10]. They discuss the many functions performed by these methods in detecting threats, including vulnerability evaluation and identifying intrusions. The article also offers an in-depth examination of the factors limiting their growth. A deep neural network-based approach to spotting network anomalies is presented by the authors[11]. They used a dataset to evaluate their method against others; however, there aren't enough samples for reliable comparisons. A recurrent neural network-based technique for identifying network anomalies is presented [12]. They used the dataset to evaluate their method against others, but the outcomes didn't show that theirs had better precision and recall.

Proposed Methodology

A. Dataset Pre-Processing

The Kaggle dataset [13] was utilized to create a profile of the network traffic used in the investigation. The effectiveness of machine learning systems relies heavily on the quality of the data acquired. Data normalization, data purification, and data transformation are only some of the pre-processing steps that will be applied to the network traffic information in this investigation. When data is cleaned, redundant or otherwise undesirable information is eliminated. As a result, the data will be more precise and simpler to understand. In order to guarantee the accuracy and consistency of the data, we will also eliminate any duplicates or incorrect entries. In order for machine learning algorithms to function, it is necessary to change data from its original category form into a numerical one. To ensure that all values are comparable and on the same scale, data normalization is conducted.

B. Selection of Features using Association Rule Mining

The computation of attribute correlation in a data set is a data mining technique utilized to identify the most potent item sets among observations involving two or more qualities.

Let F = {f1, f2, f3...........f_n} be set of features and D be dataset consisting of T transactions as {t1, t2, t3........ t_m}. Each transaction holds set of features namely antecedent and precedent. There exists conditions such that ¥ f € t and f1 η f2 = φ (disjoint sets). It computes selection of features using support and confidence as given in equations below:

$$\text{Support} = \{(t_m) (f1, f2 \in t_m)\} / N \qquad (1)$$

$$\text{Confidence} = [(t_m) (f1, f2 \in t_m) / (t_m) (fn \in t_m)] \qquad (2)$$

Association rule mining is a data mining technique that aims to discover common item groups and extract the most significant rules from these sets.

C. Using Machine Learning Classifiers

Detecting anomalies in network traffic data is a popular application of deep learning and machine learning methods. In this research, we provide two distinct classifiers that will be used to examine data on network traffic for signs of unusual behaviour.

Linear regression [14]: - It's an example of a supervised machine learning technique that estimates the linear connection between a target variable and a set of input features. The objective of the procedure is to determine which linear equation best predicts the dependent variable given the independent ones. A straight line can be drawn from the equation to depict the partnership between the dependent and independent variables. In linear relationships, the slope of the line represents the proportional change in the dependent variable for each unit change in the independent variables.

RepTree: - One such rapid decision tree learning algorithm is reduces error pruning (REP) Tree Classifier [15], which works by minimizing the error coming from variance and calculates the information gain with entropy.

Multiple trees are generated in different iterations using regression tree logic, which is applied by REP Tree. The best tree is then chosen from among those that have been regrown. Considering variance and information gain, this approach builds the regression/decision tree. This approach also does back-fitting reduced-error pruning on the tree.

D. Evaluation of Results

Following the aforementioned procedures, the outcomes are assessed using the following criteria: - *TP, TN, FP* and *FN*.

TP (true positive) is the total count of anomalies with a proper classification.

TN (true negative) is the total count of normal records when the classification was correct.

FP (false positive) is the total count of incorrectly labelled anomalies.

FN (false negative) represents the amount of typical records that were incorrectly categorized. The accuracy is the proportion of properly labeled records relative to the total number of rows in the dataset.

$$\text{Accuracy} = (TP+TN) \: / \: (TP+TN+FP+FN) \tag{3}$$

$$\text{False Positive Rate (FPR)} = FP \: / \: FP+TN \tag{4}$$

$$\text{False Negative Rate (FNR)} = FN \: / \: FN+TP \tag{5}$$

The term "**Precision** " refers to the percentage of anomaly records in which the classification was right. However, **Recall** measures how many outliers were correctly identified relative to the total number of identified and misidentified outliers.

$$\text{Precision} = TP \: / \: TP + FP \tag{6}$$

$$\text{Recall} = TP \: / \: TP + FN \tag{7}$$

Result and Implementation

Figure 30.1 shows the attributes of network profiling dataset namely protocol, source bytes, dest bytes, root-shell, hostlogin, guestlogin, server error, host rate and port rate.

Figure 30.2 shows data normalization in which all values are aligned to scale.

In Figure 30.3, feature values are generated for all attributes where first column of each attribute denotes repeated item sets and second column denotes unique item sets. Like, for protocol denoted as a0, we have 46 repeated item sets and 54 unique item sets.

Figure 30.1 Network profiling dataset attributes

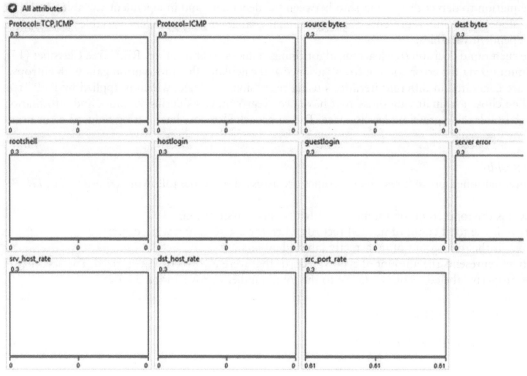

Figure 30.2 Normalized values of attributes after applying normalization

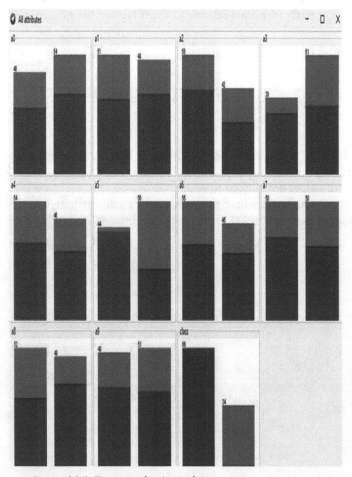

Figure 30.3 Feature selection values

Figure 30.4 shows the classifier output with linear equation in the form of y = mx + c where m is slope and c is correlation coefficient.

Here our equation is src_port_rate = -0.0003 * destbytes + 0.5788

In Figure 30.5, it is seen that information gain and variance are calculated based on the size of tree. Here, information gain and variance for first node are 6 and 0.16 respectively. Likewise, second node has information gain and variance as 4 and 0.3 respectively.

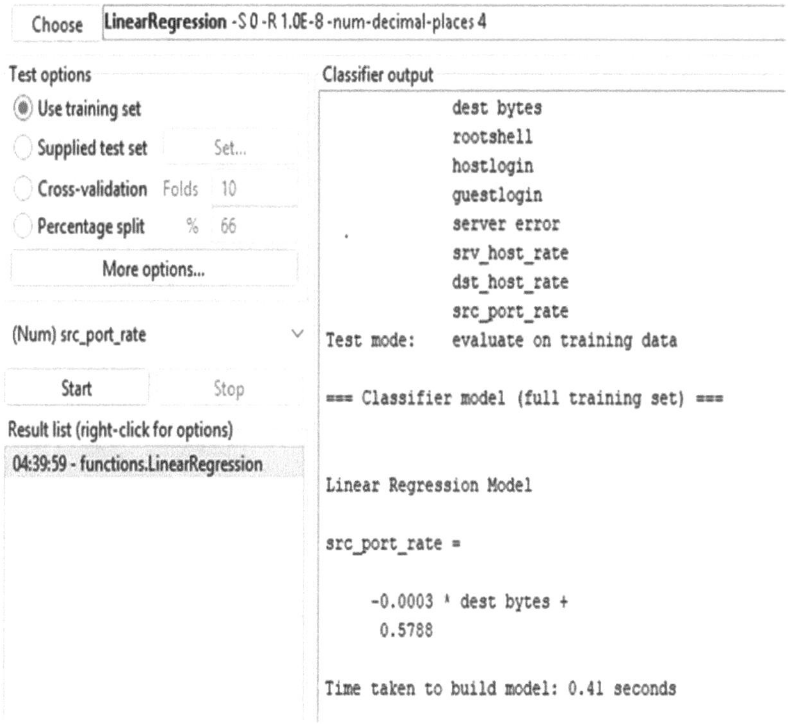

Figure 30.4 Applying linear regression on dataset

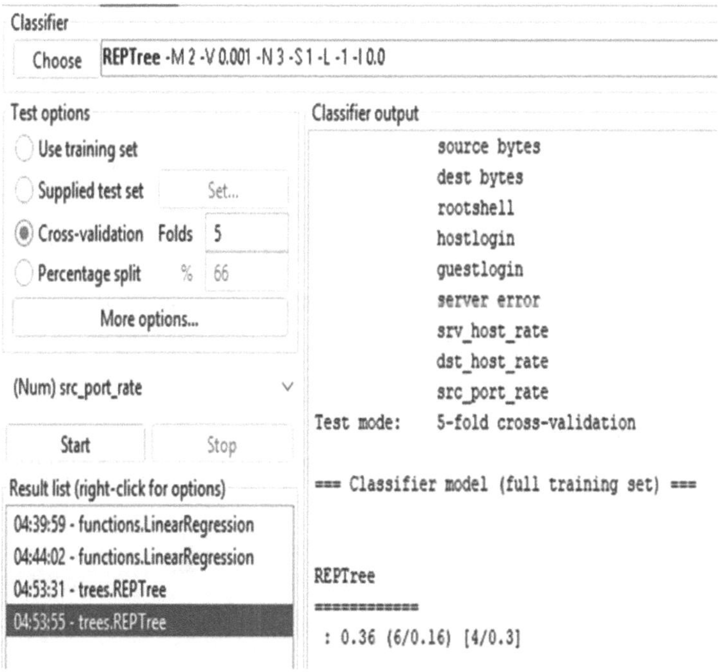

Figure 30.5 Applying REPTree on dataset

Results and Analysis

Table 30.1 shows the detailed results of linear regression classifier based on evaluation metrics.

Table 30.2 shows the detailed results of REPTree classifier based on evaluation metrics.

Table 30.3 shows the accuracy comparison of both the classifiers. It is seen that REPTree attains higher accuracy of 97% for anomalies detection in the network.

Table 30.1 Detailed results of linear regression.

Class	TPR	FPR	Precision	Recall	F1-Score	ROC
Anomaly	0.89	0.45	0.95	0.94	0.96	0.76
Normal	0.91	0.03	0.93	0.97	0.95	0.8

Table 30.2 Detailed results of REPTree.

Class	TPR	FPR	Precision	Recall	F1-Score	ROC
Anomaly	0.93	0.66	0.98	0.96	0.96	0.71
Normal	0.94	0.56	0.96	0.95	0.95	0.67

Table 30.3 Accuracy comparison.

Classifier	Accuracy (%)
Linear regression	94
REPTree	97

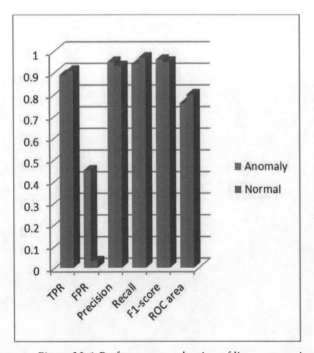

Figure 30.6 Performance evaluation of linear regression

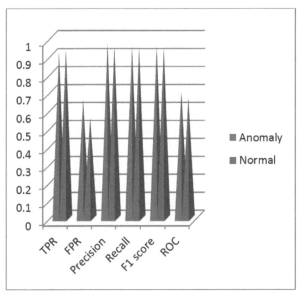

Figure 30.7 Performance evaluation of REPTree

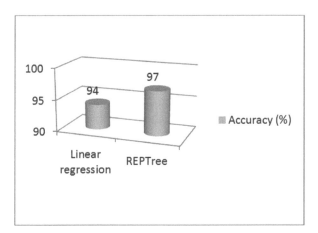

Figure 30.8 Accuracy comparison

Conclusion and Future Work

A study of how machine learning can be applied to network traffic anomaly detection is presented in this research. We used linear regression and REPTree, two very used techniques, on the network profiling dataset. To further boost performance, we also employed feature selection techniques. Our analysis showed that the anomaly detection algorithms utilized in the study achieved high levels of accuracy, recall, F1-score, and precision. Algorithm speed was also much improved because to feature selection. This research demonstrates that REPTree can effectively identify network anomalies with an accuracy of 97%.

Future studies should focus on creating models that can change in response to cyber threats. Scientists can investigate the use of deep learning techniques for anomaly detection in networks.

References

[1] Zoppi, T., Ceccarelli, A., and Bondavalli, A. (2020). Into the unknown: unsupervised machine learning algorithms for anomaly-based intrusion detection. In 50th Annual IEEE-IFIP International Conference on Dependable Systems and Networks-Supplemental Volume (DSN-S), Valencia, Spain, (pp. 81–81), doi: 10.1109/DSN-S50200.2020.00044.

[2] Dwivedi, R. K., Rai, A. K., and Kumar, R. (2020). A study on machine learning based anomaly detection approaches in wireless sensor network. In 10th International Conference on Cloud Computing, Data Science & Engineering (Confluence), Noida, India, (pp. 194–199), doi: 10.1109/Confluence47617.2020.9058311.

[3] Singh, R., Srivastava, N., and Kumar, A. (2021). Machine learning techniques for anomaly detection in network traffic. In 2021 Sixth International Conference on Image Information Processing (ICIIP), Shimla, India, (pp. 261–266), doi: 10.1109/ICIIP53038.2021.9702647.

[4] Limthong, K., and Tawsook, T. (2012). Network traffic anomaly detection using machine learning approaches. In IEEE Network Operations and Management Symposium, Maui, HI, USA, (pp. 542–545), doi: 10.1109/NOMS.2012.6211951.

[5] Amangele, P., Reed, M. J., Al-Naday, M., Thomos, N., and Nowak, M. (2019). Hierarchical machine learning for IoT anomaly detection in SDN. In International Conference on Information Technologies (InfoTech), Varna, Bulgaria, (pp. 1–4), doi: 10.1109/InfoTech.2019.8860878.

[6] Kucuk, M. F., and Uysal, I. (2022). Anomaly detection in self-organizing networks: conventional versus contemporary machine learning. *IEEE Access*, 10, 61744–61752. doi: 10.1109/ACCESS.2022.3182014.

[7] Wighneswara , A. A., et al. (2023). Network behavior anomaly detection using decision tree. In IEEE 12th International Conference on Communication Systems and Network Technologies (CSNT), Bhopal, India, (pp. 705–709), doi: 10.1109/CSNT57126.2023.10134589.

[8] Villalba, D. A. M., Varon, D. F. M., Pórtela, F. G., and Triana, O. A. D. (2022). Intrusion detection system (IDS) with anomaly-based detection and deep learning application. In V Congreso Internacional en Inteligencia Ambiental, Ingeniería de Software y Salud Electrónica y Móvil (AmITIC), San Jose, Costa Rica, (pp. 1–4), doi: 10.1109/AmITIC55733.2022.9941277.

[9] Shi, Y. and Miao, K. (2019). Detecting anomalies in application performance management system with machine learning algorihms. In 3rd International Conference on Electronic Information Technology and Computer Engineering (EITCE), Xiamen, China, (pp. 1797–1800), doi: 10.1109/EITCE47263.2019.9094916.

[10] Dmitrievich, A. G., and Nikolaevich, S. A. (2020). Automated process control anomaly detection using machine learning methods. In Ural Symposium on Biomedical Engineering, Radioelectronics and Information Technology (USBEREIT), Yekaterinburg, Russia, (pp. 0536–0538), doi: 10.1109/USBEREIT48449.2020.9117692.

[11] Das, S., Ashrafuzzaman, M., Sheldon, F. T., and Shiva, S. (2020). Network intrusion detection using natural language processing and ensemble machine learning. In IEEE Symposium Series on Computational Intelligence (SSCI), Canberra, ACT, Australia, (pp. 829–835), doi: 10.1109/SSCI47803.2020.9308268.

[12] Noor, S., Bazai, S. U., Ghafoor, M. I., Marjan, S., Akram, S., and Ali, F. (2023). Generative adversarial networks for anomaly detection: a systematic literature review. In 4th International Conference on Computing, Mathematics and Engineering Technologies (iCoMET), Sukkur, Pakistan, (pp. 1–6), doi: 10.1109/iCoMET57998.2023.10099175.

[13] Kaggle (2023). The profiling network traffic dataset uploaded from Kaggle repository (www.kaggle.com) value as on dated August 2023. https://www.kaggle.com/datasets/mandheer/profiling-network-traffic?select=Profiling.csv.

[14] Feng, Q., Zhu, Q., Yuan, C., and Lee, I. (2016). Multi-linear regression coefficient classifier for recognition. In IEEE Congress on Evolutionary Computation (CEC), Vancouver, BC, Canada, (pp. 1382–1387), doi: 10.1109/CEC.2016.7743950.

[15] Katkar, V. D. and Bhatia, D. S. (2013). Experiments on detection of denial of service attacks using REPTree. In International Conference on Green Computing, Communication and Conservation of Energy (ICGCE), Chennai, India, (pp. 713–718), doi: 10.1109/ICGCE.2013.6823527.

31 Using MLP and convolutional neural networks (CNN) to perform decision making related to skin disease infections

Neha Chauhan[1,a], Ganesh D.[2,b] and Jaymeel Shah[3,c]

[1]Assistant Professor, Department of Computer Science & Engineering, Tula's Institute, Dehradun, India

[2]Professor, Department of Computer Science and Information Technology, Jain (Deemed to be University), Bangalore, India

[3]Associate Professor, Department of Computer Science and Engineering, Faculty of Engineering and Technology, Parul Institute of Engineering and Technology, Parul University, Vadodara, Gujarat, India

Abstract

Skin diseases affect a large percentage of all living things. Keeping tabs on and identifying skin illnesses is a difficult task for the medical community. Infections leave a nearly visible mark on people's skin, but determining the precise type can be difficult due to the wide variety of people's skin tones. That's why early diagnosis and treatment of skin diseases is so crucial. There has been a recent uptick in the use of AI to healthcare. More often than not, deep learning (DL) and machine learning (ML) approaches are employed for diagnosis. The diagnostic procedure is both enhanced and accelerated by these methods. The purpose of this research is to advance skin disease categorization by creating a hybrid of DL and ML. The convolution neural networks (CNN) model is employed for the purpose of feature extraction and classification, utilizing ML models such as support vector machines (SVM) and multi-layer perceptron (MLP). In order to determine the most effective prediction model, a comparison analysis was conducted, revealing that the hybrid approach of CNN combined with MLP yielded the highest level of accuracy at 96.06%

Keywords: CNN, deep learning, MLP, skin diseases, support vector machine

Introduction

The epidermis is the body's largest and most visible skin layer, and it plays a crucial role in thermoregulation and the activation of heat and cold sensations, which in turn protects numerous internal organs from external injury and infections. The skin, however, is susceptible to change from both environmental and hereditary factors. Skin illnesses are quite widespread in the human population. Infectious skin disorders, bacterial skin disorders, and contact dermatitis disorders are the most common forms of skin issues. The texture or tone of the skin can be altered by a variety of skin conditions. Diseases of the skin are often incurable, easily spread from person to person, and even potentially cancerous. If discovered and treated early on, fungal and allergy illnesses are very simple medical conditions. However, when dealing with viral illnesses, prompt diagnosis is essential. Rapid progress has been made in the clinical sector in recent years using artificial intelligence (AI) models, machine learning (ML) [1, 2], and deep learning (DL) [3, 4]. Improved skin disease forecasts have been the focus of several ensemble based machine learning [5] and artificial neural network [6] based techniques. In this work, skin illnesses are categorised using a method that combines ML and DL models. Two ML models—SVM and MLP—were utilised to create classifiers. Convolutional neural networks (CNN) are utilised for feature extraction. Finally, a battery of tests was run to determine which prediction models performed the best. The given paper is organized into following sections. Section 2 provides a literature review of studies regarding identification and diagnosis of skin diseases. Section 3 discusses methodology of the proposed approach. Section 4 presents experimental results followed by conclusion and references.

Literature Review

The epidermis, being the biggest and most prominent layer of the skin, performs essential functions in thermo regulation and the initiation of thermal sensations. Moreover, it serves as a protective barrier against external harm and infections for many interior organs. The integumentary system, however, is vulnerable to alteration due to the influence of both environmental and inherited factors. Skin diseases are quite prevalent among the human population. The most prevalent types of skin disorders include infectious skin disorders, bacterial skin disorders, and contact dermatitis disorders. A multitude of skin diseases can lead to changes in the texture

[a]neha.chauhan@tulas.edu.in, [b]d.ganesh@jainuniversity.ac.in, [c]jaimeel.shah@paruluniversity.ac.in

DOI: 10.1201/9781003534136-31

or tone of the skin. Skin diseases are frequently characterized by their incurable nature, high transmissibility among individuals, and the propensity to develop into malignancies. When fungal and allergy disorders are identified and addressed promptly, they might be regarded as straightforward medical issues. However, in the context of viral diseases, expeditious diagnosis is imperative. Significant advancements have been achieved in the clinical domain in recent years through the use of AI models, ML techniques [7, 8] and DL methodologies [9, 10]. Several strategies based on ensemble-based machine learning [11] and artificial neural networks [12, 13] have been the primary emphasis in enhancing skin disease predictions. This study employs a methodology that integrates ML and DL models to classify skin diseases. Two machine learning models, support vector machine (SVM) and multilayer perceptron (MLP), were employed to develop classifiers. CNNs are employed for the purpose of extracting features. Ultimately, a comprehensive set of experiments was conducted in order to ascertain the optimal performance of several prediction models.

Proposed Methodology

Artificial intelligence pertains to the replication of cognitive processes shown by the human brain using computer systems. DL and ML models are commonly employed in practical applications to address real-world challenges. This study presents a novel approach that combines DL and ML models for effectively addressing the challenge of skin disease categorization. In this study, a CNN was employed as a deep learning model for obtaining features from the data sets. The classification of these samples was carried out using machine learning methods. Performance measures were utilized to evaluate the effectiveness of the input model. The detailed explanation of the steps involved in Figure 31.1 are as follows:

A. Dataset Collection

The present study utilized the publically accessible Kaggle dataset for HAM10000 [14]. It's a vast database of dermatoscopic pictures of skin discolorations obtained from various sources. Different populations' dermatoscopic pictures are obtained and preserved using various methods.

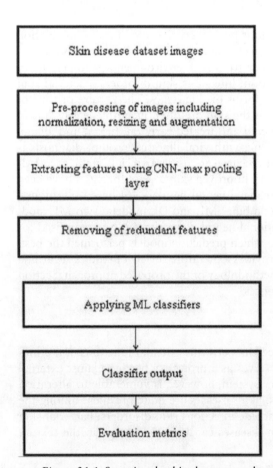

Figure 31.1 Steps involved in the proposed methodology

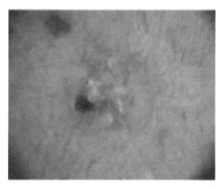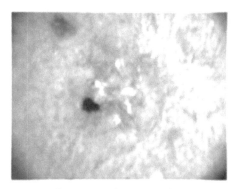

Figure 31.2 (a) Skin Disease Image from Dataset (b) Image After Normalization and Cleaning [14]

B. Pre-Processing of Images

Image data must undergo normalization, scaling, cropping, and enhancement. Data cleaning is the process of removing duplicate or inaccurate records from a dataset. In doing so, the data may be made more precise and simplified. To guarantee accuracy and consistency, we will additionally clean the data by removing any duplicates or incorrect information. To facilitate the work of machine learning algorithms, data augmentation involves translating qualitative factors into quantitative ones. When data is normalized, all the values are brought into agreement and the scale is standardized.

Figure 31.2 shows the normal image of skin lesions from the given dataset. It is said to undergo cleaning, normalization and augmentation to remove noise and complexity from image.

C. Extraction of Features Using CNN

Convolutional layers are employed to extract the salient characteristics from the input training data. Every convolutional layer is equipped with a collection of filters that aid in the process of feature extraction. The initial convolution layer is responsible for detecting and capturing elementary characteristics, whereas the final convolution layer is designed to identify and capture intricate features within the training data. Features are retrieved by the process of convolving a subset of the data sample. The quantity of data that the filter traverses during each iteration is directly proportional to the stride length and padding value. The result of the convolution is then sent into a ReLU (Rectified Linear Unit) activation unit. This component alters the information to make it non-linear. After the ReLU

D. Removing Redundant Features Using Pooling Layer

The pooling layer serves to eliminate duplicate characteristics that have been recorded during the convolution process. Therefore, this layer serves to decrease the size of the data sample. Typically, the dimensions of an input picture are halved by the utilization of a m * n filter. This cycle of feeding input to the convolution layer followed by the pooling layer is repeated until the final output is fed into the multi-layer neural network. Each individual serves as a data-carrying "feature map" for the entire group.

E. Applying MLP Classifier

The aforementioned method [15] is a neural network model that is specifically designed for the purpose of classification tasks. The architecture employed in this system is derived from the multilayer perceptron (MLP), a kind of feedforward neural networks. The MLP Classifier exhibits the ability to acquire knowledge of non-linear associations between input and output variables, hence rendering it a potent instrument for the purpose of classification endeavors.

F. Evaluation Metrics

Following the aforementioned procedures, the outcomes are assessed using the following criteria: - *TP, TN, FP* and *FN*.

"*TP* (true positive)" is the total count of anomalies with a proper classification.

"*TN* (true negative)" is the total count of normal records when the classification was correct.

"*FP* (false positive)" is the total count of incorrectly labelled anomalies.

"*FN* (false negative)" represents the amount of typical records that were incorrectly categorized. The accuracy is the proportion of properly labelled records relative to the total number of rows in the dataset.

"Accuracy = (TP+TN) / (TP+TN+FP+FN) (1)"

The term "Precision " refers to the percentage of anomaly records in which the classification was right. However, **recall** measures how many outliers were correctly identified relative to the total number of identified and misidentified outliers.

"Precision = TP / TP + FP (2)

Recall = TP / TP + FN (3)"

Result and Implementation

The implementation of the proposed methodology begins with collection of attributes from the image dataset related to skin lesions. It is followed by refining attributes using 'Remove Duplicates' filter. Then, the refined dataset is subjected to machine learning classifier named MLP for generation of results and validation of the proposed approach. Table 31.1 represents the attributes of skin lesions dataset.

Layer, the output is sent into a pooling layer.

Table 31.1 HAM10000 dataset attributes [14].

Lesion id	Type of skin disease	Age	Sex	Localization
1	Melanocytic	60	M	Scalp
2	Melanoma	70	M	Ear
3	Benign keratosis	55	F	Foot
4	Basal cell	40	F	Scalp
5	Actinic	60	M	Scalp
6	Vascular	50	F	Ear
7	Dermato	67	M	Scalp

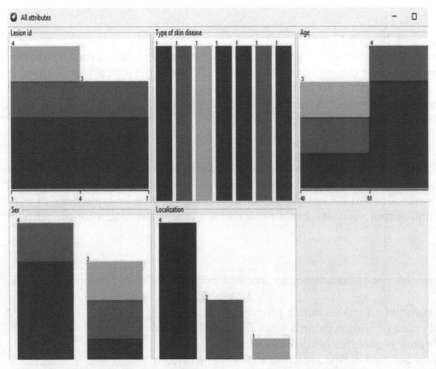

Figure 31.3 Visualization of Dataset

Figure 31.2 shows the refined and final attributes of HAM10000 skin diseases dataset by visualizing them after applying 'Remove Duplicate' filter.

Figure 31.3 shows MLP classifier output on training dataset. It leads to generation of sigmoid nodes and weights associated with each node.

Figure 31.4 shows validation of the proposed approach using MLP classifier based on testing dataset. It uses 5 folds cross validation approach to generate sigmoid nodes and their associated weights.

Figure 31.5 shows validation of the proposed approach using MLP classifier based on percentage split dataset. In this, we have assigned 80-20 distribution on training and testing dataset respectively.

Figure 31.6 shows scatterplot distribution of attributes which helps us to perform decision making in identifying parts of body affected by skin disease. In above plot, blue color channel represents scalp, red represents ear and green represents foot. Figure 31.7 and Figure 31.8

RESULTS & ANALYSIS

Table 31.2 shows the detailed parameters and description of CNN model that we have used for extraction of features in the dataset.

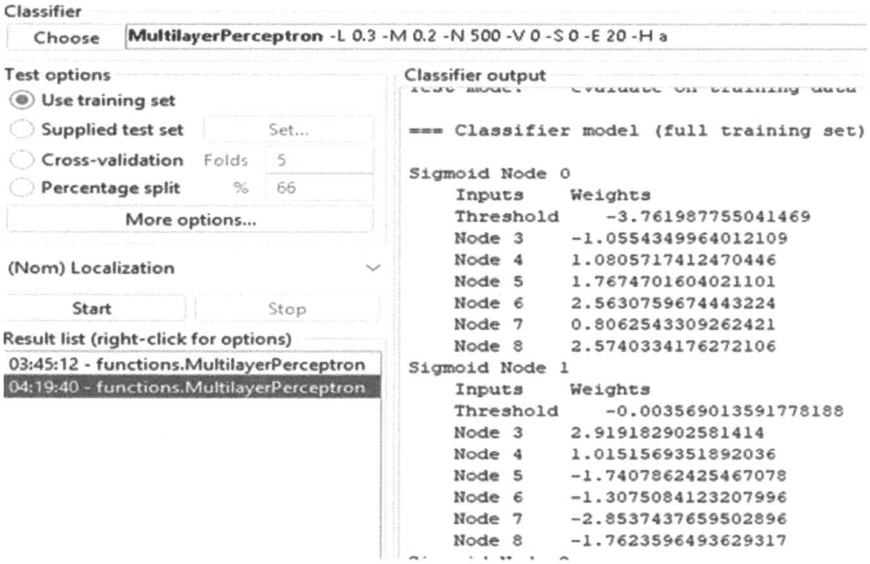

Figure 31.4 Results of MLP classifier on training dataset

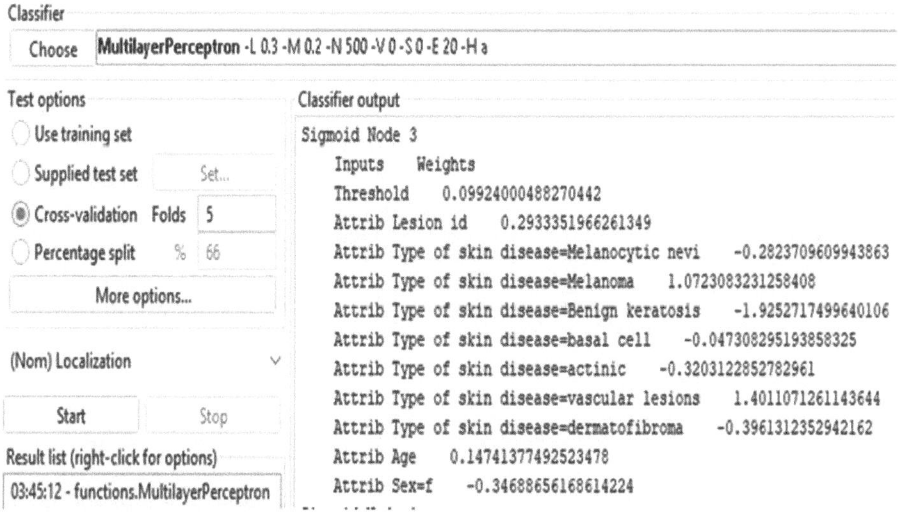

Figure 31.5 Results of MLP Classifier on Testing Dataset

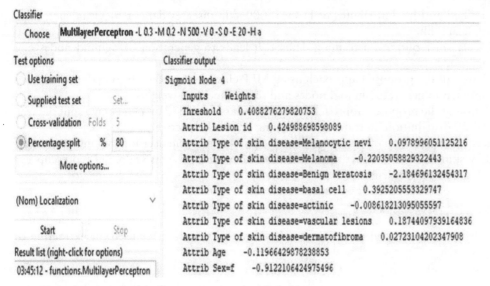

Figure 31.6 MLP Classifier Output Based on Split Test

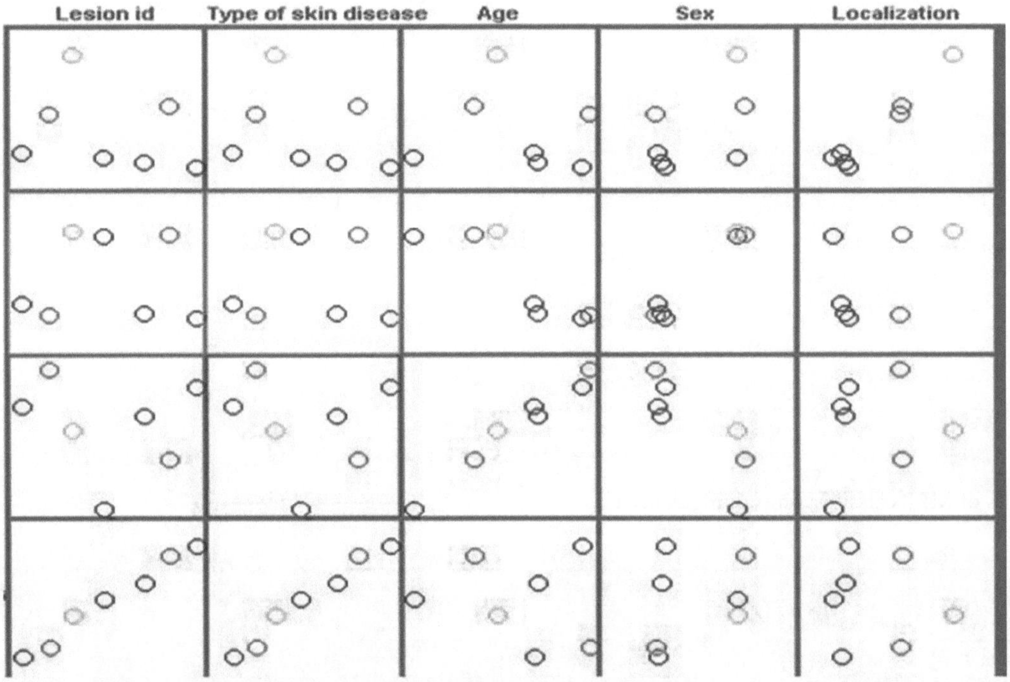

Figure 31.7 Visualization of Dataset Consisting of 5 Attributes

Table 31.2 Detailed parameters of CNN model.

PARAMETERS	DESCRIPTION
Size Of Input Images	225 * 225
Color Channels Used In Visualization	3
Size Of Filter Used In Model	4 * 4
Activator	ReLU
Pooling Layer	Max pooling
Total Layers	10

Table 31.3 Accuracy analysis.

DL + ML	Precision (%)	Recall (%)	Accuracy (%)
CNN + SVM	90	91	91.20
CNN + MLP	95	96	96.06

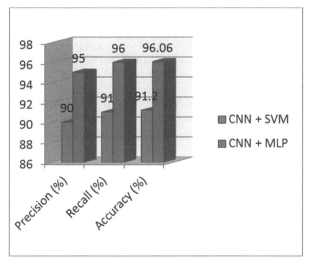

Figure 31.8 Accuracy Comparison

Table 31.3 shows accuracy comparison by using CNN with machine learning classifiers.

Table 31.3 shows the accuracy comparison of both the classifiers using CNN model as deep learning approach. It is seen that CNN along with MLP attains higher accuracy of 96.06 % for diagnosis of skin lesion diseases.

Conclusion and Future Work

The epidermis is the most substantial inherent constituent of the human body. Skin problems may arise due to a variety of internal and environmental sources. Hence, the identification and classification of skin disorders hold significant significance within the field of medical science, as it has the potential to mitigate mortality rates associated with the exposure to skin ailments or communicable infections. The therapeutic approach is characterized by a significant investment of time and resources, and the accurate identification of the condition is not always achievable. The utilization of automated categorization techniques for skin disorders might prove to be quite advantageous in such scenarios. This paper proposes an electronic approach for the diagnosis of skin problems. In this methodology, a fusion of machine learning (ML) and deep learning (DL) models was employed. The suggested strategy involved the integration of a deep learning model for feature extraction from training data with two widely recognized machine learning classifiers. Upon conducting a thorough analysis, it was determined that the Convolutional Neural Network (CNN) model, when combined with the Multi-Layer Perceptron (MLP) Classifier, yields the highest level of precision in its predictions, achieving an accuracy rate of 96.06%.

References

[1] Vasudha Rani, D. V., Vasavi, G., and Maram, B. (2022). Skin disease classification using machine learning and data mining algorithms. In IEEE 2nd International Symposium on Sustainable Energy, Signal Processing and Cyber Security (iSSSC), Gunupur, Odisha, India, (pp. 1–6), doi: 10.1109/iSSSC56467.2022.10051620.

[2] Banditsingha, P., Thaipisutikul, T., Shih, T. K., and Lin, C. -Y. (2022). A decision machine learning support system for human skin disease classifier. In Joint International Conference on Digital Arts, Media and Technology with ECTI Northern Section Conference on Electrical, Electronics, Computer and Telecommunications Engineering (ECTI DAMT & NCON), Chiang Rai, Thailand, (pp. 200–204), doi: 10.1109/ECTIDAMTNCON53731.2022.9720379.

[3] Swamy, K. V., and Divya, B. (2021). Skin disease classification using machine learning algorithms. In 2nd International Conference on Communication, Computing and Industry 4.0 (C2I4), Bangalore, India, (pp. 1–5), doi: 10.1109/C2I454156.2021.9689338.

[4] Sharma, S. D., Sharma, S., Pathak, A. K., and Mohamed, N. (2023). Real-time skin disease prediction system using deep learning approach. In 2nd Edition of IEEE Delhi Section Flagship Conference (DELCON), Rajpura, India, (pp. 1–6), doi: 10.1109/DELCON57910.2023.10127569.

[5] Hegde, P. R., Shenoy, M. M., and Shekar, B. H. (2018). Comparison of machine learning algorithms for skin disease classification using color and texture features. In 2018 International Conference on Advances in Computing, Communications and Informatics (ICACCI), Bangalore, India, (pp. 1825–1828), doi: 10.1109/ICACCI.2018.8554512.

[6] Gupta, S., Panwar, A., and Mishra, K. (2021). Skin disease classification using dermoscopy images through deep feature learning models and machine learning classifiers. In IEEE EUROCON 2021 - 19th International Conference on Smart Technologies, Lviv, Ukraine, (pp. 170–174), doi: 10.1109/EUROCON52738.2021.9535552.

[7] Janoria, H., Minj, J., and Patre, P. (2020). Classification of skin disease from skin images using transfer learning technique. In 2020 4th International Conference on Electronics, Communication and Aerospace Technology (ICECA), Coimbatore, India, (pp. 888–895), doi: 10.1109/ICECA49313.2020.9297567.

[8] Bokefode, K., and Shinde, S. (2022). Skin disease diagnosis by using different machine learning & deep learning approach. In 2022 6th International Conference On Computing, Communication, Control And Automation (ICCUBEA, Pune, India, (pp. 1–4), doi: 10.1109/ICCUBEA54992.2022.10010801.

[9] Hameed, N., Shabut, A. M., and Hossain, M. A. (2018). Multi-class skin diseases classification using deep convolutional neural network and support vector machine. In 12th International Conference on Software, Knowledge, Information Management & Applications (SKIMA), Phnom Penh, Cambodia, (pp. 1–7), doi: 10.1109/SKIMA.2018.8631525.

[10] Hasan, M. Z., Shoumik, S., and Zahan, N. (2019). Integrated use of rough sets and artificial neural network for skin cancer disease classification. In International Conference on Computer, Communication, Chemical, Materials and Electronic Engineering (IC4ME2), Rajshahi, Bangladesh, (pp. 1–4), doi: 10.1109/IC4ME247184.2019.9036653.

[11] Zhou, C., Sun, M., Chen, L., Cai, A., and Fang, J. (2022). Few-shot learning framework based on adaptive subspace for skin disease classification. In IEEE International Conference on Bioinformatics and Biomedicine (BIBM), Las Vegas, NV, USA, (pp. 2231–2237), doi: 10.1109/BIBM55620.2022.9995042.

[12] Sallam, A., and Ba Alawi, A. E. (2019). Mobile-based intelligent skin diseases diagnosis system. In First International Conference of Intelligent Computing and Engineering (ICOICE), Hadhramout, Yemen, (pp. 1–6), doi: 10.1109/ICOICE48418.2019.9035129.

[13] Adegun, A. A., and Viriri, S. (2020). FCN-based denseNet framework for automated detection and classification of skin lesions in dermoscopy images. *IEEE Access*, 8, 150377–150396. doi: 10.1109/ACCESS.2020.3016651.

[14] Kaggle (2023). The skin disease classification HAM10000 dataset uploaded from Kaggle repository (www.kaggle.com) value as on dated August 2023. https://www.kaggle.com/code/smitisinghal/skin-disease-classification#SKIN-DISEASE-CLASSIFICATION.

[15] Feng, Q., Zhu, Q., Yuan, C., and Lee, I. (2016). Multi-linear regression coefficient classifier for recognition. In IEEE Congress on Evolutionary Computation (CEC), Vancouver, BC, Canada, (pp. 1382–1387), doi: 10.1109/CEC.2016.7743950.

32 Creation of centroid clusters using canopy and cobweb clustering for likelihood of heart diseases

Shuchi Jain[1,a], A. Kannagi[2,b] and Gordhan Jethava[3,c]

[1]Assistant Professor, Department of Computer Science & Engineering, Tula's Institute, Dehradun, India

[2]Associate Professor, Department of Computer Science and Information Technology, Jain (Deemed to be University), Bangalore, India

[3]Associate Professor, Department of Computer Science and Engineering, Faculty of Engineering and Technology, Parul Institute of Engineering and Technology, Parul University, Vadodara, Gujarat, India

Abstract

Experts believe that heart attacks are the most prevalent life-threatening illness. Multiple surveys are conducted by medical experts to collect data about heart disease patients, their illnesses, and their symptoms. It might be challenging to attribute a patient's symptoms to their heart disease in the early stages of the condition. This work utilises clustering techniques to analyse a dataset with the objective of identifying latent patterns within a heart attack prediction dataset. Clustering is a commonly employed data mining approach that arranges data items according to a measurable criterion. The present study elucidated the methodology for capturing clusters and establishing new centroids through the utilisation of Canopy clustering and Cobweb clustering algorithms. Canopy Clustering is a simple and quick method for properly clustering things. Because of its ability to accommodate a non-uniform cluster, cobweb clustering is well-suited to large datasets. Both algorithms' runs were analysed, and accuracy was calculated according to the phases of clustering methods.

Keywords: Canopy clustering, cobweb, data mining, WEKA

Introduction

Heart disease has surpassed all other causes of mortality as the leading killer in the modern world. Millions of individuals are affected annually, and many of them die unexpectedly [1, 2]. Data Mining is the process of discovering previously unknown relationships and patterns within a large data set. It helps scientists draw novel conclusions from large medical datasets [3]. Data mining entails a number of steps, including selection, analysis, preparation, application, interpretation, and evaluation of outcomes [4]. Data mining techniques like clustering group data points into groups depending on how much they have in common [5]. Clustering, also known as classification without supervision or observational learning [6], is a crucial step in the data analysis process that aims to unearth data structures with underlying state by grouping data objects into related groups and expressing data in classes. Clustering is a method for grouping and separating items based on their similarities and differences. Clustered objects are identical to each other but distinct from objects within distinct clusters [7]. The purpose of this study is to provide a detailed comparison of two popular clustering methods, Canopy and Cobweb, for making accurate cardiac illness forecasts. Both of these methods cluster data from the 'Heart Attack Analysis and Prediction' set. After collecting data, it is analysed to determine which models are most accurate predictors.

The given paper is organized into following sections. Section 2 provides a literature review of studies regarding diagnosis of heart failure diseases. Section 3 discusses methodology of the proposed approach. Section 4 presents experimental results followed by conclusion and references.

Literature Review

Researchers have been inspired to conduct in-depth investigation of clinical datasets by the rising number of cardiac patients throughout the world. This section provides a summary of the published computational research on pattern recognition in cardiac illness. Finally, the research gap that prompted this investigation is discussed. The following are examples of important research:

Clustering method efficiency on a heart disease data set was proposed by the authors in [8]. Some clustering algorithms were tested for their ability to make accurate predictions. The ratio of categories to clusters will be used to determine the effectiveness of the clustering. With a prediction accuracy of 85.8%, they concluded that

[a]shuchi.jain@tulas.edu.in, [b]a.kannagi@jainuniversity.ac.in, [c]gordhan.jethava@paruluniversity.ac.in

DOI: 10.1201/9781003534136-32

make density based cluster was the best adaptable method for diagnosing cardiac conditions. The authors of [9] presented a neural network classifier for identifying cardiac conditions. using merging the posterior probability or anticipated values from numerous antecedent models, new models are generated using the ensemble-based approaches. We have developed and successfully field-tested a viable model. For the evaluation of cardiovascular risk variables [10], used WEKA to create a data mining system utilizing correlation analysis based on the Apriori algorithm. The significance of each rule that was considered was taken into account while making the final selection. The number of instances in the database was looked at to further assess the quality of each extracted rule. Consequently, several computational strategies might be used to the problem of pattern detection in cardiac illness. Other credible research on clustering methods might be listed [11–14], all of which focus on various aspects of cardiac disease across various datasets.

Proposed Methodology

Predicting when patients could get heart attacks from their data is a key to this investigation. To learn more about the features of heart disease, a model was built using a prediction technique. To forecast classes using a subset of available features, this study use data mining. Since WEKA [15] is so good in finding, analyzing, and anticipating patterns, it has been put to use in forecasting. The detailed explanation of the steps involved in Figure 32.1 are as follows:

A. Dataset Collection
In this work, researchersv utilized the 'Heart Attack Analysis and Prediction Dataset' [16] from Kaggle. The information is associated with risk factors for cardiovascular disease and heart attacks.

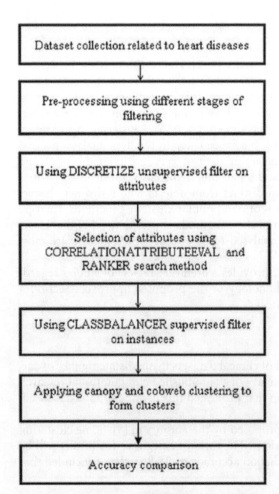

Figure 32.1 Steps involved in the proposed methodology

B. Pre-Processing of Dataset Using Different Stages of Filtering

Noise, missing information, and inconsistency are commonplace in real-world data. Therefore, data filtering is required prior to processing. By using a filter, we clean and remove any redundant or stale information from the dataset. In either the supervised or unsupervised setting, filters are applied to the data at the attribute (attribute manipulation) and instance (instance manipulation) levels to restore data parity.

C. Using DISCRETIZE Filter

The system described is an unsupervised instance filter that performs discretization on a collection of numeric characteristics inside a dataset, transforming them into nominal attributes.

D. Selection of Attributes

It is done by using CLASSIFIERATTRIBUTEEVAL that predicts the value of attributes based on user records in the dataset. This attribute classifier is used in combination with RANKER search method to rank attributes on the basis of their individual evaluations.

E. Using CLASSBALANCER Filter

The supervised instance filter is designed to adjust the weights of instances inside a dataset, ensuring that all instances are assigned equal weight. The cumulative weight of all instances will be preserved.

F. Clustering Algorithms

Canopy clustering: - Canopy clustering, as described in reference [17], is a rapid and approximate method for clustering. The input data points are partitioned into overlapping clusters referred to as canopies. Two distinct distance criteria are employed in order to estimate the cluster centroids. Canopy clustering offers a rapid estimation of the quantity of clusters and the first centroids of clusters for a given dataset.

Cobweb clustering: - Hierarchical idea clustering may be performed with COBWEB [18], an incremental system. COBWEB builds up a hierarchy of categories from a set of observations. Objects' attribute value distributions are summarized in a probabilistic concept that is assigned to each node in a classification tree, with each node representing a class (concept). The cobweb algorithm is a symbolic method of classifying data. Here, the clusters and categories are probabilistic, and the number of clusters and hierarchy depth are determined using global quality measures. COBWEB uses the likelihood of the presence of each feature value to identify category membership, rather than requiring that an item meet a predefined set of feature values. An incremental algorithm is also used. Each time we add a new classification or reorganize our taxonomy.

Result and Implementation

Figure 32.2 below shows initialization of DISCRETIZE unsupervised instance filter on heart diseases dataset.

Figure 32.3 shows 13 distinct instances after filtering of dataset. The instances are age, sex, cholesterol level, blood pressure, obesity, diet intake and types of chest pain. This filter has removed missing values and generates only nominal (unique values) to ensure transparent and refined dataset.

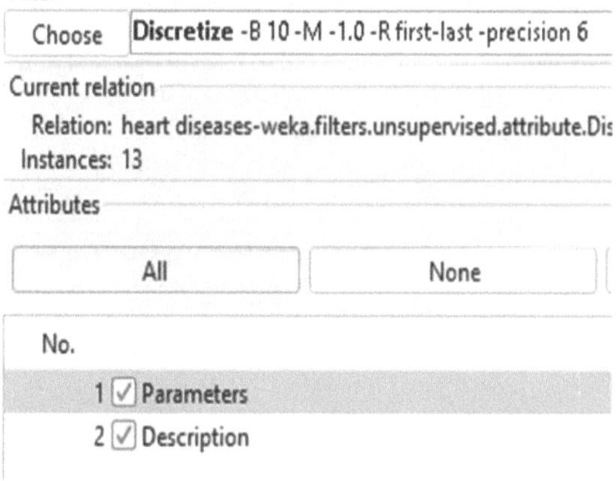

Figure 32.2 Applying DISCRETIZE filter on dataset

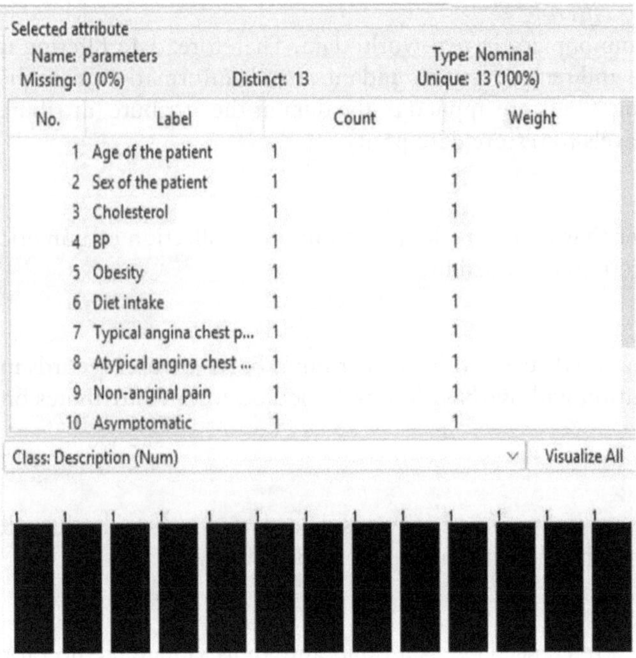

Figure 32.3 Results of DISCRETIZE filter on dataset

Figure 32.4 Results of attribute evaluator on dataset

This step is followed by selection of attributes as shown in Figure 32.4.

Figure 32.4 shows the execution of CORRELATION ATTRBUTEEVAL using RANKER as searching method. With this selection, the attributes are divided in uniform ratio of 1:1.

The filter settings are displayed in Figure 32.5. It's a form of supervised instance filtering that averages out the data's weight across all instances. All weights will continue to add up to the same amount across all occurrences.

Figure 32.6 shows working of CLASSBALANCER filter which gives weight values associated with each instance in a balanced manner. All weights are assigned similar values of 0.003 and 0.007.

It is seen in Figure 32.7 that total 14 clusters are formed using cobweb algorithm starting from leaf 1 to leaf 13.

Filter

Choose	**ClassBalancer** -num-intervals 10

Current relation

Relation: heart diseases-weka.filters.unsupervised.attribute.C
Instances: 13

Attributes

All	None

No.

1 ☑ **Parameters**

2 ☑ Description

Figure 32.5 Applying CLASSBALANCER filter

Selected attribute

Name: Parameters		Type: Nominal
Missing: 0 (0%)	Distinct: 13	Unique: 13 (100%)

No.	Label	Count	Weigl
1	Age of the patient	1	0.003
2	Sex of the patient	1	0.003
3	Cholesterol	1	0.003
4	BP	1	0.007
5	Obesity	1	0.003
6	Diet intake	1	0.007
7	Typical angina chest pain	1	0.003
8	Atypical angina chest pain	1	0.02
9	Non-anginal pain	1	0.02

Class: Description (Num)

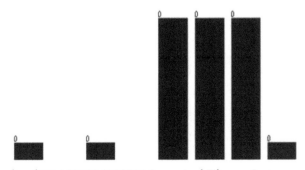

Figure 32.6 Results of 'CLASSBALANCER' Supervised Filter on Instances

Figure 32.8 shows that two canopies are formed having radius 0.382 and 0.477 respectively.

Results and Analysis

Table 32.1 gives the description about three stages of clustered filtering applied on the dataset in order to compute comparison of accuracy for canopy and cobweb.

Figure 32.7 Formation of cluster centroids using Cobweb

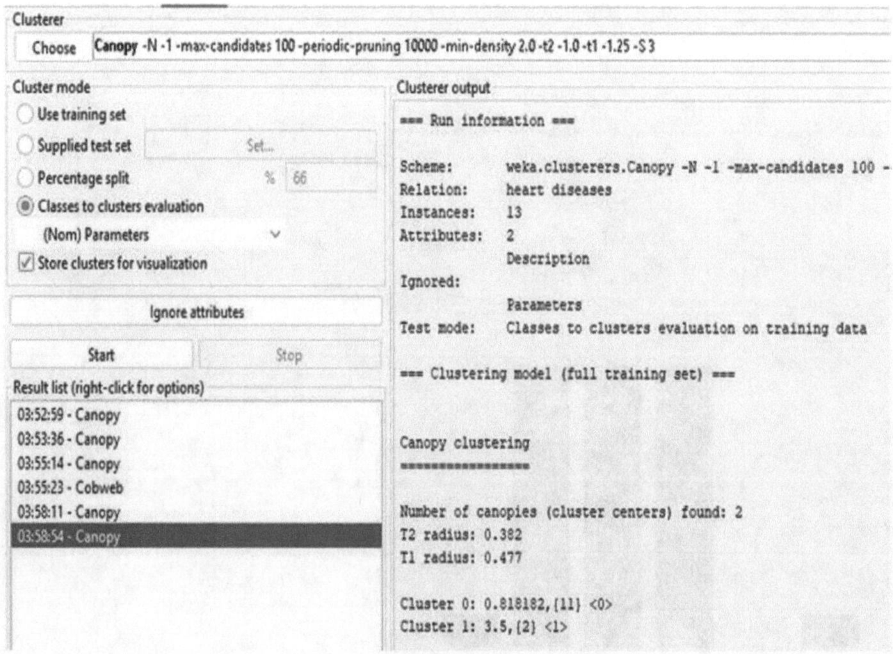

Figure 32.8 Formation of clusters using canopy algorithm

Table 32.1 Accuracy in all stages.

Clustering approaches	Stage 1	Stage 2	Stage 3
Canopy	35.65%	52.45%	73.67%
Cobweb	37.87%	56.43%	78.54%

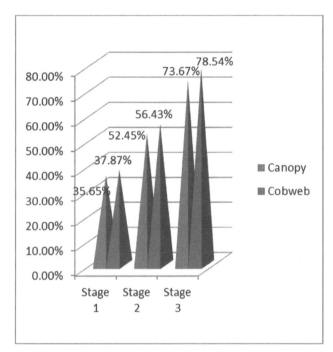

Figure 32.9 Accuracy comparison of canopy and cobweb clustering approaches

As per Figure 32.9, it is seen that Cobweb cluster provides higher accuracy (78.54%) in prediction of heart diseases.

Conclusion and Future Work

The primary objective of this study is to compare and contrast many clustering methods in quest of the optimal data mining strategy for early detection of cardiovascular illnesses. In this study, multiple clustering methods implemented in Weka are used to the dataset used for predicting cardiovascular illnesses. Clustering is an example of an unsupervised learning method that relies on seeing data. The primary goal of any clustering study is to classify data into groups based on similarities and differences. Both the canopy and Cobweb methods are compared based on how many clusters they produce and how accurate those clusters are. The study presented here showed how to obtain clusters and determine a new centroid for high-dimensional data sets. After three levels of filtering, it is clear that cobweb performs better than the other two methods, with an accuracy of 78.54%.

References

[1] Babu, M. S., and Karthick, V. (2022). Improving Accuracy in intelligent coronary heart disease diagnosis prediction model using support vector clustering technique compared over random forest classifier algorithm. In International Conference on Innovative Computing, Intelligent Communication and Smart Electrical Systems (ICSES), Chennai, India, (pp. 1–5), doi: 10.1109/ICSES55317.2022.9914283.

[2] Islam, M. T., Rafa, S. R., and Kibria, M. G. (2020). Early prediction of heart disease using PCA and hybrid genetic algorithm with k-means. In 23rd International Conference on Computer and Information Technology (ICCIT), DHAKA, Bangladesh, (pp. 1–6), doi: 10.1109/ICCIT51783.2020.9392655.

[3] Vijaya, J., and Rao, M. (2022). Heart disease prediction using clustered particle swarm optimization techniques. In IEEE 6th Conference on Information and Communication Technology (CICT), Gwalior, India, (pp. 1–5), doi: 10.1109/CICT56698.2022.9997925.

[4] Vijaya, J. (2023). Heart disease prediction using clustered genetic optimization algorithm. In International Conference on Intelligent and Innovative Technologies in Computing, Electrical and Electronics (IITCEE), Bengaluru, India, (pp. 1072–1077), doi: 10.1109/IITCEE57236.2023.10091050.

[5] Chakarverti, M., Yadav, S., and Rajan, R. (2019). Classification technique for heart disease prediction in data mining. In 2nd International Conference on Intelligent Computing, Instrumentation and Control Technologies (ICICICT), Kannur, India, (pp. 1578–1582), doi: 10.1109/ICICICT46008.2019.8993191.

[6] Goel, S., and Singh, R. (2019). Modeling of heart data using PSO and A-priori algorithm for disease prediction. In 2019 Fifth International Conference on Image Information Processing (ICIIP), Shimla, India, (pp. 475–479), doi: 10.1109/ICIIP47207.2019.8985732.

[7] Sulthana, R., Jaithunbi, A. K., and Sunraja, P. (2023). Application of machine learning algorithms in predicting the heart disease in patients. In 2023 Third International Conference on Advances in Electrical, Computing, Communication and Sustainable Technologies (ICAECT), Bhilai, India, (pp. 1–4), doi: 10.1109/ICAECT57570.2023.10117653.

[8] Umamaheswari, M., and Devi, P. I. (2017). Prediction of myocardial infarction using K-medoid clustering algorithm. In 2017 IEEE International Conference on Intelligent Techniques in Control, Optimization and Signal Processing (IN-COS), Srivilliputtur, India, (pp. 1–6), doi: 10.1109/ITCOSP.2017.8303128.

[9] Sharma, Y., Veliyambara, R., and Shettar, R. (2019). Hybrid classifier for identification of heart disease. In 4th International Conference on Computational Systems and Information Technology for Sustainable Solution (CSITSS), Bengaluru, India, (pp. 1–3), doi: 10.1109/CSITSS47250.2019.9031037.

[10] Raju, C., Philipsy, E., Chacko, S., Padma Suresh, L., and Deepa Rajan, S. (2018). A survey on predicting heart disease using data mining techniques. In Conference on Emerging Devices and Smart Systems (ICEDSS), Tiruchengode, India, (pp. 253–255), doi: 10.1109/ICEDSS.2018.8544333.

[11] Saravanan, S., and Swaminathan, K. (2021). Hybrid k-means and support vector machine to predict heart failure. In 2nd International Conference on Smart Electronics and Communication (ICOSEC), Trichy, Indi, (pp. 1678–1683), doi: 10.1109/ICOSEC51865.2021.9591738.

[12] Raman, R., Shintre, V., Joshi, K., Prasanthi, G. S. L. B. V., Kaleem, A., and Rajput, K. (2023). Smart use of machine learning in heart disease identification. In 3rd International Conference on Advance Computing and Innovative Technologies in Engineering (ICACITE), Greater Noida, India, (pp. 1169–1174), doi: 10.1109/ICACITE57410.2023.10182789.

[13] Bakhshi, M., Mirtaheri, S. L., and Greco, S. (2022). Heart disease prediction using hybrid machine learning model based on decision tree and neural network. In 9th International Conference on Soft Computing & Machine Intelligence (ISCMI), Toronto, ON, Canada, (pp. 36–41), doi: 10.1109/ISCMI56532.2022.10068473.

[14] Alkhafaji, M. J. A., Fadhil Aljuboori, A., and Ibrahim, A. A. (2020). Clean medical data and predict heart disease. In 2020 International Congress on Human-Computer Interaction, Optimization and Robotic Applications (HORA), Ankara, Turkey, (pp. 1–7), doi: 10.1109/HORA49412.2020.9152870.

[15] Duriqi, R., Raca, V., and Cico, B. (2016). Comparative analysis of classification algorithms on three different datasets using WEKA. In 5th Mediterranean Conference on Embedded Computing (MECO), Bar, Montenegro, (pp. 335–338), doi: 10.1109/MECO.2016.7525775.

[16] Kaggle (2023). The heart attack analysis and prediction dataset uploaded from Kaggle repository (www.kaggle.com) value as on dated August 2023. https://www.kaggle.com/datasets/rashikrahmanpritom/heart-attack-analysis-prediction-dataset.

[17] Zhao, H. (2021). Research on improvement and parallelization of canopy-K-means clustering algorithm. In International Conference on Electronic Information Engineering and Computer Science (EIECS), Changchun, China, (pp. 455–458), doi: 10.1109/EIECS53707.2021.9588045.

[18] Lee, K., Kim, H.-W., Moon, C., and Nam, Y. (2019). Analysis of vocal disorders using cobweb clustering. In International Conference on Artificial Intelligence in Information and Communication (ICAIIC), Okinawa, Japan, (pp. 120–123), doi: 10.1109/ICAIIC.2019.8669011.

33 A distinctive and smart agricultural knowledge-based framework using ontology

Vipul Vekariya[1,a], Sandeep Kumar[2,b] and A. Rengarajan[3,c]

[1]Professor, Department of Computer Science and Engineering, Faculty of Engineering and Technology, Parul Institute of Engineering and Technology, Parul University, Vadodara, Gujarat, India

[2]Assistant Professor, Department of Computer Science & Engineering, Tula's Institute, Dehradun, India

[3]Professor, Department of Computer Science and Information Technology, Jain (Deemed to be University), Bangalore, India

Abstract

One of the biggest problems that might arise with crop production is insect infestations. Corrective actions can be taken to reduce yield losses, but only if they are implemented quickly and accurately. By organising data in a hierarchical structure, an intelligent and novel ontological-based expert system is provided for dealing with the detection and control of insect pests and crops. The behaviour of pests and crops may now be better understood thanks to a knowledge model that incorporates the processes of information acquisition, issue identification, and knowledge retrieval. In order to boost production and quality, it is necessary to manage crops and pests effectively, and the suggested hierarchy will help farmers, extension workers, and agricultural development organisations do just that.

Keywords: Agricultural engineering, crops management, knowledge-based system, ontology development

Introduction

In the realm of smart agricultural knowledge-based service systems, such as agricultural instructional systems, agricultural language processing systems, and agricultural expert systems, agricultural knowledge is a distinct subset of domain knowledge that forms a robust basis [1, 2]. E-Agriculture encompasses several forms of information technology (IT). E-Agriculture, as described in the literature [3, 4], refers to a web-based information system that facilitates farmers' access to pertinent data in a timely manner. The web-based agricultural information system offers users a comprehensive array of resources, including crop data, farming resources, plant nutrition information, meteorological conditions specific to crops, various technologies, and market data. The syntactic resources regarding the agricultural area are provided through these systems of information [5, 6]. The language and meaning of terms in these databases, however, are not well-defined. Hence, it is not advisable to depend on the data derived from these systems for obtaining any meaningful insights. Ontologies are employed in applications developed on the internet to generate semantic data for many domains, facilitating problem-solving endeavours. The following, then, are the principal results of the cited paper:

- To provide an ontology as a knowledge model for the agricultural pest domain.
- To inculcate information about types of crops, behavior, production process and types of soil recommended for suitable production of crops.
- To inculcate information regarding pesticides and the ways to control them by taking PESTOPIA dataset [7] into consideration.

"The remaining paper is organized into following sections. Section 2 provides related works on existing E-Agriculture Systems along with ontology." Section 3 presents the proposed knowledge-based model and various phases involved in it. Section 4 provides implementation of the proposed ontological knowledge-based model followed by conclusion and references.

Literature Review

A. A Few Existing E-Agriculture Information Systems
The proliferation of web apps that may be used on mobile devices is a direct result of the fast development of wireless communications technology. To help farmers get their hands on up-to-the-minute data, the government

[a]vipul.vekariya18435@paruluniversity.ac.in, [b]sandeep.kumar.cse@tulas.edu.in, [c]a.rengarajan@jainuniversity.ac.in

DOI: 10.1201/9781003534136-33

has launched the E-choupal initiative, which involves setting up internet centers in rural regions. The E-choupal portal [8] provides rural agricultural communities with the opportunity to access information in their local languages. This includes various resources such as weather predictions, educational materials on improved farming practices, risk management strategies, knowledge development, and the ability to get better quality agricultural inputs. Another system, known as **m-Krishi** [9], was established with the aim of providing tailored advising assistance for farmers on crop productivity, market information, and weather forecasts. Additionally, this process entails the installation of several types of sensors within farmers' fields to gather data on soil moisture levels and meteorological conditions. The E-Sagu project, initiated by the Indian Institute of Technology Hyderabad, is a telephone-based agricultural initiative [10]. From planting until harvesting, this computerized system provides tailored guidance for individual farms. This service not only improves farm production and quality but also decreases the cost of agriculture.

B. Defining Ontology

Semantics, concepts, and the connections between online data are all represented by ontology [11, 12]. Applications that are driven by ontologies [13] include characteristics like high levels of expressiveness, extensibility, reusability, and support for logic reasoning. Ontologies are employed in the realm of web-based application development to facilitate interoperability and the accumulation of knowledge in a common schema. As a result, ontology offers a solid framework for modelling and reasoning about data obtained online [14].

Proposed Methodology

Ontology Web Language (OWL) [15] ontologies are employed in many web-based information systems today because of their ability to enhance information retrieval through the consistent and semantic design of data based on data already accessible on the web. The reason for this is that OWL ontologies make it possible to construct many classes, subclasses, relations, instances, and to define class axioms in any domain. E-Agriculture information systems can make use of OWL ontologies to provide consumers with meaningful data. Analyzing the stages of a farming system and the data needs of farmers at each stage is essential before constructing the data using ontology. Figure 33.1 depicts the overall structure of our suggested model.

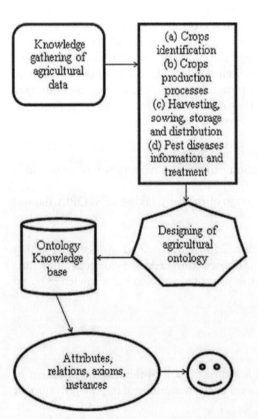

Figure 33.1 Proposed agricultural framework based on ontology

A. Knowledge Gathering
This study used publicly available Kaggle Dataset for 'PESTOPIA: Indian pests and pesticide dataset' [7]. The dataset is related to pests and pests' management practices. It also involves crop management behavior, types of crops and many more.

B. Crops Identification
At this stage, the kind of soil and climate will once again play a role in deciding which crop will be planted in a certain zone. To facilitate the retrieval of agricultural-related information, this pertinent data is loaded into an ontology that has been specifically created for that purpose.

C. Crops Production Processes
Crops are tended to and their growth is monitored throughout this time, with help from measures like watering, fertilizing, and using biocides.

D. Harvesting, Sowing, Storage and Distribution
Preparing the soil and planting the seeds occurs at this step and follows a set of guidelines.

Harvesting refers to the systematic collection of agricultural output from a farm, followed by the necessary steps to ensure its proper storage and subsequent distribution. The next step is storage and distribution, where the harvested and processed produce is packed, stored, and then made available to the general public and businesses through various distribution channels.

E. Pest Diseases Information and Treatment
In this step, a dataset created to aid academics and industry professionals in enhancing machine learning algorithms for pest identification and management is used. Also helpful for agriculturalists and pest control experts looking to expand their knowledge of India's unique pests and methods for dealing with them.

F. Designing of Ontology
Knowledge in any field may be captured using ontologies. Classes and their relationships are mapped out using the OWL ontology. Following this, the ontology for the agricultural domain will be constructed using the identified classes, subclasses, and connections. In this study, the dataset in Protégé [16] was employed to establish a knowledge-based repository using the OWL descriptive logic language (OWL DL). The class 'Thing' was chosen as the starting point, and then a class hierarchy was built by adding further classes representing things like crop types, production methods, soil types, and so on.

The created knowledge base repository is termed as ontology knowledge base (OKB) which consists of attributes, object properties, instances properties and axioms. Lastly, a user or farmer can access this ontological system to get agricultural information easily.

Result and Implementation

Figure 33.2 below shows entities related to the designed ontology named 'Agricultural_knowledge_base'.
Figure 33.3 shows classes and sub-classes of the designed ontology. Here, Agricultural_knowledge_base is super class that consists of various sub-classes namely pesticides, soil, pests and crops.

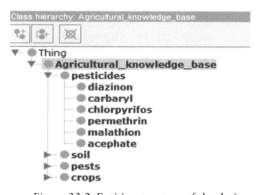

Figure 33.2 Entities structure of the designed ontology

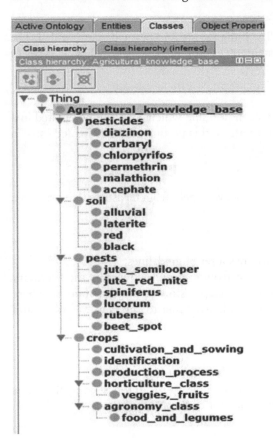

Figure 33.3 Full view of the designed ontology using PROTÉGÉ 4.3.1

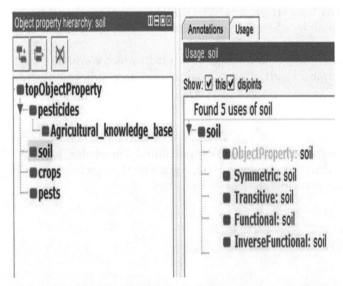

Figure 33.4 Object property hierarchy of soil as sub-class

Figure 33.4 shows distribution of attributes of the designed agricultural ontology via object property hierarchy. The properties linked with sub-classes are symmetric, transitive, functional and inverse functional.

Figure 33.5 shows annotation properties such that class of soil is annotated by property horticulture and agronomy. Similarly, label is annotated by classes and sub-classes used in the designing of ontology. VersionInfo is annotated property of tool PROTÉGÉ as 4.3.1.

Foregrounded model offers concrete description of classes given by constructed ontology. Within the ontology agricultural knowledge base ontology, we have designated the agricultural knowledge base with a depth or level of 1 as a subclass of root class Thing. Similarly the subclass pesticides and its instances are at a level 2 depth/complexity. The subclasses of soil and its instances have a third dimension or more in depth. The leaf classes within the ontology have a maximum depth or level of 5. This is shown by Figure 33.6. and Figure 33.7 Metrics distribution is been displayed.

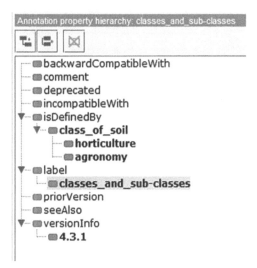

Figure 33.5 Annotation property hierarchy of the designed ontology

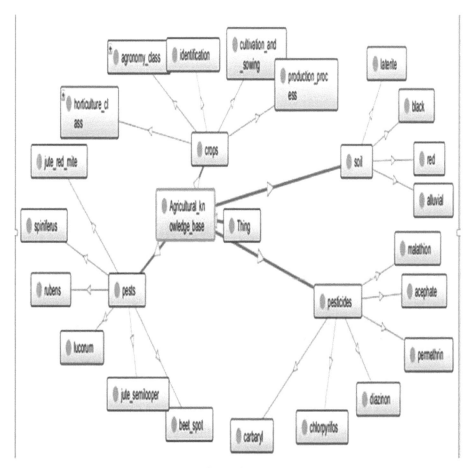

Figure 33.6 Emphasized model of complete ontology

Table 33.1 Disjoint classes.

Classes	Sub-classes	Disjoint status
Pesticides	diazinon	Disjoint with soil and pests
Pesticides	Carbaryl	Disjoint with soil and pests
Pesticides	chlorpyrifos	Disjoint with soil and pests
Pesticides	Permethrin	Disjoint with soil and pests
Pesticides	Malathion	Disjoint with soil and pests
Pesticides	acephate	Disjoint with soil and pests
Soil	Alluvial	Disjoint with pesticides and pests
Soil	Laterite	Disjoint with pesticides and pests
Soil	Black	Disjoint with pesticides and pests
Soil	Red	Disjoint with pesticides and pests
Pests	Spiniferus	Disjoint with soil and pesticides
Pests	lucorum	Disjoint with soil and pesticides
Pests	rubens	Disjoint with soil and pesticides
Pests	Jute_semilooper	Disjoint with soil and pesticides

Table 33.2 Ontology metrics count.

Parameters	Count
Superclass	1
Classes	4
Sub-classes	21
Instances	2
Object property	4

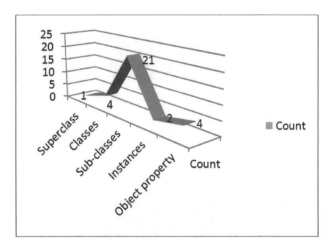

Figure 33.7 Metrics distribution

Results and Analysis

Table 33.1 gives the description about building disjoint classes in designed agricultural knowledge base. In the present ontology, several classes have been included, such as soil, pests, crops etc. The instances of these classes are now mutually exclusive, meaning that it is impossible for two classes to share a single instance. "&owl:AllDisjointClasses"is used to do this. As an illustration, the subclasses are defined as disjoint, ensuring that an instance of soil cannot simultaneously be an instance of the Pests subclass. The following syntax allows for representation of this in OWL DL:

Syntax
DisjointClasses (pesticides, soil, pests, crops): pesticides ∩ soil ∩ pests ∩ crops = { }

DisjoingInstances (diazinon, alluvial, jute semilooper, sowing): diazinon η alluvial η jute semilooper η sowing = { }

Table 33.2 presents' metrics of the designed ontology as follows:

Conclusion and Future Work

The Kaggle dataset was used to compile information about the various phases of India's agricultural industry for this study. Using issue scope identification and ontology integration into classes, subclasses, and relationships, we have analyzed the information needs of a farmer. The OWL DL ontology design language is used to create the agricultural knowledge base ontology. It also details the whole procedure for constructing an ontology, down to the individual objects, annotations, and mutually exclusive classes, all of which are necessary for effective data extraction from the system.

References

[1] Abrahão, E., and Hirakawa, A. R. (2017). Task ontology modeling for technical knowledge representation in agriculture field operations domain. In Second International Conference on Information Systems Engineering (ICISE), Charleston, SC, USA, (pp. 12–16), doi: 10.1109/ICISE.2017.18.

[2] Devi, M., and Dua, M. (2017). ADANS: an agriculture domain question answering system using ontologies. In International Conference on Computing, Communication and Automation (ICCCA), Greater Noida, India, (pp. 122–127), doi: 10.1109/CCAA.2017.8229784.

[3] Kushala, V. M., Supriya, M. C., and Divakar, H. R. (2022). Construction of domain ontology considering organic fertilizers for a sustainable agriculture. In Fourth International Conference on Emerging Research in Electronics, Computer Science and Technology (ICERECT), Mandya, India, (pp. 1–5), doi: 10.1109/ICERECT56837.2022.10060598.

[4] Saraswat, D. (2023). Ontology based agriculture data mining using IWO and RNN. In 6th International Conference on Information Systems and Computer Networks (ISCON), Mathura, India, (pp. 1–8), doi: 10.1109/ISCON57294.2023.10112187.

[5] Stoyanova-Doycheva, A., Ivanova, V., Doukovska, L., Tabakova, V., Radeva, I., and Danailova, S. (2021). Architecture of a knowledge base in smart crop production. In International Conference Automatics and Informatics (ICAI), Varna, Bulgaria, (pp. 305–309), doi: 10.1109/ICAI52893.2021.9639874.

[6] Naidoo, N., Lawton, S., Ramnanan, M., Fonou-Dombeu, J. V., and Gowda, R. (2021). Modelling climate smart agriculture with ontology. In International Conference on Artificial Intelligence, Big Data, Computing and Data Communication Systems (icABCD), Durban, South Africa, (pp. 1–9), doi: 10.1109/icABCD51485.2021.9519380.

[7] Kaggle (2023). The PESTOPIA dataset uploaded from Kaggle repository (www.kaggle.com) value as on dated August 2023. https://www.kaggle.com/datasets/shruthisindhura/pestopia.

[8] Garg, S. (2023). eChoupal: the ticker tape of agricultural markets. In 2023 International Conference on Intelligent and Innovative Technologies in Computing, Electrical and Electronics (IITCEE), Bengaluru, India, (pp. 335–341), doi: 10.1109/IITCEE57236.2023.10090873.

[9] Mittal, A., Chetan, K. P., Jayaraman, S., Jagyasi, B. G., Pande, A., and Balamuralidhar, P. (2012). mKRISHI wireless sensor network platform for precision agriculture. In Sixth International Conference on Sensing Technology (ICST), Kolkata, India, (pp. 623–629), doi: 10.1109/ICSensT.2012.6461755.

[10] Ravikumar, K. K., Ishaque, M., Panigrahi, B. S., and Pattnaik, C. R. (2023). Detection of Covid-19 using AI application. EAI endorsed transactions on pervasive health and technology, 9.

[11] Singh, G., Jain, V., and Singh, M. (2013). Ontology development using Hozo and semantic analysis for information retrieval in semantic web. In IEEE Second International Conference on Image Information Processing (ICIIP-2013), Shimla, India, (pp. 113–118), doi: 10.1109/ICIIP.2013.6707566.

[12] Yadav, U., Narula, G. S., Duhan, N., and Jain, V. (2016). A novel approach for precise search results retrieval based on semantic web technologies. In 3rd International Conference on Computing for Sustainable Global Development (INDIACom), New Delhi, India, (pp. 1357–1362).

[13] Zhou, J., Song, X., Li, Y., Gao, Y., and Zhang, X. (2021). Building real-time ontology based on adaptive filter for multi-domain knowledge organization. *IEEE Access*, 9, 66486–66497, doi: 10.1109/ACCESS.2021.3076833.

[14] Zhou, J., Song, X., Li, Y., Gao, Y., and Zhang, X. (2021). Building real-time ontology based on adaptive filter for multi-domain knowledge organization. *IEEE Access*, 9, 66486–66497. doi: 10.1109/ACCESS.2021.3076833.

[15] Santos, F., and Mello, C. E. (2022). Matching network of ontologies: a random walk and frequent itemsets approach. *IEEE Access*, 10, 44638–44659. doi: 10.1109/ACCESS.2022.3164067.

[16] Jain, S., Gupta, R., and Dwivedi, R. K. (2018). Generating patterns from pizza ontology using protégé and weka tool. In International Conference on System Modeling & Advancement in Research Trends (SMART), Moradabad, India, (pp. 126–131), doi: 10.1109/SYSMART.2018.8746935.

34 Assessment of random committee (RC) and additive regression (AR) classifiers in premature verdict of knee arthritis

Rohit Pandey[1,a], Sowmiya Kumar[2,b] and Rachit Adhvaryu[3,c]

[1]Assistant Professor, Department of UGDX, ATLAS SkillTech University, Mumbai, Maharashtra, India

[2]Assistant Professor, Department of Computer Science and Information Technology, Jain (Deemed to be University), Bangalore, India

[3]Associate Professor, Department of Computer Science and Engineering, Faculty of Engineering and Technology, Parul Institute of Engineering and Technology, Parul University, Vadodara, Gujarat, India

Abstract

Arthritis, the most prevalent form of chronic joint disease, is characterised by a wide range of symptoms that can appear at different times and in different combinations. Knee arthritis diagnosis requires consideration of several criteria, most of which are medical risk factors such as age, gender, hormonal state, body weight or size, family history of illness, etc. Given the complexity of the medical conditions that contribute to arthritis, this work aims to use classifiers as a novel, effective machine learning technique to early detection. Clinical datasets from online sources were classified to show the viability of the suggested technique. The user's text is too short to be rewritten academically. Furthermore, the validity of the methodology is established through the assessment of two classifiers, namely random committee (RC) and additive regression (AR) using metrics such as precision, recall, accuracy etc. The findings demonstrate the efficacy of machine learning techniques in the diagnosis of arthritis.

Keywords: Additive regression, classification, Machine learning, random committee

Introduction

Knee arthritis, a prevalent musculoskeletal ailment that predominantly affects elderly adults on a global scale, is distinguished by alterations in bone and cartilage structures. While a definitive solution for arthritis is currently lacking, the significance of early detection cannot be overstated. The illness is detected by clinical evaluation and X-ray examinations, while the sole efficacious intervention for the latter stages of the condition is a complete knee replacement. The user's text is too short to be rewritten in an academic manner. It is recommended to pursue early detection of knee osteoarthritis in order to reduce the need for surgical procedures and hinder the progressive degeneration of bone and cartilage. Various biological imaging techniques, such as X-ray, magnetic resonance imaging (MRI), ultrasound, and other modalities, are used for the assessment of arthritis [1, 2]. It is crucial to emphasize that a considerable number of experts in the field of artificial intelligence are interested in using this data to enhance the effectiveness of early identification of osteoporosis. The facilitation of achieving this result is made possible by the developments in medical imaging technologies and the increased accessibility of electronic health information, as shown by the osteoarthritis initiative (OAI) [3, 4]. The enhancement of job efficiency can be achieved by the classification and detection of knee arthritis using medical and imaging data. The processing of MRI photographs using different computer systems remains a significant obstacle in most research [5]. This phenomenon stimulated more investigation and advancement in the field of medical imaging techniques, resulting in a wide range of methodologies. Diagnosing early-stage knee arthritis is a significant challenge, as indicated by the findings given in reference [6]. The existing body of research highlights a clear and pressing want for clinical instruments that possess the capability to diagnose and perhaps forecast diseases in light of the acknowledged clinical and biological diversity observed in knee arthritis. Hence, the primary contribution of this study is the application of RC and AR classifiers to assess the presence of illness and mitigate the need for knee replacement surgery in patients.

The remaining paper is organized into following sections. Section 2 provides related works on assessment of methods and techniques done in this regard. Section 3 presents the proposed approach utilizing machine learning classifiers. Section 4 provides implementation of the proposed approach followed by conclusion and references.

[a]rohit.pandey@atlasuniversity.edu.in, [b]soumya.k@jainuniversity.ac.in, [c]rachit.adhvaryu24310@paruluniversity.ac.in

DOI: 10.1201/9781003534136-34

Literature Review

The authors employed convolutional neural networks (CNN) in their study, documented in reference [7], to observe and track the progression of Knee Osteoarthritis. Multiple CNN models, such as the residual neural network, visual geometry group, and densely connected convolutional networks, were used to classify the pictures of the detected knee joints. Prior to classification, the YOLO network was utilized to detect these knee joints. According to the research, a customized visual geometry group-19 model outperformed both Residual neural network and densely connected convolutional network variants in terms of prediction accuracy. The utilization of a deep learning system was employed by the authors referenced in [8, 9] for the purpose of identifying knee osteoarthritis. This identification process was conducted utilizing the MOST dataset. The accuracy of the application was 71.90%. The identification of the region of interest in X-ray pictures was accomplished by the utilization of the region proposal network technique. However, it was observed that this approach did not achieve a significant level of precision and recall. In this study, the researchers introduce the osteo high-resolution network, a novel system designed to rapidly assess the degree of osteoarthritis in the knee joint [10]. The high-resolution network was utilized to document the characteristics of knee X-ray pictures. The algorithm exhibited a 71% accuracy rate. The research conducted in reference [11] introduced a novel approach for categorizing images of knee osteoarthritis. This approach involved utilizing an unobserved local center of mass segmentation algorithm in conjunction with a deep Siamese convolutional neural network. The extraction of anatomical characteristics of Knee Osteoarthritis is accomplished through the use of the gray-level co-occurrence GLCM matrix. The clinical data undergoes training with 75 iterations and subsequent validation in order to enhance its accuracy. A CNN-LSTM based approach for knee osteoarthritis x-ray classification was proposed by the authors in [12]. Based on testing data, it is clear that the VGG-16 model achieves the best results when it comes to extracting the high-level feature by recognizing the differences in KL grading of knees.

Proposed Methodology

The layout is shown in Figure 34.1.

A. Dataset Collection

A collection of X-ray pictures and associated data characteristics are obtained from the dataset referred to as "Knee Osteoarthritis dataset with severity grading" [13]. The dataset provided encompasses knee X-ray data that serves the purpose of knee joint identification as well as knee KL grading. The grade descriptors are outlined as follows:

   Grade 0: The image depicts a knee that is in a state of good health.
   Grade 1 (Doubtful): Joint constriction, maybe due to osteophytes, is conceivable.
   "Grade 2 (Minimal)": Osteophytes are present, and there may be some narrowing of the joint space.
   "Grade 3 (Moderate)": Osteophytes are present, and there may be some narrowing of the joint space.
   "Grade 4 (Severe)": Sclerosis, joint constriction, and large osteophytes are all symptoms of this condition.

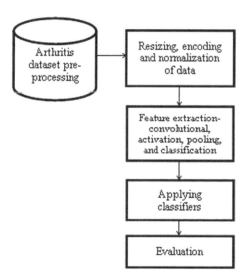

Figure34.1 Architecture of the proposed model

The knee arthritis detection dataset is a valuable resource for researchers and software engineers. Developing reliable and accurate classification models is made possible by the extensive and varied dataset.

B. Pre-Processing
Pre-processing occurs first after pictures and datasets have been loaded, and it is crucial for visual analysis and interpretation in many different types of software. Therefore, the success or failure of automated analytical techniques in these applications depends on how well image enhancement eliminates irregular illuminations and enriches images with limited contrast [14].

C. Resizing and Encoding of Images and Data
As soon as the code sees the variables for "image height" and "image width" set to 125, it scales down all of the photos in the data set to exactly 125 × 125 pixels. Images must be resized to the same dimensions before they can be used in the training of a CNN model for features extraction. Encoding is the process through which quantitative characteristics are converted into qualitative ones.

D. Features Extraction Using CNN
The convolutional layer performs a process of feature extraction on the input data, resulting in the generation of feature maps. The aforementioned feature maps are generated as a result of different feature detectors. The first convolutional layer of the neural network is responsible for extracting fundamental information, such as edges, by activating neurons. Neurons possess the capacity to gather information, which aids in the development of a more extensive comprehension of the picture inside succeeding convolutional layers. Consequently, this facilitates the identification of high-level characteristics. "The process is represented via four layers viz. convolutional layer, activation layer, pooling layer and classification layer."

Convolutional layer: - The definition of each convolutional layer encompasses several parameters, such as the input size, kernel size, depth of the map stack, zero-padding, and stride. The size of the output may be determined by the use of equations 1 and 2, which are as follows:

$$MS_x = (IS_x - KS_x) / S_x \tag{1}$$

$$MS_y = (IS_y - KS_y) / S_y \tag{2}$$

Where MS_x, MS_y denotes map stack over x and y axis respectively, IS denotes input stack, S denotes stride.

Activation layer - Once the weighted total has been computed and the bias component has been included, it becomes imperative to use an activation function. In order to augment the capacities of a neural network to act as a universal approximate of continuous functions, it is essential to include a non-linear activation function alongside the pure perceptron. This is crucial as it disrupts the linear combination of inputs, allowing for a more flexible and versatile neural network. Rectified Linear Units (ReLUs) [15] are commonly employed in neural networks as activation functions to enhance their performance.

Pooling layer - Pooling or subsampling is a process that facilitates communication and interaction among many convolutional layers. Max-pooling and average-pooling are commonly employed pooling techniques inside neural networks. Pooling is a technique that focuses on mitigating the issue of over fitting by aggregating local data inside a pooling window, hence lowering the dimensionality of the data.

Classification layer - Machine learning algorithms are utilised in this process to carry out the categorization of attributes inside a dataset. This is achieved by dividing the data into separate training and testing sets. This research employs two classifiers, which will be further upon in the subsequent sections.

Random committee classifier [16] implementation involves the creation of many base classifiers, each initialized with different random integer seed values. The ultimate classification result is derived by the computation of the standard deviation of the predictions generated by each individual base classifier. Additive regression [17] is a non-parametric approach utilized for regression analysis. The proposed model employs a one-dimensional smoothing technique to construct a constrained set of nonparametric regression models. This makes its vulnerability to the dimensionality problem much lower.

Result and Implementation

Figure 34.2 below shows a few attributes of 'knee osteoarthritis dataset with severity grading' dataset. It presents grading levels with severity associated with it.

Figure 34.3 shows refined and normalized attributes after applying normalization on dataset. These attributes play vital role in performing classification using machine learning classifiers.

Figure 34.4 shows only 2 unique attributes after replacing missing and incorrect instances.

Figure 34.5 shows classification of attributes with knee grading levels. Random tree is generated with size 6. Further, this classifier is applied on tested data as shown in Figure 34.6.

Figure 34.6 shows confusion matrix that provides a comprehensive summary of the performance exhibited by a machine learning model when applied to a specific set of test data. The measurement of classification model performance is frequently employed to assess the ability of these models to predict a category label for each input occurrence.

Figure 34.7 presents the regression classification after applying pooling and ReLU function. It generates true and false positives with different class indexes.

Figure 34.8 Graphical representation has been displayed for as a quantitative analysis and Figure 34.9 Accuracy comparison is attached to shown the clear difference for the analysis.

Results and Analysis

Table 34.1 gives the description about evaluation results based on the following metrics:

Selected attribute

Name: KL grading level			Type: Nominal	
Missing: 0 (0%)		Distinct: 5	Unique: 5 (100%)	
No.	Label	Count		Weight
1	Grade 0	1	1	
2	Grade 1	1	1	
3	Grade 2	1	1	
4	Grade 3	1	1	
5	Grade 4	1	1	

Class: Indication (Nom)   ∨ | Vis

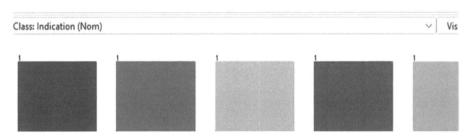

Figure 34.2 Listing of attributes of dataset

Filter

Choose **StratifiedRemoveFolds** -S 0 -N 3 -F 1

Current relation

Relation: knee arthritis-weka.filters.supervised.instance.Strat
Instances: 2

Attributes

| All | None |

No.

1 ☑ KL grading level
2 ☑ Indication

Figure 34.3 Applying 'StratifiedRemoveFolds' filter

Selected attribute
Name: KL grading level   Type: Nominal
Missing: 0 (0%)   Distinct: 2   Unique: 2 (100%)

No.	Label	Count	
1	Grade 0	1	1
2	Grade 1	0	0
3	Grade 2	0	0
4	Grade 3	1	1
5	Grade 4	0	0

Class: Indication (Nom)

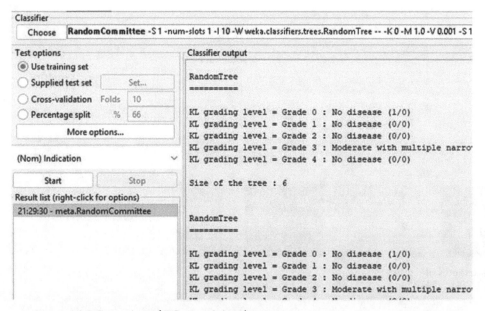

Figure 34.4 Unique attributes after normalization

Classifier
Choose   **RandomCommittee** -S 1 -num-slots 1 -I 10 -W weka.classifiers.trees.RandomTree -- -K 0 -M 1.0 -V 0.001 -S 1

Test options   Classifier output
◉ Use training set
○ Supplied test set   Set...   RandomTree
○ Cross-validation Folds   10   ==========
○ Percentage split   %   66
            More options...   KL grading level = Grade 0 : No disease (1/0)
                                       KL grading level = Grade 1 : No disease (0/0)
                                       KL grading level = Grade 2 : No disease (0/0)
(Nom) Indication   ∨   KL grading level = Grade 3 : Moderate with multiple narro
                                       KL grading level = Grade 4 : No disease (0/0)
      Start   Stop
Result list (right-click for options) Size of the tree : 6
21:29:30 - meta.RandomCommittee
                                       RandomTree
                                       ==========

                                       KL grading level = Grade 0 : No disease (1/0)
                                       KL grading level = Grade 1 : No disease (0/0)
                                       KL grading level = Grade 2 : No disease (0/0)
                                       KL grading level = Grade 3 : Moderate with multiple narro

Figure 34.5 Execution of RC on training dataset

```
=== Confusion Matrix ===

a b c d e   <-- classified as
0 0 0 1 0 | a = No disease
0 0 0 0 0 | b = Doubtful joint inflammation with lipping
0 0 0 0 0 | c = Minimal presence of narrowing in joints
1 0 0 0 0 | d = Moderate with multiple narrows in joints
0 0 0 0 0 | e = Severe with large sclerosis
```

Figure 34.6 Confusion matrix produced by RC

```
=== Classifier model (full training set) ===

Classification via Regression

Classifier for class with index 0:

M5 pruned model tree:
(using smoothed linear models)
LM1 (100/78.827%)

LM num: 1
class =
        0.1746 * a3=false
        + 0.5153 * a5=false
        + 0.2082 * a8=true
        + 0.2652

Number of Rules : 1

Classifier for class with index 1:

M5 pruned model tree:
(using smoothed linear models)
LM1 (100/78.827%)
```

Figure 34.7 Additive regression output

Table 34.1 Evaluation metrics.

Classifiers	RMSE	MAE	Computation Time
AR	0.34	0.25	0.08
RC	0.42	0.29	0.14

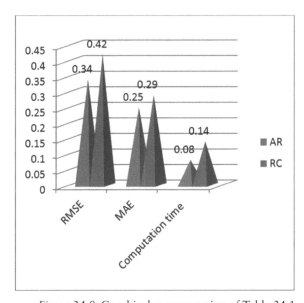

Figure 34.8 Graphical representation of Table 34.1

Mean absolute error (MAE): The metric being referred to is the average magnitude of errors observed in the gathered forecasts.

Root mean squared value (RMSE): The assessment of the dependability of a model's predictions of numeric variables is a widely used practice. The RMSE measures how well a model predicts the true value of a variable. When the RMSE is high, there is a sizable discrepancy between the residual and the true value.

Computation time (t): It is the amount of total time taken to build a trained model and testing it.

It is clearly seen from Table 34.1 that AR proves better than RC in terms of early diagnosis of knee arthritis. Lower values of RMSE and MAE indicate that there is no deviation in predicting accurate values.

Table 34.2 presents accuracy comparison of both the classifiers on the proposed model.

Table 34.2 Accuracy comparison.

Classifiers	Accuracy (%)
AR	85
RC	78

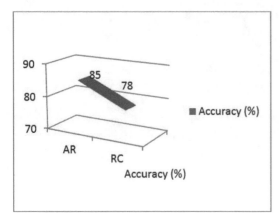

Figure 34.9 Accuracy comparison

Conclusion and Future Work

This study investigated many innovative methodologies for the automated assessment of knee severity utilizing machine learning methods. The procedure starts with the pre-processing of the dataset, which is subsequently followed by the resizing and normalization of the data. Our first attempt to classify knee injuries was using characteristics from pre-trained CNNs. The experimental results demonstrated that the features produced by the pooling and convolutional layers exhibited higher accuracy compared to the features provided by the fully connected layers. The characteristics undergo categorization using Additive regression (AR) and Random Committee (RC) classifiers. Both classifiers are subjected to confirmation employing criteria such as root mean square error (RMSE) and mean absolute error (MAE), computation time, and accuracy. The findings indicate that the use of AR yields a greater level of accuracy, namely at 85%, as well as the lowest values for both RMSE and MAE.

References

[1] Sundari. S. M., Chandra, J. V., and Pasupuleti, S. K. (2022). Machine learning methodologies for predicting neurological disease using behavioral activity mining in health care. In 8th International Conference on Advanced Computing and Communication Systems (ICACCS), Coimbatore, India, (pp. 1035–1039), doi: 10.1109/ICACCS54159.2022.9785276.

[2] Wang, X., Liu, S., and Zhou, C. (2022). Classification of knee osteoarthritis based on transfer learning model and magnetic resonance images. In International Conference on Machine Learning, Control, and Robotics (MLCR), Suzhou, China, (pp. 67–71), doi: 10.1109/MLCR57210.2022.00021.

[3] Du, Y., Shan, J., Almajalid, R., and Zhang, M. (2018). Knee osteoarthritis severity level classification using whole knee cartilage damage index and ANN. In IEEE/ACM International Conference on Connected Health: Applications, Systems and Engineering Technologies (CHASE), Washington, DC, USA, (pp. 19–21), doi: 10.1145/3278576.3278585.

[4] Du, Y., Almajalid, R., Shan, J., and Zhang, M. (2018). A novel method to predict knee osteoarthritis progression on MRI using machine learning methods. *IEEE Transactions on NanoBioscience*, 17(3), 228–236. doi: 10.1109/TNB.2018.2840082.

[5] Rehman, A., Raza, A., Alamri, F. S., Alghofaily, B., and Saba, T. (2023). Transfer learning-based smart features engineering for osteoarthritis diagnosis from knee x-ray images. *IEEE Access*, 11, 71326–71338. doi: 10.1109/ACCESS.2023.3294542.

[6] Ntakolia, C., Kokkotis, C., Moustakidis, S., and Tsaopoulos, D. (2020). A machine learning pipeline for predicting joint space narrowing in knee osteoarthritis patients. In IEEE 20th International Conference on Bioinformatics and Bioengineering (BIBE), Cincinnati, OH, USA, (pp. 934–941), doi: 10.1109/BIBE50027.2020.00158.

[7] Ganeshbabu, K., and Ilayaraja, M. (2022). Applications of machine learning in rheumatoid arthritis - an insight. In 6th International Conference on Computing Methodologies and Communication (ICCMC), Erode, India, (pp. 1161–1165), doi: 10.1109/ICCMC53470.2022.9753705.

[8] Du, Y., Shan, J., and Zhang, M. (2017). Knee osteoarthritis prediction on MR images using cartilage damage index and machine learning methods. In IEEE International Conference on Bioinformatics and Biomedicine (BIBM), Kansas City, MO, USA, (pp. 671–677), doi: 10.1109/BIBM.2017.8217734.

[9] Kumar, A., and Saxena, P. (2019). Quantification of cartilage loss for automatic detection and classification of osteoarthritis using machine learning approach. In 10th International Conference on Computing, Communication and Networking Technologies (ICCCNT), Kanpur, India, (pp. 1–6), doi: 10.1109/ICCCNT45670.2019.8944538.

[10] Nutakki, C., Narayanan, J., Anchuthengil, A. A., Nair, B., and Diwakar, S. (2017). Classifying gait features for stance and swing using machine learning. In International Conference on Advances in Computing, Communications and Informatics (ICACCI), Udupi, India, (pp. 545–548), doi: 10.1109/ICACCI.2017.8125896.

[11] Du, Y., Shan, J., Almajalid, R., Alon, T., and Zhang, M. (2018). Using whole knee cartilage damage index to predict knee osteoarthritis: a two-year longitudinal study. In IEEE International Conference on Bioinformatics and Biomedicine (BIBM), Madrid, Spain, (pp. 623–628), doi: 10.1109/BIBM.2018.8621530.

[12] Ravikumar, K. K., Ishaque, M., Panigrahi, B. S., and Pattnaik, C. R. (2023). Detection of Covid-19 using AI application. EAI endorsed transactions on pervasive health and technology, 9.

[13] Kaggle (2023). The Knee osteoarthritis dataset uploaded from Kaggle repository (www.kaggle.com) value as on dated August 2023. https://www.kaggle.com/datasets/shashwatwork/knee-osteoarthritis-dataset-with-severity.

[14] Ahalya, R., and Snekha, L. U. (2023). Integrated xception- random forest model for the detection of rheumatoid arthritis in hand thermograms. In IEEE 12th International Conference on Communication Systems and Network Technologies (CSNT), Bhopal, India, (pp. 829–832), doi: 10.1109/CSNT57126.2023.10134685.

[15] Krishnan, H., Jayaraj, A., Anagha, A., Thomas, C., and Joy, G. M. (2022). Pose estimation of yoga poses using ml techniques. In IEEE 19th India Council International Conference (INDICON), Kochi, India, (pp. 1–6), doi: 10.1109/INDICON56171.2022.10040162.

[16] Niranjan, A., Prakash, A., Veena, N., Geetha, M., Deepa Shenoy, P., and Venugopal, K. R. (2017). EBJRV: an ensemble of bagging, J48 and random committee by voting for efficient classification of intrusions. In IEEE International WIE Conference on Electrical and Computer Engineering (WIECON-ECE), Dehradun, India, (pp. 51–54), doi: 10.1109/WIECON-ECE.2017.8468876.

[17] Mirza, A. H. (2018). Online boosting algorithm for regression with additive and multiplicative updates. In 26th Signal Processing and Communications Applications Conference (SIU), Izmir, Turkey, (pp. 1–4), doi: 10.1109/SIU.2018.8404455.

35 Performance breakdown of SDG, voted perceptron and JRip classifiers in valuation of software imperfections

Amit Barve[1,a], Raghav Garg[2,b] and Gobi N[3,c]

[1]Associate Professor, Department of Computer Science and Engineering, Faculty of Engineering and Technology, Parul Institute of Engineering and Technology, Parul University, Vadodara, Gujarat, India

[2]Associate Professor, Department of Computer Science & Engineering, Tula's Institute, Dehradun, India

[3]Assistant Professor, Department of Computer Science and Information Technology, Jain (Deemed to be University), Bangalore, India

Abstract

Software engineering is a multifaceted field that necessitates effective communication among many stakeholders involved in the system development process, while also adhering to strict schedule and budget constraints. The early identification of system issues during the first phases of the project life cycle allows for more efficient allocation of project resources and software developers' efforts towards system development and quality assurance activities. The primary objective of this research was to compare three machine learning classifiers in the context of NASA datasets retrieved from a public source in order to determine which one performed the best at predicting software defects and determining the appropriate category. The classifiers used in the study are Stochastic gradient descent (SGD), voted perceptron and JRip. After evaluation and comparison, it is found that SGD attains higher accuracy of 85% in estimation of software defects correctly.

Keywords: Defects, JRip, machine learning, NASA dataset, SGD, voted perceptron

Introduction

Planning, analyzing, designing, coding, testing, integrating, and maintaining a software system is a long and laborious process [1, 2]. A software engineer's responsibilities include completing a software system on schedule and under the established budget. inappropriate design, bad functional logic, inappropriate data handling, erroneous coding, etc. can all contribute to problems during development, which in turn can raise expenses, diminish customer satisfaction, and need further labor. To better keep tabs on these issues and ultimately fix them, a defect management strategy [3, 4] should be used. It's not cheap to implement defect prevention measures in order to cut down on the number of bugs introduced during software development. It's more work, and it ends up costing more in the end, but it's worth it. Consequently, it is critical to identify software flaws early in the project life cycle [5]. Machine learning methods [6] such as the binary prediction model allow for early detection of potentially faulty parts of a software system. The purpose of this study is to compare three different machine learning algorithms in terms of their ability to forecast software defects namely SGD, voted perceptron and JRip the chosen machine learning methods for comparison are used in supervised learning to address classification challenges, using quality assurance requirements. The evaluation of software defect prediction performance metrics, such as accuracy, precision, recall, MAE, RMSE etc, in the context of NASA's software defect prediction dataset are compared and contrasted across a variety of machine learning techniques.

"The remaining paper is organized into following sections. Section 2 provides related works of studies applied to estimate defects using machine learning approaches. Section 3 presents the proposed approach utilizing machine learning classifiers. Section 4 provides implementation of the proposed approach followed by conclusion and references."

Literature Review

The study conducted by [7] utilizes logistic regression analysis to examine the relationship between a collection of object-oriented design criteria and the detection of courses that are prone to errors. The authors of [8] have conducted a study where neural networks were used to classify modules of extensive telecommunication systems as either prone to faults or not. The outcomes of this approach were afterwards compared to those obtained using a non-parametric discriminant model. Based on their research results, it was observed that the neural network model exhibited a greater level of prediction accuracy compared to the non-parametric

---

[a]amit.barve17535@paruluniversity.ac.in, [b]raghav.garg@tulas.edu.in, [c]gobi.n@jainuniversity.ac.in

DOI: 10.1201/9781003534136-35

discriminant model. The authors of [9] conducted a case study in which they used regression trees to categorize the error-prone components of massive communication networks. The developers of [10] employ a Bayesian Belief Network to detect bugs in software. However, as acknowledged by [11], this machine learning method has several shortcomings. In [12], the authors use the Random Forest algorithm to the software defect dataset presented by NASA in order to foresee error-prone components in software systems, and they compare their model to others based on statistics and machine learning. The results of this comparison reveal that the random forest algorithm has higher prediction accuracy than the other techniques studied. To deal against the noise in defect data, the authors of [13] have explored its effect on defect prediction through the use of a noise detection and removal method. The research showed that predictions for noisy cases could be made with a fair degree of precision, and that applying elimination enhanced the defect prediction precision.

Proposed Methodology

The layout is shown in Figure 35.1.

A. Dataset Collection
'NASA Software Defect Prediction Data Analysis' [14] is a dataset that collects a variety of information linked to software problems. This dataset has been released to promote reproducible, rebuttable, and upgradeable prediction models in software engineering.

B. Splitting of Dataset
The given dataset is divided into trained model and testing model. Testing is done via cross folds validation approach to validate the performance of each of the classifiers.

C. Applying Classifiers
The classifiers used in the study are SGD, Voted perceptron and JRip. They are explained as follows:

Stochastic gradient descent (SGD) is an iterative optimisation algorithm utilised to locate the optimal value (minimum or maximum) of an objective function [15]. It is often used in machine learning projects to adjust model parameters and hence decrease the value of the cost function. For best results on both the training and testing sets, gradient descent seeks to pinpoint optimal model parameters. To perform gradient descent, a vector is used that points in the direction of the functions sharpest climb at a given position. It's possible that the algorithm will start off by going in the reverse path of the gradient and then progressively descend towards lesser values of the function until it reaches the lowest value of the function.

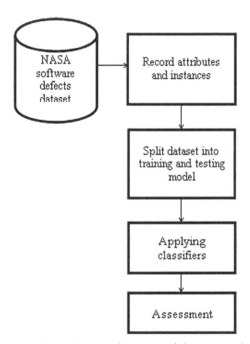

Figure 35.1 Architecture of the proposed model

One variation that makes use of many weighted perceptron's is the voted perceptron [16]. When an example is misclassified, the method begins a new perceptron utilizing the previous perceptron's weights as the beginning value for the weights vector.

JRip [17] uses association rules in combination with reduced error pruning (REP) is a routinely adopted and very efficient strategy often implemented in decision tree algorithms. The REP method uses a process of dividing the training data into two distinct sets: an expanding set and a contracting set. A heuristic technique is used to create a basic rule set over the growing set. To reduce the complexity of this excessively big collection of rules, we may regularly use one of many "pruning operators," the most common of which would be to remove a single condition or rule.

D. Assessment

The metrics that are used for comparing assessment of three classifiers are correctly classified instances, incorrectly classified instances, mean absolute error (MAE), root mean squared error (RMSE), precision, recall, and accuracy and computation time to build a model.

Result and Implementation

Figure 35.2 below shows a few attributes of 'NASA Software defect prediction' dataset. The dataset consists of 22 attributes and 10885 instances.

Figure 35.3 shows the working of SGD classifier by calculating loss function and intensity of defects related to each attribute. The negative values of some of the attributes indicate that these attributes are not subjected to over fitting to provide balanced results.

Figure 35.4 shows the total number of perceptron's formed as 4997. It indicates that there are around 4997 wrongly classified instances or defects occurred in software development process.

Figure 35.5 shows generation of rules that helps in estimation of defects occurred in software development process while utilizing machine learning classifiers. JRip generates 5 rules that act as benchmark for identification of software defects or imperfections.

Figure 35.6 shows the overall visualization plots of the entire dataset attributes. Here, blue represents false labels and red represents true labels.

Results and Analysis

This section gives the description about evaluation results of three classifiers based on the following metrics:

Mean absolute error (MAE) - It's the average magnitude of the errors in all of the forecasts taken together.

Root mean squared value (RMSE) - It is often used to quantify the precision or accuracy of a model's predictions. The RMSE measures how well a model predicts the true value of a variable. When the RMSE is high, there is a sizable discrepancy between the residual and the true value.

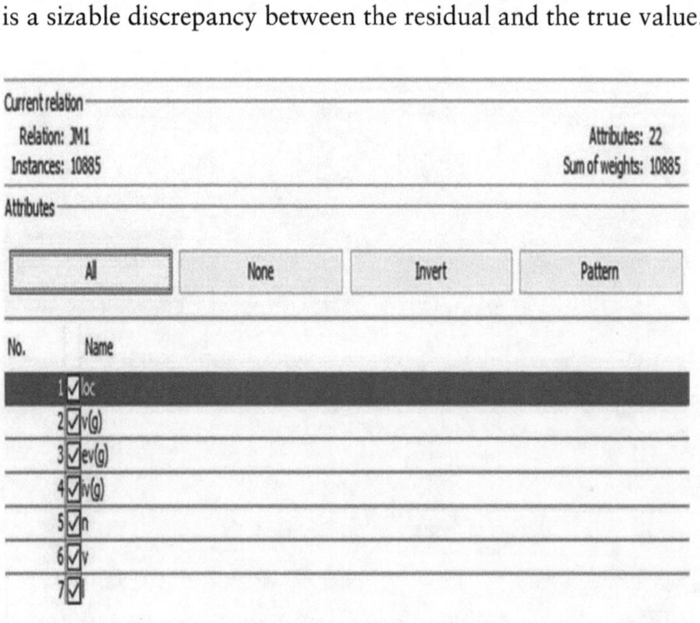

Figure 35.2 Recording of attributes and instances of the dataset

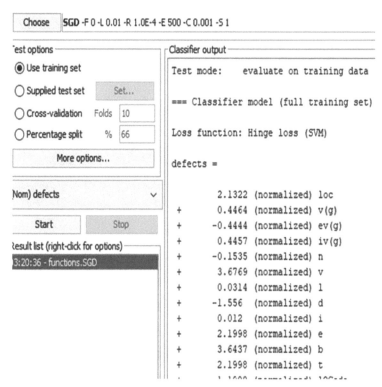

Figure 35.3 Defects estimation using SGD classifier

Figure 35.4 Execution of voted perceptron classifier

Figure 35.5 Execution of JRip classifier on training dataset

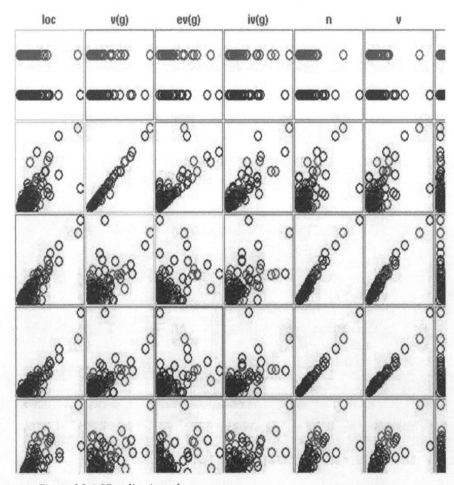

Figure 35.6 Visualization of parameters

Computation time (t) - It is the amount of total time taken to build a trained model and testing it.

While recall tells us how well our model can identify important data, precision tells us exactly which data points are important. An alternative name for recall is sensitivity.

In Figure 35.7, it is seen that SGD classifier has the lowest MAE (0.192) and RMSE (0.438) with the highest precision (0.80) and recall (0.85). It shows that SGD prove to be better than other two classifiers.

Table 35.1 Detailed classification results of SGD classifier.

Metrics	Values
Correctly classified instances	80.7%
Incorrectly classified instances	19.2%
MAE	0.192
RMSE	0.438
Precision	0.80
Recall	0.85
Accuracy	85%
Computation time	3.15 seconds

Table 35.2 Detailed classification results of voted perceptron classifier.

Metrics	Values
Correctly classified instances	50.3%
Incorrectly classified instances	49.7%
MAE	0.315
RMSE	0.560
Precision	0.74
Recall	0.78
Accuracy	75%
Computation time	7.11 seconds

Table 35.3 Detailed classification results of JRip classifier.

Metrics	Values
Correctly classified instances	76.3%
Incorrectly classified instances	23.7%
MAE	0.28
RMSE	0.48
Precision	0.78
Recall	0.82
Accuracy	82%
Computation time	5.15 seconds

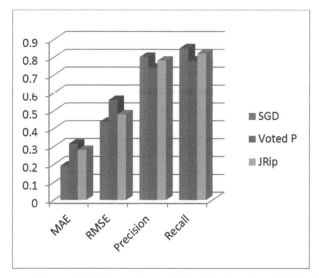

Figure 35.7 Comparison of classifiers based on MAE, RMSE, precision and recall

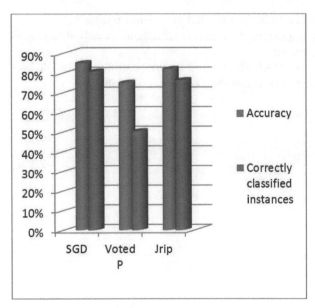

Figure 35.8 Accuracy comparison

Table 35.1 clearly displays the Detailed classification results of SGD classifier and Table 35.2 Detailed classification results of voted perceptron classifier. Which is been attached below.

Finally, Table 35.3 Detailed classification results of JRip classifier which clearly shows the values of the metrics which is been attached to the article.

Figure 35.8 shows the actual accuracy of the proposed methodologies Accuracy comparison in graphical representation.

Conclusion and Future Work

The primary objective of this experimental investigation is to assess the efficacy of three distinct machine learning algorithms in the anticipation of software problems prior to their dissemination or provision to clients. The study focuses on identifying the most proficient algorithm category by comparing their performance using software quality metrics such as "accuracy, precision, recall, MAE and RMSE." The work use the NASA software defect prediction dataset, obtained from a publicly accessible source. The results indicate that stochastic gradient descent (SGD) classifier attains the highest accuracy of 85% and the least computation time to build a model i.e. 3.15 seconds.

One potential avenue for future research is the implementation of deep learning algorithms in conjunction with existing machine learning algorithms, through the execution of an experimental study.

References

[1] Shaikh, S., Changan, L., Malik, M. R., and Khan, M. A. (2019). Software defect-prone classification using machine learning: a virtual classification study between LibSVM & liblinear. In 13th International Conference on Mathematics, Actuarial Science, Computer Science and Statistics (MACS), Karachi, Pakistan, (pp. 1–6), doi: 10.1109/MACS48846.2019.9024799.

[2] Prabha, C. L., and Shivakumar, N. (2020). Software defect prediction using machine learning techniques. In 4th International Conference on Trends in Electronics and Informatics (ICOEI)(48184), Tirunelveli, India, (pp. 728–733), doi: 10.1109/ICOEI48184.2020.9142909.

[3] Meng, F., Li, Y., and Wang, J. (2023). Research progress of machine learning in software defect prediction. In IEEE 12th International Conference on Communication Systems and Network Technologies (CSNT), Bhopal, India, (pp. 236–240), doi: 10.1109/CSNT57126.2023.10134739.

[4] Sharadhi, A. K., Gururaj, V., Umadi, K. R., Kumar, M., Shankar, S. P., and Varadam, D. (2022). Comprehensive survey of different machine learning algorithms used for software defect prediction. In International Conference on Decision Aid Sciences and Applications (DASA), Chiangrai, Thailan, (pp. 425–430), doi: 10.1109/DASA54658.2022.9764982.

[5] AlShaikh, F., and Elmedany, W. (2021). Estimate the performance of applying machine learning algorithms to predict defects in software using weka. In 4th Smart Cities Symposium (SCS 2021), Online Conference, Bahrain, (pp. 189–194), doi: 10.1049/icp.2022.0339.

[6] Meiliana, Karim, S., Warnars, H. L. H. S., Gaol, F. L., Abdurachman, E., and Soewito, B. (2017). Software metrics for fault prediction using machine learning approaches: a literature review with PROMISE repository dataset. In IEEE International Conference on Cybernetics and Computational Intelligence (CyberneticsCom), Phuket, Thailand, (pp. 19–23), doi: 10.1109/CYBERNETICSCOM.2017.8311708.

[7] Singh, R., Singh, J., Gill, M. S., Malhotra, R., and Garima (2020). Transfer learning code vectorizer based machine learning models for software defect prediction. In 2020 International Conference on Computational Performance Evaluation (ComPE), Shillong, India, (pp. 497–502), doi: 10.1109/ComPE49325.2020.9200076.

[8] Yang, K., Yu, H., Fan, G., Yang, X., Zheng, S., and Leng, C. (2018). Software defect prediction based on fourier learning. In IEEE International Conference on Progress in Informatics and Computing (PIC), Suzhou, China, (pp. 388–392), doi: 10.1109/PIC.2018.8706304.

[9] Tanaka, K., Monden, A., and Yücel, Z. (2019). Prediction of software defects using automated machine learning. In 20th IEEE/ACIS International Conference on Software Engineering, Artificial Intelligence, Networking and Parallel/Distributed Computing "(SNPD), Toyama, Japan, (pp. 490–494), doi: 10.1109/SNPD.2019.8935839.

[10] Yalçıner, B., and Özdeş, M. (2019). Software defect estimation using machine learning algorithms. In 4th International Conference on Computer Science and Engineering (UBMK), Samsun, Turkey, (pp. 487–491), doi: 10.1109/UBMK.2019.8907149.

[11] Miholca, D.-L. (2018). An improved approach to software defect prediction using a hybrid machine learning model. In 20th International Symposium on Symbolic and Numeric Algorithms for Scientific Computing (SYNASC), Timisoara, Romania, (pp. 443–448), doi: 10.1109/SYNASC.2018.00074.

[12] Suhag, V., Dubey, S. K., and Sharma, B. K. (2022). Software defect data collection framework for github. In 12th International Conference on Cloud Computing, Data Science & Engineering (Confluence), Noida, India, (pp. 82–87), doi: 10.1109/Confluence52989.2022.9734131.

[13] Assim, M., Obeidat, Q., and Hammad, M. (2020). Software defects prediction using machine learning algorithms. In International Conference on Data Analytics for Business and Industry: Way Towards a Sustainable Economy (ICDABI), Sakheer, Bahrain, (pp. 1–6), doi: 10.1109/ICDABI51230.2020.9325677.

[14] Kaggle (2023). The NASA software defect prediction dataset uploaded from Kaggle repository (www.kaggle.com) value as on dated August 2023. https://www.kaggle.com/code/semustafacevik/software-defect-prediction-data-analysis/input.

[15] Song, C., Pons, A., and Yen, K. (2020). Optimizing stochastic gradient descent using the angle between gradients. In IEEE International Conference on Big Data (Big Data), Atlanta, GA, USA, (pp. 5269–5275), doi: 10.1109/BigData50022.2020.9378007.

[16] Rojarath, A., Songpan, W., and Pong-inwong, C. (2016). Improved ensemble learning for classification techniques based on majority voting. In 7th IEEE International Conference on Software Engineering and Service Science (ICSESS), Beijing, China, (pp. 107–110), doi: 10.1109/ICSESS.2016.7883026.

[17] Luca, R., Bejinariu, S.-I., and Rotaru, F. (2019). Tree-based classifiers on human locomotion statistical parameters. In E-Health and Bioengineering Conference (EHB), Iasi, Romania, (pp. 1–4), doi: 10.1109/EHB47216.2019.8969975.

36 A reappraisal scheme for data management in IOT

Ritika[1,a] and Suneet Kumar[2,b]

[1]Research Scholar, Department of Computer Science and Engineering, MM Engineering College, Maharishi Markandeshwar (Deemed to be University), Mullana-Ambala, Haryana, India

[2]Associate Professor, Department of Computer Science and Engineering, MM Engineering College, Maharishi Markandeshwar (Deemed to be University), Mullana-Ambala, Haryana, India

Abstract

Internet of Things (IoT) is an advanced mechanics which has changed the way humans; smart devices, smart things, data, and information are connected throughout the world. IoT is a single concept of embedding everything. IoT evolution is yet in its premature steps, and there are a slew of interconnected hurdles to overcome. The IoT has the potential to boost the globe's accessibility, probity, availability, scalability, secrecy, and interoperability. Although, numerous challenges and concerns must be overcome before the IoT's full promise can be realized. Various components of IoT data are recognized and defined, including data sources, data collection, data processing, and transmitting devices. In terms of analytical and substantial data management, as well as transmission networks, the challenges that arise from the need to manage large amounts of heterogeneous data over their systems are mentioned. Sensors can be placed in isolated or far, huge, low-population localities in some applications, while sensors are used to monitor tight locations in others. Clustering the detectors lattice's nodes in multiple clusters is fundamentally beneficial clearly for scalability grounds, and it can be used to create conservation or utilization schedules that can significantly extend the lattice's life. Current study compares and contrasts common and advanced clustering schemes, as well as size, type of data collected, and performance as a function of non- uniformity and noise level. A combined metaheuristic approach, whale optimization algorithm (WOA) combined with SA, is also used in the proposed work.

Keywords: IoT clustering, metaheuristic algorithms, simulated annealing, WOA algorithm

Introduction

Recent breakthrough in implanted machinery and the Internet has authorized the interconnection of the things that surround us. It is projected that Internet of Things (IoT) devices will become a part of our surroundings in the future; generating massive amounts of data. Resource management frameworks have gotten a lot of interest as a way to deal with IoT management issues. Due to the growing complexity of IoT networks, a few of new security issues emerge. Additionally, security administration of IoT is discussed in this paper, as well as security challenges, risks, attacks, and requirements in IoT. This paper examines existing clustering approaches and employs metaheuristic algorithms to get the best optimal solution.

Big Data is a similar phrase for the massive volumes of data produced by all of these interconnected gadgets (BD). IoT-Big Data is the best sort of BD. It's also possible to argue that IoT and BD are mutually reliant mechanics that should be created together. However, in this study, we focus on a subset of the IoT , specifically "wireless sensor networks" (WSNs). They are typically made up of tiny detecting gadgets with limited assets that are linked cordlessly. These gadgets can communicate with each other as well as with the Internet and are known as wireless network nodes (WNN). They are sensory in the sense that they can gather data from their surroundings using particular detectors, which are further prepared and broadcasted to the net [1]. These applications appear to be the start of a large computing industry.

Clustering is a common strategy used at various levels of sensor network data analytics when dealing with large amounts of heterogeneous data. A notable feature of the learning of detector grids is that the characteristics of the nodes can be influenced by a number of constraints; that can influence how the aggregation stage could be approached. Few clustering jobs must be completed using small-intricacy approaches, while others should be highly suitable or conquer special challenges, such as decentralization.

Clustering in IoT

The gadgets and items that are linked to the net is continually expanding. These interconnected things produce a large amount of information that may be studied to uncover patterns data for a variety of applications. Clustering for IoT is in high demand at this point. Clustering has numerous benefits, including

---

[a]er.ritika2410@gmail.com, [b]suneetcit81@gmail.com

DOI: 10.1201/9781003534136-36

enabling IoT network scalability and reducing routing expenses by administrating routing options on the chosen cluster head (CH).

Furthermore, it aids in the reduction of communication bandwidth usage and topology maintenance costs. Furthermore, the network's backbone will consist just of Cluster-Heads (CHs) and gateways as shown in Figure 36.1, producing a streamlined configuration, decreased expenses, deluging, and crash [2]. The sole role of the end devices is to link to the CHs and convey information by not being impacted by modifications at the inner cluster-head layer. The CH's gathering of acquired information minimizes the quantity of packages sent. Ultimately, different administration measures like, scheduling, which can be executed at the CH rank, can assist to conserve power assets and increase the grid's lifespan [3–5]. Some of the clustering techniques are mentioned in Table 36.1.

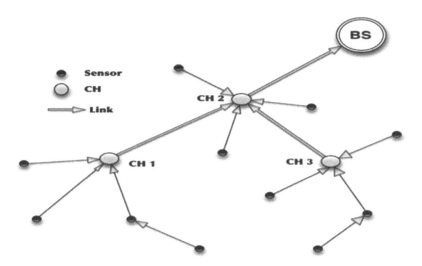

Figure 36.1 A clustering example

Table 36.1 Clustering techniques used with their description.

Clustering techniques	Description
K-Means	This method groups information by attempting to divide single information in aggregates of identical variances, reducing inactivity.
K-Medoids	The K-Medoids are an interpretation of previous clustering technique that aims to reduce the gap in the middle of cluster Area & their center. The distinction is that the medoids must be area of the collection to be grouped (that isn't always the situation with the previous clustering technique epicenters). As a result, a medoid is defined as a member of a group whom average variance to other members of the group is minutes.
DBSCAN	Another density established grouping is this technique: It seeks out high-density locations and builds clusters from there.
Hierarchical clustering	Top–down or bottom–up hierarchical clustering techniques are used: We begin with easy groups that we segregate in pairs iteratively until we achieve one group. Agglomerative hierarchical clustering is the name for this bottom–up technique, and the ranking of groups is presented as a dendrogram.
Affinity propagation	The clustering algorithm affinity propagation (AP) is established on the idea of sending messages in the middle of data points. Starting with a similarity matrix, the AP sends messages (actual numbers) between the clustering points until quality clusters emerge organically. The procedure recognizes representative location, or models, which can accurately describe a cluster during message exchange.
Constrained clustering	Clustering has a different branch that incorporates the concept of restrictions. Therefore, in this (constrained pairwise) K-means, it is defined that, this and that person must be connected, whereas min size K means mandates a minimal cluster size.

Whale Optimization Algorithm (WOA)

Whale optimization algorithm (WOA) is a metaheuristic procedure that is motivated by environment. This algorithm was developed based on humpback whale hunting behaviors. The bubble-net feeding mechanism is a whale attack method in which bubbles are formed in a circle around the victim. There are two steps to this mechanism: Attacking Prey, Encircling Prey. Whales have a unique hunting behavior that includes two techniques. The first is skyward-loop, in which the whales plunge twelve meters in the water and begin producing spirals of fizz near their enemy. Arc catch, lob tail, & arc coral are the three stages of the second technique [6].

Surrounding Enemy
The crookback whale seeks to locate its enemy & then surrounds it. The whale presumes that the finest answer at the moment is selected enemy& alerts more exploring whales to shift their positions towards the enemy. Equation [1], Equation [2] depict the encircling prey mechanism.

$$L = |v \cdot h^*(p) - h(p)| \tag{1}$$

$$h(p + 1) = h^*(p) - m. L \tag{2}$$

Where m, v are coefficient vectors, p denotes the current iteration, h* is the best solution's position vector, and h denotes the vector's location.

Exploitation Phase
There are two ways to assault a humpback whale with a bubble net. The shrinking encircling method and spiral updating are the first two approaches. The humpback whale utilizes one of these two ways to attack its prey. The chances of catching prey using these methods are roughly 50%.

First Approach–Contracting Surrounding Technique
Equation [3], Equation [4] illustrates the coefficient vectors m, v. The range [0, 1] is when the value of M steadily drops from 2 to 0..

$$m = 2M\, a - m \tag{3}$$

$$v = 2.\, \delta \tag{4}$$

The amount of 'M' starts to descend from two to zero, affecting the value of m in Equation [3.] The value of m is a random number between [–x, x]. The values for m might be anywhere between [-1, 1].

Second Approach – Spiral Updating Approach
Equation [5] is used to compute the distance between the whale and the targeted prey in this method.

$$h(p + 1) = L.\, ers.\, \cos(2\pi k) + h^*(p) \tag{5}$$

Where, $L = |v.\, h^*(p) - h(p)|$ the optimal position between the ith whale and the desired prey, r is a non-variable that describes the logarithmic loop figure, and is in the extent [-1, 1].When a crookback whale spots its enemy, it floats about it in a loop diminishing rounded figure. A spiral form or a diminishing circle has a 50 percent chance of being chosen. Equation [6] shows how to update the position of whales to the optimal solution.

$$h(p + 1) = \{h(p) - m.\, L, \quad if\ K < 0.5 \tag{6}$$

$$L.\, ers.\, \cos(2\pi k) + h^*, \quad if\ K \geq 0.5$$

Investigation Stage
During this stage, exploring agent seeks for the optimal answer around the globe at random and shifts its position in relation to other whales. The amount of X must be larger than one or smaller than -one to push the exploring agent to migrate distant away from various whales extensively. Equation [7], Equation [8] describes the random search for prey. WOA is explained in Algorithm 1.

$$L = |v.\ brand - h| \tag{7}$$

$$h(p + 1) = brand - h \tag{8}$$

Challenges Faced in IoT

Due to unique challenges, traditional network management strategies are ineffective in the IoT. IoT faces lot of challenges because of various factors. Figure 36.2 depicts the contribution of fields towards challenges of IoT. The resources available to IoT network devices are insufficient. High defect rates are common in IoT networks due to energy shortages and communication outages. The management solution for IoT should include the following set of functions:

Power Administration

IoT networks are being installed in far-flung areas. Due to the paucity of power resources in Internet of Things and its utilization in remote areas, the available energy is frequently depleted. It is unfeasible to replace power. To avoid power shortage, supply and load must be managed in a balanced manner.

Load Stabilization

Load balancing can be utilized to extend the life of IoT devices, resulting in lower energy use. Techniques like clustering can help with load balancing. Clustering organizes IoT networks into clusters, each of which is led by a cluster head.

Safety Administration

In the IoT, protection, privacy, and trust are all must-haves. Supply of security has gotten increasingly difficult due to the resource constraints of IoT devices. Because traditional security strategies are ineffective, novel security provisioning techniques are necessary. Designers of IoT management frameworks face particular issues as a result of this.

Attacks in IoT

This section is a collection of security concerns and attacks that are relevant to the IoT ecosystem. Efforts to describe IoT security vulnerabilities can be discovered in [8–13]. These dangers and obstacles are listed below:

Snooping

IoT is plainly prone to snooping because it uses a wireless communication interface. Because IoT facilities are likely to accommodate crucial information, it's critical to safeguard the information of Internet of Things linked gadgets from eavesdroppers and potential data leaks.

Destruction of Information

An assailant can attempt to change information that is transferred on-the-air among Internet of Thing machines instead of snooping or listening to it. A basic inspiration should be to disrupt communication to the point where the collecting machine is unable to comprehend and analyze the information passed by the different machine. It is a straightforward DoS attack in which the machines are unable to conduct the needed data operations. Aside from that, this approach prevents the attacker from manipulating the data itself.

Infusion Attack

Internet of Thing machines route minimal code to aid IoT approaches in detecting, collecting information, or doing a task in a certain geographical area. An attacker could inject malicious code into IoT machines that would then execute measures with the goal of disturbing the basic functioning of the IoT grid or machinery. Malicious code can potentially be used to bring down IoT devices on the network.

Insider Identification and Rejection of Service in IoT

IoT technology, which is still in its infancy, has been subjected to serious attacks. Insider attacks are one of the most damaging attacks that academics have studied. It is hoped that a mechanism will be included in the IoT security management framework to address the problem [7].

Imitation Attacks

The couple, assistance supplier and the assistance user in an IoT ecosystem must ensure that the assistance is accessible by verified individuals and is provided by a verified source. To avoid any sort of imitation, it is critical to have strong authentication systems in place.

Portability and Diversity of Devices

One of the important drivers in the emergence of IoT is the portability of smart devices. However, controlling such a large number of mobile devices becomes a critical task. Because the IoT makes use of machines with a larger rate of portability diversity, it requires devices that accommodate these machines characteristics [14, 15].

Underlying Foes

Since the underlying foe is a fragment of IoT assistance and has a better understanding of various IoT parts, the importance of an inside IoT foe strike is greater than that of an external attacker. Internal adversaries might

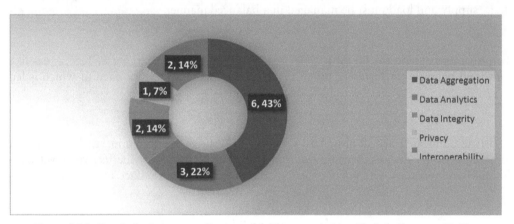

Figure 36.2 Graph depicting contribution of fields towards identified challenges of IoT

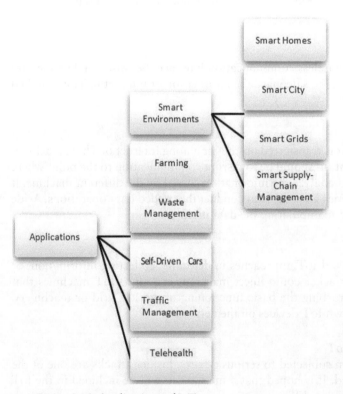

Figure 36.3 Applications of IoT

easily corrupt few device components or substantially harm machines to disturb assistance, posing an extended-term threat to the entire business.

IoT Applications

Human lives will be of utmost importance as a result of IoT technologies. The IoT can be the upcoming stage in the pouch, integrating current mobile networks, improved machines, and cutting-edge strategies. IoT machineries are designed to offer transmission data for trillions of everyday objects. Figure 36.3 depicts the many IoT application domains such as Smart Environments, Farming, Self-Driven Cars, Waste Management, Traffic Management, Telehealth, etc.

Conclusions

Internet of Things (IoT) inventor's scholars are working together to make these technologies more accessible to the general public and to help society as much as possible. However, we can only make changes if we consider the numerous challenges and faults in present technical approaches. IoT must enable seamless connection anywhere, for anybody, and with everything in order to provide intelligent services. This comprises features for detecting; sensing, networking, encoding, and visualization. This paper addresses the challenges posed by the need to administrate large amounts of heterogeneous data across heterogeneous systems. The research contrasts current and advanced clustering schemes with size, type of data collected, and performance as a function of heterogencity and noise level. A simulated metaheuristic approach, the simulated whale optimization algorithm (WOA), is also used in the proposed study.

References

[1] Plageras, A. P., Psannis, K. E., Stergiou, C., Wang, H., and Gupta, B. B. (2018). Efficient IoT-based sensor BIG data collection–processing and analysis in smart buildings. *Future Generation Computer Systems*, 82: 349-357.

[2] Guyeux, C., Chrétien, S., Bou Tayeh, G., Demerjian, J., and Bahi, J. (2019). Introducing and comparing recent clustering methods for massive data management in the internet of things. *Journal of Sensor and Actuator Networks*, 8(4), 56.

[3] Rajasegarar, S., Leckie, C., Palaniswami, M., and Bezdek, J. C. (2006). Distributed anomaly detection in wireless sensor networks. In 2006 10th IEEE Singapore International Conference on Communication Systems, (pp. 1–5). IEEE.

[4] Bakaraniya, P., and Mehta, S. (2013). K- LEACH: an improved LEACH protocol for lifetime improvement in WSN. *International Journal of Engineering Trends and Technology (IJETT)*, 4(5), 1521–1526.

[5] Pavithra, M. K., and Ghuli, P. (2015). A novel approach for reducing energy consumption using k-medoids in clustering based WSN. *International Journal of Science and Research (IJSR)*, 2(4), 6.

[6] Iwendi, C., Maddikunta, P. K. R., Gadekallu, T. R., Lakshmanna, K., Bashir, A. K., and Piran, M. J. (2021). A metaheuristic optimization approach for energy efficiency in the IoT networks. *Software: Practice and Experience*, 51(12), 2558–2571.

[7] Hu, Y., Wu, Y., and Wang, H. (2014). Detection of insider selective forwarding attack based on monitor node and trust mechanism in WSN. *Wireless Sensor Network*, 6(11), 237.

[8] Singh, J., Pasquier, T., Bacon, J., Ko, H., and Eyers, D. (2015). Twenty security considerations for cloud-supported internet of things. *IEEE Internet of things Journal*, 3(3), 269–284.

[9] Babar, S., Mahalle, P., Stango, A., Prasad, N., and Prasad, R. (2010). Proposed security model and threat taxonomy for the internet of things (IoT). In International Conference on Network Security and Applications, (pp. 420–429). Springer, Berlin, Heidelberg.

[10] Pimentel, J., Castro, J., Santos, F., and Finkelstein, A. (2012). Towards requirements and architecture co-evolution. In International Conference on Advanced Information Systems Engineering, (pp. 159–170). Springer, Berlin, Heidelberg.

[11] Suo, H., Wan, J., Zou, C., and Liu, J. (2012). Security in the internet of things: a review. In 2012 International Conference on Computer Science and Electronics Engineering, (Vol. 3, pp. 648–651). IEEE.

[12] Heer, T., Garcia-Morchon, O., Hummen, R., Keoh, S. L., Kumar, S. S., and Wehrle, K. (2011). Security challenges in the IP-based internet of things. *Wireless Personal Communications*, 61(3), 527–542.

[13] Li, S., Tryfonas, T., and Li, H. (2016). The internet of things: a security point of view. *Internet Research*, 26(2), 337–359.

[14] Zorzi, M., Gluhak, A., Lange, S., and Bassi, A. (2010). From today's intranet of things to a future internet of things: a wireless-and mobility-related view. *IEEE Wireless Communications*, 17(6), 44–51.

[15] Valera, A. J. J., Zamora, M. A., and Skarmeta, A. F. G. (2010). An architecture based on internet of things to support mobility and security in medical environments. In 2010 7th IEEE Consumer Communications and Networking Conference, (pp. 1–5). IEEE.

[16] Kumar, A., Sharma, S., Singh, A., Alwadain, A., Choi, B. J., Manual-Brenosa, J., et al. (2021). Revolutionary strategies analysis and proposed system for future infrastructure in internet of things. *Sustainability*, 14(1), 71.

37 Triple band notch and slot loaded RMPA for Wi-Fi and 5G applications

Ravi Kant Prasad[a], Manoj Kr. Vishwakarma[b], Karabi Kalita[c], Pramod Kumar[d] and Ashwini Kumar[e]

Lloyd Institute of Engineering and Technology, Greater Noida, U.P., India

Abstract

This paper presents and describes the design of rectangular shape microstrip antenna with notch and slot loaded. This proposed antenna has triple band containing resonance frequency of 3.6 GHz, 4.96 GHz and 5.2 GHz having return loss -20.15 dB, -23.33 dB and -21.08 dB respectively. The performance of analysis of antenna and impedance matching is done using inset feed and with the help of HFSS software tool. The parameters of antenna other than return loss like VSWR, radiation pattern also has been observed. The simulated results and characteristics of the presented antenna can be used for Wi-Fi and 5G applications.

Keywords: Impedance matching, notch, resonance frequency, return loss, slot

Introduction

In present time due to advancement in wireless communication system, microstrip technology grows rapidly. In this technology microstrip antenna is one of the best contender due to its attractive characteristics such as simple configuration, low cost, uncomplicated design, ease of access, high data rate as well as compatibility with IC and mechanically rugged [1]. Besides the all above positive feature, this technology has some challenges like low efficiency and multiple band communication. To overcome the challenges many more microstrip antenna has been presented for use in several wireless communication applications such as mobile, Wi-Fi, Wi-Max, radio frequency identification (RFID), GPS, telemedicine and 5G etc [2]. A fork-shaped multiband monopole antenna has been presented which cover the Wi-Max (3.5/5.5 GHz), WLAN (5.2/5.6GHz) and C frequency band [3]. For Wi-Max and WLAN application, a triple frequency band antenna having dual U-slot is proposed having % bandwidth of 3.14, 4.96 and 2.56 [4]. For WLAN and 5G application, a simple structure and compact size having monopole impedance converter triple band microstrip antenna has been proposed consisting radiating element of a Y-shaped and circular patch [5]. With dimension of 15 ? 17 ? 1.6 mm³, a hexagon shaped patch antenna is proposed and fabricated having two inclined strips and slots on radiating patch for getting the multiband frequencies which can be used for TV satellite broadcasting, 5G unlicensed band, weather monitoring application [6]. Having a defected ground and an inverted U-shaped slot radiator, a compact size antenna is designed for exciting the triple band which can be used in WLAN and WiMAX communication application [7]. A miniaturized antenna having triple band for WiMAX and WLAN applications is presented whose active radiating patch area of 9 ? 12 mm². The miniaturization and operating frequency of 2.5 GHz, 3.47 GHz and 5.75 GHz has been observed by etching H and U-shaped slots on the radiating monopole and by conjunction of E-type unit cell defected ground structure and F-shaped slot [8]. The various shaped of slotted microstrip antenna for frequency reconfiguration and many more application has been discussed [9–12].

In this paper, an inset feed rectangular microstrip patch antenna is designed with notches and slots. By using the notches and slots, a desired triple frequency band has been achieved which is for Wi-Fi and 5G wireless communication application. The simulation process of proposed antenna is done by using Ansys HFSS 19 simulator tool. The description of design procedure and geometry of the proposed antenna are given in section 2. The simulated results of the proposed antenna have been discussed in section 3 and finally overall conclusion of paper is presented in section 4.

Design Procedure and Geometry of Antenna

For proposed antenna the designing parameters are selected based on the method of transmission line model. The design resonant frequency is calculated as [1]:

[a]ravi4prasad@gmail.com, [b]manoj.rvsjsr@gmail.com, [c]karabikdas25@gmail.com, [d]kumarpramod2002@gmail.com, [e]kush.ashwini@gmail.com

DOI: 10.1201/9781003534136-37

$$f = \frac{0.5c}{w}\left(\frac{2}{\varepsilon_r + 1}\right)^{0.5}$$

where, w = width of patch, c = light's speed, ε_r = dielectric constant of substrate.
The effective dielectric constant (ε_{re}) is given as:

$$\varepsilon_{re} = \left(\frac{\varepsilon_r + 1}{2}\right) + \left(\frac{\varepsilon_r - 1}{2}\right)\left[1 + 12\frac{h}{w}\right]^{-0.5}$$

The effective patch length is given as:

$$L_e = \frac{0.5C}{f\sqrt{\varepsilon_{re}}}$$

where, h = height of the substrate
For getting the perfect impedance matching the distance from the leading edge of the patch is given by:

$$R_{in}(i = i_0) = \frac{1}{2(G_1 \pm G_{12})}\cos^2\left(\frac{\pi}{l}i_0\right) \approx R_{in}(i = 0)\cos^2\left(\frac{\pi}{l}i_0\right)$$

where, i_0 = inset feed point distance, R_{in} (i = 0) = input impedance at the leading edge of the patch, G_1 = conductance, G_{12} = mutual conductance.

The 3D view of the proposed antenna is depicted in Figure 37.1. The compact asymmetric size of the ground of the proposed antenna is 25.6 ? 34.6 mm². The radiating patch of the antenna is situated at 1.6 mm height of the ground and having area of 16 ? 21 mm². This antenna is fabricated on FR4 substrate material whose dielectric constant is 4.4. For getting the desired characteristics impedance of 50 Ω, the optimum dimension of inset feed is 3 mm × 12.6 mm.

To getting the desired frequency band for particular wireless communication application the rectangular radiating patch of basic antenna is loaded with notches and slots. The top view of proposed antenna after loading the notches and slots is shown in Figure 37.2. The two notches are loaded having different dimensions and different structure. The first notch along the both side of length is having the area 3 ☐ 2 mm² and two in number. The second notch is loaded along the width of the radiating patch with area of 5 ☐ 2 mm² and it is also two in number. Two slots also loaded on the radiating patch having same dimension. The measured value of the specifications of the proposed antenna is shown in Table 37.1 and all the values are in mm.

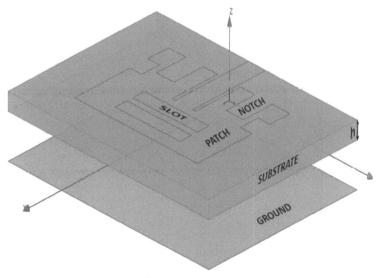

Figure 37.1 3D view of proposed antenna

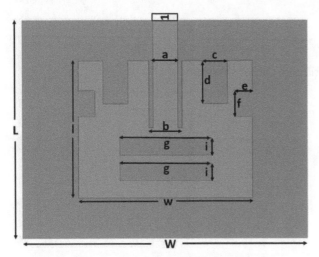

Figure 37.2 Top view of proposed antenna

Table 37.1 Specifications of proposed antenna.

S. No	Parameter	Value (mm)	S. No	Parameter	Value (mm)
1	W	34.6	8	d	5
2	L	25.6	9	e	2
3	w	21	10	f	3
4	l	16	11	g	11
5	a	3	12	h	1.6
6	b	4	13	i	2
7	c	3			

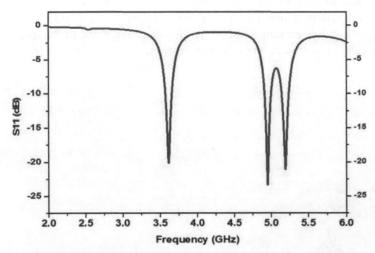

Figure 37.3 Reflection coefficient in dB of proposed antenna

Simulation Results and Discussion

For getting the simulated result and for the analysis HFSS 19 software tool has been used which is based on finite element method. Figure 37.3 shows the simulated reflection co-efficient in dB of the proposed antenna. From fig. is has been observed that the proposed antenna has triple frequency band ranging from 3.568 GHz to 3.66 GHz, 4.912 GHz to5.004 GHz and 5.14 GHz to 5.244 GHz. The center frequency of these triple bands is 3.612 GHz, 4.956 GHz and 5.192 GHz with reflection co-efficient of -20.147 dB, -23.329 dB and -21.084 dB respectively. Above triple band can be used for the Wi-Fi and 5G application in wireless communication system.

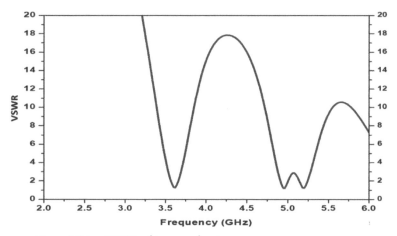

Figure 37.4   *VSWR of proposed antenna*

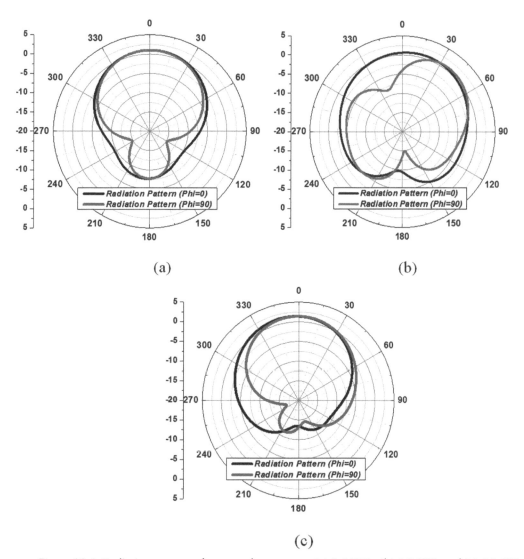

Figure 37.5 Radiation pattern of proposed antenna at (a) 3.6 GHz, (b) 4.9 GHz and (c) 5.2 GHz

The voltage standing wave ratio (VSWR) is also an important aspect of the communication system devices. The VSWR of the proposed antenna is shown in Figure 37.4. From fig. it is observed that at the center frequencies 3.612 GHz, 4.956 GHz and 5.192 GHz, the value of the VSWR is 1.25, 1.29 and 1.21 respectively. It is also observed that at the triple band frequency range of the proposed antenna the VSWR is less than 2.

The radiation pattern in 2D of the proposed antenna is shown in Figure 37.5. It is the radial distribution and function of the angular position of the antenna. It has been observed that for desired wireless application triple frequency bands i.e. at 3.6 GHz, 4.9 GHz and 5.2 GHz, proposed antenna shows the stable radiation pattern which suggest performance of antenna is good.

Conclusion

A triple band microstrip antenna loaded with notches and slots is designed and simulated. It has been observed that by loading the notches and slots of different dimensions, the antenna resonate at desired center frequencies with good reflection co-efficient which may be valuable for Wi-Fi application along with 5G network applications in wireless communication system. Impedance matching and appropriate feed network are also the two essential factors in designing the antenna. Simulation process of proposed antenna is done by Ansys HFSS 19 simulator software tool and inset feed is elected for impedance matching. For future work the simulation can also be performed by other simulation software like CST and other. The impedance matching can also be performed by using other type of feed.

References

[1] Balanis, C. A. (1997). Antenna Theory Analysis and Design. New York: John Wiley and Sons, Inc.

[2] Rahman, M. N., Beng, G. K., Samsuzzaman, M., Alam, T., and Islam, M. T. (2018). Design and analysis of an optimized S-shaped resonator based triple band microstrip antenna for satellite applications. In Suparta, W., Abdullah, M., Ismail, M. (Eds.), Space Science and Communication for Sustainability, Singapore: Springer, (pp. 253–263).

[3] Naji, D. K. (2018). Design of compact dual-band and tri-band microstrip patch antennas. *International Journal of Electromagnetics and Applications*, 8(1), 26–34.

[4] Bhagat, P., and Jain, P. (2014). Triple band microstrip patch antenna with dual U-slot for WLAN/WIMAX applications. *SSRG International Journal of Electronics and Communication Engineering*, 1(7), 19–24.

[5] Zhuang, H., Li, F., Ding, W., Tan, H., Zhuang, J., Liu, C., et al. (2022). A triple-band microstrip antenna with a monopole impedance converter for WLAN and 5G applications. *International Journal of Antennas and Propagation*, 2022, 1–9.

[6] Singh, P. P., and Sharma, S. K. (2021). Design and fabrication of a triple band microstrip antenna for WLAN, satellite TV and radar applications. *Progress In Electromagnetics Research* C, 117, 277–289.

[7] Kunwar, A., Gautam, A. K., and Rambabu, K. (2017). Design of a compact U-shaped slot triple band antenna for WLAN/WiMAX applications. *International Journal of Electronics and Communications*, 71, 82–88.

[8] Ali, T., and Biradar, R. C. (2018). A triple-band highly miniaturized antenna for WiMAX/WLAN applications. *Microwave and Optical Technology Letters*, 60(2), 466–471.

[9] Yang, S. L. S., Kishk, A. A., and Lee, K. F. (2008). Frequency eeconfigurable U-slot microstrip patch antenna. *IEEE Antennas and Wireless Propogation Letters*, 7, 127–129.

[10] Lee, K. F., Luk, K. N., Mak, K. M., and Yang, S. L. D. (2008). On the use of U-slots in the design of dual and triple band patch antennas. *IEEE Antennas Propogation Letters*, 7, 60–74.

[11] Bod, M., Hassani, H. R., and Tehari, M. M. S. (2012). Compact UWB printed slot antenna with extra bluetooth, GSM, and GPS bands. *IEEE Antennas and Wireless Propagation Letters*, 11, 531–534.

[12] Ali, M., Khawaja, B. A., Tarar, M. A., and Mustaqim, M. (2013). A dual band u slot printed antenna array for LTE and WiMAX application. *Wiley Microwave and Optical Technology Letter*, 55(12), 2879–2883.

38 Functional illiteracy and coping mechanism: a study on functionally illiterate consumers' decision making

Mohd Danish Chishti[1,a], Mohd Ijlal Anjum[2,b] and Nida Malik[2,c]

[1]Associate Professor, FMS, SRMSCET, Bareilly, India

[2]Assistant Professor, PSIT, Kanpur, India

Abstract

Purpose: To manage the self-service concept in the retail outlets, a better functional and structural knowledge is required which functionally illiterate consumers do not demonstrate, leading to face marketplace challenges, thereby ending up developing a coping mechanism [7]. Functionally illiterate consumers apply certain decision rules as coping mechanisms. The goal of study is to categorize the coping strategies employed by consumer groups with functional illiteracy.

Design/methodology/approach: The study was cross-sectional in nature. To unearth the coping mechanism used by such consumer groups, an interviewer administered questionnaire was employed. Sample size was 312. The convenient sampling was considered most suitable.

Findings: The findings showed that consumers created coping mechanisms to manage issues in the marketplace. Through such tactics, they demonstrated a desire in changing the status quo. In the backdrop of the coping strategies applied by functionally illiterate consumers in the marketplace, consumers appeared to use both confrontative and avoidant coping mechanisms.

Originality/value: The current study uncovers the coping strategies employed by functionally illiterate consumers when they encounter challenges related to marketing mix elements while taking purchase decisions for food products.

Keywords: Consumer decision making, coping mechanism, functional illiteracy, functionally illiterate consumers

Introduction

In the Indian emerging economy context, the marketplace is represented by consumers of diverse lifestyles and varying needs which are undoubtedly visible in their purchasing behavior [8]. The concept of supermarket and self-service product displays emerged and spread throughout the country due to development. To manage the self-service concept in the retail outlets, a better functional and structural knowledge is required which functionally illiterate consumers do not show, leading to face marketplace challenges, thereby ending up developing a coping mechanism [7]. The aim of the study is to find out and enumerate the coping strategies applied by functionally illiterate consumers in the marketplace. Functional literacy indicates reading abilities along with numerical skills needed for consumers in a day to day life [6]. Despite being significant in size and purchasing ability among functionally illiterate consumers, Very few researches have been conducted on them regarding their behavior in the market.

Literature Review

Functional Literacy

In the 1970s, Functional literacy made its first impression in the USA and U.K where in Number of people were found facing difficulty in reading and writing in their day to day life (UNESCO) [10]. The difference between Individual's current literacy and level required by the situation is called functional literacy [1]. A functionally literate individual should be capable of to participate in his or her social and cultural activities with the assistance of his or her reading abilities [1]. There are some fundamental components that must be included in any discussion regarding literacy and its growth. These components are as follows: 1) The significance of employing text. 2) The requirement to use text with proper comprehension. 3) Include a numeracy component in addition to text. 4) The need to investigate all of these issues that are embedded in ordinary life experiences. Food literacy, among the diverse factors influencing eating patterns, has newly been considered a key aspect in improving diet quality, health, and well-being, [4].

[a]mohddanishchishti@gmail.com, [b]Ijlalanjumm.b.a@gmail.com, [c]Maliknida.2011@gmail.com

DOI: 10.1201/9781003534136-38

According to the findings, consumer literacy should be understood as a social practice that encompasses social and personal skills, reading and writing proficiency, and the capacity to deal with the stigma associated with low literacy. (Ozanne etal,2005)

Coping Mechanism

Multinational companies progressively paying more attention on subsistence marketplaces provided their massive market potential [9]. However, this is unused because subsistence consumers encounter tremendous challenges. Such consumers require marketplace literacy to take part effectively [9]. Marketplace literacy comprises the knowledge and skills that facilitate them to participate in a marketplace as both consumers and entrepreneurs [9]. Functionally illiterate consumers use typical decision rules as coping mechanisms. This mechanism helps functionally illiterate consumers to boost their pride in the society [2]. After careful exploration of literature, the following research questions have been developed.

RQ1. What are the different types of coping strategies applied by functionally illiterate consumers in the context of selected marketing mix?

RQ2. Which one is the preferable coping strategy applied by functionally illiterate consumers in the context of selected marketing mix?

Research Methodology

The study was cross-sectional in nature because it was conducted from July 2017 to 2018 in the city of Delhi, as suggested by [3]. Three hundred and forty (340) respondents took part in the test, out of which 312 was the final sample size. An interview administered questionnaire was used. Before using the questionnaire, the respondents had to pass a screening test in order to be eligible for the main study. Eight picture and word-based questions culled from commercials made up the test. Through the test, the respondents were encouraged to carry out straightforward addition and subtraction in order to distinguish between items and gather some data. The score of four or less out of eight was the prerequisite to qualify for data collection. The questionnaire contained a set of small statements having responses on a seven point Likert type scale. Though it was developed in English but translated into Hindi as per the requirement. The convenient sampling was considered most suitable due to the nature of study and the time constraints. Functionally illiterate adults working in educational institutions, hospitals or any other organization. Doing sanitation, gardening, housekeeping, security services etc. were the unit of study. Responses were not in any way swayed in order to ensure the accuracy of the data. The majority of respondents during the pretesting appeared to have issues with the questionnaire's length. As a result, it was made easier for the respondents to a certain extent.

Results of the Study

Respondents were asked to describe the coping mechanisms they employed to deal with the issue. These coping mechanisms also have a connection to the retailer's marketing mix's components of product, price, place, promotion, salespeople, and procedure. The aggregate across all coping mechanisms is explained as follows.

- A mean of at least 4.5 indicates the dominant coping technique.
- A mean of more than or equal to 3.5 but less than 4.5 indicates the presence of a coping mechanism that is occasionally employed.
- A mean of less than 3.5 indicates a coping mechanism that is infrequently employed.

Product Associated Coping Strategy

Respondents were requested to mention the coping strategy employed to handle problems regarding food products. Findings are as follows.

Going for other stores to dodge the situation was the major strategy used by respondents (mean 5.69). Thus, individuals employed at least seven different coping mechanisms to deal with the circumstance, including avoiding purchases when unclear, buying well-known brands, asking salespeople for assistance, choosing foods based on packaging, remembering where products were located in the store, and refraining from purchasing new goods. Most of them hinted at their own resolve to find a solution. Customers avoid experimenting with new products if they can't find what they're looking for, whereas in a confrontative strategy, consumers tackle the situation, for instance, by asking the salespeople for assistance in finding what they're looking for in the store. See Table 38.1, See Table 38.2, See Table 38.3, See Table 38.4, See Table 38.5 and See Table 38.6.

Table 38.1 Product-associated coping strategies

Product associated coping strategies	Min	Max	Mean	Std. Dev
Look into other shops	1	7	5.6987	1.81250
Avoid purchasing if not clear	1	7	5.6538	1.61844
Buy well-known brands of goods.	1	7	5.6282	1.76139
Ask salesmen or other individuals for assistance.	1	7	5.4359	1.76853
Select food on packaging	1	7	4.8526	1.99293
Memorize the location in the store	1	7	4.6795	2.09420
Avoid trying new products	1	7	4.6603	2.21220
Pretend physical disability to get assistance	1	7	1.7308	1.63304

Table 38.2 Price associated coping strategies

Price associated coping strategies	Min	Max	Mean	Std. Dev
Choose other place to negotiate price	1	7	6.3462	1.256
Opt stores having easy pricing	1	7	6.3269	1.49237
Seek information from salespeople	1	7	6.1667	1.256
Complain regarding price to store in-charge	1	7	5.8077	1.49237
Skip purchasing products with percentages discount	1	7	5.0513	1.31199
Opting for shop with a friend or family	1	7	3.5	2.60965
Hand over all the money to cashier	1	7	1.9808	1.81622

Table 38.3 Place associated coping strategies

Place associated coping strategies	Min	Max	Mean	Std. Dev
Purchase from known stores	1	7	6.4295	1.02767
Purchase from nearby store	1	7	6.3141	1.42916
Seek help from salespeople or strangers	1	7	5.9231	1.27069
Buying from stores with good lighting	1	7	4.4679	1.75114
Go with friend or relative	1	7	2.9231	2.43643
Purchase from supermarkets	1	7	1.4038	1.02558

Table 38.4 Promotion associated coping strategies

Promotion associated coping strategies	Min	Max	Mean	Std. Dev
ask for help from salespeople, friends, about promoted products	1	7	5.9487	1.23609
Keep planned food expenditure before shopping	1	7	5.8910	1.27591
Purchase according to shopping list only	1	7	5.3462	2.04972
Avoid newly advertised food products	1	7	4.6026	2.09018
Try to be confirmed about price of advertised product	1	7	4.5449	1.77638
Carry limited money to avoid purchasing unnecessary food products	1	7	2.9808	2.45728

Table 38.5 Salespeople associated coping strategies

Salespeople associated coping strategies	MIN	MAX	MEAN	Std. Dev
Visit other stores to avoid bad experience from salespeople	1	7	6.0641	1.43757
Complain to store manager/shop owner in absence of help from sales people	1	7	5.5962	1.97664
Purchase from stores having familiar salesman	1	7	5.4231	2.06654
Maintain the relationship with salespeople in new stores	1	7	4.5769	2.11270
Purchase from stores where no language barrier	1	7	3.2372	2.28264

Table 38.6 Process associated coping strategies

Process Associated Coping Strategies	Min	Max	Mean	Std. Dev
Purchase from stores having better return policy	1	7	6.1154	1.78584
Purchase from other stores having better pricing	1	7	6.0385	1.79991
Purchase from stores having flexible shopping timings	1	7	2.9679	2.12902
Purchase from supermarket/organized store offering better services	1	7	1.9038	1.78157

Price Associated Coping Strategy

The table below summarizes and presents the price-related coping mechanisms adopted by respondents to deal with price-related concerns.

Respondents frequently opt to haggle the price at different locations among the tested price-related coping methods (mean 6.34). Respondents adopted other strategies such as choosing those stores having Easy pricing method (mean 6.32). They also raised the issue of price-related inconsistencies with the store manager. They decided on the products with no percentage discounts because they had inadequate math abilities. Going with a friend or family member and giving the cashier your entire wallet were deemed unimportant. Some confrontational and avoidance-related coping mechanisms were employed.

Place Associated Coping Strategies

The problems associated to place of purchase for food items were managed through the coping strategies. Such methods are summarized in the table below.

Buying from reputable retailers was a common coping mechanism employed to address location-related issues (mean 6.42). As coping mechanisms, respondents also made purchases from neighboring stores, asked strangers or salespeople for assistance, and made purchases from establishments with enough lighting inside. Going with friend or relatives was not found important strategy which does not match with the results of Viswanathan et al (2005).

Promotion Associated Coping Strategies

A summary of promotion- associated coping mechanisms is provided below.

Several coping strategies are listed to manage the problems related to promotion. Among them, asking salesmen, friends, and family for advice on the advertised product was a common tactic (mean 5.94). The two most important tactics were determined to be planning your food budget before you go shopping and just making purchases from your shopping list. Other tactics included avoiding recently promoted products and attempting to confirm the advertised product's price. The use of restricted funds to avoid making superfluous food purchases was not shown to be a useful tactic.

Salespeople Associated Coping Strategies

The responses to the series of statements that sought to elicit the coping mechanisms used by salespeople in retail stores. Results are shown in the table that is provided below.

The three main coping mechanisms were shopping at stores with well-known salespeople (mean 5.42), complaining to the store manager regarding the salespeople (mean 5.59), and visiting other stores to avoid negative experiences with salespeople (mean 6.06). Maintaining relationships with salespeople in the new store was an important strategy (mean 4.57). Purchasing from stores having no language barrier, was not a pertinent coping strategy. Here a mean of 5.59 with Std Dev of 1.97 suggests that some of them were disposed to criticize whereas others were not. Otherwise, they purchased from the store having known salespeople. Therefore, analysis approved the role of salespeople in the coping mechanism during purchase.

Process Associated Coping Strategy
Process related coping strategies used by functionally illiterate consumers are in the table that is provided below.

Buying from retailers with better return policies and better prices were the two most popular process-related coping strategies (mean 6.11, Std. Dev. 1.78; 6.03, Std. Dev. 1.79).Customers utilized avoidance coping mechanisms, which shows that customers should choose stores that advertise individualized care. Functionally illiterate consumers did not significantly use appropriate coping mechanisms such shopping at stores with flexible hours, supermarkets, or organized stores.

Conclusion of the Study

Findings showed that consumers applied a diversity of coping mechanisms to manage the issues they ran into in the marketplace. There is proof that customers who lack functional literacy adopt a variety of market coping mechanisms. Consumers can meet their daily needs by using coping mechanisms. It makes people quicker and more effective at making decisions amongst options. Even still, these coping mechanisms cannot guarantee a well-informed buying choice. The majority of respondents combined their usage of confrontational and avoidant coping mechanisms. Some of them confronted the situation by employing a confrontational strategy.

Limitations of the Study

A study would be perfect in nature if it could generalize the findings to a bigger population. The study was limited to a certain region of Delhi. The migrant population of Delhi is highly representative of the various Indian states, however, it cannot be regarded as a perfect microcosm of the entire Indian subcontinent's people. Because the study was limited to Delhi and its results cannot be applied to the entire nation. In order to incorporate as many responders as possible, the researcher tried her best. A screening exam was used to determine who qualified for the study, therefore it took a long time to conduct interviews or complete questionnaires.

References

[1] Arko, A. D. (2009). The impact of functional literacy on socio-economic lives of beneficiaries: a case study of the agona district of ghana. *Edo Journal of Counselling*, 2(2), 203.

[2] Baker, S. G. (2005). Building understanding of the domain of consuemr vulnerability. *Jornal of Macro Marketing*, 24(2), 128–139.

[3] Cooper, D., and Schindler, P. (2006). Business Research Methods. 9th edn. New York.

[4] Doustmohammadian, A., Omidvar, N., Keshavarz-Mohammadi, N. et al. The association and mediation role of Food and Nutrition Literacy (FNLIT) with eating behaviors, academic achievement and overweight in 10–12 years old students: a structural equation modeling. Nutr J 21, 45 (2022). https://doi.org/10.1186/s12937-022-00796-8

[5] Ozanne , J., Adkins, N., and Sandlin, J. (2005). Shopping for power: how adult literacy learners negotiate the market place. *Adult Education Quarterly*, 55(4), 251–288.

[6] Viswanathan, M. (2005). Functional illiteracy and nutrition education in United States: a research based approach to the development of nutritional education material for functionally illiterate consumers. *Journal of Macro Marketing*, 25(2), 187–201.

[7] Viswanathan, M. J. (2005). Decision making and coping of functionally illiterate consumer and some implications for marketing management. *Journal of Marketing*, 69(1), 15–31.

[8] Viswanathan, M. J. (2021). Marketplace literacy education and coping behaviors among subsistence consumer–entrepreneurs during demonetization in India . *Journal Consumer Affairs*, 55, 179–202. https://doi.org/10.1111/joca.12300.

[9] Viswanathan, M. U. (2021). Marketplace literacy as a pathway to a better world: evidence from field experiments in low-access subsistence marketplaces. *Journal of Marketing*, 85(3), 113–129.

[10] Records of the 20th General Conference of UNESCO: Resolutions. (PDF). 1978. p. 18.

[11] Viswanathan, M., Rosa, J. A., & Harris, J. E. (2005). Decision making and coping of functionally illiterate consumers and some implications for marketing management. Journal of Marketing, 69(1), 15-31.

39 Empowering women through FinTech: bridging the gender gap in financial inclusion

Kamakshi Mehta[a] and Umesh Solanki

TAPMI School of Business, Manipal University Jaipur, Dehmi Kalan, Jaipur-Ajmer Expressway, Jaipur Rajasthan, India

Abstract

Economic development and poverty reduction both benefit greatly from increased financial inclusion. In this context, "universal access" means people from all walks of life, including women, may use and benefit from a variety of financial services. Women in both developed and developing countries continue to be disadvantaged by a gender gap in financial inclusion, notwithstanding gains achieved in recent years. This paper looks at how FinTech may be used to increase women's access to financial services and boost their economic independence. Technology has fuelled the digital revolution and has created an opening for FinTech to disrupt the established financial system. Mobile banking, digital wallets, peer-to-peer lending, crowdfunding, and robo-advisory services are just a few financial services under the "FinTech solutions." FinTech's adaptability and low entry barrier have made it possible, especially for underprivileged women, to get access to and benefit from financial services. Financial inclusion for women can contribute in achieving sustainable development goals.

Keywords: Crowdfunding, digital wallets, financial inclusion, fintech, gender gap, peer-to-peer lending, robo-advisory services, SDG, women empowering

Introduction

The advent of the digital revolution, facilitated by technological advancements, has created opportunities for Financial Technology (FinTech) to challenge and transform the traditional financial system. In the field of FinTech, a range of novel solutions have surfaced, including mobile banking, digital wallets, peer-to-peer lending, crowdfunding, and robo-advisory services. The accessibility of FinTech, characterized by its notable adaptability and minimal obstacles to entry, has facilitated its utilization by poor women, so affording them the chance to avail themselves of financial services and derive advantages from them. In addition to promoting greater financial inclusion, the field of FinTech is significantly contributing to the empowerment of women, enabling them to break free from the cycle of poverty and develop their entrepreneurial ventures. The utilization of microloans, crowdsourcing, and digital payment solutions offered by FinTech platforms plays a crucial role in facilitating avenues for women to overcome financial limitations and engage in entrepreneurial pursuits [1]. In addition, the educational tools provided by these platforms serve to augment women's financial literacy, and hence, promote the development of economic autonomy.

Literature Review

Financial inclusion encompasses a multidimensional strategy. The primary concern revolves around the challenges faced by individuals without access to banking services while attempting to engage with established financial institutions. According to Karmakar [5], the process of financial inclusion facilitates the provision of credit to individuals across all socioeconomic groups within a nation, including those who are considered vulnerable. There is a lack of consensus regarding a universally recognized definition or metric for assessing financial inclusion [4]. However, there is a consensus that women's financial inclusion is achieved when women possess equitable access to a diverse array of financial goods and services that adequately meet their various business and home requirements.

Women who possess greater economic empowerment through higher education and employment are more inclined to exhibit informed decision-making in matters of finance, utilize financial services that they deem valuable, and exert enhanced control over their financial circumstances [12]. Legal channel/barriers: Women who possess legal empowerment experience increased levels of confidence and autonomy about their ability to access and utilize their financial assets. a more recent development, the Women, Business and the Law (WBL) project by

[a]Kamakshi.mehta@jaipur.manipal.edu, Cakamakshi.edu@gmail.com, [b]umesh.solanki@jaipur.maniapl.edu; drumesh1234@gmail.com, philanthropist_umesh85@rediffmail.com

DOI: 10.1201/9781003534136-39

the World Bank has devised a set of seven indicators to assess the legal barriers that impede women's economic empowerment. Cultural channel/barriers gender empowerment is commonly linked to cultural transformations and the elimination of societal conventions that hinder women's ability to access and utilize financial services [9]. According to a brief provided by CGAP, social norms can be defined as a set of rules and corresponding behaviors that regulate social conduct, perceptions, and behavior.

Gender financial inclusion plays a crucial role in advancing several Sustainable Development Goals (SDGs) outlined by the United Nations [6]. These linkages demonstrate how promoting financial inclusion for women can contribute to achieving broader sustainable development goals:

Gender financial inclusion can help alleviate poverty by providing women with access to financial services, allowing them to save, invest, and manage their finances effectively. This, in turn, empowers women to lift themselves and their families out of poverty (SDG 1: No poverty). When women have access to financial resources, they can invest in agricultural activities, such as purchasing seeds and tools, which can enhance food security and contribute to ending hunger (SDG 2: Zero hunger). Financial inclusion enables women to access healthcare services, purchase medicines, and afford health insurance, leading to better health outcomes for themselves and their families(SDG 3: Good health and well-being). By having access to financial services, women can save for their children's education expenses, ensuring that more girls and boys have the opportunity to attend school and receive a quality education (SDG 4: Quality education). Gender financial inclusion is inherently linked to achieving gender equality. Providing women with equal access to financial resources, credit, and banking services can help close the gender gap and empower women economically (SDG 5: Gender equality). Financial inclusion for women can lead to increased entrepreneurship and job creation, contributing to economic growth and employment opportunities, particularly in sectors where women are traditionally underrepresented (SDG 8: Decent work and economic growth). Addressing gender disparities in financial inclusion can contribute to reducing inequalities within and among countries, promoting more inclusive economic growth (SDG 10: Reduced inequalities). Women's financial inclusion can support climate action by enabling them to invest in environmentally sustainable practices, such as renewable energy solutions or climate-resilient farming techniques (SDG 13: Climate action). When women have access to financial resources, they are better positioned to engage in community development and social initiatives, promoting peaceful and just societies (SDG 16: Peace, justice, and strong institutions) [10].

Objectives

The objectives of the study are:

a. To study the impact of cultural barriers, legal barriers to behavioural intention of empowering women respectively
b. To study the indirect impact of cultural barriers, legal barriers on the behavioural intention of empowering women

Research Methodology

According to Fishbein [2], within the theory of reasoned action (TRA) framework, behavioral intention is influenced by two components, namely attitudes (the positive or negative evaluation of behavior) and subjective norms (the perception of the influence of other variables). These factors primarily impact actual behavior. Women in Rajasthan have been surveyed to determine if there is a correlation between financial inclusion and increased female agency. The study will employ primary data-gathering methods to ascertain the magnitude and characteristics of the relationships between the variables under investigation. The researchers employed a simple random sampling procedure. Subsequently, the ultimate paper-based surveys were disseminated across a collective of 650 women. Out of the total sample size of 650 women, a total of 500 replies were obtained, resulting in a response rate of 76.92%. Use this for the first paragraph in a section, or to continue after an extract.

Data Analysis and Results

The data obtained from the survey instrument has been analyzed using descriptive statistics, which are summarized in Table 39.1. The current work used a non-parametric partial least squares (PLS)-structural equation modelling (SEM) methodology, as proposed by Westland (2007). The loadings and the average variance extracted (AVE) of all latent variables to assess the internal consistency were calculated. The findings of this

Table 39.1 Profile of the respondents

Profile		
Age of respondents	Frequency	Percentage
"Less than 20 years"	25	4.8
"20 - 29 years"	188	37.8
"30-39 years"	152	30.8
"40-49 years"	96	18.8
"50-59 years"	27	5.2
"60 years and more"	12	2.6

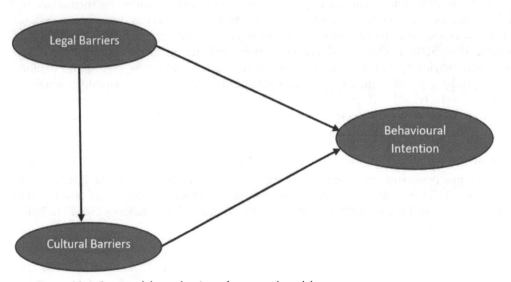

Figure 39.1 Sem model - evaluation of structural model

Table 39.2 Relationship between variables

Hypothesis	P values	Result as per p value	Final result
H01: "Cultural Barriers ® Behavioral Intention"	0.000	Significant	Reject H0
H02: "Legal Barriers ® Behavioral Intention"	0.391	Significant	Reject H0
H03: "Legal Barriers ® Cultural Barriers ® Behavioral Intention"	0.000	Significant	Reject H0

study imply that the factor loadings on their respective latent variables are statistically significant, as supported by previous research conducted by Lin et al. [7] and Hair et al. [3]. The items were also tested for multicollinearity. The estimations' stability depends on low collinearity among items [8]. The VIF scores are used to analyze the multicollinearity of the items. More multicollinearity is seen with a higher VIF score.

Coefficient of determination: R^2 is the most used statistic for evaluating structural model prediction, as with multiple regression models [11]. The calculated R^2 for the model was 0.538.

The SEM framework, as depicted in Figure 39.1, is employed to assess the interconnections among various dimensions, namely behavioral intention, cultural barriers, and legal barriers. These components are included as exogenous variables in the model. Note: In Table 39.2, the 2nd P value is 0.001 instead of 0.391 and in the above statement, it is > 2.58 instead of < 1.96, and in the last statement of this para it is ($p < 0.01$) instead of ($p < 0.001$). Please correct these. In addition to the influence of vulnerability to legal barriers, and cultural barriers on behavioral Intention, all of the direct associations observed in the study were found to be statistically significant ($p < 0.01$, T value < 2.58) as shown in Table 39.2. A thorough examination of the bootstrapping analysis reveals that the indirect result output indicates significance for the variables, which significantly influences the behavioral intention of empowering ($p < 0.001$).

The results of the analysis exhibit that all the tested relationships have proved to be statistically significant suggesting that both the cultural barriers and legal barriers have significant impact on the behavioral intention of empowering women financially. It is further observed that a partial mediating effect is being created by the mediating variable cultural barriers on the relationship between legal barriers and behavior intention.

Practical Implications

Potential beneficiaries of this research include policymakers, banks, FinTech companies, and non-governmental organizations. To effectively adapt to the rapid advancements within the FinTech sector, policymakers must undertake a comprehensive review and revision of current regulatory frameworks. Women-led FinTech firms face distinct challenges in terms of financial access and empowerment. To address these issues, several efforts such as financing schemes, incubators, and accelerator programs have been implemented.

References

[1] Demirguc-Kunt, A., Klapper, L., Singer, D., Ansar, S., and Hess, J. (2018). The Global Findex Database 2017: Measuring Financial Inclusion and the Fintech Revolution. The World Bank.

[2] Fishbein, M. (2008). A reasoned action approach to health promotion. *Medical Decision Making : An International Journal of the Society for Medical Decision Making*, 28, 834–844.

[3] Hair, J.F., Black, W.C., Babin, B.J. and Anderson, R.E. (2010). Multivariate Data Analysis. 7th Edition, Pearson, New York.

[4] Holloway, K., Niazi, Z., and Rouse, R. (2017). Women's Economic Empowerment Through Financial Inclusion: A Review of Existing Evidence and Remaining Knowledge Gaps. New Haven, CT: Innovations for Poverty Action.

[5] Karmakar, K. G. (1999). Rural Credit and Self-Help Groups: Micro-Finance Needs and Concepts in India. Sage Publications India Pvt Ltd.

[6] Kara, A., Zhou, H., and Zhou, Y. (2021). Achieving the United Nations' sustainable development goals through financial inclusion: a systematic literature review of access to finance across the globe. *International Review of Financial Analysis*, 77, 101833.

[7] Lin, A., Gregor, S., and Ewing, M. (2005). Developing a scale to measure the enjoyment of web experiences. *Journal of Interactive Marketing*, 22, 40–57.

[8] Mathieson, K., Peacock, E., and Chin, W. W. (2001). Extending the technology acceptance model: the influence of perceived user resources. *ACM SIGMIS Database: the DATABASE for Advances in Information Systems*, 32(3), 86–112.

[9] Meenai, Z. (2003). Empowering Rural Women: An Approach to Empowering Credit-Based Self-Help Groups. Aakar Books

[10] Ojo, T. A. (2022). Digital financial inclusion for women in the fourth industrial revolution: a key towards achieving sustainable development goal 5. *Africa Review*, 14(1), 98–123.

[11] Sarstedt, M., Ringle, C. M., Smith, D., Reams, R., and Hair Jr, J. F. (2014). Partial least squares structural equation modeling (PLS-SEM): a useful tool for family business researchers. *Journal of Family Business Strategy*, 5(1), 105–115.

[12] Siddik, M. N. A. (2017). Does financial inclusion promote women's empowerment? evidence from Bangladesh. *Applied Economics and Finance*, 4(4), 169–177.

40 Role of total quality management and its impact on operational performance of banks: a study

Sukhjinder S Tagger[a] and Varinderjeet Singh[b]

Assistant Professor, SBBS University, Jalandhar

Abstract

In the recent decades, the companies have been focussing on improving quality of their products and services. They have developed a system, aiming at improving the quality of a product or service at its own, called total quality management (TQM). The manufacturers as well service providers have been working on it to give the customers a great experience every time the latter buy products or avail the services, which exceed their expectations. The present study examines the relationship between the TQM and banks' operational performance; and measures the impact of TQM on the latter. The study has shown very interesting results, showing the key factors significantly affecting the banks' operational performance. It shall help the banks to examine the factors that contribute to improved performance and customer service of highest standards. The study can be extended to other service sectors to improve the performance.

Keywords: Bank performance, banks, customer satisfaction, TQM

Introduction

In the modern world with cut-throat competition, every company tries to produce and sell its quality product or service, through which it can retain its old customers and acquire new ones. The happy and satisfied customers purchase products/services repetitively and thus become loyal to it. It motivates a company to maintain quality of its products/services. The scope term 'quality' has become wider in the recent years and no more confined to a product. It has grown and developed into a full-fledged system called total quality management (TQM). The companies, irrespective of their industry/sector (manufacturing or service), have developed such systems that instils quality in their products or services right from acquisition of raw material to the delivery of the final product or service to the customers. In the recent times, the awareness of TQM has increased manifold among the business professionals. The reason for this could be assigned to the fact TQM is the one of the best ways to achieve top level of service quality and customer satisfaction which exceeds his expectations. On the other hand, it has also created awareness among the customers to ask for better product or service quality.

TQM is a philosophy of management involving a dynamic process to improve the quality through the efforts of continuous improvement. TQM is a never ending process and there are no deadlines or targets to be achieved. It must be considered to be a way of life [1]. It is a constant endeavour to exceed customer expectations at the lowest cost [2]. TQM attempts to focus on the improvement of effectiveness, competitiveness and structure of an organization [3]. It works on the data collected, which is fact based and not opinions or impressions with the goal of quality improvement [4].

Today, the service sector, including the banking, has also developed a few quality management business models on the lines of TQM practices being followed in the manufacturing sector. In the context of banking sector, TQM practices influence the service delivery and service support systems, which work as moderators and ensure that the customers get best quality of service quality. These moderators work integrally for the customers so that they can enjoy swift and effortless banking services, resulting in enhanced customer experience and satisfaction. This enhances overall business performance of the banks including operational and financial performance [5].

However, due to increase in Non-Performing Assets (NPAs), the assets and performance of the banks had been under stress. The government has been taking necessary steps to reduce the stress on assets with the merger of relatively small and less/no profitable PSBs with the bigger and more profitable PSBs having larger assets base. It is expected that due to increase in working population and growing disposable income, the demand for banking services will increase in the future and is also expected that its market size will reach US$ 83.48 billion, which comes to be INR 6.2 trillion [6]. The improved fee incomes of the banks not only improve the revenues of the banks but also will enable them to provide better services to their customers. This shall result in improved service quality, better customer experience and higher customer satisfaction [6].

[a]sstagger1@gmail.com, [b]varinderjeetsingh61@gmail.com

DOI: 10.1201/9781003534136-40

Review of Literature

TQM is a perspective–oriented concept which can be universally applied to organizations across various industries and activities [7]. The literature review suggests that TQM plays a pivot role in enhancing business performance as they have enjoyed non-inverse association between them [8]. The relationship between TQM and business performance is quite significant; leadership and customer focus and employees involvement being significant performance indicators [9] However, the workers/employees need to be trained to enhance the business performance.

The positive influence of TQM is confined not only to enhanced business performance but also results in greater customer satisfaction, increased share in the business and integrity. Such business organizations outperform through improved business processes which are specifically designed to attain higher efficiency and productivity [10].

The previous studies revealed a positive and significant impact of TQM on bank performance. The customer oriented bank processes, employees' involvement were found to be significantly affecting the bank performance. It also results in improvement in market share, competitive advantage and innovation [11].

Successful implementation of TQM in banking sector has resulted in higher customer satisfaction through better service quality delivered to the customers as well as increased the customer retention; acquired new customers resulting in enhanced performance of the banks [12]. The adoption and implementation of TQM in banking sector has widened the horizon of improving the processes, service quality, with the aim of improved performance and growth of the banks' businesses. A study concluded that the Indian banks in private sector are known for convenience, quick service and quality service culture, which is found lacking in the public sector banks [13].

Objectives and Research Methodology

Objectives of the Study
The objectives of the present study were as under:

(a) To identify TQM factors in and rate their importance in banking sector.
(b) To investigate the relationship between the TQM and operational performance of banks.
(c) To study the impact of key TQM factors on the operational performance of banks.

Scope and Period of the Study
The study was conducted on bank employees working in private commercial banks operating in the small cities in the State of Punjab (India). The duration of the study conducted was approximately four months.

Formulation of Hypothesis
As most of the review of available literature suggested that there exists positive and significant relationship between TQM and business performance, the following hypotheses were formulated:

H_1: Each TQM factor is important for operational performance of banks.
H_2: There is a significant and positive relationship between TQM factors and operational performance of the banks.
H_3: Each TQM factor significantly affects the performance of the banks.

Research Methodology
With an objective to identify the relevant TQM factors and their role in improving performance, extensive literature review was carried out to study and know more about TQM concept and other aspects related thereto. Various previous studies identified different sets of factors underlying TQM for measuring the nature and degree of relationship between TQM and performance. On the basis of available literature, five factors were identified and shortlisted, which were common and widely explored or taken up in most of the studies. Thus, these factors were selected for the study owing to (a) their wide acceptance by the authors in the past studies; (b) significantly associated with services. These factors had been found suitable for Indian banking sector in the past studies. On the similar lines, the factor of operational performance was taken into account for the current study. The present study is exploratory cum descriptive research in nature as it explains the relevance of TQM factors and also explores the factors that affect the operational performance of banks significantly. Cluster sampling method

was applied for the data collection of the sample. The entire state was divided into three clusters on the basis of its geographical landscape. From each cluster, two districts were chosen at random for the survey. Out of these districts, the rural and urban bank branches were taken for the survey.

Research Instrument

The primary data was collected using a well–structured questionnaire. The questionnaire was used to measure the perceptions of the respondents towards TQM factors. It contained perceptual statements related to the TQM factors, operational performance. In addition, the data relating to demographic profiles of the respondents was also gathered. The instrument comprised two sections– Section A and Section B. Section A contained sixty perceptual statements relating to the key TQM factors and operational performance of a bank, each factor having ten statements. The statements were rated on five–point Likert Scale, the ratings of which ranged from 1 (Strongly Disagree) to 5 (Strongly Agree). Section B was related to the demographics of the respondents, viz. age, gender, experience, etc.

Pilot Survey

Prior to the conducting the survey, the research instrument was pre–tested through a pilot survey in order to detect any ambiguity in it. The respondents included in the pilot survey were asked for any suggestions and were included in it. The results collected through the pilot survey were validated before the final survey. After incorporating the amendments, the final questionnaire was released.

Data Collection

350 questionnaires were distributed among the respondents who were bank employees and working in different branches of private commercial banks at various positions. The responses of 241 respondents were received out of which 27 were found incomplete. These 27 respondents were excluded from the survey. Thus, 214 questionnaires were found to be valid and considered for the study. The response percentage was found to be 61.1%.

Reliability, Validity and Multicollinearity

Tests of reliability and validity were carried out to measure internal consistency of the data before studying the impact of the TQM success factors. The Chronbach's Alpha Coefficient was used to measure the reliability. Validity analysis was also conducted to validate the questionnaire, which was found satisfactory for the study. The problem of multicollinearity undermines the relevance of the independent variable. The collected data for the study was also tested for multicollinearity, in which no such problem was found.

Analysis Tools and Techniques

The data collected from the respondents was compiled and entered into software for analysis. Appropriate statistical tools were applied to analyse and interpret the data. The statistical tools such as Mean Score (MS), Standard Deviation, Pearson's Correlation coefficient, Exploratory Factor Analysis and Multiple Regression Analysis were applied to test the hypothesis as well as to achieve the research objectives.

Results and Discussion

The results obtained from the data analysis using statistical tools were interpreted which have been discussed in the following paragraphs:

Identification of TQM Success Factors

The respondents were asked to rank the given TQM factors on a scale of 1 to 10, assigning 1st rank to the most preferred factor and 10th rank to the least preferred rank. After tabulating the responses, Mean Score (MS) and Standard Deviation (SD) of each factor were calculated with the objective to measure the importance of the each factor from the perspective of the bank employees. The results are exhibited in Table 40.1:

As shown in the Table 40.1, customer focus emerged as the most preferred TQM factor as it carried highest mean score (MS) of 4.516 and standard deviation (SD) of 0.492 followed by the factor of management commitment, which had MS and SD of 4.323 and 0.501 respectively. The other factors of continuous improvement, employee and strategic planning were rated as third, fourth and fifth important factors. All the above factors had mean score of 4.0 and above. However, the factor of strategic planning was ranked in 5th position, indicating the least preferred factor among the respondents. It can be observed that all the TQM factors are important as their MS vary marginally. Thus, the H_1 hypothesis was accepted. However, the respondents ranked customer

Table 40.1 Mean score (MS) and standard deviation (SD) of TQM factors

Factors	Mean score	Std Dev
Customer focus (CF)	4.516	0.492
Management commitment (MC)	4.323	0.501
Continuous improvement (CI)	4.290	0.672
Employee participation (EP)	4.258	0.653
Strategic planning (SP)	4.096	0.681

Table 40.2 Correlation between TQM factors and business performance

S. No.	Factors	1	2	3	4	5	6
		(CF)	(MC)	(CI)	(EP)	(SP)	(OP)
1	Customer focus (CF)	1.000	0.322	0.491*	0.423*	0.580*	0.895*
2	Management commitment (MC)		1.000	0.345*	0.310	0.486*	0.868*
3	Continuous improvement (CI)			1.000	0.392*	0.214	0.754*
4	Employee participation (EP)				1.000**	0.309	0.748*
5	Strategic planning (SP)					1.000	0.787*
6	Operational performance (OP)						1.000

Note: *significant value at 5% level of significance

Table 40.3 Result of analysis

TQM factor	Factor loading	Number of items	? values (original)	Items deleted	? Values (Final)
Customer focus (CF)	0.838	10	0.761	1	0.782
Management commitment (MC)	0.812	10	0.766	1	0.766
Continuous improvement (CI)	0.774	10	0.757	1	0.767
Employee participation (EP)	0.707	10	0.691	2	0.773
Strategic planning (SP)	0.589	10	0.723	2	0.732
Operational performance (OP)	0.637	10	0.712	1	0.754
Other statistics					
KMO adequacy of sampling	0.831				
Bartletts' test of sphericity	16148.61				
Total variance explained (%)	78.753				

focus, management commitment and continuous improvement in order to preference the TQM factors among the given factors.

Relationship between the TQM and Bank Performance

In this study, TQM factors were taken as exogenous (independent) variables and the operational performance as endogenous (dependent) variable. Pearson's coefficient of correlation was computed among both the independent and dependent variables to measure the degree of relationship among them. Mos of the correlation coefficients were found to be significant at 5% level of significance. Table 40.2 shows correlation matrix expressing the correlation among independent variables, *inter se,* and with dependent variable.

The above table reveals the correlation coefficient between the each of the factor and business performance ranged between 0.748 and 0.895, indicating a high degree of positive correlation. The correlation coefficients among the independent variables, *inter se,* were also found to be positive but low to moderate, which implies that these factors could influence one another in improving performance of the banks. The TQM factors were found to be significantly

Table 40.4 Impact of TQM factors on operational performance of banks

TQM factor (independent)	Dependent variable	B	S.E.	Beta	t-value
Constant	Operational performance	11.087	1.572		7.053*
Customer focus (CF)		1.638	0.300	0.263	5.437*
Management commitment (MC)		1.619	0.224	0.190	7.228*
Continuous improvement (CI)		1.631	0.253	0.204	6.447*
Employee participation (EP)		1.547	0.351	0.259	5.972*
Strategic planning (SP)		1.003	0.189	0.131	5.307*
Operational performance (OP)		0.989	0.186	0.089	5.317*

and positively correlated with operational performance. The factors also affected the performance of banks significantly. Thus the hypothesis H_2 was also accepted. It also indicated that the data is free from the problem of multicollinearity as the correlation coefficients of TQM factors, *inter se,* are less than 0.9.

Impact of Key TQM Factors on the Bank Performance
In this section, impact of TQM factors on operational performance of the banks was studied. The test of reliability and multicollinearity were also conducted to test the statistical significance of the factors. The Chronbach's alpha coefficient was calculated for each factor, which is presented in the Table 40.3.

The above table shows the original and final Chronbach's alpha values. The final values of alpha coefficient increased marginally after deleting the items which showed consistency and reliability of the data. Generally, the Chronbach's alpha value or 0.70 or above is accepted [14]. Further, the impact of the TQM on performance of the banks was also studied and thus Hypothesis H_3 was tested. In order to measure the cause and effect relationship between TQM factors and operational performance, the following equation was formulated.

$$Y = a + b_1x_1 + b_2x_2 + b_3x_3 + b_4x_4 + b_5x_5 + e$$

Table 40.4 depicts the impact of TQM factors on operational performance of banks. The table reveals the regression coefficients indicating the impact of TQM factors on operational performance of banks. The findings revealed that all the TQM factors taken in the study impact the operational performance of banks significantly.

The customer focus drives a bank to focus on its customers' needs and to provide them the timely and prompt services they require. Management commitment also plays a pivot role in adopting and implementing TQM resulting in enhanced operational efficiency of banks. Continuous improvement encourages the banks to develop improved and more convenient methods of doing business. All the factors were found significant at 5% level of significance. It implies that all the factors are equally important and significant in influencing the banks' operational performance. No factor can be afforded to be ignored, otherwise it may adversely affect operational performance of the banks. Thus the hypothesis H3 was also accepted in this case.

Conclusion

The above findings reveal total quality management (TQM) has become one of the most important element of a long term success and sustainable growth of a business. It has given new dimensions to the quality of a product/service. The present study concluded that customer focus is the most preferred TQM factor followed by management commitment and continuous improvement. TQM factors and performance of banks are positively correlated and all the TQM factors contribute and affect positively to enhance the operational performance of the banks. All the TQM factors taken for the study were found significantly impacting the operational performance of banks. Hence, adoption and implementation of TQM can be regarded of utmost importance in order to develop sustainable competitive advantage of a business.

References

[1] Mehra, S., and Ranganathan, S. (2008). Implementing total quality management with a focus on enhancing customer satisfaction. *International Journal of Quality and Reliability Management*, 25(9), 913–927.

[2] Bergman, B., and Klefsjö, B. (2003). Quality from Customer Needs to Customer Satisfaction. 2nd edn. Studentlitteratur, ASQ Quality Press, USA.

[3] Oakland, J. (1993). Total Quality Management: The Route to Improving Performance. London: Butterworth Heinemann.

[4] Morgan, C., and Murgatroyd, S. (1997). *Total Quality Management in the Public Sector.* Buckingham: Open University Press.

[5] Tagger, S. S., and Gupta, M. (2020). A study of the relationship between total quality management and business performance in the banking sector. *International Journal of Business Competition and Growth*, 7(2), 118–132.

[6] Ibef, (2021b). Indian Banking Industry Analysis, [online]   https://www.ibef.org/industry/banking–presentation.

[7] Dean, J. W., and Bowen, D. E. (1994). Management theory and total quality: improving research and practice through theory development. *Academy of Management Review*, 19(3), 392–418.

[8] Anderson, J. C., Rungtusanatham, M., and Schroeder, R. G. (1995). A path analytic model of a theory of quality management underlying the deming management method: preliminary empirical findings. Decision Sciences, 26(5), 637–658.

[9] Samson, D., and Terziovski, M. (1999). The relationship between total quality management practices and operational performance. *Journal of Operations Management*, 17(4), 393–409.

[10] Hendricks, K. B., and Singhal, V. R. (1996). Quality awards and the market value of the firm: an empirical investigation. *Management Science*, 42(3), 415–436.

[11] Srivastava, S., and Gaur, S. (2016). Quality management practices in public and private sector banks in India employees' perspective. *Research Journal of Commerce and Behavioural Science*, 6(2), 42–53.

[12] Madan, G., and Priyadharshany, J. (2018). TQM as a tool for enhancing customer satisfaction with special reference to banking industry. *International Journal of Pure and Applied Mathematics*, 120(5), 4313–4323.

[13] Selvaraj, M. (2009). Total quality management in commercial banks. *Journal of Marketing and Communication*, 4(3), 59–70.

[14] Hair, J., Black, W. C., Babin, B. J. and Anderson, R. E. (2014). *Multivariate data analysis* (7th ed.). Pearson Education Limited

41 Impact of appraisal systems on employee retention in the FMCG sector in India: a review

Vineet Mangal[a] and Somesh Dhamija[b]

Institute of Business Management, GLA University, Mathura, India

Abstract

Keeping employees in today's business world, which is marked by intense competition, is a task that is fraught with difficulty. Research of both the qualitative and quantitative variety suggests that performance reviews in India's fast-moving consumer goods (FMCG) industry are effective at retaining employees and instilling in them a sense of loyalty to the companies for which they work. Businesses need to hire employees who possess specific skills in order to maintain their position in the market. If management examines how well employees perform their jobs, they will be able to determine not only the current value of the workforce but also its potential future value. This review addresses topics such as the level of contentment enjoyed by workers, the culture of the organization, how workers evaluate their own performance, and the turnover rate of staff members.

Keywords: Appraisal system, employee performance, employee retention, employee turnover, FMCG

Introduction

Employees are precious to any company. One company focuses on retaining its talented employees and minimizing new hires [1]. This takes skilled and knowledgeable guidance in a difficult environment. Retaining top employees boosts product and service output. Thus, organizations need employee retention strategies to enhance performance [2]. Performance depends on good workers. Retaining employees boosts organizational success. Retention encourages new hires to stay. Long-term workers are more productive [3–5] added that experienced workers know how to do their jobs. Employee longevity also cuts costs. Training, replacement, hiring, productivity, and efficiency fees are examples. Cost reduction improves efficiency [6] found that employee retention strategies improved organization success globally. FMCG sales are rising in Jordan. Employee retention tactics boost company productivity. Over the past fifty years, India's FMCG sector developed. India relies on FMCG. This area affects all aspects of life. The regulated and unorganized FMCG sectors have long competed in India. Employee retention strategies have helped fast-moving consumer goods firms perform better, according to Perpetuity Research & Consultancy International [7]. The fast-moving consumer goods industry is Nigeria's largest. Lagos Business School [8] reported that 71% of FMCG firms are losing money and must reduce output costs to stay competitive [9] noted that working conditions, worker-employer relationships, training and development opportunities, job security, and company policies and processes for rewarding employees all affect employee performance. In many FMCG organizations in Uganda, there is still a high rate of employee turnover which comes with negative impact on the organization performance but organizations take employee turnover as a mean of reducing on the organization's expenditures yet in the actual sense they are losing competent and skilled labor force [10]. Thus, most FMCG companies engage in employee retention strategies to improve performance [11]. FMCG has grown faster in recent years. As the company has grown, many local and foreign companies have entered to compete [12]. Like in other countries, FMCG giants are struggling due to increased competition and creative advancements that have made some products obsolete [13]. Most workers have quit to work elsewhere. Poor results can also force firms to leave the market. Eveready in India, a FMCG leader, collapsed due to high costs and poor performance [14]. Retention strategies can boost company success. A company's employee retention plan should support its performance improvement strategy. Many companies have failed to implement employee retention strategies, despite their well-known benefits [15]. Indian retail starts in South Asia. Since 30% of Indians buy in stores, FMCGs are well supported. Thus, FMCG manufacturers have promise, but some have recently underperformed [16]. Eveready and other firms found it difficult to adapt to India's market and saw their advantage drop by 57% [17]. In 2017, Proctor and Allan income fell 3% from 2018. Employee pay, salary delays, and working conditions have been linked to declining performance [18]. Argued that employee retention strategies are necessary to attain desired performance [19].

[a]vmangal1974@gmail.com, [b]somesh.dhamija@gla.ac.in

DOI: 10.1201/9781003534136-41

Figure 41.1 Assessment of employee performance in the workplace

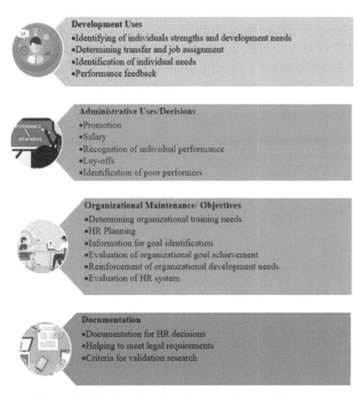

Figure 41.2 Evaluation of performance's appraisal

Performance appraisals compare an employee's work to set standards. Recording assessment results. At the end of the year, the worker gets performance feedback to help them improve. After a certain period, employees want to know their status. A systematic method must be used to track progress and results throughout the evaluation time since performance is based on actual work [20-23].

Choosing the right measurement methods is vital. It's also important to compare employee successto standardized performance. work evaluations aim to correctly assess an employee's work, provide constructive criticism, and inspire future success. Though tedious, the result is crucial. Figure 41.1 explains job evaluations.

Evaluation of the Performance Appraisal's Importance

Performance evaluations determine an employee's skill, knowledge, and output. It inspires future productivity. Good workers can get promoted or paid more. Workers can discuss personal and business issues with supervisors during performance reviews. It helps management and staff discuss job duties and issues. It shows employees where they can grow. Some jobs require formal training from the company. Figure 40.2 shows the evaluation of performance appraisal. It makes workers accountable and better equipped for future reviews. Managers can explain the company's goal and how employees can help achieve it.

Research Methodology and Data Analysis

This study's sample poll was carried out between June and August of 2021-22 at colleges and universities in the Delhi-National Capital Region. The conceptual framework included a literaturesurvey in support of objectives 1 and 2. Research was conducted on the structure of the evaluationprocess and different types of biases within it.

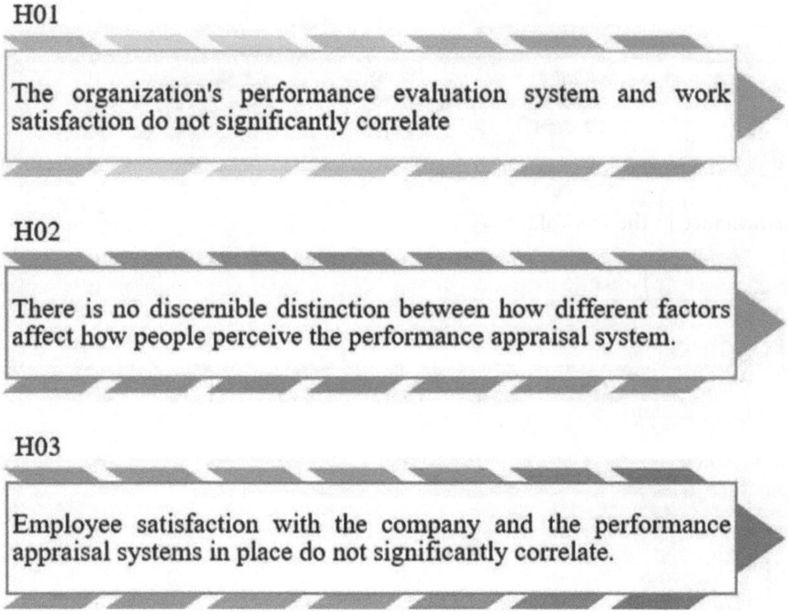

H01

The organization's performance evaluation system and work satisfaction do not significantly correlate

H02

There is no discernible distinction between how different factors affect how people perceive the performance appraisal system.

H03

Employee satisfaction with the company and the performance appraisal systems in place do not significantly correlate.

Figure 41.3 Hypothesis

Feelings Towards Current Job · Perception Towards the Appraisal Process · Career Plans in Near Future · Ability to Perform · General Feelings Towards Current Organization.

Figure 41.4 Five categories for the survey

Table 41.1 Age and gender distribution of the respondents

		Gender			Total
		Female	Male		
Age of the respondent	**21 to 25**	2	13	Count	15
		0.70%	4.90%	% Of Total	5.60%
	26 to 30	38	15	Count	53
		14.20%	5.60%	% Of Total	19.80%
	31 to 35	0	31	Count	31
		0.00%	11.60%	% Of Total	11.60%
	36 to 40	4	70	Count	74
		1.50%	26.10%	% Of Total	27.60%
	41 to 45	21	57	Count	78
		7.80%	21.30%	% Of Total	29.10%
	46 and above	15	2	Count	17
		5.60%	0.70%	% Of Total	6.30%
Total		80	188	Count	268
		29.90%	70.10%	% Of Total	100.00%

Age of the respondent *Gender cross tabulation

Created a 29-variable questionnaire with 5 categories for the original study. The split-half method was used to test questionnaire consistency during the pilot study. 268 (89.33%) of 300 individuals provided data. Table 1 shows respondents ages and sexes. The poll had 188 men and 80 women. The largest female demographic was 25–29, and the largest male cohort was 35–39. Tables 41.2 and 41.3 compare the sexes by schooling and job experience. Most women have master's degrees, and their careers reflect this. Most have 2–5 years of experience or more than 10. Performance reviews affect employees' job satisfaction and firm loyalty. 83% of the 130 male samples are doctoral- educated workers with six or more years of experience. Due to variation, descriptive numbers are usual. If only 12% of the sample is under-two-year-old, they can't influence the outcome. Seventy-five percent of the sample has been with the company for six years or more and has gone through the appraisal process, so their views can illuminate the system's effects on the business and its employees. Table 41.4 shows data factorability, KMO, and Bartlett's sphericity tests. The twenty-nine questions on the survey are broken down into five categories shown in Figure 41.4:

The constructs' reliability (0.781) across 29 elements shows good internal consistency. KMO values above 0.5 are usually chosen. According to this analysis, the correlation matrix for the population is not an identity matrix. The Chi-square value at the 0.05 level is 3451.4 with 406 degrees of freedom. The 268-column

Table 41.2 Education levels and gender of the candidates

Curriculum vitae *Gender cross tabulation

			Gender		Total
			Male	Female	
Curriculum vitae	Bachelors/masters doctorate	Count	130	40	170
		% Of Total	48.5%	14.9%	63.4%
	Masters/M.Phil.	Count	26	0	26
		% Of Total	9.7%	.0%	9.7%
	MBA/M. Com	Count	22	2	24
		% Of Total	8.2%	.7%	9.0%
	BBA/M. Tech/Graduate	Count	10	38	48
		% Of Total	3.7%	14.2%	17.9%
Total		Count	188	80	268
		% Of Total	70.1%	29.9%	100.0%

Table 41.3 Respondents' work history and gender

		Gender			Total
		Male	Female		
Work experience	Less than two years	31	3	Count	34
		11.6%	1.1%	% Of Total	12.7%
	Two to five years	0	37	Count	37
		.0%	13.8%	% Of Total	13.8%
	Six to 10 years	58	2	Count	60
		21.6%	.7%	% Of Total	22.4%
	Above 10 years	99	38	Count	137
		36.9%	14.2%	% Of Total	51.1%
Total		188	80	Count	268
		70.1%	29.9%	% Of Total	100.0%

Work experience *Gender cross tabulation

Table 41.4 KMO and Bartlett's test

3451.34	Approx. Chi-square	Bartlett's test of sphericity
406	df	-
0	Sig.	-
No. of items	-	Reliability statistics
29	0.724	Cronbach's alpha
0.781	-	Kaiser-Meyer-Olkin Measure of sampling Adequacy.

Table 41.5 The qualitative statistical analysis N = 272

S. No.	Factors	Mean	Std. Dev
1	Perceptions of one's present work	5.21	
1.1	Enjoyable	5.31	0.930
1.2	Motivational	5.17	0.860
1.3	Driving force	5.45	0.901
1.4	Meaningful	5.38	0.652
1.5	Lucky	5.47	0.755
1.6	Hobby	4.39	0.947
2	Perception towards the appraisal process	4.36	
2.1	Highly relevant	4.84	1.05
2.2	Recognition for good performance	4.36	1.08
2.3	Satisfied	4.32	1.27
2.4	Recognition for self-achievement	4.01	1.30
2.5	Proper conduct	4.21	1.28
2.6	Emphasis on positive feedback	4.46	1.28
2.7	Valuable	4.73	1.21
3	Career plans in near future	3.13	
3.1	Often think of quitting present job	3.27	1.29
3.2	No prospect in future	3.22	1.27
3.3	New Job in next 3 years	3.35	1.23
3.4	Quit present job in next 1 year	2.94	1.25
3.5	New Job in next one year	3.16	1.37
4	Ability to perform	3.86	
4.1	Often perform better	3.89	1.07
4.2	Great deal of effort	3.76	1.07
4.3	Expend extra efforts	3.79	1.13
4.4	Hard work	3.87	1.62
4.5	Quality is topnotch	3.9	1.1
4.6	Always perform better	3.93	1.03
5	General feelings towards current organization	3.12	
5.1	No feeling of belongingness	2.88	1.34
5.2	Organization has personal meaning	3.35	1.33
5.3	Do not feel as part of the Family	3.64	1.49
5.4	No emotional attachment	3.02	1.36
5.5	Enjoy discussing the organization with people outside	2.7	1.21

association matrix can be examined using factor analysis. Factor analysis is valid for this data gathering because Cronbach's alpha, a measure of scale reliability, was 0.724 for each construct. A large majority of respondents are enthusiastic about their job, but fewer are optimistic about their company. Thus, this shift in viewpoint is not just about "job." The review process's outlook matches the immediate aims and job success potential. H03: Theory As shown in Table 41.5, the general attitude toward the organization and the appraisal process are almost the same, indicating that employee satisfaction and performance review systems are unrelated. Even if they're happy in their jobs, how they're assessed affects their performance, outlook, and company satisfaction.

When factor analysis was applied to the raw data, it was possible to reduce the number of factors from 29 to a smaller set of linear composites without losing any of the information contained in the original data set (analyzed in SPSS 20.0). Two-stage factor analysis with the factor extraction method was used in this research. Nine factors were extracted from the original set of 29 using principal component analysis; these factors explained 70.54 percent of the total variation. Table 41.6 displays the early data extractions.

Second-stage principal component rotation was supposed to name and understand these early variables. Table 41.7 shows Eigen values and range for each extraction. Nine factors explain 70% of data variance. Factors 1 and 2 explain over 20% of range. Factor 1, with six variables, determines maximal loadings. The gleaned factors are summarized below. The nine factors that were extracted and their differing percentages

Table 41.6 Communalities

S.no	Communalities	Initial	Extraction
1.	Do not feel as part of the family	1	0.850
2.	Satisfied	1	0.743
3.	Always perform better	1	0.603
4.	Enjoy discussing the organization with outside people	1	0.707
5.	Meaningful	1	0.501
6.	Proper conduct	1	0.755
7.	Often think of quitting present job	1	0.752
8.	Highly relevant	1	0.821
9.	Valuable	1	0.828
10.	Hobby	1	0.677
11.	Enjoyable	1	0.639
12.	Often perform better	1	0.747
13.	Great deal of effort	1	0.701
14.	Motivational	1	0.624
15.	Recognition for good performance	1	0.630
16.	Organization has personal meaning	1	0.690
17.	No feeling of belongingness	1	0.763
18.	Hard work	1	0.662
19.	No prospect in future	1	0.668
20.	Driving force	1	0.646
21.	Expend extra efforts	1	0.770
22.	New job in next 3 years	1	0.641
23.	Emphasis on positive feedback	1	0.696
24.	Quality is topnotch	1	0.676
25.	New job in next one year	1	0.728
26.	Quit present job in next 1 year	1	0.750
27.	Recognition for self-achievement	1	0.741
28.	No emotional attachment	1	0.786

of contribution to explaining the variance demonstrate that the hypothesis H02—according to which there is no discernible difference between the contributions of different factors to the perception of the performance evaluation system—is untrue. Hypothesis of this can be seen in Figure 41.3. Self- awareness is the first factor. "Considering the task being done as extremely relevant" (.532), "recognition for good performance" (.574), and "recognition for self-achievement" (.574) make up this factor's total loadings (.611). If an employee cares about quality and works hard, his success and evaluation will be similar. H01 is not a daily occurrence because performance reviews and other feedback greatly affect job satisfaction. The second aspect is a sense of belonging. These five factors help remove this element. Job satisfaction improves company community (.471 loading). If there is no emotional commitment (loading .382) or community, employees are more apt to look for new jobs and quit within a year (loading .522). (With respective eigen values as 0.327 and 0.409 respectively). If an employee feels at home, they'll stay, but if not, they'll quit.

Thirdly, "positive attitude" contains positive feedback, motivation, and significance.

This chart shows factor eigenvalues or loadings. High contribution (0.628): positive feedback (0.569), which encourages proper behavior; meaningful job (0.445); feeling lucky (0.373); and 0.677. Four only has variables with 0.522 eigenvalues, so the new job will be filled in three years. (0.335). Thus, this is self-confidence in the

Table 41.7 Explaining total variance using principal component analysis

S. No	Initial Eigen values		
	Total	% of Variance	Cumulative %
1	4.448	15.338	15.338
2	3.760	12.964	28.302
3	2.810	9.691	37.994
4	1.975	6.811	44.804
5	1.928	6.648	51.452
6	1.698	5.855	57.307
7	1.446	4.985	62.292
8	1.310	4.516	66.809
9	1.083	3.736	70.545
10	.886	3.056	73.601
11	.799	2.754	76.355
12	.760	2.621	78.976
13	.679	2.341	81.317
14	.628	2.165	83.482
15	.569	1.961	85.443
16	.508	1.751	87.194
17	.486	1.677	88.871
18	.443	1.529	90.400
19	.380	1.309	91.709
20	.348	1.201	92.911
21	.342	1.178	94.089
22	.291	1.005	95.094
23	.259	.892	95.985
24	.244	.841	96.826
25	.222	.766	97.591
26	.268	.751	87.194
27	.321	.677	88.871
28	.385	1.321	90.400

company's value. Four factors account for nearly 40% of the variance, so far. The fifth aspect is optimistic potential. Some employees perform better consistently, while others only occasionally improve, depending on how they feel about their future with the firm. Loadings are 0.336, 0.394, 0.320, and 0.398. This is important because employees who think they can advance in their jobs are more apt to stay. Factor 6 is also linked to intrinsic variables like internal driving power (loading 0.484), which can lead us to leave our present job (loading 0.326) and work hard to find a new one. (Loadings 0.530). Company evaluations consider employees' objectives. Factor 7 emphasizes firm pride. If they found their group fascinating (loading of 0.525) and in line with their interests (loading of 0.498), they would love to talk about it with outsiders, but this loading is low. (Loading of 0.341). The company's workers and customers are satisfied. These seven factors explain 60% of the scatter. Factors 8 and 9 make for 10% of variation. Employees not feeling part of the company is the eighth reason. Its 0.819 burden is high. Our pleasure of outdoor organization debates is 0.341 for Factor 9. It contributes nearly 5% of variance. These nine extracted factors explain 70% of variation. All three ideas have been disproven. Thus, job satisfaction is linked to employee satisfaction in performance evaluations. Component Matrix for the same can be seen in Table 41.8.

Table 41.8 Component matrix

S. no	Communalities	Component								
		1	2	3	4	5	6	7	8	9
1	Satisfied	0.417	0.471	0.405	0.057	0.292	0.169	-0.114	-0.131	-0.19
2	Recognition for good work	0.574	0.204	-0.068	0.109	0.05	0.151	0.43	-0.11	0.143
3	Proper conduct	0.296	0.379	0.628	0.207	0.22	0.103	-0.104	-0.013	0.126
4	Valuable	0.36	0.136	-0.065	0.601	-0.614	-0.185	0.089	0.210	0.402
5	New job in next 3 years	0.546	0.266	-0.205	0.335	-0.064	0.207	-0.261	-0.029	-0.054
6	No prospect in future	-0.646	-0.076	0.087	-0.077	0.382	0.078	-0.089	0.223	0.218
7	Often perform better	0.173	-0.666	0.306	0.059	0.394	0.066	0.005	0.057	0.118
8	Quality is topnotch	0.496	-0.263	-0.057	-0.099	-0.383	0.418	-0.081	0.086	0.109
9	No emotional attachment	-0.079	0.382	-0.104	-0.672	0.049	0.251	0.124	0.077	0.29
10	Organizations has personal meaning	0.451	0.394	0.265	-0.314	-0.199	-0.133	-0.256	0.256	-0.221
11	Enjoy discussing the organization with outside people	-0.375	0.183	0.173	-0.166	0.121	-0.467	0.334	0.221	0.334
12	Driving force	-0.344	-0.139	0.249	0.04	-0.171	0.484	0.419	0.064	-0.036
13	Do not feel as part of the family	0.176	-0.021	0.322	-0.012	0.092	-0.165	-0.079	0.819	0.055
14	No feeling of belongingness	-0.137	0.522	-0.062	-0.634	-0.119	0.024	0.09	-0.133	0.158
15	Emphasis on positive feedback	0.300	0.486	0.576	0.297	0.045	0.043	-0.060	-0.077	0.089
16	Often consider leaving job.	-0.626	0.289	-0.207	0.15	0.244	0.326	0.031	0.172	-0.124
17	Great deal of effort	0.359	-0.121	-0.221	-0.064	-0.276	0.528	-0.20	0.369	-0.009
18	Quit present job in next 1 year	-0.520	0.410	0.280	0.100	0.140	0.30	-0.300	-0.119	0.270
19	Self-accomplishment	0.611	0.497	0.11	0.202	-0.014	-0.055	0.092	-0.034	0.234
20	New Job in next one year	-0.498	0.330	-0.230	0.390	-0.020	0.301	-0.110	0.099	0.300
21	Meaningful	-0.395	-0.061	0.445	-0.2	-0.14	0.014	-0.072	0.069	-0.269
22	Highly relevant	0.532	0.448	-0.179	0.015	0.39	0.204	-0.045	0.16	-0.287
23	Hard work	0.316	-0.445	0.02	-0.22	-0.094	0.291	-0.313	-0.257	0.241
24	Enjoyable	-0.16	-0.008	0.497	-0.137	-0.033	0.263	0.525	0.021	-0.039
25	Expend extra efforts	0.288	-0.658	0.130	-0.088	0.331	0.30	-0.052	0.060	0.210
26	Lucky	-0.404	-0.219	0.373	0.157	-0.471	0.084	0.089	0.131	-0.186
27	Hobby	0.229	0.049	-0.402	0.262	0.282	0.128	0.498	0.036	-0.216
28	Always perform better	0.009	-0.643	0.185	0.16	0.336	-0.064	-0.009	-0.057	0.093

Conclusion

Because modern work takes a lot of time and effort on the part of employees, they have higher expectations of their managers. The manager's requirement for a performance review shouldn't be seen as a burden or a waste of time. Performance evaluation needs to become a common practice and an important part of management in order for organizations to be successful at reaching their goals. Reviewing past performance is an important part of a wide range of human resources decision-making processes. Researchers have been interested in how accurate the performance appraisal system is when it is used on a global scale since the beginning of time. The answer to this question is still being looked into. Human resource development also affects how an organization measures how well employees do their jobs.

References

[1] Adam, A. (2018). Branding and business performance of fast-moving consumer goods. a case study of Muwano group of companies Kampala, Uganda.

[2] Adewuyi, A. M. (2012). Retention of employees in a professional services firm through wealth creation initiatives (Doctoral dissertation).

[3] Aduda, J. (2011). The relationship between executive compensation and firm performance in the Kenyan banking sector. *Journal of Accounting and Taxation*, 3(6), 130–139.

[4] Al-Omari, K., and Okasheh, H. (2017). The influence of work environment on job performance: a case study of engineering company in Jordan. *International Journal of Applied Engineering Research*, 12(24), 15544–15550.

[5] Amah, O. E. (2009). Job Satisfaction and Turnover Intention Relationship: The Moderating Effect of Job Role Centrality and Life Satisfaction. *Research & Practice in Human Resource Management*, 17(1).

[6] Aminu, H. (2018). Assessment of the impact of employee training on organizational performance of Vitafoam Nigeria Plc (Doctoral dissertation, Doctoral Dissertation, Department of Business Administration, Faculty Of Administration, Ahmadu Bello University, Zaria).

[7] Ampoty, J. (2018). An investigation into the effects of career development on employee retention at Anglogold Ashanti Limited, Obuasi Mine (Doctoral dissertation).

[8] Anyango, E., Walter, O. B., and Muya, J. (2018). Effects of recruitment and selection criteria on organizational performance at Kisii University, Kenya. *International Journal of Social Sciences and Information Technology*, 4(10), 271–282.

[9] Appelbaum, E., and Berg, P. (2000). High Performance Work Systems and Labor Market. New York: Structures. Kluwer Academic/Plenum Publishers.

[10] Armstrong, M. (2010). A Handbook of Human Resource Management Practice. 11th edn. Kogen Page Ltd. U.S.A.

[11] Arokiasamy, L., Ismail, M., Ahmad, A., and Othman, J. (2011). Predictors of academics' career advancement at Malaysian private universities. *Journal of European Industrial Training*, 35(6), 589–605.

[12] Balozi (2011). Influence of high-performance work practices on employee satisfaction in Tanzania Public Service College.

[13] Bruce, K., and Nyland, C. (2011). Elton Mayo and the deification of human relations. *Organization Studies*, 32(3), 383–405.

[14] Bushiri, C. P. (2014). The impact of working environment on employees' performance, the case of Institute of Finance Management in Dar es Salaam. Doctoral dissertation, The Open University of Tanzania.

[15] Čanković, V. (2015). The impact of employee selection on organisatinal performance. *SEER: Journal for Labour and Social Affairs in Eastern Europe*, 18(2), 217–230.

[16] Chepchumba, T. R., and Kimutai, B. D. (2017). The relationship between employee compensation and employee turnover in small businesses among Safaricom dealers in Eldoret municipality, Kenya.

[17] Cherono, J. (2012). Employee Development and Organizational Performance of Unilever Tea Kenya Ltd in Kericho County. Unpublished Thesis.

[18] Danish, R. Q., and Usman, A. (2016). Impact of reward and recognition on job satisfaction and motivation: an empirical study from Pakistan. *International Journal of Business and Management*, 5(2), 159.

[19] Ekwoaba, J. O., Ikeije, U. U., and Ufoma, N. (2015). The impact of recruitment and selection criteria on organizational performance.

[20] Enemuo, J. I., and Olateju, I. A. (2021). Reward management system and employee performance in the fast-moving consumer goods (FMCGS) sector in Nigeria.

[21] Eyster, L., Johnson, R., and Toder, E. (2008). Current strategies to employ & retain older workers.

[22] Dessler, G. (2012). Human Resource Management. 13th edn. New Delhi: Pearson-Prentice Hall.

[23] Disley, P., Hatton, C., and Dagnan, D. (2009). Applying equity theory to staff working with individuals with intellectual disabilities. *Journal of Intellectual and Developmental Disability*, 34(1), 55–66.

42 Performance management in the FMCG industry: an empirical analysis of its effect on employee retention

Vineet Mangal[a] and Somesh Dhamija

GLA University, Mathura, India

Abstract

The purpose of performance management is to ensure that the organization's Vision and Mission are reflected in the work of its employees. In today's global knowledge economies, survival and continued competitiveness depend on effective performance management. Employee productivity, engagement, and loyalty can all be improved with better performance management and a more robust incentive and recognition structure. The 129 participants in this study are all employees at India's largest telecom company, and their responses were collected using a structured, non- standard research tool. Partition analysis was used on the collected data to isolate the elements contributing to employee retention and their connections to performance management structures within the organization. Research shows that when workers are properly aligned with the organization's aims, the business as a whole is able to operate at a higher level.

Keywords: Performance management, employee retention, FMCG

Introduction

Monitoring, measuring, and enhancing employee performance is what performance management is all about for businesses. Because staff turnover can result in lower productivity, higher recruitment expenses, and a loss of talent, it is a pressing issue in the fast-moving consumer goods (FMCG) sector. Therefore, performance management can greatly aid in retaining FMCG workers. The Society for Human Resource Management (SHRM) found that keeping good employees is one of the biggest problems facing businesses today. In the FMCG industry, where workers are typically subjected to heavy workloads and pressure, it is especially important to keep skilled personnel [1]. Organizations can benefit from performance management systems by closing $_{performance}$ gaps, improving employee engagement and retention, and creating a more constructive work environment through effective feedback and coaching. Companies in FMCG sector often struggle to keep their best employees. The high rate of staff turnover in this industry is a major cost driver (recruitment and training expenditures) and productivity drag for businesses. By boosting productivity, morale, and engagement, performance management systems can assist overcome this obstacle. Here, we investigate how performance management might help the FMCG industry keep its best people. A study by the University of Tennessee's Global Supply Chain Institute found that retaining key employees is a major issue for FMCG businesses. Supply chain operations and production can be negatively impacted by high personnel turnover, which can lead to decreased revenue and market share [2, 3]. Therefore, in order to keep their employees and keep their business running, FMCG firms need to establish efficient performance management systems. Employees' strengths and areas for improvement can be highlighted with the aid of performance management systems, which also serve to coach workers and bring their aspirations into line with those of the company. It has the potential to create an upbeat environment in the workplace, which is good for morale and productivity. Companies in the FMCG industry can increase both staff retention and productivity by implementing performance management systems. The FMCG business has historically struggled with a serious problem: keeping competent employees [4, 5]. The high rate of staff turnover in this industry can have a negative effect on business results, including decreased productivity and higher recruitment and onboarding costs. Employee performance, engagement, and work satisfaction can all be enhanced through effective performance management, which plays a critical part in overcoming this obstacle. Therefore, the purpose of this article is to investigate how FMCG companies might better retain their employees through performance management. Deloitte found that businesses that priorities performance management have greater levels of employee dedication and loyalty. Performance management is useful in the FMCG industry because of the high stress and high demands of the work environment. Employee performance and job happiness can be boosted via performance management in the form of timely feedback, coaching, and growth opportunities, all of which contribute to greater employee retention. Aligning employee goals with organizational objectives help foster a sense of purpose and belonging in FMCG organizations thanks to effective performance management.

[a]vmangal1974@gmail.com; [b]somesh.dhamija@gla.ac.in

DOI: 10.1201/9781003534136-42

This harmony has the potential to create a supportive work environment that inspires dedication, cooperation, and loyalty from workers. Setting goals, defining employee productivity and performance measures, conducting periodic performance appraisals, providing constructive performance feedback to employees, implementing appropriate learning interventions, rewarding and recognizing employees, developing leaders, and planning for employee succession are all examples of performance management. Figure 42.1 shows a visual illustration of this concept [6-9].

Need/Importance of Performance Management on Employee Retention in FMCG

Effective performance management is a crucial procedure for increasing productivity, building staff capacity, and realizing organizational objectives. Effective performance management can be crucial to keeping skilled people and preserving a competitive advantage in the FMCG market, where competition is fierce and profit margins are low. The FMCG sector relies heavily on its employees, making performance management crucial to retaining them.

Clarifies expectations: Employees benefit from performance management because it clarifies their place in the company, their path to promotion, and the standards to which they must adhere. Employees are more likely to feel invested in their work and encouraged to provide their best thanks to this transparency, which in turn boosts job satisfaction and loyalty

Figure 42.1 Key constituents of performance management

Figure 42.2 Need/importance of performance management on employee retention in FMCG

- **Identifies training and development needs:** In order to fill in any knowledge or training gaps, businesses might use performance management. Training and development programs that target these areas have been shown to promote employee retention by improving job satisfaction, morale, and commitment.
- **Provides feedback and recognition:** Employee engagement and motivation greatly benefit from consistent feedback and acknowledgement. Managers are able to provide staff useful criticism and praise because to the structure provided by performance management. Employees are more likely to feel appreciated and satisfied in their jobs as a result.
- **Supports performance-based rewards** Performance-based awards can be especially effective in the (FMCG business, where employees' efforts have a direct impact on the company's bottom line. When top performers are singled out and rewarded for their efforts, it can go a long way towards keeping them around.
- **Facilitates career progression:** Employees can benefit from performance management by learning where they can improve their skills and advance their careers. Giving workers a defined path to advancement has been shown to boost morale and retention rates.

In conclusion, performance management is an important resource for the FMCG sector to use in retaining its employees. Organizations may boost employee engagement and satisfaction—and thus retention—by being transparent about expectations, helping workers discover areas in which they can grow, rewarding and recognizing their efforts, and creating opportunities for advancement.

Statement of the Problem Performance Management on Employee Retention in FMCG

The FMCG sector is extremely competitive and dynamic, with a strong emphasis on cost-effectiveness, innovation, and customer pleasure. For businesses to succeed in such a setting and maintain their competitiveness, they must be able to retain talented and high-performing people. However, the industry also has trouble keeping workers due to a number of issues, including a lack of career development possibilities, a strong demand for trained labor, and employee discontent with performance management procedures.

Enhancing staff productivity, building skills and competencies, and accomplishing organizational goals all depend on performance management. Performance management procedures, however, may not be in line with employee expectations in the FMCG sector, which can cause unhappiness and staff churn. The sector demands efficient performance management procedures that are open and equitable, and that are centered on employee growth, recognition, and career advancement.

Consequently, the challenge is how to establish and implement in the FMCG sector effective performance management practices that can increase staff retention by coordinating employee expectations, offering feedback and recognition, and creating possibilities for career advancement.

Research Methodology for Performance Management on Employee Retention in FMCG

Research methodology for studying the relationship between performance management and employee retention in the FMCG industry can be outlined as follows in Figure 42.3.

Figure 42.3 Research methodology for performance management on employee retention in FMCG

- **Research design:** A quantitative research design, which involves gathering and analyzing numerical data, would be used for this study. The plan would incorporate survey research, which would entail distributing a questionnaire to a sample of FMCG industry workers. For the purpose of gathering information about performance management procedures, employee satisfaction, and retention, the questionnaire would include both closed-ended and open-ended items.
- **Sampling technique:** Probability sampling will be used for this study's sampling strategy, in which a representative sample of workers in the FMCG sector will be chosen at random. In order to ensure that the sample size is sufficient to detect any significant effects, the sample size would be chosen based on statistical power analysis.
- **Data collection:** An online survey questionnaire will be used as the main mode of data gathering and given to the chosen employee sample. Data on various performance management methods, including goal-setting, feedback, recognition, training, and career development, as well as employee satisfaction and retention, will be gathered through the questionnaire.
- **Data analysis:** Statistical analysis tools like SPSS or R would be used to examine the acquired data. Inferential statistics would be used to analyses the data in order to determine the relationship between performance management strategies and employee retention. Descriptive statistics would be used to provide an overview of the data. The direction and intensity of the association between employee retention and performance management practices could be determined using regression analysis.
- **Ethical considerations:** Ethical principles for research would be followed throughout the project, including obtaining participants' informed consent, protecting the privacy of their information, and keeping them as safe as possible.
- **Limitations:** Self-reported data biases, sample size constraints, and the study's generalizability to other industries are all potential problems. Future research could expand the study's emphasis to include additional industries and use a mixed-methods approach to obtain a more complete understanding of the connection between performance management practices and staff retention in the FMCG business.

Literature Review

According to the study, employee retention in the quickly changing consumer products business is largely influenced by performance management. Armstrong and Baron [10] define performance management as "a process that aids in aligning individual and organizational goals, measures performance, and provides feedback to employees" (2014). The authors contend that effective performance management raises employee engagement, output, and loyalty.

Goyal and Chauhan [11] studied how performance management practices affected employee retention in the FMCG sector. When performance management procedures such setting goals, assessing employee performance, giving helpful criticism, and offering chances for professional advancement were used, it was discovered that employee retention increased (Table 1).

In a similar line, Nair and Vohra [12] investigated how performance management impacts employee retention in the quickly evolving consumer products sector. According to a recent study, performance management techniques including goal setting, performance evaluation, and feedback can assist the FMCG business increase employee retention. In addition, Rai et al. [13] examined the impact of performance management on staff retention in the Indian fast-moving consumer goods sector. In the Indian FMCG market, goal-setting, performance evaluation, feedback, and recognition were all discovered to have a significant impact on staff retention.

In the Sudanese fast-moving consumer goods industry, Hassan and Mohammed [14] investigated the impact of performance management on employee retention. Performance management practices like performance appraisal, feedback, and recognition have been found to increase employee retention in the FMCG sector in Sudan. Recent studies highlight the importance of performance management in keeping FMCG employees. Gamage and Harikrishnan [15] investigated how performance management strategies affected employee retention in Sri Lanka's fast-moving consumer goods sector. Performance management practices such goal-setting, performance evaluation, feedback, and training and development have been found to have a substantial impact on employee retention in the FMCG sector. Similar to this, Jain et al. [16] looked into how performance management strategies affected employee retention in India's fast-moving consumer goods business. In the Indian FMCG market, it was discovered that goal-setting, performance evaluation, feedback, and recognition all had a positive impact on staff retention.

Alqarni et al. [17] also examined the impact of performance management strategies on employee retention in the fast-moving consumer goods sector in Saudi Arabia. When performance management practices such goal

Table 42.1 Literature review on employee retention in FMCG industry

Study	Objectives	Methodology	Findings
Adekoya et al. (2022) [19]	To determine how performance management affects FMCG industry employee retention	Survey research design using questionnaires	In the FMCG sector, performance management significantly improves staff retention.
Ahmed et al. (2022) [20]	To investigate the connection between employee retention and work-life balance in the FMCG sector.	Using structured questionnaires in quantitative research	Work-life balance has a significant positive relationship with employee retention in FMCG industry
Bhattacharya et al. (2021) [21]	To examine how employee engagement affects employee retention in the FMCG business.	Mixed-method research design using surveys and interviews	Employee engagement has a significant positive impact on employee retention in FMCG industry
Goyal et al. (2021) [22]	To analyze the impact of leadership style on employee retention in FMCG industry	Qualitative research design Using semi-structured interviews	Transformational leadership style has a significant positive impact on employee retention in FMCG industry
Kumar and Jha (2021) [23]	To investigate how organizational culture affects employee retention in the FMCG sector.	Quantitative research design using structured questionnaires	Organizational culture has a significant positive influence on employee retention in FMCG industry
Nasiru and Marafa (2021) [24]	To investigate the effect of compensation and benefits on employee retention in FMCG industry	Survey research design using questionnaires	Compensation and benefits have a significant positive effect on employee retention in FMCG industry
Ogunsanmi and Adeoye (2021) [25]	To explore the relationship between job satisfaction and employee retention in FMCG industry	Quantitative research design using structured questionnaires	Job satisfaction has a significant positive relationship with employee retention in FMCG industry
Abbas et al. (2022) [26]	To research how the workplace environment affects employee retention in the FMCG industry.	Quantitative research design using structured questionnaires	The FMCG industry's work environment significantly boosts employee retention.
Chandio et al. (2021) [27]	To examine the effect of career development opportunities on employee retention in FMCG industry	Mixed-method research design using surveys and interviews	Opportunities for career development significantly increase employee retention in the FMCG sector.
Gupta and Sharma (2022) [28]	To explore the role of employee motivation in employee retention in FMCG industry	Qualitative research design using semi-structured interviews	Employee motivation has a significant positive role in employee retention in FMCG industry
Iqbal et al. (2021) [29]	To examine the connection between workplace stress and employee retention in the FMCG sector.	Survey research design using questionnaires	Work stress has a significant negative relationship with employee retention in FMCG industry
Jain and Aggarwal (2021) [30]	To examine how job security affects employee re-engagement in the FMCG sector.	Quantitative research design Using structured questionnaires	In the FMCG sector, job security has a very favorable effect on staff retention.
Kamal and Hossain (2021) [31]	To investigate how supervisor assistance affects employee retention in the FMCG sector.	Survey research design using questionnaires	In the FMCG sector, supervisor support has a very favorable impact on employee retention.
Malik et al. (2021) [32]	To examine how organizational justice affects employee retention in the FMCG sector.	Mixed-method research design using surveys and interviews	Organizational justice significantly improves employee retention in the FMCG sector.
Singh and Jain (2021) [33]	To learn more about the relationship between leadership style and staff retention in the FMCG industry.	Quantitative research design using structured questionnaires	In the FMCG sector, employee engagement mediates the connection between leadership style and employee retention.
Srivastava and Singh (2022) [34]	To examine how work-life balance and employee engagement affect FMCG industry retention	Mixed-method research design using surveys and interviews	In the FMCG sector, staff retention is significantly impacted favorably by work-life balance and employee engagement.
Yin et al. (2022) [35]	To examine how employee-organization relationships affect staff retention in the FMCG sector.	Survey research design using questionnaires	In the FMCG industry, the employee-organization connection has a substantial beneficial effect on employee retention.

setting, performance evaluation, feedback, and training and development were adopted, it was discovered that employee retention in Saudi Arabia's FMCG industry increased. Furthermore, Nasir and Abbasi [18] looked into the impact of performance management on staff retention in Pakistan's FMCG sector. In Pakistan's FMCG sector, goal-setting, performance evaluation, feedback, and recognition were found to have the biggest effects on staff retention.

According to the research, a number of factors, including the work environment, career advancement opportunities, employee motivation, stress on the job, job security, supervisor support, organizational justice, employee engagement, work-life balance, and retention efforts in the FMCG sector are heavily influenced by the employee-organizational connection. In order to retain employees and reduce turnover, businesses in the fast-moving consumer products industry might implement programs to enhance these factors.

Objectives Performance Management on Employee Retention in FMCG

The FMCG industry's goals for implementing effective performance management practices on staff retention are as follows:

- **To align employee expectations with organizational goals:** Employees should be made aware of the organization's goals and how their performance helps to achieve them through the performance management process. Increased employee engagement and motivation as a result of this alignment can enhance retention.
- **To provide regular feedback and recognition:** Employees should receive regular feedback on their performance through the performance management process, including suggestions for growth and acknowledgement of accomplishments. Employee retention and work satisfaction can both rise as a result of receiving this feedback that makes them feel valued and appreciated.
- **To identify development needs and provide opportunities:** Employees should have their training and development requirements identified as part of the performance management process, and opportunities should be provided to fill those gaps. By giving them a feeling of purpose and advancement, this support can improve employees' job happiness and increase staff retention.
- **To facilitate performance-based rewards:** Top performers should be identified by the performance management process, and they should get performance-based rewards like bonuses or promotions. This appreciation can spur workers to keep up their excellent work and boost retention.
- **To facilitate career progression:** Employees should be given a clear path for career advancement through the performance management process, including chances for promotion and development. By offering workers a feeling of purpose and direction in their careers, this support can improve job satisfaction and retention.

Effective performance management procedures in the FMCG sector aim to improve employee motivation, engagement, and development, which will ultimately result in higher retention rates and organizational success.

Findings

In the FMCG sector, performance management can have a big impact on staff retention. Several significant conclusions on this subject include:

- Regular feedback and clear performance standards can increase staff retention: When workers have clear goals to strive for and receive consistent feedback on their progress, they are more likely to feel valued and invested in their jobs. It's possible that doing so might increase their loyalty to the company and make them less likely to leave.
- Praise and prizes for successful performance can also be successful: In the FMCG sector, where competition for talent is high, workers may be more likely to stick with a business if they feel their efforts are noticed and suitably rewarded. It is conceivable in this to receive both monetary benefits (such bonuses or raises) and non-monetary rewards. (such as public recognition or opportunities for career advancement).
- Performance management can also be used to pinpoint and solve the following issues that influence turnover: Organizations can spot areas where workers may be having difficulty or where there is a high level of job unhappiness by tracking employee performance data and performing frequent performance appraisals. These problems can be resolved and overall employee retention can be increased by using the knowledge provided.

- Performance management can play a key role in keeping high-performing people on staff: Top performers are frequently in high demand in the FMCG sector and may be more prone to leaving if they feel their contributions are not acknowledged or if they are not given opportunities for growth and development. By making sure they feel appreciated and supported, effective performance management can aid in the retention of these workers.
- In the FMCG sector, performance management is a key technique for increasing staff retention. Organizations can improve employee engagement and lower turnover by defining clear expectations, offering regular feedback, and offering recognition and awards. Performance management is a crucial component of any retention plan since it helps identify and address additional elements that influence attrition.

Scope For Further Research

Performance management and staff retention in the FMCG industry have been studied, but further research is needed. Possible research topics:

- Leadership's role in performance management and employee retention: Performance management systems are necessary, but leadership's role in executing them and establishing a favorable work environment is crucial. Coaching and mentoring may affect employee retention in future study.
- Examining how performance management affects different types of employees: FMCG companies use a broad workforce with varying backgrounds and skills. Performance management systems' effects on entry-level versus managerial or culturally diverse employees could be studied in the future.
- Assessing the influence of performance management on employee motivation: Performance management is typically linked to employee retention, but its effect on motivation is unclear. Performance management systems may boost employee motivation, job satisfaction, and retention.
- Assessing performance management methods: Performance management methods include annual evaluations, continual feedback, and goal-setting frameworks. Future research could compare these FMCG industry techniques to determine which ones improve staff retention.
- Performance management's impact on organizational outcomes: Performance management research often focuses on employee outcomes like retention and job satisfaction, but it's also important to consider how these systems affect organizational outcomes like productivity and profitability. Performance management systems may affect FMCG outcomes.

Conclusion

In summary, research indicates that performance management is crucial to fast-moving consumer goods (FMCG) employee retention. Employee retention is benefited by performance management procedures such goal-setting, performance evaluation, feedback, training and development, and recognition. In order to increase staff retention and ultimately boost organizational success, FMCG sector companies should engage in effective performance management practices. Recent studies have emphasized the value of performance management in the FMCG industry for keeping employees. Employee retention is benefited by performance management procedures such goal-setting, performance evaluation, feedback, training and development, and recognition. According to the results of recent studies, FMCG companies should invest in effective performance management techniques to boost staff retention and eventually boost organizational performance. A successful PMS process promotes teamwork, ignites exceptional performance, and sustains a sense of pride and belonging. It fosters discipline and recognizes exceptional accomplishments. Employees receive constructive criticism during performance reviews, which leads to better abilities and output. It gives workers the chance to talk with their managers about both immediate and long-term professional goals that are clear, measurable, doable, reasonable, and time-bound. Any organization's success or failure depends on employee performance and the subsequent process of incentives and recognition that ensures staff retention. Evaluations are crucial for illustrating and coordinating employee contributions with the goals of the company. Disengagement encourages a lack of drive and interest, which results in staff departures. To increase employee productivity, engagement, and decrease employee turnover, performance measurement and consequence management are crucial and important. This study has confirmed the value of a strong PMS and the effect it has on staff retention in the Indian service sector.

References

[1] Society for Human Resource Management. (2021). The top HR challenges of 2021. Retrieved from https://www.shrm.org/resourcesandtools/hr-topics/talent-acquisition/pages/the-top-hr-challenges-of-2021.aspx

[2] Fitz-enz, J. (2010). Retention management: Strategies, practices, and challenges. Human Resource Planning, 33(1), 17-25.

[3] Brewster, C., Sparrow, P., and Vernon, G. (2007). International human resource management. London: Chartered Institute of Personnel and Development.

[4] Global Supply Chain Institute. (2022). Supply chain trends and challenges in the fast-moving consumer goods industry. Retrieved from https://www.supplychain247.com/article/supply_chain_trends_and_challenges_in_the_fast_moving_consumer_goods_ industry

[5] Lepak, D. P. and Snell, S. A. (2002). Examining the human resource architecture: The relationships among human capital, employment, and human resource configurations. *Journal of Management*, 28(4), 517-543.

[6] Rudman, R., Gustafson, K., and Paul, J. (2020). Employee retention in the face of an aging workforce: An examination of HR practices in the UK fast-moving consumer goods industry. *The International Journal of Human Resource Management*, 31(17), 2205-2226.

[7] Deloitte. (2021). 2021 global human capital trends. Retrieved from https://www2.deloitte.com/global/en/pages/human- capital/articles/introduction-human-capital-trends.html

[8] Kehoe, R. R. and Wright, P. M. (2013). The impact of high-performance human resource practices on employees' attitudes and behaviors. *Journal of Management*, 39(2), 366-391.

[9] Ulrich, D. (1998). A new mandate for human resources. *Harvard Business Review*, 76(1), 124-134.

[10] Armstrong, M. and Baron, A. (2014). Performance management: The new realities. London: Kogan Page.

[11] Goyal, N. and Chauhan, R. (2019). Impact of performance management practices on employee retention in FMCG sector. International Journal of Research in Management, 9(3), 13-25.

[12] Nair, S. S. and Vohra, V. (2016). Performance management and employee retention: a study of FMCG sector. *Global Journal of Management and Business Research*, 16(2), 1-9.

[13] Rai, A., Verma, R., and Chakraborty, S. (2020). Role of performance management practices in employee retention in the Indian FMCG sector. *International Journal of Management, Technology and Engineering*, 10(4), 1823-1831.

[14] Hassan, A. O. and Mohammed, M. A. (2019). The impact of performance management on employee retention in the FMCG industry in Sudan. *International Journal of Human Resource Studies*, 9(3), 150-166.

[15] Alqarni, A. M., Alzahrani, F. S., and Alqahtani, S. M. (2022). Performance management practices and employee retention in the Saudi Arabian FMCG sector. Journal of Management Development. https://doi.org/10.1108/JMD-07-2021-0275

[16] Gamage, P. P. M. N., & Harikrishnan, J. (2021). Performance management practices and employee retention in the Sri Lankan FMCG sector. *International Journal of Organizational Analysis*. https://doi.org/10.1108/IJOA-11-2020-2327

[17] Jain, P., Mittal, R., and Pathak, R. D. (2022). Impact of performance management practices on employee retention in the Indian FMCG sector. *Journal of Asia Business Studies*. https://doi.org/10.1108/JABS-06-2021-0196

[18] Nasir, M. I. and Abbasi, S. (2021). Performance management and employee retention in Pakistani FMCG sector. *International Journal of Organizational Analysis*.

[19] Adekoya, O. R., Adeniji, A. A., and Akinbode, G. A. (2022). Performance management and employee retention in FMCG industry. *Cogent Business & Management*, 9(1), 2027916.

[20] Ahmed, R., Bhatti, M. A., and Raza, S. A. (2022). Impact of work-life balance on employee retention in FMCG industry. *Journal of Organizational Change Management*, 35(1), 234-246.

[21] Bhattacharya, S., Sharma, R., and Kadian, R. (2021). Employee engagement and retention in FMCG industry: A mixed-method study. *Employee Relations*, 43(4), 1024-1044.

[22] Goyal, N., Kumar, R., and Kumar, V. (2021). Leadership style and employee retention in FMCG industry: A qualitative study. *Journal of Management Development*, 40(2), 219-232.

[23] Kumar, A. and Jha, S. K. (2021). Organizational culture and employee retention in FMCG industry: A quantitative study. *Journal of Human Resource Management*, 9(1), 1-12.

[24] Nasiru, M. A. and Marafa, L. M. (2021). Compensation and benefits and employee retention in FMCG industry: A survey study. *European Journal of Business and Management Research*, 6(2), 1-11.

[25] Ogunsanmi, O. O. and Adeoye, B. O. (2021). Job satisfaction and employee retention in FMCG industry: A quantitative study. *Journal of Economics and Management Sciences*, 6(1), 1-11.

[26] Abbas, Z., Shah, S. M. A., Ashraf, M., and Imran, M. (2022). Work environment and employee retention in the fast-moving consumer goods industry: evidence from Pakistan. *Sustainability*, 14(1), 346.

[27] Chandio, A. A., Tariq, M., Shah, S. Z. A. and Ali, A. (2021). Career development opportunities and employee retention in fast-moving consumer goods companies: the mediating role of job satisfaction. *Journal of Open Innovation: Technology, Market, and Complexity*, 7(4), 118.

[28] Gupta, N. and Sharma, A. (2022). Employee motivation and retention in the fast-moving consumer goods industry: an exploratory study. *Journal of Human Resources Management and Labor Studies*, 10(1), 61-74.

[29] Iqbal, M. Z., Adil, A., Siddiqui, S. A., and Islam, T. (2021). Work stress and employee retention in fast-moving consumer goods companies of Pakistan. *International Journal of Research in Business and Social Science*, 10(2), 123-135.

[30] Jain, R. and Aggarwal, P. (2021). Job security and employee retention in the fast-moving consumer goods industry: a study on employees' perception. *Journal of Indian Business Research*, 13(2), 267-286.

[31] Kamal, M. A. and Hossain, M. A. (2021). Supervisor support and employee retention in the fast-moving consumer goods industry of bangladesh: the mediating role of job satisfaction. *International Journal of Human Resource Management and Research*, 11(2), 1-16.

[32] Malik, M. I., Ishaq, M. I., Khan, M. A., and Javaid, U. (2021). The impact of organizational justice on employee retention in fast-moving consumer goods (FMCG) industry of Pakistan. *International Journal of Organizational Leadership*, 10(1), 51-62.

[33] Singh, K. and Jain, M. (2021). leadership styles, employee engagement and retention in fast-moving consumer goods industry: a study of Indian firms. *International Journal of Organizational Analysis*, 29(4), 800-819.

[34] Srivastava, A. and Singh, R. K. (2022). Impact of work-life balance and employee engagement on employee retention in fast-moving consumer goods industry: evidence from India. *Management and Labour Studies*, 47(1), 106-123.

[35] Yin, J., Wang, W., Zhang, Y., and Sun, Y. (2022). Employee-organization relationship and employee retention in fast-moving consumer goods companies. *Journal of Business Research*, 141, 368-377.

43 Profit analysis of linear consecutive 2:3: G system in the presence of supportive system and repairable system

Shakuntla Singla[a] and Shilpa Rani[b]

Department of Mathematics and Humanities, MMEC, Maharishi Markandeshwar (Deemed to be University), Mullana, Ambala, India

Abstract

Two out of three cold standby systems, the external supporting system with preventive maintenance, and a single server that may also fail are all subjected to reliability modeling and profit analysis in this article. This study uses two of the three units, such that when all three are operational, the system is operating at maximum efficiency. The third unit, which is in cold standby mode, is switched on with the aid of a flawless switchover system. The supporting system, which also oversees preventive maintenance for all types of units and runs a repair facility with a model for dependability performance measurements, controls the operation of these online and offline units. Numerous primary, secondary, and tertiary circuits, base states, and simple pathways about the starting and base states are listed. Four reliability measures are modeled with different path probabilities, transition probabilities, mean sojourn times, and expressions using RPGT, keeping one of the failure or repair rates of facilities units while varying the other. Sensitivity analysis is then performed by creating the appropriate tables and graphs, followed by a discussion.

Keywords: RPGT, MTSF, profit analysis

Introduction

The two out of three cold standby systems, external supporting system with preventive maintenance, and single server that may also fail are all subjected to reliability modeling and profit analysis in this article. For reliability measurements, we have modeled a two-unit cold standby system. This is a crucial need that depends on the design of the system and the individual units. In most of the studies conducted thus far by various authors, it is assumed that systems once installed for operation will continue to do so, but practically speaking it is not always necessary to manage the operation of working unit and maintenance facilities with the help of some external supporting system which system which system which system which system which system which system which system which system which system which system which system which system which may also fail, on failure of one or more units.

The necessary unbiased of the paper by Kumar et al. [1] on washing elements focuses on the investigated examination of the paper company consuming RPGT, Singla et al. [3] have discussed thresher plant steady-state behavior and profit analysis. Modibo, et al. 4] performed ability evaluation, validation, and optimization for the steam generation system of a coal-fired thermal power plant. Roy et al. [5] presented GA to address concerns with unshakable quality stochastic augmentation in a series framework with a span portion. Malik et al. [6] investigated and found that the mist group of a coal-fired thermal impact shrub was optimized. Jieong, et al [8] studies about the development and investigation of efficient GA/PSO-hybrid algorithm applicable to real-world design optimization. Majumder et al. [9] have discussed SW release models' irregular fluctuation of successive.

A steady-state transition diagram is created using the Markov process (showing transformation rates and states) utilizing the steady failure and repair rates of units and facilities. Numerous primary, secondary, and tertiary circuits, base states, and simple pathways about the starting and base states are listed. Four reliability measures are modeled with different path probabilities, transformation probabilities, mean sojourn times, and expressions using RPGT, possessing one of the disappointment or repair rates of facilities units while changeable the other. Profit analysis is then performed by creating the appropriate tables and graphs, followed by a discussion.

Assumption, Notation and Transformation Diagram

- A repairman is available 24*7.
- Failure/repair rates are constant.

[a]gargshilpa46@gmail.com

DOI: 10.1201/9781003534136-43

- m/h: Failure/Repair rates

Pleasing into reflection the upstairs assumptions and systems the Transformation Illustration of the system is certain in Figure 42.1.

$S_0 = A_1A_2(A_3)BD$, $S_1 = a_1A_2A_3BD$, $S_2 = A_1A_2(A_3)Bd$, $S_3 = a_1A_2A_3Bd$,
$S_4 = A_1A_2(A_3)BD$, $S_5 = a_1a_2A_3Bd$, $S_6 = a_1A_2A_3bD$, $S_7 = A_1A_2(A_3)bD$,
$S_8 = A_1A_2(A_3)bd$, $S_9 = a_1A_2A_3bd$, $S_{10} = a_1a_2A_3Bd$

System Description

Three production units A_1, A_2, and A_3 with similar working characteristics and constant failure and repair rates h1 are present in the system. A supporting system B manages the operation of the online and offline units with a steady failure and repair rate h_3 and a repair facility that fixes all of the online and offline units along with the supporting system but is susceptible to failure itself. In the initial working state, S_0, all units are operationally sound, A_1 and A_2 are working online, and A_3 is in cold standby mode. Supporting system B is active, and because repair facility D is not in use, it is able to manage only the preventive maintenance of operationally sound units in the initial state. Preventive maintenance is the optimal use of existing facilities since it reduces the likelihood of any unit failing and the time it takes to return from the state of S_4 during preventive maintenance to S_0 following it. When the repairing unit "D" fails with a transition rate of m_2, the system works in full capacity working state S_2, where two working units A & A_2 are online and a third unit A_3 is in cold standby mode. Because supporting system "B" is also good, the system is in a working state. However, because the repair facility is out of gear in state S_2, a specialized repair man is called in. Additionally, if the supporting system fails while the system is in state S_0, with a transition failure rate of m_3, the system enters the failed state S_7. Because the supporting system cannot regulate how the components operate, the system is inoperable. A_1, the system rejoins the operating state S_0 after a supporting system repair with a repair rate of h_3. If a working unit Ai i = 1 or 2) fails in state S_0 with a constant failure rate m1, the system joins the working state S_1 from which if working units A_1 i = 2 or 3), B, and D fail with respective failure rates m1, m_3, and m_2, the system joins the failure states S_5, S_6, and working state S_3 after these failed units are repaired with constant repair rates h_1, h_3, and h_2, the system rejoins the working state. While in state S_5 the repair facility while repairing may fail itself, then the classification intersections the state S_{10} where in state S_{10} priority in repair is assigned to repair fail 'D' by a special repairman then the system rejoins the state S_5. In state S_9 priority in repair is assigned to support service unit, and upon its repair the system joins the working state S_3. Theoretically, only one failure of a unit can occur at a time when it is in operation or idle, and neither an expert nor an ordinary repairman should be able to repair more than one unit at once. Only when every unit is in working order and the repair facility is empty can preventive maintenance is done. In the system, there are three manufacturing units A_i with comparable capacities. A supporting unit "B" that oversees the operation of units "A_i," and a 24-hour repair facility "D" that fixes the units when idle, A_i and supporting system "B" also do preventive maintenance. Two of the three units are currently operational, while the third unit, which is indicated by a simple bracket is in cold standby mode. These three units A_i have identical capacities; thus their failure rates are the same (m_1) and their repair rates are also the same (h_1) Supporting systems for controlling the operation of units Ai have a failure rate of m_3 and a repair rate of h_3. The repair facility "D" may also experience failure for any number of reasons while being serviced by outside, specialized companies, with a repair rate of h_2 and a failure rate of m_2. Preventive maintenance is therefore possible and is carried out when required and is handled by the supporting system "B" because the system is initially in state S_0, which is characterized by cold standby units A_3 and repair facility D being idle. If the supporting system "B" breaks in state S_0, the system joins the failed state S_7, where there is a repair facility that can fix the failing supporting system at a repair rate of h_3, returning the system to state S_0. From condition S_0 the system enters operational state S_2 if repair facility unit "D" fails with rate m_2. When unit "D" fails, an expert series is brought in to repair it at a rate of "h_2," bringing the system back to state "S_0." If one of the online units A_i in the working state S_0 has a failure with a failure rate of m_1, the supporting system will replace it with the standby unit, and the system will then enter the working state S_1. If unit A_i, B, and D continue to fail in working state S_1 at failure rates of m_1, m_2, and m_3, respectively, the system enters the failed state S_5, S_6, working state S_3, and upon successful unit repair at rates of n_1, n_2, and n_3, the system returns to functioning state S_1. Similar to when units fail in state S_2, the system joins state S_8 (which is failed) or state S_3 (which is functional). Captivating into thought all the notations and expectations a state transition drawing the system is haggard in figure 1 in which designates directed trails indicate disappointment/repair rates and S_i ($0 \leq i \leq 10$) denote the likely stable of the scheme:

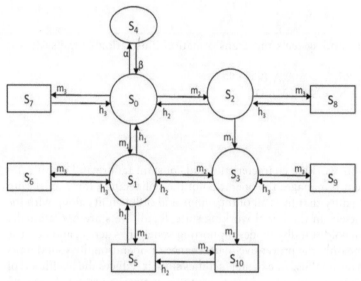

Figure 42.1 Transformation diagram

State Transformation Probabilities

$q_{i,i}(t)$

$$q_{0,1}(t) = m_1 e^{-(m_1+m_2+m_3+\alpha)t}$$

$$q_{0,2}(t) = m_2 e^{-(m_1+m_2+m_3+\alpha)t}$$

$$q_{0,4}(t) = \alpha e^{-(m_1+m_2+m_3+\alpha)t}$$

$$q_{0,7}(t) = m_3 e^{-(m_1+m_2+m_3+\alpha)t}$$

$$q_{1,0}(t) = h_1 e^{-(m_1+m_2+m_3+h_1)t}$$

$$q_{1,3}(t) = m_2 e^{-(m_1+m_2+m_3+h_1)t}$$

$$q_{1,5}(t) = m_1 e^{-(m_1+m_2+m_3+h_1)t}$$

$$q_{1,6}(t) = m_3 e^{-(m_1+m_2+m_3+h_1)t}$$

$$q_{2,0}(t) = h_2 e^{-(m_1+m_3+h_2)t}$$

$$q_{2,3}(t) = m_1 e^{-(m_1+m_3+h_2)t}$$

$$q_{2,8}(t) = m_3 e^{-(m_1+m_3+h_2)t}$$

$$q_{3,1}(t) = h_2 e^{-(m_1+m_3+h_2)t}$$

$$q_{3,9}(t) = m_3 e^{-(m_1+m_3+h_2)t}$$

$$q_{3,10}(t) = m_1 e^{-(m_1+m_3+h_2)t}$$

$$q_{4,0}(t) = n e^{-nt}$$

$$q_{5,1}(t) = h_1 e^{-(m_2+h_1)t}$$

$$q_{5,10}(t) = m_2 e^{-(m_2+h_1)t}$$

$$q_{6,1} = h_3 e^{-h_3 t}$$

$$q_{7,0} = h_3 e^{-h_3 t}$$

$$q_{8,2} = h_3 e^{-h_3 t}$$

$q_{9,3} = h_3 e^{-h_3 t}$

$q_{10,3} = 0$

$q_{10,5} = h_2 e^{-h_2 t}$

$\mathbf{p_{ii} = q^*_{i,i}(0)}$

$p_{0,1} = m_1/(m_1 + m_2 + m_3 + \alpha)$

$p_{0,2} = m_2/(m_2 + m_1 + m_3 + \alpha)$

$p_{0,4} = \alpha/(m_3 + m_2 + m_1 + \alpha)$

$p_{0,7} = m_3/(m_3 + m_2 + m_1 + \alpha)$

$p_{1,0} = h_1/(m_3 + m_2 + m_1 + h_1)$

$p_{1,3} = m_2/(m_3 + m_2 + m_1 + h_1)$

$p_{1,5} = m_1/(m_3 + m_2 + m_1 + h_1)$

$p_{1,6} = m_3/(m_3 + m_2 + m_1 + h_1)$

$p_{2,0} = h_2/(m_1 + m_3 + h_2)$

$p_{2,3} = m_1/(m_1 + m_3 + h_2)$

$p_{2,8} = m_3/(m_1 + m_3 + h_2)$

$p_{3,1} = h_2/(m_1 + m_3 + h_2)$

$p_{3,9} = m_3/(m_1 + m_3 + h_2)$

$p_{3,10} = m_1/(m_1 + m_3 + h_2)$

$p_{4,0} = 1$

$p_{2,0} = h_2/(m_3 + h_2)$

$p_{5,10} = m_2/(m_2 + h_1)$

$p_{6,1} = 1$

$p_{7,0} = 1$

$p_{8,2} = 1$

$p_{9,3} = 1$

$q_{10,3} = 0$

$p_{10,8} = 1$

$p_{0,1} + p_{0,2} + p_{0,4} + p_{0,7} = 1$

$p_{1,0} + p_{1,3} + p_{1,5} + p_{1,6} = 1$

$p_{2,0} + p_{2,3} + p_{2,8} = 1$

$p_{3,1} + p_{3,9} + p_{3,10} = 1$

Mean Sojourn Times R$_i$(t)

$\mathbf{R_i(t)}$

$R_0(t) = e^{-(m_1 + m_2 + m_3 + \alpha)t}$

$R_1(t) = e^{-(m_1 + m_2 + m_3 + h_1)t}$

$R_2(t) = e^{-(m_3 + h_2)t}$

$$R_3(t) = e^{-(m_1+m_3+h_2)t}$$
$$R_4(t) = e^{-\beta t}$$
$$R_5(t) = e^{-(m_2+h_1)t}$$
$$R_6(t) = e^{-h_3 t}$$
$$R_7(t) = e^{-h_3 t}$$
$$R_8(t) = e^{-h_3 t}$$
$$R_9(t) = e^{-h_3 t}$$
$$R_{10}(t) = e^{-h_2 t}$$

$$\boldsymbol{\mu_i = R_i^*(0)}$$

$$\mu_0 = 1/(m_1+m_2+m_3+\alpha)$$
$$\mu_1 = 1/(m_1+m_2+m_3+h_1)$$
$$\mu_2 = 1/(m_3+h_2)$$
$$\mu_3 = 1/(m_1+m_3+h_2)$$
$$\mu_4 = 1/\beta$$
$$\mu_5 = 1/(m_2+h_1)$$
$$\mu_6 = 1/h_3$$
$$\mu_7 = 1/h_3$$
$$\mu_8 = 1/h_3$$
$$\mu_9 = 1/h_3$$
$$\mu_{10} = 1/h_2$$

Analysis of Transformation Path Probabilities (TPP)

Smearing RPGT and by '0' as the initial-state of the organization as beneath: TPP issues of all the accessible states after the first state 'ξ' = '0' remain: Likelihoods after state '0' to dissimilar vertices remain assumed as

$V_{0,0} = 1$

$V_{0,1} = (0,1)/[\{1-(1,3,1)\}/\{1-(3,9,3)\}]\{1-(1,3,10,5,1)\}/\{1-(10,5,10)\}]\{1-(1,6,1)\}$
$\{1-(1,5,1)\}$

$\quad = p_{0,1}/\{(1-p_{1,3}p_{3,1})/(1-p_{3,9}p_{9,3})\}\{(1-p_{1,3}p_{3,10}p_{10,5}p_{5,1})/(1-p_{10,5}p_{5,10})\}(1-p_{1,6}p_{6,1})$
$(1-p_{1,5}p_{5,1})$

$V_{0,2} = (0,2)/\{1-(2,8,2)\}$

$\quad = p_{0,2}/(1-p_{2,8}p_{8,2})$

$V_{0,3} = ...$Continuous

TPP issues of all the accessible states after the dishonorable state 'ξ' = '1' is: Likelihoods after state '1' to dissimilar vertices stand assumed as

$V_{1,0} = (1,0)/[\{1-(0,2,0)\}/\{1-(2,8,2)\}]\{1-(0,4,0)\}\{1-(0,7,0)\}$

$\quad = p_{1,0}/\{(1-p_{0,2}p_{2,0})/(1-p_{2,8}p_{8,2})\}(1-p_{0,4}p_{4,0})(1-p_{0,7}p_{7,0})$

$V_{1,1} = 1$ (Verified)

$V_{1,2} = (1,0,2)/[\{1-(0,2,0)\}/\{1-(2,8,2)\}]\{1-(0,4,0)\}\{1-(0,7,0)\}\{1-(2,8,2)\}$

$\quad = p_{1,0}p_{0,2}/\{(1-p_{0,2}p_{2,0})/(1-p_{2,8}p_{8,2})\}(1-p_{0,4}p_{4,0})(1-p_{0,7}p_{7,0})(1-p_{2,8}p_{8,2})$

$V_{1,3} = ...$Continuous.

Modeling system parameters

MTSF(S_0) The re-forming perfect conditions to which the scheme can transit (original state '0'), previously ingoing any unsuccessful state stand: 'i' = 0 to 4 enchanting 'ξ' = '0'.

$S_0 = (V_{0,j}\mu_j)/[\{1-(0,1,0)-(0,2,0)-(0,4,0)\}]$; j = 0 to 4

Accessibility of the System (A_0)

The reformative situation at which the scheme is accessible are 'j' = 0 to 4 and the reformative situation are 'i' = 0 to 8 captivating 'ξ' = '1' the total fraction of period aimed at which the organization is accessible is certain by

$$A_0 = \left[\sum_j V_{\xi,j}, f_j, \mu_j \right] \div \left[\sum_i V_{\xi,i}, f_j, \mu_i^1 \right]$$
$$= (V_{1,1}\mu_1 + V_{1,2}\mu_2 + V_{1,3}\mu_3 + V_{1,4}\mu_4)/D_1$$
$$\text{Where } D_1 = V_{1,0}\mu_0 + V_{1,1}\mu_1 + V_{1,2}\mu_2 + V_{1,3}\mu_3 + V_{1,4}\mu_4 + V_{1,5}\mu_5 + V_{1,6}\mu_6 + V_{1,7}\mu_7 + V_{1,8}\mu_8 + V_{1,9}\mu_9$$
$$+ V_{1,10}\mu_{10}$$

Busy Period of the Server (B_0)

The reformative states where server is full are j = 1 to 8 and reformative states are 'i' = 0 to 8, captivating ξ = '0', the total fraction of period for which the waiter remains busy is

$$B_0 = \left[\sum_j V_{\xi,j}, n_j \right] \div \left[\sum_i V_{\xi,i}, \mu_i^1 \right]$$
$$= (V_{0,j}\mu_j)/D \ j = 0 \text{ to } 8$$
$$\text{Where } D = (V_{0,i}\mu_i); \ i = 0 \text{ to } 10$$

Expected Number of Inspections by the repair man (V_0)

The reformative states where the repairman appointments again are j = 1,2,4,7 the reformative states are i = 0 to 8, Attractive 'ξ' = '0', the integer of call by the overhaul man is assumed by

$$V_0 = \left[\sum_j V_{\xi,j} \right] \div \left[\sum_i V_{\xi,i}, \mu_i^1 \right]$$
$$= (V_{0,1} + V_{0,2} + V_{0,4} + V_{0,7})/ D$$

Profit function (P_0)

The organization can be prepared by used PF
$$P_0 = D_1 A_0 - (D_2 B_0 + D_3 V_0)$$
$$= D_1 A_0 - D_2 B_0 - D_3 V_0,$$
Taking D_1 = 1200;
D_2 = 100;
D_3 =200, we have

Table 43.1 (P_0)

m h	0.10	0.20	0.30
0.50	0.617	0.653	0.689
0.60	0.512	0.548	0.582
0.70	0.407	0.440	0.478

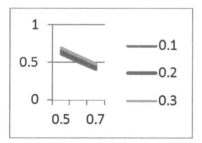

Figure 43.2   Profit function (P_0)

Conclusion

From the analytical and graphical discussion, it is noted that the values for P_0, profit table above and graph above may be set and conclusion with respect to repair and disappointment rates of units. The maximum value of profit is **689**, when disappointment rates of units are minimum and repair rates maximum.

References

[1] Kumar, A. Garg, D., and Goel, P. (2019). Mathematical modelling and behavioural analysis of a washing unit in paper mill. *International Journal of System Assurance Engineering and Management,* 10, 1639-1645.

[2] Kumari, S., Khurana, P., and Singla, S. (2022). Behavior and profit analysis of a thresher plant under steady state. *International Journal of System Assurance Engineering Management,* 13(1), 166–171

[3] Singla, S., Verma, S., Malik, S., and Gupta, A. (2022). Perform ability evaluation, validation and optimization for the steam generation system of a coal-fired thermal power plant. *Method X,* https://doi.org/10.1016/j.mex.2022.101852 (Scopus).

[4] Modibo, U. M., Singla, S., Verma, S., and Khurana, P. (2022). Mathematical model for analysing availability of threshing combine machine under reduced capacity. *Yugoslav Journal of Operations Research,* 32(4), 425–437.

[5] Roy, D., Bhunia, A. K., and Sahoo, L. (2010). Reliability stochastic optimization for a series system with interval component reliability via genetic algorithm. *Applied Mathematics and Computation,* 216(3), 929-939

[6] Malik, S., Verma, S., Gupta, A., Sharma, G., and Singla, S. (2022). Performability evaluation, validation and optimization for the steam generation system of a coal-fired thermal power plant. *Methods,* 9, 1-14.

[7] Kumari, S., Khurana, P., and Singla, S. (2021). Behaviour and profit analysis of a thresher plant under steady state. *International Journal of System Assurance Engineering and Man.,* 1-12.

[8] Jieong, S., Hasegawa, S., Shimoyama, and Obayashi, S. (2009). Development and investigation of efficient GA/PSO-hybrid algorithm applicable to real-world design optimization. *IEEE Computational Intelligence Magzine,* 4, 36-44

[9] Majumder, A. A. and Goel, P. (2021). Irregular fluctuation of successive SW release models. *Design Engineering,* 7, 8954-8962.

44 Rental Cost minimization for Two stage parallel machine FSSP with transportation time

Kanika Gupta[1,2], Deepak Gupta[2] and Sonia Goel[2,a]

[1]Department of Mathematics, DAV College For Girls, Yamuna Nagar, Haryana, India

[2]M. M. Engineering College, Maharishi Markandeshwar (Deemed to be University), Mullana, Ambala, India

Abstract

Scheduling is a great tool to handle the circumstances like dealing with organizing the jobs on machines in industries, preparing a sequence of programs that are to be performed on computers, setting up a time table, and many other similar situations. In most businesses, there are usually numerous machines working together to complete a single operation. However, the operational costs of each machine may vary. Therefore, tasks are delegated to various machines sequentially in order to minimize unit operational costs and shorten overall processing times. The current study provides a quick overview of a scenario in which jobs are first performed on equivalent machines and then transported to the machine which is rented for the second stage. The goal of this study is to organize tasks accordingly to reduce the rental cost along with overall completion time.

Keywords: Utilization time, rental cost, transportation time, earliest time

Introduction

Manufacturing Industries regularly face the challenge of job scheduling. The scheduling issue that affects the industrial sector most commonly is called the flow shop scheduling problem (FSSP). The typical problem that needs to be handled in industries on a regular basis is scheduling a work on a machine so that the time taken to accomplish all the activities can be minimized. In order to keep rental costs as low as possible while renting out machinery, one of the managers' top priorities is to do so. The basis of scheduling theory is creating a task plan so that output is maximized in the shortest amount of time and for the least amount of money. There are numerous more comparison factors that must be taken into consideration in addition to the scheduling basics. When scheduling, a variety of factors are taken into account as and when necessary, such as the requirement to finish the project by the deadline, reduce transportation costs, or spend the least amount of time in setting up the machinery.

The problems of FSS were firstly addressed by Johnsons [5] in 1954 where an algorithm was devised to solve such problems for two stage problems as well as for three stage. This algorithm was used by many other researchers to solve different types of problems under different circumstances. Another method named Branch and bound (BB) was designed by Ignall et. al. [4] for solving the problems having only two stage scheduling while by Lomniciki [7] for the problems that comprise of scheduling at three stages. The concept of parallel machines or equipotential machines is taken into consideration by Mokotoff [11] in his studies. Maggu and Das [8] extended the study of FSSP by considering the different performance measures like transportation cost, job block criteria, time lags etc. One of the important issues that is taken care of in many situations is the rental cost. Many solutions are given by different researchers under various conditions to reduce the rental cost. Singh et. al. [12] devised an algorithm to cut the rental cost. The study further continued by Gupta et. al. [3] while considering the different parameters. Goel et. al. devised the algorithm for the solution of two stage FSSP [3] with equipotential machines at first stage and both stages as well as for the three stage FSSP [1, 2]. Malhotra et. al. [9] used the BB method to solve the parallel machine FSSP.

Optimization techniques play a key role for studying FSSP. Particle swarm optimization, Genetic algorithms, Artificial Bee Colony, Ant colony optimization algorithm, teaching learning based optimization, Grover's algorithm etc. are some of the different methods that are used by different authors to solve FSSP. Mansouri et. al. [10] gave an algorithm that comprise of particle swarm optimization with tabu search method to attain more optimized results. Kianpour et. al. [6] gave the solution by using Genetic algorithm.

The present paper is an extension of BB method to solve two stage FSSP having equipotential machines at the first stage and a rented machine for the second stage. The numerical example considered is solved using the

[a]sonia.mangla14@gmail.com

DOI: 10.1201/9781003534136-44

MATLAB R2014a. The main objective is to obtain the optimal sequence of jobs so that the total elapsed time is minimized and the idle time on the rented machine is reduced to minimum to cut the rental cost.

Practical Situation

Present model is applicable in many day-to-day scheduling situations. In the food industry where different food items are prepared and then transported to the place where packing machines are taken on rent this model can be applied. Another situation can be considered in the plywood industry where logs of different kinds of wood are collected from the jungles and then sent to the industry where chippers are installed to prepare chips.

Problem Formulation

The problem being solved in this research involves parallel(equipotential) machines in the first stage and a single machine in the second. The equipment for the second stage is rented. Therefore, in accordance with the rental policies, the machine is rented when a job has to be allocated to it and returned as soon as all jobs are completed. As a result, the rent must be paid for the entire time the equipment is in use. Transportation time is also considered. Mathematical representation is given in table 44.1.

Notations
η_{ij}=Operational Cost on j^{th} machine for i^{th} job $\{(i = 1, 2, ..., p); (j = 1, 2, ..., k)\}$
κ_i = Processing time on machine M for job i
ζ_i = Processing time on machine N for job i
t_i = Cost of transportation of job i from machine M to machine N
Δ_j = Total available time of machine M_j

Methodology used
The problem is solved in 4 steps.

- **Step 1:** The problem is converted to a classical FSSP by introducing two fictitious machines H and K where $h_i = \kappa_i + t_i$ and $k_i = t_i + \zeta_i$ denotes the processing time respectively. The jobs are assigned on machines H & K in such a way that the unit operational costs of machines M_j were optimized. This is achieved using the MODI method.
  For using MODI method the condition $\sum_{i=1}^{p} h_i = \sum_{j=1}^{k} \Delta_j$ must be satisfied.
- **Step 2:** Now the two stage FSSP with parallel machines at first stage is solved using BB method by using the equation
  $l_t =$
  $\max \{\sum_{i=1}^{p} \zeta_i + \max_{1 \leq j \leq k} \eta_{tj}, \max_{1 \leq j \leq k}\{\sum_{i=1}^{p} \eta_{ij}\} +$
  $\min_{k \neq t} \zeta_k\}$
  for t = 1, 2, ..., p. and the data is prepared in form of in-out table for machines M_1, M_2, ..., M_k and N
- **Step 3:** Finding
  Earliest Time = Total elapsed time - $\sum_{i=1}^{p} \zeta_i$
  Then reform the in - out table by changing the starting time of first job on machine N to earliest time.
- **Step 4:** The total utilization time of machine N is reduced in this new in-out table. Now the rent can be calculated according to this new in-out table.

Numerical Problem

Illustration
Here is an example to illustrate the methodology that contains 5 parallel machines and 10 jobs. The data is given in Table 44.2.

Step-by-step calculations are given in the tables. After step 1 the data is represented in Table 44.3. The in-out table formed in step 2 and the modified table in step 3 is given by table 4 jointly. This table is generated by the MATLAB R2014a.The total elapsed time using BB method is 186 hrs. The table shows the difference between the results obtained using BB method and modified method. The total time for which machine N is to be rented comes out to be 133 Hrs using BB method and 87 Hrs using modified method. If the rent is considered as Rs. 500/hour then the rent is 66500/- using BB method and 43500/- from the modified version. This gap of

Table 44.1 Mathematical representation of the data

Job/Machine	M_1	M_2	M ...	M_k	P.T. on M	Transportation time	P.T. on N
1	η_{11}	η_{12}	...	η_{1k} κ_1		t_1	ζ_1
2	η_{21}	η_{22}	...	η_{2k} κ_2		t_2	ζ_2
3	η_{31}	η_{32}	...	η_{3k} κ_3		t_3	ζ_3
.							
.							
.							
P	η_{p1}	η_{p2}	...	η_{pk} κ_p		t_p	ζ_p
	Δ_1	Δ_2	...	Δ_k			

Table 44.2 Illustration

Job/Machine	M_1	M_2	M_3	M_4	M_5	P.T. on M	Transportation time	P.T. on N
1	50	55	70	29	80	50	3	2
2	30	36	59	82	96	29	5	5
3	76	63	39	48	81	80	2	7
4	85	55	47	85	38	30	4	6
5	38	74	71	62	66	46	8	3
6	49	69	46	91	69	75	7	2
7	56	52	85	23	58	25	2	8
8	46	89	75	84	55	61	1	4
9	73	87	48	62	73	54	5	1
10	29	83	56	69	74	50	3	9
	70	90	180	60	140			

Table 44.3 Processing times on fictitious machines

Job/Machine	M_1	M_2	M_3	M_4	M_5	Fictitious machine H	Fictitious machine K
1	0	20	0	33	0	53	5
2	0	34	0	0	0	34	10
3	0	0	82	0	0	82	9
4	0	0	0	0	34	34	10
5	17	0	0	0	37	54	11
6	0	36	39	0	7	82	9
7	0	0	0	27	0	27	10
8	0	0	0	0	62	62	5
9	0	0	59	0	0	59	6
10	53	0	0	0	0	53	12
	70	90	180	60	140		

Table 44.4 In-out table

Job/Machine	M					Using BB	Modified
	M_1	M_2	M_3	M_4	M_5		
10	0-53	-	-	-	-	53-65	99-111
1	-	0-20	-	0-33	-	65-70	111-116
2	-	20-54	-	-	-	70-80	116-126
3	-	-	0-82	-	-	82-91	126-135
4	-	-	-	-	0-34	91-101	135-145
5	53-70	-	-	-	34-71	101-112	145-156
7	-	-	-	36-60	-	112-122	156-166
6	-	54-90	82-121	-	71-78	122-131	166-175
8	-	-	-	-	78-140	140-145	175-180
9	-	-	121-180	-	-	180-186	180-186

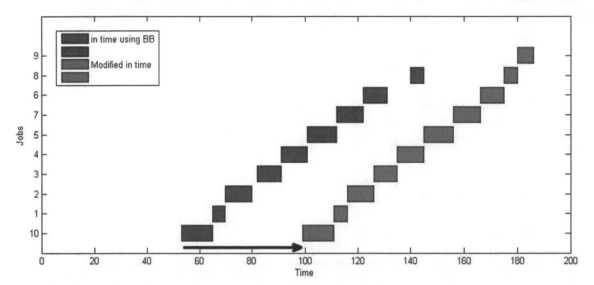

Figure 44.1 Gantt chart

in-time or the time when N is to be rented is shown by an arrow in Figure 1. The figure depicts the difference of the in-out times of jobs on machines by a Gantt Chart. The blue bars in the figure represent the in-out time obtained.

from BB method whereas the red bars show the modified in-out time. The Gantt Chart is generated using the MATLAB R2014a.

Conclusion

BB approach, which provides a more accurate solution than other methods, is used to solve flow shop scheduling problem (FSSP) using equipotential machines. However, the BB method is further optimized in this paper to obtain a more practical solution for the rental machine. The BB method can reduce make span, but sometimes unable to reduce machine utilization time. The suggested methodology is thus more helpful in these circumstances.

References

[1] Gupta, D. and Goel, S. (2020). Nx2 flow shop scheduling problem with parallel machines at every stage, processing time associated with probabilities. *Advances in Mathematics: Scientific Journal*, 9, 1061–1069.

[2] Gupta, D. and Goel, S. (2022). Branch and bound technique for two stage flow shop scheduling model with equipotential machines at every stage. *International Journal of Operational Research*, 44(4), 462-472.

[3] Gupta, D., Goel, S., and Mangla, N. (2022). Optimization of production scheduling in two stage flow shop scheduling problem with m equipotential machines at first stage. *International Journal of System Assurance Engineering and Management*, 13 (6), 1162–1169.

[4] Ignall, E., and Schrage, L. Application of the branch and bound technique to some flow-shop scheduling problems. Operations research 13, 3 (1965), 400–412. 4

[5] Johnsons, S. M. Optimal two-and three-stage production schedules with setup times included. Naval research logistics quarterly 1, 1 0 61–68.

[6] Kianpour, P., Gupta, D., Krishnan, K., and Gopalakrishnan, B. (2023). Doe-based enhanced genetic algorithm for unrelated parallel machine scheduling to minimize earliness/tardiness costs. *Journal of Optimization in Industrial Engineering*, 16(2), 99-114.

[7] Lomniciki, Z. (1965). A branch-and-bound algorithm for the exact solution of the three-machine scheduling problem. *Journal of the Operational Research Society*, 16, (1), 89–100.

[8] Maggu, P. L., Das, G., and Kumar, R. On equivalent-job for job-block in 2× n sequencing problem with transportation-times. Journal of the operations research society of japan 24, 2 (1981), 136–146.

[9] Malhotra, K., Gupta, D., Goel, S., and Tripathi, A. K. (2022). Bi-objective flow shop scheduling with equipotential parallel machines. *Malaysian Journal of Mathematical Sciences*, 16(9), 451–470.

[10] Mansouri, M., Bahmani, Y., and Smadi, H. (2023). A hybrid method for the parallel flow-shop scheduling problem †. *Computer Sciences & Mathematics Forum*, 7(1), 14413.

[11] Mokotoff, E. (2001). Parallel machine scheduling problems: A survey. *Asia-Pacific Journal of Operational Research,* 18, 2, 193.

[12] Singh, T. and Gupta, S. (2008). Minimization of rental cost in 3-stage flow shop with parallel machines including transportation time. *Acta Cinencia Indica,* 34, 2, 629–634.

45 Reliability optimization of a system under preventive maintenance using genetic algorithm

Shakuntla Singla[a] and Diksha Mangla[b]

Department of Mathematics and Humanities, MMEC, Maharishi Markandeshwar (Deemed to be University) Mullana, Ambala, India

Abstract

The production of any industry is completely dependent upon the machinery that is used to make product and the reliability of machine i.e. system have a crucial importance to increase the production. In this paper the reliability parameters such as average time to system failure and available performing time of a series system has been counted under the effect of preventive maintenance using Chapman Kolmogorov's forward equation method. The observation has been done on a system which is made up of two subsystems arranged in series manner having preventive maintenance facility of one. The variation with respect to malfunction rate and repair rate has been noticed. The genetic algorithm (GA) is applied to have an optimum value for both ATTF and availability upon the best parameters value. The results show that good maintenance plays a vital role to increase the overall availability of system.

Keywords: Average time to failure (ATTF), malfunction rate, repair rate, genetic algorithm (GA)

Introduction

Reliability can be clarified as the probability of success at time t i.e. probability of a machine intended to fulfil the purpose in provided time with given outer condition in success mode. A device or system has to be said to be more reliable or have a high reliability if it performs its function properly without failure or without having obstacles during its function. Any system can't perform very well all the time as continuously using of a system causes a tearing and outwearing of the part. These resulting in failure of parts of a system hence deficiency of reliability and efficiency.

In this paper, we discussed the reliability parameters such as average time to failure (ATTF) and available performing time of a series system having two-unit, A and B, in which B has property to failed directly with perfect repairing facility, on the other hand Unit A firstly degraded to small amount which resulting in less production. The application of preventive maintenance reverses this situation to have full working state [1]. The analysis of the reliability of induced draft fans in thermal plant using semi-Markov processes under the effect of cold standby has been done. The working efficiency of a wiping unit present in the paper industry using RPGT has been focused [2, 3]. The maintenance of turbo generator and the availability using vibration monitoring experiment has been discussed [4]. The multi-component systems with individual repairable components has been analysed under reinforcement learning approach to find an optimal maintenance action [5] The proposal of optimizing the system reliability under deterioration has given using two different techniques [6]. discussed the two type of malfunction and checked out the results for both type of failure and depicted the results to have the system reliability. The concept of Markov method has been applied to have the availability and performability of different subsystem of a coal fired thermal plant [7, 8]. A semi Marco processes with regenerative point technique has been used to understand the behavior of a system consisting of a main unit with substitute of two subunits on the demand after failing process arranged in parallel mode. A nature inspired algorithm particles swarm optimization to optimize the cost of rubber plant has been discussed [9].

Model description and Notation

System description
Two units A and B arranged in series manner and malfunction of any unit resulting in the failure of whole system.

[a]shaku25@gmail.com; [b]dikshamangla1995@gmail.com

DOI: 10.1201/9781003534136-45

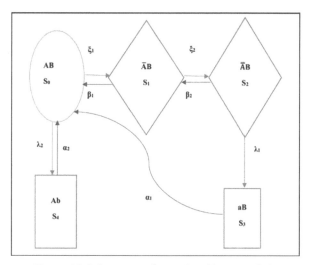

Figure 45.1 State transformation diagram of given system

Symbols and Notations

◯ -full working state   ◇ -Degraded state   ☐ -failed state

A/Ā/Ā/a = Full working state/degraded state (need preventive maintenance)/again degraded state (need preventive maintenance)/failed state.

S_i = Transformation state i = 0 to 4

λ_1/λ_2 = Malfunction rate of subsystem A/B

ξ_1/ξ_2 = Degraded rate going A to Ā / Ā to Ā

β_1/β_2 = Preventive maintenance rate from Ā to A / from Ā to Ā

α_1/α_2 = Repair rate of subsystem A / B

$P_i(t)$ = Represent the probability of different transformation state.

$P(t)/\dot{P}(t)$ = The overall probability vector/corresponding differential probability vector.

Mathematical Modelling

Average Time to Failure Analysis

For evaluating the ATTF, the commencing condition for the presented transformation from one state to another is: $P(0) = [P_0(0)\ P_1(0)\ P_2(0)\ P_3(0)\ P_4(0)] = [1\ 0\ 0\ 0\ 0]$

Using Kolmogorov's equation method, The matrix form for the differential equations can be written as

$$\dot{P} = MP \tag{1}$$

$$\text{where } M = \begin{bmatrix} -(\lambda_2 + \xi_1) & \beta_1 & 0 & \alpha_1 & \alpha_2 \\ \xi_1 & -(\beta_1 + \xi_2) & \beta_2 & 0 & 0 \\ 0 & \xi_2 & -(\lambda_1 + \beta_2) & 0 & 0 \\ 0 & 0 & \lambda_1 & -\alpha_1 & 0 \\ \lambda_2 & 0 & 0 & 0 & -\alpha_2 \end{bmatrix}$$

To eliminate the complications for evaluating ATTF, The restriction of elimination of the absorbing states has been applied and taking transpose of mentioned matrix, we get matrix N. i.e.

$$\text{MTTF} = P(0)(-N^{-1})\begin{bmatrix} 1 \\ 1 \\ 1 \end{bmatrix} \tag{2}$$

$$\text{where } N = N = \begin{bmatrix} -(\lambda_2 + \xi_1) & \xi_1 & 0 \\ \beta_1 & -(\beta_1 + \xi_2) & \xi_2 \\ 0 & \beta_2 & -(\lambda_1 + \beta_2) \end{bmatrix}$$

$$\text{MTTF} = \frac{N_1}{D_1}$$

where $N_1 = N1 = \beta_1 \lambda_1 + \beta_1 \beta_2 + \xi_2 \lambda_1 + \xi_1 \lambda_1 + \beta_2 \xi_1 + \xi_1 \xi_2$
$D_1 = (\beta_1 + \xi_2) \lambda_1 \lambda_2 + \beta_1 \beta_2 \lambda_2 + \lambda_1 \xi_1 \xi_2$

Availability Analysis
Using the same commencing condition i.e.
$P(0) = [P_0(0), P_1(0), P_2(0), P_3(0), P_4(0)] =$
$[1, 0, 0, 0, 0]$ and $\dot{P} = MP$
The stable-state availability is

$$A(\infty) = P_0(\infty) + P_1(\infty) + P_2(\infty) \tag{3}$$

In the stable state, the differential probability vector become zero, so that

$$MP = 0 \tag{4}$$

Using the following normalizing conditions:

$$P_0(\infty) + P_1(\infty) + P_2(\infty) + P_3(\infty) + P_4(\infty) = 1 \tag{5}$$

Hence, the availability of presented model is calculated as:

Table 45.1 Bounds for decision variables

$0.002 \leq \lambda_1 \leq 0.05$	$0.003 \leq \lambda_2 \leq 0.01$
$0.09 \leq \beta_1 \leq 0.95$	$0.08 \leq \beta_2 \leq 0.85$
$0.0035 \leq \alpha_1 \leq 0.99$	$0.0045 \leq \alpha_2 \leq 0.88$
$0.001 \leq \xi_1 \leq 0.01$	$0.001 \leq \xi_2 \leq 0.02$

Table 45.2 Effect of number of generations on ATTF of two-unit system

S. no.	No. of generation	λ_1	λ_2	β_1	β_2	ξ_1	ξ_2	ATTF
1	10	0.0499	0.0100	0.9403	0.0800	0.0010	0.0200	100.0407
2	20	0.0353	0.0101	0.8932	0.1021	0.0013	0.0181	100.2691
3	30	0.0448	0.0110	0.9393	0.0809	0.0011	0.0210	100.0584
4	40	0.0500	0.0100	0.9490	0.0840	0.0010	0.0200	100.1570
5	50	0.0499	0.0100	0.9496	0.0820	0.0010	0.0200	100.0412
6	60	0.0500	0.0100	0.9479	0.0825	0.0011	0.0201	100.0597
7	100	0.0500	0.0100	0.9500	0.0800	0.0010	0.0200	100.0402

Table 45.3 Effect of number of generations on availability of two-unit system

S. no.	No. of generation	λ_1	λ_2	β_1	β_2	ξ_1	ξ_2	α_1	α_2	Availability
1	10	0.0393	0.0100	0.8289	0.2867	0.0029	0.0179	0.8455	0.0015	0.1310
2	20	0.0393	0.0100	0.8531	0.0800	0.0029	0.0179	0.0963	0.0015	0.1309
3	30	0.0490	0.0100	0.9322	0.0800	0.0029	0.0179	0.0025	0.0015	0.1307
4	40	0.0493	0.0100	0.8843	0.0800	0.0058	0.0198	0.0025	0.0015	0.1306
5	50	0.0493	0.0100	0.2906	0.0800	0.0058	0.0198	0.0025	0.0015	0.1305
6	60	0.0495	0.0100	0.1031	0.0800	0.0058	0.0198	0.0026	0.0015	0.1304
7	100	0.0500	0.0100	0.0953	0.0800	0.0100	0.0200	0.0025	0.0015	0.1298

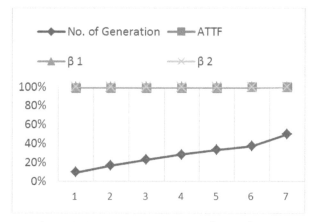

Figure 45.2. *Variation in ATTF with no. of generation and preventive maintenance rate*

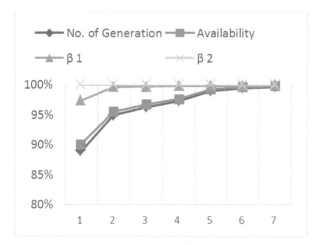

Figure 45.3. *Variation in availability with no. of generation and preventive maintenance rate*

$$A(\infty) = 1 - P_3(\infty) - P_4(\infty) = P_0(\infty) + P_1(\infty) + P_2(\infty) \tag{6}$$

$$P_0(\infty) = \frac{\alpha_1\alpha_2\,(\lambda_1(\xi_2+\beta_1)+\beta_1\beta_2)}{D}$$

$$P_1(\infty) = \frac{\xi_1\alpha_1\alpha_2(\lambda_1+\beta_2)}{D}$$

$$P_2(\infty) = \frac{\xi_1\xi_2\alpha_1\alpha_2}{D}$$

where $D = \alpha_1\,\alpha_2\,\lambda_1\,(\xi_1 + \xi_2 + \beta_1) + \xi_1\,\alpha_1\,\alpha_2\,(\xi_2 + \beta_2) + \lambda_1\,\lambda_2\,\alpha_1\,(\xi_1 + \beta_1) + \xi_1\,\xi_2\,\alpha_1\,(\alpha_1 + \alpha_2) + \beta_1\,\beta_2\,\alpha_1\,(\lambda_2 + \alpha_2)$

Methodology

In this paper GA is used to optimize the ATTF and Availability of the two-unit system. For optimize the value of parameters, the objective function is the expression for ATTF and availability.

The flow chart for the used methodology is described below to understand the logic behind the result.

Result and Discussion

In the genetic algorithm (GA) a fitness function is defined whose value is to be optimized. By defining the minor and major bounds and the Stochastic uniform approach, the best optimum result is taken over different number of generation.

Conclusions

This paper concluded that we don't have to bound the input parameters to find out the results using GA. Different set of value can be choose for better production by industries. The appropriate values of maintenance rate (preventive or corrective) can be used to have more and more availability. In this study, the mathematical expressions for ATTF and system available performance time for a two-component series system has been designed. Graph was plotted to show how the different maintenance rate put effect on the optimum value. The overall reliability of system can be enhanced by using best value for all malfunction and repair rate.

References

[1] Naithani, A., Parashar, B, Bhatia, P. K., and Taneja, G. (2013). Cost benefit analysis of a 2-out -of -3 induced draft fans system with priority for operation to cold standby over working at reduced capacity. *Advanced Modelling and Optimization*, 499-509.

[2] Kumar, A., Garg, D., and Goel, P. (2019). Mathematical modelling and behavioral analysis of a washing unit in a paper mill. *International Journal of System Assurance Engineering and Management*, 10(6), 1639-1645.

[3] Adaramola, B. A. (2020). A systematic approach of turbo generator performance evaluation maintenance for continuous power generation. *Journal of Advancement in Engineering and Technology*, 1-5.

[4] Yousefi, N., Tsianikas, S., and Coit, D. W. (2020). Reinforcement learning for dynamic condition-based maintenance of a system with individually repairable components. *Quality Engineering*, 32(3), 1-21.

[5] Modibbo, U. M., Arshad, M., Abdalghani, O., and Ali, I. (2021). Optimization and estimation in system reliability allocation problem. *Reliability Engineering & System Safety*, Elsevier, 212(C).

[6] Singla, S. and Dhawan, P. (2022). Mathematical analysis of regenerative point graphical technique (RPGT). A mathematical analysis and its contemporary applications, pp. 49-56.

[7] Singla, S., Verma, S. Malik, S., and Gupta, A. (2022). Perform ability evaluation, validation and optimization for the steam generation system of a coal-fired thermal plant. *Methods X*.

[8] Naithani, A., Khanduri, S., and Gupta, S. (2022). Stochastic analysis of main unit with two non-identical replaceable subunits working with partial failure. *International Journal of System Assurance Engineering and Management*, 13(3), 1467-1473.

[9] Kumari, S., Singla, S., and Khurana, P. (2022). Particles swarm optimization for constrained cost reliability of a rubber plant. *Life Cycle Reliability and Safety Engineering*, 11(3). doi:10.1007/s41872-022-00199-y.

46 Analysis of the constant failure density of a component and its reliability

Neeraj Singh[1,a], Nitin Kasana[2,b] and Chetan Kumar Sharma[3,c]

[1,2]Research Scholar, Department of Mathematics, Noida International University, Greater Noida, U.P., India

[3]Associate Professor, Department of Mathematics, Noida International University, G B Nagar, U.P., India

Abstract

In this manuscript, we must define when the failure rate is constant then the component must be constant throughout the procedure. Only one component is tested and repairable so that the procedure can continue after each failure. The failure rate and the unit hour's amount to the straight procedure time and define a structure that reliability (unreliability) must either decrease at the same time or must be held constant through the entire procedure.

Keywords: Random variable, probability, mean time between failures, failure rate, failure density

1 Introduction

When a component's projected failure rate remains constant over the course of equivalently lengthy operating periods [6], yet the component is solely susceptible to random failures, its reliability is:

$$R(t) = \exp(-\lambda t)$$

Where λ a constant, called the failure rate and t is the operating time. The failure rate needs to be stated in t hours, typically, and in the same time units. The reciprocal value of the failure rate that we commonly use is the mean time between failures, or m.

The MTBF is $m = 1/\lambda$

The Reliability function can be written as $R(t) = \exp(-t/\lambda)$

As discussed by Reddy [1] a component's reliability can be ascertained by comparing the proportion of components that pass a test to the total number of components at the beginning of the process. If a fixed number n_0 of components are tested there will be, after a time t, $n_s(t)$ components that survive the procedure and $n_f(t)$ components which are failed [3].

Therefore, $n_0 = n_s(t) + n_f(t)$ is a constant throughout the procedure (Tyagi et al., 2015). The reliability expressed as a fraction by the probability at any time t during the procedure is:

$$R(t) = \frac{n_S(t)}{n_0} = \frac{n_S(t)}{n_S(t) + n_f(t)}$$

According to Sharma et al. [4], the probability of failure (or unreliability) Q as

$$Q(t) = \frac{n_f(t)}{n_0} = \frac{n_F(t)}{n_S(t) + n_f(t)}$$

It is at once evident that at any time t, $R(t) + Q(t) = 1$

Working Analysis of Failure Data

Results from life tests, which involve testing a large number of models till failure and monitoring the failure rate features over time, can be used to understand the process of failures [5, 9]. Therefore, is to link reliability with

[a]nagarkoti0007@gmail.com, [b]nitingujjar2323@gmail.com, [c]cks26april@gmail.com

DOI: 10.1201/9781003534136-46

experimental or field-failure data [[8] the observation on the system at time $t_1, t_2, t_3,...$,etc. Then we can define the failure density function as follows:

$$f(t) = \frac{n_S(t_i) - n_S(t_{i+1})}{n_0(t_{i+1} - t_i)} \; ; \; t_i < t \le t_{i+1} \tag{2.1}$$

Zhou and Han [7] and Wenjuan [10] shows that failure rate over the interval $t_i < t \le t_{i+1}$ is defined as the ratio of the number of failures occurring in the time interval to the number of survivors at the beginning of the time interval, divided by the length of the time interval. It is determined as the number of failures occurring in the interval to the size of the original population divided by the length of the interval.

$$\lambda(t) = \frac{n_S(t_i) - n_S(t_{i+1})}{n_S(t_i) \, (t_{i+1} - t_i)} \; ; \; t_i < t < t_{i+1} \tag{2.2}$$

Whereas, $\lambda(t)$ measures the instantaneous speed of failures, the failure density function $f(t)$ measures the over-all speed at which failures are occurring.

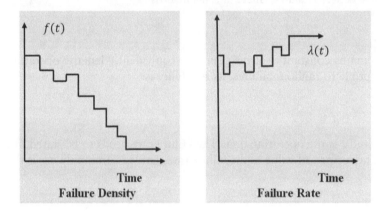

Numerical Discussion of Failure Data Analysis

The failure data for a component in time is:

Failure no.	1	2	3	4	5	6	7	8	9	10
Operating time	8	15	18	22	27	32	38	42	48	56

Table 46.1 Computation of failure density and [1]failure rate

Time interval (hrs.)	Failure density	Failure rate
0-8	0.0125	0.0125
8-15	0.0079	0.0088
15-18	0.0067	0.0091
18-22	0.0079	0.0114
22-27	0.0054	0.0093
27-32	0.0039	0.0082
32-38	0.0035	0.0095
38-42	0.0028	0.0106
42-48	0.0017	0.0106
48-56	0.0018	0.0120

---

[1] Failure Rate calculate from eqn. (2.2)

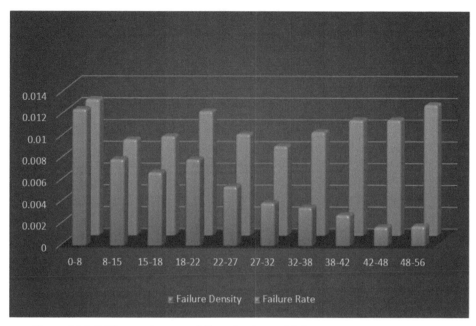

Figure 46.1 Difference between failure density and failure rate

Conclusion and Future Work

We must measure the constant failure rate of a component population conveniently and measuring a constant failure rate is to keep the number of components in the procedure constant by immediately replacing the failed components with good ones also the number of alive components $N_S(t)$ is then equal to N_0 throughout the procedure. Of course, this procedure for determining the failure rate can be applied only if λ is constant.

Acknowledgment

I would like to sincerely appreciate and express my gratitude to Prof. D K Ghosh and Prof. Ashok Kumar for their insightful advice, which helped us to conduct present work.

Author Contribution

C K Sharma organized and managed the study; Neeraj and Nitin performed the simulations and wrote the first draft of the work. After reading the manuscript, all writers accepted it in its published version.

Conflicts of Interest

On behalf of all authors, the corresponding author states that there are no conflicts of interest regarding the publication of this article.

References

[1] Reddy, R. C. (1993). Optimization of K-out of N systems subject to common cause failures with repair. *Microeiectron and Reliability*, 33, 175-183.
[2] Goel L. R., Gupta, R., and Tyagi P. K. (1995). Analysis of two stand by systems with preparation time and correlated failures and repairs. *Microeiectron and Reliability*, 35, 163-1168.
[3] Charles, E. E. (1997). Reliability and Maintainability Engineering. Tata McGraw-Hill Publishing Company Limited, New Delhi.
[4] Sharma, C. K., Gupta, M. M., and Kumar, A. (2010). Reliability analysis with an analytical discussion of the system with correlated failures. *International Research Journal of Management Science & Technology*, 1(3), 104-115.
[5] Kumar, A., Gupta, M. M., and Sharma, C. K. (2011). Reliability measurement for the exponential case of chance failures discuss with data analysis. *International Research Journal of Management Science & Technology*, 1(3), 212-218.

[6] Kumar, A., Gupta, M. M., and Sharma, C. K. (2012). Cost analysis of 2-units electronic parallel redundant system for three states. *International Research Journal of Management Sociology & Humanity*, 3(1), 290-296.

[7] Zhou, W. and Han, W. (2019). Personalized recommendation via user preference matching. *Information Processing & Management*, 56(3), 955–968.

[8] Mao, J., Lu, K., Li, G., and Yi, M. (2016). Profiling users with tag networks in diffusion-based personalized recommendation. *Journal of Information Science*, 42(5), 711–722.

[9] Guan, Y., Wei, Q., and Chen, G. (2019). Deep learning based personalized recommendation with multi-view information integration. *Decision Support Systems*, 118, 58–69.

[10] Wenjuan, Z. (2021). Learning perception prediction and English hierarchical model based on neural network algorithm. *Journal of Intelligent and Fuzzy Systems*, 40(2), 2469–2480.

[11] Tyagi, V., Kalra.B.S., Sharma, C.K., and Kumar, A. (2015). Cost Benefit Analysis of a Two Unit Parallel System with Response Period of Repair Facility. Multidisciplinary Scientific Reviewer, 2(5), 39–45.

47 A review on efficacy of gamified platforms for speech therapy

Harshita Tuli[1,a], Bibek Kumar[2] and Harshita Tuli[3]

[1]Student, Department of Computer Science and Engineering, Vishveshwarya Group of Institutions, Dadri, Greater Noida, India

[2]Associate Professor, Department of Computer Science and Engineering, Vishveshwarya Group of Institutions, Dadri, Greater Noida, India

[3]Associate Professor, Department of Computer Science and Engineering, LIET, Greater Noida, India

Abstract

Speech is a zestful, complex, and unique activity that allows a person to reciprocate thoughts and feelings. It is a neurological activity that allows us to render our views. It is a crucial process in learning and growth of any individual. Communication plays a major role in a person's societal and cognitive well-being. Any difficulty in speech can disrupt person's role in society, cordial relationships and even lead to social seclusion. The irony of current situation is many of the children suffer from speech related issues that need proper attention and measures to manage the complication. With the advent of digitalization of platforms, electronic speech rehabilitation techniques such as natural language processing, speech processing technologies have become popular. Digital games are among burgeoning methods for dealing with speech disorders. This study reviews the efficacy of intervention of digital gamified platforms and artificial intelligence techniques in facilitating the speech therapist and children dealing speech difficulties.

Introduction

Speech and language are crucial to social life and important means by which people exchange thoughts, feelings, knowledge and experiences. Children develop foundational communication skills in early childhood and because of this the ability to gain access to culturally transmitted knowledge, to reciprocate thoughts and feelings, and to participate in social interlinkage. Communication skills are most important to the match up thinking ability, a sense of self, and participation in society [1]. There was a huge increase of speech disorders among children if compared to pre pandemic era as per another study [2]. There is almost 110% increase in speech issues for children aged 0 to 12 years in 2022. Earlier, approximately 570,000 children per year were diagnosed with a speech disorder, however post pandemic these numbers raised to roughly 1.2 million [2]. The speech impairment can be categorized into broadly three types these are **fluency disorder** which can be described as continuity, smoothness, rate, and effort in speech production. **Voice disorder** where the person has an atypical tone of voice and **articulation disorder.** When the person might distort or omit certain sounds.

Speech therapy plays a crucial role in addressing articulation defects and improving communication skills, particularly in children and individuals with speech disorders. Traditional methods of speech therapy often face challenges in maintaining sustained engagement and motivation, especially among younger clients. Also, challenges that are faced by therapist include motivating the patient to maintain long and effective practice sessions at home in absence of a therapist and to make child's parent aware about the need for professional speech therapy. A big challenge in speech therapy treatment today is the lack of intensive, continuous practice (Hula, 2007). For people living in remote areas the cost usually is a lot higher and professional speech therapy can be highly inaccessible (Bourke et al, 2004). In recent years, the integration of gamified platforms into speech therapy programs has emerged as an innovative and promising approach to address these challenges. With the advent of digital tools digital gamification services have started to dominate stimulating platforms and offer a change in behavior for well-being compared to traditional persuasive technology. Gamification involves incorporating game elements to enhance user engagement and motivation. In the realm of speech therapy, this approach aims to transform traditional exercises into interactive and enjoyable activities. The gamification paradigm leverages the inherent appeal of games to create a positive and stimulating environment for speech therapy participants, particularly children who may find conventional methods less engaging. One of the key advantages of gamified platforms in speech therapy lies in their ability to captivate and sustain the interest of users. Through vibrant graphics, interactive characters, and entertaining challenges, these platforms make the learning process inherently enjoyable. The element of competition, achievement, and immediate feedback in a game setting contributes

[a]Harshita.tuli@liet.in

DOI: 10.1201/9781003534136-47

Table 47.1 Number of children having speech issues

Age group	Area	Total speech disabled children	Male	Female
0-4	Rural	22964	12788	10176
5-9		154916	88496	66420
0-4	Urban	9497	5270	4227
5-9		57902	32330	25572

to heightened motivation, encouraging individuals to actively participate in speech exercises and practice consistently. Many gamified platforms employ adaptive algorithms that personalize the learning experience based on individual performance. This ensures that users are appropriately challenged, with difficulty levels adjusting dynamically as proficiency improves. The adaptive nature of these platforms caters to the diverse needs of users, making speech therapy more effective by tailoring interventions to the specific requirements of each individual. The subsequent sections of this review will delve into empirical evidence supporting their efficacy in enhancing articulation skills, specific platforms, their features, and promoting positive outcomes in individuals undergoing speech therapy.

Review of Literature

According to statistics on children in India, 2018 out of total disabled population (different kinds) of 1291332 of 0-4 years of children 18058 males' children 14403 female children have speech disabilities. Data mentioned in Table 47.1 [3]. Speech disabilities included in table includes those people who are immobile in terms of self as well as objects due to: numbness of the limb or body (ii) stammering (iii) speaking with abnormal voice and (iv) articulation defects.

Also, according to recent research there is a 110% increase in children aged 0 to 12 years who are suffering from speech disorder, compared to the era before pandemic. It is also been observed that children who have delayed milestones with interdental articulation errors, were more likely to resolve all the errors by 7 years (67%) than those making atypical errors (35%) [4]. In a study done in [5] it has been observed that childhood apraxia of speech (CAS) causes inconstant oromotor production and suggested that expressive and receptive PRES scores of children also showed an upward trend for CAS, FAD. This results shown in this paper revealed that CAS group showed the lowest language skills. Digitalization has changed the face of almost every horizon so is suggested in next paragraph that reviews the studies done on various gamified platforms that help in improving the area of speech therapy. Another study examined the games designed for children with speech disorders and showed that English is the most acceptable language in gaming designs and commands [6]. It has also shown that PocketSphinx and the MFCC algorithm were among the commonly used technologies used for speech recognition were. Many research papers have focused on Autistic patients and children with hearing impairments. There are various challenges that designers of these games face, few of them are accents, environmental disturbances, attenuation etc. Among technical issues and attenuation, they also have to deal with a sense of irritation in children after several failures while playing game and also the incompatibility of the game level. To evaluate the linguistic competence of young children using a gamified setup a platform has been designed to administer discrimination tests [7]. The platform dynamically adapts the test according to children's performance using a Bayesian dialogue and iteratively selects the most useful stimuli to be presented. In paper [8] a HMD-based VR system has been designed to support gamified tongue rehabilitation. Any therapy prescription apps (physiotherapy, speech pathology, and occupational therapy) prescription apps will be highly engaging when they incorporate dynamic behavior change techniques (BCTs) within their design [8]. e-SpeechT designed by Bartella et al [9] is a system that offers role based functionalities and graphical interfaces for therapist, caregiver and parent. The application is highly engaging for its manifold audience, when children use these fun frolic activity-based GUI with huge interest.

Observations

Gamified platforms for speech therapy can be effective and engaging tools to help individuals, especially children, improve their articulation skills. These platforms often use interactive games and activities to make the learning process enjoyable and encourage regular practice. Here are a few examples of gamified platforms for speech therapy:

1. **Articulation station:** Articulation station is an app that offers a variety of activities and games to target specific speech sounds. It provides audio-visual feedback and allows users to record and playback their speech for self-assessment. The app includes interactive games like flashcards, sentences, and stories that make learning and practicing speech sound more engaging.

2. **Speech blubs:** Speech blubs is designed for children and uses a variety of games and videos featuring real kids to encourage imitation and practice of speech sounds. The app incorporates a reward system, where children can unlock new content and features as they progress. The engaging visuals and interactive elements help keep children motivated.

3. **Smarty ears App:** Smarty ears offers a range of apps designed by speech-language pathologists to target specific speech and language goals. Apps like "Sunny Articulation & Phonology Test" and "Articulate it!" are popular choices. The apps often include interactive games, flashcards, and quizzes that provide immediate feedback and rewards for correct responses.

4. **Constant therapy:** Constant therapy is a comprehensive therapy app that covers various aspects of speech and language therapy. It includes exercises for articulation, language comprehension, and more.

5. **Speechtastic:** Speechtastic is a speech therapy app that focuses on articulation practice. It offers a variety of games and activities for different speech sounds. The app incorporates a reward system and includes colorful graphics and animations to make the learning process enjoyable for users, especially children.

When considering gamified platforms for speech therapy, it's essential to ensure that they align with the specific needs and goals of the individual receiving therapy. Additionally, consulting with a speech-language pathologist can help determine the most suitable platform and activities for addressing specific articulation defects.

Conclusion:

The efficacy of gamified platforms for speech therapy in correcting articulation defects appears promising based on available evidence and user experiences. These platforms leverage the engaging and interactive nature of games to create a positive and enjoyable learning environment for individuals, especially children, undergoing speech therapy. Here are some key points to consider:

1. Engagement and motivation: Gamified platforms often succeed in keeping users engaged and motivated to practice consistently. The incorporation of game elements, rewards, and interactive activities can make the learning process more enjoyable, leading to increased participation and dedication to therapy sessions.

2. Immediate feedback: Many gamified speech therapy platforms provide immediate feedback on pronunciation and articulation. This real-time feedback allows individuals to self-assess and make corrections, reinforcing the learning process and promoting better understanding of correct speech patterns.

3. Personalization and adaptability: Some platforms use adaptive algorithms to tailor the difficulty levels of activities based on the user's performance. This personalization ensures that individuals are challenged at an appropriate level, promoting gradual improvement and skill development over time.

4. Data tracking and progress monitoring: Gamified speech therapy platforms often include features that allow users and, in some cases, therapists to track progress over time. Monitoring progress can be motivating and helps individuals and clinicians assess the effectiveness of the therapy program.

5. Child friendly approaches: Many gamified platforms are designed with children in mind, employing colorful visuals, engaging characters, and age-appropriate themes. This child-friendly approach can create a positive association with speech therapy, making it more likely that children will actively participate in the learning process.

Despite the positive aspects, it is important to note that gamified platforms should not replace the expertise of a qualified speech-language pathologist. These platforms are most effective when used as supplementary tools in conjunction with professional guidance. To conclude the review it can be said that gamified platforms for speech therapy have shown promise in addressing articulation defects by making the learning process enjoyable, interactive, and motivating. As technology continues to advance, ongoing research and development in this area are likely to further enhance the efficacy of these platforms in supporting individuals on their journey to improved articulation skills.

References

[1] Speech and Language Disorders in Children. Washington (DC): National Academies Press (US), ; 2016.

[2] Khan, T., Freeman, R, and Druet, A. (2023). Komodo Health. Louder than words: Pediatric speech disorders skyrocket throughout pandemic.

[3] Statistics on Children in India. National Institute of Public Cooperation and Child Development. 2018.

[4] Dodd, B., Ttofari-Eecen, K., Brommeyer, K., Ng, K., Reilly, S., and Morgan, A. (2018). Delayed and disordered development of articulation and phonology between four and seven years. *Child Language Teaching and Therapy*, 34(2).

[5] Yun, J. H., Shin, S. M., and Son, S. M. (2021). Clinical utility of repeated urimal test of articulation and phonation for patients with childhood apraxia of speech. *Children*. 8(12), 1106.

[6] Saeedi, S., Bouraghi, H., Seifpanahi, M. -S., and Ghazisaeedi, M. (2022). Application of digital games for speech therapy in children: a systematic review of features and challenges. *Journal of Healthcare Engineering*, 20. https://doi.org/10.1155/2022/4814945

[7] Origlia, A., Rodá, A., Zmarich, C., Cosi, P., Nigris, S., Colavolpe, B., and Leorin, C. (2018). Gamified discrimination tests for speech therapy applications. *Book series Studi AISV*, 4, 195-216.

[8] Rodríguez, A., Chover, M., and Boada, I. (2023). Gamification and virtual reality for tongue rehabilitation. *IEEE Access*, 11, 124975-124984.

[9] Johnson, R. W., White, B. K., Gucciardi, D. F., Gibson, N., and Williams, S. A. (2022). Intervention mapping of a gamified therapy prescription app for children with disabilities: user-centered design approach. *JMIR Pediatrics and Parenting*, 5(3), e34588. doi: 10.2196/34588.

[10] Barletta, V. S., Calvano, M., Curci, A., and Piccinno, A. (2023). A protocol to assess usability and feasibility of e-speech, a web-based system supporting speech therapies. Computer Science Department, University of Bari Aldo Moro, 70125, Bari, Italy.

[11] Hula, S. and Austermann, N. (2007). Current Directions In Treatment For Apraxia Of Speech: Principles Of Motor Learning. Perspectives on Neurophysiology and Neurogenic Speech and Language Disorders.

[12] Bourke (2004). Developing A Conceptual Understanding Of Rural Health Practice. Australian Journal of Rural Health

48 Role of consumer behavioral intensions and sustainable fashion: mapping the intellectual structure and future research trends

Mona Sharma[1,a], Yogita Sharma[2,b], Priyanka Chadha[3,c] and Amit Kumar Pandey[4,d]

[1]*Manav Rachna University Faridabad Haryana, India*

[2]*Manav Rachna University Faridabad Haryana, India*

[4]*Amity Business School, Amity University, Noida, UttarPradesh, India*

[5]*Associate Professor, Amit Business School, Amity University, Noida, India*

Abstract

One of the main causes of glasshouse gas emissions and climate change is the fashion sector. Through the design, production, and marketing of products that are both socially and environmentally responsible, sustainable fashion (SF) seeks to address this problem. In order to comprehend the patterns and future directions, this study gives a thorough assessment of the existing literature on sustainable fashion marketing. A bibliometric analysis was required to compile a summary of the sustainable fashion literature. The main goal of this study was to investigate and analyze the most recent scientific work on fashion sustainability, the most widely cited articles, the authors who have made the most significant contributions to the field, the most popular search terms. This study examines and summarizes the pertinent literature from 2016 to 2023 for the integrated analysis. The bibliometric analysis used in this work is assisted by the programs biblioshiny R and VOS viewer. From the dataset of 29 documents, various bibliometric analysis tools were used to glean insightful information. The report also offers a variety of current and upcoming sustainable fashion trends to help academics and decision-makers.

Keywords: Sustainability, sustainable fashion, consumer intention, fashion trend, consumer behavior

Introduction

In the context of the surge in fast fashion, prominent companies like Zara, H&M, Topshop, and Forever have leveraged this business approach [1]. The primary aim of fast fashion enterprises is to swiftly produce large quantities of trendy clothing within a tight timeframe. This enables consumers to keep pace with the rapid and ever-changing trends, thereby fostering increased product consumption [2].

While the economic advantages of the fast fashion model have somewhat shielded it from criticism regarding its inherent disposability and waste [3], these companies have recently begun to invest in and promote their commitment to sustainability. However, this has been occurring alongside the perpetuation of over-consumption, without any fundamental shifts in their business model [4]. Such communications typically depict sustainability as a concern tied to the company's operations, such as ethical labor practices and the use of sustainable materials, while largely sidestepping the transfer of responsibility to consumers [5].

Previous research has primarily concentrated on sustainability aspects by exploring consumers' intentions to purchase ecofriendly clothing [6-8], behaviors related to clothing recycling or donation [9-12], and the implementation of corporate social responsibility initiatives within the supply chain [13, 14]. However, limited research has been devoted to comprehending the growing problem of excessive clothing consumption [15], highlighting a gap in the literature that addresses sustainability concerns by advocating reduced and more deliberate clothing consumption.

However, this heightened environmental consciousness has yet to substantially influence purchasing decisions in the realm of fashion (Kim & Damhorst, 1998). This disconnect can be attributed to several factors, including the relatively higher cost of sustainable fashion items, a limited range of product options, challenges related to aesthetics and functionality, and an inadequacy of relevant information.

The behavioral intentions of conscientious consumers who prioritize social and ecological responsibility play a significant role throughout the entire consumption journey, spanning from pre-purchase considerations to

[a]monanps9@gmail.com, [b]yogitasharma@mru.edu.in, [c]priyanka03chadha@gmail.com, [d]*akpandey7@amity.edu*

DOI: 10.1201/9781003534136-48

post-disposal actions [16] Consumers inclined towards eco-friendly and sustainable choices actively seek clothing crafted from environmentally friendly textiles and invest in fashion offerings that provide ecological alternatives [17]. The potential for altering this trend lies in the activation of consumers, where they actively participate in creating value within the fashion system [18]. However, in order to stimulate consumer engagement with sustainable development in the fashion sector, there is a necessity to gain deeper insights into how consumers assess the practical lifespan of clothing items versus their technical durability (Zamani, Sandin & Peters, 2017).

Despite the gradual ascent of sustainability interests, it remains imperative for the apparel industry to leverage insights to formulate more potent strategies aimed at consumer education [19].

The Research Questions for this study are:

- What are the key publication trends, patterns, and shifts in research focus within this interdisciplinary domain?
- How have influential works contributed to shaping the discourse and research directions?
- What are the predominant themes and topics within research on sustainable fashion consumption?
- What are there emerging themes, cross-disciplinary collaborations, or underexplored areas that require further investigation?

The study is structured in the following manner: it commences with a succinct review of the existing literature, followed by an outline of the research methodology, presentation of findings, and subsequent discussion. The study concludes by summarizing key insights and suggesting potential avenues for future research.

Research Methodology

In this study, bibliometric analysis is employed with the support of biblioshiny R and VOSviewer software version 1.6.16 [20]. Bibliometric analysis employs quantitative techniques to examine academic literature within a specific field over a defined time frame. Within the domain of tourism studies, bibliometric analysis has gained prominence [21]. Researchers can opt for specific databases, journals, sources, and keywords to analyze, effectively organizing pertinent information such as articles, journals, researchers, institutions, and countries.

The Scopus online database was chosen for this study, given its reputation as a prominent resource for identifying institutional research output.

Subsequently, relevant keywords for the study were determined and discussed, guided by the approach of Leung et al. [22]. Keywords like "Consumer behavioral intentions for sustainable fashion" were deemed relevant, encompassing various subject areas to ensure alignment with the research field. The inclusion criteria, focused solely on peer-reviewed journals, books, and conference proceedings. Law et al. [23] posits that professional journals, books, and conference proceedings adhere to a distinct peer-review process, involving multiple rounds of review before acceptance. Only publications in the English language were considered for further analysis. This thorough screening process led to a focused collection of 29 papers that met the stipulated criteria.

The comprehensive query used is as follows: (TITLE-ABS-KEY (consumer behavioral intentions and sustainable fashion))

The titles, abstracts, and keywords of the selected articles were further scrutinized for relevance to the research topic, resulting in the exclusion of 0 articles and a final list of 29 articles for thorough review as shown in figure 48.1. Various tools for bibliometric analysis were employed to extract valuable insights from the dataset comprising 56 documents. The authors utilized VOS viewer (version 1.6.15) and Biblioshiny (version 2.0) to visualize networks involving journals, researchers, and individual publications.

A theoretical Framework of the Problem explored in healthcare

During pandemic, when entire world on halt, people in medical fraternity were working day and night for the wellbeing of the common people. It was really a difficult situation because of the nature of the virus, which was completely unknown for the world.

Discussion

A productivity analysis of publications spanning the years 2016 to 2023 reveals the dynamic evolution of research in the realm of consumer behavioral intentions and sustainable fashion. The analysis showcases a notable increase in scholarly contributions, reflecting the growing significance of this intersection. Notably, the

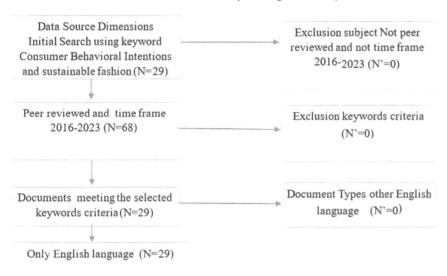

Figure 48.1 Data extraction using preferred reporting items for systematic reviews and meta-analyses (PRISMA) approach

Table 48.1 Annual scientific production

Year	Articles
2016	2
2017	1
2018	3
2019	2
2020	4
2021	2
2022	7
2023	6

year 2022 stands out with the highest number of publications as depicted in table 48.1, indicating a surge in attention to the nexus of consumer behavior and sustainable fashion. The fashion industry has been undergoing a transformation towards more sustainable practices, driven by consumer demand, regulatory changes, and corporate social responsibility efforts. As the concept of sustainable fashion is multidisciplinary, it appeals to researchers from various fields such as marketing, consumer behavior, environmental studies, and sociology. This cross-disciplinary interest contributes to a broader range of publications.

Citation Analysis
Co-citation analysis is a method used in bibliometrics and information science to identify relationships between documents based on their citation patterns as shown in table 48.2. It involves examining which documents are frequently cited together, indicating a thematic or conceptual relationship between them. To collect the data in answer each item from the respondents a Likert scale ranging from 1 (strongly disagree) to 7 (strongly agree) was employed. Total items used in the exploration survey with their references are shown. As the point above all the items used in the questionnaire were authenticated from the existing works.

Most Relevant Authors
The analysis of the most relevant authors in the field of consumer behavioral intentions and sustainable fashion highlights their contributions and impact. Notably, Marconi Freitas da Costa stands out with two articles, accounting for a substantial fraction of authorship. Other notable authors include Jordana Soares de Lira, Azenaty Alian Leite de Souza Lima, and Patrícia de Oliveira Campos, each with significant contributions as shown in table 48.3. This list encompasses researchers who have delved into diverse aspects of sustainable

Table 48.2 Average citations per year

Year	MeanTCperArt	N	MeanTCperYear	CitableYears
2016	60	2.00	7.50	8
2017	21	1.00	3.00	7
2018	54.33	3.00	9.05	6
2019	51.5	2.00	10.30	5
2020	24.75	4.00	6.19	4
2021	9	2.00	3.00	3
2022	5	7.00	2.50	2
2023	0.67	6.00	0.67	1

Table 48.3 Most relevant authors

Authors	Articles	Articles Fractionalized
COSTA MF	2	0.75
AHN J	1	0.50
ALEXANDER B	1	0.25
ALVINO L	1	0.33
BAJTELSMIT V	1	0.20
BELLI SM	1	0.50
BLAZQUEZ M	1	0.25
BLOODHART B	1	0.20
BURTON M	1	0.50
CAMPOS PO	1	0.25

fashion, including voluntary simplicity, ethics, purchase intention, and social media behavior. Identifying the most relevant authors with respect to citations is crucial for understanding the scholarly landscape and recognizing key contributors within a specific research field. To achieve this, we typically gather a collection of scholarly documents related to their research topic and retrieve citation data for each document as depicted in table 48.4.

Researchers frequently apply established theories such as the Theory of Planned Behavior and Reasoned Action to understand consumer behavioral intentions.

Most Global Cited Documents
The analysis of globally cited documents in the realm of consumer behavioral intentions and sustainable fashion provides several insights: The globally cited documents span a range of themes, from collaborative consumption and sustainable fashion adoption to the influence of self-concept, knowledge, and cultural perspectives on consumer behavior.

Studies like Blazquez et al. [24] as shown in figure 48.2 emphasized the importance of considering cultural and regional factors. Understanding consumer behavior in different contexts is crucial for effective sustainable fashion strategies tailored to diverse audiences.

Works such as Lang and Joyner Armstrong and Legere and Kang [25, 26] delved into the psychological drivers of sustainable fashion consumption. Concepts like fashion leadership, uniqueness, materialism, and self-concept play pivotal roles in influencing consumers' decisions. Gupta and Pandey [28] discussed predictive approaches offering valuable insights for marketers and policymakers.

Contributions like Kumar et al. [27] enrich established theories such as the theory of planned behavior by incorporating factors like perceived consumer effectiveness and environmental concern. These adaptations align theories with the complexities of sustainable fashion choices.

Table 48.4 Most relevant authotrs

Paper	Total Citations	TC per Year	Normalized TC
LANG C, 2018, SUSTAIN PROD CONSUM	120	20.00	2.21
DIDDI S, 2019, SUSTAIN PROD CONSUM	89	17.80	1.73
KONG HM, 2016, J GLOB FASH MARK	68	8.50	1.13
JOHNSON KKP, 2016, J FASH MARK MANAGE	52	6.50	0.87
LEGERE A, 2020, J CLEAN PROD	46	11.50	1.86
BLAZQUEZ M, 2020, FASHION PRACTICE	34	8.50	1.37
SONG SY, 2018, SUSTAINABILITY	25	4.17	0.46
KUMAR N, 2022, J GLOB FASH MARK	22	11.00	4.40
PARK H, 2017, J GLOB FASH MARK	21	3.00	1.00
JAIN G, 2018, RES J TEXT APPAR	18	3.00	0.33

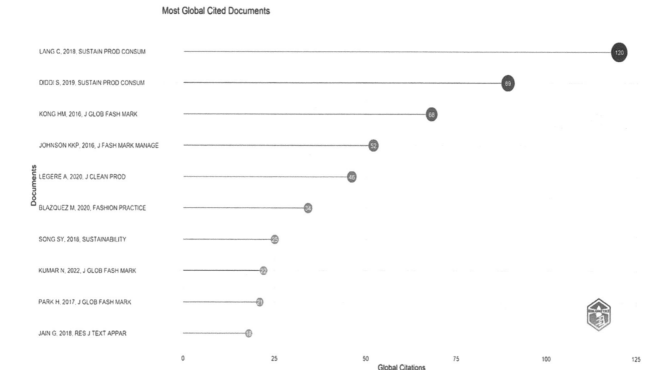

Figure 48.2 Most Global Cited Documents

Co Occurance (Author Keyword) Analysis

Co-occurrence analysis is a technique that reveals connections and associations between frequently paired keywords, shedding light on the fundamental themes and subjects within the research literature as illustrated in table 48.5. By setting a threshold of two occurrences, the authors pinpointed 23 keywords out of a total of 161 that surpassed this criterion, enabling a focused examination of the most relevant associations. This process yields valuable insights into the overall research landscape, offering guidance for subsequent exploration and analysis.

The five integrated themes illuminate the complex interplay between consumer behavior, fashion trends, sustainability, and perception within the clothing industry. These themes provide a comprehensive framework to understand the evolving dynamics, challenges, and opportunities in this landscape as shown in figure 48.3.

The theme of Navigating Sustainability and Perception highlights how consumer behavior, fashion trends, and sustainability are interconnected. It emphasizes that understanding consumer preferences can drive shifts in fashion trends, leading to a more eco-conscious marketplace.

The Sustainable Fashion Adoption in Brazil theme is Focused on Brazil's unique context, this theme explores the roles of ethics, slow fashion, and psychological models in driving sustainable fashion adoption.

Table 48.5 Authors keywrods co-occurrence analysis

Keyword	Occurrences
Sustainability	4
Sustainable development	6
Sustainable fashion	2
Marketing	4
Purchase intention	3
Behavioral intention	2
Clothing industry	3
Consumer behaviour	2
Theory of planned behaviour	2
Environmental concern	2
Perception	2
Ethics	2
Segmentation	2
Slow fashion	3
Brazil	2
Collaborative consumption	3
Fashion	3
Apparel	2
Eco- fashion	2

Collaborative Consumption, Materialism, and Segmentation Strategies: This theme highlights the transformative potential of collaborative consumption and segmentation in reshaping the industry. Collaborative models align with resource efficiency, while segmentation targets specific consumer groups with tailored messages.

Harmonizing Intentions, Behaviors, and Media is focused on behavioral intentions, consumer behavior, and social media's impact, this theme underscores the transformative power of informed consumer choices.

Navigating Eco-Fashion: Bridging Environmental Concerns and Purchase Intentions theme centers on understanding the motivations behind eco-conscious fashion choices. By bridging the gap between consumer values and ecological responsibility, it explores how environmental concerns influence intentions to make sustainable purchases.

Co- CitationAnalysis
Co-citation analysis, as a bibliometric approach, entails examining citations within a collection of documents to uncover linkages between referenced sources. A set of keywords that are relevant to our research topic. These keywords represent the main concepts or themes we want to explore as shown in table 48.6. This method considers two or more documents as co-cited when they both reference the same third document. By applying a minimum threshold of 2 citations for a specific cited reference, this study identified 38 out of 163 cited references that meet this criterion. This analysis facilitates the identification of intellectual associations among various works based on their shared citations as depicted in table 48.7. In addition to analyzing keywords, you can also conduct a co-citation analysis of references. This involves identifying which references are frequently cited together in the literature, indicating a thematic or conceptual relationship between them. Follow similar steps as outlined above, but instead of keywords, analyze the co-citation patterns of references within the documents as shown in figure 48.4.

The discussions revolve around several integrated themes, each offering a unique perspective on sustainable fashion consumption and its various dimensions.

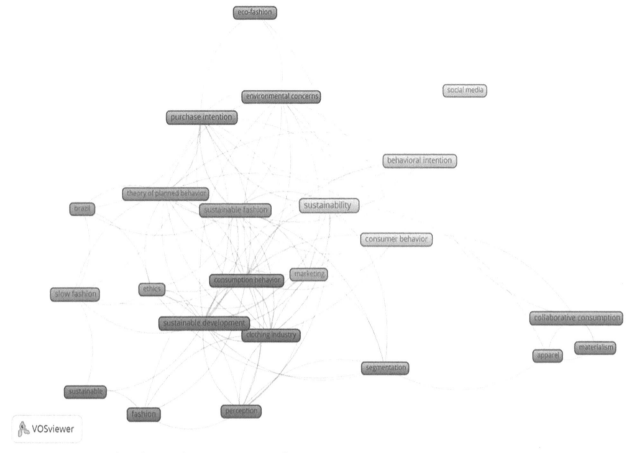

Figure 48.3 Authors keywords co-occurrence analysis

Table 48.6 CO-citation (cited- reference)

Cluster	Keyword	Themes
Red	clothing industry consumption behavior fashion perception sustainable sustainable development	The integrated theme 'Navigating Sustainability and Perception in the Clothing Industry: Consumer Behavior and Fashion's Role" encapsulates an exploration at the confluence of sustainability, consumer behavior, and fashion trends within the clothing industry. This comprehensive theme investigates how consumer choices shape fashion trends and how fashion, in turn, molds perceptions, all underpinned by the imperative of sustainable development. It encompasses an analysis of consumer motivations towards sustainable clothing, the influence of perception on fashion, and the potential of sustainable practices to transform the industry. The study delves into successful strategies that harmonize sustainability, evolving consumer behaviors, and innovative fashion approaches while considering challenges and synergies. Ultimately, this integrated approach sheds light on the intricate interplay of these factors, which collectively have the power to reshape the fashion landscape and society's perception of responsible consumption and sustainable progress.
Green	brazil ethics slow fashion sustainable fashion theory of planned behavior	Within the dynamic setting of Brazil's fashion realm, this comprehensive exploration investigates the intricate interactions among sustainable fashion adoption, ethics, the slow fashion movement, and the influential Theory of Planned Behavior. By

analyzing these facets within the Brazilian context, we seek a holistic comprehension of how ethical considerations, mindful consumption, and psychological frameworks impact the integration of sustainable fashion practices. The investigation encompasses the ethical underpinnings of sustainable fashion, the alignment of slow fashion with sustainable principles, the application of the Theory of Planned Behavior in understanding consumer adoption, and the distinct Brazilian fashion landscape. Proposed strategies for promoting sustainable fashion involve education, behavioral interventions, and fostering a lasting culture of sustainable fashion in Brazil, emphasizing cross-sector collaboration and long-term impact. This integrated approach illuminates the interwoven dynamics that shape sustainable fashion in Brazil, offering insights into motivations, challenges, and strategies within this evolving movement

Dark Blue	apparel collaborative consumption materialism segmentation	Within the shifting landscape of the apparel industry, a transformative trajectory emerges through the intricate interplay of collaborative consumption, materialism, and strategic segmentation. Collaborative consumption models, founded on shared resources and reduced ownership, are fundamentally reshaping the industry's narrative by emphasizing resource efficiency and access-driven consumption. Amidst materialism's impact on consumer behavior, a paradigm shift is sought, redirecting consumers towards quality-centric choices that align with sustainability principles. Against this backdrop, segmentation strategies prove pivotal for sustainable brands, enabling them to target distinct consumer clusters with tailored messages and offerings that resonate with ethical and environmental values. By synergizing collaborative consumption with segmentation, these strategies evolve into conduits for promoting responsible consumerism, advocating access over accumulation, and nurturing a sense of community within the domain of fashion consumption. This integrated framework delineates a path toward a consumercentric apparel industry, where the fusion of collaborative ideals, purposeful segmentation, and reframed materialistic perspectives collectively pave the way for a more sustainable and inclusive future.
Yellow	behavioral intention consumer behavior social media sustainability	"Harmonizing Intentions, Behaviors, and Media: Crafting a Sustainable Future" underscores the intricate fusion of behavioral intention, consumer behavior, social media, and sustainability that weaves together the current and future landscape of commerce. The interplay of ethical inclinations and behavioral intentions guides conscientious consumer choices, catalyzing a shift toward sustainable options and reshaping conventional consumer paradigms. Amid this transformation, social media emerges as an undeniable force, amplifying sustainability messages and molding consumer behavior through peer-driven endorsements and awareness campaigns. This orchestrated interconnection of behavioral intention, consumer behavior, and social media culminates in sustainability, as the concerted actions of mindful consumers propel industries toward ethical and eco-conscious practices.
Purple	eco-fashion environmental	. "In the realm of conscious consumerism, the integrated theme titled 'Navigating Eco-Fashion: Bridging Environmental Concerns

concerns purchase intention

and Purchase Intentions' intricately explores the synergy between eco-conscious fashion choices, environmental mindfulness, and consumer purchase motivations. This theme delves into the motivations and decision-making processes of individuals who prioritize ethical and sustainable fashion, harmonizing personal values with the imperative of ecological responsibility. Amid escalating environmental concerns, this theme investigates how these considerations shape consumers' intentions to embrace ecofriendly purchases, catalyzing transformative change within the fashion industry and nurturing a path toward a more sustainable future."

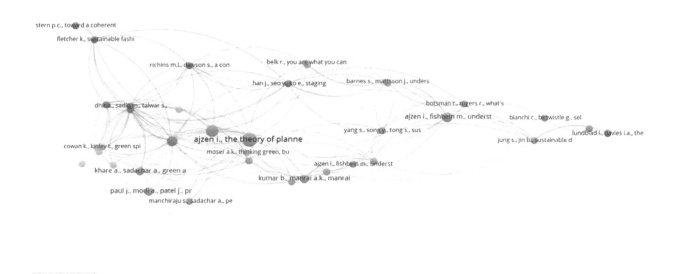

Figure 48.4 Co-citation cited reference

Bibliographic Coupling of Documents

The concept of "intellectual structure" typically refers to the organization and relationships of concepts, ideas, theories, and research within a specific field of study.

As shown in figure 48.5, Bibliographic coupling stands as a widely utilized methodology within the realms of bibliometrics and scientometrics. In the context of this study, a threshold of a minimum of 2 citations per document was chosen, resulting in 18 out of the 29 documents meeting this criterion for analysis. Out of the 18 documents, 15 were connected to each other. The integrated themes bring together diverse perspectives and insights related to sustainable fashion consumption mentioned in table 48.8 which are as follow:

Shaping Sustainable Consumer Behavior: A Tapestry of Slow and Conscious Fashion Consumption: This theme emphasizes the importance of self-concept, conscious consumption intentions, collaborative consumption, and garment life extension in shaping sustainable consumer behavior.

Sustainable Fashion Intentions: A Multifaceted Exploration through Diverse Perspectives: Diverse perspectives enrich this theme, ranging from voluntary simplicity and environmental activism to slow fashion determinants and cultural influences.

Reshaping Sustainable Fashion: Exploring Digital Strategies and Second-Hand Consumption: This theme highlights the transformative impact of digital clienteling and second-hand consumption on the fashion industry.

Collaborative Consumption and Changing Fashion Paradigms: Exploring collaborative consumption's digital antecedents and the rise of access-oriented practices, this theme showcases the transformative potential of technology and the access economy in fashion.

Table 48.7 CO-citation (cited- reference)

Cluster	Reference	Themes
Red	• dhir a., sadiq m., talwar s., sakashita m., kaur p., why do retail consumers buy green apparel? a knowledge-attitude-behaviour-context perspective, journal of retailing and consumer services, 59, (2021) fletcher k., • sustainable fashion and textiles: design journeys, (2008) • han j., seo y., ko e., staging luxury experiences for understanding sustainable fashion consumption: a balance theory application, journal of business research, 74, pp. 162-167, (2017) henninger c.e., alevizou p.j., goworek h., ryding d., sustainability in fashion: a cradle to upcycle approach, (2017) joergens c., ethical fashion: myth or future trend?, journal of fashion marketing and management: an • international journal, 10, 3, pp. 360-371, (2006) • lundblad l., davies i.a., the values and motivations behind sustainable fashion consumption, journal of consumer behaviour, 15, 2, pp. 149-162, (2016) richins m.l., dawson s., a consumer	"Sustainable Fashion Consumption: Unveiling Motivations, Values, and Environmental Impact" In the contemporary landscape of fashion, the integrated theme "Sustainable Fashion Consumption: Unveiling Motivations, Values, and Environmental Impact" delves into the intricate relationships between consumer behavior, ethical considerations, psychological dimensions, and the environmental implications of sustainable fashion choices. Through an exploration of references that span diverse aspects of this theme, this integrated perspective uncovers the multifaceted drivers behind eco-conscious consumer behavior, unveiling the motivations rooted in knowledge, attitude, and values that guide the purchase intentions of green apparel. From ethical fashion myths to luxury experiences, this theme navigates the journey of sustainable fashion, from design journeys and value orientation to upcycling approaches. By
Green	• ajzen i., fishbein m., understanding attitudes and predicting social behaviour, (1980) harris f., roby h., dibb s., sustainable clothing: challenges, barriers and interventions for encouraging more sustainable consumer behaviour, international journal of consumer studies, 40, 3, pp. 309-318, (2016) • henseler j., ringle c.m., sarstedt m., a new criterion for assessing discriminant validity in variance-based structural equation modelling, journal of the academy of marketing science, 43, 1, pp. 115-135, (2015) kline r.b., principles and practice of structural equation modeling, (2011) • kumar b., manrai a.k., manrai l.a., purchasing behaviour for environmentally sustainable products: a conceptual framework and empirical study, journal of retailing and consumer services, 34, pp. 1-9, (2017) podsakoff p.m., mackenzie s.b., lee j.y., podsakoff n.p., common method biases in behavioral research: a critical review of the literature and recommended remedies, journal of applied psychology, 88, 5, pp. 879-903, (2003) • yang s., song y., tong s., sustainable retailing in the fashion industry: a systematic literature review, sustainability, 9, 7, (2017)	Spanning disciplines of ps marketing, and sustainability, the Ajzen and Fishbein, Harris et al., H al., Kline, Kumar et al., Podsakoff Yang et al. converge to illum dynamics of understanding predicting social behavior, and sustainable choices. The theme u crux of structural equation model powerful tool for unraveling these i aligning authors' contributions principles of consumer studies, reta psychological research. In expl challenges, interventions, and b; sustainable clothing, the theme bridg between empirical studies and literature reviews. Through this sy conceptual framework emerg encapsulates purchasing beha; environmentally sustainable prod applying recommended remedies t biases, the theme enhances the reli behavioral research, providing foundation for comprehending an consumer actions. Moreover, a : literature review in sustainable further solidifies the framework, fc sustainable future for the fashion This integrated perspective serv compass, guiding scholars and pr; alike through the rich landscape of s consumer behavior, methodological the collective wisdom of influential a
Dark Blue	• ajzen i., fishbein m., understanding attitudes and predicting social behavior, (1980) bianchi c., birtwistle g., sell, give away, or donate: an exploratory study of fashion clothing disposal behavior in two countries, int. rev. retail distrib. consum. res., 20, 3, pp. 353-368, • (2010) botsman r., rogers r., what's mine is yours: the rise of collaborative	this integrated theme delves into th; tapestry of sustainable fashion con Authors' works, including Aj; Fishbein's foundational understar attitudes, interlace with con; explorations by Bianchi and I shedding light on disposal l collaborative consumption, ; transformational potential. Jung and

consumption, (2010) jung s., jin b., sustainable development of slow fashion businesses: customer value approach, sustainability, 8, 6, pp. 1-15, (2016)

of customer value steers us to sustainable development of slow businesses. The theme interweaves t collaborative consumption as her Botsman and Rogers, while Lund Davies' insights into values and moti

- lundblad l., davies i.a., the values and motivations behind sustainable fashion consumption, j. consum. behav., 15, 2, pp. 149-162, (2016) niinimaki k., eco-clothing, consumer identity and ideology, sustain. dev., 18, 3, pp. 150-162, (2010) zamani b., sandin g., peters g.m., life cycle assessment of clothing libraries: can collaborative consumption reduce the environmental impact of fast fashion?, j. clean. prod., 162, pp. 1368-1375, (2017)

weave an ethical narrative. Niinimaki's exploration of consumer identity and ideology seamlessly connects with eco-clothing choices, embracing fashion as a canvas for self-expression. Ultimately, Zamani, Sandin, and Peters' perspective on collaborative consumption's impact on environmental sustainability adds a harmonious note, guiding us toward a future where shared resources redefine fast fashion's footprint. Amid these interconnected insights, the integrated theme envisions a sustainable fashion journey, where consumer choices and societal attitudes cocreate a tapestry of conscious consumerism, propelling the fashion industry toward ethical transformation.

Integrated Theme: "Unveiling Consumer Motivations and Sustainable Fashion: Insights from Authors' Co-Citation Analysis"

Within the realm of sustainable fashion, this integrated theme unravels the intricate interplay of consumer motivations, empathies, and behaviors. Cowan and Kinley's exploration of consumer empathies for green apparel intertwines with Khare and Varshneya's investigation into antecedents for organic cotton clothing purchase behavior among Indian youth. Moser's perspective on pro-environmental purchasing behavior resonates, as it dives into the drivers behind eco-conscious choices. Furthermore, McNeill and Moore's study on sustainable fashion consumption navigates the complex fast fashion conundrum and its effects on consumer attitudes toward sustainability in clothing choices. Shen, Richards, and Liu contribute insights into consumers' awareness of sustainable fashion, underscoring the role of informed choices in reshaping the industry.

Defining Sustainable Fashion: Henninger, Alevizou, and Oates' exploration of sustainable fashion's essence underscores the foundational understanding of this evolving concept, acting as a compass guiding the investigations. The theme resonates with Tian, Bearden, and Hunter's work on consumers' need for uniqueness, which sheds light on individualistic motivations influencing fashion choices.

Yellow

- cowan k., kinley t., green spirit: consumer empathies for green apparel, international journal of consumer studies, 38, 5, pp. 493-499, (2014) henninger c.e., alevizou p.j., oates c.j., what is sustainable fashion?, journal of fashion marketing and management: an international journal, 20, 4, pp. 400-416, (2016) khare a., varshneya g., antecedents to organic cotton clothing purchase behaviour: study on indian youth, journal of fashion marketing and management: an international journal, 21, 1, pp. 51-69, (2017)
- mcneill l., moore r., sustainable fashion consumption and the fast fashion conundrum: fashionable consumers and attitudes to sustainability in clothing choice, international journal of consumer studies, 39, 3, pp. 212-222, (2015) moser a.k., thinking green, buying green? drivers of pro-environmental purchasing behavior, journal of consumer marketing, 32, 3, pp. 167-175, (2015) shen g., richards j., liu f., consumers' awareness of sustainable fashion, marketing management journal, 6, 9, pp. 134-147, (2013)
- tian k.t., bearden w.o., hunter g.l., consumers' need for uniqueness: scale development and validation, journal of consumer research, 28, 1, pp. 50-66, (2001)

Purple

- ajzen i., the theory of planned behavior, organizational behavior and human decision processes, 50, 2, pp. 179-211, (1991) fornell c., larcker d.f., evaluating structural equation models with unobservable variables and measurement error, journal of marketing research, 18, 1, pp. 39-50, (1981) khare a., sadachar a., green apparel buying behaviour: a study on indian youth, international journal of consumer studies, 41, 5, pp. 558-569,

"Empowering Sustainable Fashion Choices: Insights from Authors' Co-Citation Analysis"

This integrated theme encapsulates the collective insights emerging from the cocitation analysis of influential authors, offering a comprehensive understanding of consumer behavior in the realm of sustainable fashion. Ajzen's pivotal "Theory of Planned Behavior" serves as a cornerstone, providing a

(2017) manchiraju s., sadachar a., personal values and ethical fashion consumption, journal of fashion marketing and management, 18, 3, pp. 357-374, (2014) paul j., modi a., patel j., predicting green product consumption using theory of planned behavior and reasoned action, journal of retailing and consumer services, 29, pp. 123134, (2016)

framework to comprehend how attitudes, subjective norms, and perceived behavioral control intersect in shaping individuals' intentions. Building on this foundation, Fornell and Larcker's work emphasizes the evaluation of structural equation models, fortifying the methodological rigor required to decode the complexities of unobservable variables and measurement errors.

Youthful Perspectives on Sustainable Fashion: Khare and Sadachar's study delving into green apparel buying behavior among Indian youth adds a dynamic layer, uncovering the motivations and preferences of this pivotal consumer segment. Manchiraju and Sadachar further explore the influence of personal values on ethical fashion consumption, shedding light on the ethical dimensions intertwined with consumer choices.

Behavioral Predictors of Green Consumption: Paul, Modi, and Patel's research introduces the application of the Theory of Planned Behavior and reasoned action in predicting green product consumption, connecting theoretical foundations to actionable insights. This theme resonates with the overarching theme of empowering sustainable fashion choices, where theoretical constructs come to life in real-world behavior.

Synthesis and Future Pathways: As these threads interweave, a holistic narrative emerges, portraying a synergy between theoretical frameworks, consumer values, and real-world behaviors. The integrated theme envisions an empowered future where the Theory of Planned Behavior and its extensions serve as guiding lights, navigating consumer decisions within the complex landscape of sustainable fashion. By understanding the interplay of attitudes, norms, control, values, and intentions, this theme offers a roadmap for scholars, practitioners, and individuals to drive positive change within the realm of fashion, steering it towards a more sustainable and ethical future.

Light
Blue

barnes s., mattsson j., understanding collaborative consumption: test of a theoretical model, technological forecasting and social change, 118, pp. 281-292, (2017) belk r., you are what you can access: sharing and collaborative consumption online, journal of business research, 67, 8, pp. 1595-1600, (2014) mohlmann m., collaborative consumption: determinants of satisfaction and the likelihood of using a sharing economy option again, journal of consumer behaviour, 14, 3, pp. 193-207, (2015) piscicelli l., cooper t., fisher t., the role of values in collaborative consumption: insights from a productservice system for lending and borrowing in the uk, journal of cleaner production, 97, pp. 21-29, (2015)

Collaborative Consumption Unveiled: Values, Satisfaction, and Sustainable Practices"

Through the lens of co-occurrence analysis, this integrated theme unravels the intricate dynamics of collaborative consumption, revealing the tapestry of values, satisfaction, and sustainable practices that intertwine within this evolving paradigm. Barnes and Mattsson's theoretical model forms the core, dissecting the underpinnings of collaborative consumption, while Belk's exploration of "you are what you can access" underscores the transformative potential of sharing and collaborative consumption within the digital realm.

Satisfaction, Determinants, and Recurrence: Mohlmann's lens on the determinants of satisfaction and the likelihood of reusing sharing economy options sheds light on the intricate factors shaping consumer attitudes and behavior within collaborative consumption. Piscicelli, Cooper, and Fisher's insights into the role of values in collaborative consumption align, offering a deeper understanding of the values that drive individuals towards sustainable lending and borrowing practices.

A Sustainable Consumer Ecosystem: As these threads intertwine, the integrated theme envisions collaborative consumption as a catalyst for sustainable practices, where shared values and satisfaction act as pivotal drivers. This framework paves the way for a future where collaborative consumption thrives as a sustainable and ethical consumer ecosystem, fostering responsible sharing,

resource optimization, and reduced environmental impact.

Synthesis and Transformation: Synthesizing the interplay of values, satisfaction, determinants, and sustainable practices, this theme serves as a blueprint for individuals, businesses, and policymakers alike. By embracing collaborative consumption, replete with values and satisfaction, society can navigate towards a more equitable, resourceconscious, and sustainable future. The integrated theme resonates with the collective endeavor to reshape consumer behavior and consumption patterns, fostering a world where shared values create a foundation for conscious choices and enduring sustainability.

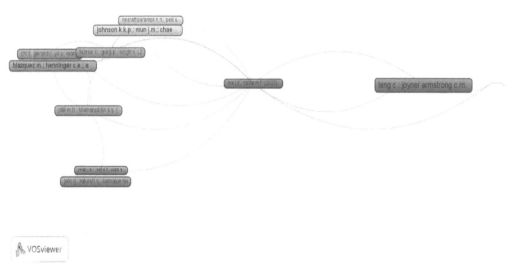

Figure 48.5 Bibliometric coupling of documents

Future Research Directions

Future research directions in the realm of consumer behavior and sustainable fashion are as follow:

Longitudinal Studies: Researchers can explore how sustained conscious choices and behaviors influence consumer attitudes, brand loyalty, and overall industry practices over extended periods.

Cultural Contexts: Researchers can compare and contrast consumer behaviors and motivations across different cultures, regions, and economic contexts to identify commonalities and unique trends.

Multi-dimensional Influences: Investigating demographic variables (age, gender, income), personal values, social influence, and psychological traits, can provide a holistic understanding of how these elements interact to drive sustainable fashion consumption.

Table 48.8 Bibliometric coupling of documents

Cluster	Document	Themes
Red	• diddi s.; yan r.-n.; bloodhart b.; bajtelsmit v.; mcshane k. (2019) kong h.m.; ko e.; chae h.; mattila p. (2016) lang c.; joyner armstrong c.m. (2018) legere a.; kang j. (2020) • • lira j.s.; costa m.f. (2022) • mcneill l.s.; hamlin r.p.; mcqueen r.h.; degenstein l.; wakes s.; garrett t.c.; dunn l. (2020)	**"Shaping Sustainable Consumer Behavior: A Tapestry of Slow and Conscious Fashion Consumption"**

Within the realm of sustainable fashion, this integrated theme weaves a narrative that encompasses the intricate threads of sustainable consumer behavior. Authors Legere and Kang explore the role of self-concept in shaping sustainable consumption through the lens of slow fashion. Lira and Costa delve into conscious consumption intentions within the context of slow fashion, employing the Theory of Planned Behavior and ethical considerations. Diddi, Yan, Bloodhart, Bajtelsmit, and McShane's exploration of the intentionbehavior gap from a Behavioral Reasoning Theory perspective resonates with the theme, bridging the gap between sustainable clothing intention and behavior.

Collaborative Consumption and Fashion Leadership: Lang and Joyner Armstrong contribute a pivotal strand, shedding light on the adoption of clothing renting and swapping. Their investigation into collaborative consumption is enriched by the influence of fashion leadership, need for uniqueness, and materialism, weaving a tapestry of motivations that influence sustainable fashion choices.

Sustainable Knowledge and Garment Life Extension: Kong, Ko, Chae, and Mattila contribute insights into understanding fashion consumers' attitudes and behavioral intentions toward sustainable fashion products. Their focus on sustainable knowledge sources and knowledge types underscores the importance of informed choices within sustainable fashion.

Garment Life Extension and Disposal: McNeill, Hamlin, McQueen, Degenstein, Wakes, Garrett, and Dunn's exploration of garment life extension practices and the factors influencing textile disposal weaves an essential layer, highlighting the behavioral intentions towards extending the life of garments and the role of brand, cost, and damage.

Synthesis of Sustainable Fashion: As these themes interlace, a holistic narrative emerges that encapsulates various dimensions of sustainable fashion, ranging from self-concept and intention to behavior, collaborative consumption, knowledge sources, and garment life extension. This integrated theme envisions a future where sustainable consumer behavior weaves a fabric of conscious choices, ethical considerations, and collaborative efforts that extend the lifespan of garments, mitigating waste and fostering a responsible fashion ecosystem.

Green	• blazquez m.; henninger c.e.; alexander b.; franquesa c. (2020) campos p.o.; lima a.a.l.s.; costa c.s.r.; costa m.f. (2023) chi t.; gerard j.; yu y.; wang y. (2021) jalil m.h.; shaharuddin s.s. (2019) kumar n.; garg p.; singh s. (2022)	"Sustainable Fashion Intentions: A Multifaceted Exploration through Diverse Perspectives"

Within the dynamic realm of sustainable fashion, this integrated theme weaves a comprehensive narrative by drawing insights from diverse perspectives. From the influence of voluntary simplicity and environmental activism on purchase intentions, as explored by Campos, Lima, Costa, and Costa, to Chi, Gerard, Yu, and Wang's analysis of key determinants driving U.S. consumers towards slow fashion apparel, a rich tapestry of consumer intentions emerges.

Eco-Fashion Consciousness and Reduction of Waste: The research by Jalil and Shaharuddin delves into consumer behaviors aligning with eco-fashion trends, emphasizing the trend's pivotal role in reducing clothing waste and fostering a more responsible fashion ecosystem.

Augmented Pathways to Sustainable Choices: Kumar, Garg, and Singh's augmentation of the theory of planned behavior, incorporating perceived consumer effectiveness and environmental concern, offers a nuanced understanding of pro-environmental purchase intentions and underscores the evolving factors shaping sustainable apparel choices.

Cultural and Regional Perspectives on Sustainability: Blazquez, Henninger, Alexander, and Franquesa's study enriches the theme by providing insights into consumers' knowledge and intentions towards sustainability from a Spanish fashion perspective, spotlighting the regional nuances that influence sustainable fashion behaviors.

Synthesis of Sustainable Fashion Intentions: This integrated theme synthesizes these diverse perspectives into a holistic narrative, envisioning a future where multifaceted consumer intentions converge towards a sustainable fashion landscape. By exploring the confluence of values, activism, awareness, and augmented theories, this theme captures the essence of conscious consumerism, underpinning a fashion industry that resonates with ecological responsibility and global ethical imperatives.

Blue	• jain g.; rakesh s.; kamalun nabi m.; chaturvedi k.r. (2018) yeap j.a.l.; ooi s.k.; yapp e.h.t.; ramesh n. (2022)	"Reshaping Sustainable Fashion: Exploring Digital Strategies and Second-Hand Consumption"

This integrated theme delves into the transformative landscape of sustainable fashion, guided by the insights extracted from bibliographic coupling analysis. The works of Jain, Rakesh, Kamalun Nabi, and Chaturvedi underscore the significance of hyper-personalization through digital clienteling in fostering fashion sustainability. This digital strategy serves as a cornerstone in redefining the fashion industry, aligning consumer preferences with eco-conscious choices.

Empowering Second-Hand Consumption: Yeap, Ooi,

Yapp, and Ramesh's investigation of predispositions towards second-hand clothing purchases on C2C platforms sheds light on the resurgence of preloved fashion. This inquiry not only elevates the ethos of sustainable consumption but also explores the evolving paradigm of circular fashion, where preloved items find new homes and appreciation.

Synthesis of Reshaping Fashion: This integrated theme weaves a narrative that envisions a sustainable fashion landscape shaped by digital strategies and renewed perceptions of second-hand consumption. By fusing technology-driven hyper-personalization with the allure of preloved items on C2C platforms, this theme captures the essence of fashion's transformative journey, where ecological consciousness and modernity harmonize. As these insights converge, the integrated theme paints a portrait of a fashion industry poised for innovation, where digital prowess and circular principles

converge, fostering a more sustainable and ethical fashion paradigm.

| Yellow | • johnson k.k.p.; mun j.m.; chae y. (2016)
• neerattiparambil n.n.; belli s.m. (2020) | "Collaborative Consumption and Changing Fashion Paradigms: Insights from Bibliographic Coupling Analysis" |

This integrated theme delves into the transformative landscape of fashion consumption, driven by the insights extracted from bibliographic coupling analysis. The work of Johnson, Mun, and Chae dissects the antecedents that drive internet use for collaborative apparel consumption, underscoring the digital underpinnings reshaping the industry. This exploration aligns with Neerattiparambil and Belli's study on the motivations behind renting fashion clothing products, shedding light on the paradigm shift towards access over ownership.

Digital Transformation of Fashion Consumption: Johnson, Mun, and Chae's research on antecedents to internet use for collaborative apparel consumption showcases the pivotal role of technology in fostering shared fashion experiences. This exploration aligns with the evolving consumer behaviors that prioritize collaborative consumption over traditional ownership.

The Rise of Access Economy in Fashion: Neerattiparambil and Belli's study on renting intention for fashion clothing products highlights the emergence of the access economy within the fashion realm. This theme resonates with the broader shift towards sustainable and conscious consumption practices.

Synthesis of Collaborative Consumption: As these insights coalesce, a narrative emerges that envisions a fashion landscape redefined by collaborative consumption and access-oriented practices. The integration of digital platforms and the preference for renting over owning reshape the industry's foundations. This integrated theme captures the essence of a dynamic and sustainable fashion future, one where technological advancements harmonize with conscious consumer choices, forging a path towards a more responsible and ethical fashion ecosystem.

Digital Platforms and Influence: Scholars can Further explore the intersection of digital strategies and sustainable fashion consumption and the role of emerging technologies such as blockchain and augmented reality.

Behavioral Interventions: Designing and testing innovative behavioral interventions based on psychological theories can effectively bridge the intention-behavior gap.

Supply Chain Transparency: Investigating the impact of supply chain transparency on consumer behavior can reveal how access to information about a product's journey influences purchase decisions.

Circular Economy Practices: Scholars can examine innovative strategies for circular fashion that extend beyond second-hand consumption.

Micro and Macro Perspectives: Balancing micro-level studies (individual consumer behavior) with macro-level analyses (industry trends, policy implications) is vital for a comprehensive understanding.

Conclusion

The analysis of scholarly productivity within the realm of consumer behavioral intentions and sustainable fashion from 2016 to 2023 offers a vivid depiction of the field's dynamic evolution.

This interconnectedness highlights pivotal years, with 2018 and 2019 standing out as periods of particularly impactful research. Moreover, the resurgence of interest in 2022 signifies the field's continuous development. The declining average citations in more recent years don't diminish the significance of these studies but rather underscore the ongoing evolution of the relationship between sustainable fashion and consumer behavior.

Notably, the consistent relevance of seminal works like Blazquez et al. [24], and Kumar et al. [27] underscores their pivotal contributions to the ongoing advancement of this field.

References

[1] Anguelov, N. (2021). The sustainable fashion quest: innovations in business and policy. CRC Press.

[2] Mehrjoo, M. and Pasek, Z. J. (2016). Risk assessment for the supply chain of fast fashion apparel industry: a system dynamics framework. *International Journal of Production Research*, 54(1), 28–48. https://doi.org/10.1080/00207543.2014.997405

[3] McNeill, L. and Moore, R. (2015). Sustainable fashion consumption and the fast fashion conundrum: fashionable consumers and attitudes to sustainability in clothing choice. *International Journal Of Consumer Studies*, 39(3), 212–222. https://doi.org/10.1111/ijcs.12169.

[4] Cavender, R. C. and Lee, M. Y. (2018). Exploring the influence of sustainability knowledge and orientation to slow consumption on fashion leaders' drivers of fast fashion avoidance. *American Journal of Theoretical and Applied Business*, 4(3), 90–101. /doi : 10.11648/j.ajtab.20180403.12.

[5] Bick, R., Halsey, E., and Ekenga, C. C. (2018). The global environmental injustice of fast fashion. Environmental Health, 17, 14.

[6] Chi, T. and Zheng, Y. (2016). Understanding environmentally friendly apparel consumption: An empirical study of Chinese consumers. *International Journal of Sustainable Society*, 8(3), 206–227. https://doi.org/10.1504/IJSSOC.2016.079080.

[7] Nam, C., Dong, H., and Lee, Y. A. (2017). Factors influencing consumers' purchase intention of green sportswear. *Fashion and Textiles*, 4(1), 1–17.

[8] Yoo, J. J., Divita, L., and Kim, H. Y. (2018). Predicting consumer intention to purchase clothing products made from sustainable fabrics. *Clothing Cultures*, 5(2), 211–224. https://doi.org/10.1386/cc.5.2.211_1.

[9] Lewis, T. L., Park, H., Netravali, A. N., and Trejo, H. X. (2017). Closing the loop: A scalable zero-waste model for apparel reuse and recycling. *International Journal of Fashion Design, Technology and Education*, 10(3), 353–362. https://doi.org/10.1080/17543266.2016.1263364.

[10] Park, J. and Ha, S. (2014). Understanding consumer recycling behavior: Combining the theory of planned behavior and the norm activation model. Family and consumer sciences research journal, 42(3), 278–291. https://doi.org/10.1111/fcsr.12061.

[11] Park, M., Cho, H., Johnson, K. K., and Yurchisin, J. (2017). Use of behavioral reasoning theory to examine the role of social responsibility in attitudes toward apparel donation. International journal of consumer studies, 41(3), 333–339. https://doi.org/10.1111/ijcs.12347.

[12] Sandin, G. and Peters, G. M. (2018). Environmental impact of textile reuse and recycling–A review. *Journal of Cleaner Production*, 184, 353–365. https://doi.org/10.1016/j.jclepro.2018.02.266.

[13] Mariadoss, B. J., Chi, T., Tansuhaj, P., and Pomirleanu, N. (2016). Influences of firm orientations on sustainable supply chain management. *Journal of Business Research*, 69(9), 3406–3414. https://doi.org/10.1016/j.jbusres.2016.02.003.

[14] White, C. L., Nielsen, A. E., and Valentini, C. (2017). CSR research in the apparel industry: A quantitative and qualitative review of existing literature. *Corporate Social Responsibility and Environmental Management*, 24(5), 382–394. https://doi.org/10.1002/csr.1413.

[15] Chang, H. J., & Watchravesringkan, K. T. (2018). Who are sustainably minded apparel shoppers? An investigation to the influencing factors of sustainable apparel consumption. *International Journal of Retail & Distribution Management*, 46(2), 148–162. https://doi.org/10.1108/IJRDM-10-2016-0176.

[16] Kim, H. S. and Damhorst, M. L. (1998). Environmental concern and apparel consumption. Clothing and Textiles Research Journal, 16(3), 126–133.

[17] Mohr, L. A., Webb, D. J., and Harris, K. E. (2001). Do consumers expect companies to be socially responsible? The impact of corporate social responsibility on buying behavior. *Journal of Consumer Affairs*, 35(1), 45–72. https://doi.org/10.1111/j.17456606.2001.tb00102.x.

[18] Ahn, J. M., Koo, D. M., and Chang, H. S. (2012). Different impacts of normative influences on pro-environmental purchasing behavior explained by differences in individual characteristics. *Journal of Global Scholars of Marketing Science*, 22(2), 163182. https://doi.org/10.1080/12297119.2012.655098.

[19] Hirscher, A. L., Niinimäki, K., & Armstrong, C. M. J. (2018). Social manufacturing in the fashion sector: New value creation through alternative design strategies? Journal of Cleaner Production, 172, 4544–4554. https://doi.org/10.1016/j.jclepro.2017.11.020.

[20] Zamani, B., Sandin, G. and Peters, G. M. (2017). Life cycle assessment of clothing libraries: can collaborative consumption reduce the environmental impact of fast fashion?. Journal of cleaner production, 162, 1368–1375.

[21] Kim, A. J. and Ko, E. (2012). Do social media marketing activities enhance customer equity? An empirical study of luxury fashion brand. *Journal of Business Research*, 65(10), 1480–1486.https://doi.org/10.1016/j.jbusres.2011.10.014.

[22] Van Eck, N. and Waltman, L. (2010). Software survey: VOSviewer, a computer program for bibliometric mapping. *Scientometrics*, 84(2), 523–538.

[23] Hall, C. M. (2011). Publish and perish? Bibliometric analysis, journal ranking and the assessment of research quality in tourism. *Tourism Management*, 32(1), 16–27.

[24] Leung, D., Law, R., Van Hoof, H., and Buhalis, D. (2013). Social media in tourism and hospitality: A literature review. *Journal of Travel & Tourism Marketing*, 30(1-2), 3–22.

[25] Law, E. L. C., Roto, V., Hassenzahl, M., Vermeeren, A. P., and Kort, J. (2009, April). Understanding, scoping and defining user experience: a survey approach. In Proceedings of the SIGCHI conference on human factors in computing systems (pp. 719728). https://doi.org/10.1145/1518701.1518813.

[26] Blazquez, M., Henninger, C. E., Alexander, B., and Franquesa, C. (2020). Consumers' knowledge and intentions towards sustainability: A Spanish fashion perspective. *Fashion Practice*, 12(1), 34–54. https://doi.org/10.1080/17569370.2019.1669326.

[27] Lang, C. and Armstrong, C. M. J. (2018). Collaborative consumption: The influence of fashion leadership, need for uniqueness, and materialism on female consumers' adoption of clothing renting and swapping. *Sustainable Production and Consumption*, 13, 37–47. https://doi.org/10.1016/j.spc.2017.11.005.

[28] Legere, A. and Kang, J. (2020). The role of self-concept in shaping sustainable consumption: A model of slow fashion. *Journal of Cleaner Production*, 258, 120699. https://doi.org/10.1016/j.jclepro.2020.120699.

[29] Pandey, A. K., Gupta, R., and Singh, A. (2020). Traditional remedies and COVID-19: A qualitative exploration of indigenous resources. *Plant Archives*, 20(S1), 2066–2069.

[30] Kumar, N., Garg, P., and Singh, S. (2022). Pro-environmental purchase intention towards eco-friendly apparel: Augmenting the theory of planned behavior with perceived consumer effectiveness and environmental concern. *Journal of Global Fashion Marketing*, 13(2), 134–150. https://doi.org/10.1080/20932685.2021.2016062.

49 Language redundancy, information entropy, and cost efficiency in digital communication

Amrita Pratap[1,a], Vijit Chaturvedi[2,b], R. Pratap[3,c] and Amit Kumar Pandey[4,d]

[1]Research Scholar Amity Business School, Amity University, Noida, Uttar Pradesh, India, Noida, Uttar Pradesh, India

[2]Professor, Amity Business School, Amity University, Noida, Uttar Pradesh, India

[3]Indira Gandhi National Open University, New Delhi, India

[4]Associate Professor, Amity Business School, Amity University, Noida, Uttar Pradesh, India

Abstract

The economics of digital communication heavily relies on file compression, which is influenced by two critical factors: language redundancy and effective communication. Language redundancy refers to the inherent property of a language, determined by the information entropy and its maximum value. Effective communication depends on the communicator's skill and knowledge to minimize superfluous information. This paper presents a novel model for estimating language redundancy in English and discusses the significance of avoiding the use of superfluous information. Our model yields information entropy 0.895 bit per letter, with a maximum value of 2.37 and a corresponding language redundancy of 62.3%, which indicates that a data file can be compressed to 62.3% of its original size. This value is comparable to the lossless compression given by WAV and ZIP file formats. Further, in contrast to Shannon's methods, our model does not require test samples of English text, nor does it suffer from the variability in human subjects.

Keywords: File compression, language redundancy, information introduction, cost efficiency, digital communication

Introduction

Digital communication has been gaining rapid momentum ever since it started and is now virtually a lifeline of corporate communication which happens most often in English language. Corporate leaders crucially depend on digital communication (online and offline) for close and continued interaction with their teams, investors and other stakeholders scattered geographically across the globe.

Software tools that effectuate data compression utilize language redundancy, an inherent property of the language in question. When a system functions with a set of rules and constraints, it is more orderly, and more organized and thus its behavior is more predictable. Curiously so, the systemic format, syntactic structure and grammatical rules of the English language build language redundancy that lends support to predict or guess the missing or illegible part of the printed text and the interrupted segments of verbal communication even in a noisy background. Language redundancy is leveraged for the compression of a data file, which can be done by a trained software. How much information in terms of bits is contained in a letter of English alphabet, and how large the redundancy in the English language is, was studied and explained by Claude E. Shannon [1] who first coined and defined the terms 'information entropy' and 'language redundancy,' and formulated the equations to determine their values as a function of probability.

Conceptual Development of Information Entropy

To gain an understanding of how classical concept of thermodynamic entropy was expanded to the field of digital communication, one needs to know how entropy, probability and information are interrelated. We walk through these terms and get to understand them qualitatively without going into the mathematical details here. If the entropy of a system of a particular configuration, and the probability of the system to assume that configuration is related to each other, and if the probability of the configuration as referred to and the informational value attached to it is related to each other, then by simple logic, entropy and information must also be interconnected [2, 3].

The term "entropy" was originally introduced by Rudolph Clausius in his work on the second law of thermodynamics [4, 5]. Thermodynamic entropy is a measure of the amount of thermal energy in a thermodynamic system that is unavailable for doing useful work. The change in entropy of a system can be calculated as the

[a]amritapratap11@gmail.com, [b]vchaturvedi@amity.edu, [c]profpratap44@gmail.com, [d]akpandey7@amity.edu

DOI: 10.1201/9781003534136-49

change in the heat content of the system divided by its absolute temperature at which the work is being done on or by the system.

In the years to follow, Ludwig Boltzmann [6] gave the following entropy equation:

$$S = K(B) \log W(E) \tag{1}$$

where S is the entropy, K (B) is the Boltzmann constant, and W is the number of all possible configurations (microstates) or arrangements across which all the constituents (molecules) could be distributed in different ways under the condition where all the configurations are equally probable and are consistent with the observable macro-state of the system having total energy content E.

J.W. Gibbs later generalized Boltzmann's idea, and characterized different configurations (micro-states) with varying probabilities [7, 8]. The reformulated Boltzmann equation is:

$$S = - K(B) \text{ Sum } (i = 1 \text{ to } n) (pi \log pi) \tag{2}$$

where the summation is done over all the configurations / microstates, pi is the probability of configuration 'i', and K (B) is the Boltzmann constant. Janes [7] says, "Disorder is a manifestation of the largeness of the number of microstates the system can have. The larger the choice of microstates, the lesser the predictability or level of order in a system." To put it in other way, the lesser the certainty in defining the parameters of a system, more is the disorderliness is present in the system.

The idea of entropy was further expanded to digital communication. Claude Shannon's groundbreaking work on information theory, published in 1948 ("A Mathematical Theory of Communication") [9] and expanded upon in 1951 ("Prediction and Entropy of Printed English") [10].

When the language is translated into binary digits for storing, and transmitting over a channel, the information entropy is expressed in bits per letter / character which implies how many bits are required to store a letter or how much information in terms of bits is generated by a letter or any other character. The transmission of a message over the channel is given in bits per second, called bit rate. Shannon presented information entropy H (X) of a discrete variable X (letter or character) as a function of probability given in the following formula:

$$H(X) = - \text{Sum } (i = 1 \text{ to } n) \, pi \log (\text{base } 2) \text{ of } (pi) \tag{3}$$

where the sum is taken over all letters (i = 1 to n); the logarithmic base is 2 and the unit of information entropy is bits per letter or character, and pi is the probability of a letter or character 'i' appearing in the string of letters/characters. The information entropy of an English letter refers to an average amount of information (minimum number of bits) that one can obtain from the letter in the context of a language model, or the minimum number of bits required to represent a letter/ variable.

Shannon's formula for language- redundancy (R) is:

$$R = 1 - H(X)/H(X)(max) \tag{4}$$

where H (X) (max) is the maximum value of the entropy associated with a variable/letter when all variables/letters are equiprobable or have uniform probability distribution in the respective probability space.

One way to assess information entropy qualitatively is by looking at the frequency of letters or words in a text. A text message with high degree of randomness/irregularity in its word- distribution will have higher entropy, while a text with low degree of randomness or less irregularity of its word-distribution will have lower entropy. Kwiatkowski [11] says, 'entropy is a measure of uncertainty or randomness in a system. High entropy means high uncertainty.' The collapse of Lehman Brothers' Holdings Inc- onetime the largest investment bank- in 2008 was not at all expected, still it happened and triggered a global financial crisis that had a major impact on the world economy.

Burton and Licklider [12] examined the statistical structure of printed English with a focus on long-range constraints: how the constraints influence the organization of words and sentences, and how they can be used to predict the probability of certain words or phrases occurring in each text.

Present Model and Approach

Our model encompasses all the 26 letters of the English alphabet. It does not differentiate between upper and lower case, and does not include characters such as punctuation marks, or other symbols that are inactive or have limited value in auditory communication (voice or videos). However, these characters have a guessable pattern of repetition in a written text, hence it easier to encode and decode them.

The model focuses on the composition of an average English word and examines the relative frequency counts of vowels and consonants present in the word to estimate the value of information entropy. Knowing the relative frequency counts, we apply Shannon's formula (Equation 3) to estimate information entropy, representing a departure from Shannon's original approach.

Another departure from Shannon's method comes in the estimation of maximum value of information entropy which appears in Shannon's language redundancy formula (Equation 4). This poses a challenge since the letters in a word belong to two distinct subgroups (vowels and consonants) of English alphabet, having different population, hence cannot be treated alike for equal probability distribution. We, therefore, treat the letter space and probability space of each subgroup separately, and then apply equiprobable condition independently.

Having obtained the probabilities as discussed earlier, Shannon's formulae are applied to calculate the values of information entropy and language redundancy which could also be termed as entropic- language - redundancy because it depends on information entropy of printed English text (Appendix B). The model yields the value of information entropy 0.895 bit per letter and language redundancy of 62.3%, based on an average word length of 6.455 letters. When the mean value of 6 letters with two vowels and four consonants for a word-length is used in the calculation, the information entropy and language redundancy change slightly to 0.916 bit per letter and 61.1% respectively. As the model does not depend on human variability which accounts for the cognition and speech characteristics, the model provides the least -biased estimate of information entropy and language redundancy both for written and spoken English.

Results and Discussion

In the following subsections, we will discuss our results and compare them with the findings of other authors as well as other compression algorithms.

Shannon's theoretical and experimental approach

Shannon used N-gram language model [Appendix A] for the estimation of information entropy of the English language, which estimates the frequency of occurrence of Nth letter in relation to the occurrences of previous N-1 letters. As N increases to letter 3 -gram, the value of information entropy approximates to 3.3 bits per letter. Shannon also calculated the frequency counts of each word of a corpus of over 8000 words, and obtained the weighted average of information entropy 11.82 bits per word. With the average word length of 4.5 letters he used, the entropy per letter turns out 2.62 bits, and the corresponding language redundancy 44.3%. From an experimental study [Appendix A] on human subject, with average good knowledge of English, based on guessing letters/words in the sentences of different paragraphs of English texts, Shannon found that the subject made 69% correct guesses, and 31% incorrect guesses. This would mean that by having to know only 31 percent of the information, the human subject could still get right understanding of the whole lot of the original text, indicating, therefore, 69% language redundancy; the reverse calculation using Shannon's redundancy formula yields information entropy 1.45 bits per letter. What is observable from the results of different procedures Shannon adopted is that the information entropy value varied from 1.45 bits to 3.3 bits per letter. Further, when the string of characters increased from 8 to over 100, the statistical fluctuation ceased and entropy reduced to the order of 1 bit per character, and redundancy rose to 78.7%.

The analysis with our model yields information entropy 0.895 to 0.916 bit per letter and the corresponding redundancy 62.3 to 61.1%. Thus, the information entropy obtained from our model approximates to 1 bit per letter and is understood to be free from statistical- fluctuation because it matches closely with Shannon's result for the long chain of characters.

LZW algorithm, ASCII representation, WAV and ZIP formats

The Lempel-Ziv (LZ) algorithm is a family of data compression algorithms developed by Abraham Lempel and Jacob Ziv in 1978. The Lempel-Ziv algorithm works by identifying repeated patterns in the data and encoding them using shorter codes. It builds a dictionary of patterns encountered in the input data and uses references to previously seen patterns to represent subsequent occurrences. By replacing repeated patterns with shorter codes, the algorithm reduces the overall size of the compressed data. Terry Welch improved Lempel-Ziv algorithm by using a specific technique of creating dynamic dictionary which keeps checking and learning in real-time from the streaming input data. By assigning shorter codes to more frequently occurring character sequences, and longer codes to less frequently occurring character sequences, the algorithm can achieve greater compression ratios, consuming less digital storage. The algorithm assigns variable-length codes to input data for reducing its entropy or, to say, the data file size. In a sense, the varying code length in the LZW algorithm can be treated as a measure of the information entropy of a language. The result is that compressed data uses overall fewer bits to represent the original data, making it more efficient to store or transmit.

If we extrapolate our model to include 256 characters of extended ASCII's coding list and then work out information entropy, we find the value falling around 9 bits per character. This is strikingly an important result because ASCII representation assigns 8 bits to each character. The average code in LZW algorithm works around 10 bits per character.

Thus, our model which is independent of approximations and human subject variability, is supported by ASCII 8-bit representation, as well as by 9-bit code length of LZW compression algorithm. Using structural nuances and rules of the language for encoding with special software tools, standard ZIP format can compress word files to 62% and retains the qualities of the original file. MP3 can shrink the digital audio file to approximately 85% but it is a lossy compression. WAV format can compress an audio file to 60% of its original size, and this compression is understood to be theoretically lossless. Our model, which is independent of text sample or audio sample, gives language redundancy 62.3 and 61.1%. This would mean that word doc or audio file can be compressed to 62.3 or 61.1% which are close to the values ZIP and WAV formats offer for lossless compression.

Conclusion

The proposed model is simple and versatile; it considers all 26 letters of the English alphabet, excluding all other characters. The letters found in an average English word are classified into two subgroups: vowels and consonants.

The information entropy per letter is estimated by separately examining the frequency counts of vowels and consonants in the average length of an English word. To estimate the maximum value of information entropy as required in Shannon's formula for language redundancy, the condition of uniform probability distribution is applied separately to both the subgroups of vowels and consonants in their respective probability spaces. Then, the weighted average is calculated by assigning the weight factors individually to the values calculated separately.

Further, we obtained language redundancy value of 62.3%, which is like the value reported by Moradi et al. who worked with different text samples and human subjects. These findings corroborate that our model is not affected by variables like text samples or human subjects.

In Shannon's experiment, when the string of characters is increased from 8 to over 100, the short-range statistical fluctuations cease, and the entropy drops to around 1.0 bit per character, which is very close to the value of 0.895 bit per letter obtained from our model. This suggests that the present model is resistant to statistical fluctuations. Unlike other models and approaches, our model does not have any theoretical or experimental constraints. The results obtained from our model are not based on any approximation, are unaffected by the length of the string of characters and are free from self-selection bias.

File compression of 62.3%, as inferred from our model, is compatible with the lossless compression provided by the WAV and ZIP file formats. When the entropy value obtained from our model is extrapolated to accommodate 256 characters, the resulting value falls around 9 bits per character. One may recall that ASCII character encoding works with 8 bits per character, while the LZW algorithm uses code lengths around 10 bits for individual characters or groups of characters. Thus, our results are corroborated by ASCII representation and LZW algorithm.

References

[1] Gallagher, R. G. (2001). Claude E. Shannon: aretrospective on his life, work and impact. IEEE Transactions on Information Theory, 47(7). 2681-2695.

[2] Gray, R. M. The Entropy and Information Theory. pp. 61-95, New York: Springer-Verlag. 2013.

[3] Jaynes, E. T. (1983). Information theory and statistical Mechanics. *Physical Review*, 106(4) 620-663.

[4] Robert, P. H., Gasser, W., and Richards, G. An introduction to statistical thermodynamics. UK: World Scientific, 1995

[5] Peter, A. The Laws of Thermodynamics. UK: Oxford University Press. 2010.

[6] Pathria, R. K. Statistical Mechanics. 2nd edt. UK: Butterworth -Heinemann. 2017

[7] Jaynes, E. T. (1965). Gibbs vs Boltzmann entropies. *American Journal of Physics*, 33, 391-398.

[8] Gianinetti, A. An Account of Thermodynamic Entropy. Bentham Science Publisher. 2017

[9] Shannon, C. E. (1948). A mathematical theory of communication. *Bell Labs Technical Journal*,27(3), 379-423..

[10] Shannon, C. E. (1951). Prediction and Entropy of Printed English. *Bell Labs Technical Journal*, 30, 47-51.

[11] Kwiatkowski, S. (2018). Entropy is a measure of uncertainty. Retrieved from https//www.towardsdatascience.com>entropy

[12] Burton, N. G. and Licklider, J. C. R. (1955). Long-range constraints in the statistical structure of printed English. *American Journal of Psychiatry*, 68, 650-653.

50 Analyzing the buy now pay later (BNPL) industry: a SWOT analysis for strategic insights

Dipti Kiran[1,a] and Ashok Kumar Mishra[2,b]

[1]Research scholar, Department of Commerce, Guru Ghasidas Vishwavidyalaya, Bilaspur, C.G, India

[2]Dean Department of Commerce, Guru Ghasidas Vishwavidyalaya, Bilaspur, C.G, India

Abstract

This study offers a thorough strengths, weaknesses, opportunities, and threats (SWOT) analysis of buy-now, pay-later (BNPL) services inside the ever-changing financial services market.

The first section of the analysis looks at the benefits of BNPL services, emphasizing their ease of use, accessibility, and attraction to younger, tech-savvy customers.

We discuss potential dangers related to BNPL services, like over-indebtedness and regulatory problems, in the Weaknesses section. BNPL services can draw new customers into the credit market and form collaborations with e-commerce platforms.

Lastly, the paper explores the Threats that BNPL encounters.

In a financial services industry that is evolving quickly, financial institutions, retailers, and consumers may all benefit from having a solid understanding of the SWOT analysis of BNPL. This understanding can help them make well-informed decisions about investment strategies, risk management, and payment options.

Introduction

A payment option called buy now, pay later (BNPL) enables customers to order products or services immediately and postpone making payments until later. Because it provides clients with a practical and adaptable payment option, it has experienced a major increase in popularity in recent years, especially in the e-commerce sector. In contrast to regular credit cards or Installment loans, BNPL allows customers to make purchases without paying the entire amount upfront [3]. The goal of BNPL is to divide the overall cost of an acquisition into smaller, more affordable installments. Customers can spread payments out over time, often from a few weeks to several months, instead of simultaneously making the whole sum payment. With this payment arrangement, customers may better plan their spending and make larger purchases without burdening their finances [2]. Creating an account with a BNPL provider or utilizing a specific retailer's service is normally required to use BNPL [5]. Customers can choose the BNPL option at the checkout when purchasing once it has been approved. The checkout procedure outlines the payment plan specifics, including the number of payments and the due dates. While other BNPL providers offer fast approval with few conditions, some may run a credit check or ask for basic personal details. The ease of use and simplicity of BNPL are two of its key benefits. Customers can experience instant pleasure by immediately obtaining the requested good or service, and the application process is frequently short and simple. If the installments are paid in whole within the predetermined time frame, BNPL also waives any interest or finance fees. This makes it a desirable choice for people who want to stay away from conventional credit cards or loans that could have high-interest rates. The capacity of BNPL to draw in a larger consumer base is another advantage. Retailers can serve consumers who might need access to credit cards or prefer not to use them for various reasons by providing this payment option [6]. Customers are more likely to finish a transaction when they have the option to spread out payments, which can enhance sales and customer loyalty. It is crucial to remember, though, that BNPL has several drawbacks and dangers that need to be considered. Customers should consider their ability to repay the installments to avoid amassing debt or financial troubles, even though it might offer short-term relief. Some BNPL providers may disclose a customer's payment history to credit bureaux, which could impact the customer's credit score. Late or missed payments may incur fines or additional fees. BNPL is so simple that people can be persuaded to buy things they cannot afford in the long term.

Growth of BNPL in India

BNPL services have expanded dramatically in India in recent years. Because of its practicality, adaptability, and capacity to increase purchasing power, this payment method has become increasingly popular among Indian consumers. Let us investigate the main elements influencing the expansion of BNPL in India.

---

[a]diptikiranchoudhary@gmail.com, [b]hudcoashok@gmail.com

DOI: 10.1201/9781003534136-50

Digital revolution: With rising internet penetration and smartphone use, India has seen a substantial digital revolution. The proliferation of e-commerce platforms and digital payment methods has created a favorable atmosphere for expanding BNPL services. With easy access to internet buying, consumers now favor practical payment methods that suit their financial circumstances [1] [7].

The influence of millennials and Gen Z: India's population is primarily young, with a sizeable chunk falling within the millennial and Gen Z groups. These tech-savvy generations favor frictionless purchasing occasions and are receptive to cutting-edge payment methods. Since BNPL provides a more flexible alternative to conventional credit choices and enables them to make purchases without experiencing a huge financial strain, it aligns with their philosophy.

Improved shopping experience: BNPL services provide clients with a seamless and improved shopping experience. Customers who don't have the cash upfront can still purchase the things they want by having the option to pay in installments. This feature increases customer pleasure and loyalty by doing away with the need to save money or wait for the ideal occasion to buy something.

Increase in online shopping: With a boom in online retail platforms, India's e-commerce has grown exponentially. For online shoppers, BNPL services have developed into a desirable method of payment that enables convenient shopping—especially during holiday and promotions seasons. While delaying their payments, customers can take advantage of discounts and offers.

Partnership with shops: BNPL service providers have partnered with several shops and e-commerce sites in India. Through this partnership, BNPL choices can be seamlessly incorporated into the checkout process, increasing customer visibility and allure. Consumers like the flexibility and convenience of deferring payment, while retailers profit from better conversion rates and average order values.

Consumer attitudes are changing: Traditional financial practices have focused on saving and cash-based transactions in India. Consumer attitudes regarding accepting credit and installment-based payment options have changed, nevertheless. By providing a more up-to-date and approachable method of financing goods, BNPL services take advantage of this shift in mentality.

The competitive environment: With numerous domestic and foreign firms joining the market, the BNPL market in India is experiencing fierce rivalry. Consumers now find BNPL services more enticing thanks to innovation, better terms, and low-interest rates brought forth by this competition. Customers now have more freedom to select the provider that best meets their needs because of the growing variety of options accessible [9].

COVID-19 impact: In India, the use of digital payments and e-commerce has accelerated due to the COVID-19 epidemic. Consumers turned to online purchasing for both their vital and non-essential requirements due to the lockdowns and social isolation measures in place. BNPL services developed become a desirable alternative, enabling customers to better manage their money while adjusting to the new normal.

Competition in the BNPL Market

As more businesses enter the market to profit from its rising popularity, competition in the BNPL sector has increased recently. The possibility to capture a sizeable portion of the market and the chance to satisfy shifting customer demands for flexible payment choices fuel the rivalry. Let's examine the specifics of the rivalry in the BNPL market.

Domestic players: Several domestic players have appeared on the Indian BNPL market, vying for market share while providing creative solutions. Businesses like Slice, LazyPay, ZestMoney, Simpl, and ePayLater have flourished by offering Indian customers simple and practical BNPL services. These businesses form alliances with merchants, internet platforms, and e-commerce marketplaces to increase their consumer base.

Global powerhouses: Global businesses have entered the BNPL sector after realizing the potential of the Indian market. Utilizing their international experience and well-known brands, businesses like Klarna, Afterpay, and Affirm have expanded their operations to India. The skills heighten the competitiveness of indigenous firms and experience these foreign competitors bring to the Indian market.

Financial institutions: Well-known financial institutions have also entered the BNPL market, including banks and non-banking financial corporations (NBFCs). These organizations have a solid foundation in the financial industry and can use their current clientele to provide BNPL services. They benefit from trust and reputation but struggle to keep up with the innovation and agility that agile startups offer [1].

E-commerce platforms: To keep customers and increase sales, e-commerce behemoths like Flipkart and Amazon have introduced BNPL services. The "Pay Later" and "Amazon Pay EMI" options from Flipkart and Amazon are two of their BNPL offers. These e-commerce businesses want to offer a seamless purchasing experience and foster consumer loyalty; therefore, they have integrated BNPL into their platforms.

Retailer-tied BNPL solutions: To increase client loyalty and boost sales, retailers are also providing their own BNPL solutions. Businesses like Myntra, Tata CLiQ, and BigBasket have made it simpler for clients to make purchases and pay overtime with installments by introducing BNPL services. Retailer-tied BNPL solutions give businesses more control over the payment process and enable them to make customized offers to their clients.

Expansion into offline retail: Although BNPL services first became well-known in the e-commerce industry, several providers are now extending into offline retail. Thanks to their partnerships with physical stores, customers can use BNPL companies' services for in-store purchases. This action expands the client base while also giving customers a smooth experience.

User experience is a priority: BNPL providers are investing in enhancing the user experience by creating intuitive web and mobile interfaces. An easy-to-use interface, rapid clearance procedures, and clear terms and conditions enhance the user experience. User experience-focused providers gain a competitive advantage and draw in more clients.

Customer education and trust: To succeed in the competitive environment, customers must be educated about the advantages and responsible usage of BNPL services. A solid foundation of trust is built by service providers who value open communication, unambiguous terms and conditions, and proactive customer support. Their position in the market is further bolstered by educating consumers about the possible dangers of taking on debt and advocating responsible borrowing.

Different Types of BNPL Providers

Different kinds of suppliers have developed in the quickly growing BNPL market to meet the wide range of needs of consumers and enterprises. These service companies have various target markets, tactics, and services. Let's look at a few of the main categories of BNPL providers:

Standalone BNPL providers: These are standalone businesses just focused on providing BNPL services. They concentrate on giving customers a simple and adaptable payment option across various businesses and sectors. These providers frequently have platforms, mobile apps, and alliances with online shops and physical stores. BNPL providers that operate independently of other companies include LazyPay, Slice, Afterpay, Affirm, and Klarna.

Credit card companies with BNPL services: Many credit card companies have incorporated BNPL services into their portfolios to compete with independent suppliers. These businesses offer possibilities for installment payments by utilizing their current client base and infrastructure. Customers can purchase with their credit cards and then choose the BNPL option to break the transaction into payments. The Pay It Plan It option from American Express and Citi Flex Pay are two examples of credit card issuers that offer BNPL services [4] [8].

E-business platforms with in-house BNPL: Major e-commerce platforms have introduced their own in-house BNPL choices after realizing the popularity of BNPL services. These systems provide customers with a seamless purchasing experience by immediately integrating the payment option into their checkout procedure. Customers who want to pay in installments might choose the BNPL option. Examples of e-commerce sites using internal BNPL services include Amazon Pay EMI and Flipkart's "pay later." [2]

Mobile wallets with BNPL: Companies that offer mobile wallets, which are well-liked in nations like India, have begun providing BNPL services. These companies allow clients to pay for products using their mobile wallets, breaking them into payments. To increase their reach, they frequently collaborate with shops and e-commerce platforms. Ones that come to mind are Paytm Postpaid, PhonePe's "PayLater," and Mobikwik's "BNPL."

Local and regional BNPL providers include: Regional and local BNPL providers have also developed in addition to the well-known national and international players. These companies concentrate on a single area or city, addressing regional customer preferences and networking. They might have fewer clients, but they provide specialized, regional services. To increase their visibility and offer a more individualized experience, regional and local BNPL providers frequently work with local stores and enterprises.

Research Design

The current study focuses on doing a SWOT analysis of the Buy Now Pay Later (BNPL) industry and extracting strategic insights from the analysis. Descriptive research design will be employed for SWOT Analysis studies [8]. Descriptive research seeks to provide a detailed account of the qualities of a phenomenon or the correlation between variables. Within the framework of a SWOT analysis, this design facilitates a methodical examination and presentation of the internal and external elements that impact an organization.

SWOT Analysis of BNPL

Strengths:

- Convenience and flexibility: BNPL offers customers a simple and adaptable payment method. It allows customers to divide payments into manageable installments and make purchases without making an immediate complete payment.
- Higher sales and conversion rates: It has been demonstrated that BNPL services increase sales and conversion rates for retailers. By allowing installment payments, BNPL services can draw clients who might otherwise be reluctant to purchase due to financial concerns.
- Client loyalty and repeat business: BNPL services can promote client loyalty. Customers are more likely to make subsequent purchases and show loyalty to the retailer or platform that provides the service when they have a positive BNPL experience.

Weaknesses:

- Impulsive buying: More often use of BNPL may lead to aggressive, impulsive buying, creating trouble for people managing their finances.
- Potential user identification is difficult: BNPL attracts a lot of users. Some may not be financially sound enough to avail the scheme's benefits. In such conditions, it is difficult to identify real potential users.
- Possibility of overborrowing and debt accumulation: If BNPL services are not used appropriately, it is easy to over-borrow and accumulate debt. Customers might be persuaded to incur more debt than they can manage, which could put them in a difficult financial situation and cause them to miss payments.
- Late payment and penalty fees: Customers who cannot meet the payment dates may be subject to additional fees and penalties for making late payments on BNPL installments. The cost of using BNPL services may increase due to these surcharges.
- Limited chances to build credit: Unlike credit cards, BNPL services sometimes fail to record payment history to credit bureaux. A customer's credit history or score may not be built or improved due to using BNPL services responsibly.

Opportunities:

- Market expansion and adoption: There are chances for providers to broaden their clientele and boost adoption rates as a result of the BNPL market's rapid expansion. Partnerships with merchants, e-commerce platforms, and financial institutions to provide BNPL services to a larger clientele can accelerate this expansion [5].

- Vertical expansion and diversification: BNPL suppliers can broaden and change their product offerings from what is typically found in retail. They can look into joint ventures and target particular markets, including healthcare, travel, education, or home renovation, opening up fresh growth prospects.
- Integration with existing payment platforms: BNPL service providers can connect their products to e-commerce, mobile wallets, and existing payment platforms. By enabling a seamless and user-friendly checkout process, this connection increases the audience for BNPL services.

Threats:

- Increasing regulatory monitoring: As BNPL services become more popular, regulatory monitoring will also grow. The profitability and operations of BNPL providers could be impacted by governments and regulatory agencies introducing harsher regulations, consumer protection measures, or interest rate limitations.
- Competitive Environment: With the introduction of new companies and reputable financial institutions offering comparable services, the BNPL market is getting more and more competitive. Price wars, reduced profit margins, and the requirement for ongoing innovation to set oneself apart from rivals can all result from intense rivalry [2].
- Economic downturn and default risks: For BNPL providers, economic downturns or financial crises can raise the risk of default. Higher default rates may result from job losses, decreased consumer spending, and unstable economies, which could affect the profitability and sustainability of BNPL services.

Remembering that different BNPL providers may have distinct strengths, limitations, opportunities, and dangers is crucial. A specific SWOT analysis based on the distinctive qualities and placement of a single BNPL supplier might offer more precise insights into their particular circumstance.

References

[1] Alcazar, J., and Bradford, T. (2021). The rise of buy now, pay later: bank and payment network perspectives and regulatory considerations. *Payments System Research Briefing* , (December 1, 2021), 1–6. (Federal Reserve Bank of Kansas City).

[2] Berg, T., Burg, V., Keil, J., and Puri, M. (2023). On the rise of' buy now, pay later'. *Pay Later'(May 15, 2023)*. (https://ssrn.com/abstract=4448715) JEL: D12.G40.G50

[3] Danes, S. M., and Hira, T. K. (1990). Knowledge, beliefs, and practices in the use of credit cards. *Home Economics Research Journal*, 18(3), 223–235.

[4] Di Maggio, M., Williams, E., and Katz, J. (2022). *Buy Now, Pay Later Credit: User Characteristics and Effects on Spending Patterns* (No. w30508). National Bureau of Economic Research.

[5] Gerrans, P., Baur, D. G., and Lavagna-Slater, S. (2022). Fintech and responsibility: Buy-now-pay-later arrangements. *Australian Journal of Management*, 47(3), 474–502.

[6] Guttman-Kenney, B., Firth, C., and Gathergood, J. (2023). Buy now, pay later (BNPL)... on your credit card. *Journal of Behavioral and Experimental Finance*, 37, 100788.

[7] Lee, J., and Kwon, K. N. (2002). Consumers' use of credit cards: store credit card usage as an alternative payment and financing medium. *Journal of Consumer Affairs*, 36(2), 239–262.

[8] Wulandari, R. T., and Damayanti, S. M. (2022). The importance of digital financial literacy to anticipaye impulsive buying behavior in buy-now-pay-later mode. *International Journal of Business and Economy*, 4(3), 170–182.

[9] Lux, M and B Epps (2022): Grow now, regulate later? Regulation urgently needed to support transparency and sustainable growth for buy-now, pay-later, *Harvard Kennedy School M-RCBG Associate Working Paper Series*, no 182, April.

51 Solar heat utilization and storage using solar cookware setups

Rishabh Chaturvedi[1,a] and Manish Saraswat[2,b]

[1]GLA University, Mathura, India

[2]LLOYD Institute of Engineering and Technology, Greater Noida, India

Abstract

Around the world, cooking is an essential requirement for people. It makes up a sizable portion of the energy consumed in emerging nations. As a result, in these nations, residential use of solar cookers is quite prevalent. The benefits of using solar cookers would reduce the amount of CO_2 released into the atmosphere. Even if there are many solar cookers that have been researched and designed by researchers and scholars around the world, their use is still insufficient. There are a variety of factors that contribute to the limited use of solar cookers, including their large size, massive weight, lack of open space, slow cooking, set cooking times and poor knowledge. A greater awareness of solar cookers, such as parabolic cookers, box-type solar cookers, panel-type solar cookers is provided by the presented work.

Keywords: Box type, concentrating, cook-wares, heat storage, parabolic, solar irradiation

Introduction

Nowadays fossil fuels are put to extensive use. The use of energy that is derived from fossil fuels continues to account for the largest percentage of the total worldwide energy demand. The generation of clean energy, on the other hand, is becoming more and more important on a daily basis due to the increasing significance of environmental challenges. Long-term, future generations will be forced to contend with a number of challenges, including environmental contamination, a dearth of accessible energy sources, and the occurrence of catastrophic disasters [1]. Therefore, the greatest alternative choice for culinary purposes in rural families is to use renewable energy rather than traditional resources. Designers as early as the nineteenth century saw the potential in using the energy from the sun to supply heat for preparing food and other uses and they created the necessary equipment to do so. Reduced reliance on fuel sources is often touted as a major benefit of solar cookers. It's good for consumers because they'll spend less on fuel, and it's good for the environment because it will cut down on deforestation (in areas where wood is used as a cooking fuel) and pollution from burning [2]. Solar cooking has the possibility to minimise the ingestion of smoke along with associated health concerns because so much wood-based cooking is done indoors with insufficient airflow. Providing energy that can meet our demands in the future is essential. Solar power is superior to the other options because it doesn't is cost effective to use the energy from the sun. Solar energy was probably used for cooking far earlier than that. Individuals and the natural world both stand to gain from the widespread use of solar cookers. The kitchen is one potential application field for solar thermal systems. Concentrating solar power is one technique that accomplishes this transformation from solar radiation to thermal energy. Conventional solar energy conversion systems made use of reflector materials to focus the sun's rays and turn them into usable heat [3]. The focal point is a small area where all the heat is concentrated. At last, those underprivileged populations may easily boil water or cook meals using the concentrated heat from that point of focus.

The configuration of the cooking surface determines how effective a mirror with high reflectance is at concentrating sunlight on a compact hob. On a bright day, most solar cookers can reach temperatures between 650 and 4000 degrees. Solar cookers focus sunlight directly onto a cooking surface. Sunlight is converted into thermal energy when it encounters with a receiver material. Black is the only acceptable colour for kitchen cookware. Using a glass lid on the pot is a simple way to insulate the cooker. It helps keep the solar cooker's heat from escaping through convection. Although the exact mechanism by which each solar cooker heats food may vary, most of them operate on the same premise. Cutting food into smaller pieces speeds up the cooking process. Typically, solar ovens are used for cooking very little portions of food. A household may use one or more solar cookers, depending on the size of the family and the amount of food that needs to be cooked [4]. In a solar oven, stirring the food is usually not necessary. Not only does the method of cooking matter, but so does

[a]rishabh.chaturvedi@gla.ac.in, [b]manish.saraswat@lloydcollege.in

DOI: 10.1201/9781003534136-51

Figure 51.1 Steps included in operation of solar cookware [2]

the amount of food, the weather, the wind, and the latitude. Figure 51.1. depicts steps included in the operation of solar cookware setups.

Heat Storage Methods

Practical heat storage involves capturing the temperature change that occurs during the heating or cooling of either a liquid or a solid thermal storage medium to store thermal energy. With regard to their exceptional thermal conductivity, low specific heat, good thermal stability at elevated temperatures, and lack of combustibility and adverse effects, molten salts are considered a suitable material for usage in solar energy facilities. When certain chemical bonds are broken or formed in endothermic or exothermic reactions, particular substances may soak up or release a great deal of thermal energy. The chemical heat storage technology was developed due to these factors. Chemical heat storage can be accomplished using either organic or inorganic materials, provided that their reversible chemical reactions absorb/release a significant quantity of heat [5].

As the phases of their geometries are transformed by melting/solidification, gasification/liquefaction, and other processes, phase change materials (PCMs) can hold/release an immense amount of heat. It is substantially more efficient to store heat as latent heat than actual heat since the phase-transition enthalpy of PCMs is often much higher than practical heat. The latent heat of these materials varies from 124 to 560 kJ/kg, and their phase change temperatures go from 100 to 897 degrees Celsius [6]. Latent heat retention can function in an almost isothermal manner due to the phase change procedure, in contrast to practical heat storage, in which solids have a considerable temperature surge/drop when capturing/releasing thermal energy. This makes latent heat storage a good option for uses that have very specific temperature requirements. However, low thermal conductivities are latent heat storage's biggest drawback [7]. The basic objective of the cooker was to focus on sun radiation and use various reflective materials to transform it into heat. The reflector's surface needs to be glossy and smooth, and both controllable (by loading, tracking, and temperature monitoring) and unrestrained (by wind, etc.) aspects were taken into attention.

Solar Cook-Ware Setups

(1) Solar Parabolic Cookware:
When compared to panel or box cookers, solar parabolic cookers don't require a particular cooking container and may reach very high temperatures in a short amount of time. Nevertheless, because of the focused power, food cooked in a parabolic cooker runs a possibility of being burned if left unchecked for too long. A solar parabolic cooker is no more complicated than a parabolic reflector, a base, and a pot to cook in placed at the cooker's focal point. The main benefits of this steel are its ability to resist corrosion and its quality as a reflector. It also has a low electrical conductivity. Stainless steel can be divided into five categories. Austenitic, Ferritic, Martensitic, Duplex, and Precipitation Hardening are the other four. Molybdenum, Nickel, Manganese, and Chromium Alloy are the Main Components. In addition to being easily formed, it also welds well. Stress corrosion cracking is a common failure mode in these steels. Steel with no magnetic properties. The focal point is the point where a ray reflected from the surface meets the axis of symmetry [8]. The focal length is the distance between the lens's optical centre to its focal point. At the apex, the focal length is double the radius of curvature.

$$F = \left\{ \frac{D_a^2}{16h} \right\} \tag{1}$$

Where, 'D_a' is dish's aperture diameter,
'h' is depth of focal point inside the dish.
and 'F' is the focal length.

Parabolic dish collectors concentrate sunlight onto the receiving device at the collector's focal point with the help of a row of mirrors in the configuration of a parabolic dish. For the generation of electricity, a tiny engine is

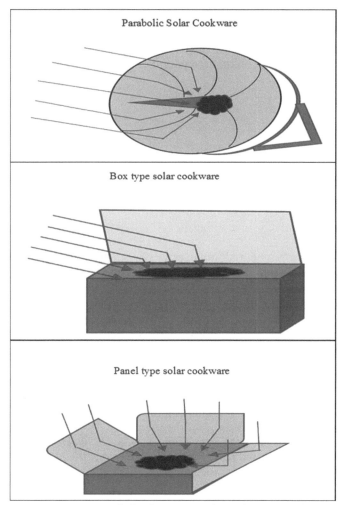

Figure 51.2 Parabolic, box type and panel type portable solar cookware systems

connected to the receiver and heated to working temperatures and pressures using heat transfer fluid contained in the receiver. Diverse reflecting materials, including stainless steel, aluminium foil, and mylar tape, were devised for use in a number of parabolic solar cookers. All the three types of solar cookware setups are illustrated in Figure 51.2.

(2) Solar panel cookware:
Because of their inexpensive cost and ease of assembly, solar panel cookers are often considered the easiest option. Solar panel cookers focus sunlight from the sky. Flat panels on panel cookers concentrate and reflect sunlight for use in the kitchen. This solar approach to cooking is not recommended due to its low efficiency [9].

(3) Solar box cookware:
The most popular and affordable solar ovens. A black coated metallic trapezoidal tray (cooking tray) and a pair of glass pane are the primary components of these low-priced and straightforward box cookers. It is protected by a metal or fibre -glass exterior and insulated with glass wool to prevent heat transfer between the cooking tray and the exterior. The pots and tray, which have become blackened from exposure to the sun, are hit directly by the rays as they pass through the double glass lid [10]. While short-wavelength radiation from the sun can pass through the glass covers, low-temperature radiation from the box is almost completely blocked. This causes the internal temperature of the box to increase until the heat gained from the glass and the heat lost from the exterior surfaces cancel each other out (greenhouse effect). In addition, the aperture area is supplemented with solar radiation using a plane reflecting mirror (booster mirror) of almost the same size. Insulation lines the underside and sides of the cooking tray. The food within the pots is cooked more quickly because the blackened top absorbs more heat.

The solar box cooker may get as hot as 15°C (300°F) [11]. Although it won't get as hot as a conventional oven, this will nonetheless do the trick over a longer length of time. It is not usually required to prepare foods at the exceptionally high temperatures specified in typical manuals, especially since food comprising a lot of liquid cannot become much hotter than 100°C (212°F). Due to the low cooking temperature, dishes might be left in the slow cooker all day without risk of burning [3].

$$P_d = P_t (700/I_t)$$ (2)

where:
   P_d = standard cooking power (W)
   P_t = Power available in interval for cooking (W)
   I_t = average solar insolation (W/m^2).

Conclusion

Providing energy that can meet our demands in the future is essential. Solar power is superior to the other options because it doesn't is cost effective to use the energy from the sun. The greatest alternative choice for culinary purposes in rural families is to use renewable Energy rather than traditional resources. In supplying the needed energy, solar cookers can fully or partially replace the use of firewood for cooking in many developing regions. Solar cooking has regularly been viewed as a solution looking for a problem, or a technological solution developed without sensitivity to user needs. In this paper an analysis of different solar cookers has been done on the basis of their feasibility, design and operation.

References

[1] Hosseinzadeh, M., Faezian, A., Mirzababaee, S. M., and Zamani, H. (2020). Parametric analysis and optimization of a portable evacuated tube solar cooker. *Energy*, 194, 116816.

[2] Ahmed, S. M. M., Al-Amin, M. R., Ahammed, S., Ahmed, F., Saleque, A. M., and Rahman, M. A. (2020). Design, construction and testing of parabolic solar cooker for rural households and refugee camp, *Solar Energy*, 205, 230—240.

[3] Saraswat, M., and Chauhan, N. R. (2020). Comparative assessment of butanol and algae oil as alternate fuel for SI engines. *Engineering Science and Technology, an International Journal*, 23(1), 92–100.

[4] Sharma, H. K., Kumar, S., and Verma, S. K. (2022). Comparative performance analysis of flat plate solar collector having circular &trapezoidal corrugated absorber plate designs. *Energy*, 253, 124137. https://doi.org/10.1016/j.energy.2022.124137.

[5] Tian, Y., and Zhao, C. Y. (2013). A review of solar collectors and thermal energy storage in solar thermal applications. *Applied Energy*, 104, 538–553.

[6] Dong, S., Al-Zahrani, K. S., Reda, S. A., Sharma, K., Amin, M. T., Tag-Eldin, E., et al. (2022). Investigation of thermal performance of a shell and tube latent heat thermal energy storage tank in the presence of different nano-enhanced PCMs. *Case Studies in Thermal Engineering*, 37, 102280. https://doi.org/10.1016/j.csite.2022.102280.

[7] Singh, S. K., Verma, S. K., and Kumar, R. (2022). Thermal performance and behavior analysis of SiO2, Al2O3 and MgO based nano-enhanced phase-changing materials, latent heat thermal energy storage system. *Journal of Energy Storage*, 48, 103977. https://doi.org/10.1016/j.est.2022.103977.

[8] Kumar, P., Singh, P. K., Nagar, S., Sharma, K., and Saraswat, M. (2021). Effect of different concentration of functionalized graphene on charging time reduction in thermal energy storage system. *Materials Today: Proceedings*, 44, 146–152.

[9] Chaturvedi, R., Sharma, A., Sharma, K., and Saraswat, M. (2022). Tribological behaviour of multi-walled carbon nanotubes reinforced AA 7075 nano-composites. *Advances in Materials and Processing Technologies*, 8(4), 4743–4755.

[10] El-Sebaii, A. A., and Ibrahim, A. (2005). Experimental testing of a box-type solar cooker using the standard procedure of cooking power. *Renewable Energy*, 30(12), 1861–1871.

[11] Sharma, A., Chaturvedi, R., Sharma, K., and Saraswat, M. (2022). Force evaluation and machining parameter optimization in milling of aluminium burr composite based on response surface method. *Advances in Materials and Processing Technologies*, 8(4), 4073–4094.

52 Deterioration of solar cells performance due to presence of cracks

Arti Badhoutiya[1,a] and Birendra Kr. Saraswat[2,b]

[1]GLA University, Mathura, India

[2]Raj Kumar Goel Institute of Technology, Ghaziabad, India

Abstract

Wrapping materials retain the broken cells of a crystalline solar cells together when they break. The photovoltaic (PV) industry is currently conducting extensive study on microcracks at the user end in bulk solar cells. Cell fragments shift as a result of variations in thermal performance, allowing fractured metallization to lose and reestablish contact. The aluminum bridges protect against fatigue failure with more cycling. The impacts of cracks on PV cells are justified by comparing the performance parameters observed before and after occurrence of cracks. Evaluation of the effect of microcracks on the physical and electrical functionality of silicon solar cells has been done in this paper.

Keywords: Fabrication, fissures, metallization, microcracks, subfascial cracks

Introduction

Throughout their lifetime, photovoltaic (PV) modules are subjected to a variety of mechanical stresses, including transit from the factory to the site where it is installed, different environmental factors, and changes in the ambient temperature. Solar cells made of crystalline silicon are prone to cracking after being assembled into PV modules. Solar cells that are fractured but still connected to the module are frequently still functional [1]. Parts of the cell may become segregated from the external circuit when fractured metallization disrupts current flow, lowering the energy output of the cell. Power loss and heating can result from electrical mismatches between cells in the same series string [2]. This dissipation occasionally poses a risk to safety. These loads can damage the cell connectivity and reduce the electrical output of PV modules made of crystalline silicon, which can result in fractures and hotspots. Detecting changes in metallization resistance between cell fragments during variations in module temperature can be done via electroluminescence (EL) imaging. EL images exhibit great contrast over a fracture when damaged metallization obstructs current passage there. When the temperature of the module changes, cell pieces move. In some circumstances, the metallization's irregular fracture surfaces allow it to continue to be electrically linked during this movement [3]. In other situations, electrical continuity is sporadic or nonexistent. These surfaces may come into touch and shift, resulting in wear and a gradual loss of electrical continuity. Operators of industrial PV systems have become more conscious of these loads during the past few years. The output power generated by the PV installations is continuously monitored and recorded, and it is compared to theoretical projections for health and safety precautions. Throughout their lifespan, PV modules are subjected to a variety of compressive loads, including when they are transported from the factory to the project location, dirt, ice, or high winds.

The PV business is extremely sensitive to how solar panels operate under standard testing conditions (STC). Pmax normally relates to the maximal power point at STC, and these conditions equate to the efficacy at a temperature of 25°C and an irradiance of 1000 W/m². Any given measurement will take place at various temperatures and levels of light, but sophisticated formulae have been created to precisely return each point on the I-V curve to STC conditions [4]. The literature usually ignores this effect, which can have significant economic effects, because degraded panels may degrade particularly distinctly at low irradiances than at 1000 W/m². Cross-sectional view of a solar module arrangement is shown in the Figure 52.1 given below.

Identification of Cracks

Depending on the size of the fracture, it is possible to classify cracks as macro- or micro cracks. Typically, a crack that is less than 30 m wide is referred to as a -crack. The cracks are categorized as facial or sub-facial cracks depending on where they are located. Facial cracks are cracks that appear on the silicon wafer's surface [5]. These face fissures are difficult to measure with bare eyes owing to their size. Subfascial cracks are those

[a]arti.badhoutiya@gla.ac.in, [b]saraswatbirendra@gmail.com

DOI: 10.1201/9781003534136-52

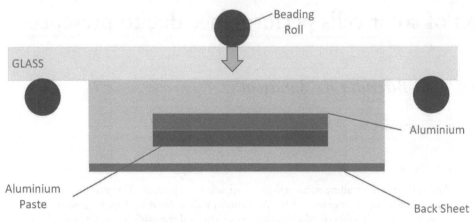

Figure 52.1 Cross-sectional view of a solar module arrangement

that originate on a wafer's surface and spread in the depth direction, or those that start on the surface and do the opposite [6]. Subfascial cracks may be additionally categorized as deep or shallow cracks depending on the severity of the fracture.

Severe ohmic shunts may be caused by microcracks that are inherent in the beginning wafer or develop while fabrication before screen-printing metallization. When the operational current of a model surpasses the minimized short-circuit current of a fault cell, a module's defective cell or group of cells may cause hot-spot overheating issues. Grunow et al. applied substantially changing fractures patterns to an exemplar cell module to ascertain the impact of the location of the fissures on the electrical properties of each of the cells [7]. Only a small power loss of less than 4% resulted if the fissures were parallel and located in the middle of the bus bars. Perhaps, however, a significant power loss of 60% happened if the fissures were in parallel position with respect to the bus bars and are present on both the sides of bus bars.

Levels of Cracking

1. State 1 is the intact specimen from the initial loading cycle. Al-paste is here electrically and physically active, just like it was when it was manufactured.
2. Except for the bridges that structurally and electrically link the two cell components, the Al-paste is fractured. The present pathways are roughly shown by the blue lines. Due to the presence of Al-paste in the Al-bridges for conduction throughout the cross-sectional, the resistance does not vary from state 1 to state 2. The bridges distort with each loading cycle, which causes them to get weaker and eventually shatter [8].
3. In an unloading state, the damaged bridges could not electrically recouple. The bridges in condition 3 also exhibit mechanical fatigue as a result of additional circulation [9]. The bridges can change from the loaded condition to state 4 in the unloaded condition over a specified level of this weariness.
4. When loaded or unloaded, the bridges electronically and mechanically recuperate. A bridge can arbitrarily shift between states 3 and 4 after its initial transition from state 3 to 4 [10].

The J_s, which is dependent on the photon flux incident on the cell surface, corresponds to the quantity of current density that passes across the external circuit when the terminals of the cell are shorted.

$$J_s = J_p - (R_s {}_* J_s)/ R_{shunt} \tag{1}$$

This finding supports the idea that localized cracks could lower the Voc.

$$\% \text{ Loss of open circuit voltage} = (V_{ocmax} - V_{ocmin}) \text{ of cracked area}/V_{ocmax} \tag{2}$$

Results

Figure 52.2 depicts the graphical representation of impact of cracks on the performance parameters of the solar cell. It shows how the current density and output voltage drops after the introduction of cracks.

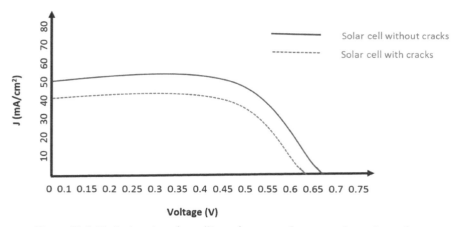

Figure 52.2 Variations in solar cell's performance due to cracks on its surface

Conclusion

In this paper, cracks on the surface of PV cells are analyzed as identification of the type of crack appeared, the severity of the crack can be checked by assuring under which level of crack does it fall. The impacts of cracks on PV cells can then be justified by comparing the performance parameters observed before and after occurrence of cracks. Fissures in solar cells are frequently securely sealed, and STC measurements show negligible loss. Contrary to the front side, conducting aluminum bridges on the back side connect the fractured cell pieces both electrically and mechanically. These aluminum bridges protect against fatigue failure with more cycling. A clear deterioration in the performance of solar cell can be seen in the graphical comparison. The PVs sector may be interested in this paper's key results because a sizable portion of the products have fabrication time fissures.

References

[1] Gabor, M., Eric J. Schneller, Hubert Seigneur, Michael W. Rowell, Dylan Colvin, Michael Hopwood and Kristopher O. Davis. (2020). The impact of cracked solar cells on solar panel energy delivery. In 2020 47th IEEE Photovol-taic Specialists Conference (PVSC), (pp. 0810–0813), doi: 10.1109/PVSC45281.2020.9300743.

[2] Schneller, E. J., Frota, R., Gabor, A. M., Lincoln, J., Seigneur, H., and Davis, K. O. (2018). Electroluminescence based metrics to assess the impact of cracks on photovoltaic module performance. In 2018 IEEE 7th World Conference on Photovoltaic Energy Conversion. IEEE, Jun. 2018, (pp. 0455–0458).

[3] Sharma, A., Chaturvedi, R., Sharma, K., and Saraswat, M. (2022). Force evaluation and machining parameter optimization in milling of aluminium burr composite based on response surface method. *Advances in Materials and Processing Technologies*, 8(4), 4073–4094.

[4] Yao, G., and Wu, X. (2019). Halcon-based solar panel crack detection. In 2019 2nd World Conference on Mechanical Engineering and Intelligent Manufacturing (WCMEIM), 2019, (pp. 733–736), doi: 10.1109/WCMEIM48965.2019.00154.

[5] Chaturvedi, R., Sharma, A., Sharma, K., and Saraswat, M. (2022). Tribological behaviour of multi-walled carbon nanotubes reinforced AA 7075 nano-composites. *Advances in Materials and Processing Technologies*, 8(4), 4743–4755.

[6] Grunow, P., Clemens, P., Hoffmann, V., Litzenburger, B., and Podlowski, L. (2005). Influence of micro cracks in multicrystalline silicon solar cells on the reliability of PV modules. In Presented at the 20th Eur. Photovoltaic Solar Energy Conf., Barcelona, Spain, Jun 6–10, 2005.

[7] Kumar, P., Singh, P. K., Nagar, S., Sharma, K., and Saraswat, M. (2021). Effect of different concentration of functionalized graphene on charging time reduction in thermal energy storage system. *Materials Today: Proceedings*, 44, 146–152.

[8] Sharma, H. K., Kumar, S., and Verma, S. K. (2022). Comparative performance analysis of flat plate solar collector having circular &trapezoidal corrugated absorber plate designs. *Energy*, 253, 124137, ISSN 0360-5442, https://doi.org/10.1016/j.energy.2022.124137.

[9] Dong, S., Al-Zahrani, K. S., Reda, S. A., Sharma, K., Amin, M. T., Tag-Eldin, E., et al. (2022). Investigation of thermal performance of a shell and tube latent heat thermal energy storage tank in the presence of different nano-enhanced PCMs. *Case Studies in Thermal Engineering*, 37, 102280, ISSN 2214-157X.

[10] Sanfeng Dong, Khaled S Al-Zahrani, Shaker A Reda, Kamal Sharma, Majdi Talal Amin, Elsayed Tag-Eldin, Mohammad Mehdizadeh Youshanlouei, Investigation of thermal performance of a shell and tube latent heat thermal energy storage tank in the presence of different nano-enhanced PCMs, Case Studies in Thermal Engineering, Volume 37, 2022, 102280, ISSN 2214-157X.

53 Technical advancements in parking area management system (PAMS)

Arti Badhoutiya[1,a] and Nathiram Chauhan[2,b]

[1]GLA University, Mathura, India

[2]Indira Gandhi Delhi Technical University for Women, Delhi, India

Abstract

In this paper, a low-cost, barely perceptible system for effectively managing parking places on both public roadways. To assist drivers in finding the ideal parking place for their vehicles, automated smart parking technologies must be developed. A lot of material has been written about the installation of smart parking systems, but it does not include real-time detection of problems like automated parking fee administration and illegal parking. Internet of things (IoT)-based parking systems are considered in the concept that is presented. The initial version uses a centralized parking meter to overcome all of the aforementioned issues and help manage the SPS in urban areas. The parking meter uses an ultrasonic sensor node to determine whether or not a car is there. Light indicators are used to show if a parking space is reserved or available, depending on the situation. The alarm that will play a warning sound for inappropriate parking is set using a micro-controller.

Keywords: Licence plate recognition, manual entry, mechanical car-parking, technological solutions, urbanization, wireless sensing

Introduction

A contemporary developing aim is to contribute attempts to efficiently and intelligently automate the monitoring, access, and utilization of the infrastructure supporting the key services provided to inhabitants of a smart cities. The major enablers of secure and efficient administration of the frequently scarce city resources include advanced wireless sensing technologies, machine learning methodologies, 5G networks, and big data analytics tools [1]. If its use is correctly optimized, such resources can greatly aid in altering the lives of the people through facilitated healthcare, cheaper, more eco-friendly education, and more comfortable transportation. The necessity to save time in hunting for available parking places is one of the factors that contribute to this excessive amount of time spent driving in private road transportation. Many authors have considered creating sensor-based technological solutions to enhance parking spot utilization [2].

With affordable sensors along with backing technology, Internet of things (IoT) enables smart parking alternatives. Different intelligent parking systems that can identify vacant spaces were recently presented. Parking places are found using scanned camera footage. Identical to this, sensors are installed, empty spaces are found, and the consumer is informed of the specifics of the parking places that are vacant [3]. These parking alternatives, however, emphasize a single parking place. An integral part of an IoT-based parking platform is its incorporation of a record-keeping system. The implementation of a reliable database system is required due to the room for storage needed to manage the enormous quantities of data produced by IoT devices, such as parking place information and data about users [4]. Figure 53.1 depicts various technologies applied for parking area management.

The requirement for residential land, industry, and agriculture is growing due to the global increase in human demographic and urbanization which puts a significant amount of stress on obtaining property designated for car parking [5]. Additionally, searching for a parking space takes up a lot of time for automobile owners in the parking lots.

Steps Included in Operation of PAMS

Parking area management system (PAMS) sends the image to Licence Plate Recognition (LPR), which executes an algorithm and keeps processing, to verify the car number plate of the parked vehicle. If ALPR is unable to obtain the LPN, the site officer is notified via SMS that the plate number is not available. A GSM module that is inline attached to the PMS is used for this message communication [6]. The LPN is then manually entered into the system by the site officer. If the system malfunctions in both scenarios, PAMS receives a signal that incorrect

[a]arti.badhoutiya@gla.ac.in, [b]nramchauhan@gmail.com

DOI: 10.1201/9781003534136-53

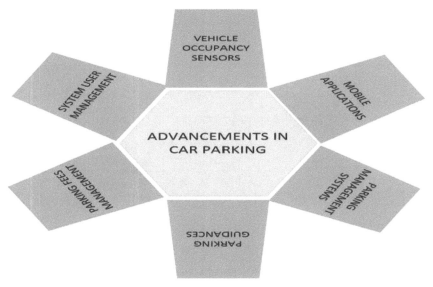

Figure 53.1 Various technologies applied in parking management

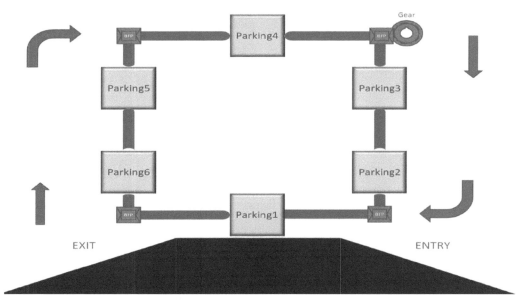

Figure 53.2 Central parking system (CPS)

parking has occurred, and a buzzer rings to alert drivers to their error, as indicated in the flowcharts of Figure 533. If the linked vehicle's license plate number is obtained easily, the record is updated to reflect the vehicle's information and to change the "available" indicator to a "not available" indicator. Following the car's departure, PAMS sends information about how long the vehicle was parked for [7]. The driver is then informed of the total amount due for parking and given a transaction choice. When the system of centralized parking receives a request to reserve a parking space, initially it determines which lot is empty and has available parking spaces before instructing the appropriate PAMS to make the reservation. The detailed record for the relevant parking space is updated to depict the information of the reservation and to include further information if the PAMS confirms it [8]. Following that, the PMS notifies the CPMS of the confirmed reservation and the quantity of available parking spaces. When a parking lot is full, PMS notifies Central Parking Management System (CPMS) that there are no open spots in that parking lot. The CPMS is installed on a top-of-the-line CPM server with a global IP address so that it may be accessed through the Internet [9]. It can therefore be distributed online. Each parking facility's free lots are kept up to date. As a result, a handheld device with a GUI will provide information on the parking facilities and open spaces that are available [10]. The vehicle's driver must reserve a free parking

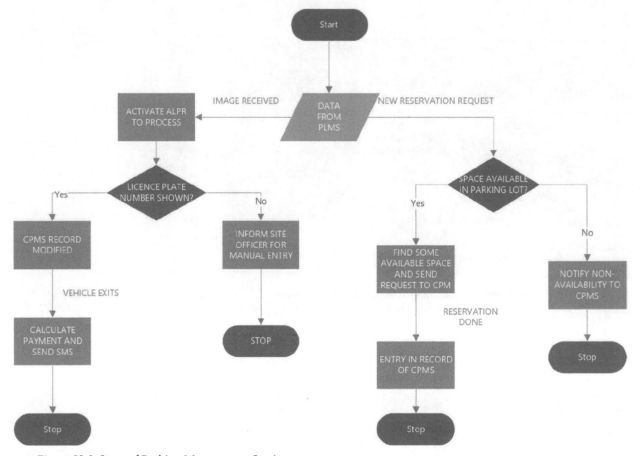

Figure 53.3 Steps of Parking Management Service

space inside the specific parking facility in order for LMPS to receive a request for that space [11]. CPMS may send the booking verification and transaction choices to the user's software once the spot for parking has been assigned by the LMPS and has received notification as well. Figure 53.2 shows the architectural diagram for Central Parking System (CPS).

Conclusion

This method will provide a creative answer to the city's widespread parking problems. By utilizing reservation-based management for parking facilities, this suggested SPS enables the vehicles to learn about the availability of parking spaces and, with the aid of a GUI, book a place in a parking lot. Every parking place has a distributed installed part called a parking meter (PM). This suggested technique can quickly identify illegal parking within the parking area and aids in determining how long each car has been using it. The planned system allows for the automatic collection of parking fees, and drivers have access to advanced payment choices.

References

[1] Anand, A., Kumar, A., Rao, A. N. M., Ankesh, A., and Raj, A. (2020). Smart parking system (S-Park) – a novel application to provide real-time parking solution. In 2020 Third International Conference on Multimedia Processing, Communication & Information Technology (MPCIT), (pp. 93–96), doi: 10.1109/MPCIT51588.2020.9350429.

[2] Chaturvedi, R., Islam, A., Singh, P. K., and Saraswat, M. (2023). Nanotechnology for advanced energy system: synthesis & performance characterization of nano-fuel. In AIP Conference Proceedings (Vol. 2721, No. 1). AIP Publishing.

[3] Anwar, A., Ijaz-ul-Haq, Saeed, N., and Saadati, P. (2021). Smart parking: novel framework of secure smart parking solution using 5G technology. In 2021 IEEE International Smart Cities Conference (ISC2), (pp. 1–4), doi: 10.1109/ISC253183.2021.9562776.

[4] Kumar, P., Singh, P. K., Nagar, S., Sharma, K., and Saraswat, M. (2021). Effect of different concentration of functionalized graphene on charging time reduction in thermal energy storage system. *Materials Today: Proceedings*, 44, 146–152.

[5] Ampuni, A., Fonataba, S., Fitrianto, A., and Wang, G. (2019). Smart parking system with automatic cashier machine utilize the IoT technology. In 2019 International Conference on ICT for Smart Society (ICISS), (pp. 1–4), doi: 10.1109/ICISS48059.2019.8969793.

[6] Al-Kharusi, H., and Al-Bahadly, I. (2014). Intelligent parking management system based on image processing. *World Journal of Engineering and Technology*, 2(2), 55–67.

[7] Chaturvedi, R., Sharma, A., Sharma, K., and Saraswat, M. (2022). Tribological behaviour of multi-walled carbon nano-tubes reinforced AA 7075 nano-composites. *Advances in Materials and Processing Technologies*, 8(4), 47432–4755.

[8] Gandhi, B. M. K., and Rao, M. K. (2016). A prototype for IoT based car parking management system for smart cities. *Indian Journal of Science and Technology*, 9(17), 1–6.

[9] Elsonbaty, A., and Shams, M. (2020). The smart parking management system. arXiv preprint arXiv:2009.13443.

[10] Sharma, A., Chaturvedi, R., Sharma, K., and Saraswat, M. (2022). Force evaluation and machining parameter optimization in milling of aluminium burr composite based on response surface method. *Advances in Materials and Processing Technologies*, 8(4), 4073–4094.

[11] Padmaja, M., Shitharth, S., Prasuna, K., Chaturvedi, A., Kshirsagar, P. R., and Vani, A. (2022). Grow of artificial intelligence to challenge security in IoT application. *Wireless Personal Communications*, 127(3), 1829–1845.

54 Smart air and noise pollution monitoring systems

Rishabh Chaturvedi[1,a] and Manish Saraswat[2,b]

[1]GLA University, Mathura, India

[2]LLOYD Institute of Engineering and Technology, Greater Noida, India

Abstract

Due to extremely high concentration of toxic gases that are present in our environment, air and noise pollution have developed into a very serious problem in modern times in large urban areas. Pollution has a great impact on human health and thus has to be dealt with utmost attention. Internet of things (IoT) technology can be used to develop a system where data can be uploaded on the server with the correct date and time, making the data accessible to all users. In this work, IoT based solutions for observing environmental condition like air pollution and sound pollution have been studied. Additionally, the various hardware elements employed in the design of such a system are explained. The IoT technology provides remote access to any environmental data by storing it in a database or on cloud.

Keywords: Air pollution, Arduino, IoT, monitoring system, node MCU, noise pollution, raspberry Pi, sensors

Introduction

In day to day, new technologies came across all over the world. These advance technologies help in effectively keeping track of the pollution level in the environment. Internet of things (IoT) is one such technology that can help in air and noise pollution monitoring. IoT involves the interaction of humans with machines over the internet. The main factor for the tremendous success of IoT is its efficiency that provides a feasible solution to most of the common problems at low cost. The air and sound pollution monitoring systems can detect wide range of gases with the help of sensors that have long life time, are easily available, have less cost, and are compact and easy to handle. Individuals and the entire planet are negatively impacted by both air and noise pollution. Table 54.1 gives the pollution level at day time and night time which is faced by the human beings [5].

To monitor the pollution level, different sensors are used that measure the noise level and the level of gases like N_2O, CO and SO_2 which are harmful and cause air pollution. Using the technology of IoT a system can be designed where the data can be uploaded on the server with proper date and time, so that the data is available to all the users. Moreover, a danger limit can be set that can be used to inform authorities to take future actions for well-being.

Air and Noise Pollution Monitoring Approaches

Sumithra et al. [1] use air and sound sensors to provide a pollution free city. The authors upload the monitored data on cloud storage for analysis and subsequent notification to the users connected to the cloud server. Singh et al. [2] use sensors to monitor air and noise. Authors use Raspberry Pi to collect the data of the sensors and send it to the application. Sindhu et al. [3] describe the concept of air monitoring with the help of a PIC microcontroller which senses the atmospheric signals for measuring the pollution level in the air. The monitored data is then uploaded on internet for viewing through an application. Kim et al. [4] design an environmental monitoring system and transmit the results to a server. Authors compare their system with the National Ambient air quality Monitoring Information System (NAMIS). Aarthi et. al. [5] use LM393 sound sensor, MQ135 gas sensor, DHT11 temperature and humidity sensor and buzzer along with Rasperry Pi interfaced with GPRS module and WIFI module to design an air and noise pollution monitoring system. Dhruvil Shah et al. [6] propose a real time system with visual output to check the quality of indoor as well as outdoor air. Chandana et al. [7] develop an air and noise quality monitoring system where the monitored data is available to the user over Wi-Fi where the analysis can be done. Anushka Sharma et al. [8] propose a method where the tracked data is transferred from the city's stationary nodes to the nodes in motion stationed aboard public transit. Lipane et al. [9] present a live air and noise quality monitoring system. The data over remote location is transmitted using Wi-Fi module. Joshi [10] propose a system for monitoring the pollution parameters of a particular region so as to make the region smart and pollution free.

[a]rishabh.chaturvedi@gla.ac.in, [b]manish.saraswat@lloydcollege.in

DOI: 10.1201/9781003534136-54

Table 54.1 Standard noise level limit in distinct zone.

Area	Day Time	Night Time
Factorial zone	75	70
Commercial Area	65	55
Dwelling zone	55	45
Hospital area	50	40

Table 54.2 Microcontroller/microprocessor used.

Microcontroller/microprocessor	Specification
Raspberry Pi	A microprocessor that runs a suite of open source software.
Arduino	Single-board microcontrollers which can connect multiple digital and analog sensors.
Xmega 2560	The high-performance, low-power Microchip 8-bit AVR RISC-based microcontroller.
Node MCU	A microcontroller that has **ESP8266** as a low-cost Wi-Fi chip.

Table 54.3 Sensors/actuators used.

Sensors/actuator used	Specification
MQ 2	Used to detect methane, butane, LPG, smoke
MQ-3	Used to detect alcohol, ethanol, smoke
MQ 7	Used for detecting CO gas.
MQ 135 sensor	Used to measure air quality. It is used to detect low conductivity tin oxide (SnO_2).
Sound sensor	Used to detect the presence of sound waves.
DHT11	This is digital temperature and humidity sensor.
Buzzer	An actuator for producing an alarm sound.

Table 54.4 Integration module used.

Integration module used	Specification
Wi-Fi module	Used to provide Wi-Fi connectivity to the Arduino board.
GPS module	To get position, speed, date and time.

Traditional methods involve physical labour where data fellers would physically gather the data, examine it, and utilise analogies to produce an output that was lengthy and time-consuming while also being unproductive [11]. Actuators used in the monitoring model can detect harmful gases like carbon dioxide (CO_2), sulphur dioxide (SO_2), etc. For high values of a variable, such as sound, CO, and pollutant levels, a mark will be given. When nearby objects, sometimes referred to as the perceptive environment, function as a self-defence and observation environment [4] [12-14], they are outfitted with actuators, gadgets, microcontrollers, and various software programmes. It assists in assessing numerous characteristics and transferring data continually into storage.

Hardware Description

This section gives a description of the different hardware components used in designing an IoT based air and noise pollution monitoring system [15]. Table 54.2 gives a brief description of the microcontroller/microprocessor used in designing an IoT based solution.

Table 54.5 Air quality index, effect on health.

Air index	Effect on health
Good (0-50)	Very less risk
Moderate (51-100)	Overall, the Air quality is acceptable. However, there is moderate risk from few pollutants to some highly sensitive people.
Unhealthy for sensitive groups (101-150)	Acceptable by the people in general, but problematic to sensitive people.
Unhealthy (151-200)	Problematic to the people in general; serious risk for sensitive people
Very unhealthy (201-300)	Health warning of emergency conditions.
Hazardous (301-500)	Very serious health effects.

Table 54.3 gives a brief description of the various sensors/actuators that can be used in designing an air and noise pollution monitoring system.

Table 54.4 gives a brief description of the other hardware components used to provide network connectivity.

Table 54.5 gives a brief description of the different air quality index values and their impact on health.

Conclusion

The noise and air pollution monitoring system provides a solution to one of the biggest problems faced by mankind on the earth. It used the latest technique of Internet of Things (IoT) to provide an effective system to support a healthy lifestyle. The Municipal Corporation representatives and the general public can both utilise such an arrangement to receive notifications of the extent of pollution on their mobile devices. In the present work, we have discussed a number of different strategies that have been suggested in the previous research for the development of a similar system utilizing IoT. The different hardware components that are used in the development of such a system are also discussed. As the awareness about the pollution is increasing among people day by day, this concept of IoT provides an effective solution for the welfare of the society.

References

[1] S. Jiyal, J. Sheetlani and R. K. Saini. (2022). Internet of Things: A Survey on Air Pollution Monitoring, Challenges and Applications. 7th International Conference on Computing, Communication and Security (ICCCS), Seoul, Korea, Republic of, 2022, pp. 1–6, doi: 10.1109/ICCCS55188.2022.10079635.

[2] Singh, A., Pathak, D., Pandit, P., Patil, S., and Golar, P. C. (2017). IOT based air and sound pollution monitoring system. *International Journal of Advanced Research in Electrical, Electronics and Instrumentation Engineering*, 6(3), 1273–1278.

[3] Chaturvedi, R., Islam, A., Singh, P. K., and Saraswat, M. (2023). Nanotechnology for advanced energy system: synthesis & performance characterization of nano-fuel. In AIP Conference Proceedings (Vol. 2721, No. 1). AIP Publishing.

[4] Kim, S. H., Jeong, J. M., Hwang, M. T., and Kang, C. S. (2017). Development of an IoT based atmospheric environment monitoring system. In International Conference on Information and Communication Technology Convergence (ICTC), 2017.

[5] Kumar, P., Singh, P. K., Nagar, S., Sharma, K., and Saraswat, M. (2021). Effect of different concentration of functionalized graphene on charging time reduction in thermal energy storage system. *Materials Today: Proceedings*, 44, 146–152.

[6] Prasad, P. & Rani, Maddasani & Keerthana, Garimella & Kumar, Kollu & Bhargav, Uppalapathi. (2021). IOT BASED SOUND AND AIR POLLUTION MEASURING TEMPERATURE AND HUMIDITY MONITORING SYSTEM. International Journal of Innovative Research in Computer Science & Technology. 9. 10.21276/ijircst.2021.9.4.5.

[7] Parmar, C., Patel, S., Shah, R., and Bhelande, M. (2020). Air and Sound Pollution Detector. Recent Innovations in Wireless Network Security, 2(3).

[8] Chaturvedi, R., Sharma, A., Sharma, K., and Saraswat, M. (2022). Tribological behaviour of multi-walled carbon nanotubes reinforced AA 7075 nano-composites. *Advances in Materials and Processing Technologies*, 8(4), 4743–4755.

[9] Borate, T., Lipane, M., Kale, M., Pardeshi, V. and Jawalkar, P. (2019). IoT Based Air and Sound Pollution Monitoring System. Open Access Journal of Science and Engineering, 4(2), 8–11.

[10] Mohan, Lalit. (2017). Research paper on IOT based Air and Sound Pollution Monitoring System. *International Journal of Computer Applications*. 178. 36–49. 10.5120/ijca2017915840.

[11] Sharma, A., Chaturvedi, R., Sharma, K., and Saraswat, M. (2022). Force evaluation and machining parameter optimization in milling of aluminium burr composite based on response surface method. *Advances in Materials and Processing Technologies*, 8(4), 4073–4094.

[12] Kumar, S., and Jasuja, A. (2017). Air quality monitoring system based on IoT using raspberry Pi. In International Conference on Computing, Communication and Automation (ICCCA), 2017.

[13] M. Meli, E. Gatt, O. Casha, I. Grech and J. Micallef. (2020). A Low Cost LoRa-based IoT Big Data Capture and Analysis System for Indoor Air Quality Monitoring, *International Conference on Computational Science and Computational Intelligence (CSCI)*, Las Vegas, NV, USA, 2020, pp. 376–381, doi: 10.1109/CSCI51800.2020.00070.

[14] Swaminathan, B., Palani, S., Vairavasundaram, S., Kotecha, K., and Kumar, V. (2023). IoT-driven artificial intelligence technique for fertilizer recommendation model. *IEEE Consumer Electronics Magazine*, 12(2), 109–117. doi: 10.1109/MCE.2022.3151325.

[15] Khan, S. (2022). Barriers of big data analytics for smart cities development: a context of emerging economies. *International Journal of Management Science and Engineering Management*, 17(2), 123131. DOI: 10.1080/17509653.2021.1997662.

55 Sensor based detection of the space availability in buildings

Rajat Yadav[1,a] and Birendra Kr. Saraswat[2,b]

[1]GLA University, Mathura, India

[2]Raj Kumar Goel Institute of Technology, Ghaziabad, India

Abstract

Building occupancy is very important for controlling buildings in a way that saves energy. There have been a lot of works made to estimate and find out if a building is occupied. Sensor fusion techniques are a way to make up for this, with the goal of using a number of different indoor climate variables to more accurately figure out if a room is occupied. Since combining multiple sensors is a common way to estimate and find out who is in a building, a review is done in this paper on the systems that use different combinations of sensors. By making occupancy predictions more accurate, the difference between predictions and reality could be cut down by a large amount. This paper comprises different methods of occupancy detection mainly employing IR and CO_2 sensors.

Keywords: Detection, environmental sensors, illumination, occupant behavior, ventilation

Introduction

Over the course of the last decade, a significant number of studies have concentrated on sensor technologies for occupancy detection. Nevertheless, there is no standardized or directed selection procedure integrated into the monitoring method. In addition, there is an absence of specific standards for the various combinations of building sensors, which may result in the collection of data that is less than ideal as well as increased expenses associated with experimental installation. Because of its low cost and simple operation, passive infrared, sometimes known as PIR, has seen widespread application. On the other hand, in a prior investigation, the occupancy model was unable to be developed since the delay of passive infrared (PIR) led to inaccurate estimation [1]. Even if the methods of modelling are always the same, the methods of data collection are always different. The PIR sensor is an electronic device that can determine the presence of other things based on the amount of energy that they produce. It has a detection accuracy that falls somewhere between 80% and 90%. The PIR sensor has quickly become the most popular type of sensor due to its low cost and ease of installation. This has led to its widespread application in the detection of occupant movement. Before being sent back to the gateway, the signal from the PIR sensor was run through a filter and an amplifier, which resulted in a significant improvement in the accuracy of the occupancy detecting.

In context-aware computer systems, it is critical to extract insights and useful details from the data collected by sensors. For example, much research has been done on extracting sensor records for context-aware computing, such as estimating occupancy in residential contexts using a range of sensors; occupancy can be recognised by analysing sensor data. To be more particular, data from the detection of occupancy and occupant behavioural variations can be analysed in order to autonomously manage and control buildings for air circulation, air conditioners and heaters, and efficiency in terms of energy use.

The IoT paradigm and its technologies enable things (items) to be connected over the medium of the internet as well as interact with one another in online environments all around the world. Because the Internet of Things connects people and things in omnipresent surroundings, it allows them to share information at any point in time or place, with anything or anybody.

IR Based Occupancy Detection

A number of experiments on occupancy detection have been undertaken utilising traditional sensors such as carbon dioxide (CO_2) gas, ultraviolet (UV) rays, temperature, and moisture sensors. Light sensors and PIR sensors are affordable; however, their detection performance is limited. Through model training, the IR sensor system estimates the density of persons in a specific observation area. This scheme's detecting area is relatively limited, and its mobility is likewise weak [2]. By comparing the aforesaid techniques, we discover that low-resolution

---

[a]rajat.yadav@gla.ac.in, [b]saraswatbirendra@gmail.com

DOI: 10.1201/9781003534136-55

IR sensors can overcome the prior schemes' drawbacks of high incursion, problematic implementation, and low level of detection accuracy. A single IR array sensor can be put in a doorway to compensate for the prior systems' limited mobility and tiny observation areas.

The PIR sensor is probably the most widely used method of detection in buildings for occupant sensing, particularly for illumination control. Despite a substantial body of research on occupant sensing in building contexts over the past couple of years, technological limitations with PIR sensors continue to impede the exploration of novel occupancy sensing solutions [3]. The potential use of PIR sensing in buildings is well recognised to be limited due to numerous fundamental limitations. (a) PIR sensors are capable of delivering only rough binary data (occupied or unoccupied) (b) PIR sensors necessitate a straight line of vision from the location of the sensor and people in the vicinity of a place [4]; (c) PIR sensors demand continual movements to function properly (i.e., occupants must remain seated or the sensor's view is obstructed by obstacles such as objects) (d) PIR sensors can be affected by different thermal currents such as heated coffee/tea, electrical gadgets, and heating & ventilating systems.

Applications of Carbon-Dioxide Sensors

The amount of CO_2 in a space goes up directly when people are there. It has been shown that the CO_2 sensor is the best environmental sensor for figuring out how many people are in a room [2]. It can find things between 85% and 95% of the time. Statistical pattern matching was used by Szczurek et al. to come up with a simple way to estimate the number of occupants [5]. First, the researchers had been using a time sequence technique to measure and record the Concentration of carbon dioxide. Then, they used pattern matching to look at the relationship between the framework of the time series and the availability.

Dong [6] also used a mix of sensors (temperature, moisture, CO_2, and light) to find out if there were people in a room. He observed that the CO_2 sensor data had the most impact on the findings of the prediction. Above figure shows the two most common ways that sensors can be put together. The first one has a camera, a PIR sensor, and a CO_2 sensor. A CO_2 sensor is set up in the room to find out how many people are in there. On the seat of the occupant, a PIR sensor is set up to check if the person is there. The camera records how the person actually moves. Figure 1 depicts applications of sensors in availability detection. This fusion is good for figuring out if there will be more than one person in an office building. Arora et al. showed a system for estimating occupancy by combining data from many sensors, such as temperature, humidity, CO_2, lighting, PIR, door state, and energy utilization [7].

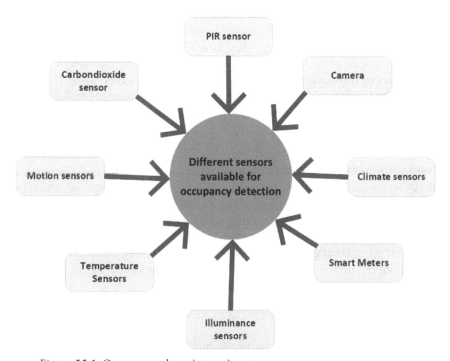

Figure 55.1 Occupancy detections using sensors

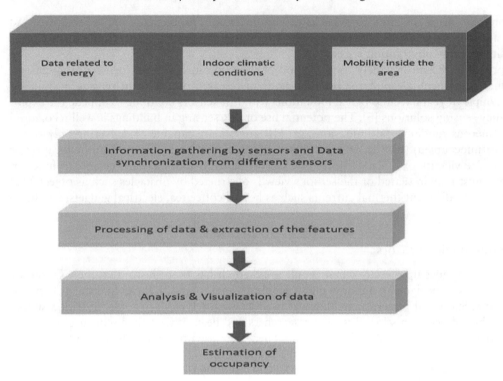

Figure 55.2 Steps included in sensor-based occupancy detection

Using environmental sensors to guess the number or variety of people in a room is more difficult. Since the raw sensory data is loud and not useful for estimating occupancy, study aimed to use a technique called "feature engineering," which is often used for machine learning models [4]. The two parts of feature engineering are feature extraction and recovery of features. Using domain knowledge, feature extraction is the process of making some informative representations of the raw data. Feature selection is the process of choosing some features that are more insightful based on certain parameters. Zhang et al. used statistical modelling to combine CO_2 and power consumption data to estimate how many people were in a building [8]. First, they used a physical diffusion model to pull out some features from CO_2. For occupancy prediction with restricted training data, statistical distribution was used with two models: maximum a posteriori probability (MAP) estimation of HMM and multiple-hypothesis sequential probability ratio test (MSPRT). First, they took the raw sensory data and pulled out some relevant properties. Then, information gain theory was used to choose which features to use. Using the chosen features and a DT algorithm, the number of occupants was finally found. In their other work, [9], they also added a microphone that can measure the room's sound level. The same method for choosing features was used. The DT and RF learning algorithms were used to estimate how many people were in the room [10]. Figure 2 shows how sensor-based occupancy detection works.

Conclusion

Occupancy detection in buildings is beneficial in controlling things like illumination and ventilation, which saves energy and keeps the building comfortable. But because of their limitations, PIR and environmental sensors always make mistakes in detecting people and collecting data. By making occupancy predictions more accurate, the difference between what actually happened and what was predicted could be cut down by a lot. When CO_2 sensors and cameras are used to record data, the accuracy of the data is high. Light has a big effect on how well a camera can see, but a CO_2 sensor can compensate for this. The article discusses many methods of detecting occupancy, primarily using IR and CO_2 sensors.

References

[1]   Wang, D., Federspiel, C. C., and Rubinstein, F. (2005). Modeling occupancy in single person offices. *Energy and Buildings*, 37, 121–126.

[2] Candanedo, L. M., Feldheim, V., and Deramaix, D. (2017). A methodology based on hidden Markov models for occupancy detection and a case study in a low energy residential building. *Energy and Buildings*, 148, 327–341.

[3] Sharma, A., Chaturvedi, R., Sharma, K., and Saraswat, M. (2022). Force evaluation and machining parameter optimization in milling of aluminium burr composite based on response surface method. *Advances in Materials and Processing Technologies*, 8(4), 4073–4094.

[4] Amayri, M., Arora, A., Ploix, S., Bandhyopadyay, S., Ngo, Q.-D., and Badarla, V. R. (2016). Estimating occupancy in heterogeneous sensor environment. *Energy and Buildings*, 129, 46–58.

[5] Chaturvedi, R., Sharma, A., Sharma, K., and Saraswat, M. (2022). Tribological behaviour of multi-walled carbon nanotubes reinforced AA 7075 nano-composites. *Advances in Materials and Processing Technologies*, 8(4), 4743–4755.

[6] Dong, B., Andrews, B., Lam, K. P., Höynck, M., Zhang, R., Chiou, Y. S., and Benitez, D. (2010). An information technology enabled sustainability test-bed (ITEST) for occupancy detection through an environmental sensing network. *Energy and Buildings*, 42(7), 1038–1046.

[7] Kumar, P., Singh, P. K., Nagar, S., Sharma, K., and Saraswat, M. (2021). Effect of different concentration of functionalized graphene on charging time reduction in thermal energy storage system. *Materials Today: Proceedings*, 44, 146–152.

[8] Liu, Z., Zhang, J., and Geng, L. (2017). An intelligent building occupancy detection system based on sparse auto-encoder. In IEEE Winter Applications of Computer Vision Workshops (WACVW), 2017, (pp. 17–22).

[9] Chaturvedi, R., Islam, A., Singh, P. K., and Saraswat, M. (2023). Nanotechnology for advanced energy system: synthesis & performance characterization of nano-fuel. In AIP Conference Proceedings (Vol. 2721, No. 1). AIP Publishing.

[10] Liu, H., and Motoda, H. (1998). Feature Extraction, Construction and Selection: A Data Mining Perspective, (Vol. 453), Springer Science & Business Media.

56 Fire detection & fighting using deep learning method

Aman Sharma[1,a] and Nathiram Chauhan[2,b]

[1]GLA University, Mathura, India

[2]Indira Gandhi Delhi Technical University for Women, Delhi, India

Abstract

Abstract. An industrial fire catastrophe would be extraordinarily hazardous and expensive. Accidental industrial fires would cause significant damage and pose a considerable risk to human life. Small firefighting efforts and early fire discovery could stop considerable loss of property and save lives. This is simple due to developments in sensing, information, and communication technologies, Early fire detection and small-step firefighting techniques taking action could prevent catastrophic loss and save lives. many people. If there is effective firefighting, fire accidents won't result in significant loss. There has been a significant advancement in fire sensing and firefighting technology in recent years. This paper includes the methods for detecting fires using deep learning method and also android in mobiles helpful in monitoring robots for firefighting.

Keywords: Android, deep learning, detecting, fire, raspberry-pi

Introduction

Fires are generating serious [1] consequences in companies like those that handle nuclear power plants, refineries, petroleum, chemical factories, and fuel tanks. Due to the fact that human involvement is decreasing daily as a result of advancements in the field of robotics, robots are widely used for safety purposes. The firefighting robot helps to put out fires quickly and safely, rescue individuals from potentially dangerous fires, and relocate them to a safer location. And the fire-fighting robot was sent out to detect the fire and put it out before it spread. Due to its low danger of injury, this firefighting robot can replace actual firefighters. Additionally good for commercial fire safety [2] is a crucial factor to consider since it can prevent businesses from suffering significant losses and contribute to the preservation of human life. To stop fires from starting uncontrolled, many businesses should have fire safety measures. The fire prevention measures prevent the surrounding and the environment from suffering significant damage. Incidental fires have the potential to cause severe damage to both property and human life. It would be extremely advantageous to have an automaton capable of detecting and extinguishing fires under these circumstances. Historically, burn robots identified peril using flame sensors and other detection mechanisms. Obstacles were detected by firefighting robots by means of their ultrasonic sensors. The distance between the robot and the barrier was ascertained through the measurement of the detector's pulse's return journey from the object to the sensors. The precise reference point for this measurement was a cutoff point. Nuclear power plants, refineries, fires, and petroleum accidents all have a significant impact on the chemical and fuel tank industries. Due to the fact that technological advancements are decreasing the need for human interaction, robots have found extensive application in the realm of safety. With the aid of the robotic firefighter, flames are extinguished. Efficiently and effectively extinguish the fire while assisting individuals in evacuating the hazardous vicinity to a more secure area. In addition, the dispatch of the firefighting automaton is intended to detect the fire prior to its propagation. This struggle against the flames Firefighters is being replaced by robots due to the reduced risk of injury they present. Also effective in commercials. When the distance between obstacles fell below the specified threshold, the robot would proceed in a reversing direction towards the fire in order to locate the path with the fewest obstructions [4, 3]. This study implements a Deep Learning methodology for fire detection and suppression robotics operating on the Android platform. In this regard, deep learning methodologies may be implemented to classify photographs with the intention of identifying objects. A subset of deep learning neural networks consists of convolutional neural networks (CNNs), for instance. An input image is modified by means of filters or kernels. The purpose of each filter is to accentuate a distinct attribute, such as the contours of the cheekbones or eyes [5, 6]. Table 56.1 shows Fire types with their extinguishable system.

[a]aman.sharma@gla.ac.in, [b]nramchauhan@gmail.com

DOI: 10.1201/9781003534136-56

Table 56.1 Fire types with their extinguishable system.

Fire type	Description	Examples	Safe way of extinguishing
A	Flammable gasses	Methane butane	Dry powder
B	Electrical equipment's	Computers generators	CO_2, dry powder
C	Combustible material	Paper wood	Wet chemical, dry powder, water
D	Flammable liquids	Paint, petrol	Foam, CO_2, dry powder
E	Flammable metals	Lithium potassium	Dry powder

Figure 56.1 Fire detection using deep learning method

Fire Detection using Deep Learning Method

In this study, the YOLOv3 model was previously trained, and deep learning was used to teach it to recognize fire and its coordinates. Transfer learning was used to expedite learning and guarantee that the models trained were more effective at detecting objects. There are 533 images in the collection overall. Using LabelIng, bounding boxes around objects in the dataset's pictures were labelled [7, 8].

The training code was utilized to educate the model. We developed a model capable of precise item detection through iterative refinement of the sample size and experimentation count. We utilized a group size of 8 and 100 experiments for model training [9, 10]. In order to select the optimal model, its mean average precision (mAP) was computed. The 89th epoch model was selected as it produced the highest value compared to all other models [11]. Subsequently, the model proceeded to produce bounding box regions with a minimum probability of 30% [12]. The present investigation utilized a pre-existing iteration of the YOLOv3 model, which had been trained to identify fire and its locations via deep learning. Transfer learning was implemented to accelerate the learning process and improve the object detection performance of the trained models. The collection contains 533 images. Item bounding boxes were applied to the photographs in the dataset, which were annotated with Labelling. Using deep learning to detect fires (Figure 56.1). The training code was utilized to educate the model. We developed a model capable of precise item detection through iterative refinement of the sample size and experimentation count. We utilized a group size of 8 and 100 experiments for model training [9, 10]. In order to select the optimal model, its mean average precision (mAP) was computed. The 89th epoch model was selected as it produced the highest value compared to all other models [11]. Subsequently, the model proceeded to produce bounding box regions with a minimum probability of 30% [12].

Using Android Designing of Fire Fighting Robots

Due to its low danger of injury, this fire fighting robot can replace actual firefighters. Additionally helpful for industrial use [13].

Used Components are

a. *Rasberry pie.* The single-board Raspberry Pi 3 computer is popular in robotics. Additionally, research projects employ it. The Raspberry Pi is affordable and lightweight. That is the raspberry Pi is employed for managing the project. robot movement and for water spraying when the button is depressed.

b. *Temperature sensor.* A cheap digital temperature sensor is the DHT11. Thermistor is used to measure the air quality and convert it to a digital signal. Data is used to transmit the digital signal pin. Although it is easy to use, it must be handled carefully. To pull up from data, a 4.7k or 10k resistor is needed the VCC pin [14].

c. *Flame sensor.* A flame sensor is used to find fires when they start. The term "flame sensor" refers to the sensor's high sensitivity to ambient light. This sensor finds fire within the vicinity of from 760 to 1100 nm. The sensor's output is digital. This robots employ sensors for things like alarms [15].

d. *Node Mcu.* Node mcu is an open source IoT platform. The node mcu is the name of the inexpensive firmware device. Both IoT applications and prototypes are developed using it. The ESP32 microcontroller in the mcu node has Bluetooth and WiFi. Ethernet as well. It uses 7 to 12 volts to work.

Working Model of Fire Fighting Robot

Wherever there is a chance of a fire accident, the sensor module is installed. The module is made up of a Node mcu for data transfer and sensors for temperature, smoke, and flame. Node mcu will send data to the firebase as soon as the fire is discovered. The receiver is made up of two components: an Android application and a Raspberry Pi in the first half. The raspberry pi receives data from the pi camera, which is used by the android application to display video. A WIFI module is part of the Android application and is used to connect the robot and android application. Through the android application, commands are transmitted to the robot to move forward, left, right, and put out fire. The robotic vehicle is equipped with a water tanker and a wirelessly operated water-throwing pump. Using an Android application device, commands are transferred from the transmitting end to the receiver to direct the robot's movement in various directions, including forward, backward, left, and right. Three motors are connected to the Raspberry Pi at the receiving end; two of them are used to move the vehicle, while the third one is used to move the robot's arm. Any smartphone is capable of remote operation. Figure 56.2 shows the flowchart of the working model [16].

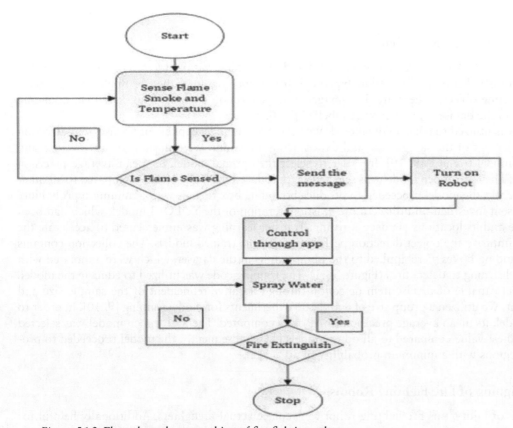

Figure 56.2 Flow chart shows working of fire fighting robot

Applications
Used as a fire extinguisher.
  Used in home security.
  Used in server rooms in offices.

Conclusion

As a consequence of mechanical progress, the need for human involvement has diminished, and robotics are currently being implemented across diverse sectors, including human welfare. Constantly occurring fires pose a significant hazard to individuals and their assets, and they have the potential to claim the lives of firefighters endeavouring to extinguish the blaze. Incidental fires have the potential to cause severe damage to both property and human life. In such circumstances, an autonomous firefighting device with the ability to detect and extinguish fires would be of the utmost importance. Earlier designs for firefighting robots significantly relied on sensors, such as flame detectors, to detect fire. This paper develops a framework for fire protection and detection utilizing mobile Android robots and deep learning. We implemented deep learning and its algorithms, in addition to an Android-operable firefighting device, in order to avert fires. The most prevalent locations for these fire detection and prevention systems are in residential buildings and fire extinguishers.

References

[1] Ramasubramanian, S., Muthukumaraswamy, S. A., and Sasikala, A. (2020). Fire detection using artificial intelligence for fire-fighting robots. In 2020 4th International Conference on Intelligent Computing and Control Systems (ICICCS). IEEE, 2020.

[2] Chaturvedi, R., Islam, A., Singh, P. K., and Saraswat, M. (2023). Nanotechnology for advanced energy system: synthesis & performance characterization of nano-fuel. In AIP Conference Proceedings (Vol. 2721, No. 1). AIP Publishing.

[3] Raj, P. Anantha, and M. Srivani. (2018). Internet of robotic things based autonomous fire fighting mobile robot. IEEE international conference on computational intelligence and computing research (ICCIC). IEEE, 2018.

[4] Raj, P. A., and Srivani, M. (2018). Internet of robotic things based autonomous fire fighting mobile robot. In 2018 IEEE International Conference on Computational Intelligence and Computing Research (ICCIC). IEEE, 2018.

[5] Kumar, P., Singh, P. K., Nagar, S., Sharma, K., and Saraswat, M. (2021). Effect of different concentration of functionalized graphene on charging time reduction in thermal energy storage system. *Materials Today: Proceedings*, 44, 146–152.

[6] Raj, P. A., and Srivani, M. (2018). Internet of robotic things based autonomous fire fighting mobile robot. In 2018 IEEE International Conference on Computational Intelligence and Computing Research (ICCIC). IEEE, 2018.

[7] Chaturvedi, R., Sharma, A., Sharma, K., and Saraswat, M. (2022). Tribological behaviour of multi-walled carbon nanotubes reinforced AA 7075 nano-composites. *Advances in Materials and Processing Technologies*, 8(4), 4743–4755.

[8] Bansal, S., and Tomar, V. K. (2022). Challenges & security threats in IoT with solution architectures. In 2022 2nd International Conference on Power Electronics & IoT Applications in Renewable Energy and its Control (PARC). IEEE, 2022.

[9] Sowah, R. A., Ofoli, A. R., Krakani, S. N., and Fiawoo, S. Y. (2016). Hardware design and web-based communication modules of a real-time multisensor fire detection and notification system using fuzzy logic. *IEEE Transactions on Industry Applications*, 53(1), 559–566.

[10] Sharma, A., Chaturvedi, R., Sharma, K., and Saraswat, M. (2022). Force evaluation and machining parameter optimization in milling of aluminium burr composite based on response surface method. *Advances in Materials and Processing Technologies*, 8(4), 4073–4094.

[11] Fadlullah, Z. M., Tang, F., Mao, B., Kato, N., Akashi, O., Inoue, T., and Mizutani, K. (2017). State-of-the-art deep learning: Evolving machine intelligence toward tomorrow's intelligent network traffic control systems. *IEEE Communications Surveys & Tutorials*, 19(4), 2432–2455.

[12] Taiwo, O., Ezugwu, A. E., Oyelade, O. N., and Almutairi, M. S. (2022). Enhanced intelligent smart home control and security system based on deep learning model. *Wireless communications and mobile computing*, 2022, 1–22.

[13] Bansal, S., and Tomar, V. K. (2022). Simulation and analysis of 11T SRAM cell for IoT-based applications. In Advances in Communication, Devices and Networking. Singapore: Springer, (pp. 329–340).

[14] Wu, X., Dunne, R., Zhang, Q., and Shi, W. (2017, October). Edge computing enabled smart firefighting: opportunities and challenges. In Proceedings of the Fifth ACM/IEEE Workshop on Hot Topics in Web Systems and Technologies (pp. 1–6).

[15] Agrawal, R., and Tomar, V. K. (2018). Analysis of low power reduction techniques on cache (SRAM) memory. In 2018 9th International Conference on Computing, Communication and Networking Technologies (ICCCNT), (pp. 1–7). IEEE.

[16] Zhang, Qingyang, et al. Edge video analytics for public safety: A review. Proceedings of the IEEE 107.8 (2019): 1675–1696.

57 Controlling jatropha seed distribution through graphic solution

Rajat Yadav[1,a] and Manish Saraswat[2,b]

[1]GLA University, Mathura, India

[2]LLOYD Institute of Engineering and Technology, Greater Noida, India

Abstract

When biodiesel comes from jatropha and pong, alternating fuels produce more returns. This bioenergy is a substitute and is particularly important for petrol-diesel. However, the collection of olive oilseeds is a highly complicated activity. The following algorithms were used by the current supply chain system: Bender's decomposition, Programming based on Markov chain process, etc. For the use of the corresponding systems, the algorithms provided positive values. Consequently, the planner must bear in mind social and economic problems associated with the development of a bioenergy system and the unique challenges each country faces. Through an integrated unilateral graphical approach, possible and required constraints, the models proposed recommend the optimum Jatropha seed district. The cycle takes four different levels of the module. In the graphical method for designing the correct delivery solution, the paper focuses on the initial process level. The solution will be transferred to the next stage of the supply chain network module.

Keywords: Bi-lateral graph, biodiesel, Jatropha seed, Signed graph, supply chain, unilateral graph

Introduction

The fall in oil production raises global oil prices and decreases the global economy [1]. This Jatropha cruces seed was considerable political and social constraints in favor of India's development as a way of stimulating the economy, social employment and alleviating poverty in disadvantaged communities [2]. Jatropha is a rare, multi-purpose plant that can be used for bioenergy to mitigate soil erosion, desertification and deforestation. A supply chain is the network of seed procurement, transformation into oil for these seeds and delivery to consumers of these producers, warehouses or distribution networks [3]. This network planning decides on the network configuration, i.e. the number, location, power and equipment. Optimal seed collection center sites, facilities scale, stockpiling and traffic offs are taking the opportunity to decide. A network architecture method and a solid structure function for the execution of the operational supply chain must be modeled and tested Costs are estimated to be approximately equal to those of petroleum diesel for biodiesel generated by transesterification of oil obtained from Jatropha Cruces oleaginous seeds.

Petroleum Diesel demand is forecast at 52,33 million tons by the end of Plan 10 (2006-07). A total of 2.29 million ha under Jatropha cruces plantation is required to substitute petroleum diesel with biodiesel by 5% by the year 2006-07. Unnecessary land will become productive farmers and farmers can be assured that their goods would be costly. The seed of Jatropha contains 27 to 31% extractable oil. The Jatrofa plantation is estimated to yield over 100 000 hectares of jatropha crude petroleum from 250 000 to 300 000 tons per year. The original Jatropha farm is expected to produce revenues of 100,000 hectares of USD per year.

Factors Influencing Distribution Network Design

Includes vendor needs, which are met, and the expense of meeting and supplier are needs [4]. The delivery network efficiency measured in two dimensions at ground level. Ø Network-influenced supplier service elements such as well as time, quality of the commodity, supplier experience, visibility of orders, modes of transport [5]. Ø Network structure-influenced supply chain charges include, seed inventory or storage, transportation, equipment and management, details, transport process. When pickup sites are chosen by the teacher, the decision taking issue occurs. The graphic method has overcome this.

Preliminary Definitions

$G = (V(G), E(G), G)$ is a commanded threefold composed of a non-empty set $V(G)$ a set $E(G)$, a $V(G)$ disjoint and the βG incidence feature, that combines an un-compared pair of $V(G)$ elements with each element of $E(G)$. V

---

[a]rajat.yadav@gla.ac.in, [b]manish.saraswat@lloydcollege.in

DOI: 10.1201/9781003534136-57

(G) is defined as the vertex set with the edge set of G and E(G). V (G) elements are known as the G vertices (also known as G points or nodes), and E (G) elements are known as the G edges.

Example: 1
G= (V (G), E (G), ÷G) where V (G) = {V1, V_2, V_3, V_4},

E(G) = {e_1,e_2,e_3, e_4, e_5, e_6} and $÷_G$, is defined by $÷G_{(e1)}$ = V_1, V_2, $÷G_{(e2)}$) = V_2V_3 $÷G_{(e3)}$ = V_3V_4 $÷G_{(e4)}$ =V_4V_1, $÷G_{(e5)}$ =V_2V_2, $÷G_{(e6)}$ =V_3V_4

Let G be a p-vertical graph and q-edge diagram described as the V1, V2,V3 ... Vp and e1, e2, e3, ... ep. The matrix incident to G1 is p X q matrix M (G) = (mij) where mij is a quantity of incidents that occur in Vj and Ex that can provide an extension up-to:

i = 1, 2, 3, 4, 5, 6.....m

j = 1, 2, 3, 4, 5, 6....n

Algorithm of Graphical Chain
This algorithm defines a number of Phases to be taken to solve a certain problem in a certain sequence chain in a limited number. The problem of an algorithm is the f(n) function, that allows the algorithm to run or store the information in the size n. If the input size, n, is a polynomial, or if the data is bound to n, the algorithm is efficient. If the problem is solved by an efficient algorithm, the code issue is called tractable. A computational problem can be found if no effective problem-solving algorithm exists [6]. This kind of classification is not well understood for many problems.

Graph Theory -Binary Trees Fundamentals
D = (V(D), A(D), D) can be seen here.
   If e = (u, v) is a Darc it is said that u is annexed to v1. We often claim that the Arc E is an accident and an occurrence from u. Number of the vertices adjacent to the V is known as the v outdegree and the adjacent vertices are identified by v index. The v index, outdeg and vertex grades are defined by indeg v, outdeg v, and deg vor d(v) respectively.
   The D digit walk is an alternation of a series of vertices and arcs (finite and not null) W: v0, e1, v1e2v2 ...... even such that ei = (vi-1) for 1d I d n.The distance is defined as n. We define road, route and cycle in the same manner as in a graph [7]. On a walk, if you are at the halfway point, you will be referred to as an ei = (Vi-1, Vj) or (Vi, Vj,-1).

Constraints on Decision Making
As a result of distribution network problem the constraints on decision making can be seen in Figure 57.1.

   a. Distance
   b. Cost of seed
   c. Mode of Transport
   d. Others

Figure 57.1 Constraints on Decision making

Hypothesis Fixing

* **Instance (1)**
   All constraints are met in the connection from F1 to C1. Indeg (C1) = 4, therefore;

Ind(F1) = 0. Index As formers (F1) wanted adjacency to the collection centers in general in relation to the limitations a, b, c, d. That's good. In other words, index (F1) < index (C1) is + ve. It shows in Figure 57.2

Figure 57.2 Constraints on Decision making

- **Instance (2)**
  F1 with first 3 conditions C1 fulfilled, i.e. index (C1) = 3; index (F1) = 1.
  Indicator (F1) <Indeg (C1),It shows in Figure 57.3.
  As illustrated in Table 58.1, all levels give positive results to choose the collection center C.

- **Instance (3)**
  Here F1 has only 2 fulfilled C1 terms While C1 also has two satisfied F1 conditions, the decision is only taken by F1. The decision to choose pickup sites or collection centers for customers is therefore focused exclusively on the preferences of the four restrictions: distance, expense, transport methods and psychological factors. It is shown in Figure 58.4.

The following table shows the decision tree with the four limitations. The decision tree is simplified by constructing binary [9–11] decomposition.

Table 57.2 clearly shows that the first two restrictions, namely distance and expense, have been prioritized and that collection centers, can be selected if both or the first or only level 5 of the first two limitations are met [12]

- **Instance (4)**

  Index (F1) = 3; Index (C1) = 1

Since F1 only has one with C1, according to our priority in this Instance, with regard to a, b , c, d, selection of collection center fails. It shows in Figure 58.8.

Graphical Approach Used in Selection Priority
After all, F1 may or may not have adjacency to C1. The figure below shows the preference of collection centers for the constraints of the correct formers [13, 14].

Table 57.1 Positive results description.

S. No.	Status	P(d)	T(c)	C(b)	D(a)
1	+ve	1	1	1	0
2	+ve	1	1	0	1
3	+ve	1	0	1	1
4	+ve	0	1	1	1

Table 57.2 For instance 3 negative results description.

S.No.	Status	P(d)	T(c)	C(b)	D(a)
1	-ve	0	1	0	1
2	-ve	1	1	0	0
3	-ve	0	0	1	1
4	-ve	1	1	0	0
5	-ve	1	1	0	0

Special Instance

Here C1 wanted adjacency with F1 in 4 ways. The above Table 58.3 summarized by the following JDS-algorithm. It shows in Figure 58.9.

JDS-algorithm

The Jatropha seed distribution strategy as Jatropha distribution system (JDS) has an algorithm developed for decision-making [15].

Phase 0: Measure the formers and retailers initialize

Phase 1: A previous relation to n number

Table 3: Summarized outcome

The four Instances will be followed by each distributor in phases 1 to 5.

Phase 1: For all input units, it is positive.

Table 57.3 Comparison of F1 and C1.

S.No.	Instances	Index of F_1	Index of C_1	Comparison of F_1 with C_1
1	Instance 1	0	2	$F_1 < C_1$
2	Instance 2	1	4	$F_1 < C_1$
3	Instance 3	4	4	$F_1 = C_1$
4	Instance 4	5	2	$F_1 > C_1$

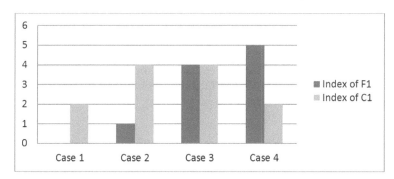

Figure 57.3 Comparison of C1 and F1

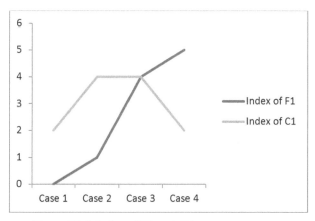

Figure 57.4 Index of F1 and C1

C1(4)>0 Positive

C1(4)=0 Negative

Phase 2: If any three input units are applicable it is positive i.e.

C2 (3)>0 Positive

C2(3) =0 Negative

Phase 3: The cost and distance priority that must be taken into account. It is good if costs and distances apply. i.e.,

C3 (2)>0 Positive

C3 (2)=0 Negative

Phase 4: If only one input limit exists, it is negative. i.e.,

C4 (1)>0 Positive

C4(1) =0Negative

Phase 5: If the trader (customers) meets all of the Instances in a dealer, the former selects the nth dealer.

Then take Phases 1 to 5 until the distributor is identified. It shows in Figure 58.10.

Conclusion

The results show clearly the network based on a unilateral diagram. This graphic approach creates outgoing logistics options, which look at ways to find the best way to choose suitable collection centers or pick-up sites. Identification of a variety of variables causing the decision-making difficulties. With capacity restrictions and balanced restrictions both, for a problem of allocation, the algorithm proposed can be generalized. Jatropha seed distribution strategy (JDS) has an algorithm developed to help make decisions. The decision has taken to choose pickup sites or collection centers for customers is therefore focused exclusively on the preferences of the four restrictions: distance, expense, transport methods and psychological factors. The advantage of this algorithm is tackling of cost and distance, it is good in managing both the factors.

References

[1] Ge, S., Yek, P. N. Y., Cheng, Y. W., Xia, C., Mahari, W. A. W., Liew, R. K., ... and Lam, S. S. (2021). Progress in microwave pyrolysis conversion of agricultural waste to value-added biofuels: a batch to continuous approach. *Renewable and Sustainable Energy Reviews*, 135, 110148.

[2] Bansal, S., and Tomar, (2022). Challenges & security threats in IoT with solution architectures. In 2022 2nd International Conference on Power Electronics & IoT Applications in Renewable Energy and its Control (PARC). IEEE, 2022.

[3] Sharma, A., Chaturvedi, R., Sharma, K., and Saraswat, M. (2022). Force evaluation and machining parameter optimization in milling of aluminium burr composite based on response surface method. *Advances in Materials and Processing Technologies*, 8(4), 4073–4094.

[4] Badhoutiya, A., Shivhare, N., and Goyal, S. (2021). An Intelligent traffic control prototype for smooth vehicular flow based on FX5U-32MT PLC. In 2021 International Conference on Simulation, Automation & Smart Manufacturing (SASM), (pp. 1–5), doi: 10.1109/SASM51857.2021.9841181.

[5] Chaturvedi, R., Sharma, A., Sharma, K., and Saraswat, M. (2022). Tribological behaviour of multi-walled carbon nanotubes reinforced AA 7075 nano-composites. *Advances in Materials and Processing Technologies*, 8(4), 4743–4755.

[6] Kumar, P., Singh, P. K., Nagar, S., Sharma, K., and Saraswat, M. (2021). Effect of different concentration of functionalized graphene on charging time reduction in thermal energy storage system. *Materials Today: Proceedings*, 44, 146–152.

[7] Sriprapakhan, Preecha, Ritchard Artkla, Santipong Nuanual, and Pisit Maneechot. (2021). Economic and ecological assessment of integrated agricultural bio-energy and conventional agricultural energy frameworks for agriculture sustainability. *Journal of the Saudi Society of Agricultural Sciences*. 20(4), 227–234.

[8] Srinivasan, S. P., and Deenadayalan, G. (2020). A decision support strategy for Jatropha seed collection for biodiesel making through graphical approach. *International Journal of Services Operations and Informatics*, 10(3), 190–206.

[9] Ge, S., Yek, P. N. Y., Cheng, Y. W., Xia, C., Mahari, W. A. W., Liew, R. K., ... and Lam, S. S. (2021). Progress in microwave pyrolysis conversion of agricultural waste to value-added biofuels: a batch to continuous approach. *Renewable and Sustainable Energy Reviews*, 135, 110148.

[10] Chaturvedi, R., Islam, A., Singh, P. K., and Saraswat, M. (2023). Nanotechnology for advanced energy system: synthesis & performance characterization of nano-fuel. In AIP Conference Proceedings (Vol. 2721, No. 1). AIP Publishing.

[11] Rith, M., and Biona, J. B. M. M. (2021). Development of mathematical models for engine performance and emissions of the producer gas-diesel dual fuel mode using response surface methodology. *Engineering and Applied Science Research*, 48(1), 18–32.

[12] Yu, Fengbo, Xiangdong Zhu, Wenjie Jin, Jiajun Fan, James H. Clark, and Shicheng Zhang. (2020). Optimized synthesis of granular fuel and granular activated carbon from sawdust hydrochar without binder. *Journal of Cleaner Production*. 276: 122711.

[13] Srinivasan, S. P., and Deenadayalan, G. (2020). A decision support strategy for Jatropha seed collection for biodiesel making through graphical approach. *International Journal of Services Operations and Informatics*, 10(3), 190–206.

[14] Yadav, K., and Agrawal, R. (2022). Ethical hacking and web security: approach interpretation. In 2022 Second International Conference on Artificial Intelligence and Smart Energy (ICAIS), (pp. 1382–1384), doi: 10.1109/ICAIS53314.2022.9742736.

[15] Singh, Digambar, Dilip Sharma, S. L. Soni, Chandrapal Singh Inda, Sumit Sharma, Pushpendra Kumar Sharma, and Amit Jhalani. (2021). A comprehensive review of physicochemical properties, production process, performance and emissions characteristics of 2nd generation biodiesel feedstock: Jatropha curcas. *Fuel*. 285: 119110.

58 Evaluation of soil fertility using multi-SVM and K-means

Saloni Bansal[1,a] and Birendra Kr. Saraswat[2,b]

[1]GLA University, Mathura, India

[2]Raj Kumar Goel Institute of Technology, Ghaziabad, India

Abstract

Farmers always play a significant role in the Indian economy, but occasionally they experience distinct financial difficulties owing to unfavorable weather. Farmers also deal with a variety of problems when choosing crops based on the soil's fertility. Different types of fertility and minerals are present in the soil at various soil locations throughout India. Farmers constantly struggle to choose the optimal crop based on soil fertility and mineral content. A crop's growth is largely dependent on the properties of the soil. For crop selection based on soil test results, the paper used Multi-SVM (support vector machine) and the K-means clustering technique. K-means and Multi-SVM algorithms create clusters according to the classification of the dataset. In the paper, a connection between the Multi-SVM and K-means algorithms was proposed. Multi-SVM implementation is significantly more difficult than K-means but gives greater quality. Multi-SVM had an accuracy rate of 80% whereas K-means clustering had an accuracy rate of 62%. Larger databases perform better than tiny databases when using the Multi-SVM algorithm. In order to study the weather, the report also suggested a module for weather forecasting. Finally, producers can select a crop based on the qualities of the land and the weather.

Keywords: Crop, fertilizers, K-means clustering, multi-SVM (support vector machine)

Introduction

Farmers constantly struggle to choose the optimal crop based on soil fertility and mineral content. Crop growth mostly depends on the properties of the soil. For crop selection based on soil test results, the paper used multi-SVM (support vector machine) and the K-means clustering technique [1]. K-means and multi-SVM algorithms create clusters based on the classification of the dataset. In the paper, a connection between the multi-SVM and K-means algorithms was proposed. Multi-SVM implementation is slightly more challenging than K-means but provides better accuracy. Multi-SVM has an 80% accuracy rate whereas K-means clustering had a 62% accuracy rate. There are five different diseases that might reduce apple yield: Alter aria leaf spot, mosaic, grey spot, rust, and brown spot. However, the current approaches are unable to timely and accurately identify these disorders. The goal of this study is to use CNN and deep learning to quickly identify this issue [2]. The disease dataset was created utilizing data augmentation and picture annotation techniques, and it includes sophisticated laboratory images. Several human and material resources are being used to collect data on apple leaf disease because there aren't enough datasets accessible for real-time detection. Temperature, brightness, and humidity all affect the disease patterns on leaves. Labeling positions and areas on photographs of diseases is the major goal. There is an algorithm in Python that performs the function of frame selection.

Related Work

One of the most productive fruit in the world is apple and with a quality of high nutrition and medicinal value. On a large production of apple, various diseases occur which also creates a problem of economic loss. Therefore, the timely detection of apple diseases is very necessary for healthy environment and apple industry. There is error because of subjective perception in previously [1], plants diseases were diagnosed by visual observation and spectroscopic technique, which was not very effective and took high cost. After coming of digital camera and electronic devices, they were used as satisfactory alternative to detect plant diseases using machine learning [2]. Previous techniques like K means and SVM were not very effective. Machine learning methods are more effective in uniform background image disease detection. Deep learning and convolution neural network have enabled an improved method of disease detection. CNN can extract feature directly from input images and do not required preprocessing which make them very effective [3]. This leads to a plenty of research in diseases detection using CNN. Apple leaf diseases detection are still very difficult because of various factors such as multiple disease on same leaf, varying size of disease on leaves and other environmental factors like illumination

[a]saloni.bansal@gla.ac.in, [b]saraswatbirendra@gmail.com

DOI: 10.1201/9781003534136-58

and shadow. This paper uses improved CNN, detects real time diseases, and overcomes above challenges. The proposed model of apple leaf dataset detection is providing a surety of generalization capability. The image of diseases apple with complex background are collecting for increase the robustness of CNN model. The diseases apple image have insufficient and over fitting of the CNN based model, which is used to solve the problem of leaf diseases. The real time detection of apple leaf disease by CNN. The discriminative feature of apple images are automatically identify with high accuracy by using deep learning. The proposed approach is very beneficial because it can do much work at the same time not only identify the various diseases in the same diseases image but also can detect the different diseases in the same diseases image. The collection of apple leaf disease by many human and material resources because for real time detection the few dataset is available. Disease patterns of leaves changes with factors such as humidity, luminance and temperature. Disease of apple image is divides into five parts first is Alternaria leaf spot, which is caused by Alternaria alternate f.sp mali, second is Brown spot which is caused by *Marssonina coronaria*, third is Mosaic which is caused by Papaya ring spot virus, fourth is grey spot which is caused by *Phyllostictapirina Sacc.* and *Coryneum folii colum* and last is rust which is caused by *Pucciniaceae glue rust*. There are two reasons of selected these five common types of apple diseases first it is identified by visually from leaves which is important for application of CNN and other reason is they are helps to sustainable reproduction in apple industry. The leaf rust of causal agent is Puccinia triticina Eriks. (Pt), the three mostly distributed diseases of wheat are more common. The geographical variation of leaf rust caused grain losses. In [4–6] pathogen, displays high diversity cause dangerous diseases of leaf rust and wide range of climates have high adaptability exhibits pathogen. In [7] Due to race specific or non race specific resistance identify the rust infection of genetic resistance. The wheat or wild relatives defined more than 150 genes of wheat resistance and it is sure in race specific resistance [8]. Race specific genes the one of the most widely utilized is Sr31 against pgt [9]. The adult plants resistance is a non race specific resistance sure quantitative resistance against rusts wheat [10]. Lr34 and Lr67 respectively encode an ATP-binding cassette transporter and hexose transporter [11].

Methodology Used

K-means clustering technique and multi-SVM were employed in this study to choose the crop based on the results of the soil test [12]. K-means and multi-SVM algorithms create clusters based on the classification of the dataset. The link between the multi-SVM and K-means algorithms is provided in this study. Multi-SVM implementation is slightly more challenging than K-means but provides better accuracy. Multi-SVM had an accuracy rate of 80% whereas K-means clustering had an accuracy rate of 62%. Larger databases perform better than tiny databases when using the multi-SVM algorithm.

Multi SVM Algorithm
Crammer and Singer's multi SVM algorithm is proposed. It is also an algorithm for unsupervised. We can use the multi-SVM algorithm to address the optimization problem. There are modules for learning in this algorithm. New data was loaded by these components. It is done by breaking down a single class SVM into numerous binary classifications. Figure 59.1 displays the multi-SVM algorithmic block diagram.

K-Means Clustering
K-means algorithm categorizes the data sets from observations into k groups 13]. The algorithms base their decisions on clusters that K-means' algorithm produces. In this lesson, a soil test dataset with characteristics is utilized to learn about the characteristics of soil, including its PH value, P and K content, and other information. The K-means clusters are employed to train the classification model. According to the clustered data, the method obtained an accuracy of 56.08%. Based on data gathered from various sources, Figure 59.1 depicts the cluster of acidic and basic soil. Acid soil is represented by blue dots, while base soil is represented by pink dots. Figure 59.2 displays the K-clustering algorithmic block diagram.

Experimental Analysis

This paper should include a component for weather forecasting, which was carried out using a public API [14]. A website called OpenWeatherMap.org offers free public APIs for various types of weather forecasting. This module will only be able to provide forecasts for up to 7 days, and Java script has been used to read that JSON data and display the desired output on the web GUI. Paper presents multi-SVM and K-means clustering techniques for the soil classification module. Multi-SVM produces the superior outcomes of the

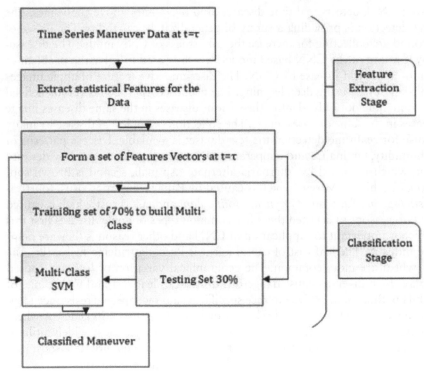

Figure 58.1 Algorithmic block diagram of multi-SVM

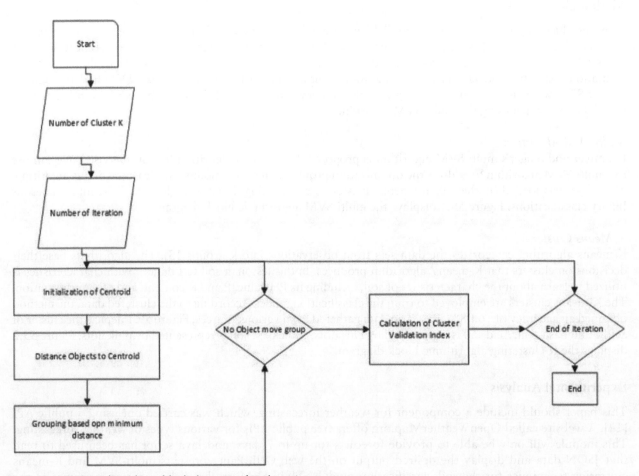

Figure 58.2 Algorithmic block diagram of K-clustering

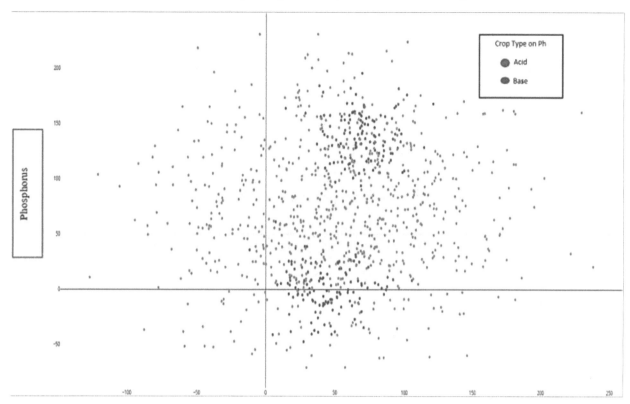

Figure **58.3** Cluster of acid and base soil

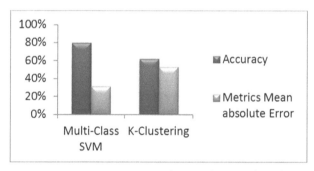

Figure **58.4** Comparison of crop selection algorithms

Table **58.1** Comparison of crop selection algorithms

Algorithms	Multi support vector machine	K means clustering
Accuracy	80 %	62%
Metrics mean absolute Error	31%	53%

two algorithms. (Figures 59.3 and 59.4) Table 59.1 displays a highly accurate comparison of crop selection algorithms.

Conclusion

Multi-SVM (support vector machine) and K-means clustering were chosen as the two techniques for the crop selection module in the paper (Table 59.1). The suggested method uses K-means clustering and multi-SVM for crop selection based on soil test results. K-means and multi-SVM algorithms create clusters based on the classification of the dataset. In the paper, a connection between the multi-SVM and K-means algorithms was proposed. Multi-SVM implementation is slightly more challenging than K-means but provides better accuracy. Multi-SVM had an accuracy rate of 80% whereas K-means clustering had an accuracy rate of 62%. Larger databases perform better than tiny databases when using the multi-SVM algorithm.

References

[1] Arnal Barbedo, J. G. (2019). Plant disease identification from individual lesions and spots using deep learning. *Biosystems Engineering*, 180(2016), 96–107.

[2] Chaturvedi, R., Islam, A., Singh, P. K., and Saraswat, M. (2023). Nanotechnology for advanced energy system: synthesis & performance characterization of nano-fuel. In AIP Conference Proceedings (Vol. 2721, No. 1). AIP Publishing.

[3] Ashqar, B., and Abu-Naser, S. (2018). Image-based tomato leaves diseases detection using deep learning. *International Journal of Advanced Engineering Research (IJAER)*, 2(12), 10–16.

[4] Kumar, P., Singh, P. K., Nagar, S., Sharma, K., and Saraswat, M. (2021). Effect of different concentration of functionalized graphene on charging time reduction in thermal energy storage system. *Materials Today: Proceedings*, 44, 146–152.

[5] Agrawal, R., (2022). Low-power SRAM memory architecture for IoT systems. In Recent Advances in Manufacturing, Automation, Design and Energy Technologies, (pp. 505–512). Singapore: Springer.

[6] Bansal, S., and Tomar, V. K. (2022). Challenges & security threats in IoT with solution architectures. In 2022 2nd International Conference on Power Electronics & IoT Applications in Renewable Energy and its Control (PARC). IEEE, 2022.

[7] Chaturvedi, R., Sharma, A., Sharma, K., and Saraswat, M. (2022). Tribological behaviour of multi-walled carbon nanotubes reinforced AA 7075 nano-composites. *Advances in Materials and Processing Technologies*, 8(4), 4743–4755.

[8] Periyannan, S., Milne, R. J., Figueroa, M., Lagudah, E. S., and Dodds, P. N. (2017). An overview of genetic rust resistance: from broad to specific mechanisms. *PLoS Pathogens*, 13, e1006380.

[9] Azadbakht, M., Ashourloo, D., Aghighi, H., Radiom, S., and Alimohammadi, A. (2019). Wheat leaf rust detection at canopy scale under different LAI levels using machine learning techniques. *Computers and Electronics in Agriculture*, 156(September 2018), 119–128.

[10] Sharma, A., Chaturvedi, R., Sharma, K., and Saraswat, M. (2022). Force evaluation and machining parameter optimization in milling of aluminium burr composite based on response surface method. *Advances in Materials and Processing Technologies*, 8(4), 4073–4094.

[11] Dodds, P. N., and Lagudah, E. S. (2016). Starving the enemy. *Science*, 354, 1377–1378.

[12] Bashir, K., Rehman, M., and Bari, M. (2019). Detection and classification of rice diseases an automated approach using textural features. *Mehran University Research Journal Science and Technology*, 38(1), 239–250.

[13] Bai, X., Li, X., Fu, Z., Lv, X., and Zhang, L. (2017). A fuzzy clustering segmentation method based on neighborhood grayscale information for defining cucumber leaf spot disease images. *Computers and Electronics in Agriculture*, 136, 157–165.

[14] Ali, S., Gladieux, P., Leconte, M., Gautier, A., Justesen, A. F., Hovmøller, M. S., et al. (2014). Origin, migration routes and worldwide population genetic structure of the wheat yellow rust pathogen Puccinia striiformis f. sp. tritici. *PLoS Pathogens*, 10, e1003903.

59 Utilization of IoT in smart irrigation system (SIS)

Saloni Bansal[1,a] and Nathiram Chauhan[2,b]

[1]GLA University, Mathura, India

[2]Indira Gandhi Delhi Technical University for Women, Delhi, India

Abstract

Automation currently plays a significant role in human life. It not only makes you more comfortable, but it also saves time and energy. now that Industries use expensive automation and control equipment that is not appropriate for usage on a farm field. Therefore, a smart irrigation system that is affordable and useful by Indian farmers is also designed here. The core brain of the entire system is the Raspberry Pi. To maximize the utilization of irrigation water for agricultural crops, an automated irrigation system was created. We can automatically control appliances thanks to automation. The autonomous management of the water motor, webcam monitoring of plant growth, and live broadcasting of the farm on Android mobile devices were the goals of this research. Our study aims to reduce the farmer's human labor in two ways: 1) by preventing unforeseen water use, which prevents a lot of water from being wasted. 2) Farmers can save a lot of time by using irrigation as the only option when the soil is not sufficiently moist. The threshold value determines when the pump should be switched on or off.

Keywords: Android, connected farm, irrigation, raberry pi, wifi

Introduction

India's economy is largely based on agriculture, and the country ranks second globally in terms of farm outputs. As of 2018, 17% to 18% of the GDP of India comes from agriculture, which employs 50% of the labor force. In India, much of the irrigation system is manually operated. Our nation is in a position to save every drop as water becomes more scarce [1-2]. Water is a very important component of irrigation systems, so new irrigation techniques should be implemented in a way that uses less water than outdated ones. Smart irrigation means that in addition to using less water, it also supplies water as needed. Increased agricultural productivity and risk-reduction potential result from this. Using wireless sensors, this system remotely monitors weather conditions, plant soil conditions, and reservoir water levels. While traditional methods produce water wastage of between 20% and 70%, smart irrigation solutions can reduce it by up to 95%. To water the plants, additional laborers are needed in our traditional farming approach. minimizing farmer involvement and transforming this procedure into an many sensors, such soil moisture sensors, temperature sensors, and others, are employed in an automated system, and the output of these sensors is connected to the microcontroller. The primary flaw in a typical irrigation system is the loss of water during reservoir filling, and overwatering of plants is another factor. It is the most likely scenario in which there will be a water shortage [3-4]. The crucial component of a plant soil moisture is being monitored by a smart watering system. Depending on this, one may determine whether or not the plant is receiving enough water for its growth. Many people neglect to water their plants throughout daily chores, making it difficult to maintain their plants' health and life. To stay clear of these issues and an automatic irrigation system is created to boost plant growth. Therefore, the goal of our project is to offer intelligent irrigation systems for watering plants while also informing the customer via message. The user will additionally benefit from this project's information on the water level in the tank and the soil's moisture content. This research also aids in determining the environment's humidity and temperature.

Methodology

In this work, we suggest the following components for measuring soil moisture and temperature are Sensors, Rasberrypi, Android

i. *Sensors*

Sensors are classified into two categories.

1.1: Temperature Sensor. When the weather grows cooler and less water is required, the temperature sensors are required to cut back on watering periods. Then, as the climate starts to warm, to extend the irrigation period. Figure. 59.1 shows soil Moisture sensor.

[a]saloni.bansal@gla.ac.in, [b]nramchauhan@gmail.com

DOI: 10.1201/9781003534136-59

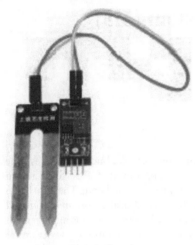

Figure 59.1 Soil moisture sensor

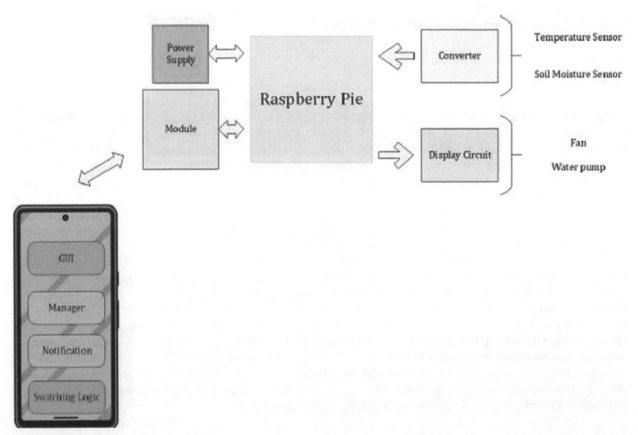

Figure 59.2 System architecture

1.2: Soil Moisture Sensor. The volumetric water content of the soil is determined using the soil moisture sensor. In order to manage irrigation in greenhouses, it is utilized to monitor soil moisture content. The amount of moisture in an irrigation field is detected using a moisture sensor. It has a level detection module where a reference value can be set. Figure. 59.2. shows system architecture.

ii.   *Rasberry pi.* An example of a Raspberry Pi computer is. It has both internal and external memory of its own. In that, any operating system, such as Linux or Unix, is installed. soil and temperature. Raspberry Pi is connected to a moisture sensor, which sends signals to it. Sensor readings are compared to a user-provided or defined threshold value [5-6].

iii. *Android App.* This module will be in charge of gathering user input and the client will be an android-based application.XML is used to construct the GUI. input from a Raspberry Pi will be guided by this GUI.

Uses

Farmers will love the low-cost deployment solution. Alerts for quick time provisioning automatically variances in climatic parameters. Analysis of numerous environmental and climate variables, such as temperature, humidity, and soil moisture level. Using solar energy, a sustainable resource, to power the devices during the day.

Working

Webcam is connected to Raspberry Pi in this setup using a WiFi module. The system's beating heart is the Raspberry Pi. There are several improvements and additional features included in the Raspberry Pi model B+. enhanced power [6-7-8]. This potent, compact, and light ARM-based computer has been improved in terms of consumption, connection, and IO. The relay cannot be operated directly by the Raspberry Pi.

To setup all of the hardware, utilize the system configuration module. Wi-Fi module, temperature sensor, and soil moisture sensor are all. Linked to the principal Raspberry Pi component, we originally needed to install the Raspbian operating system on the Raspberry Pi and related gpio connections with soil moisture sensor, temperature sensor [9-10]. To setup all of the hardware, utilize the system configuration module. Wi-Fi module, temperature sensor, and soil moisture sensor are all linked to the principal Raspberry Pi component, we originally needed to install the Raspbian operating system on the Raspberry Pi and related gpio connections with soil moisture sensor, temperature sensor. When sensor values fall below or rise over a certain threshold, a Wi-Fi-based offline alert message is sent to the user's mobile device. module (automatic/manual) mode. Automatic system switches ON/OFF will let users turn the system ON/OFF as it suits them [11-12]. System ON/OFF switches. control equipment. Figure. 59.3 shows system architecture.

Algorithm

a. Start
b. Using a temperature sensor, temperature can be determined.
c. Using a soil moisture sensor, moisture content in the soil is determined.

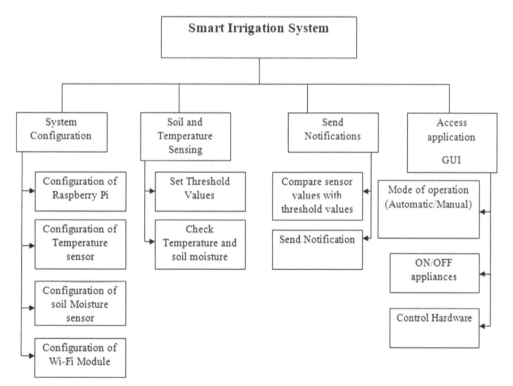

Figure 59.3 Working architecture

d.   Send alert message to owner phone when sensor values condition is met.
e.   The following decision will be made in accordance with user modes, which are automated and manual.
f.   If automatic, then the system is automatic. Turns will switch the system ON or OFF.
g.   Additionally, if the mode is manual, system ON/OFF commands will be made utilizing input from the user's application.
h.   When a user launches an app, the following option is displayed.
i.   The user will act appropriately in a specific circumstance.
j.   Stop

Conclusion

The countries whose economies are focused on agriculture and where the meteorological circumstances cause a lack of rain and water scarcity served as the inspiration for this article. The rains and bore wells are the only sources of irrigation for the farmers who operate on the farmlands. Despite the water pump on the property, manual intervention by Farmers must switch the pump on and off as needed. The design includes an Android app that allows users to operate the raspberry from their android phone. raspberry pi, which will control sensors, also monitors the surroundings. Thus, utilizing an Android mobile device, the user may manage their farm from a distance.

References

[1]   Karpagam, J., I. Infranta Merlin, P. Bavithra, and J. Kousalya. (2020). Smart irrigation system using IoT." In 2020 6th International Conference on Advanced Computing and Communication Systems (ICACCS), pp. 1292–1295. IEEE.

[2]   Pernapati, K. (2018). IoT based low cost smart irrigation system. In 2018 Second International Conference on Inventive Communication and Computational Technologies (ICICCT). IEEE, 2018.

[3]   Sharma, A., Chaturvedi, R., Sharma, K., and Saraswat, M. (2022). Force evaluation and machining parameter optimization in milling of aluminium burr composite based on response surface method. *Advances in Materials and Processing Technologies*, 8(4), 4073–4094.

[4]   Krishnan, R. Santhana, E. Golden Julie, Y. Harold Robinson, S. Raja, Raghvendra Kumar, and Pham Huy Thong. (2020). Fuzzy logic based smart irrigation system using internet of things. *Journal of Cleaner Production*. 252: 119902.

[5]   Darshna, S., Sangavi, T., Mohan, S., Soundharya, A., and Desikan, S. (2015). Smart irrigation system. *IOSR Journal of Electronics and Communication Engineering (IOSR-JECE)*, 10(3), 32–36.

[6]   Chaturvedi, R., Sharma, A., Sharma, K., and Saraswat, M. (2022). Tribological behaviour of multi-walled carbon nanotubes reinforced AA 7075 nano-composites. *Advances in Materials and Processing Technologies*, 8(4), 4743–4755.

[7]   García, Laura, Lorena Parra, Jose M. Jimenez, Jaime Lloret, and Pascal Lorenz. (2020). IoT-based smart irrigation systems: An overview on the recent trends on sensors and IoT systems for irrigation in precision agriculture. Sensors 20(4): 1042.

[8]   Kumar, P., Singh, P. K., Nagar, S., Sharma, K., and Saraswat, M. (2021). Effect of different concentration of functionalized graphene on charging time reduction in thermal energy storage system. *Materials Today: Proceedings*, 44, 146–152.

[9]   Agrawal, N., and Smita, S. (2015). Smart drip irrigation system using raspberry pi and arduino. In International Conference on Computing, Communication & Automation. IEEE, 2015.

[10]   Kumar, B. H. (2017). WSN based automatic irrigation and security system using Raspberry Pi board. In 2017 International Conference on Current Trends in Computer, Electrical, Electronics and Communication (CTCEEC). IEEE, 2017.

[11]   Chaturvedi, R., Islam, A., Singh, P. K., and Saraswat, M. (2023). Nanotechnology for advanced energy system: synthesis & performance characterization of nano-fuel. In AIP Conference Proceedings (Vol. 2721, No. 1). AIP Publishing.

[12]   Imteaj, Ahmed, Tanveer Rahman, Muhammad Kamrul Hossain, and Saika Zaman. (2016). IoT based autonomous percipient irrigation system using raspberry Pi. In 2016 19th International Conference on Computer and Information Technology (ICCIT), pp. 563–568. IEEE.

60 Optimising efficiency by drive cycle control in parallel hybrid electric vehicle

Aman Sharma[1,a] and Manish Saraswat[2,b]

[1]GLA University, Mathura

[2]LLOYD Institute of Engineering and Technology, Greater Noida

Abstract

In HEVs, maintaining high energy density is a necessity while demanding higher peak power as well thus this results in doubling the incremental cost of the vehicle if approx. 15 % of all electric range is demanded. The SOC of the vehicle directly affects the economy and the emission rates. In this work the parallel HEV is modelled and Different SOC limits are taken for testing the performance and fuel economy for the same designed driving cycle. The usable SOC range will be determined in order to obtain the various ESS capacities. The different energy storage systems are taken for the examination with 150 V of terminal voltage and 100 HP of engine with an electric motor of 40 KW. The simulation is performed by taking repetitive velocity profiles (drive cycles) of different curves i.e. UDDS and HWFET. The operating effectiveness of the parts must be optimised by taking the system as a whole into account. The forward-looking approach will be used to carry out the control strategy. In this technique, the operating efficiency is maximised in order to maximise fuel economy; other strategies do not have this additional component. In order to improve fuel economy, the ability controller for parallel hybrid automobiles is mentioned in this study. The older power controllers that were installed optimise operation but do not fully utilise the possibilities.

Keywords: Control strategy, electric range, operating efficiency, performance, state of charge, velocity profile

Introduction

The majority of commercially available HEVs have an all-battery ESS that is connected by a bidirectional converter to a high-voltage dc bus. In order to expand the range of electric vehicles, the battery pack's capacity must be increased to store adequate energy [1]. In electric vehicles, ESS should be able to meet the total power consumption of the vehicle. Several authors have developed topologies to hybridise ESSs for EVs, HEVs, FC hybrid vehicles (FCHVs), and PHEVs in order to increase miles per gallon efficiency. The Toyota Prius, Honda Insight, and Ford Escape are examples of commercially available HEVs with fuel efficiency of about 40 mpg. In order to increase fuel efficiency and reduce emissions, hybrid electric vehicles provide additional flexibility [2, 3]. In order for the HEV to operate effectively, an electric motor is linked with the electrical energy storage. Due to the linkage of the bidirectional converter, a two-power path was made available, allowing the engine to be cut off during low power operation as well as the use of a smaller, more efficient engine for this kind of vehicle. This is possible while maintaining the average power carrying capacity of the vehicle [4]. By accepting the extra power generated by the engine's effective operation, the electrical energy in the battery or any other energy storage device is kept constant during this process. Regenerative braking, in which kinetic energy is converted into electrical energy and stored, also aids in recharging the energy storage system [5]. One of the ESS that is utilised the most is batteries. A battery-based ESS, however, has a variety of challenges, leading researchers to look for alternatives. The power density of the batteries used in battery-based ESSs must be sufficient to meet the peak power demand.

Parallel HEV Basic

A parallel hybrid vehicle's IC engine, transmission, and EM connections are shown in Figure 60.1 as a block diagram. The power flow affects how various systems function, including: battery charging, where one part of the ice power is used to drive the EM as a generator and another part is used to drive the wheels; and regenerative braking, where the vehicle is slowed down and the EM is used as generator [6, 7]. We can provide power with only ice, with only an electric motor, by using the internal combustion engine and the EM simultaneously.

It suggests that a parallel HEV system's performance is significantly influenced by how this power split is managed. Simple rule-based or map-based heuristic control strategies seem to be falling behind controllers that

[a]aman.sharma@gla.ac.in, [b]manish.saraswat@lloydcollege.in

DOI: 10.1201/9781003534136-60

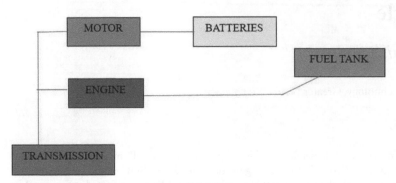

Figure 60.1 Schematic of Parallel HEV

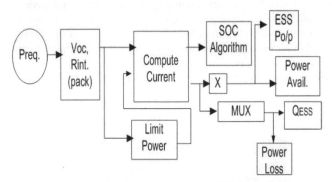

Figure 60.2 Schematic Block Diagram of ESS Model

are oriented on minimising fuel consumption [8]. The latter, commonly known as optimal controllers, actually provides more generality and reduces the need for significant adjustment of the control parameters [9].

System Configuration

The system configuration is shown in the schematic Figure 60.2, where the battery pack is represented by the charge reservoir and the remaining charge is the circuit parameter [10]. The charge that an ESS contains is thought of as a constant amount, and the coulombic efficiency is what determines how well batteries are refilled. The only amount that can be provided by the battery is the maximum amount of power that the equivalent circuit or controller can tolerate under the circumstances of the lowest voltage requirements [11].

Hybrid electric vehicles offer extra flexibility in order to improve fuel economy and emissions. For the HEV, the electrical energy storage is coupled with an electric motor so that the vehicle can operate efficiently. The two-power path, which is possible due to coupling of bidirectional converters, makes it possible to shut down the engine during low power operation and also the more efficient and smaller engine can be used for this type of vehicle. This can be done while maintain the vehicles average power carrying capability. During this process the electrical energy in the battery or any other energy storage system is maintained by accepting the excess power during the efficient operation of engine [12]. The process of regenerative braking in which the kinetic energy is stored in the form of electrical energy, also helps to charge the energy storage system. Batteries are one of the most often used ESS. However, a battery-based ESS faces a number of obstacles, prompting researchers to seek alternative methods. In battery-based ESSs, the battery's power density must be sufficient to fulfil the peak power demand.

Simulation Results

The parallel hybrid electric vehicle is modelled for different drive cycles as shown in Figure 3 and the two limits of state of charge value are taken for testing the fuel economy. The usable SOC range will be determined in order

Table 60.1 Vehicle parameters.

Vehicle weight	15000 Kg
Motor ratings(power)	43 KW
Torque	200 nm
Engine ratings	120 hp
Battery pack	VRLA
Battery capacity	110 Ah
Terminal voltage	145 V

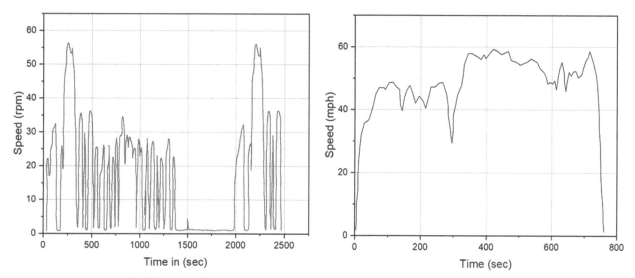

Figure 60.3 (a) and 3(b) Figure Showing Drive Cycles for Simulation

to obtain the various ESS capacities. The different energy storage systems are taken for the examination with 150 V of terminal voltage and 100 HP of engine with an electric motor of 40 KW

The vehicle is simulated with the following parameters given in the below Table 60.1 -

One half of the simulation is performed for the lower limit of SOC, and the other part is performed for the top limit of SOC. As too low or too high a value of SOC can harm the battery, it is necessary to maintain the practical limits of 20 to 80 percent. We form groups for the upper limit, or the end point, run separate simulations, and attempt to determine which group's soc range is optimal. As it depends on the initial values of SOC, the two crucial aspects that are taken into consideration are the engines' operating procedure and overall fuel usage.

Conclusion

For the HEV to operate effectively, an electric motor is linked with the electrical energy storage. In order to increase fuel efficiency and reduce emissions, hybrid electric vehicles provide additional flexibility. Due to the linkage of the bidirectional converter, a two-power path was made available, allowing the engine to be cut off during low power operation as well as the use of a smaller, more efficient engine for this kind of vehicle. This is possible while maintaining the average power carrying capacity of the vehicle. Energy storage units are charged when there is a low demand for electricity, and they are discharged when there is a high demand. The component that controls the electric range and fuel economy is the ESS. UDDS and HWFET are two different curves whose repetitive velocity profiles (drive cycles) are used to run the simulation. The system as a whole must be taken into consideration in order to optimise the operating effectiveness of the parts. The control strategy will be implemented using the proactive approach. While other techniques do not include this additional element, this technique maximises operating efficiency in order to maximise fuel economy. The ability controller for parallel hybrid vehicles is mentioned in this study as a way to increase fuel economy. The installed older power controllers optimise operation but do not utilise all of the potential.

References

[1] Schaltz, E., Khaligh, A., and Rasmussen, P. O. (2009). Influence of battery/ultracapacitor energy-storage sizing on battery lifetime in a fuel cell hybrid electric vehicle. *IEEE Transactions on Vehicular Technology*, 58(8), 3882–3891.

[2] Song, Z., Hofmann, H., Li, J., Hou, J., Han, X., and Ouyang, M. (2014). Energy management strategies comparison for electric vehicles with hybrid energy storage system. *Applied Energy*, 134, 321–331.

[3] Chaturvedi, R., Islam, A., Singh, P. K., and Saraswat, M. (2023). Nanotechnology for advanced energy system: Synthesis & performance characterization of nano-fuel. In AIP Conference Proceedings (Vol. 2721, No. 1). AIP Publishing.

[4] Beck, R., Richert, F., Bollig, A., Abel, D., Saenger, S., Neil, K., et al. (2005). Model predictive control of a parallel hybrid vehicle drivetrain. In Proceedings of the 44th IEEE Conference on Decision and Control, (pp. 2670–2675). IEEE, 2005.

[5] Kumar, P., Singh, P. K., Nagar, S., Sharma, K., and Saraswat, M. (2021). Effect of different concentration of functionalized graphene on charging time reduction in thermal energy storage system. *Materials Today: Proceedings*, 44, 146–152.

[6] Saxena, A., Kumar, J., and Deolia, V. K. (2021). Optimization of NPIC controller using genetic algorithm. *IOP Conference Series: Materials Science and Engineering*, 1104(1), 012001. IOP Publishing, 2021.

[7] Beck, R., Richert, F., Bollig, A., Abel, D., Saenger, S., Neil, K., et al. (2005). Model predictive control of a parallel hybrid vehicle drivetrain. In Proceedings of the 44th IEEE Conference on Decision and Control, (pp. 2670–2675). IEEE, 2005.

[8] Chaturvedi, R., Sharma, A., Sharma, K., and Saraswat, M. (2022). Tribological behaviour of multi-walled carbon nanotubes reinforced AA 7075 nano-composites. *Advances in Materials and Processing Technologies*, 8(4), 4743–4755.

[9] Bhangu, B. S., Bentley, P., Stone, D. A., and Bingham, C. M. (2005). Nonlinear observers for predicting state-of-charge and state-of-health of lead-acid batteries for hybrid-electric vehicles. *IEEE Transactions on Vehicular Technology*, 54(3), 783–794.

[10] Sharma, A., Chaturvedi, R., Sharma, K., and Saraswat, M. (2022). Force evaluation and machining parameter optimization in milling of aluminium burr composite based on response surface method. *Advances in Materials and Processing Technologies*, 8(4), 4073–4094.

[11] Kumar, Y., Pushkarna, M., and Gupta, G. (2020). Microgrid implementation in unbalanced nature of feeder using conventional technique. In 2020 3rd International Conference on Intelligent Sustainable Systems (ICISS), (pp. 1489–1494). IEEE, 2020.

[12] Han, S., Han, S., and Aki, H. (2014). A practical battery wear model for electric vehicle charging applications. *Applied Energy*, 113, 1100–1108.

61 Auxiliary source optimisation for charging systems in electric vehicle

Kanchan Yadav[1,a] and Birendra Kr. Saraswat[2,b]

[1]GLA University, Mathura

[2]Raj Kumar Goel Institute of Technology, Ghaziabad

Abstract

Aside from the fact that nearly every automobile has its own battery charging system, only a few permits the use of a separate system to charge an auxiliary source, which is typically batteries. Controlling the AC-DC power circuit of this charging system is necessary to preserve nominal qualities and extend battery life. Additionally, it should ensure that the batteries remain undamaged throughout the charging and discharging processes. The relationship between the number of charge-discharge cycles a battery undergoes and its cycle life is inverse. The cost of degradation and battery cycle life should be meticulously accounted for when optimizing V2G operations. Battery charging and discharging practices that are executed with caution consider not only the vehicle owner's convenience but also the capacity and requirements of the power grid. In this situation requiring real-time control, energy cost, battery SoH and SoC, and additional variables must be taken into account.

Keywords: Battery charging, discharging, grid system, lifespan, power circuit, state of charge, state of health

Introduction

The transportation sector's oil consumption has increased more rapidly than any other sector in recent decades. This growth has mostly resulted from increased consumer demand for personal-use vehicles using standard internal combustion engines (ICEs). Different ground vehicles use the majority of the petroleum [1]. The world Vehicles will grow from 700 million to 2.5 billion in number. Since they use no oil and emit no pollutants locally, battery-powered electric vehicles (BEVs) look like the perfect solution to the energy crisis and the problem of global warming. The drawbacks of these vehicles have been brought to light by aspects including their high initial cost, limited driving range, and lengthy charging times [2, 3]. The new topology of the battery combined with the bidirectional ac/dc-dc/dc converters for PHEVs is being studied by researchers. The suggested architecture can be used in four different ways, including bidirectional power transfer between the battery and the dc connection and charging and discharging the battery from/to the grid.

An electric motor that draws electricity from a rechargeable battery propels electric vehicles (EVs). The performance requirements for many EV specs much surpass what traditional battery systems are capable of. Due to the high voltages and currents involved in the system as well as the advanced charging algorithms, however, as battery technology advances, charging these batteries becomes increasingly difficult [4]. The two methods by which electric vehicles (EVs) can be linked to the grid are indirect and direct. The direct design dictates that the electric vehicle and the grid system operator can only communicate via a single path. Interaction between the grid operator and an intermediary system is required for the indirect design to function [5]. The central argument of this essay pertains to the initial arrangement. By cycling their batteries frequently, electric vehicles (EVs) are capable of performing a variety of vehicle-to-grid (V2G) operations. The financial implications associated with battery degeneration can cause considerable concern among electric vehicle (EV) owners [6, 7]. Consequently, it is imperative to elucidate the cycle life (CL) of the battery when assessing its degeneration.

Optimization Parameters

The service of V2G is participated in the cycle life of battery for the model optimization by considering the signals of frequency regulation and degradation of battery cost [8].

Cycle Life

Battery degradation, or the volume and rate of energy lost in batteries, is a factor in CL. The DOD and cycle frequency are additionally employed in the computation of the utmost charge-discharge cycles that an electric

---

[a]kanchan.yadav@gla.ac.in, [b]saraswatbirendra@gmail.com

DOI: 10.1201/9781003534136-61

vehicle (EV) battery can endure prior to malfunctioning. 80% DOD is considered the optimal degradation condition for a Li-ion battery [9].

$$CL = (L100)\ e\beta(1-DoD)$$

where, CL is the cycle life of a battery, L100 is the value of

The decay factor is and the CL at 100% DOD. For various batteries, the decay coefficient, which measures the exponential decline in the value of the cycle count, ranges from 3 to 6.

The Iterative Algorithm with Dynamic Cycle Life

Approaches for iteratively determining the CL of electric vehicle batteries while they are operating in V2G mode have been proposed. The associated DOD is employed to initialize the CL of the electric vehicle battery [10], in adherence to the framework. Therefore, communication with the electrical supplier is required to obtain information regarding the electricity's cost and regulatory requirements. By simulating the EVCD optimization process, it is possible to ascertain the optimal charge and discharge patterns, thereby minimizing expenses associated with battery degradation.

Source Modelling

This battery model should meet your needs if you are looking for one that considers the non-linear charging and discharging characteristics of the battery in addition to its state of charge. The open circuit voltage characteristics of self-discharge resistance (Rs), discharge resistance (Rd), and charge resistance (Rc) vary in accordance with the charging and discharging currents. A substantial increase in overcharge resistance (Rco) and overdischarge resistance (Rdo) is induced by the battery's intrinsic chemistry [11].

Modelling of battery capacity (Ah) that varies with SOC and the expressions for the auxiliary source i.e battery charging and discharging characteristics are as follows:

The maximum power limit is determined by using the following formula: Maximum power limit

$$P = V_{bus} \times \frac{V_{oc} - V_{bus}}{R}$$

Where V_{bus} is either VOC/2 or minimum battery voltage. Applying KVL to the above power equation will come as -

$$\frac{P_{max}}{I} = V_{oc} - (R \times I)$$

Multiplying with I on both sides of the expression -

$$P_{max} = (V_{oc} \times I) - RI^2$$

$$RI^2 - (V_{oc} \times I) + P = 0$$

The lesser requirement of voltage is needed for obtaining equal amount of power and the allowable voltage value is achieved by not exceeding the minimum value of raw current-

$$I = \frac{V_{OC} - V_{max}}{R}$$

The algorithm for SOC profile is taken and it uses the unit of residual capacity in terms of Amp-hrs. The estimation is performed by taking the maximum capacity and columbic efficiency as the temperature functions and a series of steps is used for approximation [12]. In order to calculate initial non-zero value of SOC the below given expression is used -

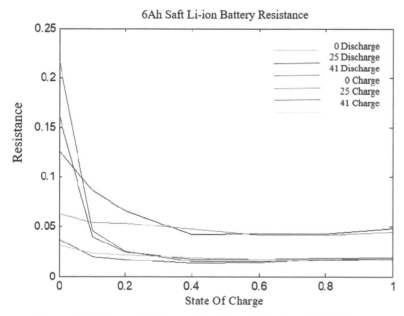

Figure 61.1 Charge /Discharge Condition Variation with SOC

$$SOC = \frac{C\max - Ah}{C\max}$$

Where, Cmax- Maximum capacity

Ah- Amp-hr used

For different time instants, the SOC for different time instants (t) is calculated by the expression below-

$$SOC(t) = SOCi + \frac{1}{3600}\frac{\eta bat(i(t),T)}{Cap(T)}\int_{t0}^{t} i(t)dt$$

Where, columbic efficiency is denoted by □bat(i(t),T) and Cap(T) is the capacity.

Result and Discussion

Internal resistance decreases during discharge and reaches its lowest value at half charge. After a complete charge and discharge, the resistance reading is greater. When a Li-ion battery is charged from empty to full, its internal resistance value is largely flat. When SOC is between 0 and 70%, the battery power declines, with the biggest drop occurring between 0 and 30% of SOC.

The batteries are carefully charged or discharged based on the state of charge condition as shown in Figure 1. Several factors need to be considered in this real-time control scenario. It includes state of charge and state of health for battery, battery lifetime, energy price etc. In ground vehicles, batteries are the principal ESS. Increasing the AER (All Electric Range) of cars by 15% nearly doubles the ESS's added cost. This is because the ESS of HEVs maintains a high energy density while necessitating a higher peak power. The battery power decreases when SOC is between 0 and 70%, with the biggest loss occurring between 0 and 30% of SOC.

Current energy and environmental issues have been effectively addressed by EVs, HEVs, FCHVs, and PHEVs. Electric drive trains completely or largely replace ICEs in these vehicles thanks to the breakthrough power electronics and ESSs. The goal of advanced ESSs is to meet the energy needs of hybrid power trains. At this time, the majority of commercially available EVs and hybrid cars lack hybrid ESSs. Advanced hybrid electric drive trains could not be equipped with just one ESS component, such as batteries, UCs, or FCs. Researchers are looking at hybrid ESSs that have a huge capacity, quick charging and discharging, a long lifespan, and are inexpensive. More research should be done to introduce transformative ESSs into future advanced vehicles to lower costs, boost efficiency, and extend electric driving range in order to make HEVs and PHEVs competitive with conventional vehicles on the market.

Conclusion

Cycle life is an inverse relationship between the number of charge-discharge cycles a battery undergoes and the number of cycles it remains charged. When optimizing the operation of V2G, it is critical to consider both the cost of degradation and the cycle life of the battery. In this investigation, we employ a novel iterative methodology to predict the impacts of dynamic power, regulation pricing, battery cycle life, and static and dynamic power. In an effort to optimize the charging and discharging process of electrical devices, we consider day-ahead real-time pricing, frequency regulatory signals, and the anticipated cycle life. A significant proportion of the electrical power supplied onboard is derived from batteries characterized by their elevated energy density. On the other hand, UCs have gained acclaim due to their exceptionally high power densities, swift charging and discharging cycles, exceptional efficiency, and extended operational lifespans. Due to these qualities, they have gained widespread acclaim. The primary mechanism by which ground vehicles store their energy is through the utilization of battery packs. A 15% increase in the All Electric Range (AER) of vehicles results in an almost twofold increase in the supplementary expense of the ESS. Consequently, for HEV ESSs to sustain high energy densities, a greater peak power requirement is required. Between 0% and 70% of its capacity, the battery's power decreases, with the most substantial reduction occurring between 0% and 30% of its capacity.

References

[1] Hill, Electric car sales predictions are all over the map. [Online]. Available: http://thehill.com/blogs/pundits-blog/transportation/315958- forecasts-for-electric-car-sales-are-all-over-map.

[2] Sharma, A., Chaturvedi, R., Sharma, K., and Saraswat, M. (2022). Force evaluation and machining parameter optimization in milling of aluminium burr composite based on response surface method. *Advances in Materials and Processing Technologies*, 8(4), 4073–4094.

[3] Wang, R., Li, Y., Wang, P., and Niyato, D. (2013). Design of a v2g aggregator to optimize phev charging and frequency regulation control. In Smart Grid Communications (SmartGridComm), 2013 IEEE International Conference on. IEEE, 2013, (pp. 127–132).

[4] Chaturvedi, R., Sharma, A., Sharma, K., and Saraswat, M. (2022). Tribological behaviour of multi-walled carbon nanotubes reinforced AA 7075 nano-composites. *Advances in Materials and Processing Technologies*, 8(4), 4743–4755.

[5] Tang, L., Rizzoni, G., and Onori, S. (2015). Energy management strategy for HEVs including battery life optimization. *IEEE Transactions on Transportation Electrification*, 1(3), 211–222.

[6] Kumar, P., Singh, P. K., Nagar, S., Sharma, K., and Saraswat, M. (2021). Effect of different concentration of functionalized graphene on charging time reduction in thermal energy storage system. *Materials Today: Proceedings*, 44, 146–152.

[7] Monteiro, V., Gonçalves, H., Ferreira, J. C., Afonso, J. L., Carmo, J. P., and Ribeiro, J. E. (2012). Batteries charging systems for electric and plug-in hybrid electric vehicles. *New Advances in Vehicular Technology and Automotive Engineering*, 149–168. InTech, 2012.

[8] Chaturvedi, R., Islam, A., Singh, P. K., and Saraswat, M. (2023). Nanotechnology for advanced energy system: Synthesis & performance characterization of nano-fuel. In AIP Conference Proceedings (Vol. 2721, No. 1). AIP Publishing.

[9] Kumar, Y., Pushkarna, M., and Gupta, G. (2020). Microgrid implementation in unbalanced nature of feeder using conventional technique. In 2020 3rd International Conference on Intelligent Sustainable Systems (ICISS), (pp. 1489–1494). IEEE, 2020.

[10] Dixit, K. K., Yadav, I., Gupta, G. K., and Maurya, S. K. (2020). A review on cooling techniques used for photovoltaic panels. In 2020 International Conference on Power Electronics & IoT Applications in Renewable Energy and its Control (PARC), (pp. 360–364). IEEE, 2020.

[11] Beck, R., Richert, F., Bollig, A., Abel, D., Saenger, S., and Neil, K., et al. (2005). Model predictive control of a parallel hybrid vehicle drivetrain. In Proceedings of the 44th IEEE Conference on Decision and Control, (pp. 2670–2675). IEEE, 2005.

[12] Li, Q., Chen, W., Li, Y., Liu, S., and Huang, J. (2012). Energy management strategy for fuel cell/battery/ultracapacitor hybrid vehicle based on fuzzy logic. *International Journal of Electrical Power and Energy Systems*, 43(1), 514–525.

62 Heuristic routing technique in optimizing energy utilization

Kanchan Yadav[1,a] and Nathiram Chauhan[2,b]

[1]GLA University, Mathura

[2]Indira Gandhi Delhi Technical University for Women, Delhi

Abstract

Communication is one of the most significant parts of today's technological advancements. Efficiency, energy savings, delay, throughput, range, and other factors all affect communication performance. Wireless sensor networks are one type of communication in which energy conservation optimization is a primary focus because there is a limited power resources for many embedded sensor nodes. In this study, increasing lifetime and reducing delay is the goal which has been achieved by reducing the energy consumption and finding the minimum path between the available nodes. The heuristic routing technique is used here to take the decisions related to the multiple hoping of data relay in the nodes while taking the residual energy of nodes. The distance between the source and destination is also considered. The Energy Saving via Heuristic Routing (ENSHR) algorithm was created to lower the energy costs associated with data relay while also providing a node with less residual energy. Graph simulation results show that the suggested algorithm, ENSHR, can significantly increase network lifetime and result in energy savings.

Keywords: Energy efficiency, energy saving, energy saving, Heuristic routing, hopping, network lifetime, optimization, residual energy

Introduction

There are a variety of environmental and physical conditions which need to be controlled and thus the embedded sensors have been taken which are employed by WAN (Wireless Sensor Networks) [1]. Wireless sensor networks have a wide range of applications in medical care, military applications, traffic monitoring, and industry, among others. The invention of effective wireless communication, as well as the current trend in electronic upgrading, has resulted in the development of low-cost, low-power, and multifunction devices.

Many nodes in wireless networks are equipped with sensors and deployed in severe settings, with limited battery capacity, making it impossible to replace energy by replacing batteries. In order to maintain the functionality of these environmental and physical conditions, the data must be accumulated and delivered in a systematic manner by using the sensors equipped in nodes [2]. When the sensor nodes are operated, the data receiving takes lesser energy than sending. This leads to the more consumption of time, reduction in lifetime of network. To overcome this issue and to increase the energy efficiency, there is a need to find the shortest distance which will consume lesser energy while data transmission and receiving. There are a number of energy efficient routing protocol techniques to achieve the goal of least energy consumption and efficient data transmission. The algorithm used for this purpose must be multifunctional as it has to find out the minimum distance for routing while considering the balance between residual energy of the sensor nodes [3].

Packet loss and multiple transmission of packets along a pre-selected good path are also caused by network outages and network partitions. Retransmission of packets on a pre-selected good path consumes a lot more energy. This indicates that maximising energy consumption reduces network life time and vice versa. As a result, energy usage as well as network lifetime must be balanced.

Robots, domestic industries, and other civil applications are just a few of the uses for one-dimensional (1-D) queue networks that are constructed and developed [4, 5]. Take a look at the diagram of the traffic information acquisition system below, which is based on a linearly spaced (1-D) queuing network. Power-saving management features are lacking in a large number of the traffic acquisition systems currently in use. due to the various smart city developments' increasing demands. Low energy utilisation strategies are one of the main factors taken into account for smart traffic acquisition. Each node that detects motion within its sensing range needs to have motion sensors attached so that it can gather data on traffic, such as traffic density and vehicle velocity. These motion sensors gather information, transmit it to a relay sensor, and the relay sensor then notifies the traffic control centre of the most energy-efficient route to the target node. Relevant data is selected by the traffic

---

[a]kanchan.yadav@gla.ac.in, [b]nramchauhan@gmail.com

DOI: 10.1201/9781003534136-62

management centre and sent over the network to clients [6]. Therefore, a clever traffic acquisition system can aid in extending the life of a (1-D) queue network while also helping wireless sensor nodes conserve energy [7].

In this study, the shortest route between nodes is determined by using the heuristic routing protocol. For this operation the energy balance is maintained by considering the nodes having the energy equivalent situation. In order to increase the lifetime of the network and to save energy, this protocol has been used and it will calculate the transmission range between the nodes which is considered as the ideal for operation. For determining the shortest path between these sensor nodes, there is a set of information for each sensor node like the residual energy of nodes, the minimum distance between source and sink node and network traffic etc.

Survey of Previous Work

Numerous studies on network routing protocols, including those on node density, probability of network problems connecting, and queue networks, have been conducted in the past. The probability of the entire network has been clarified by the studies [8, 9]. Here, there are several clusters that make up the one-dimensional wireless ad hoc networks. It fully explains the network's probability of connectivity. Many energy-related protocol designs are extracted from papers [12, 14].

In networks during data transmission, the nodes which are sending data takes significantly more energy than those taking/receiving data. This technique has the main goal to save this energy and make an energy balance by finding the shortest path between nodes through WSN. For the ideal power control, a conceptual analysis has been performed for energy hop by H. Liu et al [12]. WSN make use of only single cell and thus for a given time frame, the simultaneous transmission is possible in only single direction. The solution to this problem is the multi-hop relay concept. For the hop lengths that are longer and higher power operation, the operating cost in this concept is less than that when the lower power and lesser hop length is used [10]. The energy consumption can be reduced by using this method when the sensor nodes are held for ideal distance during transmission [13]

D.Bruckner et al. [1] explain how data acquisition using multidomain data acquisition works. This study combines data from multimodal sensor nodes to explain surveillance networks. The ability to gather information about the sensed environment is improved by the inclusion of both audio and video data in this method as opposed to previous ones that only used visual data. This system picks up information about typical behaviour and can identify a predefined set of behaviours [11]. A smart architecture with actual sensor nodes is the smart embedded network of sensing entities.

Opportunistic routing theory, which provides routing in wireless networks, was described by H. Liu et al. [12] for unrealistic wireless links. When compared to other routing techniques, opportunistic routing has the advantage of enabling packet forwarding for many neighbours and transmission nature for greater distances of wireless media. Examples of opportunistic routing include geographic random forwarding, highly opportunistic routing, and QOS aware geographic opportunistic routing.

The effectiveness of the entire network or specific nodes can be increased using the routing protocol designs listed below. Other elements like node residual energy, network lifetime, delay, and so forth must also be prioritized [14]. As a result, the major metric to be looked at must be the residual energy of the sensor nodes [15].

Proposed Methodology

The methodology used in this study for increasing the lifetime of network and reducing the consumption of energy have two techniques known as heuristic and greedy routing. The block diagram of the proposed

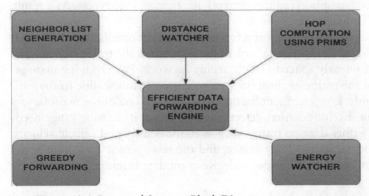

Figure 62.1 Proposed Strategy Block Diagram

method is shown above in the Figure 62.1 consists of the effective data forwarding engine, energy watcher, distance watcher, hop computation, list generator [16]. The nodes present in this list are placed nearer to each other having just one hop distance. The distance watcher placed in the block is used to assign the nearest node to the sink node. Hop calculation block is used to count for the number of hops which are needed when the travel from one node to other is done. Energy watcher select the coming node in forward face and while doing so it maintain the highest residual energy in the node next to the chosen. The energy watcher and distance watcher are used accordingly to the integer based on the threshold count. The control packets have been used during route discovery process.

Heuristic Routing Technique

Each node in this method will receive an equivalent amount of energy; this type of node is known as an equivalent energy node (EEN) [17]. A sink will check the energy of a neighbouring node and compare it to a threshold value before sending a packet. The packet is forwarded if it is within the limit and uses less energy than other nodes. The following terms are defined.

The Ideal Energy Approach
The equivalent energy node is introduced when the data transmission process is performed for the network so that it will in turn help in maintaining minimum consumption of energy . In this scenario , the curves of optimal transmission help a lot and as a result the lifetime of the network is depleted and also the energy associated with the nodes is also depleted quicky . For example , when there is transmission between the nodes which are in range of destination node , the data relay which is near to this equivalent energy node will attempt for the quicker depletion of energy .

The Best Energy Plan for Choosing the Forwarder Set
In the case of a potential node, the number of hops is convex with respect to energy consumption. Here, selecting the right number of ideal hops will help you determine the right transmission range distance. There are additional factors, such as balanced network energy and node residual energy.

Choosing Energy Nodes Using Heuristic Routing
This section explains how to prioritise and choose the forwarder set while taking an appropriate transmission energy method into account [18]. It explains how to choose the best data relay nodes from a list of potential forwarders.

Greedy Algorithm

The greedy method is used when the heuristic routing protocol fails to route a path. Finding a different route that uses the least amount of energy is helpful for energy-efficient routing.

1. The sensor node will keep a table with a single hop list containing the IDs of all nodes within its transmission range.
2. If a source node needs to send a control packet to a destination, it will assign each control packet a threshold with an initial value of M [19].
3. The hop list includes the request packet.
4. The node that will receive request packets from neighbors and has the most battery power.
5. If the threshold value of the packet is zero, an algorithm that allows the sink node to use the Prims algorithm to find the shortest path is used.

Table 62.1 Table showing proposed results.

Parameters	Conventional Approach	Proposed Approach
Energy consumed	75 J	120 J
Throughput value	162 Kbps	168 Kbps
delay	10 ms	12 ms

Experiment Results

The major goal is to use as little energy as possible while extending the life of the network. NS2 software is used to conduct the simulation results. By using the equivalent energy node concept , the neighbor nodes have been provided with the packets of information which will help in finding the shortest path between source and destination nodes , the network lifetime , throughput, delay , energy consumption . here in the below given table , there is a comparative analysis shown for the heuristic and greedy techniques while showing the improved results with the proposed technique. The outcome is shown in the Table 62.1

Conclusion

In WSN, the optimization for energy saving plays a vital role due to a number of nodes which have very limited resources for power . The significant advantages (such as easy maintenance, easy deployment , low cost and low power) of WSN makes it proper tool to be used in monitoring and controlling .this study mainly aims for increasing the lifetime of network and reduce the consumption of energy for a network which has fixed and preset sensors . Firstly , the network efficiency is maintained through heuristic approach by considering two parameters i.e. the residual energy and distance between source to sink node while taking the varied features of embedded sensor nodes. To discover the shortest path between sink and source, the usual technique and greedy algorithm are applied, resulting in lower energy consumption and longer network life. The practical results demonstrate that using the EEN and greedy algorithm improves energy savings and consumption significantly. This paper can be improved in the future by include error packets to reduce errors and making the nodes mobile to increase communication flexibility.

References

[1] Bruckner, D., Picus, C., Velik, R., Herzner, W., and Zucker, G. (2012). Hierarchical semantic processing architecture for smart sensors in surveillance networks. *IEEE Transactions on Industrial Informatics*, 8(2), 291301.

[2] Pottie, G. J., and Kaiser, W. J. (2000). Wireless integrated network sensors. *Communications of ACM*, 43(5), 5158.

[3] Chaturvedi, R., Islam, A., Singh, P. K., and Saraswat, M. (2023). Nanotechnology for advanced energy system: Synthesis & performance characterization of nano-fuel. In AIP Conference Proceedings (Vol. 2721, No. 1). AIP Publishing.

[4] Hoang, D., Yadav, P., Kumar, R., and Panda, S. (2014). Real-time implementation of a harmony search algorithm-based clustering protocol for energy efficient wireless sensor networks. *IEEE Transactions on Industrial Informatics*, 10(1), 774783.

[5] Kumar, P., Singh, P. K., Nagar, S., Sharma, K., and Saraswat, M. (2021). Effect of different concentration of functionalized graphene on charging time reduction in thermal energy storage system. *Materials Today: Proceedings*, 44, 146–152.

[6] Behnad, A., and Nader-Esfahani, S. (2010). Probability of node to base station connectivity in one-dimensional ad hoc networks. *IEEE Communications Letters*, 14(7), 650652.

[7] Piret, P. (1991). On the connectivity of radio networks. *IEEE Transactions on Information Theory*, 37(5), 14901492.

[8] Chaturvedi, R., Sharma, A., Sharma, K., and Saraswat, M. (2022). Tribological behaviour of multi-walled carbon nanotubes reinforced AA 7075 nano-composites. *Advances in Materials and Processing Technologies*, 8(4), 4743–4755.

[9] Ramaiyan, V., Kumar, A., and Altman, E. (2012). Optimal hop distance and power control for a single cell, dense, ad hoc wireless network. *Transactions on Mobile Computing*, 11(11), 16011612.

[10] Sharma, A., Chaturvedi, R., Sharma, K., and Saraswat, M. (2022). Force evaluation and machining parameter optimization in milling of aluminium burr composite based on response surface method. *Advances in Materials and Processing Technologies*, 8(4), 4073–4094.

[11] Keshtkarjahromi, Y., Ansari, R., and Khokhar, A. (2013). Energy efficient decentralized detection based on bit-optimal multi- hop transmission in one dimensional wireless sensor networks. In Proceedings of the International Federation for Information Processing, Wireless Days (WD), 2013, (p. 18).

[12] Liu, H., Zhang, B., Mouftah, H. T., Shen, X., and Ma, J. (2009). Opportunistic routing for wireless ad hoc and sensor networks: present and future directions. *IEEE Communications Magazine*, 47(12), 103109.

[13] Biswas, S., and Morris, R. (2005). Exor: opportunistic multi-hop routing for wireless networks. *Association for Computing Machinery, SIGCOMM Computer Communication Review*, 35(4), 133144.

[14] Zorzi, M., and Rao, R. R. (2003). Geographic random forwarding (geraf) for ad hoc and sensor networks: Multihop performance. *IEEE Transactions on Mobile Computing*, 2(4), 337348.

[15] Cheng, L., Niu, J., Cao, J., Das, S., and Gu, Y. (2014). Qos aware geographic opportunistic routing in wireless sensor networks. *IEEE Transactions on Parallel and Distributed Systems*, 25(7), 18641875.

[16] Kumar, Y., Pushkarna, M., and Gupta, G. (2020). Microgrid implementation in unbalanced nature of feeder using conventional technique. In 2020 3rd International Conference on Intelligent Sustainable Systems (ICISS), (pp. 1489–1494). IEEE, 2020.

[17] Dixit, K. K., Yadav, I., Gupta, G. K., and Maurya, S. K. (2020). A review on cooling techniques used for photovoltaic panels. In 2020 International Conference on Power Electronics & IoT Applications in Renewable Energy and its Control (PARC), (pp. 360–364). IEEE, 2020.

[18] Saxena, A., Kumar, J., and Deolia, V. K. (2021). Optimization of NPIC controller using genetic algorithm. In IOP Conference Series: Materials Science and Engineering, 1104(1), 012001. IOP Publishing, 2021.

[19] Badhoutiya, A., Chandra, S., and Goyal, S. (2020). Identification of suitable modulation scheme for boosted output in ZSI. In 2020 4th International Conference on Electronics, Communication and Aerospace Technology (ICECA), (pp. 238–243). IEEE, 2020.

63 Design challenges for automotive application with wide-band-gap & scalable power electronic devices

Yogendra Kumar[1,a] and Manish Saraswat[2,b]

[1]GLA University, Mathura

[2]LLOYD Institute of Engineering and Technology, Greater Noida

Abstract

Despite the relatively small size of the high-temperature electronics market, there are probably numerous systems that could derive substantial economic benefits from their implementation. However, low power transistor applications will be the primary use for these wide band gap semiconductor devices (WBG devices). Subsequent to attaining the universally acknowledged temperature threshold, these devices based on semiconductors can operate without the need for external cooling. They could find extensive application in the automotive, aerospace, and energy generation industries, among others. In order to operate at elevated temperatures, partially constructed Si-based WBG has been created. Due to their ability to operate at elevated power and temperature levels, WBG devices have been implemented in an overwhelming majority of electronic subsystems. This study examines the application of WBG devices as components of energy storage and presents an exhaustive summary of the technological obstacles involved.

Keywords: Automotive, high power, high temperature, integrated circuits, large scale, semiconductor, temperature, wide band gap

Introduction

The utilization of high-temperature electronics holds promise for numerous systems from an economic standpoint, despite the relatively small market for such products. The global market for high-temperature electronics is anticipated to be worth $400 million in 2003 and $900 million in 2008 [1]. This represents less than 0.1 percent of the worldwide semiconductor electronics market. Power electronics for a multitude of original equipment manufacturer (OEM) automobile applications have been developed by Magna Electronics. At present, there are electronic control modules that are designed for use in power plants, electric and hybrid vehicles, and dc/dc charger converters.

Electrical properties hold equivalent significance when driving inductive loads; mechanical packaging has the capability to enhance them. At this time, specific connection techniques for IGBT power modules ensure minimal parasitic inductance. Die attachment materials and construction have a direct bearing on the dependability of the device [2]. Testing the packages, materials, topologies, and other components to ensure they can endure the hostile environment will facilitate the design's acceptance for subsequent uses.

Wide Band Gap Devices

Power electronic devices have significantly influenced conventional social norms by contributing to the improvement of the environment by mitigating the adverse consequences of industrialization, including but not limited to greenhouse gas emissions and climate change. Power electronic devices featuring a broad Band Gap have the potential to revolutionize efficiency and functionality in comparison to those built on mature silicon. Silicon carbide and gallium nitride, which are WBG materials, are capable of exceeding the performance thresholds of Si switching devices. By utilizing these WBG devices, power converters can be manufactured with increased efficiency, decreased power losses, accelerated switching, and greater power density. Further reading will enlighten you on the benefits and drawbacks of prevalent SiC and GaN power devices, as well as their power electronics applications.

The construction of an energy-independent planet requires state-of-the-art materials, including wide band gap (WBG) semiconductors. Energy electronic converters and interior weather monitoring serve as the foundation of building energy consumption and management. Approximately 60% of the energy required to generate electricity is lost during the conversion process [3], contrary to conventional belief. Before power electronics converters can even put to use the energy they produce, they waste a substantial amount of energy undergoing these

[a]kumar.yogendra@gla.ac.in, [b]manish.saraswat@lloydcollege.in

DOI: 10.1201/9781003534136-63

inefficient processes. Denoting a WBG semiconductor, the band gap, which represents the energy demanded for electrons to transition from the valence band to the conduction band, is an indispensable physical characteristic. The electrical and optical properties of a semiconductor are determined by this energy. The capacity of a power device to reduce eddy current and hysteresis losses is significantly influenced by the magnetic characteristics of the semiconducting material.

Semi-Conductor Power Devices

While SiC and GaN are the most suitable WBG semiconductor materials for high-power applications, there are a few others that are more suitable. An example of such a situation is the ongoing discourse surrounding Schottky diodes and their silicon equivalents. Due to the superior performance of SiC in comparison to Si diodes, SiC-fabricated devices can sustain higher current densities while employing more compact cooling systems. The broad band gap characteristics of GaN and SiC devices render these materials resistant to thermal and radiation-induced changes in their electrical properties. SiC exhibits superior efficiency, faster switching capabilities, and higher voltage tolerances when compared to Si. This is because SiC possesses a significantly wider bandgap. The effects of power semiconductor devices on key performance indicators (KPIs) of power electronic systems, including efficiency, weight, volume, cost, and cost, can only be determined through modeling. For instance, the existence of elevated power densities indicates the implementation of high switching frequencies, potentially leading to a decline in efficiency [4]. A relationship exists between the aforementioned indexes [5]. The application of modeling enables one to perform a precise analysis of innovative device structures before they are produced. These models are constructed upon an electrical equivalent circuit composed of aggregated circuit components. These constituents consist of capacitors, inductors, and controlled voltage or current sources.

WBG Devices for Automotive Applications

Power electronic components can be more compact, swifter, dependable, and efficient than those based on silicon (Si) thanks to wide bandgap (WBG) semiconductor materials. With these abilities, a variety of power applications can reduce weight, volume, and life-cycle costs. In the near future, WBG devices will break into the automotive industry, where the risk of change is low [6]. Time will be required to convince the automotive industry of the long-term advantages that would accrue from the widespread integration of WBG devices. As opposed to utilizing the currently available Si technology, designing with WBG devices provides a number of advantageous characteristics. Further advantages encompass enhanced inverter efficiency, reduced conduction losses, and decreased resistance. Nevertheless, potential adjustments to the cooling mechanism may be necessary to accommodate significantly elevated junction temperatures. WBG materials are favored over silicon for electric vehicle construction on account of their reduced cost, reduced size, decreased weight, and increased energy efficiency. In the below given Table 63.1 wide band gap material properties have been given.

DC/DC Converters: The car's main inverter, which controls the electric motor and returns energy recovered from regenerative braking to the battery, is a crucial part. The type of electric motor used can be brushless DC, synchronous, or asynchronous [7]. The DC-DC converters in EVs are responsible for converting high voltage battery energy into low voltage for the power system bus. Auxiliary systems like air conditioning, electronic power steering, cooling pumps, and oil pumps receive power from the high voltage battery via the auxiliary inverter or converter [8].

Table 63.1 Si based wide band Gap material properties.

Properties	Si	4H-SiC	6H-SiC
Thermal conductivity (W/cm K)	1.5	4.9	4.9
Band gap (eV)	1.12	3.26	3.03
Dielectric constant	11.9	9.7	9.66
Breakdown field (MV/cm)	0.3	2.2	2.5
Intrinsic carrier concentration (cm−3)	0.1	$10-6$	$10-9$
Electron mobility (cm2/Vs)	1500	800	400
Drift velocity (107 cm/s)	1.02	2.0	2.0

Battery Management System: During charging and discharging, the battery state is managed by the battery management system. This can be accomplished in a clever manner to increase the battery's lifespan. Cell usage needs to be optimised as battery ages by balancing performance during charging and discharging cycles. The on-board battery charger is essential in this situation because it enables battery charging from a regular power outlet. Given that the same circuit must support various voltage and current levels, this is seen as an additional requirement for the designers [9].

Switch Mode Power Supply: By combining switches with energy storage components, switched-mode power supplies (SMPS) are known to achieve voltage or current regulation. The 20th century saw the initial introduction of this technology, with mechanical switches, vacuum tubes, and ultimately semiconductor-based switches being used. The energy storage requirement, which is determined by the converter power requirement and operating frequency, directly relates to the size of the storage elements [10]. As a result, increasing the operating frequency of the converter enables it to decrease the size of the energy storage components, which directly affects the converter's volume, power density, and cost. Using wide bandgap (WBG) semiconductor devices can help with this.

Conclusion

Electric motors with increasingly small sizes and higher performance are needed for automotive applications. Since they have historically been silicon semiconductor-based, motor driver circuits struggle to meet these demanding specifications. With restrictions on power density, breakdown voltage, and switching frequency, the silicon technology is actually approaching its theoretical limits, which has an impact on power losses. These restrictions primarily manifest as a less-than-optimal level of efficiency. Additional potential issues could arise, particularly during operation at high temperatures and rapid switching rates. The energy storage requirement, which is determined by the converter power requirement and operating frequency, directly relates to the size of the storage elements. As a result, increasing the operating frequency of the converter enables it to decrease the size of the energy storage components, which directly affects the converter's volume, power density, and cost. Wide bandgap (WBG) semiconductor devices can be used for this.

References

[1] Su, M., Chen, C., and Rajan, S. (2013). Prospects for the application of GaN power devices in hybrid electric vehicle drive systems. *Semiconductor Science and Technology*, 28(7), 074012.

[2] Sharma, A., Chaturvedi, R., Sharma, K., and Saraswat, M. (2022). Force evaluation and machining parameter optimization in milling of aluminium burr composite based on response surface method. *Advances in Materials and Processing Technologies*, 8(4), 4073–4094.

[3] Chemali, E., Preindl, M., Malysz, P., and Emadi, A. (2016). Electrochemical and electrostatic energy storage and management systems for electric drive vehicles: state-of-the-art review and future trends. *IEEE Journal of Emerging and Selected Topics in Power Electronics*, 4(3), 1117–1134.

[4] Hamada, K. (2008). Present status and future prospects for electronics in electric vehicles/hybrid electric vehicles and expectations for wide-bandgap semiconductor devices. *Physica Status Solidi (b)*, 245(7), 1223–1231.

[5] Chaturvedi, R., Sharma, A., Sharma, K., and Saraswat, M. (2022). Tribological behaviour of multi-walled carbon nanotubes reinforced AA 7075 nano-composites. *Advances in Materials and Processing Technologies*, 8(4), 4743–4755.

[6] Kumar, P., Singh, P. K., Nagar, S., Sharma, K., and Saraswat, M. (2021). Effect of different concentration of functionalized graphene on charging time reduction in thermal energy storage system. *Materials Today: Proceedings*, 44, 146–152.

[7] Xing, Y., Ma, E. W., Tsui, K. L., and Pecht, M. (2011). Battery management systems in electric and hybrid vehicles. *Energies*, 4(11), 1840–1857.

[8] Chaturvedi, R., Islam, A., Singh, P. K., and Saraswat, M. (2023). Nanotechnology for advanced energy system: Synthesis & performance characterization of nano-fuel. In AIP Conference Proceedings (Vol. 2721, No. 1). AIP Publishing.

[9] Yadav, K., and Maurya, S. (2020). A comparative study on the performance of energy storage systems for hybrid electric vehicles. In Advances in Energy Technology: Select Proceedings of EMSME 2020, (pp. 795–803). Springer Singapore, 2022.

[10] Badhoutiya, A., Chandra, S., and Goyal, S. (2020). Identification of suitable modulation scheme for boosted output in ZSI. In 2020 4th International Conference on Electronics, Communication and Aerospace Technology (ICECA), (pp. 238–243). IEEE 2020.

64 Neural system model & effect of soiling on PV modules

Yogendra Kumar[1,a] and Birendra Kr. Saraswat[2,b]

[1]GLA University, Mathura

[2]Raj Kumar Goel Institute of Technology, Ghaziabad

Abstract

Soiling loss occurs when the accumulation of dirt and debris on PV surfaces over time reduces the amount of sunlight that reaches the panels. Due to the direct correlation between the efficacy of a PV system and the efficiency of solar energy conversion, soil loss is a significant factor in estimating PV system losses. The rapid progress of photovoltaic cell technology has significantly simplified the process of installing and utilizing solar energy. Due to the use of semiconductors in solar cell fabrication, PV system efficiency has decreased by 15–2 percent. Dust accumulation or soiling further degrades the performance of solar panels. This research paper introduces a Levenberg-Marquardt (LM) neural network-based automated windshield wiper control system designed for the purpose of washing solar panels. A pattern recognition LM-based network model is trained and assessed using expert information data. In the absence of a formal model, the outcomes demonstrated that this LM neural network-based model can comprehend the uncertainties and nonlinearities of an automatic windshield wiper system.

Keywords: Algorithm, dust, pattern recognition, performance, PV system, semiconductor, soiling

Introduction

In order to convert sunlight into electricity, photovoltaic (PV) technology employs semiconductors and the photovoltaic effect. Solar power and other forms of clean, alternative energy have recently garnered international attention [1]. Soiling loss occurs when the accumulation of dirt and debris on PV surfaces over time reduces the amount of sunlight that reaches the panels. Due to the direct correlation between the efficacy of a PV system and the efficiency of solar energy conversion, soil loss is a significant factor in estimating PV system losses. The rapid progress of photovoltaic cell technology has significantly simplified the process of installing and utilizing solar energy. In order to ascertain soiling and shading losses, calculate a ratio (t) between the actual DC power generation of the plant and the DC power it would generate in the absence of these factors [2].

When designing solar panels, achieving optimal performance is a primary objective. The factors that impact this output can be classified into two groups: those that are modifiable, including the tilt angle, and those that are immutable, including the number of solar cells in a panel and the distance between each cell. The arrangement and construction of solar panels are influenced by numerous variables, some of which are non-variable and others of which are. Mutable variables permit variable system supply design flexibility, whereas immutable variables are inherently in a state of constant change [3].

"Soiling" denotes the accumulation of diverse particulates on the glass surfaces that comprise solar panels. Potential surface stains include, apart from dirt accumulation, plant detritus, soot, salt, bird droppings, and the proliferation of organic organisms. Energy consent is significantly impacted by soiling loss, which subsequently diminishes the efficacy of solar modules [4] due to diminished light absorption and dispersion. Researchers are currently focused on addressing the significant concern of energy loss that arises from the accumulation of grime on the glass surfaces of solar panels.

Soil Accumulation

The act of contaminating or polluting; including unwanted substances or factors (either intentionally or unintentionally). contamination by dust. contamination is when dust is introduced. Days that are cloudy or rainy also make dusty panels less effective at capturing sunlight. The impact of soiling on solar output varies according to the season. For example, the air is denser in the winter, which reduces efficiency [5]. The air's uppermost layer also has more contamination, which has an impact on emissions. Because of the climate's tendency to be windy in the autumn, pollution levels are frequently higher than they are in the winter. When installed in the spring, solar panels have a greater tilt angle, which maximizes efficiency because rainy weather washes away

[a]kumar.yogendra@gla.ac.in, [b]saraswatbirendra@gmail.com

DOI: 10.1201/9781003534136-64

Table 64.1 Investigation of selected polluting elements.

composition	Type	Solar technology
Sand particle	Natural	Solar collector
Natural dust	Natural	PV System
suspended dust	Natural	Glass Plate
Ash	Artificial	PV System
Red soil	Artifical	PV System
Used clay	Artificial	PV System
Sand soil	Natural	PV System
Fine and coarser dust	Artificial	Photovoltaic concentrators
Biological plants	Natural	Natural

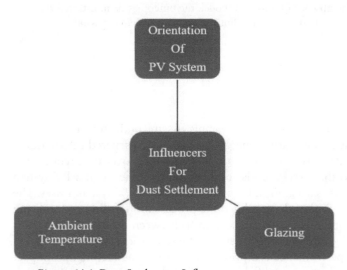

Figure 64.1 Dust Settlement Influencers

dirt. The selected elements with their type and solar technology used have been given in the following Table 64.1 and the influencer for the dust settlement have been illustrated with the Figure 64.1.

Small solid particles carried by air currents make up dust pollution. These particles can be created in a number of ways, including milling, breaking up the solids into smaller pieces, and other techniques [6]. Dust is defined by the Mine Safety and Health Administration (MSHA) as finely divided solids that have only undergone fracture and are present in the atmosphere in their original form. Micrometers are typically used to measure dust particle size. With time, the amount of dust on the solar panel thickens.

The prominence of solar photovoltaic has increased as an environmentally responsible, long-term option. As of now [7], advancements in materials research have failed to substantially enhance the conversion efficiency of commercial PV modules. When strategizing the installation of a photovoltaic system, the quantity of available solar insolation, latitude, inclination, and orientation of the site are the most crucial factors. However, once these parameters are attained, additional variables that impact the efficacy of the system (such as output and efficiency) come into play. Unbeknownst to the majority, grime significantly reduces the performance of PV systems. The solar panel with jet sprayer is shown in the below Figure 64.2 and the measured data during different time period of the day is shown in the Table 64.2.

Affecting Parameters

The consequences of dust accumulation on photovoltaic (PV) systems are contingent upon the dust's characteristics and its interaction with the surrounding environment. Orientation, height, surface coatings, and other

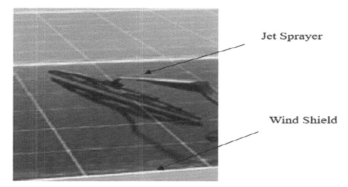

Figure 64.2 Solar Panel with Jet Sprayer

Table 64.2 Measured data on different time period of cloudy, dust accumulated and sunny days.

Time	Day	current	voltage	Power	Module temperature	Irradiance
11:00 a.m	Cloudy	3.11	9.38	29.2	24.4	150
12:00 p.m	Cloudy	2.91	13.9	13	27.2	200
11:00 a.m	Sunny	6.6	13.8	91	43	465
12:00 p.m	Sunny	7.6	18.7	142	48	764
11:00 a.m	Dust accumulated	2.58	12.9	33.5	46.1	564
12:00 p.m	Dust accumulated	3.15	13.5	42.5	46.4	793

characteristics of the built environment interact with natural elements such as vegetation type and weather to define the local environment. The site-specific elements of the local environment are also influenced by the prevailing human activities. In addition to dust collection or aggregation, characteristics including type, size, shape, and weight are crucial.

The PV surface refinement of the settling surface is an additional critical factor. A smoother, less sticky surface attracts less grime than an adhesive surface. Additionally, it is widely acknowledged that the process of dust settling on a surface promotes additional dust accumulation by rendering the surface more conducive to dust collection [8].

System Model and Results

When a control signal has been sent by the model, the wiper motor starts as soon as the windscreen received the signal. The windscreen has received the control signal for the wiper motor to operate and then the process initializes in which small jet like structure sprays water . This is based on the solar panel's current profile , power and voltage . There are three layers which are the basic structure of ANN model i.e. input , hidden and output layers. The input layer receives control signal based on solar insolation, irradiance, module temperature, PV power, current and voltage. There is only one node in output layer which indicates that dust is accumulated in the panel. The 0 and 1 values have been sent as the control signal for indicating soil accumulation, 0 indicates that there is not any dust accumulation on the panel and then the windscreen wiper will have no need to operate [9].

The trained pre setup has consists the following modelling data for input and output performance measure of the system

$$E = \frac{1}{\eta}(\gamma \sum_{i=1}^{n} e_i^2 + (1-\gamma)\sum_{j=1}^{n} w_j^2$$

The above expressing is the modified error which has been as the performance character for the feed forward training of the model [10]. The LM algorithm uses two or more variables that are expressed as the sum of squares of non-linear real-valued functions.

Conclusion

When dust and grime accumulate on PV surfaces over time, less sunlight is able to reach the solar panels, causing soiling loss. Because the performance of a PV system is directly impacted by the solar energy conversion efficiency, soil loss is an important factor in calculating PV system losses The PV cell technology has been developed rapidly and simplified the solar plant installation. With the system model proposed, the module has been simplified and generate the signal for the wiper motor to the windscreen. The advantage of this model is that it does not require any additional parameters, in contrast to couched systems that do, making calculations more difficult because the parameters are not readily available.

References

[1] Koca, A., Oztop, H. F., Varol, Y., and Koca, G. O. (2011). Estimation of solar radiation using artificial neural networks with different input parameters for mediterranean region of anatoliain Turkey. *Expert System Application*, 38, 8756–8762.

[2] Kalogirou, S. A. (2000). Applications of artificial neural networks for energy systems. *Applied Energy*, 67(1-2), 17–35.

[3] Chaturvedi, R., Islam, A., Singh, P. K., and Saraswat, M. (2023). Nanotechnology for advanced energy system: synthesis & performance characterization of nano-fuel. In AIP Conference Proceedings (Vol. 2721, No. 1). AIP Publishing.

[4] Kumar, P., Singh, P. K., Nagar, S., Sharma, K., and Saraswat, M. (2021). Effect of different concentration of functionalized graphene on charging time reduction in thermal energy storage system. *Materials Today: Proceedings*, 44, 146–152.

[5] Badhoutiya, A., and Yadav, A. (2017). Boost control for PV applications using impedance source inverter. In 2017 2nd IEEE International Conference on Recent Trends in Electronics, Information & Communication Technology (RTEICT), (pp. 1967–1970). IEEE, 2017.

[6] Chaturvedi, R., Sharma, A., Sharma, K., and Saraswat, M. (2022). Tribological behaviour of multi-walled carbon nanotubes reinforced AA 7075 nano-composites. *Advances in Materials and Processing Technologies*, 8(4), 4743–4755.

[7] Chowdhury, M. S., Rahman, K. S., Chowdhury, T., Nuthammachot, N., Techato, K., Akhtaruzzaman, M., et al. (2020). An overview of solar photovoltaic panels' end-of-life material recycling. *Energy Strategy Reviews*, 27, 100431.

[8] Maghami, M. R., Hizam, H., Gomes, C., Radzi, M. A., Rezadad, M. I., and Hajighorbani, S. (2016). Power loss due to soiling on solar panel: a review. *Renewable and Sustainable Energy Reviews*, 59, 1307–1316.

[9] Caron, J. R., and Littmann, B. (2012). Direct monitoring of energy lost due to soiling on first solar modules in California. *IEEE Journal of Photovoltaics*, 3(1), 336–340.

[10] Sharma, A., Chaturvedi, R., Sharma, K., and Saraswat, M. (2022). Force evaluation and machining parameter optimization in milling of aluminium burr composite based on response surface method. *Advances in Materials and Processing Technologies*, 8(4), 4073–4094.

65 Diagnosis and controlling neurodegenerative disorders using machine learning methods: a review

Krishna Kant Dixit[1, a] and Manish Saraswat[2, b]

[1]GLA University, Mathura, India

[2]LLOYD Institute of Engineering and Technology, Greater Noida, India

Abstract

To diagnose, treat and control neurodegenerative disorders such as Parkinson's disease (PD), artificial intelligence (AI), can be used particularly machine learning (ML). The tasks are difficult because there are many similarities between how many diseases manifest in the body, but there are also many differences between people. The purpose of this research is to recapitulate the parametric analysis of neurodegenerative disorders especially for PD using machine learning methods to apply artificial intelligence. Artificial Intelligence is mainly used to find and evaluate PD. The kinematics of the body are used to determine how far someone has moved. Several machine learning methods produced promising results, particularly when it came to detecting PD early on. The study investigates whether it is possible to collect information using low-cost and easily accessible technologies. Researchers, doctors, and medical institutions must collaborate more comprehensively, in order to fully utilize artificial intelligence technologies in the future. It is critical to keep the data collection processes in sync, as well as to share and combine the various data sets.

Keywords: Parkinson's disease, diagnosis, machine learning, artificial intelligence

Introduction

The subfield of study known as artificial intelligence (AI) is expanding at a rapid rate and encompasses a wide variety of approaches that attempt to simulate the ways in which intelligent humans think and behave [1]. Augmented reality (AR), virtual reality (VR), 3D printing, AI, wearable sensors, and a wide variety of other cutting-edge and innovative technologies are currently being developed for use in the medical field. AI is a reality that is all around us right now, and it is doing amazing things in many fields, such as robotic surgery and cars that drive themselves. AI is a reality that is all around us right now. Recent developments in machine learning, such as new discoveries and improvements, have contributed to the expansion of the field of AI, despite the fact that AI encompasses a diverse array of subfields. Machine learning (ML), is a subfield of artificial intelligence that consists of powerful algorithms that give computers the ability to explore data and find patterns. These algorithms give machines the ability to learn. Through learning via experience, classify and anticipate outcomes. In addition to detection, outcome prediction, progression tracking and disease management, machine learning has found a position in healthcare. This method has also made its way into neurology [2]. Wearable technology and machine learning algorithms have tackled a variety of difficulties related to neurodegenerative movement diseases, including PD is a brain disease that is affecting people. According to a study employing post-mortem neuro-pathological testing to investigate the efficiency of conventional clinical diagnostics methods and it is observed that clinical detection of PD has specificity and sensitivity of around 68% and 88% respectively. The untreated or unresponsive patients are only about 26% and around 53 % are those who were responsive to treatment, were appropriately diagnosed as having Parkinson's disease. prescription drugs Tremor is one of the most prominent clinical characteristics of PD. The goal of this paper is to provide a broad perspective about the improvements that AI and, in particular, ML has brought to the management and diagnosis of Parkinson's disease, as well as instruments and technology which made it possible. Tremor, bradykinesia, stiffness, and postural instability are the most general clinical characteristics of PD [3]. These symptoms affect both the lower and upper extremities, making it difficult for patients to do daily chores during the disease's initial phases. As a result, assessing these symptoms using body movement analysis is a crucial aspect of the detection and clinical assessment of Parkinson's disease.

Upper Extremities

Use of Advanced Hand Motion Analysis Techniques in assisting Diagnostic.
Machine learning algorithms, according to the literature, gradually increase distinction between healthy participants and PD patients in comparison with results obtained during previous studies of clinical application.

---

[a]krishnakant.dixit@gla.ac.in, [b]manish.saraswat@lloydcollege.in

DOI: 10.1201/9781003534136-65

The number of people enrolled, illness stages, applied methodology, and apparatus vary between studies, but all indicate improved classification accuracy between healthy controls (HC) and PD patients for larger datasets & later stages of disease. Figure 66.1 depicts the installation of ML methods for diagnosing PD and the obtained results are applied to upper panel of kinematic data [4]. The performance indicators - accuracy (A), have been used to describe the performance. The diagram depicts the most used or successful supervised methods. A selection that indicates all reviewed ML algorithms was obtained from published works. The used Algorithms are shown in the columns including TREE, SVM, NB, LR, KNN, EVOL, ENS and ANN in reverse alphabetic order.

Figure 65.1 shows the algorithms that were used, along with the abbreviations that were used for each algorithm. The leading ML algorithms (one in each column), FOG detection (lower panel), implementation of ML on lower extremity kinematic data for diagnosis (upper panel) and showing the number of patients (shown by the size of the marker), the instrumentation that was used (shown by the shape of the marker), and their performance (the horizontal axis shows the presented measure and the vertical axis shows its percentage value), Naïve Bayes (NB), artificial neural network (ANN), ensemble (ENS) of different algorithms, evolutionary algorithms (EVOL), logistic regression (LR), support vector machine (SVM), k-nearest neighbors (KNN),– tree-based algorithms (TREE). The other parameters include electromagnetic (EM) tracking and inertial measurement unit (IMU).

Monitoring the progression of disease response to treatment

Researchers [5] have offered features indicating clinically significant factors, such as amplitude of repeated movements, rhythm city, frequency, tremor frequency, as input to such intelligent algorithms. In Figure 65.1 the results show the supervision of ML algorithm to assess PD patients by taking kinematic data for upper panel and in Figure 65.2 the results are shown by taking lower extremity. For examining the patients, Cloud based applications have been developed by utilizing ML, in order to increase the efficiency of patient examining process. Some other applications included are finger tapping, remote recording of UPDRS tasks, symptoms severity, tremor etc. For differentiating low- and high-quality recordings, the deep learning algorithm is also integrated with this system. For the detection of patient's conditions and everyday activities, ML is used. It will also help in providing the report of medications and thus help in making patient tolerable plant for treatment.

LOWER EXTREMITIES

Furthermore, using advanced algorithmic processes, new methods of diagnosis and evaluation based on lower extremity mobility have been developed. These techniques rely on the mobility of the lower extremities.

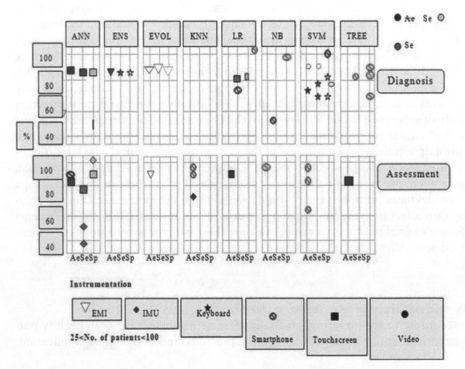

Figure 65.1 Performance measures based on upper extremities

Alternative methodologies have been used, which may include a wide range of instrumentation and algorithms [6]. This study discusses the use of machine learning algorithms in diagnosing, particularly early-stage detection, assessment of therapeutic response, prediction of disease severity, and detection of major symptoms that interfere with normal walking (such as gait, freezing, and falling). The importance of early disease detection is emphasized in particular. An emphasis is placed, in particular, on detection in its early stages.

Group of Advanced Information Technology in assisting Diagnostic

Different ML algorithms have been applied to datasets acquired from infrared cameras in order to find the best method for reliable PD diagnosis (motion capture or Kinect with optical marker) [7-9]. Studies focusing on algorithms for early PD diagnosis, where the kNN algorithm achieved Ac=85.5 percent, made a substantial contribution. Using SVM resulted in an accuracy of 85 percent or higher, as evidenced by many research. The obtained Spas for LDA is 86%:88%. For earlier detection of PD (UPDRS value is below 15), for mild PD score is more than 20 and about 100% features can be extracted. When moderate stage of PD is taken for analyzing around 93 patients with the help of RBF NN, the value of Ac is 96.39%. For generally used ML algorithms, the results of PD diagnosis are shown in Figure 66.2 for Lower panel of kinematic data.

Track of disease's progression & reaction to treatment

The identification and estimation of freezing of gait (FoG) falls is another key application for machine learning techniques. Due to their adaptability, wearable sensors have been extensively utilized, for usage at home and recording along winding, difficult paths narrow passageways and doorways. Sensors are commonly placed on the waist and legs [10], although they can also be found on the chest & wrist. As cell phones have become increasingly integrated into our daily lives, they also found their job to be unobtrusive thanks to integrated inertial sensors. The Figure 66.2 depicts the most commonly used or successful supervised methods. A selection that indicates all reviewed ML algorithms was obtained from published works. The used Algorithms are shown in the columns including, ANN, KNN, LDA, LR, NB, SVM, and TREE.

Figure 65.2 shows the used algorithms are abbreviated as follows k-nearest neighbors (KNN),– atificial neural network (ANN), linear discriminate analysis (LDA), Naïve Bayes (NB), logistic regression (LR), support vector machine (SVM), tree-based algorithms (TREE). The other parameters include inertial measurement unit (IMU) and electromagnetic (EM) tracking.

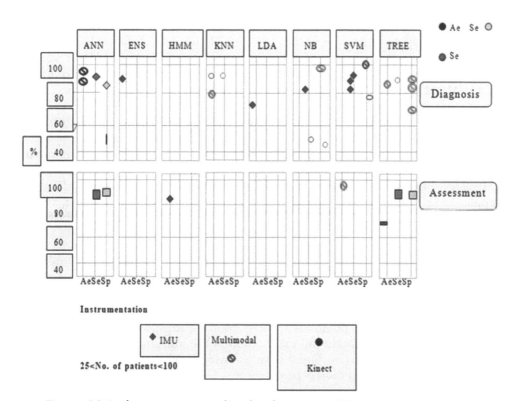

Figure 65.2 Performance measures based on lower extremities

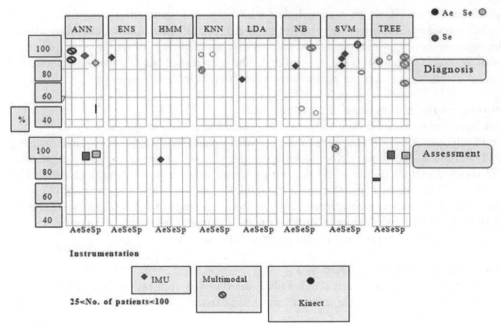

Figure 65.3 Performance measures based on both upper and lower extremities

Upper and Lower Extremities

The data is recorded with some sensors (ambient light, magnetic door, infrared, vibration) on the dominant arm and inertial sensors on the dominant limb, for the differentiation between patients having cognitive impairments but no PD, having PD with or without cognitive impairments, HC [11-12]. By using Ada Boost DT algorithm, the accuracy of around 86 5 can be achieved for these above-mentioned groups, as reported from the obtained results. The accuracy range achieved for comparing PD and HC patients with DT, SVM (both non-linear and linear), KNN, NB, and LDA is approx. 79.62-84.1%. On the other hand, the accuracy of classifiers can be above 90% [13-14]. If we make use of other algorithms like H&Y III, H &Y II and H&Y I, the achieved accuracy can be 93.63%, 87.75%, and 94.5%, resp. In some other studies, kNN, PNN and EML classifiers [13] are used to compare the three stages (severe, moderate and mild) of PD which is based on UPDRS and H& Y scores. The achieved accuracy of HMM is around 87% for predicting severity of tremor for both the upper & lower extremities [15-16]. By using SVM [14] and DNN [15] above 90% performance can be achieved for accessing dyskinesia, bradykinesia, and tremor. For different classifiers like RT, DT, RF and NB, Figure 66.3 will indicate the diagnosis assessment of PD patients by using ML algorithms and the data for lower and upper extremity is included in kinematic set [17-18].

Figure 65.3 ML implementation for diagnosis of kinematic data on both the lower and upper extremities in which the performance indicators, accuracy (A), has been used to describe the performance. The diagram depicts the most commonly used or successfully supervised methods. A selection that indicates all reviewed ML algorithms was obtained from published works. The used Algorithms are shown in the columns including, TREE, SVM, NB, LR, kNN, ENS and ANN, LDA, IMU, HMM [19-20-21].

Conclusion

The purpose of this in-depth review is to provide an overview of the research that has been carried out regarding the application of machine learning strategies within the realm of artificial intelligence. The upper and lower panels each contain a significant amount of kinematic data, which can be used to derive information about movement analysis, full-body kinematics, and the prognosis for Parkinson's disease. No matter how much effort is put into assured testing, the size of the sample and the location of the instruments could potentially differ from one another. A common issue that arises in clinical trials is having an excessive number of participants with a diverse range of symptom severity and disease progression. A lack of uniformity in the reporting of results, as well as the assessment of validity, outcome measures, and other metrics, is another problem that needs to be addressed. In light of these limitations, it would be helpful to validate sensor-derived assessments of PD characteristics by increasing the amount of collaboration between studies, standardizing data collection methods, and improving data quality. This would be helpful in validating sensor-derived assessments of PD characteristics. gathering information from a variety of sources and exchanging it with one another.

References

[1] Jiang, F., Jiang, Y., Zhi, H., Dong, Y., Li, H., Ma, S., Wang, Y., Dong, Q., Shen, H., and Wan, Y. (2017). Artificial intelligence in healthcare: past, present and future. *Stroke and Vascular Neurology*, 2(4).

[2] López, W. O. C., Navarro, P. A., and Crispin, S. (2019). Intraoperative clinical application of augmented reality in neurosurgery: a systematic review. *Clinical Neurology and Neurosurgery*, 177, 6-11.

[3] Sharma, A., Chaturvedi, R., Sharma, K., and Saraswat, M. (2022). Force evaluation and machining parameter optimization in milling of aluminium burr composite based on response surface method. *Advances in Materials and Processing Technologies*, 8(4), 4073-4094.

[4] Jain, V., Agrawal, M., and Kumar, A. (2020). Performance analysis of machine learning algorithms in credit cards fraud detection. In 2020 8th International Conference on Reliability, Infocom Technologies and Optimization (Trends and Future Directions), pp. 86-88. IEEE, 2020.

[5] Chaturvedi, R., Sharma, A., Sharma, K., and Saraswat, M. (2022). Tribological behaviour of multi-walled carbon nanotubes reinforced AA 7075 nano-composites. *Advances in Materials and Processing Technologies*, 8(4), 4743-4755.

[6] Singh, P. K. and Sharma, K. (2018). Mechanical and viscoelastic properties of in-situ amine functionalized multiple layer grpahene/epoxy nanocomposites. *Current Nanoscience*, 14(3), 252-262.

[7] Kostikis, N., et al (2015). A smartphone-based tool for assessing parkinsonian hand tremor. *IEEE journal of Biomedical and Health Informatics*, 19(6), 1835-1842.

[8] Djurić-Jovičić, Milica, et al. (2014). Implementation of continuous wavelet transformation in repetitive finger tapping analysis for patients with PD. *2014 22nd Telecommunications Forum Telfor (TELFOR)*.

[9] Kumar, P., Singh, P. K., Nagar, S., Sharma, K., and Saraswat, M. (2021). Effect of different concentration of functionalized graphene on charging time reduction in thermal energy storage system. *Materials Today: Proceedings*, 44, 146-152.

[10] Djurić-Jovičić, Milica, et al. (2018). Finger and foot tapping sensor system for objective motor assessment. *Vojnosanitetski pregled (VSP)*, 75(1), 68-77.

[11] Baron, L. and Braune, A. (2016). Case study on applying augmented reality for process supervision in industrial use cases. In *2016 IEEE 21st International Conference on Emerging Technologies and Factory Automation (ETFA)*, pp. 1-4

[12] Sharma, A., Chaturvedi, R., Singh, P. K., and, Sharma, K. (2021). AristoTM robot welding performance and analysis of mechanical and microstructural characteristics of the weld. *Materials Today: Proceedings*, 43, 614-622.

[13] Bazgir, O. et al. (2018). A classification system for assessment and home monitoring of tremor in patients with Parkinson's disease. *Journal of Medical Signals and Sensors*, 8(2), 65.

[14] Sharma, A., Sharma, K., Islam, A., and Roy, D. (2020). Effect of welding parameters on automated robotic arc welding process. *Materials Today: Proceedings*, 26, 2363-2367.

[15] Rajpoot, V., Agrawal, R., Chaturvedi, A., and Goyal, K. (2021). An empirical study of sentiment analysis on movie review using machine learning based classification approach. *In 2021 5th International Conference on Information Systems and Computer Networks (ISCON)*, pp. 1-4. IEEE, 2021.

[16] Chaturvedi, R., Islam, A., Singh, P. K., and Saraswat, M. (2023). Nanotechnology for advanced energy system: synthesis & performance characterization of nano-fuel. In *AIP Conference Proceedings*, 2721(1).

[17] Jeon, Hyoseon, et al. (2017). Automatic classification of tremor severity in Parkinson's disease using a wearable device. *Sensors*, 17(9), 2067.

[18] Oung, Qi Wei, et al. (2018). Empirical wavelets transform based features for classification of Parkinson's disease severity. *Journal of Medical Systems*, 42(2), 29.

[19] Cuzzolin, Fabio, et al. (2017). Metric learning for Parkinsonian identification from IMU gait measurements. *Gait & Posture*, 54, (127-132.

[20] Kumar, A., Sharma, K., and Dixit, (AR). (2020). Carbon nanotube-and graphene-reinforced multiphase polymeric composites: review on their properties and applications. *Journal of Materials Science*, 55(7), 2682-2724.

[21] Belić, Minja, et al. (2019). Artificial intelligence for assisting diagnostics and assessment of Parkinson's disease—A review. Clinical Neurology and Neurosurgery, 184, 105442.

66 The influence of artificial intelligence on the the diverse financial sector

Garima Singhal[1,a], Aniket Singh[2,b] and Bhawna Kaushik[3,c]

[1]Department of Management of Business Administration, IIMT Group of Colleges, Greater Noida, Uttar Pradersh, India

[2]Department of Computer Science, Delhi Technical Campus, Greater Noida, Uttar Pradersh, India

[3]Department of Computer Science Lloyd Institute of Engineering and Technology Greater Noida, Uttar Pradersh, India

Abstract

The trend of financial automation is rising as businesses look for more economical and effective methods to handle their accounts and provide the right services. Businesses can expedite decision-making and automate a multitude of financial tasks thanks to artificial intelligence. Artificial intelligence (AI) should not take the place of human intelligence and judgment in the financial industry. As AI algorithms advance, financial knowledge will be required to guarantee that the judgments made by AI are accurate and consistent with the objectives of the business. AI is capable of digital assistant customer support, fraud detection and prevention, loan risk assessment, and automated client onboarding. When evaluating client data, AI systems could look for two-communicative threat patterns. These changes could have to do with spending, credit, and income. Additionally, AI may forecast user behavior and provide recommendations for the customer experience. This is achieved by using many data sources. This study looks at the impact of financial market automation on the financial industry, the main applications and domains that influence the use of AI in financial services, regulatory frameworks, and AI limitations. A self-contained financial summary wraps up the study. The results show that technology and automation may enhance the banking industry's accuracy, transparency, cost-effectiveness, and client happiness. Financial institutions need to continuously assess how they use AI to satisfy customer needs and maintain their competitive edge.

Keywords: Artificial intelligence, financial services, finance, artificial intelligence

Introduction

The phrase artificial intelligence (AI) was first used by Stanford University computer and cognitive scientist John McCarthy to characterize a machine's remarkable capacity to mimic human behavior and cognition. AI is able to evaluate situations and determine the best course of action. Given the options available to it, AI may need to make perfect and logical judgments in order to accomplish a goal. AI is able to create sophisticated systems that can decode, understand, and analyze complicated data in addition to provide very specialized answers to challenging issues and tasks. These days, artificial intelligence is used by a variety of enterprises beyond financial institutions. Banks use AI for a variety of tasks, including recordkeeping, stock investment, activity planning, and real estate management. Robots defeated humans in a simulated financial trading competition in August 2001. Fintech fraud has dropped as AI keeps an eye on user behavior to spot unusual changes. AI regularly examines bank accounts. AI analyses vast amounts of data quickly. AI improves security, reduces audit risk, and speeds up audits for banks, insurance businesses, and real estate corporations. The impact of artificial intelligence has led to the use of the term "finance automation" by the financial sector. Finance automation is the use of technology to automate administrative labor and financial functions like cash flow forecasting. This creative strategy promotes worldwide financial liberty and has revolutionized the banking industry. Automating time-consuming tasks like bookkeeping and accounting allows firms to focus on activities that generate money. More money is accessible to people and organizations for both initial investments and sporadic spending. Financial automation has reached a significant size and will only get larger. It makes achieving financial stability and independence easier.

The majority of insurers and DACH institutions are evaluating AI's business potential: 50% of CEOs think AI will make legal compliance easier, while 73% want to save costs. CEO interest in improving digital effectiveness is 79% [1].

Among these CEOs, over half have used AI for automation, chatbots, and predictive marketing. Sadly, a lot of possibilities are lost. Advanced data analysis, for instance, may make risk assessment and decision-making easier. AI automation has completely changed the banking industry, along with the economy's overall technological

[a]garima4137_gn@iimtindia.net, [b]aniket@delhitechnicalcampus.ac.in, [c]bhawna.Kaushik@liet.in

DOI: 10.1201/9781003534136-66

growth. Now that financial data is managed more efficiently, banks and corporations can make more responsible financial choices. AI automation can forecast, identify financial trends, and find fraud by using machine learning algorithms. Both cost reductions and higher customer satisfaction may result from this. Despite its benefits, adopting financial technology raises ethical questions and raises the possibility of data breaches and fraud. Data breaches damage companies' reputations, result in financial losses, and present legal challenges for banks and insurers. To avoid any risks, financial organizations need to protect their data. Role-based permissions and access controls are used to limit access to data, while classification and sensitivity analysis protect sensitive data. Both in transit and at rest, data is encrypted. DLP keeps an eye on and blocks the flow of illegal data. AI, however, aims to address problems in the integrated banking industry and among customers by integrating diverse technologies to the benefit of financial institutions.

Literature Review

Finance with AI

In domains such as automated task processing, chatbot assistants, and fraud detection, artificial intelligence is transforming financial resource management and accessibility. 80% of financial organizations believed AI had potential in the banking industry, according to Insider Intelligence. Regulation, customer acceptance, and technology will steer FLS's AI implementation. Artificial intelligence has the capacity to enhance the customer experience in financial institutions by presentment of automated processes, round-the-clock account access, and financial consulting services. This research looks at how the acquisition and administration of financial resources are being affected by artificial intelligence. In order to promote the use of artificial intelligence by financial institutions, this paper highlights three key factors: technological development, user acceptability, and regulatory adjustments. Finance applications for artificial intelligence are discussed in this paper's conclusion, including robo-advisors, chatbot assistants, automated task processing, credit scoring, fraud detection, and natural language processing for data analysis. By automating processes, enhancing customer support, and offering 24/7 account and financial advising services, AI has the capacity to exceed to upend the commercial and financial industries. The potential benefits of artificial intelligence have several financial institutions looking at methods to employ it. This paper discusses AI's pros and cons in finance to help firms make educated choices [2].

AI Implementation in Financial Literacy

Both the study and use of financial AI are growing more quickly. Among the industries that use AI are risk management, banking, and customer service. The efficiency of financial institutions, the timeliness of risk assessments, and mitigation techniques are possible areas for development. AI improves the offering by giving customer care 24/7 access to account information and financial support. Banking AI is influenced by many factors, including customer adoption, changing regulatory environments, and technology breakthroughs. Innovative financial institutions employ ecosystems to provide individualized, customer-focused services by integrating AI into their production processes. Monetary AI lowers risk, boosts operational effectiveness, and enhances customer service. Both the study and use of financial AI are growing more quickly. Among the industries that use AI are risk management, banking, and customer service. The efficiency of financial institutions, the timeliness of risk assessments, and mitigation techniques are possible areas for development. AI improves the offering by giving customer care 24/7 access to account information and financial support. Banking AI is influenced by many factors, including customer adoption, changing regulatory environments, and technology breakthroughs. Innovative financial institutions employ ecosystems to provide individualized, customer-focused services by integrating AI into their production processes. Financial AI reduces risk, improves operations, and improves customer service. This study examines AI's usage in insurance, financial management, and finance to cover gaps in understanding and examine its possibility across sectors. The writers examine significant banking, insurance, and financial monitoring themes to determine the pros and cons of adopting artificial intelligence. The multidisciplinary nature of the issue and the rising interest in AI-driven solutions provide new study opportunities [3].

Examining the Prospects and Obstacles of Implementing AI in the Financial Industry

AI in finance offers advantages as well as disadvantages. By automating time-consuming processes and offering financial advice, AI has the potential to improve customer service. The impact of artificial intelligence on financial services is examined in this paper. AI is widely used by financial organizations to increase efficiency, make better decisions, and satisfy customers. Artificial intelligence finds use in risk assessment, fraud detection, investment management, and customer service. Data privacy, ethics, and security are a few of the new issues with AI. Other challenges include job loss, transparency, and the need to defend AI choices. Technology, law, and ethics must all be carefully evaluated and discussed in order to manage the benefits and drawbacks of artificial intelligence in the financial services industry, according to the report.

finish with the paper examines the moral and legal implications of AI for the financial services sector. Data privacy, transparency and accountability, fairness and nondiscrimination, and individual rights are examples of ethical issues. It makes sense to investigate data ownership and implement suitable data protection measures to maintain privacy and empower individuals with more control over their data. The research concludes that variety and objectivity in training data are essential for removing bias in AI decision-making. Make AI decisions clearer and more exciting to foster confidence. The study also emphasizes the need of accountability protocols for AI errors. Research may be done on how AI impacts financial market equity and how to deal with the social injustices that AI's decisions create. [4].

Financial Inclusion with AI

Research suggests that AI may improve financial access for underrepresented groups. Studies suggest that AI has the capacity to enhance financial inclusion by making banking more accessible to under banked and un banked people. This is an example of how artificial intelligence might alter financial solutions to help the underprivileged. The research also looks at how AI may enhance low-income banking services. This research also reveals basic obstacles to the broad use of AI for financial inclusion. Since accurate predictions depend on high-quality data, data availability and quality are issues. Complex constraints and mysterious AI algorithms reduce openness. Important answers are given in the report. Governments and politicians need to control AI if they want to encourage financial inclusion. Fintech data quality and infrastructure improvements are required for AI integration. AI-powered financial services must adhere to open and fair ethical norms. AI has the ability to transform the financial industry and promote financial inclusion, but before it is widely used, research challenges must be overcome [5].

AI in Financial Sectors in Developing Nations

Many developing nations, notably South Sudan and Latin America, lack access to financial institutions and mobile money providers, based on the Global Findex database provided by the World Bank, Financial services are inaccessible to There exists a significant number of micro, small, and medium-sized businesses, approaching an aggregate of 200 million. in developing countries. Paper conclusions According to the Global Findex database of the World Bank, a considerable proportion of the populace in developing nations such as South Sudan and Latin America lacks access to formal banking services. Up to 200 million SMBs in developing countries could not have financial insulation.

According to research, AI may make it possible for those without bank accounts to use digital payment methods and mobile banking. Chatbots and machine learning algorithms have the potential to improve financial inclusion, accessibility, and literacy for loans in poor countries. The study makes the claim that AI in finance might make it easier for businesses and citizens of poor countries to get formal financial services [6].

AI on the Financial System with Risk Considerations

The IMF studies AI's potential to improve financial sector efficiency, risk management, customer service, and innovation. AI in banking, insurance, asset management, and payments is extensively investigated. The research found that AI improves financial innovation and efficiency. AI improves financial risk assessment and mitigation. AI chatbots and virtual assistants provide 24/7 customization and quick problem resolution. AI develops financial goods, services, and investment strategies based on market developments and client wants. AI is transforming the financial industry, presenting many potentials to improve efficiency, lower costs, and generate new products. Financial services will grow with AI. The report advises financial institutions to study, develop, and use AI to maximize its disruptive potential. Forward-thinking regulators should promote AI ethics and innovation. For financial industry AI adoption, stakeholders should establish AI frameworks, standards, and best practices. Finally, financial institutions should train and retrain AI personnel. AI principles may improve financial sector efficiency, client happiness, and service [7].

Risk and Challenges in Finance wih AI

AI may enhance financial services judgment, efficiency, and satisfaction. This article examines AI in fraud detection, risk assessment, investment management, and customer service. AI creates ethical, security, and privacy problems. How to overcome AI decision-making explain ability and transparency is covered in this paper. The report recommends regulating financial services AI to balance its advantages and hazards. It advocates studying finance-specific AI use for moral and legal solutions. The study examines AI in financial risk assessment, fraud detection, investment management, and customer service also discusses AI's general influence and pros and cons in financial services, not particular applications and AI might enhance financial services decision-making, efficiency, and customer service. The research recommends examining financial services AI to use and regulating the AI ethics [8].

The Utilization of AI in the finance instituations

AI has the implicit to ameliorate banks' operating effectiveness in several areas, including client service and executive operations. AI gathers and analyzes data, looks for trends, and produces accurate vaticinations. According to a recent PwC analysis, artificial intelligence may boost the world frugality by around$ 16 trillion by 2030. also, a PwC report projects that by 2030, when its GDP is anticipated to expand by 26, China will benefit economically the most from the deployment of AI. An analogous significant growth in GDP of 14.5 is projected for North America. These two diligences are anticipated to contribute $10.7 trillion to global frugality overall, counting for further than 70 of the prognosticated effect of enforcing AI. Artificial intelligence is being used by banks to improve customer service, risk management, fraud detection, analytics, and financial advising. The "ETBFSI" research states that 71.7% of account payment transactions in India employ modern AI technology. Banks' and other financial companies' finances may be altered by AI's automated, data-driven decision-making and financial advising [9]. Financial institutions are predicted to be significantly impacted by AI; thus, in order for the sector to adapt and stay competitive, it must make rapid investments in AI.

Automatic Trading System-
Notably, two major players in the global financial markets are automatic trading (AT) and high-frequency trading (HFT). According to Cartea et al. (2015), algorithmic trading (AT) is the process of carrying out trading operations by use of complex systems that integrate financial principles. Both AT and HFT have advanced significantly in the contemporary period. According to Kuroda (2017), a significant percentage of financial market activity, namely 60% of futures trade, has been observed. More specifically, records of between fifty and seventy percent of financial market activity exist. This results in the company's AI algorithms operating at a very high speed, which makes it possible for them to handle trade orders much faster than human traders.

The United States is the country where this phenomenon is most noticeable, however emerging nations such as India have a considerably lower percentage of 40%. Kuroda (2017) lists the advantages of AT and HFT as obtaining the best possible transaction prices, reducing instances of human mistake, efficiently managing large amounts of data, and concurrently keeping an eye on several markets. Reducing temporal discrepancies and using significant automation and consolidation capabilities are critical to improving the efficiency of the stock market. The practice of diversifying assets across a range of financial instruments, including equities, corporate bonds, exchange-traded funds (ETFs), futures, and government bonds, is known as HFT. International trade organizations are the main entities involved in this kind of business. Important players in the HFT space, such as hedge funds, corporations, and enterprises. The minute price fluctuations seen in their tick-by-tick data at various time intervals demonstrate the SPDR S&P 500 ETFs' current millisecond transaction execution capabilities.

Automation of often performed operation by Robotic Process Automation-
The rise of robot technology, which can progressively mimic human intellect and capacities, is causing a significant paradigm to change in the financial and insurance services industry. Two instances of how robotics is impacting the financial services sector include automation in the automobile sector and industrial robots. One example of such an application is robotic process automation (RPA), which is being used in the banking industry to automate laborious and repetitive processes. These procedures include, but are not limited to, creating invoices, clearing checks, and handling deposits and withdrawals.

Tasks that need to be repeated or come up again may be automated using a program called robotic process automation (RPA). Many tasks, like data input, processing invoices, and bank reconciliation, may be automated by putting RPA into practice. Operations may be carried out more precisely, with fewer mistakes, and more efficiently by using this technology. Moreover, robotic process automation has the potential to reduce risk and

Figure 66. 1 Architecture of an algorithmic trading system

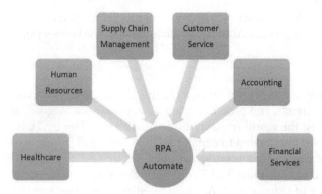

Figure 66.2 RPA automate can automate the different parts of the financial industry like bank

fraudulent activities, improve customer service, and provide financial savings linked to labor-related costs. RPA has the potential to revolutionize the financial sector by setting new benchmarks for accuracy, efficacy, and total productivity worldwide. The banking industry has seen a significant increase in the use of RPA, which allows employees to focus on more important tasks by automating repetitive and tedious tasks. Technology has also made it possible to reduce error rates, increase productivity, and implement process automation.

RPA is essential to the financial sector for a number of reasons, some of which are as follows:

1	**Increased operational efficiency**	Robotic process automation (RPA) improves operational efficiency by automating rule-based and repetitive procedures. The deployment of process optimization, the decrease of human error rates, and the reallocation of workers to strategic, higher-value jobs are the means by which financial institutions accomplish these goals.
2	**Cost reductions**	RPA helps financial organizations reduce the costs that are associated with labor-intensive manual operations by automating regular activities. When it comes to an industry in which operational efficiency has a direct impact on the bottom line, cost-effectiveness is of the utmost importance.
3	**Error reduction**	Error reduction is a fundamental goal of robotic RPA systems, which are designed to carry out tasks with extraordinary precision and consistency. RPA systems are designed to reduce errors. By lowering the chance of mistakes that typically occur during the manual entry and processing of data, this strategy improves the quality of the data and reduces the possible risks that may be incurred.
4	**Increased compliance**	The financial sector is subject to a comprehensive set of regulations. Robotic process automation makes it easier to verify that tasks have been completed in a reliable manner and in accordance with regulatory rules. It enables financial organizations to offer regulatory evidence of compliance by facilitating audit trail followability and making it easier to follow audit trails.
5	**High speed and scalability**	RPA helps to speed up the execution of financial activities, which in turn improves responsiveness and makes decision-making easier. Furthermore, RPA systems may be scaled up via the use of human labor in order to meet increasing responsibilities during times of high demand.
6	**Improved customer experience**	By using the automation capabilities of RPA, financial institutions are able to provide their customers with services that are both timely and accurate. An overall improvement in the quality of the customer experience is the consequence of this, which in turn leads to higher levels of customer satisfaction and loyalty.
7	**Data security**	Robust security measures that are included into RPA systems have the ability to protect sensitive financial information. This is essential in a sector were protecting one's privacy and the confidentiality of one's data is of the highest significance.
8	**Legacy system integration**	Legacy system integration is a common practice among financial organizations, which commonly use antiquated systems that provide difficulties when it comes to making the move to more modern options. By acting as a bridge, RPA makes it possible to streamline integration with pre-existing systems, hence eliminating the need for a comprehensive redesign.
9	**Solutions that are adaptable and scalable**	Solutions that are adaptable and scalable business RPA solutions may be adapted by financial institutions to meet their particular requirements. Businesses are given the opportunity to react to developing technical breakthroughs and shifting customer tastes as a result of their capacity to provide adaptability and expandability.
10	**Reallocating human resources to strategic initiatives**	RPA facilitates the reallocation of human resources to strategic undertakings like as customer relationship management, innovation, and the creation of unique financial products and services. This is accomplished by the automation of repetitive operations.

CB Insights research indicates that the robotics business has seen a significant rise in financing agreements in recent years. Global commitments of investments exceeded 273 million USD in 2014. This value almost quadrupled to $587 million by 2015, an increase of 115% over 2014 when compared to the 55% growth seen in 2014.

This shows that more companies are realizing the promise of robot's technology and that the robotics sector is becoming more appealing to investors [10]. Robotic process automation (RPA) has the potential to provide substantial advantages for financial institutions looking to streamline their processes, save expenses, and boost output.

Continuing to Improve the Quality of the Insurance Experience

The insurance sector uses modern technologies to solve significant client issues. AI, ML, and NLP may help insurance companies decrease fraud and improve customer service. Additionally, firms' ambition to start new insurance companies has caused unprecedented financial difficulties. This article examines in the insurance industry, highlighting its main benefits and uses.

Insurance companies may now manage policies and claims more accurately and effectively using artificial intelligence. This technology has proved especially effective in underwriting, as companies must understand each customer's individual needs and circumstances. Because it swiftly analyzes vast volumes of data. Several American startups have incorporated artificial intelligence-powered technologies that can resolve claims in seconds to better serve clients. Insurers may be able to anticipate client needs by employing artificial intelligence to foresee risks and opportunities. As a consequence, artificial intelligence might cause the biggest insurance sector disruption. Insurers that adopt it will be in a unique position to gain from greater accuracy and security.

Creditworthiness scoring and prediction using alternative data

The rate of financial exclusion is rising, especially in emerging countries like India. Millions of individuals and small companies lack credit history, which prevents them from being able to receive bank credit and financial services. FinTech companies are using AI and predictive analytics to authorize loans even in the lack of credit history in order to get around this problem. Fintech businesses are increasingly using alternative data to assess creditworthiness. Internet use, social media presence, and other digital traces might provide more details about a borrower's financial situation and character. Fintech companies use alternative data to assess borrowers' creditworthiness. Lenders may use this information to assess the borrower's capacity to repay the loan. Alternative data that reveals the borrower's spending and saving habits in addition to their credit history may help predict default.

Table 66.2 The potential advantages of AI use within the insurance sector

1	Increase the precision of policy underwriting	AI can analyze large datasets in-depth, making it easier to find intricate relationships and patterns that human analysts would find challenging to identify. With this skill, insurers can more accurately evaluate risk and set rates that correspond to the assessed degree of risk.
2	Boost the effectiveness of processing claims	AI has the ability to automate a wide range of claims processing tasks, including data input, verification, and adjudication. This invention has the potential to improve the workflow of human adjusters by allowing them to concentrate on more difficult jobs, which will raise the caliber of customer care.
3	Fraud detection	AI has the ability to distinguish and recognize applications and claims that are fake. For insurers, this might result in significant financial gains, translating into yearly losses in the millions of dollars.
4	Provide customized customer support	One benefit of using AI-enabled chatbots is their ability to provide customized customer support. The chatbots may provide clients with round-the-clock support by addressing issues related to policy, invoicing, and claims. This technology has the ability to increase client satisfaction while reducing the burden of customer service representatives who are human. Additionally, insurers may efficiently gather underwriting data and unearth previously undiscovered sources of information by relying on computer
5	Developing better risk management techniques	Developing better risk management techniques is one area that needs improvement. With its capacity to facilitate the creation of predictive models that may foresee approaching threats, such as those associated with natural catastrophes or cyber-attacks, AI holds great promise for this Endeavor. The information that has been supplied has the potential to assist insurers in developing risk management techniques that are more efficient.

Fintech businesses also use alternative data to determine what their customers need. These companies are in a position to provide more specialized services, products, and programs thanks to their understanding of their clients. Finally, alternative data may be used to identify wrongdoing. Fintech companies can identify fraud and suspicious activity faster thanks to alternative data. Not only does this protect the company against future losses, but it may also improve customer happiness. Alternative data is becoming more and more important to fintech companies as a way to improve their services and decision-making processes. It makes it easier for them to understand their customers and helps them provide services that are better suited to their individual needs.

Prevention, detection, and compliance of money laundering, fraud, and regulations

Artificial intelligence is becoming more and more prevalent in banking because of its capacity to precisely identify and reduce fraud. Banks and other financial firms can reliably and swiftly evaluate massive quantities of data thanks to AI. This aids in identifying fraudulent transactions. An AI program known as "decision intelligence" at MasterCard generates a "default transaction." This "default transaction" is then evaluated in comparison to new customer transactions. According to the 2015 Javelin Strategy Study, one of the biggest problems facing the financial services industry is erroneously disallowed transactions.

AI may be able to assist in discovering and resolving these transactions. Many financial institutions are using AI systems with advanced analytics to evaluate transaction risk as a result of this challenge. Businesses may lower risk and inappropriate transactions by doing this, increasing consumer satisfaction.

AI may also assist companies in adhering to industry standards and laws by lowering the likelihood of fines. For banks and other financial institutions, the Basel Accords make regulatory compliance and risk management challenging. AI can resolve the issue, however with a great deal of paperwork and a lengthy process. The operational burden for banks is significantly reduced by this technology. Artificially intelligent anti-fraud systems might potentially pick up on minute differences in human behavior, which would raise questions. The detection and prevention of fraud and other crimes is made easier by automated teller machines equipped with image and face recognition AI. Financial services companies and banks have benefited from AI technology. These companies may reduce risk and adhere to rules by using AI.

Wealth Management and Portfolio Management for High-Net-Worth Individuals

AI is revolutionizing portfolio and wealth management, allowing financial services firms to provide personalized, data-driven recommendations. BlackRock, a big financial business, has an AI lab, and many other corporations use AI to improve client estimations. For instance, UBS built two new trading floor AI systems. The first algorithm discovers trading associations in enormous data related with market and gives bank clients strategies to generate profits and the second method accommodates UBS clients post-trade allocation preferences.

AI helps wealth and portfolio management firms improve estimates and provide customized recommendations to boost investor returns. As it grows, AI will help banks and clients achieve financial independence with excellent services [12].

Key Factors for Implementating Artifical Intelligence Framwork into Financial Services.

AI's progressive development is revolutionizing the finance sector. Whoever implements this technology will reap substantial benefits. AI might help with payments, insurance, and asset management, as well as provide new goods and services, increase efficiency, and reduce costs in the banking and financial businesses. Applications of AI that demonstrate its adaptability include chatbot-based customer service, increased risk management tools, and real-time fraud detection. However, obstacles such as data silos, complex regulatory compliance, and the requirement for trained personnel prevent the financial industry from implementing AI. To make maximum use of the opportunity of AI in finance, these challenges must be overcome. Financial institutions that effectively overcome these obstacles will achieve triumph in the domain of financial services propelled by AI.

Vision and strategy of organization for Artificial Intelligence

Critical elements of the management process include setting firm goals and achieving agreement between the technical and commercial leadership teams recognizing the need of a specific AI strategy. the procedure for understanding what it is that a company hopes to accomplish. Through the use of proof-of-concepts (PoCs) to plan investments in AI and the parallel use of the champion/challenger paradigm. The formulation of broad objectives for the integration of artificial intelligence across the whole organization Methodically demonstrating prior accomplishments and return on investment may help get sponsorship from CxOs for artificial intelligence projects. Making the most of the momentum gained to investigate new methods for achieving AI-driven improvements to operational efficiency and financial performance complete artificial intelligence integration for synergistic outcomes.

Data For Artificial Intelligence to be train on

Organization should prove assessing the volume, caliber, uniqueness, and accuracy of the information that the organization has gathered by identifying the data requirements required for the brand's success. The procedure for standardizing the gathering and preparation of company data.

Efficiency and quality are prioritized throughout the data consolidation process, along with identifying the key connections, tools, and methods for gathering more data. High-automation central data repository; long-term data platform that searches both within and outside the company for new, relevant data sources Effective data governance requires both data privacy and data catalogs, which track the provenance of data for the successful AI Implementation.

Modelling the AI practices in financial sectors

Fraud detection, portfolio management, customer enrollment, and experience improvement are some of the applications of AI in the financial services. One of the most important aspects of service quality is the level of engagement and happiness that customers have with the financial institution. The functions of artificial intelligence to improve client registration at financial institutions leads to higher customer engagement. It is possible that the organization may obtain success by using straightforward AI testing in order to identify use cases and make rapid progress. There is a possibility that artificial intelligence models will grow more centralized if the most efficient algorithms and technical solutions are identified in order to accomplish modest goals. For the best possible outcomes, it is important to utilization of the governance tools to monitor the performance and acceptability of AI models [11].

Infrastructure of the Artificial Inteligence

Early testing infrastructure is needed to employ artificial intelligence effectively. Scalability requires a core design that can allow operational extension as new use cases and demands develop. Further experimental development necessitates frequently upgrading the infrastructure with cutting-edge AI technologies. This dynamic approach ensures that the firm keeps ahead of technological advances by continuously improving infrastructure to effortlessly integrate cutting-edge artificial intelligence. To guarantee the long-term viability and scalability of the present infrastructure over five to 10 years, the emphasis must expand beyond urgent needs. This involves introducing components that make it simpler to incorporate cutting-edge AI tools and methodologies, creating a flexible and forward-thinking framework that represents AI's dynamic field.

Navigating the Triad: People, Policies, and Processes

Financial services must intentionally increase and maintain their personnel to become AI-capable. Leadership must foster an AI learning culture in corporate organizations. This involves identifying AI roadmap risks and creating key performance metrics to track progress. A center of excellence (CoE) strengthens these endeavors. To teach employees AI, HR processes must be streamlined. All employees should learn technical and non-technical AI skills in an inclusive curriculum. In this changing context, robust governance structures are needed to design and explain new paradigms that ensure regulatory compliance. AI in financial services requires a fully established machine learning (ML) operations infrastructure with continuous integration and deployment capabilities to be swiftly deployed.

Implementing AI in financial sectors:- Challengence and risks

AI technology has the potential to drastically change how financial services are provided and used if it is incorporated into the financial sector. But putting AI into practice comes with a lot of risks and complications that need careful consideration.

1.   *There are obstacles in the financial sector when it comes to using AI.*
     * A significant quantity and quality of data are required for the efficient functioning and training of AI systems. Financial institutions need to gather, store, and analyze massive amounts of data in order to use AI successfully.
     * Comprehending and explaining AI systems: it may be challenging due to their complex features. This may make it more difficult for financial institutions to ensure the fairness and integrity of the decisions made by AI and to provide an explanation for their progress.

- **Regulatory compliance:** Financial organizations are required to adhere to a complicated set of standards that control regulatory compliance. Strict adherence to all relevant legal requirements is required while developing and deploying AI systems.
- **Abilities and expertise:** implementing AI effectively requires a certain set of abilities and expertise. It may be necessary for financial organizations to hire or train more employees in order to develop and manage AI systems.
- Cybersecurity: AI systems may be the target of cyberattacks. Financial institutions must put strong cybersecurity safeguards in place to prevent hackers from accessing their AI systems.

2. *Risk Factors Related to AI Integration in the Financial Sectors*
- Discrimination and bias: AI systems that are trained with biased data have the potential to reinforce preconceived notions. This can lead to certain customer types being treated unfairly.
- Privacy concerns: Large amounts of personally identifiable data are gathered and analyzed by AI systems. Financial organizations must create and implement thorough data privacy policies in order to guarantee the privacy of their clients.
- Inadequate implementation, development, and supervision of AI systems may give birth to operational risks and introduce new dangers to operations.
- If AI is heavily incorporated into the financial industry without sufficient safeguards against failures and disruptions, new systemic risks might emerge.

3. *Taking Care of the Challenges and Risks Associated with AI Application in the Financial Sectors*
- Financial institutions need to come up with a thorough AI strategy that outlines the use of AI in order to achieve their objectives. It is essential that this strategy include a plan for reducing the risks and challenges related to the use of AI. Financial organizations must set aside funds for the creation and implementation of data governance procedures in order to ensure the highest levels of integrity as well as moral and responsible management.
- Financial institutions should invest in the creation of explainable AI solutions in order to foster a better understanding of the mechanics behind AI judgments.
- Employee education and training: To guarantee that employees are aware of the challenges and possible risks associated with the use of AI, financial institutions are required to provide AI training.
- Strong cybersecurity protocols must be put in place by financial organizations to prevent assaults on their AI systems.
- Financial institutions need to keep a close eye on AI systems to make sure any possible problems are found and fixed.

AI is a promising tool for financial institutions to enhance their operations, provide superior goods and services to their consumers, and improve risk management via comprehensive evaluations of related risks and difficulties.

Conclusion

Artificial intelligence (AI), albeit yet in its infancy, has already had a big influence on the banking sector. The many benefits of this cutting-edge technology will be felt by users. Though AI seems to be promising in banking and finance, there are still issues. Despite concerns, artificial intelligence will transform financial management and communication inside the sector. Particularly outside of the IT industry, the use of AI to overcome obstacles to financial inclusion is still in its infancy. Even though Artificial Intelligence has been providing so many different benefits like chatbot or automated robotic process automation and providing the customer support 24*7 in the several financial industries, yet the problems with complicatedness with the implementation and data privacy still need to be addressed. AI integration with the financial system necessitates a thorough infrastructure upgrade. Understanding how AI will affect financial markets and create its scope in the banking sector is crucial. It is necessary to consider the reskilling the financial industries to create the financial workforce comfortable with AI technologies and Financial Sector needs to invest into AI technologies to get the trending services provided by AI. Future planning needs to identify AI-driven financial services roles and competences as well as the deployment of retraining and workforce transformation programs. The article explains how AI is changing the financial industry by promoting the creation of new goods and services, boosting productivity, and reducing costs. AI's incorporation into financial services is anticipated to transform the industry as technology develops.

References

[1] Artificial Intelligence in Financial Services (n.d.). PwC. https://www.pwc.de/en/finanzdienstleistungen/artificial-intelligence-in-financial-services.html

[2] Mehndiratta, N., Arora, G., and Bathla, R. (2023). The use of artificial intelligence in the banking industry. *2023 International Conference on Recent Advances in Electrical, Electronics & Digital Healthcare Technologies (REEDCON)*, New Delhi, India, 2023, pp. 588-591. doi: 10.1109/REEDCON57544.2023.10150681.

[3] Aleksandrova, A., Ninova, V., and Zhelev, Z. (2023, May 11). A Survey on AI Implementation in Finance, (Cyber) Insurance and Financial Controlling. Risks. https://doi.org/10.3390/risks11050091

[4] Han, Y., Chen, J., Dou, M., Wang, J., and Feng, K. (2023). The impact of artificial intelligence on the financial services industry. *Academic Journal of Management and Social Sciences*, https://doi.org/10.54097/ajmss.v2i3.8741

[5] Mehrotra, A. (2019). Artificial intelligence in financial services – need to blend automation with human touch. *2019 International Conference on Automation, Computational and Technology Management (ICACTM)*. https://doi.org/10.1109/icactm.2019.8776741

[6] Kshetri, N. (2021). The role of artificial intelligence in promoting financial inclusion in developing countries. *Journal of Global Information Technology Management*, https://doi.org/10.1080/1097198x.2021.1871273

[7] Boukherouaa, G. S. B. (2023). Generative artificial intelligence in finance: risk considerations. IMF. https://www.imf.org/en/Publications/fintech-notes/Issues/2023/08/18/Generative-Artificial-Intelligence-in-Finance-Risk-Considerations-537570

[8] Fernández, A. M. C. (2019). Artificial intelligence in financial services. *Social Science Research Network*, https://doi.org/10.2139/ssrn.3366846

[9] PwC's Global Artificial Intelligence Study: Sizing the prize. (n.d.). PwC. https://www.pwc.com/gx/en/issues/data-and-analytics/publications/artificial-intelligence-study.html

[10] The AI In Fintech Market Map: 100+ Companies Using AI Algorithms To Improve The Fin Services Industry. CB Insights Research. https://www.cbinsights.com/research/ai-fintech-startup-market-map/#:~:text=The%20AI%20In%20Fintech%20Market%20Map%3A%20100%2B%20Companies%20Using%20AI,Improve%20The%20Fin%20Services%20Industry&text=Startups%20are%20using%20AI%20to,finance%20services%2C%20and%20regulatory%20software.

[11] Carter, D. (2018). How real is the impact of artificial intelligence? The business information survey 2018. *Business Information Review*. https://doi.org/10.1177/0266382118790150

[12] Mehrotra, A. (2019). Artificial intelligence in financial services – need to blend automation with human touch. *2019 International Conference on Automation, Computational and Technology Management (ICACTM)*. https://doi.org/10.1109/icactm.2019.8776741

[13] Kuroda, Haruhiko. (2017). The Role of Expectations in Monetary Policy: Evolution of Theories and the Bank of Japan's Experience. Bank for International Settlements. https://www.bis.org/review/r170612d.pdf.

67 Diagnosing cardiomegaly with the help of support model based on CNN using RES-NET

Aniket Singh[1,a], Ritika Rai[2,b], Anita Chaudhary[3,c], Pankti patel[4,d] and Bhawna Kaushik[5,e]

[1]Assistant Professor, Department of Computer Science, Delhi Technical Campus

[2]Assistant Professor, Department of allied healthcare sciences, Vivekananda Global University Jaipur

[3]Assistant Professor, Department of MCA, ABES Engineering College, Ghaziabad

[4]Assistant Professor, Department of Allied Healthcare Sciences, Vivekananda Global University, Jaipur

[5]Assistant Professor, Department of BCA, Llyod Institute of Engineering and Technology, Greater Noida

Abstract

Clinical master emotionally supportive networks utilizing clinical information fundamentally add to the field of medication by using wise picture examination innovation. Such clinical frameworks should be approved and should have a straightforward inward construction. Hence, the procedure of investigating the consequences of the clinical framework is a significant component. This paper presents a cardiomegaly conclusion support model based on CNN, ResNet, and logical component map. To set up the model, first a ResNet-based cardiomegaly prediction model is created, then a chest X-beam informational index is used and scholarly. As the outcome changes resulting from the model's information adjustments for model finding support are distinguished, a reasonable highlight map for examination is carried out. Every matrix of the needed picture is switched in grouping, and the progressions of the brain network yield layer are saved money on the component map, resulting in model information alterations. Thus, the designed examination strategy gives data inside the brain organization through an exactness result near 80% and an outwardly communicated highlight map. Specifically, this translation strategy can be reached out to a broader structure in a clinical emotionally supportive network that investigates designs.

Keywords: ResNet, Cardiomegaly, Cardiac disease, Xrays, Heart Size, Imaging

Introduction

With an incidence of at least 1 in 500 in the general population, cardiomegaly is one of the most prevalent hereditary cardiovascular diseases. It is a sign. cardiac insufficiency, the result of increased biomechanical loads brought on by a range of external and internal stressors on the heart. Although hypertrophy gradually normalizes wall tensions, it is linked to negative outcomes and poses a risk of sudden mortality or the development of overt heart failure for those who are afflicted [1].

Artificial intelligence is becoming increasingly important in a variety of sectors [2]. Algorithms like contemporary DNNs, use a massive pixel form, and image scanning system include hundreds layer and variable related to this. As a result, many AI - powered algorithms that have lately been commercialized are called as such black box models [3]. As that of the amount of black box designs used grows, so does the number of people who use them. there is a growing desire for openness among various AI-related interest groups [4]. Medical diagnosis assistance systems, in particular, for health expert diagnosis support, must give a variety of information about result interpretation [5].

Because a patient's inner-body environment varies depending on the ailment, a medical specialist decides the value of each aspect based on the circumstances. Typical CNNs pool layers to aggregate the context. CNNs, however, ignore the pictures' geographic coordinates. Therefore U-NET was used to try to replace conventional CNNs for diagnosing cardiomegaly. Whenever the machine learning model assesses a patient's attributes, it must provide the most essential judgement grounds. A medical specialist can only identify the strategy so that it can acknowledge each of the components and the dependability of the outcomes of the models after going through this process. The radiographic images for cardiomegaly judgement are utilized as the basic data to create a diagnostic support model utilizing an understandable feature map. Cardiomegaly is a condition that causes heart enlargement in general. It is linked to a variety of cardiac disorders, physiological states, and hereditary [6].

---

[a]aniket@delhitechnicalcampus.ac.in, [b]ritikarai1210@gmail.com, [c]anita.chaudhary@abes.ac.in, [d]panktiapatel96@gmail.com, [e]Bhawna.kaushik@liet.in

DOI: 10.1201/9781003534136-67

The research suggests a cardiomegaly diagnostic support model established on Residual Network (ResNet, convolutional neural network (CNN) and a descriptive feature map. This technique uses an excellent CNN algorithm to classify illnesses using just X-ray pictures and an understandable feature map to explain the classification. This technique uses an excellent CNN algorithm to classify illnesses [7]

Method

The properties of CNN consist of several different component's successive types of layers, several of them are replicated. There are three layers that are the most prevalent layers: 1. Input layer which Specifies data input for most pictures with deep RGB color representation of standard dimensions (width* length). 2. Extraction of features or learning sequence in this Every algorithm checks for similar features at this stage and rank them with an increasingly important order. The example of this layer we have is convolutional layer and pooling layer. 3. The layer of classification (fully connected) i.e. the mechanism links all neuron with one layer to each and every neuron in another layer after a few layers of flexibility and integration.

Relevant Work

Evaluation of Image Based on CNN and XAI

Machine learning methods such as CNNs are steadily improving in accuracy. According to diverse perspectives, (explainable artificial intelligence (XAI) was examined as the first AI research, despite the fact that Fisher, Rudin, and Dominic precisely described it in 2004. Recent XAI is described as process and strategies for using technology like artificial intelligence in like a way that the solution's outcomes can be comprehended, and it is seen as a vital component of the future, alongside AI. An analogous state-led initiative is being carried out Defense Advanced Research Project Agency in the USA (DARPA). This program ran through 2021 and contains 11 comprehensive initiatives. According to research by DARPA, XAI is determined on improving the AI scenario by adding description and human computer interaction (HCI) features to a fundamental model. To put it another way, by using XAI, the customer ensures transparency in the process of decision-making of the support system, makes the process of interpretation easier, allows for the prediction of unspecified effects and establishes the causal relationship between the model's logic. Recently, black box explanations using transparent approximations (BETA), as well as local explicable model diagnostic explanations, have become popular (LIME). generalized additive models (GAMs), for example, are being investigated. Moreover, while this method compensates for the shortcomings of the feature importance strategy, the calculating process is excessively lengthy. This method allows learning without existing understanding of the models and is divided into global proxy analyzing system, which uses all learning data, and local proxy analysis, which uses only the training data, 21 and localized substitute assessment, which interprets just single learning data. This strategy is applied to any form of machine learning, makes implementing a substitute analysis model straightforward, and simplifies the description. The outcome reading may differ slightly because that's not a direct evaluation by the model. Local interpretable model-diagnostic explanations (LIME) is the delegate approach in local substitute analysis, and several research has been completed recently. LIME is a method for examining how an artificial intelligence model understands a single piece of data. In the case of a picture, the pixel that is most impacted by the outcome is chosen like the super pixel. The region around the super pixel is then expanded, and the places with the similar impact are chosen. The following are LIME's operational procedures: the original document is first entered into the system, and then the predicted value is calculated. The manufactured data is then enrolled into the black-box model in a similar fashion to the genuine data. The information that has been created is progressively modified.

Cardiac Hypertrophy Cause and Reading

Physiological, hemodynamic, hormonal, and pathological stressors all affect the heart. As a result, several factors trigger a hypertrophy reaction, which changes heart load needs by expanding cardiac muscle mass. Cardiomegaly happens if the heart repeatedly overworks owing to a condition which amplifies the cardiac impulse, and it's linked to a variety of disorders, physiologic situations, and hereditary variables. It might happen as a result of physiological function such as manual workers or athlete' aerobic fitness. It is also affected by practically many cardiovascular illnesses, hypertension, myocardial infarction, arrhythmia, hormone abnormalities, and genetic alterations.

23 people in the United States are classified with heart failure, with a fatality rate of nearly 50%. The cardiac hyperplastic reactions are a compensatory mechanism that tends to increase cardiac output in the early stages.

Breathing difficulties, palpitation, chest congestion, and chest discomfort are all indications of this condition. When a moderate intensity physical activity begins quickly, such symptoms may appear or become worse. Heart muscle cells in this scenario, the ability to reliably discern standard training effects is critical, because an inaccurate diagnosis has a significant impact on the sports organization and society. An anomalous electrocardiogram may be included in diagnosis of heart hypertrophy if an enlargement in wall thickness of ventricles is indicated. relying on what classification of disorder, myocardial fibrosis, morphological heart diseases, anomalous coronary artery and other structure circulation, and other factors, as well as a unique ECG, are all covered. Several imaging modalities, including chest radiography, electrocardiography, echocardiography, 24 and angiography, are currently available.

Since magnetic resonance imaging (MRI) scan for the heart is seldom utilized to determine the etiology of cardiac hypertrophy, it can help with diagnosis by indicating the dispersion and level of hardness for myocardial morphology. The use of MRI in the current diagnosis of patients with cardiac hypertrophy is crucial because it allows for precise evaluation of total left ventricular wall repair, as well as the propagation and pattern of cardiac hypertrophy. The phase shift of signals formed by protons in a nucleus is detected by cardiac magnetic resonance, which is a tool for assessing structural factors and blood flow status. CMR is by far the most effective supportive imaging test method for diagnosing selected patients with cardiac hypertrophy, and it is capable of detecting regions of left ventricular hypertrophy that are not easily recognized by echocardiography testing. Echocardiography is useful as a first assessment technique because it could be utilized to assess anomalies related to hemodynamics in the cardiovascular system. It can be utilized to validate the form, location, size, connection with neighboring organs, and fluidity of the tumor. As a result, echocardiography is helpful in identifying a future treatment strategy for heart hypertrophy as well as doing post-treatment evaluations. supplementary examination

Moreover, while echocardiography has a high specificity and sensitivity for visualizing the left ventricular wall, it can't tell the difference among the hypertrophy due to inability of filtration or accumulation in the metabolic organ cells. Chest X-ray, on the other hand, is a reasonably inexpensive test that has been utilized in the past and can be performed anywhere, and it can diagnose cardiac hypertrophy by calculating the cardiothoracic ratio (CTR). CTR technique for diagnosing cardiac hypertrophy using chest ratio graphs, and it is calculated with the formula.

CTR = (MR+ML)/TD. The right heart's maximum circumference is MR (Maximal Right), while the left heart's maximum diameter is ML (Maximal Left) (Maximal Left).

A CTR of more than 50% is considered abnormal, while the thoracic diameter is the greatest diameter of the thorax. Latest discoveries from molecular genetic studies have altered our basic knowledge of ventricular hypertrophy, and a medical accord has been established. The gene testing are relevant in the case of patients found with cardiac hypertrophy.

Diagnosis of Cardiomegaly using Support Model Based on CNN And Understandable Feature Map III
The three-step approach is necessary to set up the diagnostic support model for cardiomegaly. In order to recognize X-ray images, the first step is to set up a ResNet. The data collection for the ResNet's teaching is all set and pre-possessed, and the teaching process is carried out. Step 2: When learning is complete in a neural network, the target photos categorized as cardiovascular patients are collected, together with SoftMax values, of output layers. These values are also kept distinct in the database. A feature map will also be created. The impact of each portion on the output layer is correlated using the image's partial reversal technique. Step 3: The imaging is carried out in such a way that give permission to visible expression.

Data Collection and Pre-Processing of Radiographic Image Data
The Baseline Data for measuring heart hypertrophy is X-ray pictures. To properly analyze the data that attained from X-ray image and explain the cause for these kinds of readings, an algorithm assessing chest radiographic images of limited results and patients with heart hypertrophy is needed. A sophisticated algorithm must be able, to discern between the respective shape and size of the heart, as well as determine whether or not relationship to cardiac hypertrophy is substantial. For cardiac hypertrophy differentiation, a CNN-based ResNet is deployed. The teaching-completed differentiation system discriminated patients by categorizing fresh radiographs, and the differentiating process learned images labelled as cardiovascular and normal using CNN. The chest radiograph data set given by the National Institute of Health (NIH) is utilized as the learning baseline. The following data is known as image data in PNG format, having resolution of 1024X1024 pixels per picture. A total of 112,121 data points is categorized and anonymized for each condition. The data for learning and assessment is compiled first. The first 112,121 photos are divided into 14 illness categories and one 'No Finding' category. For effective

learning data sorting, 20,797 data with an 'Overlapping illness' were eliminated from the classification. A total of 1,000 data from the remaining 91,324 data are chosen from a total of 1,093 data identified as patients of cardiomegaly. The 'Technique of under sampling' is then utilized to alleviate the problem of class instability. To accomplish so, 1,000 data points are chosen at random from the 60,361 data points classed as no-findings. Table 1 shows the data that were eventually chosen. The data used for learning, and the data used for assessment. Individuals who have been definitively diagnosed with cardiomegaly are studied using 900 data points for teaching and 100 data points for analysis. The same is true for data marked as 'minimal Finding.' A total of 1,800 data points are employed in the training process. The size meets the minimal requirements for learning. Although, because some photos are unclear or include partially skewed data or empty spots, there is a chance that these issues will affect accuracy.

Image Conversion for Composition of Explainable Feature Map
The healthcare expert should be able to explain why the ultimate medical decision was made. The description employs a variety of metrics after the artificial neural network's assessment, including text statement, visual statement, partial statement, statement through example, statement through simplification, and function-related statement. The visual statement is the best approach for explaining the complex interactions inside the model to individuals who don't know about the neural network. XAI, like LIME, is commonly used as a visual statement method. Such findings are useful for identifying items, but not so much for a medical system that is analyzing specific patterns. The basic notion of LIME is supplemented, and its functional form is broadened in this work. The main idea is to invert the images of X-ray input value per place and apply a technique to identify changes in the neural network's nodes of output. The visual description approach is used to provide the detection findings to an expert in image form. To accomplish so, the ResNet structure is first created, followed by the learning process [19]. The learning completed neural network is given an X-ray picture that requires diagnosis. The sum of MaxN, the node with the highest value among the finalized output nodes, is validated. The image's pixels are then inverted in order, and the adjustments in MaxM, the output node's maximum value, are evaluated. The formula for computing Pixel P's Positive Factor value is as follows: PF = Relu (Max N Max M). The highest range after inverting the pixel set of input picture is Max M, while the node's value with the prior maximum value is Max N. PF represents the positive effect of the pixel on illness assessment. When the input value is less than 0, Relu that is Rectified Linear Unit is transmitted as 0, and when the input range is more than 0, it is delivered as it is. This formula may be used to represent the position on the picture that serves as the basis for diagnosing the condition. Through the picture shapes, the healthcare professional may visually grasp the forms connected with illness incidence.

Result

In general, the form of configuration layers, the selection of specific functions, the learning rate, and other factors influence the assessment outcomes of an artificial neural network. As a result, the internal configuration must be changed, modelled, evaluated, and tested. It is feasible to design a model that demonstrates the best accuracy using this method. Furthermore, a CNN-based image analysis model rapidly increases the number of operations it can do dependent on the number of nodes employed in the pattern type. As a result, it's critical to finish the teaching process within the allotted learning time. As a result, a form with a sufficient operation quantity to superb precision ratio must be set.

Evaluation of Result Based on Accuracy
The established neural network's function correctness is assessed. The AdaGrad, SGD, Adam functions and RMSProp, are employed, with the 'Accuracy' function used to evaluate certainty. Reliability relates to the total test findings' right response rate, and it is the most widely used term since it is obvious. The precision is computed as follows:

$$Accuracy = \frac{TP + TN}{TP + TN + |FP + FN}$$

AdaGrad, SGD, RMSProp, and Adam are used to assess correctness. The accuracy and incidence of the overfitting problem are proven after the 160 epochs. Figure 68.5 depicts the assessment findings involving SGD and Adam.

After 50 epochs, SGD and Adam both have results near to 80%. After 100 epochs, no performance improvement has been made. Over-fitting appears to occur in the case of Adam in particular. Figure 68.1 depicts the performance assessment results combining AdaGrad and RSM Promp.

After 100 epochs, both RMSProp and AdaGrad indicate a result of around 75% but after, 100 epochs, negligible improvement in performance is made. Because the general look of RMSProp is unstable, it appears that bringing it to functional use would necessitate prudence.

On the above picture, as visual in Figure 68.3, the general shadows and appearance of the heart denotes as key criteria for cardiomegaly assessment, which gets clearer as the learning amount grows. This component is compatible with the technique of diagnosing cardiomegaly by calculating the cardio-thoracic ratio, which is the gold standard for determining true cardiomegaly, and it implies that the real surgery is normal. The component that has a detrimental impact on illness judgement is shown in the lower picture. The factor picture can be used as a criterion for judging whether the patient is recovered or not, regardless of the type of condition.

Adjusting the size of pixels can produce more smooth results when presenting the positive factor image to a healthcare professional. Figure 68.4 depicts the outcomes for the two input types of 1 × 1 and 2 × 2.

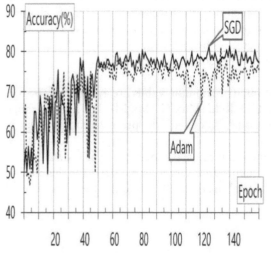

Figure 67.1 Evaluation results using Adam and SGD

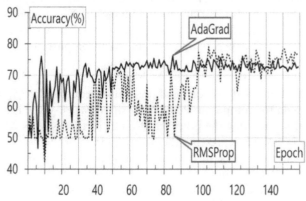

Figure 67.2 Evaluation results using RMSProp and AdaGrad

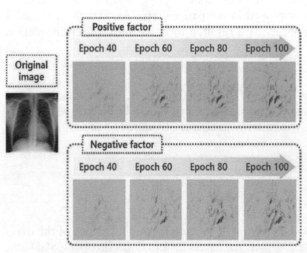

Figure 67.3 Changes in factor map image based on amount of learning

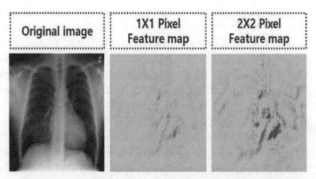

Figure 67.4 Once input pixels are set to 1 × 1, the pattern form is studied on the picture, as illustrated in Figure 67.4, the results are not smooth and non-clear. The same image becomes smooth and better when input pixels are adjusted to 2 × 2. Relying on the structure of the neural network, the final printed pixel pattern may vary. As a result, the size is determined experimentally. A smooth form was presented in most cases when input pixels with a size of 2 × 2 were utilized. The final cardiomegaly diagnostic impact analysis result is shown in Figure 67.5.

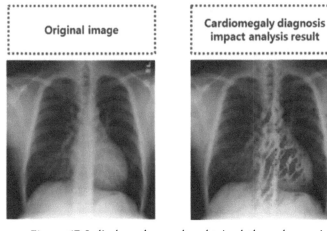

Figure 67.5 displays the results obtained through merging all the understandable feature map. On a red picture, Figure 67.5 displays the results obtained through merging all the understandable feature map elements influencing the ResNet outcomes.

Conclusion

The study suggests integrating support algorithms like the deep learning algorithm like ResNet with understandable feature map to create a mutually supportive system. The suggested approach can improve cardiomegaly judgement efficiency while also providing internal information to the neural network. In order to successfully applying a more adequate model, the accuracy and trait of the teaching data, as well as various forms of learning the data according to race, age, and sex of patients suffering from cardiac hypertrophy, as well as the quantity of learning on the scale of big data sampling and related assessments are needed, must be increased. The method of teaching and learning should be expanded to include a more thorough neural network architecture and other research on hyper parameter adjustment. Integrating an intelligence system that requires interpretation with a healthcare support system is predicted to turn into a critical step in the development of future healthcare intelligence system.

Reference

[1] Que, Q., Tang, Z., Wang, R., Zeng, Z., Wang, J., Chua, M., et al. CardioXNet: automated detection for cardiomegaly based on deep learning. *In: 2018 40th Annual International Conference of the IEEE Engineering in Medicine and Biology Society (EMBC)*. IEEE; 2018.

[2] Russell, A. (2014). Research resource review: introduction to sustainability – a massive open online course (MOOC). *Progress in Physical Geography*, 38(6):827–829. Available from: http://dx.doi.org/10.1177/0309133314541600

[3] Chung, K. and Yoo, H. (2020). Edge computing health model using P2P-based deep neural networks. *Peer-to-Peer Networking and Applications*, 13(2):694–703.

[4] Preece, A., Harborne, D., Braines, D., Tomsett, R., and Chakraborty, S. (2018). Stakeholders in explainable AI. arXiv [cs.AI]. Available from: http://arxiv.org/abs/1810.00184

[5] Kim, J.-C. and Chung, K. (2020). Knowledge-based hybrid decision model using neural network for nutrition management. *Information Technology and Management*, 21(1), 29–39.

[6] He, K., Zhang, X., Ren, S., and Sun, J. (2016). Deep residual learning for image recognition. *In Proceedings of the IEEE conference on computer vision and pattern Recognition (CVPR)*. p. 770–778.

[7] Schoenborn, J. M. and Althoff, K. D. (2019). Recent trends in XAI: A broad overview of current approaches, methodologies and interactions. *In Proceeding ICCBR Workshops*. p. 51–60.

[8] Grajewski, K. G., Stojanovska, J., Ibrahim, E.-S. H., Sayyouh, M., and Attili, A. (2020). Left ventricular hypertrophy: evaluation with cardiac MRI. *Current Problems in Diagnostic Radiology*, 49(6), 460–475.

[9] Kim, J.-C. and Chung, K. (2020). Neural-network based adaptive context prediction model for ambient intelligence. *Journal of Ambient Intelligence and Humanized Computing*, 11(4), 1451–1458.

[10] Russell, S. J. Artificial Intelligence: A Modern Approach. Pearson Education, Inc., 2010.

[11] Preece, A., Harborne, D., Braines, D., Tomsett, R., and Chakraborty, S. (2018). Stakeholders in explainable AI. arXiv Prepr. arXiv1810.00184.

[12] Chung, K. and Yoo, H. (2020). Edge computing health model using P2P-based deep neural networks. *Peer-to-Peer Networking and Applications*, 13(2), 694–703.

[13] Holzinger, A. (2018). Explainable ai (ex-ai). *Informatik Spektrum*, 41(2), 138–143.

[14] Arrieta, A. B. et al. (2020). Explainable artificial intelligence (XAI): concepts, taxonomies, opportunities and challenges toward responsible AI. *Information Fusion*, 58, 82–115.

[15] Ravindra, K., Rattan, P., Mor, S., and Aggarwal, A. N. (2019). Generalized additive models: building evidence of air pollution, climate change and human health. *Environment International*, 132, 104987.

[16] Lakkaraju, H., Kamar, E., Caruana, R., and Leskovec, J. (2017). Interpretable & explorable approximations of black box models. arXiv Prepr. arXiv1707.01154.

[17] Peltola, T. (2018). Local interpretable model-agnostic explanations of Bayesian predictive models via Kullback-Leibler projections. arXiv Prepr. arXiv1810.02678.

[18] Palladino, N. (2021). The role of epistemic communities in the 'constitutionalization' of internet governance: the example of the European Commission high-level expert group on artificial intelligence. *Telecommunications Policy*, 45(6), 102149.

[19] Petrauskas, V. et al. (2020) XAI-based medical decision support system model. *International Journal of Scientific and Research Publications*, 10, 598–607.

68 Fuzzy logic-based approach for real-life applications in IoT: enhancing intelligence and adaptability

Savita Singh[1,a], Anita Chaudhary[1,b], Aniket Singh[2,c] and Bhawna Kaushik[3,d]

[1]ABES Engineering College, Gzb

[2]Assistant Professor, Delhi Technical Campus

[3]Assistant Professor, Llyod Institute of Engineering and Technology, Greater Noida

Abstract

Internet of Things (IoT) in the present scenario, is one of the most prominent buzzing terminologies in the field of Information Technology. IoT, *"as it is the powerful present of these times; surely promises to be an empowering future with the speedy advancements and transformation of reality into virtualization"*.

With an efficient vision of technological unification, Internet of things (IoT) has established itself as a specific domain enlightening world by making lives better and much more effectively easier than ever and, with the usage of different set of concepts and techniques for the purpose of invention and advancements; IoT indeed succeeds by modern combinational accommodations. In the light of this, the paper presents real-life applications successfully transformed into reality with the help and usage of fuzzy logic concepts or features. With the brief introduction to IoT and Fuzzy logic as a modern and efficient combinational technique for developing smart applications; the paper also discusses a systematic and literature review through a variety of scholarly and academic research papers, online databases and professional expert discussions. The foremost objective of this paper is to represent an overview and provide the in-detail briefing of two most prominent IoT applications in the market developed with the help of fuzzy logic methodology and concepts. As conclusion is concerned, the paper highlights the stand-outs of the developed technologies based on fuzzy logic with a concise representation of home survey reports and future work.

Keywords: Fuzzy logic, IoT, smart home systems, wearable devices

Introduction

*"A popular technology, a solution to the diversified needs of people, or the newest wave of rising connectivity, collectively determined and recalled as **Internet of Things (IoT)** is without any doubt fulfilling the world these days."* With the numerous amount of smart applications being launched on constant basis, Internet of Things (IoT) is surely convincing enough to accomplish the plethora of needs and demands (as in requirements) of the various people.

In the realm of IoT, numerous companies belonging to the IT sector are ambitiously developing and launching new technologies with the vision of achieving a name in the IT sector. A step ahead of the traditional technological methods, it is factual to say that *"IoT with other modern technologies like soft computing, fuzzy systems (to name a few) is rising beyond human expectations and fulfilling our increasing imaginations."* With that, the paper is deterministically focused on representing a detailed view of the real-life applications launched or being processed to be launched in the market, designed and accomplished by inheriting and utilising fuzzy logic system. More specifically, the techniques and theories involved in the IoT applications with fuzzy logic usage have proved themselves to be efficiently successive for the purpose of resolving the numerous complex problems with the enhanced tools and techniques.

Internet of Things (IoT)

Internet of Things basically comprises of 2 prominent words, i.e. **INTERNET** and **THINGS** can be simply explained or defined as the combined interaction between these two terms i.e. the *interaction between the Internet or more precisely the digital world and the thing which represents the physical world*.

Moreover, the basis of the interaction between the two is accomplished by utilising numerous of sensors, embedded processors and communication hardware. Statistically, more and more organisations (representing diverse industries) have been utilising IoT applications and technology as an effective solution for successively achieving the following agendas:

- *Accomplishing efficient operations*
- *Enhancing Customer Service (CS) capabilities (with the improvement of customer understanding process)*

[a]savita.singh@abes.ac.in, [b]anita.chaudhary@abes.ac.in, [c]aniket@delhitechnicalcampus.ac.in, [d]Bhawna.kaushik@liet.in

DOI: 10.1201/9781003534136-68

- *Enhanced Decision-making criteria*
- *Improving organisational value and efficiency*

Fuzzy Logic

Fuzzy Logic, also known as one of the main paradigms under Computational Intelligence (CI) and a well-known mathematical term, is a problem/query solving technique or methodology that offers a sufficient and straight forward way of drawing unquestionably-accurate conclusions from a wealth of ambiguous and ill-defined information.

Fuzzy logic introduces the concept of approximate reasoning Particularly, fuzzy logic applications now-a-days include:

- *Framework/Prototyping*
- *Analysis and Development*
- *Decision making*
- *Supervision and Identification*
- *Information*

Review of Literature

A literature review on the fuzzy-based approach for real-life applications using IoT (Internet of Things) devices explores existing research and scholarly articles in this field. This review aims to gather and analyze relevant literature to gain insights into the application of fuzzy logic in addressing real-world challenges within IoT-driven environments. By examining the existing body of knowledge, the review aims to identify key findings, methodologies, limitations, and potential future directions in the field of fuzzy-based approaches for IoT applications.

Internet of Things (IoT)

Internet of Things (IoT) describes systems and devices that are intelligently connected and that collect data from embedded sensors, actuators, and other physical items. IoT is anticipated to quickly spread in the upcoming years, opening up a new dimension of services that enhance consumer quality of life and business productivity. Moreover, Paper [1] explores the necessary conditions for implementing the Internet of Things (IoT), which include dynamic resource requirements, real-time capabilities, availability of applications and many more. Paper [2] highlights about technological communities that are currently investigating the research fields that support the Internet of Things (IoT). As sensing, communication, and control technologies evolve, these societies frequently have similar interests but slightly different viewpoints. Fostering greater coordination between these communities is essential. The foundation for debating open IoT research challenges and imagining how IoT can revolutionise the world in the far future will be laid by this partnership.

In the present era, IoT has the potential to revolutionize various research fields. This literature categorizes these fields into several domains, including massive scaling, knowledge generation through big data, the structure and connections between different elements, resilience, accessibility, safeguarding, confidentiality, and human engagement.

Fuzzy Logic

According to paper [3], Fuzzy logic is a type of logic that falls under the category of many-valued logic. It differs from traditional binary logic, which only allows for fixed and precise reasoning. In contrast, fuzzy logic deals with interpretation that is estimated and allows for degrees of truthfulness. Variables in fuzzy logic can have truth values that range from 0 to 1, unlike variables in binary sets, which can only be true or false. The concept of partial truth has also been added to fuzzy logic, allowing truth values to range from completely true to completely false.

In mathematics, variables typically involve arithmetic values. However, fuzzy logic introduces the concept of non-numeric linguistic variables, which are frequently utilized to express rules and facts more effectively [4]. A Fuzzy Logic System comprises four essential components: fuzzifier, rules, inference engine, and defuzzifier. Designing systems that incorporate fuzzy logic to leverage human knowledge and experience can be a challenging endeavour, as it involves tackling engineering issues encountered in real-world systems [5].

Table 68.1 Elements of a smart home system

Element in Smart Home system	Example
Sensor	Temperature monitoring, Fire detection, Home Surveillance
User interface devices	Remote control, computer, Smartphone, Tablets
Types of Networking	Wireless-Bluetooth, WiFi, ZigBee, RF
Centralizing control	Micro controller, PLC, Computer, FPGA

Table 68.2 Inputs & outputs of lighting control system [fuzzy logic usage]

INPUTS	OUTPUTS
Light Level Received (from Outdoors)	Daylight Adjustments (Daylight Harvesting)
Various Human Activities	Space Occupancy (using Sensors)
Time	Chronological and Solar scheduling

IoT Applications (with Fuzzy Logic Usage)

The numerous applications of IoT from time-to-time, have been designed and developed with the simple vision of making devices smart enough so as to make human lives better with the deduction in the labour effort. With the approximate reasoning methodologies and modern logic system, [6] fuzzy logic in the last decades has widely been used due to its successful application to control and predict the behaviour of dynamic system. Therefore, *following are some of the most visionary real-life IoT applications based on fuzzy logic usage*:

Smart Home Systems
In today's era, Smart Home stands out as the highest Internet of Things application across all assessed channels. More businesses are engaged in the smart home market than any other IoT application [17]. For a better clarification or summarization of *Why* Smart Home systems are proving out to be such a success, following are the essential elements of a Smart Home System that clearly justifies its importance Table 68.1.

With the numerous functionalities (*remote access, wireless capabilities, to name a few*) it comes along, there are always the chances of ambiguity if the system do not perceive the environment (*of their existence*) as similar as we do.

As a solution, many Smart Home Systems now-a-days, are using fuzzy logic as a prominent and behavioural solution to the uncertainty problem. *As the modern approach of handling uncertainties, fuzzy logic overcomes the two most specific obstacles which are:*

Learning (*through observation, brief analysis, etc.*) from the actions of the user.
Actively **foreseeing the needs** of the users (calculated through the observed data).

Lighting Control System: Smart Home Application (With Fuzzy Logic Usage)

- A lighting control system is a smart network of lighting controls that enables you to have command over the lights in a particular area. A conventional switch in your home that turns a light on or off represents a type of lighting control. Similarly, the driveway flood lights that activate when they detect motion as someone approaches your house also serve as a form of lighting control.
- The following table represents the number of Inputs along with the desired outputs of a Lighting Control System with the usage of Fuzzy Logic Table 68.2.
- Wearable Biosensors composed of two prominent terms i.e. Wearable and Biosensors; are the devices that allow data and information like blood pressure, blood- glucose level, heartbeat rate, perspiration levels and other biometric information to be calculated through sensors and software and then measured on a constant basis.

- Lighting Control System, as an essential part of Smart Home Systems provide the users with an eminent advantage i.e. end-user convenience. With fuzzy logics' modern reasoning algorithms hence making lives better and easier.

Wearable Devices

Wearable devices concisely are the devices that help in the collection and organisation of data and information about the specific users they are connected or worn by for the purpose of pre-processing the collected data for extracting out the important statistical details of the user. Wearable devices from quite a few time has been proving out as an emerging trend for youth due to the numerous areas it is applicable for (like entertainment, health requirements, fitness status, etc.)

This IoT technology is a success as it accomplishes the two major pre-requisites i.e. (a) It proves out to be a high *energy-efficient application* with less power consumption, and (b) It provides user the facility of wearing devices comfortably due to their *small sizes*. As wearable devices are as close as to be the heart of in- particularly every discussion about IoT, some discussions amongst all often represent possibilities or objectifying questions rather than providing solution.

Wearable Biosensors – (Wearable Device With Fuzzy Logic Inheritance)

- As the name suggests, this technology due to the many facilities it provides is recognised as one of the most important and efficient developments made in the Medical and Health technology sector.
- Afterwards, the information measured and calculated i.e. in itself a real-time information gets transferred to the specific health or medical concerned authorities allowing a two-side communication between the medical authorities i.e. Doctors and the user or the applicant i.e. the Patient. For better understanding, the following Figure 68.1 shows exactly how Wearable Biosensors operate (*during an uncomfortable situation or emergency*).

Commerce : Fuzzy logic has found various applications in the field of commerce. Here are some examples of how fuzzy logic is used in commerce:

- Customer Segmentation
- Pricing Optimization.
- Fraud Detection
- Inventory Management
- Customer Satisfaction Analysis
- Decision Support Systems

The continued development of Business to Customer Electronic Commerce (B2C EC) is widely acknowledged to depend on trust. There have been many trust models developed, but the most of them are subjective

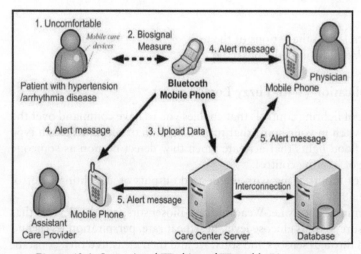

Figure 68.1 Operational Working of Wearable Biosensors

and do not account for the EC trust's ambiguity and vagueness as well as the customers' intuitions and experiences when making online purchases [7]. Online transactions also depend on the personality and experience of the customer. Some factors could be more important to some clients than others. As a result, we think that in the future systems, users should be allowed to rate trust variables based on their own view and experience [8].

Environment: Fuzzy logic finds applications in a wide range of environments due to its ability to handle imprecise and uncertain information. Here are some examples of how fuzzy logic is used in different environments:

- Environmental Monitoring and Control
- Energy Management
- Traffic Control
- Robotics and Automation
- Healthcare Systems
- Agricultural Systems
- Industrial Control Systems

Fuzzy-based models can handle uncertainty in medical data and assist healthcare professionals in making accurate and personalized decisions. Paper [9] provides an explanation of healthcare services designed for elderly individuals who desire to maintain their independence. The method for remote health monitoring is described in paper [10]. In this method, wearable technology is utilised to measure fundamental indicators of health state.

These are just a few examples of the diverse applications of fuzzy logic in various environments. Fuzzy logic's ability to handle imprecision and uncertainty makes it suitable for addressing real-world challenges in dynamic and complex systems.

Engineering

Fuzzy theory was initially introduced in the nineteenth century, opening the door for ongoing study and application in numerous domains. Geotechnical engineering has utilised fuzzy set theory on a global scale, and research in this area is still ongoing. The fuzzy inference system is a commonly employed approach to tackle geomechanical challenges encountered in both surface and underground excavations. The purpose paper [11] is to expand the creative use of the same approach specifically in tunnel geomechanics by delving into fuzzy theory-based approaches in mine geomechanics.

Conclusion

Needless to say, through the research we can surely conclude that IoT and the day-by-day emerging hype around numerous of its relative discussions and work including applications, advancements, etc. is both comparatively huge and productively strong.

Through the analysis, it's a strong and clear indication that IoT applications (being high on demands) developments with the inclusion of more and more complex and high- end solution producing concepts, methodologies and techniques are surely going to revolutionize the entire IT sector along with the various companion sectors. The inclusion of Fuzzy logic concepts and techniques is one step forward of what IoT has been taking to connect devices with people for making their lives not just better but meaningfully well. And, as the analysis represents, Smart Home Systems and Wearable devices stands out to be the most efficient and strong IoT applications amongst the numerous rankings and surveys conducted by *Google* and other Prominent websites. With the strong advancements in IoT technology and its applications based on such methodologies; it won't be wrong at all to quote that *"these applications are making lives smarter, better and growth faster and efficient."* Therefore, we can conclude that with the era enhancing and enriching IoT to one more step forward, the world is all set to experience a highly advanced network, devices and systems connectivity like *Smart Homes, Smart Cities,* etc.

References

[1] Madakam, S., Ramaswamy, R., and Tripathi, S. (2015). Internet of things (IoT): a literature review. *Journal of Computer and Communications*, 3, 164–173. DOI: 10.4236/jcc.2015.35021.

[2] Stankovic, J. (2014). Research directions for the internet of things. *Internet of Things Journal, IEEE*, 1(1), 3–9.

[3] Shruti, SS Jamsandekar, RR Mudholkar. (2013). Performance evaluation by fuzzy inference technique, *International Journal of Soft Computing and Engineering*, 3(2), 306–320.

[4] Patidev, D., and Sohani, N. (2013). Green supply chain management: a hierarchical framework for barriers. *International Journal of Engineering Trends and Technology*, 4(5), 2172.

[5] Deepak, K., Ramakrishna, H., and Jagadeesh, R. (2011). Assessment of supply chain agility using fuzzy logic for a manufacturing organization. *International Journal of Software Engineering and Computing*, 3(1), 25–29.

[6] Burnett, M. M., and Myers, B. A. (2014). Future of end-user software engineering: beyond the silos. In FOSE 2014: Future of Software Engineering Proceedings, (pp. 201–211), 2014.

[7] Vairal, K. L., Kulkarni, S. D., and Basotia, V. (2020). Fuzzy logic and its applications in some area: a mini review. *Journal of Engineering Sciences*, 11(8), 85–96. ISSN NO:0377-9254.

[8] Meziane, F., and Nefti, S. (2007). Evaluating e-commerce trust using fuzzy logic. *International Journal of Intelligent Information Technologies (IJIIT)*, 3(4), 25–39. DOI: 10.4018/jiit.2007100102

[9] Basanta, H., Huang, Y. P., and Lee, T. T. (2016). Intuitive IoT-based H2U healthcare system for elderly people. In IEEE Conference on Networking, Sensing, and Control Mexico City, Mexico, April 28-30, 2016.

[10] Kulkarni, C., Karhade, H., Gupta, S., Bhende, P., and Bhandare, S. (2016). Health companion device using IoT and wearable computing. In International Conference on Internet of Things and Applications (IOTA) Maharashtra Institute of Technology, Pune, India 22 Jan – 24 Jan, 2016.

[11] M. M. Burnett and B. a. Myers. (2014). Future of end-user software engineering: beyond the silos, Proc. Futur. Softw. Eng. - FOSE 2014, no. April 2016, pp. 201–211.

69 Renewable energy technology

Bhawna Kaushik[1,a], Pramila Chandel[1,b] and Mayank Saini[2,c]

[1]Assistant Professor, Lloyd Institute of Engineering and Technology

[2]Assistant Professor, G.L.Bajaj Institute of Management

Abstract

This research explores the imperative need for transitioning to renewable and sustainable energy sources in response to global challenges such as climate change, volatile oil prices, and increasing energy consumption. With the Paris accord's call to limit global temperature rise, it is evident that a substantial shift away from fossil fuels is essential, aiming for at least 50% renewable energy by mid-century. The study examines various renewable energy sources, including solar, wind, hydropower, tidal, geothermal, biomass, fusion, and fuel cells, assessing their economic viability through Energy Return on Energy Invested (ERoEI). While renewable energy technologies hold promise, they face technical, economic, and societal challenges that must be overcome to ensure a sustainable energy future. As the world invests in research, development, and renewable energy infrastructure, achieving a favorable ERoEI and energy security remains paramount in our journey toward a cleaner, greener, and more prosperous future.

Keywords: Energy sources, ERoEI, hydropower, renewable energy, solar energy, sustainable energy systems, tidal energy, wind energy, etc

Introduction

Additional investigations are now being undertaken in the realm of alternative energy sources and the production of sustainable energy, primarily driven by the need to address the challenges associated with a sustainable long-term energy supply [1]. The phenomenon of global warming is influenced by several factors, including greenhouse gas emissions, variable oil prices, and the escalating electrical consumption seen in rising countries. Extensive study has shown the pressing need for innovative strategies to address this issue. The Paris Agreement, which was ratified by 196 countries in December 2021, stipulates a target of limiting the rise in global average temperature to a maximum of 2 degrees Celsius over pre-industrial levels by the conclusion of the current century. Hence, it is evident that expediting the cessation of our dependence on fossil fuels is imperative [2]. It is imperative that a significant proportion, if not a majority, of our energy requirements be met by renewable sources by the middle of the century. Nuclear power accounts for a mere "2.2% of global energy consumption, whilst the other 79.5% is derived from sources such as oil, gas, coal, and other non-nuclear alternatives. Solar energy"", hydroelectric power, wind power, geothermal energy, biomass, and emerging energy sources such as hydrogen storage and nuclear fusion provide a selection of renewable energy resources that we briefly discuss before delving into more sophisticated advancements within this domain.

The significance of renewable energy in the global energy mix cannot be overstated. However, achieving this objective requires increased commitment, advancement in state-of-the-art technology, and the implementation of an energy-efficient strategy and financial framework. This is particularly viable for several uses, such as transportation using electric vehicles and liquid biofuels, power generation for industrial purposes, renewable energy for heating and cooling of buildings, and other comparable applications. This objective may be achieved by the acceleration of the use of renewable energy sources.

Alternative and Sustainable Energy Systems

The Energy Reimbursement on Energy Expended (ERoEE) metric is a resilient indicator of the economic viability of an energy source. In accordance with the dominant perspective among experts, it is widely concurred that the Energy Return on Energy Invested (ERoEI) must surpass a threshold of 3:1. The juncture at which the break-even transpires lacks economic viability. Notwithstanding the ecological damage it inflicts, the observed ERoEI ratio of 80:1 implies a substantial degree of cost-efficiency. Table 69.1 exhibits a juxtaposed examination of the Energy Yield on Energy Expenditure (ERoEI) for diverse types of sustainable energy (RE) in connection with coal. The present condition of the energy industry is encountering a noteworthy revival, with a substantial journey remaining before it becomes economically feasible without depending on sustainable energy sources.

[a]Bhawna.Kaushik@liet.in, [b]Pramila.Chandel@liet.in, [c]Mayank.Saini@glbim.ac.in

DOI: 10.1201/9781003534136-69

Table 69.1 ERoEI of different energy sources [11], [12].

			ERoEI
Coal			80: 1
Biomass	Solid	Wood	25: 1
	Liquid	Biodiesel	1.3: 1
		Corn	1.3: 1
		Sugar canes	8: 1
Hydropower			100: 1
Solar	Thermal		1.9: 1
	Concentrated		9: 1
	Photovoltaic		6.8: 1
Tidal / wave			15: 1
Wind			18: 1
Geothermal			9: 1

This is transpiring alongside a worldwide decrease in the expense of sustainable energy deployment, which is additionally facilitating the embrace of diverse technologies in both countryside and metropolitan regions.

Emerging research indicates that some types of renewable energy sources may not possess unlimited sustainability. Biomass derived from wood, as an example, has the characteristic of being renewable but lacks sustainability. Moreover, should the use of renewable energy sources occur at an accelerated rate that surpasses their capacity for replenishment, their sustainability becomes compromised. Hence, it is imperative that sustainable energy sources has the capacity to meet both present and future energy requirements [3].

Solar Energy

At a temperature ranging from around 10 to 15 megakelvin, a fusion process occurs where 600 million metric tons of hydrogen nuclei combine to produce gas, thereby releasing an energy output of one septillion (10^{24}) joules per day [16]. The amount of energy provided is sufficient to meet the global energy demand for a 24-hour period. However, it is estimated that only around 5.108 percent of this energy reaches the Earth's surface, as a result of absorption by the atmosphere and the vast expanse of space beyond 150 million kilometers [4]. The principal utilizations of the Sun's essential energy are either:

Passive Solar Energy

The success of such a strategy relies on carefully planning the layout of the structure to take use of as much sunshine as feasible. Such a system relies on the principles of both climatology and thermodynamics. When solar radiation is captured and amplified, it produces heat that may be used to power generators. The process involves heating a certain fluid to create steam, which may then be utilised either immediately to warm a structure or later stored in a thermally insulating salt to spin turbines and generate energy. Otherwise, photovoltaic cells are used to convert the sun energy.

Photovoltaic Plants (PV)

Light may be directly converted into power by PV devices. Typically, semiconducting materials (silicon) are used in their construction. Different models of CSP systems have different risks, cost implications, and operational and technical requirements [5]. For example, solar towers, parabolic troughs/dishes, and linear Fresnel reflector designs all have the potential to generate electricity, but each has its own unique configurations and design constraints. Concentrated solar PV is a promising new development in the field of photovoltaics. In its most efficient configuration, "the CPV system generates electricity by transferring heat from a heat receiver module to a thermal collector, which then transfers the heat potential (depending on the design) via a designated working fluid to spin a turbine." Although parabolic trough technology is currently the most widely used and reliable system, linear Fresnel designs are rapidly progressing and hold even greater potential because of their lower material requirements, lower costs, better land management, greater operational efficiency, improved thermal storage capacity, etc. However, in order to maximise their performance, CPV technologies are often needed to function as hybrids and be connected with energy storage systems.

North and South America's western states, Spain, the United Arab Emirates, a few of Asian nations including India and China, and, most notably, Morocco and South Africa on the continent of Africa all make use of such technology."

Figure 69.1 An Illustration of Solar Reflector Technology, Including the Solar Tower, Parabolic Troughs, and Linear Fresnel Mirrors [6]

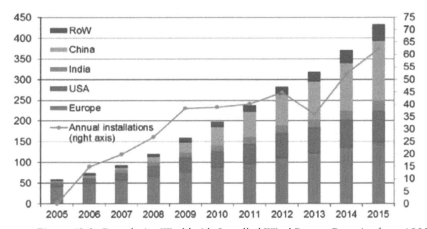

Figure 69.2 Cumulative Worldwide Installed Wind Power Capacity from 1990 to 2021, and Annual Installed Capacity, in Gigawatts (GW) According to Author [7]

Wind Energy

This is especially true near the equator, where more land is available to absorb the infra-red solar radiation that is used to heat buildings. The produced heat gradient forces air to flow in the form of wind. Wind power makes use of this occurrence by means of wind devices (turbines). There are two main types of turbines: those with a horizontal axis and those with a vertical axis. When a significant number of these turbines are grouped together, they are called wind farms. Despite the noise impact and the observed incidence of birds dying as flying over agricultural land, the ERoEI for wind energy is 18:1, making it economically feasible with increased interest, as seen in Figure 69.2. This formula may be used to approximate a wind turbine's output power:

$$P = \frac{1}{2}\rho \times A \times V^3 \tag{1}$$

"Where A is the area scanned by a rotor: $\pi \times R^2$ (m2), R is the pale radius, V speed of the wind (m/s) and ρ is air density (1.23 kg/m3 at 15 °C, 1.0132bar)."

Hydropower Energy

Water's potential energy, whether from a river's flow or a lake's drop, may be converted to mechanical energy and then to electricity by rotating a large electromagnet rotor housed inside a cylindrical stator itself constructed of coils. The kinetic energy of the water turns the turbine's blades, which in turn spin the rotor in accordance with Faraday's law. Consequently, a change in the strength of a magnetic field causes a current to be produced (Figure 69.3). Among renewable energy sources, this is by far the most widely used today; its popularity spans both developing and industrialised nations. However, the technique has a severe effect on the ocean's ecology, from the pollution of the water supply to the loss of marine life due to building and maintenance operations at the dam. The energy that a dam generates may be measured as:

$$P = \phi \times g \times h \times \eta_{elec} \times \eta_{hyd} \tag{2}$$

"where P: power (W), ϕ: water flux (m3/s), h: fall height (m), g: gravity 9.8 (m/s2), ηelec: electrical conversion efficiency (0 - 1), and ηhyd: turbine efficiency (0 - 1)."

Tidal and Wind Energy

The continual oscillation of the ocean, resulting from the gravitational forces exerted by the Earth, sun, and moon, generates tidal effects that give birth to currents. This phenomenon serves as the guiding principle behind the operating mechanism of a tidal energy system, which harnesses this natural process to create electricity. The phenomenon of the periodic fluctuation of sea water levels is attributed to a gravitational force exerted by celestial bodies, namely the Sun (30%) and the Moon (70%), acting differentially on the Earth. The flow effect is a phenomenon that produces mechanical energy with the capacity to rotate turbines. It may be categorized into two types: tidal assault and stream systems (see Figure 69.4). Therefore, the movement of the ocean is transformed into electrical energy by means of magnetic induction. Extensive coverage has been provided on the conditions, fields and technologies employed for the utilization of tidal power in the conversion of tidal and currents energy. These encompass various methods such as the "Oscillating Hydrofoil, Vertical Axis Turbine, Venturi Effect Turbine, Horizontal Axis Turbine, as well as the horizontal, cross-flow, and vertical tidal current converter devices [8]. The technology" exhibits characteristics of sustainability, reliability, and predictability. However, its widespread adoption is hindered by the associated expenses of building, installation, and maintenance, as well as the potential adverse impact on marine ecosystems.

Geothermal Energy

The name "geothermal" is derived from its Greek roots, with "geo" referring to the Earth and "thermo" denoting heat. As an individual excavates farther "into the Earth, the temperature progressively increases towards the

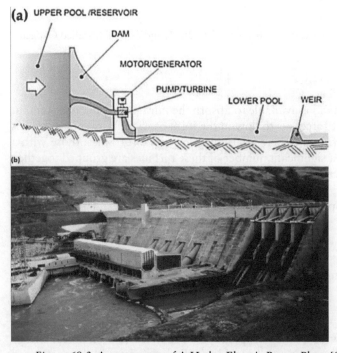

Figure 69.3 Arrangement of A Hydro Electric Power Plant [8]

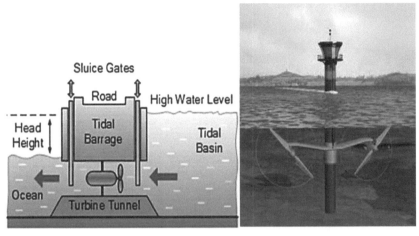

Figure 69.4 Illustration; 1) Tidal Barrage, 2) Tidal Stream Power Generation [9]

Step 1	Step 2	Step 3
Identify/Characterize a Site	**Create a Reservoir**	**Operate the Power Plant and Maintain the Reservoir**
• Develop a geologic model of a potential site using surface, geologic, geophysical, and remote sensing exploration. • Assess the temperature gradient, permeability, in-situ stress directions of the resource, rock mechanical properties, and whether fluid is present. • Determine if the necessary characteristics to create an EGS reservoir are present.	• Drill an injection well into hot rock with limited fluid content and/or permeability. • Inject water at sufficient pressure (or temperature differential) to create fracture network. • Continue volume to create a reservoir (flow rate, temperature, volume, and sustainability). • Drill a production well into the fracture network, intersecting the created flow paths. The resulting circulation loop allows water to flow through the enhanced reservoir, picking up in situ heat. The hot water is then pumped to the surface through the production well (see diagram below).	• At the surface, the water transfers to steam, or it heats a working fluid that produces vapor. • The steam/vapor turns a turbine to create electricity. • The original geothermal water is recycled into the reservoir through the injection well to complete the circulation loop.

Figure 69.5 Steps for Engineering of an EGS Reservoir, and Operation

planet's core. Thermal energy, in the form of pressured heat, is transported by continuous translational motion from the center to the surface of the Earth. The steam and heat generated are used for direct heating of buildings or, in the event of an indirect application, for power production. The technical prerequisites and conditions pertaining to future development have been thoroughly examined in previous studies [9]. Current research is exploring new findings that go beyond the difficulties of laborious exploration for naturally occurring hot spots. Instead, the focus is on the artificial drilling of geothermal wells to reach the depths where hot rocks are located. This drilling process aims to stimulate thermal energy, which can then be harnessed for the purposes of power generation or heating. These systems, known as enhanced geothermal systems, represent a promising avenue for

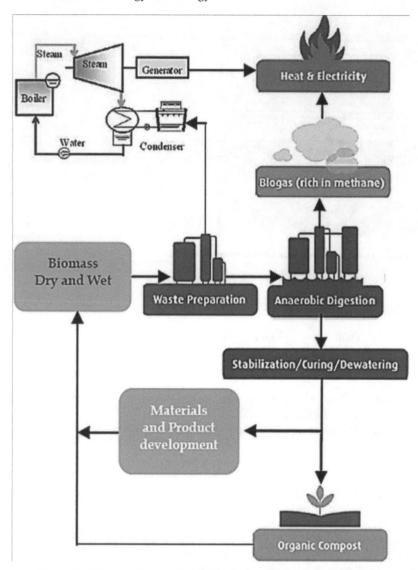

Figure 69.6 Energy Process from Biomass

the utilization of geothermal energy. The engineering process for constructing reservoirs, as seen in Figure 69.5, involves a series of necessary procedures."

Energy from Biomass

Biomass energy is mostly derived from organic materials derived from animals and plants [10]. Wood is the prevailing kind of biomass, but its sustainability is questionable. Conversely, biofuels like ethanol and biodiesel are altering the prevailing viewpoint on the effective use of agricultural resources and trash in order to revolutionize the energy industry. The use and implementation of bio-gas as a means to fuel automobiles and provide sustainable energy on isolated islands and tiny communities has grown more prevalent. Renewable resources are available in a somewhat constant and plentiful manner, making them readily accessible for harnessing.

The two primary uses of biomass energy, as seen in Figure 69.6, are the utilization of a boiler for power generation via turbine operation, and the production of renewable fuels such as biogas, bioethanol, and biodiesel through the process of anaerobic fermentation. The concept of producing biofuel from cellulosic plant-derived materials, such as long grasses, woody plant cell walls, wood debris, and agricultural and urban waste, signifies a noteworthy technological advancement. This methodology deviates from the conventional approach of using botanical substances such as fruits and seeds for the production of biofuel. The efficacy of this alternative method, however, yet to be shown in the commercial sphere. The research and development of this particular renewable energy technology is progressing significantly.

Prospects and Perspectives

The exponential decline in the cost of renewable energy technology is being seen worldwide, coinciding with increased investment in this sector. The advancement and deployment of requisite technology, as well as the execution of emerging efforts aimed at addressing the aberrations of climate change, hold promise for the establishment of an environmentally sustainable society in the next years. Consequently, this results in a decrease in power costs and the emission of carbon into the environment as a result of fossil fuel use. The Western scholars assert that the evidence supporting the existence of continued global warming is indisputable, and thus, urgent measures must be implemented to prevent reaching a critical threshold beyond which reversal becomes impossible [11, 12]. On the contrary, and with the intention of maintaining objectivity, it is essential to also consider the opposing perspective. The majority of the technologies examined in this research encounter similar technological, socio-economic, and environmental difficulties. Technical concerns within the realm of developing systems include several aspects such as load balancing, performance optimization, material selection, and the challenges associated with procuring these materials for establishing and sustaining the operational processes of each given technology. In addition, the inclusion of essential skillsets and the design of systems are anticipated to be integral components in the development of technologies, among other potential alternatives. These factors are likely to be taken into account when implementing supporting policies. The manner in which individuals respond to novel concepts and advancements is a potential risk to the achievement of projects and has the potential to compromise a significant financial investment. Additional economic indicators, such as operational costs and topological location, are also significant factors that influence technical advancement and energy prices. Nevertheless, similar to past initiatives in the field of alternative energy, these projects have facilitated the creation of employment opportunities on a global scale. Therefore, the global effort to address the challenges posed by the use of fossil fuels and its associated technologies via the implementation of green energy programs and a willingness to invest in sustainable solutions is imperative. Furthermore, it is crucial to underline the timely and vital nature of evaluating and monitoring progress.

Conclusion

In conclusion, the urgent need for transitioning to renewable and sustainable energy sources to combat global warming and secure our energy future is undeniable. As we strive to meet the goals set forth in the Paris accord and reduce our reliance on fossil fuels, it is evident that renewable energy technologies play a crucial role. From solar and wind power to hydropower, geothermal energy, biomass, fusion, and fuel cells, a wide array of options exists to harness clean energy. These technologies have the potential to not only reduce greenhouse gas emissions but also create economic opportunities and pave the way for a greener and more sustainable future. However, challenges such as technical complexities, material sourcing, and societal acceptance must be addressed. As we continue to invest in research, development, and the expansion of renewable energy infrastructure, achieving a favorable Energy Return on Energy Invested (ERoEI) and ensuring energy security should remain paramount. The journey towards a sustainable energy economy requires dedication, innovation, and a concerted global effort, but the benefits in terms of environmental preservation and a cleaner, more prosperous future are well worth the investment.

References

[1] Popescu, G. H., Mieila, M., Nica, E., & Andrei, J. V. (2018). The emergence of the effects and determinants of the energy paradigm changes on European Union economy. *Renewable and Sustainable Energy Reviews*, 81, 768–774.

[2] Onu, P., and Mbohwa, C. (2018). Future energy systems and sustainable emission control : Africa in perspective. In Proceedings of the International Conference on Industrial Engineering and Operations Management, (pp. 793–800).

[3] Olivier, J. G. J., Schure, K. M., and Peters, J. A. H. W. (2017). Trends in Global CO2 and Total Greenhouse Gas Emissions. PBL Netherlands Environmental Assessment Agency.

[4] Onu, P., and Mbohwa, C. (2018). Sustainable oil exploitation versus renewable energy initiatives : a review of the case of Uganda. In Proceedings of the International Conference on Industrial Engineering and Operations Management, 2018, (pp. 1008–1015).

[5] IREN. (2021). Renewable Energy Capacity Highlights. *International Renewable Energy Agency*, vol. 00, no. March 2021, 2021, pp. 1–3, https://www.irena.org/publications/2021/March/Renewable-Capacity-Statistics-2021.

[6] Raji, O., and Onu, P. (2017). Untapped wealth potential in fruit for Uganda community. *International Journal of Advanced Academic Research*, 3(February), 17–25.

[7] Onu, P., and Mbohwa, C. (2018). Green supply chain management and sustainable industrial practices : bridging the gap. In Proceedings of the International Conference on Industrial Engineering and Operations Management, 2018, (pp. 786–792).

[8] Akiyode, O. O., Tumushabe, A., Hadijjah, K., and Peter, O. (2017). Climate change, food security and environmental security : a conflict inclination assessment of Karamoja region of Uganda. International Journal of Scientific World; 5 (2), 172–176.

[9] IRENA (2016). Roadmap for a Renewable Energy Future, 2016. [Online]. Available: http://www.irena.org/document-downloads/publications/i rena_remap_2016_edition_report.pdf. [Accessed: 09- Sep-2018].

[10] Peter, O., and Mbohwa, C. (2019). Sustainable production : new thinking for SMEs. In IOP Conference Series: Materials Science and Engineering, 2019.

[11] Hall, C. A., Lambert, J. G., and Balogh, S. B. (2014). EROI of different fuels and the implications for society. *Energy policy*, 64, 141–152.

[12] King, L. C., and Van Den Bergh, J. C. (2018). Implications of net energy-return-on-investment for a low-carbon energy transition. *Nature energy*, 3(4), 334–340.